D0983837

ARCHIPELAGIC ENGLISH: LITERATURE, HISTORY, AND POLITICS 1603–1707

ARCHIPELAGIC ENGLISH: LITERATURE, HISTORY, AND POLITICS 1603–1707

JOHN KERRIGAN

OXFORD
UNIVERSITY PRESS

OXFORD
UNIVERSITY PRESS

Great Clarendon Street, Oxford OX2 6DP

Oxford University Press is a department of the University of Oxford.
It furthers the University's objective of excellence in research, scholarship,
and education by publishing worldwide in

Oxford New York

Auckland Cape Town Dar es Salaam Hong Kong Karachi
Kuala Lumpur Madrid Melbourne Mexico City Nairobi
New Delhi Shanghai Taipei Toronto

With offices in

Argentina Austria Brazil Chile Czech Republic France Greece
Guatemala Hungary Italy Japan Poland Portugal Singapore
South Korea Switzerland Thailand Turkey Ukraine Vietnam

Oxford is a registered trade mark of Oxford University Press
in the UK and in certain other countries

Published in the United States
by Oxford University Press Inc., New York

© John Kerrigan 2008

The moral rights of the author have been asserted
Database right Oxford University Press (maker)

First published 2008

All rights reserved. No part of this publication may be reproduced,
stored in a retrieval system, or transmitted, in any form or by any means,
without the prior permission in writing of Oxford University Press,
or as expressly permitted by law, or under terms agreed with the appropriate
reprographics rights organization. Enquiries concerning reproduction
outside the scope of the above should be sent to the Rights Department,
Oxford University Press, at the address above

You must not circulate this book in any other binding or cover
and you must impose the same condition on any acquirer

British Library Cataloguing in Publication Data

Data available

Library of Congress Cataloging in Publication Data

Data available

Typeset by Laserwords Private Limited, Chennai, India
Printed in Great Britain
on acid-free paper by
Biddles Ltd., King's Lynn, Norfolk

ISBN 978–0–19–818384–6

1 3 5 7 9 10 8 6 4 2

For Niamh

Preface

Historians increasingly recognize that early modern England, Scotland, Ireland, and Wales were in different degrees and for a variety of reasons, but sometimes to crucial effect, interactive entities. During the period 1603–1707, the islands of the North-West Atlantic constituted, culturally as well as politically, a linked and divided *archipelago*. This term, as used by the historians, and redeployed in my title, does three related things: it designates a geopolitical unit or zone, stretching from the Channel Islands to the Shetlands, from the Wash to Galway Bay, with ties to North America and down to the Caribbean; it does so neutrally (avoiding the assumptions loaded into 'the British Isles'); and it implies a devolved, interconnected account of what went on around the islands. The contention of this book is that an archipelagic approach not just to seventeenth-century history but to the anglophone literature of the period can yield valuable insights.

Archipelagic English is more extensively historical than my earlier work. In this it follows a trend in literary studies, yet it owes more to mainstream historiography than to the theoretically and anthropologically driven methods of last century's 'new historicism'. It may be that the historicizing tendency in literary scholarship has started to become restrictive, but it has opened up issues that cannot be probed in other ways and equipped us more fully to make judgements about the value of texts. This is all that *Archipelagic English* seeks to achieve. It does not offer itself as the best way of thinking about seventeenth-century literature, nor as providing a full toolbox for reading, say, *Cymbeline* or *Colonel Jack*—works whose peculiarities require a mix of approaches. The aim is to add to our understanding of such works by recovering the circumstances of their composition and reception.

The book also contributes to the geopolitical turn in literary studies. If it does not talk much about cartography—probably a relief, given how fashionable that topic has become—it does, in some sense, remap the English- and Scots-speaking cultures of seventeenth-century Britain and

Ireland. This shift to the geographical owes something to the general loss of belief that history has a providential or progressive direction. *Archipelagic English* does hazard a few generalizations about the overall course of events, and it unpicks some knots of connection and conflict, such as were generated by the long, involved relationship between English, Scottish, and Dutch Protestantism, which throw up repeated crises that had literary as well as military-political aspects. But the geocultural cast of this book has reinforced the impulse—understandable in any case, given the relative novelty of my subject—to proceed in an essayistic manner. I have selected texts or clusters of texts, often related thematically, and sought to probe them in context, rather than attempt to construct overarching historical narratives, which are so often contradicted by local variation.

Historians frequently adopt a deep-litter approach to the page, piling up footnotes into running bibliographies. At times, especially when entering areas new to me, I have been grateful for this, but the effect can be cumbersome, and, in an age of electronic searches, it is less and less necessary. In the introduction, I do list further reading in notes as a way of condensing essential, preliminary information. Elsewhere, debts are signalled, but scholars not mentioned should not assume that their work has gone unread. For similar reasons, the bibliography lists only Primary Sources; secondary works should be readily locatable given the division of topics by chapter. To assist the reader, all the sources cited in a chapter are given in full detail on first mention. Because of the book's historical tenor, it has seemed right to use old spelling. I have made a few silent corrections, and lightly regularized titles. Ligatures have been removed from 'ae' and 'oe', and such forms as '&' and 'ye' expanded where appropriate. When the background is Scottish, members of the royal family are likely to be called Stewarts not Stuarts. Whether a monarch is referred to as James VI or James VI and I, or Willem van Oranje or William of Orange or William II and III, depends on context, which is often debatable. Because location is a leading concern, place as well as date of publication is specified whenever possible for pre-1800 texts. The Bible is quoted from the Authorized Version.

I am grateful to the British Academy for awarding me a Research Readership (1998–2000) which allowed work on this book to begin, and to St John's College, Cambridge and to the Cambridge English Faculty for additional support. Chapters were tried out as lectures, conference and seminar papers at the following universities: Aberdeen, Bangor, Cambridge, Exeter, Hull, Liverpool, London, Oxford, Queen's (Belfast),

Sussex, Swansea, Trinity College Dublin, Ulster (Derry), University College Dublin, York; Bologna, Copenhagen, Fribourg (Switzerland), Leiden; Chicago, Columbia, Harvard, McGill, Princeton, Toronto, and Wisconsin-Madison. Peter Burke, Andrew Carpenter, Jo Eastwood, Alan Fletcher, Germaine Greer, Rod Lyall, Caroline Macafee, James McGuire, Femke Molekamp, Eiléan Ní Chuilleanáin, Máire Ní Mhaonaigh, Jane Moody, Jacinta Prunty, Colm Ó Baoill, Rory Rapple, John Ross, Jonathan Scott, Jenny Wormald, and Andrew Zurcher made fruitful suggestions or provided information, as did others mentioned in the notes. Chapters were kindly read by Toby Barnard, Michael Brown, Philip Connell, Robert Cummings, Eamon Duffy, David Finnegan, David Hayton, Clare Jackson, Michael and Peter Kerrigan, John MacCafferty, Scott Mandelbrote, Susan Manning, David Loewenstein, John Pitcher, Deana Rankin, Nigel Smith, Paul Stevens, and the editors of collections mentioned below. Even warmer thanks must go to Andrew McNeillie and John Morrill for commenting on an early, full draft, to Colin Burrow and Willy Maley for doing that and more, and to Helen Small, who read material repeatedly as well as acutely, and who was supportive through a period whose challenges for me included chairing the Cambridge English Faculty.

My first thoughts on this topic were aired in the *London Review of Books*, 5 June 1997, under the editor's cross-bred title 'Birth of a Náison', and a progress report appeared as 'Ulster and the New British Histories: Milton to Mitchelbourne', in Edna Longley, Eamonn Hughes, and Des O'Rawe (eds.), *Ireland (Ulster) Scotland: Concepts, Contexts, Comparisons* (Belfast: Cló Ollscoil na Banríona/Queen's University Belfast, 2003). Slightly different versions of chapters have been published as follows: 3 in Glenn Burgess, Rowland Wymer, and Jason Lawrence (eds.), *The Accession of James I: Historical and Cultural Consequences* (London: Palgrave, 2006), 4 in my *On Shakespeare and Early Modern Literature: Essays* (Oxford: Oxford University Press, 2001), 8 in David Baker and Willy Maley (eds.), *British Identities and English Renaissance Literature* (Cambridge: Cambridge University Press, 2002), 10 in Liam McIlvaney and Ray Ryan (eds.), *Ireland and Scotland: Culture and Society, 1700–2000* (Dublin: Four Courts, 2004), and 11 in Simon Mealor and Philip Schwyzer (eds.), *Archipelagic Identities: Literature and Identity in the Atlantic Archipelago, 1550–1800* (Aldershot: Ashgate, 2004).

Liverpool—Cambridge—Co. Mayo

Contents

List of Illustrations

I

Introduction

(i) Scope

O ver the last few years there has been a significant devolution of power within the United Kingdom. What the outcome of this process will be remains, for the moment, unclear. The future shape of Ireland, north and south of the border, depends on many factors, and while nationalists looking for independence are entrenched in the Scottish Parliament and (to a lesser extent) the Welsh Assembly, the long-anticipated 'break-up of Britain'[1] is by no means inevitable. Within England itself—a country that is often but unconvincingly said to have escaped the imprint of nationalism—there has been a growing, unresolved debate not just about the wisdom of granting self-determination to Scotland, Wales, and the six counties of Ulster which did not go into the Irish Free State, but about where devolution leaves Englishness. Should the country shake off the legacy of Britishness and assert its national identity?

Across swathes of British and Irish life, these issues are either dormant or overtaken by more immediate pressures and distractions. Yet the past informs the present even of those who ignore it, and, as this book shows, the fraught, bloody, but often creatively productive relations between different ethnic and religious groups around the islands are deeply installed in the culture. So if the arguments made for devolution and its big sister separatism sometimes run ahead of popular aspirations on the ground, there is nothing unusual about that in the history of social change, and it does not make those arguments, which are part of the evolving dynamic, less challenging—especially as they become entangled with multi-culturalist vs integrationist debates about the African, Caribbean, and Asian communities that have built up in Britain and Ireland in the aftermath of empire. Devolution matters because it has encouraged the peoples of the islands to imagine different relationships with one another, and with the peoples of Europe—the future of the European Union providing one horizon—but also because of the opportunity it gives the anglophone world as a whole to reconfigure its understanding of where it comes from. The incentive to strip away modern Anglocentric and Victorian imperial paradigms to recover the long, braided histories played out across the British-Irish archipelago between three kingdoms, four countries, divided regions, variable ethnicities and religiously determined allegiances is there even for those who are sceptical about the desirability of Scottish or Welsh independence. Yet the response of intellectuals to this chance to reassess the past has been uneven in quality. And the challenge has only been partially met for one of the most important periods of literary production and, connectedly, nation and state formation: the seventeenth century.

This book is designed to make good some of that deficiency. It does so by recognizing that the current devolutionary process—a development partly driven by plays, poems, and novels (from Seamus Heaney to James Kelman)—has thrown into relief distortions in the received picture of seventeenth-century literature. There have, of course, been shifts of late in the way this field is construed. Feminist scholars have retrieved and explored the work of dozens of women writers, from Lady Mary Wroth to Jane Barker, and changed the way male-authored texts are read. Waves of critical theory running through the academy, and the postmodernizing of culture at large, have eroded the once-vaunted autonomy of the literary object and toppled the hierarchy of genres which put tragedy and lyric poetry at the top of an aesthetic pyramid and pamphleteering somewhere near the bottom. A related historicizing tendency in English studies has drawn into the sphere of analysis traditionally reserved for literary artefacts a wide range of materials from medical treatises to heraldic devices. These changes have in principle left all early modern writing open to scrutiny. Yet the geopolitical parameters of enquiry remain substantially unrevised. Even within the UK, where devolution is a growing reality, students of the period continue to operate within a dated construction of 'Eng. Lit.'.

This state of affairs has been surprisingly little affected by the growth of postcolonial studies. That scholars of Renaissance literature are now keen to talk about plantation treatises, *The Tempest*, and *Oroonoko* shows that they have been affected by the tremendous access of new thinking that postcolonialism has unleashed.[2] Voices can now be heard protesting that the conditions of modern imperialism are being projected back into a period in which colonial adventures were (initially, at least) limited and had little impact on literary texts.[3] While anachronism is indeed a danger, one should also not be purist, and, tied to the history of ideas, or vocabulary, miss how protean empire can be. In the century covered by this book, plantations, the growth of the slave trade, and the activities of trading companies from America to the East Indies made their often shameful mark on literature. I shall return to the issue of imperialism in Section (iv) of this introduction. What needs noting immediately is that, while postcolonial analyses have been valuably brought to bear on how, for instance, Ireland is represented in *The Faerie Queene*, or Wales in *I Henry IV*,[4] the gross effect of the turn towards the study of empire and its aftermath has been to overlook the uneven, inherited relationships between the parts and peoples of Britain and Ireland in order to concentrate on ill-defined 'English' or 'British' penetration of the New World, Africa, and South Asia. The incentive has been reduced to explore the cultural specificity and heterogeneity of the advocates of overseas empire, the identity of the colonizers, and the feedback effects of colonization on their difference.[5]

Students of later periods would be less surprised by a call to devolve, and less in need of hearing it. Anyone seriously interested in English Romanticism reads Ossian; experts on literary modernism know about Joyce's Dublin as well as David Jones's London Welshness. Why are those working in the seventeenth century by comparison relatively uninterested in Scottish, Welsh, and even Irish angles? It was not always so. When the advanced study of Eng. Lit. began in mid-eighteenth-century Scotland, under the tutelage of Adam Smith and Hugh Blair (admirer of the Scots poet Allan Ramsay, and Ossian, as well as of Swift and *The Spectator*), and when, a few years later, Thomas Warton wrote in Oxford the first substantial *History of English Poetry*, with accounts of Welsh-Britonic romance and chapters on the Scottish poets, there was a British and Anglo-Irish aspect to the depiction of medieval and early modern literature.[6] During the Victorian period, as 'English Language and Literature' became established in English universities, Scotch professors were influential.[7] Such men as David Masson—eminent in both London and Edinburgh—gave the seventeenth century a Scottish accent.[8]

Meanwhile, the primers consulted by those cramming for civil service exams, or just eager for self-improvement, could be impressively inclusive.

Robert Chambers' *Cyclopaedia of English Literature*, the Norton Anthology of its day, published in 1844 and expanded through several editions until 1938, gave extracts from, information about, and portraits of, Scottish, Welsh, and Irish as well as Anglo-English authors, including many from the seventeenth century unfamiliar to most modern readers: Alexander Hume, Sir Robert Ayton, James Howell, Lord Herbert of Cherbury, the Earl of Roscommon, Lady Rachel Russell.... [9] Chambers, a Scot, and author of *Vestiges of Creation*, was a high-profile man of letters,[10] and those involved in selecting and introducing extracts in later editions—Stopford Brooke, Sidney Lee, S. R. Gardiner, Edmund Gosse—were also major figures. The *Cyclopaedia* became the Authorized Version of Eng. Lit. Expanding to take in work by American, Canadian, and other English-speaking peoples, it also became paradoxically more Anglo-Saxon. The sections on Old English and early medieval literature—entrenching *Beowulf* and King Alfred at the head of a story which swept up Scots and Anglo-Irish writing—were enhanced, and a Teutonizing, high-imperial ethos crept over the editorial outlook. In the edition of 1901—fronted by another Scot, David Patrick—the arguments advanced for regarding Scottish Highland and Irish culture as 'English' are implausibly, racially unionist.[11] But if the predicates of the project became dubious, its scope remains an example.

English became more narrowly English at a time when humane literary studies of a broadly Arnoldian stamp were weakening the hold of medieval philology in major universities in Britain and North America and were being laid down, within England, as a main plank of the school curriculum.[12] In a summary such as this, 1921 is the date to conjure with, because the publication of 'The Newbolt Report' in that year is conventionally identified as the start of modern, institutionalized English. *The Teaching of English in England*, as the government report was officially called, is an enlightened, liberal document. It does reflect, however, the patriotic ethos which the First World War encouraged around the study of England's history and its literature.[13] Nineteen twenty-one was also the year when the Anglo-Irish War of Independence ended in the partition of Ireland and the establishment of the Free State. The remapping of Irish culture, begun during the Irish Literary Revival, was now entrenched in the twenty-six counties and taken further by such republican scholars as Daniel Corkery,[14] while, in England, the setback to imperial unionism both reinforced 'little Englandism' and, with the withdrawal of the least Anglo- (rural Catholic, Gaelicizing) section of the UK, made it easier to think of

'Britain' as England writ large.[15] (In Scotland cultural nationalism reclaimed literature over the same period, from the founding of the Scottish Text Society (1882) through G. Gregory Smith's classic account of the 'Caledonian antisyzygy' in *Scottish Literature: Character and Influence* (1919),[16] but there was no Easter Rising in Edinburgh, no Treaty of Secession, little reaction south of the border, and, as in anglophone Wales,[17] the fostering of national traditions through advanced literary study would be delayed.)[18] Finally, 1921 was the year in which T. S. Eliot published his review article on 'The Metaphysical Poets'—a lightning-bolt of critical modernism shot into conventional views of the seventeenth century.[19]

Eliot was not the first critic to internationalize Jacobean culture, placing it in the Europe of Dante, St John of the Cross, and Port Royal.[20] Nor was he the first to identify a 'dissociation of sensibility' in the early modern period,[21] finding breaks in the literary tradition between Donne, Milton, and Dryden. His cutting across the periodization favoured by English Whig historians (1603 to 1688 or 1707 or 1714) reinforced an existing and still current impulse, which derives from Burkhardt and late Victorian aestheticism, to distinguish between an 'English Renaissance'—that took its bearings from Petrarch, Ovid, and Titian, and that manifested itself in the production of artefacts rather than events—and the later phase of civil war and Restoration, characterized as an epoch of commerce, science, and modernity. Nonetheless, Eliot's carve-up of the period in favour of Donne, early Marvell, and certain Jacobean divines was perceived by contemporaries as radical.

That makes it the more striking that his analysis was so quickly absorbed back into a longer-reaching Anglo-English account of the seventeenth century. Eliot himself was partly the master of this process, reconciling himself in his later essays to Dryden and Milton (no longer agents of dissociation) and, with an assurance verging on presumption, defining the essentials of English identity and reconciling the warring parties of the mid-seventeenth century in *Four Quartets*.[22] (The European and transatlantic ambit within which all this went on did not diminish—if anything, it exacerbated—his reduction of Ireland, Scotland, and Wales to provincial outposts of England.)[23] The strongest critical effect can be found in F. R. Leavis and others associated with *Scrutiny*, whose preoccupation with Englishness has become something of a derisive commonplace though its permutations were complex. In Leavis's 'A Sketch for an "English School"' (1943) Eliot's arguments in 'The Metaphysical Poets' are worked into a restatement of the claims of the entire century.[24] Outlining a programme thick with the matter of Anglocentric Whig historiography ('Tolerance', 'The Causes of the Civil War', 'the Revolution of 1688 and its significance'), Leavis cites the historians Macaulay, Tawney, and the Hammonds in support of his belief that the study of specifically English seventeenth-century culture—diversified only by an optional 'comparison with French development'—should be central, and compulsory.[25]

The role of the historians in this was significant. Across nineteenth-century Europe the growth of literary studies, and, in particular, the writing of literary history, was interwoven with nationalism. In Britain, and even more potently in the Ireland of the Revival, similar energies were at work. But the geocultural complications involved in constructing 'Eng. Lit.', already apparent to Hugh Blair and Thomas Warton, were highlighted for Victorian literary scholars by the relatively *Archipelagic* approach—to introduce a title word that is glossed in my preface and unpacked in Section (iii)—of the leading historians of the seventeenth century, Macaulay and S. R. Gardiner. Both were in different ways preoccupied with the destiny of the English nation. But Macaulay's outlook was qualified by his Scottish family background, by the influence on his procedures of the novels of Sir Walter Scott, and by his commitment to the great liberal causes of Catholic emancipation and the disestablishment of the Church of Ireland.[26] Gardiner, in turn, followed Gladstone in converting to Irish Home Rule, and he came to favour a fully federal constitution for the UK.

Like many of their contemporaries, Macanlay and Gardiner were drawn to the seventeenth century because it was seen as the origin not just of the political blessings enjoyed by the English people, including parliamentary government, but also their unresolved problems: how to settle the conflicts in Ireland, how to respect Dissent without damaging the established church.[27] (Macaulay's attraction to the period was also strongly literary; his influence on the construction of what he called 'British Literature'[28] was exercised through his role in shaping the Indian education system, and civil service exams, as well as through his critical essays.)[29] As a result both were impelled to take in Scotland, Wales, and Ireland. The siege of Derry and Glencoe are among Macaulay's most celebrated set pieces. Though sometimes more aggregating and sectionalized than interconnected and explanatory, Gardiner's multi-volume account of the civil wars was open to the whole archipelago.[30]

The outlook after 1921 was by comparison limited, especially in England. As John Morrill has pointed out, the most influential early-twentieth-century account, G. M. Trevelyan's oft-reprinted *History of England under the Stuarts* (1904), was constrictingly Anglocentric. Thereafter, half-a-dozen factors kept the range narrow.[31] Historians inspired by positivistic, Christian-socialist and Marxist ideas set out to establish the economic and sociological determinants of seventeenth-century events. With the data available for Scotland, Wales, and Ireland being so limited, the story of how social change led to civil war in the 1640s 'became an exclusively *English* story'. Then, the growing fascination on both sides of the Atlantic with radical movements thrown up by the war led to a concentration on the English Levellers and Ranters, with 'a resulting de-emphasis on the popular cultural responses to the collapse of royal and noble power in Scotland and Ireland'.[32] Again, the civic and county communities, which became the focus for those researching seventeenth-century attitudes away from Whitehall, were more densely available and representative in England than in Scotland, Wales, and Ireland, where patterns of settlement had been more dispersed, and pastoral. To these shaping factors, Morrill would now add two more:[33] that English public and private records were relatively better catalogued, just as books and pamphlets printed in seventeenth-century London (e.g. the Thomason tracts) were more readily available to researchers on microfilm than those produced elsewhere in the islands, and that the hiring of early modern historians in small academic departments in Britain and overseas gave an advantage to those working on 'mainstream' English topics. All this encouraged Irish, Scottish, and Welsh historians—who were usually writing in a nationalist framework, which emphasized differences from England—not to connect with a well-resourced, politically powerful, and restrictively English discourse.

So if English (and American) critics of Leavis's generation were not encouraged by the historians they read to broaden their picture of seventeenth-century anglophone writing beyond England, the same was equally true of those who were stimulated from the 1960s onwards by Christopher Hill and Lawrence Stone.[34] The results are depressingly apparent in the standard literary-historical surveys, from the American Douglas Bush's *English Literature in the Earlier Seventeenth Century, 1600–1660* (1945), through the relevant volumes in the *Pelican History of English Literature* and the more promisingly titled *Sphere History of Literature in English* from the 1950s to the 1980s. Only in the last few years have devolutionary flickers begun to appear in literary-historical round-ups of the seventeenth century.[35] Because more of the literature produced in early modern Wales, Scotland, and Ireland employed the Celtic languages than would later be the case, as English spread around the islands, a large proportion of the period's anglophone writing is indeed Anglo-English.[36] If that sort of calculation makes Eng. Lit. assumptions seem more viable, however, it can never make them sufficient.

This is not to say that my topic is untouched. *Archipelagic English* discusses anglophone (including Scots/Inglis) literature written in Britain and Ireland between the accession of James VI of Scotland to the English throne in 1603—a succession which brought with it the incorporated Principality of Wales, and the Kingdom of Ireland—and the 1707 Anglo-Scottish Treaty of Union. To get greater interpretative and explanatory purchase, it ventures before and after those dates. Much of relevance can be found in recent books on Spenser, Shakespeare, and 'the Elizabethan writing of England',[37] while, post-1707, work on Jacobitism, Whig historiography, and British identity formation during a century of Anglo-French conflict, is informative (see Chapter 12). Anthologists have started to represent the literature of 1603–1707 more adequately.[38] Deana Rankin has produced a germinal account of war-related texts from Ireland.[39] And, closest to my own subject, David Baker and Willy Maley have published impressive books on seventeenth-century literature in a British-Irish framework.[40] Both, however, stop around the middle of the period, and both, frustratingly, deal only with English authors (Shakespeare to Marvell)—a limitation that also prevails in the small number of articles and essays that have sought to devolve the field.[41]

The lack of a full, circumstantiated account of anglophone literary production in 'the three kingdoms'—to use the standard seventeenth-century formula for England/Wales, Scotland, and Ireland—makes it the less surprising that the taught canon should have changed so little. There is a complex geocultural legacy to deal with, yet in the core zones of Anglo-British and American intellectual life it is viewed through blinkers. (What is taught in certain North American universities as 'British Literature' turns out, especially for the period between Shakespeare and Defoe, to be 'Eng. Lit.' by another name.) I hedge that observation because the scholarship generated by Irish studies worldwide, in departments of Scottish Literature, and in the Welsh universities where Anglo-Welsh material is taught, is often profound as well as committed. One purpose of this book is to connect readers schooled in an Anglo-restricted version of Eng. Lit. with texts, resources, and debates which are on the menu elsewhere. Cultural nationalism can produce its own distortions, however, and, even in the so-called Celtic fringe, scholarship has far to go in understanding the make-up of anglophone writing during the period in which the modern British-Irish state system began erratically to cohere.

That much remains to be explored can be seen not just in the narrowness of the canon but in the inconsistencies that bedevil it. While some writers have been excluded, others have been included on the wrong terms. Henry Vaughan, for instance, author of such lambent, devotional lyrics as 'They are all gone into the world of light!',[42] has been read by Anglo-American scholars as a mainstream Eng. Lit. figure, a successor of Donne and Herbert. Even from this point of view, he is an intricate, haunting poet. One good effect of literary historicism, however, has been to draw attention to the poet's background in bilingual Brecknockshire (Brycheiniog, modern Breconshire).[43] Some of the most inward, loaded specificities of his writing, as well as larger aspects of style and spirituality, spring from the predicament of Welsh Anglicanism during and after the civil wars of the 1640s.

The situation is complicated by the way Vaughan has figured in disputes within Wales about the status of Anglo-Welsh writing.[44] An argument has long raged between those who hold that the Welsh language is the stem of the nation and those more pluralistic souls, often from the southern, more anglophone areas, who see Anglo-Welsh literature as integral to the national heritage. Vaughan has been a prize in these controversies because, if his Welsh credentials could be established, then an indigenous, Anglo-Welsh tradition would have a very early and distinguished representative. As it happens, the case against his Welshness has been most thoroughly made by a scholar-poet who did much to demonstrate the contribution of Anglo-Welsh literature to Welsh identity: Roland Mathias.[45] As I show in Chapter 6, however, the arguments for reading Vaughan as 'No Englishman' are strong and can be developed. Wherever the balance of truth lies, the importance of the debate in clarifying the nature of his achievement is indisputable.

Yet if nationalism can bring to bear on authors such as Vaughan genuinely critical questions about ethnicity, tradition, and idiom, it can also be prejudicial. Hence the predicament of William Drummond of Hawthornden, a fine Scottish poet who has for generations been passed over by the canon-builders. While Vaughan remains misunderstood because his British-Welsh affiliations have been sold short, Drummond has been neglected for more contradictory reasons. The Victorians admired his lyricism, but his Scottish taste for French Petrarchanism led him to write verse very different from the English 'metaphysical' poetry that was favoured by T. S. Eliot and his followers. (Long before Dryden quipped that Donne affected the metaphysics and perplexed the minds of the fair sex with nice speculations, Drummond expressed disapproval of 'metaphysical *Ideas* and *Scholastical Quiddities*' in verse.)[46] As a result he was sidelined by English and American critics and assumed to be a poet for specialists in Scottish literature—an ironic fate given that, for anachronistic reasons, such readers were keener to disown than read him.

As I show in Chapter 4, it is hard to place Drummond summarily. When he praised James VI for visiting Scotland in 1617 by emphasizing the success of his Scottish kingship up to 1603, or gave the Dunfermline-born but anglicized Charles I a crash-course in Scottishness in the *Entertainment* that he wrote for his belated coronation in Edinburgh, Drummond looked at events from a Caledonian point of view. But he was cold-shouldered by later Scottish intellectuals because he purged his texts of Scots vocabulary and wrote in Southern English. This was pragmatic of him, not unpatriotic; he was adding another tongue to a repertoire that, for lairds of his generation, had to be plural, and keeping up with the language used at the Scottish king's court (now in London). Yet he abandoned Scots at the very moment when the accession of James to the English throne initiated, or anticipated, the incorporation of Scotland into a British state, and the accident of being in on that moment left him open to the charge of contributing to a history of lost national self-determination, even though that history was driven by (mostly later) economic and political forces which owed nothing to him.

This gets me towards the core of my topic. I am interested in seventeenth-century writers who are anglophone but not necessarily English and who often have no place in the canon, or, more insidiously, are there on the wrong footing. The *English* of my title thus performs several tasks (layered as the word is with meanings left by the conflicted, appropriative history excavated by this book). It is a linguistic term broad enough to encompass Hiberno-English and Scots—the latter often known to its early modern speakers as Inglis.[47] It refers to a discipline ('the author teaches English at Cambridge') in need of devolution in its account of the seventeenth century. And it points to the mutual implication of English as a language with English ethnicity, nationhood, and the related beliefs and social practices that spread through seventeenth-century Britain and Ireland by means of plantation, legal reform, evangelization, trade, and so on.

I use *English* as plurally as this to free myself to range about, not to signal any intention to make a comprehensive survey of the literature of the period. A huge amount of writing goes undiscussed in this book because it does not highlight the devolutionary and interactive dynamics that most concern me (those dynamics that are evoked by my other title word, *Archipelagic*); yet in principle a place could be found for all seventeenth-century anglophone literature within its framework. Topics that preoccupied readers right across Britain and Ireland, issues that might be thought 'universal' (witchcraft, for instance, or cookery),[48] often turn out to be geoculturally variable in the treatment writers accord them. However one defines literature—a category which, in this book, includes sermons, chronicles, and polemics, in line with seventeenth-century usage—it is stuff made out of language, and the appearance in a text of south-eastern, Hiberno-English, Scots, or Anglo-Welsh vocabulary can have potent implications regarding affiliation and identity. It should also be emphasized that although this book is large it does not begin to exhaust the stock of works from the period which are self-conscious about the make-up of the British-Irish entity. The sheer quantity of such material is hardly surprising given that the compound, unresolved nature of British-Irish geopolitics was such an involving and troublesome matter. Neither is it strange that writers who strike us as in other respects ambitious and engaged (Shakespeare, Morgan Llwyd, Defoe) should show, in some part of their output, a preoccupation with these issues, nor that this preoccupation should feed back into areas of their work that primarily deal with other subjects.

With writers who inhabit the centre—to assert a simplistic topology for the time being—such as the Londoner Ben Jonson, we need to remind ourselves that divisions and connections run everywhere, both genealogically and in microgeography. Thus, when James VI became king of England, Jonson, already connected to Welsh literary circles,[49] got interested in his own Scottish-border ancestors, moved into Scottish households in London, went on a walking tour to Edinburgh,[50] and wrote masques about Anglo-Scottish union and the place of Ireland and Wales in the Jacobean system.[51] His case is far from unique. For example, his friend, the antiquarian Robert Cotton, renamed himself Robert Bruce Cotton after 1603 and made himself an authority on the history of Scotland. Seventeenth-century Anglo-English writers often situated themselves more self-consciously within British-Irish diversities than modern scholars have noticed. And the reassertion—which always means the reinvention—of English identity, customs, and chronicle history, among common lawyers, dramatists, poets, and others, in the wake of James I's arrival in London, or among parliamentarian apologists during the British-Irish wars of the 1640s, should be understood not as a mere recrudescence of old formations but as flexible, contingent responses to the pressures of impending plurality.

If Anglo-Eng. Lit. is as amenable to archipelagic re-reading as texts from Wales, Scotland, or Ireland, it also, as urgently, requires it. A devolutionary approach can recover the ethnic affiliations, the pride in ancient institutions (courts of law, crown in parliament), and the growing confidence in vernacular literary achievement that contributed to the configuration of early modern Englishness. It can strip from seventeenth-century formulations—always inflected by gender, status, region, age-related and other factors—the accretions which built up later as England became the centre of an international empire (one largely administered by Scotsmen).[52] The potency of English identities, and their expansive influence around the archipelago, can be critically represented without the overall perspective becoming Anglocentric. What one discovers is that Englishness was a contested resource as much for writers engaging with readers as for leaders mustering armies, and that 'England' was a shifting entity, open to reconceptualization, defined against and meshed with its neighbours. That is why this book includes chapters on such figures as Milton and Marvell (7 and 9) whose Englishness is often taken as given, rather than historical, inherited, and refashioned.

More is usually known about the circumstances of authors like Jonson, Milton, and Marvell than is the case with anglophone writers outside England. For the latter, fresh research is needed to reconstruct their literary environments. And then one finds that to devolve Vaughan to Brecknockshire or the Irish Protestant Roger Boyle, Earl of Orrery to County Cork (Chapters 6 and 8) is not to arrive at points of resolution but to discover, within the local, signs of those larger perplexities which produce such hybrid phenomena as Vaughan's Welsh Anglicanism and Orrery's Anglo-Irish and British politics (working for Cromwell in Scotland, for the Duke of Ormond in Dublin, for Munster Protestants in Westminster, and for himself everywhere he went). The seventeenth century saw a plethora of cultural as well as geopolitical interactions that drew many parts of the Stuart kingdoms into new relationships.

(ii) Elizabethan to Jacobean: Shakespeare

Though a distinctively post-1603 British-Irish matrix took time to develop, its imminence could be anticipated and in some measure encouraged by writing. Many historians would date the beginnings of Anglo-Scottish union back to policies, pamphlets, and poems framed on both sides of the border in the 1540s, reinforced by diplomatic realignments in 1558–60.[53] It was announced, however, in the panegyrics[54] and treatises[55] that greeted James's arrival in England and his state entry (delayed by plague) into London.[56] Well-established genres were hospitable. Anthony Munday's city pageant, *The Triumphes of Re-vnited Britania* (1605), for instance, revives the legends about ancient British unity set out in Geoffrey of Monmouth's twelfth-century *Historia regum Britanniae*. Though Galfridian myths about Britain faded out of civic entertainments, they persisted in court masques right through the Caroline period.[57] The resources of Jacobean unionism were not entirely legendary and secular. Protestant opinion in Scotland had often been more favourably inclined to Britishness than had the Catholic allies of France. This fed into royalist discourse as a whole after 1603. Finding in the Old Testament a divinely sanctioned, auspicious precedent for regal union, orators and clerics likened James to David, the heroic king who commanded the loyalty of both Israel and Judah.[58]

State construction always involves a degree of ad hoc fabrication. Thus the coinage issued under James brought the Scottish lion into what must have been for contemporaries a disconcerting conjunction with the Irish harp and the English rose, circulating miniature, valuable images of union across the islands. The 'half laurel', worth ten shillings (alluding to a wreath shown on the king's head) and the 'unite', worth twenty-two shillings (its name picking up the coin's celebration of union) carried the legend, in Latin out of Hebrew, 'Faciam eos in gentem unam' ('I will make them one nation'—Ezekiel 37: 22). As with coins, so with flags. It was now, in 1606, after several discarded designs, that the cross of St George gules was imposed on a white saltire cross of St Andrew, against a blue background, to make the 'Union Jack'. (North of the border, the Scots had a way of surmounting the saltire over the red cross.)

Yet if Britishness invented icons and disseminated inscriptions of unity, it also claimed relics and ruins. Antiquarians dug around in the records, not always to the advantage of union. William Camden's *Britannia* (1586) was enlarged, translated, and reprinted; his *Remaines of a Greater Worke, Concerning Britaine*, which appeared in 1605, was expanded in 1614, and several times reissued. Both were followed by James Ussher's *Discourse of the Religion Anciently Professed by the Irish and Brittish* (1622/1631), John Spottiswoode's *History of the Church of Scotland* (1655), and a dozen similar treatises.[59] At the cheap end of the market, almanacs came to declare their Britishness on title pages, and provided tide-tables and astrological predictions that covered the whole island.[60] In ballads and drinking songs, the field of reference expanded, as it did on stage, where a late-Elizabethan taste for English chronicle history gave way to such Stuart-British works as *King Lear*.

To throw the implications of 1603 into relief—1707 and its aftermath will be looked at in Chapters 11–12—I want to pause for a moment over Shakespeare, who is in this as in other respects acutely responsive to his time and place.[61] *King Lear* (1606) is merely the most conspicuous example of his turn to British and archipelagic subject matter after 1603. Though alert, during the 1590s, in *Richard II* and the *Henry IV* plays, to rebellion and cross-border encroachment coming out of Ireland, Scotland, and Wales—material which reflects indirectly on Hugh O'Neill, Earl of Tyrone's revolt in Elizabethan Ulster[62]—he focussed on England itself, both as a power in France and a scene of internal division. The first and second tetralogies of history plays have behind them the civil strife that flared up along regional and religious lines in the England of Shakespeare's childhood.[63]

It is true that the Scots are prominent in *Edward III* (1590–4), which I take to be partly Shakespearean,[64] but as old enemies of England and allies of the French. When King David declares that his 'bonny riders', with their 'byting whinyards', will make Edward cry for mercy,[65] his pride comes before a fall. After spilling across the border in search of easy spoils, the Scots show their mettle by fleeing from an approaching English army. If *Edward III* was written with James's aspirations to succeed Elizabeth in view (ambitions that had been strengthened by his marriage to Anne of Denmark in 1589), it would have to be categorized as hostile.

bonny: comely   *whinyards*: short swords

In this it shares an outlook with such early 1590s works as Peele's *Edward I* and Greene's *George a Greene*. Even plays of this period which include advocacy of Anglo-Scottish union—Greene's *James IV*, for example—tend to be cross-cut with anti-Scottish, if not anti-Jacobean, sentiment.[66] By 1598, the year in which *Edward III* was published, Elizabeth's agent in Edinburgh was writing to her to say that offence was being taken 'that the comedians of London should in their play scorn the King and people of this land'.[67]

In *Henry V* (1600), by contrast, with a Jacobean succession not only likely but supported by patrons such as Essex with whom Shakespeare has been associated, the tone is different. In Act I, Edward III's conflict with the Scots is spoken of as well as his victories against the French, and 'the Weazell (Scot)' is noted as a possible threat to English security if Henry takes his army to France.[68] It is, however, a threat which seasoned observers discount, and it does not materialize. As the play moves forward, it leaves behind the legacy of medieval Anglo-Scottish antagonism and introduces Captain Jamy as a peacemaker among a group of Scottish, Irish, and Welsh officers who caricature, in their fractiousness, the difficulties that James VI would have to deal with when he came to power in England/Wales and Ireland. The irenic manner of Jamy the Scot has not been picked out by commentators, but audiences would have recognized it as one of James VI's most vaunted qualities. Equally conspicuous is his swearing by the mass and by Our Lady. This might be merely a sign that the north is linguistically old-fashioned, but it could also, more insinuatingly, play on James's association with his Catholic mother, Mary Queen of Scots, and the belief that he would extend toleration to recusants if he inherited the English throne. That the sequence involving the captains appears only in the 1623 Folio of Shakespeare's plays (III.iii. TLN 1192–258), and is absent from a quarto (1600) which reflects early performance, suggests that it was never staged—a victim of the sensitivity of Anglo-Scottish and British-Irish relations during Elizabeth's declining years.[69]

Hamlet (1601?) is equally though less explicitly alive to the prospect of union. That the tragedy has a Scottish background has long been recognized, because of the closeness with which the Old Hamlet-Claudius-Gertrude triangle shadows the relationship between Mary Queen of Scots, her murdered husband, Darnley, and her later husband, his killer, Bothwell.[70] To return the play to its moment, however, we need to be conscious not just that the Danish practice of elective monarchy was bound to interest audiences given the reluctance of Queen Elizabeth to nominate a successor but that Denmark was part of a Norwegian-Danish state which provided a model for Anglo-Scottish Britain. When, at the end of the play, the young Norwegian Fortinbras assumes the crown of Denmark, the Scandinavian kingdoms move towards the compound form that would characterize them throughout the medieval and early modern periods. (It was a state structure which, for a time, incorporated a third kingdom, Sweden—a point not lost on the Irish dramatist, Henry Burnell, when, in 1640, he drew on sources close to those of *Hamlet* to explore the three-way conflicts between the Stuart kingdoms.)[71] The analogy with a Scottish prince claiming rights of memory in England, and threatening to take the throne, if necessary by force,[72] would have struck Shakespeare's audience. Even the north-south geography of Norway-Denmark supported the analogy.

After James's accession we have *King Lear*, about the break-up of Britain into three realms (then two), a play which engages, scholars agree, with the debate about Anglo-Scottish union that raged between 1603 and 1607, when the king's own ambitious scheme for full political union (*una rex, una lex, una grex*),[73] itself perhaps a bargaining gambit, was rejected by the House of Commons. It would be fatuous to claim that the irregular, overloaded, speculative world of this tragedy can be reduced to topicality. Yet Lear's 'diuision of the Kingdome' (or, as the quarto puts it, 'kingdomes')[74] is what triggers the action, and the issue, disconcertingly, returns in the closing moments of the drama. Shakespeare wrote *King Lear* as one of a company known as The King's Men; he and his fellow-actors were members of the royal household, and the play was premiered, in all likelihood, at court. There are telling points of contact between James's intellectual obsessions (with prophecy, astrology, number) and the tragedy,[75] but the primary connection is geopolitical. With controversy going on in pamphlets and parliament about the innate unity or plurality of Britain, the audience was invited to gauge how wise Lear was to split it into the traditional realms of the north (the Duke of Albany's portion with Gonerill), the Celtic West (Cornwall and Regan), and fertile southern England, intended for Cordelia.

The major elements of *Lear*—division, filial ingratitude, the king's madness and death—come from medieval legend. The initiating act of the play is not just derived from Geoffrey of Monmouth but echoes the origins of British history as Geoffrey described them. In the *Historia*, he tells how Brut, the grandson of Aeneas (Roman hero and fugitive from Troy),

after many adventures in North Africa, the Mediterranean, and Gaul, took
command of the island that subsequently bore his name. His legacy was
problematic. In the royal conduct book, *Basilikon Doron*, first privately
printed in Scotland in 1599, King James warned his eldest son, Henry, that
if he came to power in England he should not break up Britain when he
died: 'otherwayes by deuiding your Kingdomes, yee shall leaue the seede of
diuisione and discorde among your posteritie'. A London edition of 1603
adds: 'as befell to this Ile: by the diuision and assignement thereof, to the
three sonnes of *Brutus, Locrine, Albanact*, and *Camber*'.[76] The addition shows
the king appealing to English readers as well as instructing Henry. It reflects
a greater liking for Geoffrey south of the border, because his account of
Brut's succession granted the English crown suzerainty of Scotland.

Yet if *Lear* is, like Munday's *Triumphs of Re-vnited Britania*, a Galfridian
text about British antiquity, its subplot uses names that were prominent in
more recent, Anglo-Saxon history: Edmund and Edgar. The collaging of
periods becomes more explicable when one notices that Jacobean pamphlets
about union often cite Edgar (who ruled 959–75) as the monarch who
drew the seven kingdoms of Saxon England into a single polity while
also laying claim, like James, to a more extensive, British imperium. At
the end of the quarto, which was printed from a manuscript written in
about 1605–6, the legendary ruler of the north, the Duke of Albany (one
of James's own titles), reluctantly takes up the mantle of authority; in the
Folio, which derives from a later, revised text, Edgar is assigned the last lines
of the play, given to Albany in the quarto, and implicitly takes command.[77]
Two models of monarchical union, Scoto-Britannic and Anglo-Scottish,
compete within the fraught, exhausted density of the tragedy's ending. Are
we looking, here, at two stages of composition, or at versions of the play
aimed at different audiences, at court and in the Globe theatre?

The impact of Jacobean union is as evident where it is most diffusely
felt, in Shakespeare's growing interest in how different kinds of state
structure deal with unrest and change. As early as *Titus Andronicus* he
had explored (perhaps in collaboration with Peele) the choice between
patrilineal primogeniture and election as a way of selecting monarchs,
and he had shown, in the rule of Saturninus, how damaging the former
arrangement, orthodox for England, could be. But there was a new
concentration, from the late 1590s, on dispensations very different from
those found in the early history plays. The presence of *Henry VIII* in
the later Jacobean output shows that the shift was incomplete between

plays which assume (however disruptedly) a dynastic, national order of
things and the more heterogeneous, imperial state structures explored in
Anthony and Cleopatra and *Cymbeline*. But Shakespeare's response to the
conditions of James's multiple, imperial monarchy goes far beyond the
three-kingdoms resonance of Octavius Caesar's declaration, at the end
of *Anthony and Cleopatra*, that 'the three ... nook'd world | Shall beare the
Oliue freely' (IV.vi. TLN 2582–3). Certainly, *Coriolanus*, which works
with London perceptions of Anglo-Scottish difference in the polarity that
it establishes between the fractious, politically complex world of Rome
and the more archaic, aristocratic, and militaristic milieu of the Volscians,
responds to the stubbornness of MPs in the Commons (Tribunes of the
people) during the union debate as it reached its climax in the parliamentary
session of 1607.[78]

As the issues of representation and authority in *Coriolanus* show, the
formation of a state involves more than constitutional machinery. It is
bound up with the disposition and legitimation of power throughout an
entire social order, which is why the best account of the subject for the
early modern period in England (and to some extent Scotland and Wales)
is more concerned with local office-holding than with the higher reaches
of authority or with Renaissance political theory.[79] This is one direction
in which we should look for evidence of a response to regal union and
its associated debates in Shakespeare, and we find it in *Macbeth*, which, as
I show in Chapter 2, ties the destiny of Scotland, and of Anglo-Scottish
alliance, to the rules, favours, and deceptions that govern the distribution
of titles and offices, and the connected, ostensibly more exalted question
of whether kings should be in some measure chosen (according to Gaelic
tradition) or inherit their royal authority by patrilineal right.

With *Macbeth*, however, we are back with drama which deals explicitly
with the British-Irish polity. Often called 'The Scottish Play', this composite, highly political tragedy, with its English scenes and its Danish and
Irish aspects, is not confined to the Scotland of Holinshed's *Chronicles* but
deeply implicated in archipelagic issues. As I show in my analysis, the play's
response to its moment is so searching that it sees beyond the horizon of
Jacobean geopolitics to the playing out of British-Irish problems in the
1640s and far beyond—not only staging the witches but appropriating
their prophetic power. In its account of the kerns and gallowglasses led
against Duncan by Macdonwald, and later headed by Macbeth, it reaches
into questions about the 'pacification' of Ulster and its reduction to a

British enclave—an objective not yet achieved, despite (and because of) the plantations imposed during Shakespeare's lifetime. As it happens, the play most often correlated with Ireland is not, however, literally about kerns and gallowglasses, but a magical island in the Mediterranean which is fused with the colonial conditions of Virginia and the Caribbean. Head-on declarations that Caliban is a Gaelic Irishman, Prospero an English planter, and so on, cannot be persuasive. But quantities of critical scholarship have built the case that Ireland does not fade out of Shakespeare after *Henry V*, but draws its kingdom-and-colonial, its ethnic/class and linguistic conflicts into *The Tempest*—the play most often taken (with some disregard of *Henry VIII* and *The Two Noble Kinsmen*) as Shakespeare's final, summary achievement.[80]

Early modern Ireland has also been claimed as a context for *Cymbeline*,[81] but this late, inventive tragicomedy more evidently explores the legendary bases of Britishness. Along with *Lear* it shows how attracted Shakespeare was after 1603 to what medievalists call 'the matter of Britain'.[82] This extravagant, syncretic mixture of romance, psychological intrigue, hard pastoral, and chronicle drama is also (by general consent) topical. Like the well-known map in John Speed's *Theatre of the Empire of Great Britaine* (1612) that is reproduced as Fig. 1, it construes the regal union of James VI and I through the prism of Cunobelinus—a pre-Christian British monarch credited by scholars of Shakespeare's generation with reigning over a period of harmony and increasing civility. Speed's map presents an eclectic surface, ornamented with cherubs, compass-points, and elaborate calligraphy, but it translates division into balance by pairing, west and east, the arms of James VI and I with the Orkneys—whose incorporation was in hand (below, p. 43)—views of London and Edinburgh, and two sides of a quasi-imperial ancient British coin. Shakespeare's play has a similar drive to order and reconciliation, but it turns to dramatic advantage (among other sublunary irregularities) the difficulties of regal union by exposing what was mixed and unresolved in 'the Empire of Great Britaine'.

It is often rather smoothly argued that *Cymbeline* was written to coincide with the investiture of James's eldest son as Prince of Wales in 1610. Yet Henry was, strictly speaking, invested as Prince of Wales and of Britain, a title which reflects the peculiar position of Wales. Unlike such Elizabethan plays as *I Henry IV* and *The Merry Wiues of Windsor*, where Welshness is linguistically alien (Mortimer's wife) or troublesomely

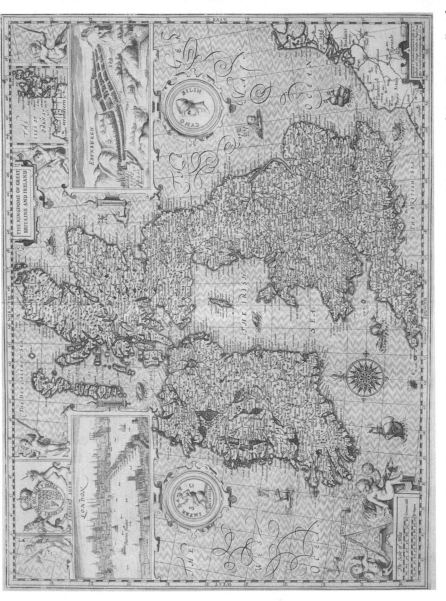

Fig. 1. 'The Kingdome of Great Britaine and Ireland', in John Speed, *The Theatre of the Empire of Great Britaine* (London, 1612). The Jacobean imperium, stamped with ancient legitimacy by Cunobelin, Shakespeare's Cymbeline, the king of south-east Britain (fl. 9 AD–42 AD).

rebellious (Glendower) or ludicrous (Parson Evans),[83] *Cymbeline* seeks an accommodation between the invented Britishness of the 1603 union and the claims to ancient British survivalism that were particularly made for Wales. As I show in Chapter 3, the play's pan-British design helps explain why it absorbs into Welsh-Britonic events an episode from Holinshed's *Historie of Scotland*. That this synthesis was achieved, however, by excluding even from scenes set around Milford Haven (or should that be Aberdaugleddyf?)[84] any characters born and bred in what would later become 'Wales' is a sign of how artifical, selective, and uncertainly founded—how compatible with the ethos of tragicomedy—Jacobean Britishness could be.

(iii) Problematics

Though literary scholars have neglected the archipelagic scope of seventeenth-century anglophone writing, historians have been more as-siduous in pursuit of their material. Over the last decade or so there has been an explosion of interest in 'the new British history' and 'the British problem'. It is usual to trace these developments back to J. G. A. Pocock's call in the 1970s and early 1980s for a 'British history [that] denotes the historiography of no single nation but of a problematic and uncompleted experiment in the creation and interaction of several nations'.[85] Pocock was hardly the first to notice that different parts of the Atlantic archipelago (the neutral term he substitutes for the so-called British Isles) 'interacted so as to modify the conditions of one another's existence'.[86] As I have said, Macaulay and Gardiner wrote with an expansive sense of the canvas on which the multi-stranded stories of the islands were worked out.[87] Yet the dismissive response to Pocock's initial proposals[88] shows that he was not pushing at an open door.

As a New Zealander, Pocock felt moved to reassess British history at a time when the United Kingdom was turning its back on the Common-wealth and joining the European Economic Community. It was as though Britain deserved one last look as it put its empire behind it; there was a case for reviewing the origins and growth of the overseas expansion which such late Victorian historians as Seeley had made their triumphalist theme. If this put Pocock out of phase with UK historians, their own history caught up with them in the 1980s, when the protracted agony of Northern Ireland, where the Troubles had restarted in 1969, and growing pressure for

devolution in Scotland and Wales, against a background of harsh and assertively English Thatcherite government from Whitehall, combined with
a crisis in historical scholarship itself to give Pocock's call for a new British
history fresh appeal and put the British problem on the table.

That crisis within the discipline stemmed from the success with which
a group of revisionists put in doubt received explanations for the outbreak
of the English civil war.[89] Having discredited, to their satisfaction, both the
Whig account, which emphasized the disruptive effect of quarrels between
crown and parliament, and the more broadly based Marxist analysis, which
cited the decay of feudalism, economic restructuring, dearth, and class
conflict, the revisionists had to explain why the political order collapsed
so quickly in 1641–2. Conrad Russell and others showed that the finances
of the crown had been weakened by the conservatism of Queen Elizabeth
(who limited expenditure rather than increasing taxation), so that James and
Charles inherited an underfunded state. It was agreed that developments in
legal and constitutional thought (jurisprudence, republican theory, history
of the common law) made the limitation of royal prerogative defensible
for those in the kingdoms who resisted the expediencies to which the early
Stuart monarchs were driven. There were long-standing conflicts within
the British and Irish churches about the proper limits of reformation,
and Arminian innovations in England sponsored by the crown triggered
reactions that seem less disproportionate if one shakes off a modern secular
perspective and empathizes with the beliefs of the period. There was,
however, a further factor, evident to historians once they looked beyond
the islands and noted the instability, all over seventeenth-century Europe,
of the compound states known as multiple monarchies.[90]

While Charles I was losing control in Scotland and Ireland, in 1638–41,
Spain, at odds with Portugal, had to cope with a separatist rebellion in
Catalonia, a rebellion encouraged by France much as Catholic unrest in
Ireland was fostered by Spain. Was this not a clue to how the Stuart
state unravelled? A new historiographical paradigm developed in which
'the British problem'—the difficulty of managing the three kingdoms in
a single state system—had a leading role in explaining the breakdown
in royal authority.[91] An archipelagic approach to what was now called,
not the English civil war, but the war of the three kingdoms[92]—or,
more convincingly, given the elements of civil strife within each of the
Stuart realms, and the conflict's chronological phases, the *wars* of the
three kingdoms—became de rigueur for many. But the scope of enquiry

enlarged, because the challenges encountered by Charles I in Scotland and Ireland were long-standing (recall Tyrone's rebellion in the 1590s) and continued beyond the Restoration. So the British problem of the late 1630s and early 1640s began to cast its shadow over the entire seventeenth century.[93]

From the outset it was clear that there were problems with the British problem. The most glaring of them is apparent—as a literary critic might be expected to say—in the language of the formula. Why use 'the *British* problem' to cover all three kingdoms? The failure to mention Ireland, even though turbulence in Ireland most immediately triggered the crisis of 1641–2,[94] betrays an Anglo-British bias that has often been complained of in work associated with the project. Conrad Russell's too glancing recantation of 1995, where he replaces 'the British problem' with 'a British and Irish problem', makes for piquant reading.[95] Even the term that the formula does use is potentially misleading. 'British' was not widely current in the seventeenth century and it had specialized, now subsumed, meanings. The word 'Britain' goes back to ancient Greek and Latin. It was not, however, until the early sixteenth century that it was used with any regularity to designate the interlinked Anglo/Welsh-Scottish polities; and despite James VI and I's attempts to put 'Great Britain' into circulation ('Great' to distinguish his British state from Brittany), it was only after 1707 that it came into everyday speech. 'British' had related but subtly different implications; it was used, for instance, by Welsh literati to claim descent for their countrymen from the Brythonic peoples who survived west of the Severn after the Anglo-Saxon invasions. Britishness of this sort was attributed to Harri Tudur (Henry VII) and his progeny, until James VI and I, who had his own descent from Harri, could be said to have brought about what Merlin had prophesied in Geoffrey's *Historia*: the return to power of British/Welsh stock in an island that had long been dominated by their English neighbours.

The word 'British'—though hard to avoid, and in some contexts legitimate—carries further dangers. It tends to imply if not the existence then the inevitability of a state that was only just, unevenly, forming, in the seventeenth century, and it suggests that there was more cultural Britishness around the islands than can be found. While literature of the period includes officially sponsored accounts of imaginary, often antique Britishness (as in court masques), and testifies to the existence of vital interfaces which encouraged hybridization (e.g. Anglo-Welsh puritan writing), the record is also riven—especially in texts from Ireland—with inter-ethnic strife. Overall there are few signs of a newly synthesized identity; and it is questionable how complete that synthesis would ever become.[96] As Chapter 12 brings out, the Anglo-Scottish union of 1707 did not generate a fully integrated British nation, any more than the British-Irish union of 1801 settled 'the Irish problem'. There were several versions of Britishness—regionally, confessionally, and institutionally various—and they overlaid or accompanied other affiliations and identities. Hence the later, centrifugal dynamics of the wishfully named United Kingdom. After World War I, the violent birth of the Irish Free State was associated with the stirrings of secession in Scotland and Wales (cf. Hugh MacDiarmid and Saunders Lewis), and the pressure for devolution grew during the 1970s with a rapidity that was symptomatic of underlying fragmentation, as the advantages of joint involvement in the British empire evaporated in the wake of decolonization and as the prosperity of heavy industry in South Wales and on the Clyde declined. At that point entities that had been relatively distinct in the seventeenth century began to reassert themselves—though irreversibly modified by interaction, and the conditions of modern nationalism—as small nations.

Outside Wales, the first group of people to be both identified, and, at times of crisis, to identify themselves, as 'British', were the English and Scottish settlers who established, after 1609, those plantations in the North of Ireland which lie somewhere behind the bombings and shootings that started in Belfast and Derry in 1969—events in a 'British' statelet notoriously unassimilable to Britain. Far from being produced on the 'mainland', out of a blend of traits from both sides of the Tweed, Britishness was projected into Ulster,[97] a feature of what many would call colonial identity. Before it became, after 1707, a common word in Scotland or (a little later) England to describe people north and south of the border, 'British' was used of settlers in the sugar islands of the Caribbean, a part of the early empire which drew in large numbers of Scots and Irish (many transported there by Cromwell) as well as English fortune-hunters. Later in the seventeenth century, there was a great deal of multi-ethnic emigration to the middle Atlantic colonies, and there again the settlers were known as 'British'.

A second problem with the British problem is that the formula is singular while its applications have become plural. The webs which entangled Charles I may connect with the archipelagic issues his father dealt with three decades earlier and those which brought down his son James II and VII in 1688–91, but it takes a degree of reductiveness to extract a common principle. Of course, contemporaries *could* be reductive, and they tended, especially in England, to blame popish plots for three-kingdom instability,[98] but paranoia, though historically significant, and a vital force in literary representation, is never more than a partial explanation for how events panned out. This is one reason why, although seventeenth-century observers often write with an acute sense of the problematic interactiveness of the three kingdoms,[99] they do not have an agreed term to designate the evolving perplexities.

At the same time, the single formula drew on, developed, and has transmitted several different accounts of what exactly was problematic. Since the publication of Michael Hechter's *Internal Colonialism* in 1975—a book with a century of Marxist historiography behind it—conflict in the early modern archipelago has often been seen as a consequence of English expansion.[100] The story can be told (as Steven Ellis has told it) as one of imperial state-building: denied a continental outlet by the growing power of France, the English (Tudur/Tudor) crown extended its power into Wales at the expense of marcher lords, then into Ireland on similar terms; after threatening the independence of Scotland, it advanced in the seventeenth century by the paradoxical means of two Scottish-born monarchs, James VI and Charles, asserting English dominance. It reached its fullest extent not under a Stuart king but in the Cromwellian union of 1654. In some versions of this account, core zones of 'civility' in southern England, Lowland Scotland, and Leinster extended their influence into Gaelic Irish, Welsh, and Highland peripheries or frontiers or marchlands. In others, Ireland is viewed as anomalous among the three kingdoms, a site of colonial exploitation which shows in advance the strategies by which England and later Britain would become global imperial powers.

A further perspective again emphasizes religion. In charting this difficult territory, John Morrill led the way,[101] though the idea that British-Irish difficulties were geared to confessional difference had been part of the historiography since David Hume. This account of the archipelagic problem noted how the Reformation produced dissonance within each of but also between the three kingdoms, which the European-wide early modern principle, that the monarch's religion would determine the official faith of his realm (*cuius regio, eius religio*), could not settle. Like the expanding-English-imperium thesis, the religious-dissonance explanation will be sifted, along with much literary evidence, in Section (iv) of this introduction, and throughout the book. What needs stating at this point is that it is itself potentially problematic that analyses of 'the British problem' should turn out to involve any one of several explanatory schemes, or a mixture of them, because the forces said to be decisive were not always complementary; yet it is overall a strength of the scholarship that it has drawn in such a range of factors. The most persuasive accounts of events in the seventeenth-century archipelago recognize that no single paradigm is sufficient.

A question that follows is whether the overlapping, sometimes jarring problematics pushed the three kingdoms towards conflict, or only came to life when animated by other factors that more radically motivated unrest. My own reading in literature has encouraged me to be wary of attributing primacy to the rather piecemeal set of explanatory devices associated with 'the British problem'. It has also reinforced my sense that, as Pocock himself has stressed,[102] we should not be so dogmatically anti-Anglocentric as to deny that among the wars of the three kingdoms was a serious, bloody process, highly generative of literary material, that can be called 'the English civil war' (1642–6). (That this war, from the outset, involved Welsh and Cornish troops, and thus anti-Welsh and anti-Cornish writing in England, only slightly blunts the point.) Although an author such as Drummond presents in his career and writings an almost textbook example of the British problem working itself out, during its classic early Stuart phase, most writers of the period between Shakespeare and Swift are more unevenly involved with geopolitical issues.

The wisest historians of the British problem are always willing to concede that 'there is no point in trying to force a Three-Kingdoms approach where one does not make sense. Sometimes the appropriate unit of inquiry might be the nation or a locality. On occasion the trans-national perspective that beckons might be continental European or trans-Atlantic rather than British and Irish.'[103] The same holds, only more so, for the necessarily—linguistically—hybridized, inherently absorptive, always incipiently deterritorialized anglophone literary text. *Archipelagic English* does not assume that talk of a British problem answers the major questions in seventeenth-century historiography, and it is decidedly not a set of literary illustrations of the thesis; it mounts a broader, less doctrinal, investigation, in the course of which issues underlined by the new British history come into view meshed with others which also impelled the production of literature across the three kingdoms.

A third problem with the British problem is strictly speaking incidental, but it damaged the working-out of the approach in ways which have still not been entirely rectified. In the hands of English historians especially, the analysis was almost on principle top-down. The focus was on affairs of state to the neglect of *mentalité* and those socio-economic difficulties that helped incite the common people into fighting for crown, parliament, and (most often on the parliamentarian side) one or more forms of religion. Such second-wave contributors as Jane Ohlmeyer and Colin Kidd have shown what can be achieved when intellectual and cultural history are investigated in a three-kingdoms matrix,[104] but there is still plenty of scope for literary scholars to make a difference, as Mark Netzloff has shown in his bold, innovative study of *England's Internal Colonies* (2003), which cuts down through the social strata to examine 'Piracy, Conversion, and Nation Space', 'Discourses of Colonial Labour', the role of Gypsies in Anglo-Scottish union, and so on.[105]

There does remain a danger that three-kingdoms literary criticism will inherit the relative indifference to collective consciousness and social division that the once-new British history inherited too freely from high-flying revisionism (with its emphasis on the workings of government). This is so because the temptation is always there to interpret signs of conflict in literary texts along national or ethnic lines even when they have more universal, or pointedly local, socio-economic and ideological determinants. Such a distortion is the more likely because it serves the interests of modern nationalism. My hope is that *Archipelagic English* avoids falling into this trap, and provides a framework that will encourage others to go deeper into popular culture, to probe the entire matrix in which writing was done across the seventeenth century (Netzloff's study is chronologically restricted). The key is no doubt to recognize how overdetermined conflicts were.

Thus, as William Lithgow, Henry Vaughan, Alexander Griffith, and others discussed in Chapters 4 and 6 show, there were ethnically and nationally inflamed disputes, not ethnic or national in origin, around hierarchy, deference, taxation, the imposition of puritan Godliness, and so on, in Scotland and in Wales, as potent as those that have been identified in England—where they for the most part lacked ethnic exacerbation—by social historians from Christopher Hill to Ann Hughes[106] and by a series of literary scholars.[107] In Ireland, perhaps most complexly, status and ethnicity were mutually implicated without the latter erasing the former. A straightforward case would be Thomas Cobbes's 'A Poeme uppon

Cromuell and his Archtrayterous Rabble of Rebellious Racailles, and Englandes Jaolebirdes', in which an Irish Catholic's denunciation of the 'impious' and 'hedge borne' regicides, whose depredations have left 'deere Irelande, sole Relict of the three | Faire Puissant Monarchyes', combines religious dismay with a reassertion of hierarchy.[108] More disconcerting, especially for ethnically inclined nationalists who want to think of Irish as the language of solidarity, is a text such as the *Pairlement Chloinne Tomáis* [*The Parliament of Clan Thomas*] (*c.*1608–15), in which ill-bred Irish upstarts are satirized for speaking uncouth English.[109] Modern readers are likely to sympathize with the view that Irish should be upheld against the encroachments of English, yet the contempt that the author lavishes on his inferiors makes the impurity of their jargon attractively insubordinate. Perhaps the 'Rebellious Racailles' associated with Cromwell had a point when they said that the Irish peasantry should be educated, anglicized, and turned against landlords who wanted to preserve an exploitative Gaelic order for the sake of their own status.

The capacity of literary scholarship to fill out and in some areas challenge the findings of the new British history is particularly clear when it comes to gender. The bare grammatical fact—if there can be such a thing—that the words Hibernia, Britannia, Scotia, and so on have feminine endings does not explain why civic pageants, the iconography of frontispieces, or the profile on page and stage of such women leaders as Boadicea should so obsessively gender nationhood female. Claire McEachern may be italically over-insistent when she writes of 'the *absolutely fundamental quality of gender to national identity*' in Tudor England, but there are reasons to agree that 'For the Tudor-Stuart nation... the volatile contours of female figurality draw the permeable borders of the domestic.'[110] When Britain walked down the aisle, as, in James's account of the union, the wife that he would marry,[111] Ireland was seen as, among other things, a 'yong wenche that hath the greene sicknes for want of occupying',[112] while the linguistic opacity and supposed unruliness of Scottish Gaeldom elicited, from the rhymer John Taylor, on a walking tour from London to Edinburgh, a lurid, frightened, and comic account of how a screeching deaf and dumb girl with breath like sugar-carrion clambered into his bed (a nightmare of coercive union?).[113]

Such loaded, even loathsome, projections of the patriarchal imaginary should be put into conjunction with the realities of cultural access allowed to women across the archipelago. Contrary to the mute, appetitive monstrousness that Taylor found in the Highlands, 'Scottish Gaelic society would seem to have been the culture, out of the three kingdoms and the four nations, where women could function as poets in the most unproblematic way.'[114] This functioning was only ever more or less unshackled because, as the anglophone Scottish poet Mary Oxlie, praising William Drummond for his local patriotism, lamented:

> Perfection in a Woman's worke is rare;
> From an untroubled mind should Verses flow;
> My discontents makes mine too muddy show;
> And hoarse encumbrances of houshold care
> Where these remaine, the Muses ne're repaire.[115]

Yet if women writers were distracted by household care, they were also, more often than men—with positive consequences for historians and literary scholars—tied by that to far-flung estates and parishes: they left plentiful traces of their work in local manuscript networks; they wrote about the places, languages, and families that surrounded them; and they could become, as a result, self-consciously engaged with the politics of location—all of which one sees with Katherine Philips in Chapter 6.

The strongest resistance to talk of a British problem came from those Scottish and Irish historians who complained that the new British history was not genuinely archipelagic but was raiding the record of England's neighbours in order to explain events in English history that were not explicable from internal data. It was a tacitly unionist approach which cut across the integrity of Irish, Scottish, and Welsh histories, and distorted the evidence that was being lifted from 'the Celtic fringe'. It also threatened to interrupt the programmes of research that Irish, Scottish, and Welsh scholars needed to undertake if they were to illuminate the history of their own peoples, including their relationships with England.[116] Against this it was objected that, because of the relative power of the English during the seventeenth century, other peoples on the archipelago were forced to monitor, react to, and live with the consequences of what the English did: a degree of Anglocentrism is legitimate because it is a feature of the period. It was also tendentiously added that those who overlooked this in the rush to avoid the charge of Anglocentrism were misdescribing the period in the interests of modern Scottish, Welsh, and Irish nationalisms.[117]

Returning to these issues in a recent collection of his essays, J. G. A. Pocock has noted that, while the 'enriched' English history produced by early exponents of the British problem was no substitute for fully devolved enquiry, the subsequent tendency of three kingdoms' history to underinvestigate the dominant, incorporating role of England—a role which has long made reflexive political analysis difficult for the English—has left the motor of archipelagic change, and obstacles to adaptation, misunderstood.[118] That strikes me as true, and I agree with Pocock that we need—though this has begun to happen[119]—more writing about the role of England in archipelagic history by Welsh, Scottish, and Irish historians, as well as a willingness to trace the imperial ideology of what would become Great Britain back through James VI and I to Henry VIII. Related challenges face the literary scholar, because devolving seventeenth-century Eng. Lit. requires one to look back from a variety of post-1707 perspectives to understand how English writing of the period came to dominate an Anglo-British canon which also distorted it.

(iv) Localities, ethnicities, nations, empires

In a celebrated, early account of the British problem, Conrad Russell compared the three kingdoms to clashing billiard balls—distinct, dynamic, reactive.[120] Is that how the seventeenth-century polity operated, or was there an untidy patchwork of local, overlapping allegiances? How did literary texts reinforce or reformulate identities? Did the peoples of the islands constitute nations at this date, and has the preoccupation with literature and nationhood which runs through much recent scholarship obscured processes better understood by a focus on state construction? Was the archipelago a self-determining system, or a theatre in which European-wide dynastic struggles and religious wars were fought out? And what of the westward, colonial enterprise in which Ireland ('this famous island in the Virginian sea')[121] could figure as the stepping stone to America? Does the growth of commercial and, during the 1650s, military imperialism from Jamaica to North Africa and eastward to the Indies not weaken the explanatory power of a British-Irish frame of reference? These questions are intractable, and I can only review them briefly, but my conclusion is that key literary and historical vectors converge on the archipelagic.

Seventeenth-century literature does reinforce local attachment, perhaps with heightened particularity in a century which saw so many gentlemen becoming antiquarians.[122] Jacobean readers of Camden, the poetry and prose of Samuel Daniel, Drayton's verse chorography *Poly-Olbion* (1612–22), and many similar texts, were alerted to the intricacy of a multiple monarchy that included not just ancient kingdoms which had themselves been composite (the British tribes reported by the Romans, the Anglo-Saxon Heptarchy, Scots and Picts to the north), but the anomalous kingdom/colony of Ireland, the principality or dominion of Wales, the palatinates of the north and in Ireland, and the scattering of insular lordships and debatable lands that ran from Orkney and Shetland, through the Solway Firth and Man to the Scillies and Channel Islands. When such large questions of union as the relationship between England and Wales were reopened (1603–24), poems and plays harked back to the mosaic of half-traceable entities that underlay the Stuart state system. In *The Welsh Embassador* (1624?), for instance, probably by Thomas Dekker, ancient Britons and Saxons share a cast list largely made up of dukes, princes, and earls representing such residually distinct units as Cornwall, Kent, Chester, and Wales itself.[123]

Yet the hold of inherited divisions on early modern hearts and minds should not be overstated, especially for long-centralized England. It is counterfactually possible that, if Owain Glyn Dŵr, Earl Percy, and Douglas had succeeded in the rebellions against Henry Bolingbroke that Shakespeare dramatizes in *I Henry IV*, a band of principalities reaching from Wales through Northumbria to south-west Scotland would have broken the advance of royal authority both north and south of the Anglo-Scottish border.[124] By the seventeenth century, however, the palatinate jurisdictions of Durham, Cheshire, and Cornwall (with its Duchy and stannary parliaments) had become vehicles for administering royal policy rather than semi-autonomous authorities.[125] At times of crisis, self-interest and loyalty were often locally determined.[126] Yet defining the *extent* of the local has proved a difficult business; attempts to show that the English shire was a natural unit of community have not been successful for any but the greater gentry (most people's outlook was both more parochial and more national).[127] And although the patterns of allegiance show regional variation,[128] no English, Scottish, or least of all Irish gentleman would have calculated the chances of holding onto his lands by considering only the local picture.

If one turns to estate poetry, as a genre with classical sources which was nonetheless an invention of the period covered by this book, the impulse to set the immediate within larger frames is clear. In what is arguably the earliest such poem, Aemilia Lanyer places Cookham—a little lamely—in an expanding, even European context: 'thirteene shires ... all in your sight, | Europe could not affoard much more delight'.[129] As it developed, estate poetry took to using its characteristic, Virgilian motif of *multum in parvo* to process British problems. Thomas Carew's 'To My Friend G. N. from Wrest', for example, gives a finely wrought account of one Bedfordshire estate, but the writing is coloured throughout by the circumstances of its composition in the wake of the First Bishops' War. As the poet declares in his opening lines, the temperate, well-ordered fertility of Wrest Park is the more welcome because he has just returned from serving the king on the cold and mountainous banks of the Tweed. The balmy English midlands provide a haven from the spiky Scottish thistles and brambles that trouble Charles I in 'thc wildc North'. In the absence of royal success, Carew is pointedly reduced to finding images of British security in the moat which encircles the house, like the seas around the Stuart island, and in hunting ('th'embleme of warre').[130]

The very intensity of local identity construction could encourage people to define themselves within national frames. The pageant *Chesters Triumph*, for instance, performed in honour of Prince Henry's investiture as Prince of Wales in 1610, though full of civic pride, makes St George's Day its occasion and the deeds of that English saint its theme.[131] Chester is close enough to Wales to be assertive about not belonging to it. Since this was the period of the Four Shire Controversy, when the English border counties sought to escape Welsh jurisdiction (see Chapter 3), we are not allowed to forget, as viewers or readers of the entertainment, that Chester, brought under the control of the Council in the Marches in the process of incorporation that subsequently became known as the Anglo-Welsh Acts of Union (1536–43), had been released in 1569. As in West Belfast today, where Irish tricolours flutter defiantly along the Falls Road, while the Shankill (scarcely an English street) sports the cross of St George, an identity defined against neighbours employs iconography that brings with it larger attachments.

The prominence of civic pageants in the Elizabethan and early Stuart periods shows that local elites put considerable resources into making cities magnets for loyalty.[132] Symptomatically, however, the pageants looked at in this book deal with more than local issues—with the past and future of Scotland (pp. 153–6) and with relations between the crown in Ireland and Catholic landowners threatened with plantation (p. 170). During the period 1603–1707, larger cities mushroomed, drawing in workers and servants from all over the English and (less so) Scottish,

Welsh, and Irish countrysides, as people travelled further in search of employment;[133] this made it easier to project them not just as historic sites of civility, manufacture, and consumption, but as microcosms of the kingdoms, and as points in an urban web that tied the realms together. Canterbury, Edinburgh, and Dublin were the carriers of meanings generated by the national histories in which they figured, and each of them housed institutions with functions in the multiple polity.[134]

In the case of the metropolis, London, which had built up its own literary ecosystem, around theatres, booksellers, Inns of Court, coffee houses (after the 1650s), and so forth,[135] there were larger resonances, because, as a hive of industry with its own citizen ethos, but also many incomers from all over the archipelago, it could stand for the condition of England, or, as the seat of crown and parliament, the plight of all three kingdoms. During the revolutionary mid-century, as again during the Exclusion Crisis and the ousting of James II and VII, London was a hive of radicalism, as well as of royalist reaction.[136] When the English Republic (the Rump parliament) needed insignia, it adopted the arms of the city.[137] Hence the extrapolating dynamics of such works as Milton's *Areopagitica* (1644), which shifts from a celebration of puritan, intellectual London to a magniloquent appeal to the English people as a whole, and Hester Pulter's 'The Complaint of Thames 1647 When the Best of Kings was Imprisoned by the Worst of Rebels at Holmbie'. Anti-metropolitan complaint and satire had been a feature of English writing since Langland, but the mid-century saw such economically informed thinkers as James Harrington blaming London for bleeding wealth and population away from the rest of the country.[138] The form of regional government introduced by Cromwell under the Major-Generals (1655–7) was an expedient superimposition on older, indigenous structures,[139] but it does reflect a long-standing 'country' distrust of government from the corrupting capital. By the end of the century, the gigantism of London had become, for many, obscene; a dispersal of authority and wealth was called for, and neo-Harringtonian arguments began to modulate, most eloquently north of the border, into anti-unionism.[140]

So while properly grounded accounts of seventeenth-century literature need to be locally informed, national and three-kingdom factors repeatedly impinge. We need to notice how the Cornish appear in Ford's *Perkin Warbeck* or Cowley's broken epic *The Civil War*, as a distinct, unassimilated people,[141] and how events specific to the West Riding of Yorkshire contributed to Marvell's 'Upon Appleton House'.[142] Yet it would be a mistake to overlook how Ford and Cowley's Cornishmen are participants in pan-British conflict, and how Marvell expects readers to know that Fairfax's retirement to Nun Appleton was prompted by his reluctance to attack the Scots, whose royalist-Presbyterian army was poised, at just that time, to march southwards, quite likely into Yorkshire. 'See how the Flow'rs, as at *Parade*, | Under their *Colours* stand displaid.'[143] Though city, parish, townland, county, and regional conditions can be crucial, we are likely to misunderstand them if we do not know what was going on elsewhere in Britain and Ireland.

Fairfax's sympathy with the Scots was not unusual in the north country,[144] where attitudes were shaped by steady contact in the way they were not in London or Bristol. The case is a salutary reminder both that generalizations about English views of the Scots (or the Welsh or even the Irish) are subject to regional qualification—and this is yet more the case, given the Highland-Lowland divide, the other way round—and that proximity to borders complicates perceptions. A border can polarize identities, yet it can also simultaneously create zones, levels, and modes of negotiation and mutual interest. These effects were reinforced in Stuart Britain by the way sovereignty operated. In the modern nation state, authority expands to fill the space of the territory, but during the seventeenth century it still radiated from sites of royal power and faded towards the edges of the realm—where magnates, gentry, gallowglasses, or reivers could prevail. The borders within the archipelago should not be thought of as lines but as elongated regions of weak royal authority (we still speak of 'the Scottish borders' when we mean extensive borderlands); it has been calculated that these areas constituted about half the extent of the Tudor state,[145] and the picture changed only gradually between 1603 and 1707. As the imaginative literature makes clear, the cultural consequences were profound. In plays and poems, the borders were inhabited by the likes of Milton's Comus. The weakness of the crown in the western Highlands and Ulster meant that the areas connected by the North Channel were transit zones for troublesome texts and armaments (e.g., pp. 79, 166, 304–5).

When James succeeded to the English throne, medieval antagonisms still persisted along the Anglo-Scottish border—the ballad of *Chevy Chase* was current for more than epic-heroic reasons (below, p. 277)—but the area was also one of constructive ambiguity. An exasperated official described the people as 'Scottishe when they will, and English at their pleasure'.[146] Like the border counties of Wales, and the margins of British settlement in Ulster, the territory which they occupied was neither internally consistent nor scaled with steady gradations.[147] The resulting ethos of disorder meant that Scottish incivility could be associated not just with the Highlands and Western Isles but with districts close to the supposedly civilizing influence of the south. It could even be associated with border areas which were technically part of England. The broad-tongued, jigging exemplar of Scottish rudeness in Greene's *James IV* is a Redesdale man, from Northumberland.[148]

Pacifying these borders, renamed 'the middle counties', was a priority of James on his arrival in London.[149] His policies enjoyed some success—they built on measures predating regal union[150]—but steps were still being taken more than a decade later to transplant troublemakers to Virginia.[151] That much remained to be done can be deduced from the fulsome complacency of John Taylor's rhyming account (published in 1618) of how he crossed the Esk into Scotland and felt as though he were still on English ground. The district in which he found himself—the Avondale from which Ben Jonson claimed descent—had once been, Taylor remarks, 'the curst climate of rebellious crimes', but now, thanks to the union of the crowns, the borders have been calmed and are 'almost the Center of the land'.[152] Half a century later, Marvell was still urging readers of 'The Loyall Scot' not to sing *Chevy Chase*, and arguing that physical continuity validated union (see Chapter 9). As late as the lifetime of Defoe (below, pp. 341–3), jurisdiction along the border was still not quite resolved and animosity hung in the air.

There were more borders within the archipelago than those between kingdoms. The English Pale around Dublin, for example, had, shrinkingly since the Middle Ages, sustained its own part-Gaelicized culture, and, as poems and pamphlets show, it had a self-defining sense of the unruliness of such abutting Irish districts as the Glens of Wicklow. More diffusely, a frontier consciousness governed the attitude of Scottish Lowlanders to the Western Isles, and of Tudor and Stuart English settlers to the unplanted reaches of Ireland. In the Statutes of Iona (1609), James VI and I outlawed many of the customs of Scottish Gaeldom, and, by the end of his reign, the clans had become more tractable.[153] As late as the 1640s, however, Irish lords retained bards and swordsmen, levied their people, held great feasts; cattleherders practised transhumance, lived in temporary shelters called boolies, and so on. This lifestyle was preserved by a physical inaccessibility to crown agents which the culture did nothing to ameliorate. According to Jane Ohlmeyer, 'it was not until after 1690, and the completion of the Williamite conquest, that the Protestant interest finally closed the frontier in Ireland'.[154] For much of the century parts of the archipelago were if not mutually exclusive then relatively impenetrable. The field of interactivity was not open and single.

What of the peoples whose habitats were inscribed with these borders and frontiers? Ethnic solidarity could be formidable. Language, dress, diet, custom, and popular beliefs about historical origin might divide even small communities (as in villages along the Anglo-Welsh border) and turn them against one another. Most of the English and Irish nobility accepted a Scottish king in 1603. Yet culturally inherited differences between James on the one hand and English courtiers and MPs on the other contributed to friction. That Charles I, decades later, was denigrated as a Scot is telling.[155] When the Commonwealth was threatened, russet-coated captains asserted their freeborn Englishness with an ethnic as well as a common-law thrust.[156] Nor did the shape of the kingdoms neatly coincide with ethnicities; they contained different groups or cut across them. Scotland, for instance, was a jigsaw of Gaelic, Saxon/Norman/Lowland, and Scandinavian-derived peoples, while continuities that ran from Kerry to Inverness meant that the affinities of the *Gaedhil* still cut across the demarcations of multiple monarchy, though with declining potency over the course of the century.[157]

Early modern ethnicity should not be invested with later ideologies of *race*. That difficult word was used to designate the posterity of an ancestor—the British were 'the race of Brut'—but it was not until the late eighteenth century that it acquired the meaning 'One of the great divisions of mankind, having certain physical peculiarities in common' (*OED* n.[2] 2.d), and it was only after Darwin that evolutionary biology gave it a sharper definition again. During the period covered by this book, generalizations were aired about the fickleness of island peoples (a charge often levelled against the English, especially by disappointed Englishmen) and the sluggishness of bog-dwellers, but scholars were caught between an inherited, classical impulse to contrast the civil with the barbarous (a dichotomy which fed into later, indeed modern discourses of race) and an emphasis on common origins, similarity, and relatedness.[158] According to the Bible, all humankind descended from Noah and his family, sole survivors of the flood, and Acts 17: 26 was widely cited: '[God] hath made of one blood all nations of men for to dwell on all the face of the earth, and hath determined the times before appointed, and the bounds of their habitation.'

The Victorian division of the archipelago into Saxon and Celtic peoples had not yet been consolidated by 'the twin influences of romanticism and racialism',[159] though war in Ireland and, to a lesser degree, the Scottish Highlands, did encourage polarization between Gaels and Sassenachs. Antiquarians were interested in what the Saxon invasions had brought to Britain, and new developments in historical philology, from the Scottish humanist George Buchanan in the mid-sixteenth century to the Welsh polyglot Edward Lhuyd in *Archaeologia Britannica* (1707), were teasing out the relationship between different branches of the Celtic tongues.[160] There is some evidence that the word 'Celt' developed ethnically charged implications as the result of a Welsh-inspired reaction to Whig appropriation of the term 'British' after 1688,[161] but most writers in the period, programmed by Old Testament, Noachite beliefs, looked for connections rather than contrasts. It was consistent with royal plans for fuller political union that George Saltern should find, in 1605, that all the peoples of Britain descended from 'branches of the same stock, namely the Cimbri of Gomer, and likewise the Saxons and Danes of Ashkenaz, and of the Scots, of Iberi, of Gubal, and all of Japhet',[162] but the thesis was too ubiquitous to be merely opportunistic.

That ethnic difference remained a source of friction is clear from the way it figures in satire, stage comedy, jestbooks, and the 'character' writing that grew out of classical models in the seventeenth century. This bulky, repetitive body of discourse reassured Englishmen that the Scots were lice-infested, lived on oatmeal, and refused to doff their blue bonnets to their superiors, that the Welsh kept goats, loved cheese, and drank a honey-based brew called metheglin, and that the unkempt Gaelic Irish were partial to bonny-clabber (fermented milk) and papistical superstition. This literature has been sifted by a number of scholars[163] and several points are clear: that the stereotypes were crude and relatively stable (their comic value depended on recognition); that they were reasserted at moments of crisis (as when anti-Welsh feeling flared up among English parliamentarians in 1642); and that changes in the writing—the softening, for example, of images of the Irish after the Restoration, a process interrupted by the Williamite campaigns of 1688–91—reflect large-scale shifts in power relations and security.

To this one can add that such books could be uneasy about their own rationale. The preface to *Bogg-Witticisms* (1682), for instance, explains that it is purveying Irish bulls because the Scots and the Welsh have been mocked in earlier publications (it is, as it were, only fair for the Irish to take their turn), and, implausibly enough, that no national slurs are intended, since generalization about entire peoples would, by implication, affront both taste and reason. Going further, *Wallography: Or, The Britton Describ'd* (1682), by William Richards of Helmdon(?), though classified as anti-Welsh by the older scholarship, can be read as quietly subverting the conventions of ethnic character writing and pricking the complacency of English readers.[164] John Evelyn (if it was he) went so far as to write a pejorative *Character of England* (1659) using the persona of a Frenchman. It shows that the genre had not dissolved into self-parody that within months Anon had published *A Character of France to which is added, Gallus Castratus: Or, An Answer to a Late Slanderous Pamphlet, called the Character of England* (1659).

While the English mocked their neighbours, Scottish and Welsh literati, pushing their respective claims to King Arthur and the Stuart genealogy, plunged into mutual abuse which had an ethnic-national flavour. When paper bullets gave way to real ones, during the 1640s and early 1650s, Presbyterian Scotland and royalist Wales were peculiarly antagonistic and reluctant to join forces. It is symptomatic that Charles I, seeking to galvanize support in 1645, should warn the Welsh gentry that their country had been promised to the invading Scots as a 'prey and reward'.[165] North of the border, Gaelic disdain for kale-eating Lowlanders (below, p. 166) was more than matched by the animus that generated the infamous jibe that God made the first Highlander out of a horse turd.[166] Scottish-Irish antipathies ranged down from elevated arguments about the nationality of Duns Scotus[167] to bitter violence in Ulster between Covenanters and Gaelic Catholics (despite the initial willingness of the 1641 rebels to spare Scottish settlers while pillaging the English). Even within Gaeldom, divisions began to open between the clans and septs across the North Channel. And a visceral dislike of the Irish, as 'wild and savage barbarians, no better than the fearsome Turks', was widespread in Wales[168]—sustained on little contact, though fuelled by anti-papist fears. Among the permutations of hostility, however, the originally medieval but renewed and religiously polarized one between Gaelic Catholic Irish and Protestant incoming English was the most heated and the closest in tone and psychology to modern racism.

It may be quite a step from the dehumanizing picture of the Irish that early modern English commentators revamped from the writings of Giraldus Cambrensis (*c*.1147 − *c*.1220) to Jimmy Rabbitte's quip in Roddy Doyle's *The Commitments* (1987) that 'The Irish are the niggers of Europe', but Spenser was not alone in believing that, since the Gaels by their own account had reached Ireland (those in Connacht, at least) from Spain, then they were, like the haughty Spanish, polluted with Moorish blood.[169] This gave a learned gloss to the folk syllogism that, since good things were fair, and the Irish were bad, it was right to call them 'black'.[170] And the slur gained extra potency from the willingness of English colonizers to learn from the Spanish *reconquista* of Moorish Andalucia, first, that force could legitimately be used to oppress and transplant people of a different faith, who were occupying land in Ireland that, according to many chroniclers, had once been held by ancient Britons,[171] and, second, that Gaelic customs that were infecting the English in Ireland (long hair, easy divorce, and so on) should, like the Morisco traits that had tainted Christians in Andalucia, be outlawed.[172]

There are signs that the Irish at all social levels responded to the racialized hostility of the incomers. We hear, for instance, of rebels in County Mayo picking out 'the English breed of cattle' and putting the beasts through mock-trials. Like Gaels denied the Brehon laws and forced into anglophone courts, where they could not read the 'neck verse' in the Bible that would save them from hanging, the English cattle were given 'the book' to read and when they failed the test were executed.[173] One pro-Gaelic account of the wars that followed the 1641 rising was even more derisive. Describing with grim relish the aftermath of the Battle of Benburb (1646), in which the Ulster Gaelic army won a victory over Protestant forces, the *Aphorismical Discovery of Treasonable Faction* (*c*.1652−9) said that the fallen English were found to be sporting tails and attributed to the Scots sexual organs that were as blue as their bonnets and circumcised like those of Jews ('The tail behinde made knowen the English race, | The blue chopt yarde bewrayed the Scottish face').[174] As for the Irish and blackness, the *Aphorismical Discovery* rebutted any such association when it described how 'a blackamoore, an ould beaten souldier' fought so vigorously for the English at a siege in County Kildare that he was 'either possessed by a deuill or a witche'. The only way of stopping him was to mark the Irish bullets with crosses and kill him with the power of white, Catholic magic.[175]

How readily did ethnicity translate into nationhood? The question is such a semantic and methodological minefield that it is impossible to give an unqualified answer. For 'primordialist' historians, nations grow out of long-established (even ancient) mentalities, ethnically and dynastically configured; hard-line 'modernists', by contrast, insist that nations were constructed over the last couple of centuries to provide a focus of loyalty for populations deracinated by industrialization.[176] Alert to the kitsch and fakely folkloric, a modernist like Ernest Gellner has no difficulty in finding nations which made themselves up only decades ago.[177] This approach is attractive to liberal and many left-wing critics because, by stressing that nations are, in Benedict Anderson's phrase, 'imagined communities',[178] it brings out the capacity of fictions to glue societies together, while encouraging us to despise nationalism as a form of right-wing delusion ripe for deconstruction.

Nothing is easier to mock than the late invention of clan tartan and the iconography of toby jugs, yet there are ethno-symbolic features of dress and diet, architectural style, flag design, coinage, and heraldry within Ireland and Britain which long pre-date the eighteenth-century emergence of nationalist ideology across Europe, and which still mark national attachment. The modernist analysis has lost some of its persuasiveness as old national loyalties have reasserted themselves in Europe in the aftermath of the Cold War. In any case, when the modernist package is tested against the seventeenth century, elements of it can be found in England—where capitalism started early, where the Reformation facilitated the making of a polity more centralized and self-determining in religious as well as secular affairs than late medieval England had been, where the vernacular and its literary achievements were consolidated by print, and where the spread of newsbooks from the 1620s (they emerged later elsewhere in the islands)[179] anticipated the ethos of the modern national society in which, as Hegel noted, the reading of the morning papers replaced the saying of morning prayers.[180]

Fortunately, it is not my remit to determine when 'the English nation' first took shape—a judgement which would have to be hedged about with all manner of definitional caveats—though I am willing briskly to declare that those who date its birth to the Reformation[181] are putting it rather late, while those who locate it before 1066 are probably claiming too much for a late-Saxon kingdom which undoubtedly had a shared sense of ethnicity and legal culture.[182] The great Victorian historians, much preoccupied with this question, from Macaulay through Stubbs to Freeman, argued that the thirteenth century was the period in which a national consciousness emerged. Yet despite—or because of?—the Norman Conquest's imposition of a divided, trilingual society (Latin, Norman French, English),[183] there are signs of a national identity being innovatively worked out in insular French texts as well as in such vernacular romances as *Horn* within decades of 1066.[184] The popularity of Geoffrey of Monmouth—the manuscript legacy is huge—shows that the idea of Britain, its antiquity and uniqueness, was powerful for English readers throughout the Middle Ages. Yet the reality of Anglo-Norman expansion into Wales and Ireland involved a hardening into socio-cultural defensiveness as the military strength of the centre waned. By the thirteenth century the archipelago was thought of as a collection of four countries and English identity was becoming 'raucously strident'.[185]

During the period covered by this book, the dynamics were rather different. The preaching of Protestant divines instilled a belief across all social ranks that the English were an elect (if not *the* elect) nation[186]—a second Israel, favoured by the Lord but sinful.[187] This religiously informed patriotism ('God is English', in Bishop Aylmer's celebrated gloss), reinforced by Spanish threats during the reign of Elizabeth, was challenged in some respects by James's aspirations to union. Yet the Britishness promulgated by James, which became, in the Caroline period—most resplendently in such court entertainments as Carew's *Coelum Britannicum*—a badge of royalist affiliation, was transposed into the vocabulary of mid-century English republicans (hence the title of their newsbook, *Mercurius Britanicus*) because the fate of the Commonwealth was so bound up with Wales and Scotland, as they fell under English sway. At the same time, the civil wars strengthened the association between self-conscious English ethnicity and loyalty to parliament[188] because Charles I drew so much of his support from Wales, Scotland, and Catholic Ireland, and because his defeat shifted power from a Scoto-British dynasty to the New Model Army, which recruited from the English heartlands.[189] For these and other reasons, the 1640s was a vital period of English nation-building.[190] The Commonwealth reinforced structures of attachment that might be local or civic in base and royalist as well as parliamentarian in expression, but which could be harnessed to national allegiance. They could be whipped into xenophobia and exploited in the interests of crown and commerce during the wars against the Netherlands and France that followed the Restoration.

England's closest neighbours present very different pictures. Split by the Anglo-Norman invasion into a principality in the west and marcher lordships to the east,[191] and reduced to semi-colonial status after the suppression of Owain Glyn Dŵr,[192] Wales was given administrative unity at the moment of its incorporation with England (1536–43). As a result, the development of collective consciousness among its newly empowered gentry proved inextricable from British state-formation.[193] This process had a literary aspect. All over Renaissance Europe, scholars were bringing accounts of lands, peoples, and customs into chronicles previously dominated by kings and their wars. The Welsh were no exception, and such works as David Powel's *Historie of Cambria* (1584) can stand beside Buchanan's *Rerum Scoticarum historia* (1582), Edward Hall's English *Chronicle* (1548),[194] Philip O'Sullivan Beare's *Historicae Catholicae Iberniae compendium* (1623), and Seathrún Céitinn's *Foras feasa ar Éirinn* [Geoffrey Keating's *A Compendium of Knowledge about Ireland*] (c.1618–34). Yet, from Sir John Prise's *Yny lhyvyr hwnn [In this book]* (1546) through Arthur Kelton's *A Commendacyon of Welshmen* (1546) and Humphrey Llwyd's *Commentarioli Britannicae descriptionis fragmentum* (1572), the trilingual resources of Wales were used to reassert the legendary British history set out by Geoffrey of Monmouth.[195] The Welsh projected themselves as representatives of a Britishness that the Tudors were bringing to fulfilment. Once again, the ideology of union both enabled and limited the realization of what we would now call national identity.

The Welsh gentry remained attached to such crypto-national institutions as the Council in the Marches and the established church in Wales. Although the Council, set up by Henry VIII, was based in the English border-town of Ludlow, it gave devolved, locally informed attention to Welsh affairs. Englishmen with attitude could represent the Lord President of the Council as a neo-medieval border baron, a bulwark against an alien people.[196] But hostility towards the Welsh, with their devoted royalism and reputation for unreliability, keen in the early 1640s, more typically found expression in calls for the Council to be abolished—an outcome not secured until another revolutionary period, 1689. As the civil war writing of Henry Vaughan shows, Welsh resistance to English encroachment could be intense, but it matters that the poet's Welshness should turn out to be more locally than nationally identified (Chapter 6).

Any realization of nationhood—to lapse into teleological shorthand—was disrupted by the very factors which preserved the vitality of Welshness.

First, linguistic division: the use of Welsh had been limited by Henrician legislation,[197] yet although English was acquired by the *Cymric* gentry, it did not spread out of the south, the border counties, and Pembrokeshire, to become the general tongue, in part because Welsh also became the language of the established church. Compared with the sustaining presence of a vernacular Bible (from 1588), the patronage of bardic poetry by the landed elite in the seventeenth century[198] was a minor factor in preserving the language, but the latter is evidence of the social conservatism that prevailed in rural Wales (where authority lay in the hands of local, intermarried families, acutely conscious of lineage) and that militated against the formation of a national community. Equally and more visibly obstructive was the mountainous topography. It was easier for a mid-seventeenth-century Welsh MP like James Philips—who, not uncharacteristically for his social group, married an English wife, the poet Katherine Philips (Chapter 6)—to take the road from Cardigan to London than it was for him to penetrate the fastnesses of North Wales. The result is clear from such texts as *Wallography*: Welsh culture remained distinctive even as it assumed a provincial status.

Historians often cite the Declaration of Arbroath (1320) as the founding declaration of the Scottish political nation.[199] It is indeed a statement of independence from English control. Yet the plurality of the kingdom's origins (Pictish, Dalriadic, Saxon, Norman, and so forth) long continued to divide it.[200] As in the north of England, though for generations longer, magnate power localized loyalty.[201] And the borders of the kingdom were still unfinished business during the period covered by this book: the Donald Lordship of the Isles had only been incorporated in 1493,[202] and, as *Macbeth* reminds us, unrest in Western Gaeldom remained an issue for James VI and I (see Chapter 2); Orkney and Shetland (which had their own micropolitics and revolts) were annexed from Norway-Denmark as late as 1611–14; it was not entirely incredible for both English royalists and parliamentarians to assert that the other side had promised the Scots the right to govern the four northern counties of England in return for military support.[203] Whereas the Welsh and the Cornish were small minorities under the English crown, half of the Scottish population, and more than half its land, was occupied by Gaelic-speaking clans whose social organization and literature were inimical to the development of a large-scale structure of allegiance. That the Highlanders and Western Islanders were known as 'Irish' by Lowland Scots during the seventeenth century summarily indicates their problematic place neither within nor forthwith the nation.

During the reign of James VI, Scotland was dominated by the crown and nobility. In the absence of such 'representative' organs as the House of Commons, and the literary output associated with it (dialogue, satire, newsbooks), and of such cultural institutions as theatre—which it acted vigorously to suppress—the Kirk took a leading role, especially through its General Assembly, in the process of national self-definition. The embattled righteousness of Scottish Calvinism found expression in severe declarations which proved the more challenging for the Stewarts once they became British monarchs. Sympathy for Charles I in the face of Covenanter demands has consequently never been restricted to Laudians.[204] Yet if the Kirk could adopt a defensive, even an anglophobic posture in its attempts to strengthen itself within a Scotland that was confessionally more divided than we are inclined to remember—Episcopalianism and pockets of Catholicism remaining strong into the eighteenth century—it also had a strain of (for the most part confederating) unionism that was not just tactically open to a self-protective alliance with puritanism in England but was militantly, even apocalyptically, attracted to the construction of a Protestant Britain strong enough to defeat Antichrist in Europe.[205]

This ideology and its literary manifestations[206] lent support to James VI's aim of succeeding to the English crown,[207] though Scottish royalists had a more Constantinean, imperial conception of Britannia.[208] Regal union encouraged such men to contribute to the cultural fabrication of Britishness.[209] At times of difficulty, however—as the later works of Drummond show (Chapter 3)—they harped on the ancient loyalty of Scotland to its own kings and were less enthusiastic about Stewart claims to Britain. During the mid-century crises, support for the Solemn League and Covenant made with English parliamentarians in 1643 did more to keep Scotland tied into three-kingdoms conflict than ultra-royalist support for Charles I and II (Chapter 7). For many the model was biblical: a league between Godly nations resembling the Old Testament covenants between Israel and Judah.[210] After the internal unrest of the 1670s, loyalist writers like Sir George Mackenzie stressed the autonomy of Scotland to bolster the traditional absolutism of free monarchy north of the border (Chapter 9). It was an argument about lineage and authority which brought Mackenzie into conflict with such Irish antiquarians as Roderic O'Flaherty as well as with home-grown Calvinists and historically minded Englishmen who still rested their assumptions about the make-up of Stuart and Williamite Britain on medieval claims to suzerainty over Scotland. Despite long-running impulses towards integration, divergence between the nations was the background of the union of 1707 (below, pp. 329–30).

The relationship between national sentiment and three-kingdom inter-action was sharply refracted in Ireland by ethnic and religious factors.[211] Contemporaries identified four main groups: the indigenous, almost en-tirely Catholic, Gaelic (or mere or Old) Irish, oppressed and given to rebellion; the Old English descendants of medieval settlers, also mostly Catholic but traditionally loyal to the crown; the largely Protestant New English progeny of Tudor and Stuart planters (eventually known as Old Protestants) and, after them, the Cromwellians; and the waves of Scot-tish, mostly Presbyterian colonists, who came to Ulster after 1609. The eighteenth-century triumph of Protestant Ascendancy has retrospectively given centrality to such forerunners of Anglo-Irishness as Spenser, Barnaby Riche, William Molyneux, and Jonathan Swift. It is impossible to make sense of Ireland and its literature without reflecting on the issues which Molyneux and Swift addressed at the end of the period covered by this book, and they are both discussed in my epilogue (Chapter 12). During the period itself, however, it was the Old English who were most often caught in the conflicted circumstances that spur creativity. Protestants with this ethnic background, such as James Ussher, Archbishop of Armagh, interfaced with Catholic friends, kin, and fellow-scholars. They shared a lineage with Old English Catholics so extensively Gaelicized that they have been dubbed the New Irish (Geoffrey Keating, i.e. Seathrún Céitinn, author of *Foras feasa ar Éirinn*, belongs to this category).[212] On the con-tinent, such Counter-Reformation Old English clerics as Luke Wadding associated with mere Irish militants.[213] And in the middle were men like Richard Bellings, gifted poet, diplomat, and historian, who published in 1624 a frequently reprinted conclusion to Sidney's unfinished *Arcadia*—the classic tale of Protestant chivalry, penned by the son of a Lord Deputy in Ireland—yet who went on to become secretary to the Council of the Confederate Catholics of Kilkenny during the civil wars.[214]

Scholars of Gaelic Ireland now argue that late sixteenth-century bards encouraged their patrons to develop a crypto-national response to English violence[215] and that Counter-Reformation Catholicism fostered an ide-ology of faith and fatherland.[216] Whatever the sources were for the new political thinking (and, if some of it was continental, some was archipelagic, brought in by English/Scots settlers), a change is signalled by the appear-ance of the word *náision* in early seventeenth-century Irish writing.[217] As I show in Chapter 5, the attempt in the 1640s to forge a common front out of Old Irish and Old English Catholics was incompletely successful (and foundered on more than ethnic difference); but a Catholic nation was imagined during these years of conflict and opportunity by scholars, poets, and playwrights, and it was partly realized in the Confederate polity centred on Kilkenny—an expression of what historians of seventeenth-century Europe call national constitutionalism.[218] Ireland remained, for all that, a site of overlapping, incompatible affiliations, with those of Protestant descent still calling themselves English or Scots, long after the Restoration, and Catholics—indurated by defeat, as they had earlier been animated by the prospect of religious toleration—seeking alternatives. By the end of the period, in a work such as *A Light to the Blind*, probably written by the Old Englishman Oliver Plunkett of Dunsoghly,[219] the word 'nation' is freely used to include both Old English and mere Irish Catholics, but it does not yet encompass the Protestant precursors of Swift.

The building of this nation owed a great deal to the experiences of exiles in Catholic Europe. Some were soldiers, others clerics, but all were exposed to some level of continental thought about the legitimacy of multiple monarchy. When Conor O'Mahony, a County Cork Jesuit based in Lisbon, contended, in his *Disputatio apologetica* (1645),[220] that the Irish people had the right to cast off Charles I and choose a ruler for themselves (he had in mind Owen Roe O'Neill), he was adapting Portuguese arguments in favour of independence from Castile.[221] Groups within the archipelago reinforced their ethnic, national, and confessional interests along competing international axes. The Gaelic Irish—despite O'Mahony—were traditional allies of Spain. The auld alliance between the Scots and the French resonated into the 1630s,[222] and revived in a divisive form during the Jacobite campaigns discussed in Chapter 11. Swedish-Scottish relations were also richly significant, especially in the military-diplomatic sphere,[223] and they could cut across Anglo-British interests,[224] though they remained secondary in importance—within a spread of Scottish settlement that reached from Lithuania to North America[225]—to the Scoto-Dutch axis explored in Chapter 7.

It was once fashionable to argue that the English civil war was a symptom of a 'general crisis' that swept across mid-seventeenth-century Europe.[226] That connections can be traced between revolutionary events in England

and those in, for instance, France, is clear,[227] and although few now accept that the same causal mechanisms were operating from Prague to Lisbon, it would be wrong to deny the extent of the unrest in the interests of an archipelagic focus. When it comes to Britain, and more intriguingly Ireland, however—which was early on assessed for inclusion in 'the general crisis'[228] —literary works that manifest the importance of European contexts often bear out a thesis of archipelagic historians, that the exploitation of existing tensions around the islands was regarded by continental powers as the best way of weakening the authority of the crown. Distinctions need to be sought,[229] first, between events and ideas, insofar as these are separable, because the people who shaped British and Irish culture were often heavily indebted to continental accounts of absolutism, classical republicanism, theology, natural law, and so on, and, second, between crises, for if it attributes too much to Europe as the *primum mobile* of events to interpret the wars of the three kingdoms as a branch of the Thirty Years War, it is broadly the case that the Williamite struggles of 1688–91 were, as J. G. A. Pocock—no friend of continental contexts—concedes, 'the archipelagic face of a European conflict'.[230]

'Broadly the case' rather than completely because, as any reader of the plays, poems, and tracts generated by the Williamite wars will agree, the face presented by the conflict was so different in Ireland from that shown in England, where the struggle was largely constitutional, thanks to a Protestant majority and a pre-emptive Dutch invasion, as to make specifically Irish issues—around religion, ethnicity, landholding—formative not just of how the antagonisms were fought out but of how different factions made their case to British readers (Chapter 10). In this, the wars of 1688–91[231] continued a pattern established in the representation of conflict during the 1640s and 1650s. The period covered by this book saw a series of multifaceted exchanges between internationally conditioned archipelagic crises and literary production. Thus, to stick with Ireland, the Earl of Orrery, who mustered troops and built fortifications to defend Restoration Munster first against the Spanish then against the Dutch and the French, fed his writing on the same priorities (see Chapter 8). Anti-Spanish anxiety is clear in his tragicomedy *The Generall*, while his history plays *Henry V* and *The Black Prince*, though welcome to a London public fearful of Louis XIV, were written in Ireland and designed to encourage policies that would frustrate alliances between the French and the Catholic Irish.

Nor were Britain and Ireland merely objects of foreign ambition: they had international designs of their own. Orrery's plays about France had behind them a long line of patriotic-expansionist texts, including *Edward III* and Shakespeare's *Henry V*, which all sustained the idea that England's military strength and dynastic inheritance required it to have at least a foothold on continental Europe. In his 'Panegyrick to my Lord Protector' (1655), a poem much preoccupied with union (below, p. 85), Waller said that Cromwell had made Holland England's 'Out-guard on the Continent'.[232] As I indicate in Chapter 7, the States of Holland did become, at least virtually, in the early to mid-1650s, part of an extended archipelago, because, although the English Republic felt obliged, for security reasons, to protect itself against royalism by stamping out resistance across the three kingdoms (creating, between 1654 and 1660, a union even more comprehensive than that achieved in 1707),[233] the union that it aspired to was with the Netherlands, and when the Dutch proved reluctant they were defeated in the naval war that provides one backdrop to Waller's poem. The potential for Dutch-British convergence, which long engaged the attention of poets and pamphleteers, including Wither and Marvell, culminated in the arrival in 1688–9 of the Dutch Stadholder, Willem van Oranje, as monarch of the three kingdoms (Chapter 9).

To understand what was involved, psychologically as well as politically, in the watery, shoal-scattered union proposed with the Dutch it is necessary to remember the importance of the sea to British identity formation—from the defeat of the Spanish Armada to the Battle of Trafalgar. Within the archipelago, water was connective. The standard route from Edinburgh (Leith) to London was through coastal waters, not on horseback along difficult roads. The seas which we view on maps as surrounding and dividing the islands drew them together, and opened them to continental and Atlantic worlds. My title is maritime, because *Archipelagic* derives from Greek *archi*, 'chief, primary', and *pelagos*, a word for 'sea'. According to the *OED*, 'archipelago' came into English in 1502 to designate the Aegean. But in Hakluyt's *Voyages* (1600)—on cue for the period covered by this book—the modern sense emerges: 'Any sea, or sheet of water, in which there are numerous islands; and *transf.* a group of islands'. It is as though the three kingdoms grew out of the watery medium of the seas. If this sense of the archipelago appealed to sea dogs of Hakluyt's generation, it became even more potent after the Restoration as the maritime English turned into full-blown commercial imperialists. The crowning expression arrives in

1740, in 'Rule Britannia': 'When Britain first, at heaven's command, | Arose from out the azure main'.[234]

Stuart writing is full of islands: far-flung and fantastic (*The Tempest, The Isle of Pines*), actual, proximate, and contested (Lundy in Drayton's *Poly-Olbion*, caught between England and Wales); often classical in origin (Ariadne's Naxos, Circe's Aeaea), they can also, more surprisingly, be anglophone Gaelic (the legend of *Hy-Brasil* retold by the Ulster-born Richard Head).[235] There are even floating islands, as in Jonson's *Masque of Beautie* (1608) and *The Fortunate Isles and their Vnion* (1624), where pieces of drifting territory link up with the British mainland and blend the iconography of union with the notion that the three kingdoms are a version of the Hesperides.[236] (At the other end of the period, in his paraphrase of Horace's Odes I.xiv, Swift would compare Ireland, cast adrift on a sea of misfortune by a united, indifferent Britain, with the floating island Delos.) In both those Jonson entertainments, the sea is more than a foil to set off the quality of the islands. It is a visible, elaborately represented, source of wealth and power. This prominence owes something to the fact that arguments about sovereignty of the sea had implications for the authority of the crown.[237] One reason for the ubiquity of King Edgar in seventeenth-century literature is that, like the Stuart monarchs, he asserted his claim to empire over the British seas. Equally important, however—especially in the second half of the period—was the practical realization of an English variety of imperialism through overseas commerce. 'It is no Paradox to say that England hath its root in the Sea', declared Halifax in 1690, 'and a deep root too, from whence it sendeth its branches into both the Indyes.'[238]

What were the origins of this empire? Drawing on definitions derived from classical Rome, late-medieval and Renaissance kings of Scotland and England had declared their crowns imperial. By this they meant that their authority within their respective kingdoms was unqualified by that of rival monarchs or the Pope. Hence Henry VIII's declaration, in the Act in Restraint of Appeals (1533): 'this realm of England is an empire.'[239] Once the English medieval claims to suzerainty over Scotland were translated into this idiom, it became natural to talk of a 'British empire'. A step was taken towards realizing this potent but insular entity in the Anglo-Welsh union of 1536–43; it was variously promulgated in texts associated with Anglo-Scottish and Scoto-Britannic Protestant unionism in the 1540s;[240] and it was given a more expansionist cast when Humphrey Llwyd and John

Dee argued for Elizabeth I's claims to the pseudo-historical empire of King Arthur in Northern Europe and Virginia in the New World.[241] During the period covered by this book, *empire* as 'imperial rule or dignity' (*OED* 1–2), and 'a country of which the sovereign owes no allegiance to any foreign superior' (*OED* 7) lost primacy to the originally thirteenth-century meaning 'An extensive territory (*esp.* an aggregate of many separate states) under the sway of an emperor or supreme ruler [or] sovereign state' (*OED* 5a)'.[242] Yet the overseas British empire remained a nascent phenomenon. Even after the Restoration, a writer who refers without qualification to 'the Empire' will have in mind the continental remnants of the Holy Roman Empire.

If one looks at Jacobean texts which adumbrate the attitudes that inform later, full-blown imperialism, they often fold back into the empire which was Britain. Jonson's *Masque of Blacknesse* (1605), for instance, opens with a maritime scene, across which two sea horses carry Oceanus and Niger. Oceanus asks Niger why he has journeyed so far west, 'And, in mine empires heart, salute me thus?'[243] This may be the the growth-point of future imperial discourse, but Britain is at the heart of Ocean's empire; whatever the implicit trope, it cannot yet be said to be at the heart of an oceanic empire of its own. As the narrative unfolds, moreover, an insular message emerges. The daughters of Niger, regretting their blackness (there are far-reaching imperialistic implications in that), have been encouraged by a vision to seek a country '*Whose termination (of the* Greek) | *Sounds*—TANIA' (897). There they will find a monarch whose temperance in government fosters beauty. Niger and his daughters have gone from Mauritania to Lusitania and Acquitania, each country lighter in its hues, and have now reached Britannia. Yet again reversing what we might expect, Britain is not internally threefold and globally powerful but 'a blest Isle' admired by 'the triple world' (897–8).

So *The Masque of Blacknesse* is not concerned with British overseas settlement, but with how regal union has won global admiration for an island which has in its reunification recovered its classical identity as a world apart: 'With that great name BRITANIA, this blest Isle | Hath wonne her ancient dignitie, and stile. | *A world, divided from the world*' (898).[244] That James can assimilate to his own mode of 'triple' government even those of a black-skinned race may anticipate the later claims of colonialism in Africa and the Caribbean, but in the masque it represents in heightened form the ability of the British monarchy to turn the most uncouth, tawny, even barbarous peoples (bog-trotters, Highlanders) into candid subjects of Albion. The masque asserts James's self-sufficient, imperial efficacy in the eyes of an uneasily mixed audience of English, Scottish, and Irish courtiers, and ambassadors from countries overseas where there would be, for quite some time, little understanding of what the three-kingdom polity amounted to.[245]

Seventeenth-century models of empire did not always turn on monarchy. Elizabethan colonial tracts had drawn on the example of the Roman republic, whose expansion was characterized by the incorporation of conquered territory and the granting of rights of citizenship to the defeated.[246] In the union debates around 1603 and 1707, these precedents were invoked despite the presence of Stuart monarchs on the throne. More stringently and classically republican was the language used in 1651–2, by such writers as Marchamont Nedham, to justify the English Commonwealth's policy towards Scotland.[247] Under the Protectorate, parallels were drawn between Cromwell and triumphant Roman generals—as in Waller's 'Panegyrick', where the victor of Drogheda and Dunbar is praised for enfranchising the Irish and the Scots and giving their representatives seats at Whitehall: 'So kinde Dictators made, when they came home, | Their vanquish'd Foes, free Citizens of *Rome*' (6). Encouraged by Tacitus and Suetonius, English republicans were suspicious of imperialism within and beyond the archipelago because they associated empire with decadence. The Protectorate, however, advanced a Western Design, sending troops and naval forces to the Caribbean, and this expansionist policy has been identified as the source of the Whig ideology of empire which found expression in such post-Restoration plays as Dennis's *Liberty Asserted*.[248]

Another reason why the growth of empire is inextricably archipelagic lies in the uneven development of colonialism in relation to programmes of union.[249] In Chapter 4, I show how Scottish fears that its possessions in North America were being given away by Charles I mobilized discreet protests even from the royalist Drummond (pp. 155–6). At the end of the period, as Defoe brings into focus (Chapter 11), it was the hope of gaining access to English colonies in the New World that inclined many Scots towards union. The Treaty of 1707 was not agreed, however, without the Scots making one last, bankrupting effort to acquire an empire of their own. In 'The Golden Island or the Darian Song' (1699), an anonymous

'Lady of Honour' applauds Scottish attempts to establish a colony at Darien
on the Isthmus of Panama:

> Some slumbring thoughts possess'd my brain,
>   was Prophecied of Old,
> That Albanie should Thrissels spread,
>   o're all the Indian Gold.[250]

The poet's view of England is competitive to the point of hostility. The
nations are poles apart, and not just because the Scots have now planted
a colony so far south: 'The *Thristle* and the *Reed Lyon* | will Crush our
Enemies. | We're Antipods to England now'. This exudes a violence not
wholly directed at the unnamed Spanish ('our Enemies') who happened to
claim Darien. Yet the poet's combative assurance

> King William did Encourage us
>   against the *English* will.
> His words is like a Statly Oak,
>   will neither Bow nor Break. ...

shows why the colony would fail. Such lines would not be in the poem if
royal support could be taken for granted. In the event, William II and III
sacrificed Scottish interests to English diplomacy with the Spanish, and the
colony's demise became inevitable.

Why look forward to Darien, or back to medieval disputes about English
suzerainty over Scotland, when the origins of the British empire are so
viciously apparent in sixteenth-century Ireland? In practice the Elizabethan
reconquest was plurally motivated and unevenly realized: it carried over
from England and Wales late medieval strategies for breaking magnate
power in the interests of the crown; it denied Counter-Reformation
missionaries and Spanish troops a gateway into the three kingdoms; and
it imposed through the system of plantation schemes of agricultural improvement that were spreading in Britain.[251] It also gave scope to the
time-honoured, not specifically archipelagic acquisitiveness of courtiers,
merchants, and arrivistes.[252] If this was a colonizing process, it was an erratic
and overdetermined one. The most far-reaching, punitive expropriation of
Irish Catholic estates followed the Cromwellian invasion;[253] this carving up
of the country along religious lines was barely moderated at the Restoration and it was taken further after the triumph of Willem van Oranje over
James II and VII in 1688–91.[254] According to the traditional estimates, the
proportion of land held by Catholics fell from 61 per cent in 1641 to 22

per cent by 1688 (and 15 per cent after 1703). But historians cannot agree how far the redistribution associated with Cromwell was the product of an imperialist agenda,[255] and how far it was designed to seal the victory of the English parliament over an English monarch by defeating royalists across the water.[256]

The tendency of the new British history has been to think of Ireland as more a kingdom than a colony. In narrowly constitutional terms, this is accurate enough, but only with the caveat that, unlike Scotland and England, with their long history as kingdoms, and their (reputedly) ancient, imperial crowns, the Kingdom of Ireland was widely acknowledged to be a recent invention. Though the title *Ard Ri* (High King) had early medieval currency, it was never borne by a single, overall monarch of Gaelic Ireland;[257] and, after the Anglo-Norman invasion of 1169–71—licensed by a papal bull,[258] the validity of which some post-Reformation Irish Catholic writers contested—the country, which meant in practice those regions that came under Anglo-Norman control, had the status of a lordship, subsumed, on the accession of King John, under the crown of England. After the introduction of a far-reaching measure known as Poynings' Law, in 1494, royal control was tightened. The Lord Deputy and his council now needed the king's consent before summoning an Irish parliament—an arrangement which, during the period covered by this book, unevenly blocked legislation in Dublin which was not generated, or approved, by the crown.[259]

It was only in 1541, when an Act for Kingly Title was passed by the Irish Parliament, that an English monarch—Henry VIII—formally became King of Ireland, and even then the sovereignty was 'united and knit to the imperial crown of England'.[260] The constitutional difficulties implicit in this arrangement quickly became apparent. Henry revisited the terms of his title within months of its proclamation; it was probed by later Irish Catholic scholars, and dealt with contentiously by such Protestant patriots as Swift (see Chapter 12, Section (ii)). In effect, however, as their regalia indicated, the Stuarts after 1603 enjoyed three kingdoms but only two crowns. That the Kingdom of Ireland was annexed to the English monarchy did not prevent the Gaelic Irish as well as the descendants of the Anglo-Normans having legal rights, a parliament subject to Poynings' Law, and, in some cases, feudal titles. But the realm remained subsidiary, and that generated contradictions.

One way of putting this is to say that Ireland was accorded the status of a kingdom not out of respect for its cultural distinctiveness (hardly a decisive

factor in early modern constructions of the state) but because England was
not strong enough to incorporate it as Wales had been incorporated. It
was a kingdom because it was more than a colony but not a dominion
that could be absorbed. And this had the paradoxical effect of leaving
England looking less than self-sufficient when it was most assertive about its
authority. The principality of Wales could be occluded in the iconography
of the state, and taken for granted, often enough, in literary representations
of England. But Ireland had a way of remaining visible, attesting to English
power when displayed as an acquisition yet acting as a reminder that the
state was not simply unitary. Hence the flags, coins, arms, and seals of the
English Republic, which show the cross of St George with the Irish harp
prominently attached. When Milton declared to all Europe the legitimacy
of self-determination and the military prowess of the Commonwealth in
his *Pro Populo Anglicano defensio* (1650), his work bore on its title page this
double heraldry of English and Irish devices.

   These constitutional facts were important to literary as well as political
writers in seventeenth-century Ireland, but they would not have been so
much discussed had they not meshed with the nature of experience in a
country which in economic, religious, and military terms could seem so
dependent on England as scarcely to be a kingdom. An archipelagic account
can elucidate these aspects of Irish life without playing down the existence
of a long-running, colonialist design to plant and anglicize the country,[261]
but its three-kingdom agenda will predispose it to cut across the transatlantic
routes and links along which the British empire spread.[262] This is an ironic
outcome, given the westward sweep of Pocock's original vision of a new
British history, his willingness, at times, to include the eastern American
seaboard in his definition of the Atlantic archipelago. In Chapter 10, I argue
that Ireland moved against the direction of development one might expect,
becoming less a kingdom and more a colony as a result of processes sealed
by Anglo-Scottish union.[263] What is beyond dispute is that this diverse,
split-up country—in so far as it was thought about whole—was seen
through a number of shifting, often simultaneous perspectives, from the
Elizabethan periods of plantation, with their neoclassical treatises, through
the efforts of the native elite to accommodate itself to the new Gaelic
monarchy (as they chose to see it) of James VI and I, the attempt of
Franciscans and Jesuits to claim Ireland as a piece of Counter-Reformation
Europe, the languages of puritan hostility and commercial development in
the 1650s and 1660s, and so on.

Whether or not they saw themselves as contributing to a global imperial enterprise—and few of them will have—English, Welsh, Scots, and Irish settlers, mariners, religious exiles, and indentured servants took their hopes, grudges, and cultural programming across an early modern Atlantic that we are learning to think of as more British than English, and arguably more European than either, as well as, increasingly over the seventeenth century, Black. There is no point in underestimating the English connection that WASP America has made so much of.[264] Puritan colonists could think of old England as Egypt, a locus of persecution from which they had organized an exodus, but they also looked upon it as another Zion where their brethren bore witness.[265] The poet Anne Bradstreet—traditionally regarded as one of the founders of a distinctively American canon—shows the ties to have been strong. In 'A Dialogue between Old England and New; concerning their present Troubles. Anno 1642',[266] she explores them at a time of crisis. Why did Bradstreet gender the speakers of this dialogue female? That male writers routinely personified countries as women (above, p. 28) might be a more misleading than sufficient answer. By projecting female voices, in some sense versions of her own, Bradstreet must have found it easier to engage with the mass of historical and political material which makes up the core of her poem; but the strategy also allowed her—given early modern gender roles—to bring out qualities elsewhere under-represented in texts about Old England: its vulnerability to abuse by those careless of its constitutional and cultural fabric, the pathos of its suffering, even a certain passivity (born of political stalemate) which allowed it to slide into war. Meanwhile, New England's femininity squares with her inability to take up arms and sail to the rescue.

As the poem begins, New England does not know why Old England hangs her head and weeps, while the latter is critical of her child for being ignorant of her woes. The gap in understanding is in part a necessary fiction, because it gives Old England an opportunity to explain to the reader what has gone wrong. Interestingly, however, she picks out structural tensions that were latent in the transatlantic relationship by asking whether New England imagines that she can survive without her support, or hopes to profit from her afflictions. The old country then reviews her history, concentrating on threats to her peace from Hengist to the Armada, and blaming Laudianism and prerogative government for the difficulties of the hour. It is striking that, in all this chronicling, no attempt is made to highlight markers of ethnic distinctiveness, or to claim genealogical purity; Englishness is felt to derive from shared experience and developing institutions. This is characteristic of English self-description at this date.[267] Britishness, by contrast, is nowhere. Scotland and Ireland figure on the same basis as continental states. The civil war is very much an English, parliamentarian cause. Only when victory leads to justice in the Commonwealth and simplicity in the church will England take on a broader mission by sending men forth to fight the Turks and bring on the Second Coming of Christ.

The poem's lack of interest in archipelagic complexities is partly a product of its moment; it was written early in a conflict which would become more intractably multiple as the 1640s went on. This is reflected in the writing that came out of New England, which becomes more troubled by the divisive ramifications of the crisis. But it is also symptomatic of an Anglo-American indifference to Old England's neighbours which was as contributory within England itself as were Scottish and Irish Catholic antipathy to the English church and state in bringing about the wars of the three kingdoms. That the 'Dialogue' is in this respect no less English for having been written in America returns us to the question of why *Archipelagic English* does not revert to Pocock's initial, Atlanticist formulation of the new British history?[268] For a circum-Atlantic story can be told about the period 1642–60, as it can around the crises of 1688–91, when colonies were again caught up and mutated by their involvement in the British-Irish problematic.

During the 1640s, the lines of communication remained open. New England divines returned to the old country to advise on the reform of the church, generating such London-published texts as *New Englands Lamentation for Old Englands Present Errours and Divisions* (1645) by Thomas Shepard. After the regicide, writers like Bradstreet muted their support of parliament. Six of the colonies, from Newfoundland down to Barbados, rebelled against the republic, and, by declaring for Charles II, brought down upon themselves a milder form of the repression inflicted on Scotland and Ireland. During the Western Design, the colonies were enlisted in support of the Protector's ambitions. And the Restoration settlement, which returned Scotland and Ireland to the status of kingdoms within a multiple monarchy, left the plantations tied to the English state. 'With a monarch now at its head, the Restoration empire inherited most of its features from the interregnum. It was recognizably the entity that would later be known as the "first British empire".'[269]

So why *not* include in *Archipelagic English* the literary and cultural worlds of Bradstreet and her contemporaries in America? There are, first, considerations of scale and attenuation. That 'Really, universally, relations stop nowhere'—as the great transatlanticist Henry James put it—yet they have to in a book,[270] is one factor. That the literature of America did not, despite such luminaries as Edward Taylor and Jonathan Edwards, have anything like the mass and quality of that of the British–Irish archipelago, until well after 1707, is another. A weightier argument, audible in the period, is that the status of the three kingdoms distinguished them categorically from the settlements in America. As William Molyneux put it in 1698: 'Do not the Kings of *England* bear the *Stile of Ireland* amongst the rest of their Kingdoms? Is this Agreeable to the nature of a *Colony*? Do they use the Title of Kings of *Virginia, New-England*, or *Mary-Land*?'[271] It is true that, as a Dublin Protestant, complaining of crypto-colonialist treatment by the English parliament, Molyneux had particular reason to press this distinction. The rhetorical insistence of his questions reads like an attempt to bolster a claim that did not strike English MPs as self-evident. That said, constitutional difference had a slow, erratic, but cumulative effect on the way authority was exercised on both sides of the Atlantic, and thus on socio-economic and cultural development, making it right to conclude that 'As kingdoms in their own right, Ireland and Scotland each had its own specific relationship to the Stuart monarchy, and they were not directly analogous to the king's dominions of Bermuda and beyond.'[272]

Another set of reasons for regarding America as semi-detachable from archipelagic Englishness stems from the relative degrees of European involvement. That there was a matrix of commercial, cultural, and colonizing activity that can be called 'the British Atlantic' is indisputable,[273] at least after the mid-seventeenth century,[274] though given the heavy transportation of Irish Catholics to the Caribbean—Montserrat became crowded with Gaelic-speakers[275]—it would be more accurate to speak of a 'British–Irish Atlantic'. The logistics of migration brought people from the archipelago into new conjunctions in the Old World (heading for ports like London and Bristol) as well as the New. This was one of the ways in which British identities began minimally to coalesce.[276] As I have indicated, however, there are reasons for regarding the Atlantic as too multiply European, and, as the seventeenth century went on, too involved in African slavery,[277] to be defined as British–Irish. Hence the role of the Spanish and of plantation slavery in Defoe's *Colonel Jack* (see Chapter 11). That an archipelagic analysis of events in the three kingdoms has enough internal logic to be complemented by a European perspective does not mean that the same is equally true across the Atlantic. One should not exaggerate the level of interaction between English and Scottish plantations and French or Spanish colonies on the ground. In the large dynamics of empire, however, migrations from the three kingdoms were entwined with streams of people leaving continental Europe and Scandinavia. Spain, Sweden, and even more the Netherlands were inextricable from British overseas adventures. The settlement of North America required co-operation as well as competition, and the resulting interpenetration had far-reaching cultural as well as economic consequences.[278]

We are back with the crucial, though not straightforward, criterion of *interactivity*. This term will be subjected to clarifying pressure in Section (vii) of this introduction. For now, how does the picture look if one seeks to triangulate the colonies with Britain and Ireland? The flow of people, books, and beliefs westwards across the Atlantic was uneven but over the seventeenth century as a whole substantial. From the late 1630s onwards, there was also growing communication between the American colonies—induced, in part, by the archipelagic wars which forced the plantations to take sides with reference to one another.[279] Yet poems by Anne Bradstreet, or the presence of New England divines in British debates about the future of the church, do not constitute an equivalent counter-flow. That colonists returned to England during the mid-century is acknowledged.[280] But the evidence that British-Irish issues were influenced by events or literary texts produced in America is slight. We seem to have a two-sided triangle, with the third, west-east axis looking much more sketchy. This was true even towards the end of the period 1603–1707, when the colonies were both more prosperous and more closely knit into the British imperium. As Eliga H. Gould notes: 'the two great colonial upheavals of the later seventeenth century—King Philip's War in New England (1675) and Bacon's rebellion in Virginia (1676)—made little difference to the conduct of politics in England, although they carried dire implications for the status of Indians and the growth of African slavery in North America. Whereas political unrest in Scotland and Ireland repeatedly encroached on English affairs, the American colonies were juridically and geographically remote.'[281]

Just as significant in cultural terms is the lack of interactivity between American colonists and the tribes they dispossessed. (In the Caribbean, osmosis was ruled out entirely by extermination.) This was apparent socially, in patterns of habitation, sexually, in the refusal of the authorities officially to countenance relations with the natives, and, interfusing it all, in attitudes to religion. On that front, anglophone America was quite different from the empires to the north and south. Protestant ministers were not interested in superficial conversion. They dismissed the missionary achievements of Catholics in Spanish America and New France because they did not instil a complete programme of re-education. And they were shocked by the willingness of Jesuits, in particular, to accommodate Native American beliefs. They did not want to co-opt indigenous religion, but to destroy and replace it.[282] Attitudes seem to have hardened after the 1620s,[283] and, although exceptional individuals can be found expressing sympathy for native Americans (Mary Rowlandson, for example), it is distressingly evident from the literature that 'redskins'—as they would come to be known—were categorized as a barbarous, ungodly Other.

This does not mean that *othering*, that much-touted anthropological phenomenon, played no part in the construction of identities within the archipelago. Such groups as Gypsies, the 'mountain Welsh', Cornish tin-miners, and the inhabitants of the Derbyshire Peak District, not to mention the wild Irish, were on a spectrum with native Americans, and could be equated. As Roger Williams put it, in a now-famous observation, 'We have Indians at home—Indians in Cornwall, Indians in Wales, Indians in Ireland'.[284] Yet the proportion of Old and New English to the Gaelic Irish, for instance, was much greater than that of the New England colonists to the Amerindian nations, and their circumstances were more tightly bound together. People identifying themselves as English had lived among the mere Irish, reading and writing about them, for centuries, not just for decades. And the Gypsies who travelled the north country, or the targe-bearing, fierce-looking Highlanders who intermittently descended on Edinburgh, impinged much more immediately on core English/Scots-speaking communities than native Americans could, even when one takes into account the profile of the latter in travel narratives, woodcuts, and pageants. Leaving out America is thus consistent with the rationale of this book, focussed as it is on the cultural layerings, fusions, and conflicts that characterize the long-anglophone and proximate areas of Britain and Ireland, where mixed inheritances were lived through and transformed.

(v) Languages

How can one analyse the make-up of something as diverse and variously embedded as archipelagic English—a language known in the period to have itself been pulled together from Saxon, Norman, French, Latin, Dutch, and other tongues—without attending to texts written in Welsh, Irish, Cornish, Manx, Scottish Gaelic or, come to that, Norn? Not to mention Latin—so active and prestigious,[285] so visible in the output of anglophone authors, that it would be artificial entirely to ignore it (see the discussion of Marvell's 'Scaevola Scoto-Brittannus' in Chapter 9). On the one hand, the tie between language and culture was strong enough to make the English/Inglis archipelago a coherent unit of study. On the other, discussion can only be complete when fully polyglot because important controls, perspectives, and elements of inter-ethnic dialogue lie in the Celtic tongues. Yet the high quality of such cross-linguistic work as has been done[286] so clearly depends on its in-depth bilateral understanding as to suggest that it would be misguided for any scholar to sacrifice particularity and inwardness to the heroic task of acquiring all the tongues used around the islands—a competence that seventeenth-century individuals did not possess. That being the case, it must be acceptable to push forward what is going to be a piecemeal, collaborative project, involving scholars from quite different backgrounds, some more polyglot than others, by concentrating on English/Inglis texts. It is to be hoped that this book will be followed by others more philologically specialized, drawing out the various strands within archipelagic English and situating writers of Hiberno-English, Scots, and the like in the habitats which they shared with the Ulster Irish, North Welsh, and so on.

In any case an anglophone account inevitably draws in words, phrases, and difficulties that move between languages. After the Cromwellian invasion, for example, macaronic texts enact as well as lament the penetration of Irish by English culture.[287] To understand how potently these poems register this trauma through their use of English words one needs to recall both how deeply schooled Gaelic poets were in the patterning of their language and the strength of their belief that Irish was free of loanwords. Here is a sample from a Gaelic poem written in County Cork, c.1658. The language of the text is Munster Irish but it incorporates phrases uttered by the hated English:

> Le *execútion* bhíos súil an chéidfhir,
> costas buinte 'na chuinne ag an ndéanach.

Transport, transplant, mo mheabhair ar Bhéarla.
Shoot him, kill him, strip him, tear him.
A Tory, hack him, hang him, rebel,
a rogue, a thief, a priest, a papist.
Bíd na mílte dínn i n-aonacht,
iad 'na mbanna dá dtarra[i]ng 'na gcéadaibh
chum gach cuain ar fuaid na hÉireann,
dá gcur don Spáinn ar áis nó ar éigin.[288]

The English in the poem is spectacularly archipelagic not just because it was written by an Irish speaker but because, within it, there are tracks of interaction. The word 'Tory' had crossed from Gaelic *tóraidhe, -aighe* ('pursuer, rebel') into English in the 1640s,[289] and it returns here barbed with negative connotations ('outlaw, thief'), meanings that would run into the long future of the word in British politics during the crisis of royal succession in 1679–82. Interestingly, during that Exclusion crisis 'Tory' was polarized against a word that had first been used in Scotland in the late 1640s to describe rebellious Presbyterians, 'Whig'.[290] The Whitehall party system was injected from the outset with implications from the archipelagic margins.

Though the Irish liked to believe in the ancient purity of their language, there were, in practice, imports, and that languages were felt to be distinct was not the same as mutual obscurity. In the *Pairlement Chloinne Tomáis*, the satire of the English argot spoken by ill-bred, tobacco-smoking upstarts depends on readers knowing both tongues. Monoglottism could be a useful fiction.[291] Contemporaries make it clear that bilingualism was routine among the Old English of the Pale (though English-speaking might be shunned),[292] as it was in West Cornwall, in much of Wales, especially in the later seventeenth century, and along the Highland line, where borrowing between Scots and Gaelic, and, increasingly, English and Gaelic, was common.[293] That such Irish poets as Ó Bruadair kept Anglo-English vocabulary out of their work does not mean that they were ignorant of the writing of men like Cowley.[294]

What incited bilingualism? War, with its need to communicate between allies and across battle-lines, was one spur, especially in Ireland. The use

---

Le execútion ... *ar áis nó ar éigin*: The first man's expectation is with execution, | The last with costs awarded against him. | *Transport, transplant*, is my recollection of English. | *Shoot him, kill him, strip him, tear him.* | *A Tory, hack him, hang him, rebel,* | *A rogue, a thief, a priest, a papist.* | Thousands of us together, | Being sent willingly or unwillingly to Spain. | They in groups descending in their hundreds | On every harbour throughout Ireland. (tr. Meidhbhín Ní Úrdail)

of interpreters in the Nine Years War[295] finds an echo in the role-shifting
of Darby in John Mitchelbourne's *Siege of London-Derry* (see Chapter 10).
Cross-linguistic fluency spread quickly when deprivation incited it, as
among Irish speakers in Ulster after the plantation:[296] the native Gaels had
to work with incoming strangers, whose dress and some of whose customs
they also started to acquire. Religious zeal was another factor; linguistic
barriers were crossed by English- and Scots-speaking churchmen, who were
willing to use Welsh in Wales, prepared, with less enthusiasm, to employ
Gaelic in the Western Isles, and, more unusually, persuaded to learn Irish,
as the much-admired William Bedell did,[297] to convert the peasantry.[298]
Such variables in the progress of the vernacular Reformation[299] reflect
inter alia the differing levels of security felt by anglophone groups outside
England—insecurity, it would seem, inciting a sense of cultural superiority
which made it harder to adopt the local language. They also demonstrate,
yet again, that the use of English/Inglis was a locally contingent, not a
consistent, phenomenon.

What are the English equivalents of the macaronic lines I quoted
above? Scots and Anglo-Welsh poetry differ—the verse of Morgan
Llwyd, for instance, includes exalted, even visionary, Welsh phrases (see
Chapter 6)—but if one is looking for strictly Anglo- or Hiberno-English
incorporations of Irish the characteristic tone is satirical if not sadistic. Here
is a stanza about the Irish in *A Medley of the Nations* (1655):

> O hone, O hone, poor Teg and Shone,
>   O hone may howl and cry,
> St Patrick help dy country-men,
>   Or fait and trot we dye;
> De English steal our hoart of Usquebagh,
> Dey put us to de Sword all in Dewguedagh:
> Help us St Patrick we ha no Saint at all but dee,
> O let us cry no more, O hone, a cram, a cree.[300]

Divergence from the writer's own Anglo-English is an index of weakness
and defeat. It would be naive to look for sympathy in 'poor Teg and Shone',
which flags up Irish indigence and self-pity, much as the propensity to
'howl and cry' reflects a long-running English prejudice against keening as
infantile, barbarous, and subversive.

Oh hone: Alas   *Teg and Shone*: Taigue and Sean (stereotypical Irish names)
Usquebagh: whiskey   *Dewguedagh*: Drogheda (Cromwellian victory/massacre)
a cram, a cree: my dear (Gaelic *grád mo croidhe*, 'love of my heart')

To move onto Irish ground is to find the linguistic energies of archipelagic English shifting. *Lilli burlero* (1688), for instance, which was almost certainly (as early printings assert) composed in Ireland then exported to England, centres on James II and VII's appointment of the Old English Catholic, Tyrconnell, to the Lord Deputyship:

> Ho, brother Teague, dost hear de decree,
> > Lilli burlero, bullen a-la;
> Dat we shall have a new debittie,
> > Lilli burlero bullen a-la,
> > Lero lero, lero lero, lilli burlero, bullen a-la;
> > Lero lero, lero lero, lilli burlero, bullen a-la.[301]

The staple of the song is a convincing Hiberno-English, of the sort that would be uttered by an ill-bred Catholic Irishman, but what of the refrain? The contemporary Ulster-born poet and linguistic trickster, Paul Muldoon adopts the traditional view when he takes it to be fermented Gaelic with archipelagic English thrown in:

> 'Bullen a-la' ... is a corruption of *Baineann an la*, a phrase having to do with taking, or carrying the day. Some version of this phrase had supposedly been used by native insurgents in the great revolt of 22 and 23 October 1641. .... *Lilly* may also refer to William Lilly (1602–81), the [English, never in Ireland] astrologer who predicted the defeat of the Royalists, ... Another reading, therefore, of the phrase 'Lilli burlero' would be 'Lilly, *ba léir dó*' or, 'it was clear, or evident, to Lilly'.[302]

Some texts of *Lilli burlero* are further diversified by two stanzas of Anglo-English: 'There was a prophecy lately found in a bog, | That Ireland should be rul'd by an ass and a dog; | This prophecy's true, and now come to pass, | For Talbot's the dog, and Tyrconnel's an ass.'[303] Whatever its provenance or function in the song, this throws into relief the interconnective role of Hiberno-English. The simple polarities of *A Medley* break down as we see how Anglo-English will absorb Irish through Hiberno-speak:

> Now Tyrconnel is come a-shore,
> > [Lilli burlero, bullen a-la;]
> And we shall have commissions gillore.
> > [Lilli burlero, ...]

What language is *this* written in? The word Tyrconnell is as Gaelic ('land of O'Donnell') as William Lilly is English, but Talbot's elevation to the Earldom of that title in 1685 made it current in Anglo-English. 'Gillore', i.e.

galore, was also *en route*, the *OED* recording it from 1675 as an importation from Irish or Scottish Gaelic (*go léor* 'sufficiency'). The word's subsequent, lively future in standard English helps discredit for us the contempt the poem hangs upon it.

The absorbency of Hiberno-English, and its capacity, as a result, to enrich or contaminate Anglo-English, had been a feature of the dialect for generations. It was a complaint of the New English against their Old predecessors that, along with assuming Irish dress and sexual mores, they had let their language degenerate by cross-breeding with Gaelic. Yet the philological picture was complex, with Hiberno-English showing characteristics that were older, more Chaucerian, than the continentally influenced English (with its Ulster admixture of Scots) brought in by Tudor and Jacobean planters. At the northern edge of the Pale a tongue known as Fingalian intrigued both New English settlers and travellers in search of curiosities. Fingalian combined highly conservative, ultimately Middle English traits with elements of local Irish, showing that large-scale archipelagic transits were not the only means by which linguistic hybridization took place.

We can get no closer to Fingalian now than is allowed by a celebrated passage in John Dunton's 'Letters from Ireland' (1698), a work which attests to the survival of this dialect long after Catholic Ireland had been subjected to execution and transplantation. 'In a small territorry called Fingaal neare Dublin', Dunton reports, 'they have a sort of Jargon speech peculiar to themselves, and understand not one word of Irish, and are as little understood by the English.'[304] This claim of two-way incomprehension need not be taken on trust, from a passing English visitor, but the poem which Dunton then approximately reproduces shows not just the imprint of Gaelic but the influence on an Old English community of the mere Irish custom of keening: 'I'le give a sample of it in a lamentation which a mother made over her sons grave, who had been a greate fisher and huntsman: Ribbeen a Roon, Ribbeen Moorneeng, thoo ware good for loand stroand and mounteen, for rig a tool and roast a whiteen, reddy tha taakle, gather tha Baarnacks, drink a grote at Nauny Hapennys.'[305] It has been said that 'This pathetic doggerel is

---

Ribbeen ... Moorneeng: Robin my love, Robin my dear   *for rig*: (*good*) at using
whiteen: whiting   *reddy tha taakle*: prepare your gear   *Baarnacks*: bannocks
grote: groat   *Nauny Hapennys*: Nanny Halfpenny's (alehouse)

clearly assonantal, as is Celtic poetry, rhetorically structured, and dependent on Irish: as such, it is a rare record of a tradition at the point of extinction, expiring in English with memories of Irish words and Irish verse-forms.'[306] The judgement has some validity, yet it is too pessimistic about the extinction of Gaelic tradition. Dunton's passage shows that Irish was still strong enough to transmute English rather than expire in it.

What of the languages of Britain? Though the English spoken in Wales was subject to regional variation[307] and local peculiarity (e.g. in Pembrokeshire), it broadly derived from medieval and early modern England. It also showed, however, the influence of the Celtic tongue which it displaced, supplemented, and neighboured. The poetry of Henry Vaughan has elements of vocabulary and rhyme which indicate that his English was coloured by the Welsh that he spoke from infancy.[308] Welsh-speaking was being eroded by the advance of English, both geographically (chiefly from the East) and socially (in the anglicization of the gentry). There is also evidence of degradation as ancient Welsh vocabulary became the province of the elderly, and of country folk, then passed out of use as English-derived terms were incorporated.[309] At the start of the period covered by this book, we hear of Cornish speakers unable, or defiantly unwilling, to use English;[310] by the middle of the century, the old tongue had retreated to the Western edge of the county. In Scotland the situation was different again. Though Scots-Inglis and Southern English were both encroaching on Gaelic, which would be further beaten back after 1707, and though all three tongues were engaged in a degree of trading, the primary linguistic drama centred on the anglicization of Scots. During the Middle Ages, the varieties of Old English used north and south of the Tweed diverged into Early Scots and Middle English, but the Scots tongue began to move back towards what Inglis-speakers called 'sudron' during the sixteenth century.[311] When James VI wrote, in *Basilikon Doron*, of 'this Ile of Brittane ... al-ready ioyned in vnitie of Religion, and language',[312] he was forcing the linguistic (as well as the religious) evidence in order to support his case for succession, but he was also responding to a process which 1603 would advance, not initiate.

This is a difficult topic, best taken up in the context of writings by such anglicizers as Drummond, his fellow-poet Sir William Alexander (who started life as 'MacAlistair'), and James himself, and I return to it in Chapter 4. One generalization worth making, however, is that, although language could be regarded by early modern Inglis/English, Welsh, and Irish-speakers alike as a component of cultural identity—contributing to group loyalties, and transmitting beliefs and customs—the assumption of many post-eighteenth-century nationalists that language is constitutive of national consciousness was not yet entrenched. It should also be pointed out that, although Scots attracted opprobrium in Jacobean England, or at least became the focus for resentment at the visibility and success of Scotsmen at court, the language could also claim a certain prestige, which made it easier, on occasion, for the Scottish king to be granted respect. Among sixteenth-century humanists, a patriotic search for the pure springs of English led back to northern dialects. Though Puttenham, for instance, values the south-eastern norm, he concedes that the language of the north 'is the purer English Saxon at this day'.[313] Most advocates of fuller union who got into the politics of language backed the king's claim that the same language (Saxon) was spoken in both parts of the island, but the theory was also aired, on the basis of northern purity, that English derived from Scots.[314] In a sense just short of flattering delusion it was possible to believe that James was more anglophone than the English.

During the seventeenth century English was not much spoken outside Britain, Ireland, and the American colonies, though it had a presence in the Low Countries (see Chapter 7). Yet visionary or wishful individuals were already anticipating its transformation into a global language. In a now-celebrated passage, published in 1619, Alexander Gill declared: 'Since in the beginning all men's lips were identical, and there existed but one language, it would indeed be desirable to unify the speech of all peoples in one universal vocabulary; and were human ingenuity to attempt this, certainly no more suitable language than English could be found'.[315] It is one of the ironies of humanism that Gill made this observation in Latin. Two decades later, condemning the pagan classicism of men like Gill, the puritan James Hunt went further:

> God will gather all Nations into Religion one
> So by degrees all shall be taught the English tongue;
> For the Word which proceedeth from the God of peace,
> Doth plainly say, that *tongues shall cease*: I Cor. 13.[316]

What sort of English would fill the world? Gill, who opposed affected pronunciation, and Hunt, who praised 'plaine English', would have been conscious of standardization around the language spoken in London that derived from an East Midlands dialect of Middle English. The norm was being developed in the fifteenth century and it was established by 1553 when Thomas Wilson brought the phrase 'the kynges English' into use.[317] It was possible in the sixteenth century for Gavin Douglas and Richard Stanihurst to translate *The Aeneid* into Scots and an almost Joycean, neologizing Hiberno-English with no apparent anxiety about losing classical dignity. By the seventeenth, this was not an option because of changing attitudes to 'dialect'.[318] Modern scholars disagree about how negatively regional English was regarded. The variousness of the tongue[319] could be interpreted, along humanist lines, as a symptom of desirable abundance, a sign of linguistic wealth. As Richard Carew put it: 'the Copiousnes of our languadge appeareth in the diuersitye of our dialectes, for wee haue court, and wee haue countrye Englishe, wee haue Northern, and Southerne, grosse and ordinary, which differ ech from other, not only in the terminacions, but alsoe in many wordes, termes and phrases, and expresse the same thinges in diuers sortes, yeat all right Englishe alike'.[320] Against this can be set Aubrey's comment on Sir Walter Raleigh, 'that notwithstanding his so great Mastership in Style and his conversation with the learnedest and politest persons, yet he spake broad Devonshire to his dying day'.[321] There is room for uncertainty about what Aubrey is describing (vocabulary, accent?), and about how exceptional Raleigh was in combining high status with 'broad' speech, but it is hard to read 'notwithstanding... yet' without feeling that the great man's language was judged by some to be beneath him.

Aubrey's is a late seventeenth-century gloss on characteristics that Raleigh's contemporaries may have noted with less surprise. Dialectal variation declined within educated English over the period covered by this book, as the south-eastern norm became normative. It was rare for printed texts to incorporate dialect, and when it appears it is usually attributed to the inferior, the culturally peripheral, and/or the potentially troublesome—the Welsh and Catholic Irish scoring high in all three categories. The broadness of the Scots attributed to Lauderdale in *A Dream of the Cabal* (1672), quoted in Chapter 9, is a measure of the author's animus. North of the border, Scots remained current in everyday speech through the eighteenth century and beyond, but its literary scope narrowed—educated prose became self-consciously anglicized—despite the vigorous survival of the ballads, and the reinvigoration of the poetic vernacular by Allan Ramsay, Robert Fergusson, and Burns. A further development within England was for dialect features to become conventionalized, approximate markers of divergence from the norm, rather than accurate representations of speech. This was the period which saw the birth of stage 'mummerset'. Like most general shifts, the movement towards standardization was not the result of a single change but the confluence of various pressures, some of them English-patriotic. After the Restoration, there was, for example, hostility to the fashionable borrowing of words from the national enemy, France.

One counter-effect of standardization was a growing interest in dialect among antiquarians. John Ray's *A Collection of English Words* (1674), for instance, lists terms collected on Ray's 'travels through several parts of *England*' and supplied by friends. According to the preface, his prospectus of 'the Language of the common people' would be valuable for a traveller heading north—leaving the province of the King's English. Ray lists the names of birds and beasts and the language of trades (always defined in relation to place, from 'The Smelting and Refining of Silver, at the Silver Mills in Cardiganshire' to 'The Making of Salt at Namptwych in Cheshire').[322] Such was the success of the *Collection* that a new edition was called for, and Ray filled it out with communications from such scholars as Francis Brokesby, Rector of Rowley in Yorkshire, and Edward Lhuyd, the Celtic philologist. Lhuyd's contribution was a list 'of *British* [i.e. Welsh-Britonic] Words parallel to some of the Northern Words in this Collection, from which probably the Northern might be derived'.[323] This catalogue was part of a collective enterprise by antiquarians to explore the Celtic, Cimbric, and Gothic strains in the language. There was nothing new in the recognition that English was 'part *Dutch*, part *Irish, Saxon, Scotch, Welsh*, and indeed a gallimaffry'.[324] But the drive to highlight the mongrelism of even standard English ran symptomatically against the polite consolidation of the norm.

The literary effects of this drive can be seen in the overlap between Ray's *Collection* and what is generally regarded as the first self-consciously English dialect poem to get into print, George Meriton's *A Yorkshire Dialogue* (1683):

> D[aughter]. Mother our Croky's Cawven sine't grew dark,
> And Ise flaid to come nar, she macks sike wark;

M[other]. Seaun, seaun Barn, bring my Skeel and late my tee
Mack hast, and hye Thee ore to'th Laer to me: ...³²⁵

Locally published, this work was composed (as its title page put it)
*In its pure Natural Dialect: As it is now commonly Spoken in the North
parts of Yorkshire*. For those unfamiliar with the idiom, editions from
1685 included a glossary, while the third edition of 1697 reprinted
Brokesby's 'Observations concerning the Dialect and Various Pronunciation of words in the *East-Riding* of *Yorkshire*' from the 1691 version
of Ray's *Collection*. It has been said that 'Ray's scholarly interest in and
Meriton's use of dialect for "literary" purposes are very early compared to other European countries.'³²⁶ But there were developments
elsewhere in the islands that parallel, or even anticipate, Meriton's
poem—the staggered dates, and varieties of implication, reflecting local
conditions.

Thus in Ireland scholarly curiosity was tainted by an urge to mock
and, at times of danger, discredit ordinary Catholics. This is apparent in
the textual history of a 'travesty' of the *Aeneid* which also shows how
much had changed since Stanihurst used Hiberno-experimental English
as a vehicle for translating Virgil. Probably composed in about 1670, and
circulated in manuscript as 'Purgatorium Hibernicum',³²⁷ this send-up of
the customs and linguistic peculiarities of Fingal recasts Aeneas and Dido as
Nees the oafish Old Englishman and a crude ex-nun called Dydy. Aeneas's
descent into the underworld is turned into a journey by Nees into a
cave at St Patrick's Purgatory, the old Catholic shrine in County Donegal
that remained a site of contention between religious groups throughout
the period of this book. Expanded as 'The Fingallian Travesty', another
manuscript text, incoherently related to the 'Purgatorium', the work was
revised and updated with allusions to the Jacobite-Williamite crisis of
1688–9, calculated to demean the supporters of Tyrconnell, and printed in
London as *The Irish Hudibras* (1689).³²⁸

The author, or authors, and revisers of the 'Purgatorium', most likely
New English Palesmen, went to so much trouble to annotate the evolving
poem with glosses, historical sources, and cross-references to Virgil that
the whole enterprise now seems paradoxical. Their assiduity manifests

---

Croky: little Scottish cow   *Cauven*: calved   *flaid*: afraid   *sike wark*: such work
Seaun, seaun Barn: quickly, quickly child   *Skeel*: milk pail
late: find   *tee* string used to tie a cow's legs together during milking   *Laer*: barn

a perverse respect for the life and language that are mocked, and the multilingual competence assumed in readers of the manuscript texts—the printed version of 1689 comes with a glossary of Irish words aimed at a less capable, English audience[329]—attests to a cultural richness in the mix of classical and church Latins, Hiberno-English, Irish, and Anglo-English that the work aims to deride as inchoate (even while it ingeniously puns between languages), that it tries vainly to put into hierarchies, and seeks politically to polarize. One of the most peculiar features of *The Irish Hudibras*, indeed, is that, despite its governing assumption that Fingalian words and customs need explaining for civilized readers, it can assume greater familiarity with Irish vocabulary than with British—as when '*Coge*' (a north-country word, in Hiberno-English usage, meaning 'wooden drinking-vessel') is glossed in the margin '*Vsquebagh*',[330] an Irish term for distilled spirits that would not become English (according to the *OED*) until the eighteenth century, when a truncated form came in from Scottish Gaelic as *whisky*. How archipelagic is that.

(vi) Textual circulation

That 'The Fingallian Travesty' went into print in England after circulating in manuscript in Ireland surely owes more to the ambition of its sponsors to reach a large, influential readership swiftly than to a lack of press capacity in Dublin. Yet the London publication of the text does form part of a larger, uneven pattern of book production, trade, and reception around the archipelago in which a relative shortage of printers in Ireland was a factor. For decades after 1603, production was limited to a single press in Dublin operated by the King's Printer. Books and pamphlets were published in Waterford, Cork, and Kilkenny during the Confederate wars,[331] but the establishment of a sustainable provincial printing industry had to wait until the 1690s. By the early eighteenth century, there were presses in such towns as Belfast and Limerick, and Ireland, already engaged in reprinting English books and exporting them back across the water, was positioned to profit from loopholes in the Copyright Act of 1709 (effective from 1710), which restricted printing in Britain. From being a net importer of books, Ireland became a substantial exporter. It is hard for historians to be sure what proportion of the huge list of works published in Hanoverian Dublin—from Samuel Richardson's *Pamela* to Gibbon's

Decline and Fall—were read by Irish people and how many were shipped overseas.[332]

The restricted basis of print culture during the period 1603–1707 affected Catholics disproportionately. Works by Irish papists, often composed in Latin, were more typically produced on the continent. Texts by English recusants could follow the same path,[333] and Scottish Presbyterian material was often printed in the Low Countries.[334] But Irish book production was peculiarly diasporic, especially for those active in Gaelic. Such a major work as Céitinn's *Foras feasa ar Éirinn* was available (at least in Irish) only in manuscript.[335] There was printing in Irish at Louvain, and, towards the end of the century, in Rome,[336] but the failure of Catholic Ireland to develop its own industry, whether at home or abroad—partly the product, as in Scottish Gaeldom, of thinly spread population, economic backwardness, and low levels of literacy (though the Welsh, under similar conditions, published many books in their own language)[337]—has been plausibly seen as contributing to its inability to consolidate a 'national' identity in the face of English aggression.[338]

The English print industry was, by contrast, buoyant and expansive, and far into the seventeenth century books and pamphlets shared the market with the socially exclusive or politically expedient custom of manuscript circulation.[339] Of the hundreds of works quoted and noted in this book, the great preponderance were printed in London even when written elsewhere.[340] This was not a supply-led process, though publishers were aware of the need to cultivate their publics; the appetite for print was voracious, as became only too clear to the authorities during periods when licensing lapsed. The grass-roots vitality of English textual culture is evident, at a pre-literary level, in the growth in letter-writing and the related spread of newspapers. Schemes for a letter office were afoot by 1635,[341] but it was the eruption in correspondence and newsbook publication during the civil wars that set off new developments.[342] The Protectorate instituted a post office, where letters were covertly opened, decoded, and copied.[343] An Act of 1657 anticipated the post-Restoration growth of the postal service, while the secret state continued its monitoring. Now the post office did not just fillet out intelligence from intercepted letters but marketed the information it gathered, becoming a centre for the collation, copying, and forwarding of restricted-circulation newsletters.

At this date, the bulk of the mail passed at some point through London, radiating out along six main routes through Kent, Yarmouth, Chester,

Bristol, Plymouth, and the North, with letters going three times a week to Dublin and Edinburgh, plus daily transport to Dover for the continental pacquet boats.[344] New routes and post towns opened up, networking the English nation along with guidebooks and maps. By the 1680s, most market towns were connected into the service—a process impeded beyond England, notably in rural Ireland, by the poor state of the roads. Postmasters were caught into the loop of spying and news distribution; they were rewarded for intelligence-gathering with copies of newsbooks (especially the *London Gazette*) and the right to circulate them free of charge. For this and other reasons the development of the newspaper industry ran in parallel with the postal service.[345] As government press controls were lifted during the Exclusion Crisis, there was a step-up growth in titles, while William Dockwra—himself associated with 'Whig' political forces—introduced the Penny Post. Waves of newspaper production followed the Revolution of 1688–9 and the lapse in licensing in 1695. This was also the moment at which Scottish conditions changed, with the licensing of newspapers from 1699 and their distribution out from Edinburgh by employees of the office of the Postmaster General, set up four years earlier. During the union controversies of 1705–6, this new matrix of print would be vigorously active[346] and cross-border. As Defoe discovered when he attempted to partition English and Scottish readerships, the impact of pamphlets and newsprint depended on the range of circulation as much as what was argued (below, pp. 335–6).

How were those readerships constituted? Literacy rates are hard to determine, and historians dispute the figures. It should also be remembered that, even among the literate, the hearing and learning by heart of ballads, drinking-songs, jests, prayers, hymns, and catechisms spread information, inculcated prejudice, and consolidated religious communities. So did dramatic performance, whether staged by local people, or by travelling players (we have recently learned a great deal about theatre in the English regions, in Wales and Ireland, and an account of Scotland is imminent).[347] Those caveats and qualifications aside, the standard view is that, in England, some 30 per cent of men and 10 per cent of women could read in the early 1640s (taking the ability to sign one's name as evidence of literacy)[348] and that these proportions rose to about 45 and 25 per cent by 1714.[349] Rates varied considerably according to region, however, and even more so by habitat. Towns were good for literacy, and so were trades which required record-keeping. In London, with its large, mixed, and shifting, often socially ambitious population, nearly 80 per cent of male adults could apparently sign their names by the outbreak of the civil wars.[350] In urban and Lowland Scotland, literacy also reached high levels by the 1670s and 1680s—providing a ready audience for the Covenanter tracts, printed ballads, and satires discussed in Chapter 9. As in England, regional and status-related differences were marked; books in any language were not common in the Highlands, and across Scotland as a whole more than 80 per cent of labourers were illiterate in the second half of the century.[351]

Enough library catalogues survive from seventeenth-century Ireland for us to know that, among the elites, reading was a prestigious as well as informative practice.[352] That wealth was patchily spread inhibited general literacy, but reading was incentivized by the struggle for advantage in a country subject to the rigours of agricultural revolution, religious controversy, and litigation. There are reasons for believing that literacy rates in Ireland were higher—among the native, Gaelic Irish as well as the New English gentry[353]—than historians have customarily assumed. Among the urban affluent and tradesmen of the middling sort whose everyday language was English there were demonstrable concentrations of ability. One study has found two-thirds of those providing sureties in Dublin signing their names (as against making their marks) in the early 1650s, rising to more than three quarters in the 1690s. Another, focussed on the Adair estates in County Antrim, in the later decades of the century, indicates that, whereas only 33 per cent of farmers and yeoman could sign their names, 94 per cent of those in trade were capable.[354] Literacy, in short, was unevenly distributed in Ireland as well as Britain; but there was plenty of it across the archipelago.

As the contrast sketched out above between Irish and English textual conditions suggests, economic and cultural geographies affected how literary works were circulated in each of the kingdoms. The structure of the print industry also made a difference. Though London had a concentration of commercial scriptoria, it was many times more prolific in the publication of books. English printing was largely a metropolitan operation; that was where the Stationers' Company, and the licensing authorities, were based—though the example of Menston's *Dialogue* points to an expansion in provincial publishing in the later part of the century.[355] Ireland presented a similar picture, in the dominance of Dublin—though not in the rate of print production—and in the role of the London Stationers as they attempted to establish a book trade in that city during the early Stuart period. In Scotland the situation was otherwise because there was no commercial, regulatory body as powerful as the Stationers. As in Ireland, the office of King's Printer had influence, and there was centralized control by the state, in the form of the Scottish Privy Council, until it was abolished in the wake of the 1707 union, but superintendents (after 1612, bishops) of the Kirk, and the burghs of Aberdeen, Edinburgh, and Glasgow all had significant, localized input into licensing and trade regulation.[356]

Until recently, historians of the book obscured what was distinctive about Scottish conditions by eliding them with those of England, or by ignoring them altogether. We are now much clearer about the role of burgh magistrates and councillors in licensing—a procedure which had no parallel in England. Over the first half of the seventeenth century the power of the London Stationers' Company, consolidated by King James in 1603, spread into Scotland; the process was advanced by the granting of a 'Scottish Patent' by Charles I. Cromwellian union abolished the Privy Council in Scotland, and put English judges and magistrates, and town councils, in charge of licensing. Yet these reforms were short-lived, and the return of the Privy Council at the Restoration re-established a pattern which anticipated arrangements that would apply across Britain as a whole during the eighteenth century. With the arrival of the Copyright Act under Queen Anne, 'the law of the United Kingdom [of Great Britain] was brought back to an older commercial, and still current Scottish idea—that on the "publication" of intellectual property or an invention, the only copyright possible was that granted by the state for a limited period. ... The copyright system embedded in Scotland by the 1670s seems to have a closer relationship to the later developments of copyright in the United Kingdom than the history of an Elizabethan corporation.'[357]

During the period covered by this book, the diversity of licensing authorities within Scotland—though the long arm of the Privy Council was usually ready to pressurize local magistrates during periods of upheaval—and the differences between Scotland and England, allowed cultural particularities to show through. Take the case of the Book of books. South of the border, the Authorized Version (1611) quickly spread into use. In Scotland, despite the passing of a canon law in its favour, it was not ubiquitous until the Restoration. Until then, the more stringently Protestant Geneva Bible, long orthodox in the Kirk, was dominant. There was no equivalent in Scotland of the English High Commission action against the importation of Geneva bibles in 1632, nor of Laud's Star

Chamber decree in favour of the Authorized Version. In this as in other respects more internationalized than their neighbours, the Scots freely imported bibles. There were, however, paradoxes. Many of the bibles traded into Scotland from the Low Countries, for instance, were set from the Geneva Bible produced in Edinburgh by Andro Hart in 1610. And at the other end of the period, as the 1707 union was poised to legalize the flow of books from England which already threatened the profitability of Scottish publishing, Agnes Campbell produced in Edinburgh a bible that declared on its title page, 'London, printed by Charles Bill'. It was one way of capitalizing on the Scottish appetite for imported bibles.[358]

The history of the Irish print industry is usually said to start with the arrival of Humphrey Powell from London supported by a grant from the English Privy Council and the title of King's Printer, 'an office probably created by the government to regulate the trade'.[359] Within months, Powell had published in Dublin the first Edwardian Book of Common Prayer (1551). This conjunction of London commerce with royal authority, control of the press, and the inculcation of reformed religion through the medium of English, established a structure which prevailed during 1603–1707. Whereas the influence of the Stationers' Company was limited in Scotland by the vitality of the indigenous book trade, in Ireland the Stationers took over the role of King's Printer in 1618 and escalated publishing output fivefold by the late 1630s. Even so, the relative weakness of the market for books, in what was in many respects a garrison and plantation society, meant that the Stationers were willing to sell their monopoly in 1639. Until 1663, the purchaser William Bladen acted as printer to both king and Commonwealth. Beneath his even-handed, or opportunistic, industry was a field of book production polarized by war. In Waterford, and then Kilkenny, Thomas Bourke printed official matter for the Catholic Confederation, works of contemporary controversy, and the summary of *Titus: Or, The Palme of Christian Courage* that is discussed in Chapter 5. London, at this date, saw an eruption of unlicensed printing. In Dublin, the government was able to keep the much smaller book trade on a tight leash. The rolling back of Catholic authority by the English army under Cromwell led to the closure of the Kilkenny press, and the removal of printing from Waterford to parliamentarian Cork.[360] By the late 1650s, Protestant dominance was re-secured, and print once again promulgated the belief systems and legal instruments of a semi-colonial state.

Inevitably, the pattern was frayed by exceptions, imports, and commercially motivated initiatives. Ulster drew in large numbers of books from Presbyterian Scotland. Although the Scottish trade with Ireland was worth only 15 per cent of the English one, it was much more specifically devoted to religious and political works. Bibles, catechisms, testaments, and copies of the Westminster Confession flowed into Belfast and Derry. There were complaints even in the 1690s about a Scotch Directory and the Solemn League and Covenant being hawked about Ireland by chapmen.[361] After the Restoration, the Dublin book trade, which had developed during the 1630s in the same district as the Werburgh Street theatre (below, pp. 170–81), enlarged and became more adventurous. Up to a third of the books produced in the second half of the century were unlicensed reprints of English works aimed at the English market.[362] But the sheer quantity and variety of titles published during this period[363] testifies to a craving for print in a country convulsed by war and new waves of anglophone settlement. That Restoration Ireland was securely in the orbit of England brought its output, and its imports, closer to the London market. Yet it was possible for Catholic readers, especially during the reign of James II and VII, to find congenial religious works even in Dublin bookshops. Often enough through England, though also direct from the continent, Catholic bibles, prayerbooks, and iconography made their way into the country. Meanwhile the dominance of the King's Printer was eroded not just by competition from rival publishers in Dublin, but by the import of books from Britain through such seaports as Galway and Cork.[364]

So the plurality of jurisdictions did not preclude the movement of books around the archipelago—though censorship often cut across their production at source.[365] By the end of the seventeenth century, Ireland was drawing in quantities of English printed matter,[366] while London and Lowland Scotland were tied into 'an expanding domestic and international book market which showed scant respect for territorial boundaries and intellectual property'.[367] This was an outcome with several origins, some of them continental. Imports of print from Bristol to the Irish ports had grown substantially as the country settled into the uneasy peace that followed the end of Tyrone's rebellion and the Nine Years War in 1603.[368] Under-used capacity in Dublin then allowed the printing of the 1621 edition of Sidney's *Arcadia* for the English trade.[369] It may be that the Stationers' Company set itself up in Ireland with a view to just such an arrangement. As noted in Chapter 7, Scottish books poured into England from the late 1630s—in the hope of influencing opinion—both direct from Edinburgh and Glasgow and out of sympathetic presses in the Low Countries. After the 1641 rebellion,[370] as in 1688–91 (see Chapter 10), Protestant Ireland was equally ready to keep the English informed. Meanwhile, London publishers kept farming out work to Dublin. By the 1640s, books printed in Dublin were commonplace in England,[371] and, for the remainder of the century, printed matter flowed both ways.

Manuscript was similarly mobile. Spenser's *Vewe of the Present State of Ireland* was apparently written in London, but it circulated on both sides of the Irish Sea before coming back to Dublin for discreetly edited publication in Sir James Ware's 1633 compilation, *The Historie of Ireland*—a book (or series) which also had a London issue.[372] It was presumably along the same sort of network that the 'Purgatorium Hibernicum' made its way, among Leinster gentlemen and their friends and relatives in England. The second extant version of the text, 'The Fingallian Travesty', survives in the papers of Sir Hans Sloane, an Irishman in England.[373] Yet manuscripts did not always come well out of archipelagic circulation. When Sir Thomas Urquhart marched south from Scotland with Charles II in 1651, he brought with him in manuscript 'a hundred severall bookes, on subjects never hitherto thought upon by any' (as he modestly put it), intending to have the texts printed in London. After the rout of the royalists at Worcester, he could only recover a tiny fraction of the 'sixscore and eight quires and a half' that he had carried down from Cromarty.[374]

If books travelled, so did printers. By the end of the century, the propaganda value of print was so obvious that, when the 9th Earl of Argyll rebelled in 1685, he took care to have a *Declaration* printed in the West of Scotland (by a Dutchman brought over with materials, specifically for the purpose), while, to cite a better-known case, Willem van Oranje invaded Ireland with a London printer in his entourage.[375] As printers moved about, they took conventions with them. When the Englishman Robert Waldegrave became King's Printer in Edinburgh, in 1590, he anglicized his books—in line with James VI's unionist ambitions—not just linguistically but in the employment of such paratextual features as dedications. This sort of bibliographical coding could prove explosive when texts were resituated. One reason why the Scots found the crypto-Anglican prayerbook of 1637 an imposition is that it was set in black letter, whereas Scottish Protestant religious texts had for decades preferred roman.[376] The Bishops' Wars were fought over more than a typeface, but the appearance of the book displayed in black and white English insensitivity to cultural difference.

It is often forgotten that the controversial service-book was not precisely the one used in England. Charles wanted to exploit what he took to be an opportunity to Laudianize British religion by including 'higher' elements than were current south of the border. The intention was to use Scotland, as it would be used again, as an arena for testing out measures that might then be applied to England. Yet Laud and his allies in the Kirk were also canny enough to realize that Scottish susceptibilities needed consideration, and so, in other respects, the Anglicanism of the prayerbook—a throwback to 1549—was muted (lessons from the apocrypha, for instance, current in England, were taken out). The text went through several stages of annotation and revision; even while it was being printed, changes were made.[377] The variant nature of the book both across the border and within the Scottish print-run bears out a common tendency for texts to metamorphose as they moved around the archipelago. The effect has already been noted in the addition of the story of Brut's division of Britain to a London edition of *Basilikon Doron*. It is probable that *Lilli burlero* picked up its stanzas in standard English once the body of the song—the 'first part' of it, anyway—arrived in England. 'The second part', attached to most early editions,[378] has an English setting, a later implied date, and an even coarser, more triumphalist stereotyping of Catholic Irishness that seems to stem from a perception of the Irish as an internal minority easily disposed of at Tyburn rather than the dangerous besieging people that Irish Protestants felt them to be.

Accretions of this sort develop even in texts that, as far as we can tell, were confined in their circulation to English, or at least British, ground. The case of Marvell's 'The Loyall Scot' has general enough implications to bring this section to a close. As I explain in Chapter 9, this apparently downright, devious satire was written during a period in which Charles II's policy of extending toleration to Dissenters, while ostensibly exploring the possibilities of Anglo-Scottish union (*c*.1669), was distancing him from the Anglican establishment. Marvell, who had Presbyterian sympathies, seized the opportunity to deride the bishops as opponents of the royal will and dividers of the island. Yet the make-up of his poem, which is variant both between manuscripts and between manuscripts and (decades later) print, appears to reflect a process rather than a moment of composition. Thus, some texts of 'The Loyall Scot' include a long, abusive passage on the bishops which is missing in others. So far, so unsurprising, for a late seventeenth-century satire which was passed around in manuscript. What should we make, however, of the inclusion, in the most anti-Episcopalian texts, of an eight-line translation of a Latin epigram by Marvell (with its own, independent, manuscript life) about the Irish Dissenter Thomas Blood? Infuriated by the Restoration settlement that gave a modest amount of appropriated land back to Catholics, the Presbyterian Blood had plotted with Ulster Covenanters to seize Dublin Castle in 1663,[379] and, in the escapade celebrated by Marvell, stole the crown jewels from the Tower of London to make up for his lost Irish rents.

As it passed into 'The Loyall Scot', the fabric of the epigram became archipelagically variant: the ground of Blood's complaint was distinguished from the site of his theft by the insertion of the word 'English'.[380] That is but a salient detail. What should be noted more largely, is, first, that it is not anomalous, in the context set out by this book, for an Irish-angled epigram to slip into a poem about Anglo-Scottish relations. Blood was one of many involved in a Scoto-Irish radical network that ran from Ulster (where he was active) across the channel to Galloway. He was a thorny branch of Scottish influence in a kingdom that had long been subject to the English crown. Second, if one follows the tracks of interaction with the receptiveness proposed by *Archipelagic English* one finds that Ulster Presbyterianism contributed more extensively to 'The Loyall Scot' because it shaped the high-flying Anglicanism of Marvell's episcopal enemies. It was the bruising experience of dealing with the Ulster Scots in Derry and in Down and Connor that made John Bramhall and Jeremy Taylor such uncompromising and influential Anglican divines after the Restoration. From such figures, propagandists like Samuel Parker took their cue, and created the English context for Marvell's poem.[381] The circulation of texts around the archipelago was inextricable from the creation of meanings which the processes of interaction compounded.

(vii) Devolutionary interactivities

This book deals with a wider range of texts and issues than have been caught up in debates among historians about the British problem. But that does not free it from the risk of falling into the Anglocentrism that has been imputed to the new British history. To select material for discussion on the grounds of its having been written in English/Inglis may in fact pull discussion more strongly towards the heartland of anglophone literary production—roughly the triangle that runs between Hull, Stratford, and London—than state papers draw historians to Whitehall. Yet because literary criticism is more descriptive and explicatory than is historical scholarship on the lookout for causes and consequences, it has been possible in some measure to proportion my own mix, choosing texts written in or beyond England on grounds of literary quality, cultural resonance, or representative range, without being constrained by the demands that historians labour under when they hunt out the origins of the Root and Branch Petition or the effects of 1688.

To devolve is to shift power in politics or scholarly analysis from a locus that has been disproportionately endowed with influence and documentation to sites that are dispersed and more skeletally understood. How can the impulse to do this be honoured given the difficulties that are dragged in by the associated, implicit topology of centre and margin, core and periphery? Let me unpack the question by citing an example not pursued in the body of this book. The Isle of Man lies at the centre of the archipelago geographically, and it was microcosmic both in its mix of Norse, Manx-Gaelic, and English ethnicities and in the nature of the events which unfolded there during the mid-seventeenth century.[382] When James, Lord Strange, inherited the Lordship of Man in 1627, he governed it through a deputy, preferring to reside (like his Stanley forebears) on the family estates in Lancashire. After backing Charles I against the Scots, Strange was active in the Long Parliament until he joined the royalist army. Ineffective in battle, he was ordered to Man by the king in 1643 to suppress a threatened revolt. From that point on, despite further forays into the English theatre of war, *Yn Stanlagh Mooar* (the Great Stanley) turned Man into a royalist haven. He exercised in his petty regality a version of Stuart prerogative government, quashing unrest about land tenure and tithes, and facing down demands—with the help of English soldiers—that the leaders of the Manx community (the twenty-four 'keys') and its judges ('deemers') be chosen by the people.

What happened on the Isle of Man—too abruptly summarized here—is deeply interesting and representative, but it is hardly ever mentioned in textbooks because so incidental to the huge conflicts that racked Britain and Ireland. Parliament did not trouble to claim the island until 1649, nor seriously attempt to invade it till March 1651, a few months before the Earl of Derby (as Strange had become) brought his interventions into Anglo-Scottish warfare to a disastrous close by joining up with Charles II shortly before the battle of Worcester. In the wake of that swingeing defeat for royalism he was executed. Yet the conclusion of the *Oxford Dictionary of National Biography*, that 'Derby's violent death ended an undistinguished career' can be qualified by recognizing what the *DNB* does not even mention, that this pious writer-earl, who left a number of devotional works, a commonplace book, a collection of anecdotes, and a 'Discourse Concerning the Government of the Isle of Man',[383] and who was the subject or addressee (in both English and Manx) of other men's songs, theatrical performances, and elegiac verses,[384] kept the culture of the Caroline court alive in his regality.

In the wishful words of a 'Prologue to a Play Acted in Castle Rushin, before the Right Hon*our*able Iames Earl of Derby', the Isle of Man was a 'Little Quiet Nation', safe from the mercenary turmoil of the English revolution, from 'the Troubles of pale Gold' and the dangers of 'Loose Freedom', and the 'change' sought by fools who would do away with old traditions and bring in 'Excise & Committee Men':

> Let the World run round,
> Let the World run round,
> And know neither End nor Station;
> Our Glory is the Rest [of],
> Of a Merry, Merry Breast,
> In this Little Quiet Nation.

'Lhig da'n Seighl tchindah my-geart'—as the stanza began in Manx. The poet snatches pleasure from the jaws of defeat in Britain and Ireland by arguing that the threats to royalism that were running round the world should inspire Stanley and his followers, in the spirit of Herrick or Lovelace, to an appetite for life, a devotion to *carpe diem*:

> We Eat, we Drink, we Dance, we Sing,
> To morrow freely Comes & Goes;
> We Strike up Musick's gentle Strings,
> And Understand no other Blows.
> [Chorus] Let the World run Round &c[385]

Derby was open enough to this advice to sponsor glittering entertainments. On Twelfth Night, 1645, for example, the earl and his countess (who had appeared in Jonson's *Chloridia* at court in 1630) invited all the Officer*es* Temparall and Spirituall The Cleargie the 24 Keyes of the Isle the Crowners with all theire wives & likewise the best sort of the rest of the Inhabitance of the Isle to a great maske; where the right ho*nourab*le Charles lo*rd* Strange w*i*th his traine the right ho*nourab*le Ladies w*i*th theire attendance were most gloriously decked with silver and gould broidered workes & most Costly ornaments bracelletts on there hands chaines on there neckes Jewels on there foreheads, earrings in there eares & Crownes on there heads and after the maske to a feast which was most royall & plentifull w*i*th shuttinge of ornans &c[386]

That Derby was able to uphold the ethos of Caroline Whitehall precisely because Man, though geographically central, was marginal to the civil wars shows that assumptions about core and periphery can be compound and reversible. The topology is sometimes useful, but researching this book has made me sceptical about the general application of a paradigm which can be distorting and is so susceptible to switching around (the margin becoming the centre) that the capacity of that manoeuvre to surprise is lost. The cultural and literary field opened up by *Archipelagic English* was never entirely free from the gravitational pull of south-east England, but a devolutionary approach needs to avoid being tied to a core-and-periphery schema so as to bring out those aspects of the field which were expansive, multilevelled, discontinuous, and polycentric.

I have said that I want to 'highlight the devolutionary and interactive dynamics' of anglophone writing (above, p. 11). If the example of Derby on Man shows that literary scholarship can extend and give sharp local focus to the devolved approach proposed by the new British history, there are difficulties associated with the related principle of interaction which cannot be dispatched so swiftly. For one thing, how *much* interactivity is needed to make a text archipelagic? Does devolution to local conditions not sufficiently dismantle monolithic approaches to Eng. Lit. without texts needing to be resituated within a larger dynamic? Does the promotion of interaction, however adjusted to the particularities of given poems, plays, or romances, not install a master-trope, and obscure entities and forces better identified through other conceptual schemes? Examples can be found of the values of the *Gaidhealtachd* passing into anglophone discourse—as in the political thought of the Covenanting 8th Earl of Argyll:[387] but are these not exceptions to a flow which was more often one-way, a

---

shutting of ornans: shooting of ordnance, firing of heavy guns

matter of English and (in Ulster) Scottish encroachment? Does the process by which colonists appropriate the icons of those they subjugate (harps, wolfhounds, words like *Tory* and *whiskey*) count as interactivity? Does a stress on interactivity not risk undervaluing both the tenacity of grass-roots traditions and, contrariwise, the capacity of broadly held conventions to signify differently on a local basis? Does it smuggle in assumptions about literary value, as though hybridization were inherently good? There are, clearly enough, methodological dangers.

J. G. A. Pocock, who encouraged three-kingdom historians to privilege interaction (above, p. 21), recently complained that his formulation ' "the Atlantic archipelago" … has failed to catch on: partly for the rather interesting reason that you cannot form a generic adjective from it, partly for contrary reasons having to do, as I see it, with a general invective against naming or defining or having any identity at all, which is part of the politics of post-modernism.'[388] Obviously, once this book is published, the adjective *archipelagic* will carry all before it—context usually determining whether the Atlantic or the Pacific, or indeed the Aegean, is being discussed. Pocock may be right to believe that a suspicion of naming has rendered some readers sceptical about 'the Atlantic archipelago' as a definable entity. Given that postmodernism itself made so much of interactivity, however, it is likely that the intellectual climate of the late twentieth century did more to advance than discourage archipelagic thinking.

Certainly, there is a correlation between a three-kingdoms approach to the mid-seventeenth century, with its anti-Whig, anti-Marxist, revisionist impulse to discredit large-scale, causal explanations, its anti-teleological ethos, and the rejection of grand narratives that was a feature of the postmodern condition as much as it was an explicit element in 'the politics of postmodernism'. Common to both was a desire to decentre, to see the historical and the cultural fields as matrices rather than arenas dominated by a controlling focus. They were in different ways suspicious of essentialist claims about motivation (e.g. that the Irish were bound by race or destiny to rebel against the English), preferring the hybrid and contingent. Because new British historians tended to concentrate on the activities of elites, which had many values and interests in common across the archipelago, they were as predisposed as postmodernists in another key to deconstruct identities based on oppositions, stressing mutual implication. As the Scottish historian Keith Brown notes, it is now routine to think of Scots identity as 'defined in terms of [its] relationship' with Englishness.[389] John Morrill is no more a postmodernist than is Brown, but when he writes of 'the partly successful processes of acculturation of the Celtic peoples of the Atlantic archipelago into lowland English systems of law and inheritance, language, religion', there are undertones of the *Zeitgeist*: 'The result was the creation of new English, Irish, Scottish, and Welsh identities very different from older English, Irish, Scottish, and Welsh identities. It also resulted in the creation within the peoples of the island of Britain, but not amongst most of the peoples of the island of Ireland, of an additional *British* identity.'[390]

Morrill's statement is not offered as complete and it strikes me as far more substantive than merely a symptom of its moment because it is compatible with the sweep of literary evidence. As the epilogue to this book will emphasize, however, it is misleading to speak of 'an additional *British* identity' in the singular; and English cultural encroachment did not so extensively reach into even anglophone Ireland, Scotland, and Wales as to transform identities wholesale, especially where communities were largely illiterate. Here we are back with the question about degrees of interactivity, and it does seem clear that scholarship risks distortion when it foregrounds mutual modification at the expense of the locally fixed. (On the other hand, we should acknowledge how continuity, e.g. in Welsh Anglican royalism during the 1640s, was relativized by change elsewhere, and was in consequence experienced differently by its adherents.) Furthermore, while an emphasis on interactivity should not obscure the locally constant, neither should it make us look straight through the ubiquitous. The variables do not diminish the importance of the existence of certain modes of writing across anglophone Britain and Ireland. To take a minimal case, the following lines from a gravestone are archipelagically interesting because they come from County Kilkenny in 1646 yet could equally come from Kent, and not because they comment on, say, Charles I's inability to enjoy good relations with both Scotland and Ireland until his head had been chopped off: 'Both wifves at once alive he could not have: | Both to injoy at once he made this grave.'[391]

This raises another point. That Burnell's *Landgartha* presents Charles's difficulties with Scotland and Ireland as a love-triangle (Chapter 5) does not make it more legitimate to read the Kilkenny epitaph as a political allegory. Interpretation should not too briskly reduce poems, plays, or romances to the dynamics that shaped the archipelago. It is true that a number of works were written to be read, if only in sections, in just this way. When Harrington says in his treatise *Oceana* that Marpesia, to the north of Oceana/England, 'is the dry nurse of a populous and hardy people', and that Panopea 'is a neighbour Island, anciently subjected by the Arms of *Oceana*', the countries referred to are obvious (though Harrington's reasons for believing that Panopea would flourish best if 'farm'd out unto the Jews, and their heirs for ever' are less so).[392] Three-kingdom ingredients go with almost equal directness into Orrery's *Parthenissa* and Mackenzie's *Aretina*.[393] But even *romans à clef* are not necessarily best understood by taking them as they ask to be taken. The danger is not so much that of missing the productive complexity in which such romances were embedded, nor of overlooking how historical narratives now received as common wisdom were being fabricated even as what they concerned took place (a process in which literary texts played a part), but of pulling the same sort of story out of artefacts which did very different kinds of work, and which harnessed archipelagic issues to indirect ends—as when Waller in his 'Panegyrick' praises the Cromwellian union of what had been three Stuart kingdoms not because he was enthusiastic about Irish and Scottish MPs voting at Westminster during the First Protectorate Parliament but in order to press for unity within England,[394] or when Shakespeare is inspired by the titles of Anglo-Scottish union to explore the valency of greeting in *Macbeth* (Chapter 2).

Waller uses the presence of MPs representing Ireland and Scotland in the parliament of 1654–5 to advance the claim that Cromwell can secure 'the ... Union ... of the English nation'. Why would the inclusion of outliers add to internal unity? It is a relevant, tough-minded subtlety—characteristic of this poet—that most of the MPs for Irish, Scottish, and in many cases Welsh constituencies, were, in practice, Englishmen, so that the archipelagic imperialism of the notion that England is inwardly strengthened by incorporating its neighbours is underpinned by the knowledge of Waller and his contemporaries that the Protector and his allies had made the reformed House of Commons safe for England.[395] A deeper historical consideration, however, springs from what union could mean in the early modern period. The Cromwellian union of three nations—the phrase is widely used in the 1650s—that was enacted by the 1654–5 parliament is on a spectrum with 'the ... Union ... of the English nation' because the semantic field of *union* included what we would call unity.[396] This was a reality of the state system, as well as a fact of language, because the three nations—plus or including Wales, Man, the Channel Islands, and so on—were not yet socio-political units (never mind modern nation-states) that could act as coherent blocks capable of being slotted into a single entity. The fiscal-administrative and military infrastructure took a leap forward during the Protectorate because that impulse was there, but it was not an achievable condition. Union in its early modern sense had to operate along networks of unity, hegemonies of allegiance, affinity, and interest that were different from the ties which bind up and demarcate modern bureaucratic states.

In other words, just as anachronistic ideas about what a *nation* was in the early modern period will impede our understanding of the cultural dynamics of the archipelago (above, pp. 40–46), so will the model of *union* that has reached us from the period when the United Kingdom of Great Britain and Ireland was at its most capacious (1801–1922). The forms of nationalism that developed across Europe during and after the late eighteenth century and the ideology which is still appealed to in one part of Ireland as unionism are in that respect two sides of the same distracting coin.[397] As should be apparent, from the shifting, qualified way in which the term has been used so far ('regal union', 'incorporating union', 'confederating union'), the word union could denote a number of modes of interaction in the period covered by this book. At one extreme was the sort of 'entire union' that Defoe argued for around 1707 (Chapter 11). He believed, or purported to believe, that full parliamentary Anglo-Scottish union would create a new British nation. Further down the scale, there was the federative union that Presbyterian Scots fought for in the wake of the Solemn League and Covenant (see above, p. 44), and that leading English statesmen and poets advocated with the Dutch (Chapter 7), followed, even less insistently, by varieties of alliance and co-operation between states which we would simply not now call union. All these meanings were current to 1707,[398] coloured, it may be, by further ideas about union in the visual arts and Scottish Law.[399]

The problem of seeing clearly what was meant in the seventeenth century by such still-active, evolving words as *nation* and *union* is inextricable from a further difficulty. All thematic accounts of literature are necessarily selective, and the risk of reductiveness is compounded by a danger of distortion when the theme has a modern resonance. In the case of *Archipelagic English*, the fascination of three-kingdom interaction is heightened by the way in which alliances and incompatibilities within present-day disputes about devolution and separatism often go back to 1603–1707. This book is not a manual for devolutionary politicians, yet it will in my eyes fail if does not give its readers some of the background they need for understanding the current circumstances of Britain and Ireland, and what the options are for change. There must relatedly be a trade-off between the demands of historical placing in the analysis of literary texts and an awareness that some works have exceptional lasting value. A chapter such as 'The Romans in Britain' respects the efficacy of William Rowley's *A Shoo-maker a Gentleman* (1608), as a play about Anglo-Welsh-British relations written for a popular audience after a period of debate about union, but it also embraces the opportunity to explore, at greater length, how similar contexts shaped the more renewably effective *Cymbeline*. More renewably effective because more fully engaged with the diversities of human experience (sexual, linguistic, touristic) in which ethnic, national, and imperial ideologies are installed.

Even if one resists the urge to reduce seventeenth-century texts to recensions of the same narrative of archipelagic interactivity, there is another, more insidious temptation, that of framing a literary character or episode and deciding that he, she, or it should be taken as historically topical. Such a tactic is usually misplaced, yet a complication needs to be acknowledged: some writers do create, for analytical purposes, as well as to avoid censorship, deniable and even contradictory topical effects. I mentioned, above, that aspects of Shakespeare's Henry V resemble features of James VI. The Salic Law speech, for example, about Henry's claim to the crown of France, offers a critical sidelight on the claim of James Stuart to the crown of England[400]—a succession which, at least in theory, would bring with it the crown of France because the Anglo-Norman claim to rule on both sides of the channel had become fossilized into the titles of the King of England. This analogy can be extended if one remembers that, behind the scenes, James was applying military pressure, threatening to destabilize England if his bid for the crown were rejected,[401] as Henry V brought havoc to France. But James's more public avowal of peaceable ways and means, audible as we have noted in the speeches of Captain Jamy, is obviously incompatible with the militarism of Henry V; James was never rebuked with having had a delinquent adolescence (Esmé Stuart was no Falstaff), he did not marry a French princess, and so on. To conclude that we are dealing, in the case of *Henry V*, with a topicality which at some point fails would be to start from too mechanical a set of assumptions. The differences between James VI and Henry V helped Shakespeare's audience focus on what did connect the two. The play is analytical in that sense, highlighting the problem of succession, as prior to yet bound up with union, in a way which isolates and focuses the issue. A character like Henry V is good for audiences to *think with*.

The revisionism which gave rise to the new British history was often most arresting when it showed that 'what really happened' in the seventeenth century was different not just from what Whig historians later claimed but from what people believed at the time. Some accounts of the British problem follow suit, demonstrating with too much knowingness how social and geographical distance prevented participants from understanding a situation that the modern historian can scan. Yet what really happened must include what people thought was happening not just because the latter is an historical phenomenon—and one integral to literary production—but because it so often went on to influence events. To understand why relations broke down between crown and parliament in England we must be aware not only of the brutal, unanticipated actuality of the Catholic rising in Ireland in 1641 but of how it was exaggeratedly depicted in pamphlets which despite their (to our eyes) obvious scaremongering appear to have had a lurid plausibility for readers as informed as Milton.[402] Literary critics are well placed to remind anyone who needs the prompt that history is always, as etymology attests, a story, even when it is happening—that events by themselves are not history—and that texts are enablers, not simply reflectors. In the case of the Irish Rebellion, this should draw attention to the generic modes and belief paradigms which printers took advantage of when marketing atrocity stories (murder pamphlets, Foxean martyrology, popish-plot literature), all bringing in train conventions which affected the packaging and consumption of what the rebels were said to have done.[403]

Historians can lose sight of the realities bundled up into the word 'interaction' and play down damage and loss. My own use of Pocock's term tries to avoid euphemism, and starts from a recognition that, while it must be permissible to use a guiding concept, no one interaction in history is the same as any other, and that some are horribly violent. (Come to that, no interaction can strictly be one, i.e. single, given the overdetermined nature of motivation and the differing perspectives of agents.) If this airbrushing tendency was encouraged by the top-down priorities of revisionism, it also owes something to the temptation—which revisionism, creditably, resisted—to look for the causes of historical change by thinking back from outcomes, rather than forward, from the position of participants in events, often through suffering, to uncertainty. The present condition of Ireland, scarred and unhappy enough, can be thought of as pluralistic by liberal historians just long enough for the horror of such 'interactions' as the massacre of Protestants in the 1641 rising and of Catholics at Drogheda to be softened and subconsciously processed as one of history's birth-pangs. It should be our aim to understand the past, not to exculpate it.

Archipelagic issues could hardly be ignored by James VI and I's clerk of star chamber, Sir Francis Bacon,[404] or Sir George Mackenzie, lord advocate of Scotland (Chapter 9). British–Irish problems came to them. But the crises of the period more often impelled writers to make unpredictable journeys across the islands, and into exile in Europe and the colonies, coming into conjunction with new people and ideas. After 1603 Scottish poets migrated to London, exposed to alien scenes and idioms (Chapter 4). When the poet and playwright Elizabeth Cary went from England to Ireland in 1622 as the wife of a Lord Deputy (Viscount Falkland) she taught herself Irish and took Catholic spiritual counsel ahead of a high-profile conversion announced shortly after her return to London (1626).[405] There were the British and continental tours of the self-consciously Anglo-Welsh James Howell, extensively registered in his writings.[406] All such interactions had the potential to reinforce received ideas, but also to cross-fertilize. Meanwhile the make-up of the archipelago out of distinct, interpenetrating zones situated men like Robert Kirk, the anglophone Scottish Gaelic scholar and collector of Highland superstitions, as connectors and mediators,[407] and facilitated the rapid shift of writers out of one belief system into another—as in the case of John Toland, who moved from the Gaelic Catholicism of rural Donegal, through the Ulster-Scots Presbyterianism of Derry, and higher education in Glasgow and Edinburgh, into freethinking pantheism.[408]

The capacity of the archipelago to foster fusions and transformations is worth stressing in conclusion because there is a danger in a book of this sort of crying up difference as in itself a source of value. Scholars must make distinctions, but this should not unquestioningly reinforce a post-Enlightenment liberal bias in favour of pluralism and identity politics. English/Inglis was not the only connective medium in a century riven by strife. Religious doctrine and practice forged links between ethnic groups (e.g. the Calvinism shared by parts of Gaelic Argyll and the Lowlands), and so did economic interest and status (e.g., on occasion, between Old and

New English landowners in Ireland). There were also phases of toleration, if only as a species of neglect. With the arrival of William III, diversity within Protestantism was officially sanctioned.[409] The legacy of the Revolution would give succour to mid-eighteenth-century Irish Catholics seeking a relaxation in the penal laws (see below, pp. 376–7). Yet the peoples of Britain and Ireland did not have a social order that resembled modern, multi-faith, multiculturalism. As for the politics of identity, although this was a period in which legal precedent, old lineages, and ancient rights were venerated, origins were not valued in a post-Romantic, essentialist or racial way.

Identities get wired up, but they are not congenital. Exchange babies in a Belfast hospital and the child of Catholics brought up on the Shankill will become a Protestant loyalist. If identities are circumstantial, they are also dynamic. Invade Iraq and Muslims in Leeds change their relationship with Britishness. One way of responding to these facts is reverently to embrace difference and talk about respect, but a more constructivist critique is inevitable once history is introduced and it becomes apparent that allegiances were ordered otherwise in the past. From both Catholic and Protestant pulpits, the people of Northern Ireland should be reminded on a regular basis that, in 1689, the Pope supported King Billy. Literary texts help show—as when the spies in Mitchelbourne's *Siege of London-Derry* slip between rival armies—how such alliances had within them the potential to be turned around, and how all can turn round again. One hope of this book is that literature can be re-engaged with the evolving and devolving interactivity of the Irish-British archipelago and help change the past in the future.

2

Archipelagic *Macbeth*

One speech of Mackbeth's has been neglected by Shakespeare scholars. It comes as English forces mass against the Scots. To the sound of ominous drumbeats, the warrior comes on stage with a couple of battle-ready companions. 'Wher's our Generall, | The hopefull *Wallace*?', asks Wintersdale. 'Gone in quest of death, | Firme as his fate', Grimsby replies. Hearing that Wallace has infiltrated the enemy camp, to spy out their plans, Mackbeth declares:

> So *Hercules* sought honour out in Hell.
> He not deserves, the name of Generall,
> Dares not face danger, and out-do the Devill.[1]

As will be apparent, this is not strictly Shakespeare's protagonist, though the defiant, almost satanically competitive lines might be his, but a character of the same name, rallying to the support of the Scottish national hero, William Wallace, in J. W.'s *The Valiant Scot*. This play, published in London in 1637, is influenced by Shakespeare's first tetralogy of history plays as well as by *Macbeth*. Its immediate source, however, is the Scottish patriotic epic, Blind Harry's *Wallace*, composed in the late fifteenth century and reprinted north of the border right through the early modern period.[2]

Like the epic, J. W.'s play deals with Wallace's rising against the English (Anglo-Norman) overlord of Scotland, Edward I. It dramatizes his loyalty to Robert the Bruce—a king of Scotland in waiting, who fights alongside Edward—and his betrayal by fellow Scots. Wallace has good reason to be up in arms. The play starts with Englishmen depriving his father of his inheritable shrievedom and lands, and, just before Mackbeth comes into the action, they murder Old Wallace, the protagonist's wife Peggy, and a sympathetic Friar. In a campaign which combines patriotism with revenge,

Wallace threatens to carry the war to London. He is, however, defeated, and the play ends in an uneasy peace.

It is impossible to determine precisely when this old-fashioned yet evidently Caroline play was composed,[3] but its publication in 1637 could hardly have been more timely. This was the year in which the regal union of 1603 began to fragment. On top of decades of distant, sometimes uncongenial government from London, the Scots were now required to accept a crypto-Anglican prayerbook (above, pp. 77–8). By 1638 many had signed a national Covenant to defend the religion of the Kirk, and both sides began to recognize what the Bishops' Wars of 1639–40 brought to pass, when a royal army twice went north, and was both times repelled by the Scots, who in turn invaded northern England, that the issue would come to blows. Just as, in *The Valiant Scot*, such Englishmen as the Earl of Clifford believe that the Scots are best dealt with generously, there was considerable support for the Covenanters in England. Given the stubbornness of the king, the best that could be hoped for was a stalemate.

Hence, in 1639–40, the players of the Fortune Theatre staged *The Valiant Scot* with success. As a sympathetic pamphlet called *A Second Discovery* (1642) explains, it ran for five days—a long innings for a play, especially an old, revived one—fuelled by interest in Anglo-Scottish conflict and popular hostility in London to the Laudian English bishops. 'Well,' says the Scotsman Willie, in the pamphlet, 'let the Bishops be angry as they will, we have acted the valiant Scot bravely at *Barwicke*, and if ever I live to come to *London*, Ile make one my selfe to make up the number, that it may be acted there too, and that with new addition.'[4] Willie and his friends had been valiant Scots when they put Charles's army to flight and occupied the English border town of Berwick. Now, like William Wallace, Willie is threatening to come to London.

My leading claim in this chapter is that *The Valiant Scot* dramatized tensions within Scotland and between Scotland and England that were already registered in *Macbeth*—an equally topical dramatization of medieval material that is calculated to explore the heterogeneity of the archipelago at the very moment (1605–6) when James VI and I was trying to go beyond regal union and develop an integrated British state. The appearance of a character called Mackbeth in *The Valiant Scot*, when no one of that ilk is in Blind Harry's *Wallace*, is but one sign of this continuity. Between 1639 and 1642, for example, when Milton was making notes about subject matter for possible plays—including a work about 'Adam unparadiz'd' which eventually took another form—he proposed a series of 'Scotch [hi]stories—or rather brittish of the north parts'. The qualification is revealing, given the Anglo-Scottish crisis of the moment—the unfolding 'brittish' problem—which, as his early prose works show, Milton was fully aware of. He noted that Holinshed provides materials for a tragedy about 'Macbeth beginning at the arrivall of Malcolm at Mackduffe. The matter of Duncan may be express't by the appearing of his ghost.'[5] This would have altered Shakespeare's and the chronicles' order of exposition by starting with a scene in England (it would, in that sense, have been a very British *Macbeth*), but the scope of the action would have been the same as in Shakespeare's play.

My second contention is that both *Macbeth* and *The Valiant Scot* are led by Anglo-Scottish dis/union to engage with the related topic of titles and offices. As we have seen, J. W.'s action is triggered by the confiscation of Old Wallace's heritable office of sheriff. That *Macbeth* is concerned with titles, from the protagonist's first greeting by the witches, as Thane of Glamis and Thane of Cawdor, who will be king hereafter, to the celebrated lines in Act V, in which Angus declares, 'Now do's he [Macbeth] feele his Title | Hang loose about him, like a Giants Robe | Vpon a dwarfish Theefe',[6] is equally obvious—though its significance has not been grasped. Since Alan Sinfield and David Norbrook opened up the anti-absolutist, Buchananite strand in the sources used by Shakespeare, scholars have been alert to the debate behind the play between patrilineage and the older Scottish and Irish system of tanistry, between Stewart 'free monarchy' and aristocratic-republican notions of how power should be allocated.[7] But the crucial promotion of Malcolme to Prince of Cumberland by his father, Duncan, while connected to this debate, is tied into the play's union-related attention to how titles and offices are acquired. Following from this is a third contention (my fourth will follow soon, a fifth at the end of the chapter), that, while *The Valiant Scot* is alert to how office-holders are addressed, as well as how they enjoy their rights, the topic more profoundly informs *Macbeth*, as Shakespeare explores the valency of titles through a rhetoric of greeting, hailing, and welcoming.

★ ★ ★

Macbeth grew out of a moment in which the problems of union threw the whole issue of offices and titles into relief. After a long, conservative

reign during which preferment was hard to come by, James's accession
offered hope to many. The king was lavish in bestowing honours—partly,
as satirists pointed out, because selling knighthoods brought him revenue[8]
—but it was impossible to satisfy the appetite for office. The influx
of ambitious Scots became the more controversial as it grew apparent
that, with two courts, in effect, collapsing into one, preferment would
be harder to secure under the very union which offered the prospect
of advancement.[9] James's attempt to use the honour system to create a
renovated, British aristocracy began to undermine itself when disappointed
English nobles, noticing the disproportionate success of the Scots at court,
used their influence over parliament to frustrate union legislation. By 1612
a pause became necessary because 'beggarly' Scots—as the English saw
it—were being promoted beyond their means, and were unable to fill their
offices with dignity (another factor which threw the meaning of titles into
question). Despite these and other problems, however,[10] James continued
to favour the construction of a pan-British nobility. He wanted the Stuarts
to build support among such men as the dedicatee of *The Valiant Scot*, Duke
of Hamilton north of the border and Earl of Cambridge in the English
peerage.

His motives for doing this went back to Scotland, where magnates were
powerful in the localities and the authority of the crown was limited. This
long-standing situation had been exacerbated by the frequency with which
Scottish monarchs (including James himself) began their rule as minors, but
it was grounded in the dynamic, kin-based, competitive ethos of Scottish
society. 'To refuse to compete', a historian explains,

> was to invite predators and lose support which naturally gravitated to those
> lords who could deliver. ... power was not so structured and apportioned that
> it was closed off to ambition, but rather it remained fluid and there for the
> taking. ... feuds were rarely fought out in isolation, but were ... linked ... to
> the politics of the royal court where local and national issues were meshed in
> a complex web of loyalties, rivalries and factional conflict.[11]

Source-hunters have related *Macbeth* to notable manifestations of this
ethos—to the Bothwell and Gowrie plots.[12] While it can be instructive to
connect *Macbeth* with particular events,[13] it is more important, however, to
track its realization of this feuding, competitive dynamic, which impelled
the elite but also infected lesser men worsted by the system with the sort
of resentment which the murderers in *Macbeth* hold against that supposedly

admirable ancestor of the Stuarts, Banquo (III.i. TLN 1064–149). Even
Duncan, seen by too many critics as representing kingly order, pushes the
interests of his family and followers, in a world where there is no safety in
stasis—a point grasped by Macbeth in his tortured rhetorical relationship
with prolepsis.

James saw in union a way of stabilizing this system. First, and ponderably
for a scholar-king with a taste for political theory, union grafted the Scottish
crown, whose (absolutist) claims had to be constantly argued for, into a long
English tradition which derived legitimacy from custom and law. Second,
the resources of Britain made this King of Scotland far more powerful than
any of his nobility. And third, because he was based in Westminster, he was
freer from immediate pressure.[14] The obvious danger, of course, was that an
absentee Scottish king would lose touch with his natural, noble supporters
north of the border. This was undoubtedly a factor in the breakdown of
royal authority in Scotland under Charles I. It is echoed in the way Scottish
noblemen such as Grimsby turn against Edward I and join Wallace in *The
Valiant Scot*. Such was the disaffection among the Scottish elites that some
contemporaries suggested that the anti-prayerbook riots of 1637 had been
orchestrated by noblemen.[15]

Among the sources of local power that James warned his son Henry
to resist, in his guidebook to kingship, *Basilikon Doron*, were 'heretable
Shirifdomes and Regalities, which being in the hands of the great men
wracketh the whole country'. A wise Scottish king, he advised, would hold
sheriffs to account, and refuse to let their offices pass from father to son.
After the hoped-for regal union, the English custom of appointing sheriffs
by the crown could be introduced to Scotland.[16] James sought to follow his
own advice, establishing an itinerant commission to buy out sheriffdoms,[17]
but Charles went even further. When he came to the throne in 1625 he
issued a Revocation of all measures passed on his behalf but against his
interests not just during his minority (the usual limit of such revocations)
but reaching back several generations. This included a reclamation of
heritable offices. The policy could have appealed to the Scottish gentry,
since it promised to curb the power of high-handed magnates; but it was
taken to be part of an across-the-board assault on the security of property.
It was also seen as damaging the traditional fabric of local government.[18]

While *Macbeth*, as I shall show, responds to the crisis around titles
and offices that followed the union, *The Valiant Scot* reflects the related
controversy sparked by the Revocation. Thus, when Wallace's father is

deprived of his heritable shrievedom by royal command, this is followed by a typically Caroline assault on property when Old Wallace admits that he holds his castle and lands by tradition not charter or service. In the legal idiom of the time, his title is defective, and his estate, at the mercy of the crown, falls into the hands of English agents. His fellow-Scotsman, Sir John Graham is told that he can keep his lands, but only if he makes them a dowry for his daughter Peggy—with her 'true Scotties feace' (B1r-v), broad Scottish speech,[19] and loyalty to her lover Wallace, the epitome of her country[20]—to marry the young Englishman, Selby.

The dedicatee of J. W.'s play, with his titles from both sides of the border displayed for the reader (A2r), showed his loyalty to the British monarchy by surrendering, in 1629, a heritable sheriffdom, and by relinquishing, six years later, his rights to the Abbey of Arbroath, to set an example to others.[21] But the topic of heritable offices was not the only feature of *The Valiant Scot* that would have made Hamilton an interested reader. In the early 1630s, the Duke had mustered an Anglo-Scottish force to fight with Gustavus Adolphus in Germany. Rumours began to circulate that he would use these men to kidnap the royal family and, by invoking a heritable claim of the Hamiltons more potent than that of any shrievedom, become King of Scotland.[22] This chimes suggestively with the role of Robert the Bruce in the play, who fights for Edward I before apparently being condemned to execution by the king under his English title:

> You hence sir, from this houre I sweare,
> Never to see thee Earle of *Huntingdon*, …
> Your head shal feel our meaning, see it dispatch'd.   (K3r)

In the event this is merely a ploy designed to show that Edward has power over Bruce (that the English have suzerainty over Scotland); the Earl's head is not chopped off but returns wearing the crown of Scotland.

I can now announce my fourth contention which is that topicality is most formidable in drama not when it is immediate (as with the probable influence of the Gunpowder plot on *Macbeth*) but when it is sufficiently invested in an analysis of its moment to have prophetic power. Thus, after *The Valiant Scot* was published, Hamilton was obliged by his Anglo-Scottish entitlements to become even more like Bruce by leading Charles's army against the Scots in the Bishops' Wars.[23] The parallel is the more striking given the neo-medieval character of the royal army, which was led by the same border families—the Percies, the Cliffords—as figure in *The Valiant Scot*, and equipped with such archaic weaponry as bows and bills.[24] The Hamilton/Bruce parallel can only have been reinforced for audiences at the Fortune Theatre by Wallace's Covenanter qualities. If the old nobility led Charles's army, the Scots gave command to proven soldiers who, in the words of J. W.'s Mackbeth, 'deserve[d] the name of Generall'.[25] And if Hamilton later remembered the play whose dedication he had apparently accepted, he will have been struck by an irony as dark as the coming of Birnam wood to Dunsinane. When tried as a stubborn royalist by parliament in 1649, he argued that as a Scot he was beyond English jurisdiction.[26] Like Bruce, however, his English title left him subject to his accusers. Only, whereas the head of Bruce felt in a benign sense Edward's assertion that he would not be seen again as Earl of Huntingdon, Hamilton, sentenced under the title Earl of Cambridge, had his head cut from his shoulders.

★ ★ ★

Let me start again, from the top. What were the titles of King James? When he rode on a progress into Oxford in 1605, he was met, outside the gates of St John's College, by three boys, dressed as sibyls, who recited some Latin verses composed by Matthew Gwinn.[27] Identifying themselves as the 'three same Fates' who 'once foretold | Power without end' to Banquo and his heirs (the weird sisters of *Macbeth*), they saluted the king as follows:

> [1]   Hail, whom Scotland serves!
> 2 Whom England, hail! 3 Whom Ireland serves, all hail!
> 1 Whom France gives titles, lands besides, all hail!
> 2 Hail, whom divided Britain join'st in one!
> 3 Hail, mighty Lord of Britain, Ireland, France![28]

Shakespeare did not need to know this pageant to recognize the dramatic potential of the episode in Holinshed which was Gwinn's source as well as his own for the scene between Macbeth, Banquo, and the witches.[29] It is a striking analogue, however, because it points to one of the springs of the obsession with triplicity that runs through Shakespeare's tragedy from the witches' opening question, 'When shall we three meet againe?', through the three murderers who dispose of Banquo, to the twofold balls and treble sceptres held by James and his successors in the vision of the Stuart line that appals Macbeth in Act IV.[30] Gwinn's sibyls double with toil and trouble the threeness of James's kingdoms—England/Wales, Scotland, Ireland, but also France, Britain, Ireland—and they present his place in the world (the more obviously because the claim to France was empty) as a list of titles.

Yet Gwinn, like Shakespeare, was aware that threeness gave an incomplete account of the new Stuart polity. A Danish element, for instance, was important in James's genealogy and the disposition of the Stuart realms. Freshly prominent because of his marriage to Anne of Denmark, this connection was also present in James's descent from a king who had earned a place in the history of multiple monarchy by governing both England and Denmark and by splitting the former into four earldoms for efficient government during his periods of absence:

> Thou dost restore the fourfold glory of Canute,
> Great ancestor, his crowns and royal thrones.
> Nor shall we bear wars, slaughter, anxious hearts,
> Or fury 'gainst ourselves; but we'll grow warm
> With love and peace ...

In Elizabethan propaganda, unity was the sovereign protection against civil strife. Though Gwinn is not so rash as to draw attention to Canute's record as an absentee monarch, one who divided his time (as James seemed likely to) between England and another country, he does boldly stress the 'glory' of multiple government, and adds, not perhaps causally enough, that love and peace will follow. It is hardly surprising that the king, a reader of Holinshed who was as fond of Scottish history as he was of being eruditely flattered, was gratified by the entertainment.[31]

The prospect of British union repeatedly generated prophecies, both north and south of the border, partly as a way of freeing up, by riddling means—since questioning royal intentions could be dangerous—analysis and debate about how union might be achieved.[32] Though James disapproved of prophecy,[33] he could not stop the ferment associated with his arrival in London, and there are signs of an attempt to harness it to his advantage. Thus Robert Waldegrave, the king's printer, published *The Whole Prophesie of Scotland, England, and Some-part of France, and Denmark, Prophesied bee Meruellous Merling, Beid, Bertlingtoun, Thomas Rymour, Waldhaue, Eltraine, Banester, and Sibbila, All According in One* (1603). The title of this compilation of union-related prophecies reminds us that such texts could, like James's claims to legitimacy, reach beyond Britain to France and Denmark. It should also connectedly alert us to the transnational range of *Macbeth*. This means, among other things, recognizing that the tragedy involves all of the three kingdoms governed by King James (as when Malcolme and Donaldbain flee Scotland to England and Ireland—destinations specified more than once).[34] It also means resisting any impulse to assume a tidier, more completed British polity than is appropriate for 1605–6, and a more coherent Scotland. From the start, Duncan's realm is a threatened, embattled entity, attacked by Irish kerns and by Scandinavians who, throughout the medieval period, had held Shetland, Orkney, and Caithness, and who still laid claim to Scottish territory.

The first scene of *Macbeth* is given over to the witches. In the second, the bleeding sergeant draws us into the political action:

> The mercilesse *Macdonwald*
> (Worthie to be a Rebell, for to that
> The multiplying Villanies of Nature
> Doe swarme vpon him) from the Westerne Isles
> Of Kernes and Gallowg[la]sses is supply'd,
> And Fortune on his damned Quarr[el] smiling,
> Shew'd like a Rebells Whore: ...   (I.ii. TLN 28–34)

In Holinshed, as in the play, Macdonwald is called a rebel, but Shakespeare firmly associates him with islands which had long been unassimilable to the British-Irish state system, even after the independent Lordship of the Isles was forfeited to the Scottish crown in 1493. It is no accident that James, who was especially hostile to the Gaels of the Western Isles,[35] was in the process in 1605 of using his newly extended authority to suppress the insubordination of their leader Angus Macdonald by sending troops to Kintyre.[36] The issue was archipelagic because the pacification of the Western Isles had to involve Ulster. Civility could not be planted in the Isles without the suppression of the Irish lords who employed redshanks from Scottish Gaeldom as soldiers beside their own kerns and gallowglasses. So the campaign of 1605 (which coincided with the king's progress through Oxford and the gestation of *Macbeth*) was the thin end of a Jacobean policy of driving a wedge into the Gaelic zone that ran from Donegal to the Scottish Highlands—a policy that led to the Ulster plantation, with what consequences history still shows. In that sense *Macbeth* helped pave the way for British colonialism in Ireland.

I have said that topical drama can be informed enough about its moment to generate prophetic insights. *Macbeth* is so impressive in this regard that it can be interpreted as not merely staging the witches but as co-opting their powers. Just as the kerns (not beaten after all) return to battle at the end of *Macbeth*, so the campaign of 1605 did not neutralize the Western Islesmen. As conspiracy and rebellion would prove in 1615 and 1641, not even the Ulster Plantation could defuse the disobedience of the Gael. Moreover, just as the kerns fight at the end of the play for the leader (Macbeth) who opposed them at the outset, so, during the Bishops' Wars, the Ulster branch of the Macdonalds would back the Stuarts against the Covenanters, in pursuit of their own claims on Kintyre,[37] and indeed their kerns and gallowglasses would support Charles in 1644 by fighting alongside the Scottish royalist, Montrose.[38]

Because it is so deeply invested in the dynamics of archipelagic history, topicality in *Macbeth* can be productive even in the questions it generates. Is Macdonwald a rebel? Maybe so in 1605, less clearly in the medieval world of Scotland and the Western Isles derived by Shakespeare from Holinshed. This is not a problem but an enabling doubt for an audience because the sergeant's denunciation of Macdonwald is the first of several in which rebellion, like treachery, is imputed by those who happen to have authority or are on the winning side. Macduffe, for instance, is called a rebel and a traitor, yet he is true to his country and a future king. Holinshed shows us Macdonwald rising against the king to pre-empt a punishment which his people deserve for killing a royal messenger. Shakespeare avoids explanation. What, the play makes us wonder, once we are habituated to its archipelagic, multiple, politically competitive setting, were Macdonwald's grievances against Duncan, and was his campaign justified?

Once the challenge from the Western Isles was beaten off by Macbeth, a new threat reared its head. The bleeding sergeant explains:

> No sooner Iustice had, with Valour arm'd,
> Compell'd these skipping Kernes to trust their heeles,
> But the Norweyan Lord, surueying vantage,
> With fur[ni]sht Armes, and new supplyes of men,
> Began a fresh assault.   (I.ii. TLN 48–52)

What looks like a triumph for Macbeth turns (fair is foul) into another onslaught. Rosse reports this development and its outcome:

> *Norway* himselfe, with terrible numbers,
> Assisted by that most disloyall Traytor,
> The *Thane* of Cawdor, began a dismall Conflict,
> Till that *Bellona's* Bridegroome, lapt in proofe,
> Confronted him with selfe-comparisons,
> Point against Point, rebellious Arme 'gainst Arme,
> Curbing his lauish spirit: and to conclude,
> The Victorie fell on vs.　　　(I.ii. TLN 76–83)

Some editors have taken 'him' in 'Confronted him' as Cawdor. To hear it that way has the merit of abruptly labelling Cawdor (like Macdonwald) 'rebellious'. Yet the syntax seems to make Norway a more natural candidate for 'him'. Macbeth struggled hand to hand with '*Norway* himselfe'. That, however, leaves 'rebellious Arme 'gainst Arme' not just subject to the irony (available whoever is 'him') that Macbeth is tacitly rebellious even while he acts for Duncan,[39] but open to an even stronger form of the Macdonwald question. For how can Rosse call Norway a rebel when he is a monarch in arms—a more acceptable role by any early modern measure, and particularly for King James who claimed descent from the King Fergus who invaded northern Britain from Ireland.[40]

Holinshed says that Sueno, the Norwegian king, was followed by Danes.[41] No doubt it would have been impolitic to play up the Danish dimension given James's marriage to Anne of Denmark, especially if, as has been proposed,[42] *Macbeth* was premiered during the visit of her brother, Christian IV, to London. If the issue was so sensitive, however, why were the Norwegian/Danish incursions mentioned? The dramaturgy is of its moment. Denmark-Norway-Sweden had not relinquished possession of the far north of Scotland until the late fifteenth century, and the status of Orkney and Shetland was still disputed in 1605–6 (the islands were not fully incorporated into Scotland until 1612). And here again the archipelagic dynamics were persistent enough for topicality to have a prophetic function. During the late 1630s, the period when *The Valiant Scot* was published and performed, the Danish-Norwegian state sought to recover Orkney as the price of helping Charles pacify Scotland. In 1643, Charles again asked for Danish troops, and used the northern isles as security against the loan-aid of military supplies.[43]

Shakespeare's treatment of the Danes helps clarify how England is represented as the story of *Macbeth* unfolds. In Holinshed, Edward the Confessor can only entertain Malcolme on his escape from Scotland after he has 'recouered the dominion of England from the Danish power'.[44] Shakespeare could have repeated the ploy of calling the Danes Norweyans. By avoiding reference to this conflict altogether, he heightened a contrast between insecure Scotland and stable, united England. The solidity of England is suggested not just by the absence of foreign predators but the impression of cohesion. That a core, unitary Scotland—'O Nation miserable!'[45]—exists in the play is not in doubt. But it is weakened (and left vulnerable to incursions) by magnate rivalries. Shakespeare's primary motive for removing from the narrative the many years of good government which Macbeth brought to Scotland before he sank into tyranny may have been dramaturgical (in this play about acceleration and over-leaping), but one consequence of the change is that Scotland is never shown as a properly functioning state. It seems to be waiting for English intervention to stabilize it. I shall return to Anglocentrism later. For now it is enough to observe that, if Shakespeare's adaptation of his sources to achieve this contrast reflects an English bias, it also jibes with the Scottish point of view of his patron, King James, given his experience of magnate unrest.

The contrast is the more striking because *Macbeth* represents England as more culturally benign than its sources entirely credit. When Macduffe turns on Malcolme, for instance, after the latter has claimed to be too lustful and avaricious to deserve the Scottish throne, he does not accuse him of being 'replet with the inconstant behauiour and manifest vices of Englishmen' as the same figure does in Holinshed.[46] The vices of soft living and treachery imputed to the English in such works as Blind Harry's *Wallace*, accusations that filter into Holinshed through his use of Scottish texts, are not only not depicted in *Macbeth*: they are spoken of only by an increasingly embattled Macbeth ('English Epicures')[47] when, in Act V, he displays a self-interested patriotism.

Patriotism in this play is a conditional good. Macbeth's appeal to it is partly a tactical response to the fact that Malcolme arrives with an English power. He needs to rally his dwindling forces. How deeply does it authenticate his Scottishness that he should suddenly come out with a word that was current in English representations of the Scots tongue (it is used by J. W.'s Peggy) in the play's rudest greeting: 'The diuell damne thee blacke, thou cream-fac'd Loone'?[48] Since the late eighteenth century, when productions began to be affected by a Romantic valorization of Celtic ethnicity,[49] there has

---

Loone: rascal

been an anachronistic risk of indulging Macbeth's late-found rhetoric. This has been compounded by a post-Ossianic tendency to identify Scottishness with the Gaeldom that Macbeth is aligned with when he hires the followers of Macdonwald to fight on his side. It has to be remembered not just that patriotic Scots such as Macduffe oppose him, but that early audiences, both English and Scottish at court, would have viewed with disapproval his willingness to buy in the kerns that he had originally fought.[50]

In any case it comes to nothing. Prophecy has its cryptic way, and a murderous king is killed by a man not of woman born. Like Macdonwald, whose head is set upon the battlements after being defeated by Macbeth, the head of Macbeth is brought in by Macduffe. But if the dead king now acquires the titles 'Vsurper' and 'Butcher',[51] what of Malcolme and his followers? Macduffe greets Malcolme with the words 'Haile King, for so thou art' (V.vii. TLN 2505). This is not in Holinshed. It has been transferred from his account of the witches' hailing of Macbeth and Banquo. Not unusually for Shakespeare, this casts a less than happily legitimate light upon the denouement. Doubt is reinforced by the fact that, like the witches' greeting of Macbeth as Thane of Cawdor, Macduffe's entitling of Malcolme is premature, prophetic, in that it precedes a decision of the thanes. In a very *Macbeth* way, Macduffe pressures the nobles by anticipation into delivering what he wants, saying that he already hears what is in their minds (again, in a minor key, like Macbeth's ambition educed by the witches).

This is the cue which prompts the thanes to a chorus of salutation:

> [*Macduffe.*]   Behold where stands
> Th'Vsurpers cursed head: the time is free:
> I see thee compast with thy Kingdomes Pearle,
> That speake my salutation in their minds:
> Whose voyces I desire alowd with mine.
> Haile King of Scotland.
> *All.* Haile King of Scotland.   *Flourish.*   (V.vii. TLN 2506–12)

Those with an ear for irony will hear the insubstantiality of 'voyces' (like the 'Voyces' of election that Coriolanus scornfully calls for).[52] Those with an eye for it will be struck by the way the witches' 'All haile' (a phrase with overtones of betrayal elsewhere in Shakespeare)[53] returns to the page through a Folio speech prefix ('*All.* Haile King of Scotland'). It is in the hands of directors whether the flourish sounds from the tiring house unannounced, as the play's endorsement, as it were, of Malcolme's new title, or whether Macduffe signals the trumpeters, to orchestrate this relatively benign coup or assertion of heritable principles. What it remains for criticism to do is to analyse the connection between the hailing of the witches and that of the nobles. To undertake this task is to return to the topic of offices and titles highlighted by *The Valiant Scot*.

★   ★   ★

That the word *hail* occurs far more often in *Macbeth* than in any other play by Shakespeare cannot be entirely explained by the freedom with which the witches use it in Act I and the thanes echo them in Act V. Hardly has the action begun than Malcolme greets the bleeding sergeant with a 'Haile, braue friend' (I.ii. TLN 23). There is no doubt, however, that the witches give hailing prominence:

> *Mac.* Speake if you can: what are you?
> *1.* All haile *Macbeth*, haile to thee *Thane* of Glamis.
> *2.* All haile *Macbeth*, haile to thee *Thane* of Cawdor.
> *3.* All haile *Macbeth*, that shalt be King hereafter.   (I.iii. TLN 147–50)

Requesting a greeting for himself (a curious gambit), Banquo is rewarded with a similar, yet developing, refrain, as 'Hayle' repeated by each of the witches turns into riddling doublets:

> *3.* Thou shalt get Kings, though thou be none:
> So all haile *Macbeth*, and *Banquo*.
> *1. Banquo*, and *Macbeth*, all haile.   (I.iii. TLN 167–9)

By means of these repetitions, *hail* gains cumulative weight, yet it also evolves in significance. The process starts as the witches use 'haile' not only as a greeting but as an imperative to one another to hail their visitors and then as a description of what they are doing.[54] As one witch hails she hails another to join her in hailing; and if uttering the word binds them together, as their broken, choric utterances repeatedly do, so does its semantic field, since 'all haile' could mean 'all whole'. As figures of inversion—a Shakespearean anti-masque—the witches parody in their three-in-oneness the constitutional theology of the Jacobean threefold monarchy. *Hail* implies 'whole' because it also means, especially in northern usage, 'health'—being sound and whole in body.[55] At the start of a play preoccupied with insanity and disease, the witches mockingly wish upon Macbeth and Banquo all the health they set out to subvert with the bad medicine they brew up in what they say as well as their cauldron.[56] This is one reason why their greeting sounds like a charm. Another is that the weird sisters wish the travellers 'luck'—an archaic meaning of *hail*, as it is of weird (i.e. 'wayward/weyard').[57] Wholeness can be projected upon Macbeth and Banquo because they are, like those who greet them—Jacobean versions of the three fates[58]—joined in their 'lot' or 'destiny'. The ambiguity of welcome is underwritten by the slipperiness of the word.

Macbeth has another question:

> Stay you imperfect Speakers, tell me more:
> By *Sinells* death, I know I am *Thane* of Glamis,
> But how, of Cawdor? the *Thane* of Cawdor liues
> A prosperous Gentleman: And to be King,
> Stands not within the prospect of beleefe,
> No more then to be Cawdor. Say from whence
> You owe this strange Intelligence, or why
> Vpon this blasted Heath you stop our way
> With such Prophetique greeting?   (I.iii. TLN 170–8)

The play's concern with how fathers relate to sons has led critics to make much of Macbeth's lack of an heir. Yet the role registered in his name (Mac-, 'son of') is also striking, since he has come to lack a father. By that death he inherits the title Thane of Glamis. Did Cawdor not have a son? (How many children had Lady Cawdor?) Perhaps the treachery imputed to the father has been punished in his heir. Perhaps the lack of an heir made the Thanedom ripe for redistribution. Either way, *Macbeth* starts with a heritable title being allocated by order of the king. In this the play, like *The Valiant Scot*, is potently of its period. It is a strategy that Duncan will revisit, obscured from the sight of most modern commentators because passed off as not allocation at all, but inheritance, when he settles the estate of kingship, over which by Scottish custom he has no particular rights, upon his firstborn, Malcolme.

Before that, Macbeth receives official news of his own promotion. Giving *hail* another twist, Rosse tells him how reports of his success in battle came 'thick as hail' to Duncan.[59] Heralds announcing success approached the king with so many greetings (hailings), one upon another, that there was a blizzard of welcomes mixed with welcome reports. Because of this, Macbeth is to be not just thanked and heralded into the king's presence but *greeted*.[60] This is a more handsome reward than it sounds because the greeting includes a title (we often hail a named addressee), and the anticipated form of that title (Cawdor) makes what Rosse obscurely says about this being 'earnest of a greater Honor' provocative because it is bound to put Macbeth in mind of the royal title that has been prophesied:

> And for an earnest of a greater Honor,
> He bad me, from him, call thee *Thane* of Cawdor:
> In which addition, haile most worthy *Thane*,
> For it is thine.   (I.iii. TLN 209–12)

Rosse's hailing is as insidious as that of the witches.

When Shakespeare's contemporary, Simon Forman, made notes on a performance that he had seen of *Macbeth* he remembered from the next phase of the play the 'kindly wellcome' that Duncan gave to Macbeth and Banquo;[61] and it is indeed remarkable how elaborately Macbeth is welcomed. Duncan lavishes upon him the sort of fulsome greeting—'Thou art so farre before,|That swiftest Wing of Recompense is slow,|To ouertake thee', and so forth (I.iv. TLN 299–301)—that seventeenth-century conduct-book writers, such as the Scotsman John Cleland, warn against.[62] After fewer words of welcome to Banquo, marked as warmer by a physical embrace, Duncan seizes the chance to capitalize on the victories that Macbeth has won him:

> Sonnes, Kinsmen, *Thanes*,
> And you whose places are the nearest, know,
> We will establish our Estate vpon
> Our eldest, *Malcolme*, whom we name hereafter,
> The Prince of Cumberland: which Honor must
> Not vnaccompanied, inuest him onely,
> But signes of Noblenesse, like Starres, shall shine
> On all deseruers.   (I.iv. TLN 322–9)

Favouring Malcolme with estate, name, and honour, Duncan gives him at least the prospect of solid advancement. In his capable way, he makes it clear that others—those who deserve it, those who have backed him—will also be promoted, though 'signes of Noblenesse, like Starres' has a superficial air which suggests that the recognition may not eat much into the king's purse. As for Macbeth, his new title (entirely cost-free to Duncan) is confirmed at the end of this sequence:

> *King.*   My worthy *Cawdor.*
> *Macb.* [aside] The Prince of Cumberland: that is a step,
> On which I must fall downe, or else o're-leape,
> For in my way it lyes.   (I.iv. TLN 335–8)

Duncan's 'My' implies possession as well as familiarity; by reassigning the title, the king has a claim over Macbeth that he did not when he was simply Thane of Glamis, enjoying his heritable rights by Sinel's death. The juxtaposition of '*Cawdor*' with 'Prince of Cumberland', rearticulated by Macbeth *as* a title, quoted from Duncan, is potent, for it is this invented title, and only as its holder the youth that bears it—'*that* is a step', not 'he ...'—that is the obstacle to his realization of the witches' prophecy. That the title also lays claim to what was for Jacobean audiences a piece of northern England continues, from the opening scenes, the idea of Duncan's Scotland as provisionally bounded, intermeshed with other polities, and, in a word, archipelagic.

It is a commonplace of criticism that the witches colour the play rhetorically through the incidence of doubling and trebling. What has been overlooked is the similar taint they leave on the ubiquitous practice of greeting. I have noted how Rosse's hailing of Macbeth as Thane of Cawdor must work on his psyche like venom. This is how Lady Macbeth now welcomes her husband to Dunsinane: 'Great Glamys, worthy Cawdor, | Greater then both, by the all-haile hereafter' (I.v. TLN 406–7). What she echoes from the witches is precisely the formula of greeting. It is a rhetoric which becomes more significant because the practice of welcome is discussed. This is most obvious in the banquet scene, but it is first explored when Lady Macbeth describes the ethos of the time to her husband:

>   to beguile the time,
> Looke like the time, beare welcome in your Eye,
> Your Hand, your Tongue: looke like th'innocent flower,
> But be the Serpent vnder't.   (I.v. TLN 418–21)

Alerted by this the audience can hardly overlook the serpent under her welcome to Duncan, a few stage minutes later. When she describes her and her husband's labours to serve the king, the witches' doing and doing and doubling and troubling are ominously audible:

> All our seruice,
> In euery point twice done, and then done double,
> Were poore, and single Businesse, to contend
> Against those Honors deepe, and broad,
> Wherewith your Maiestie loades our House:
> For those of old, and the late Dignities,
> Heap'd vp to them, we rest your Ermites.
> *King.* Where's the Thane of Cawdor?   (I.vi. TLN 450–7)

Her welcome acknowledges old favours as well as new. He highlights
his latest generosity by stressing Macbeth's acquired title. He is also, in
his vigilant way, wondering, sharply and out loud, why the lord of the
house is not there to greet him—a breach in the code of welcome which
an audience will find eloquent of Macbeth's state of mind and intentions.

The infrastructure of titles and offices is highlighted at Dunsinane, where
it will also be betrayed. First there is Macbeth's soliloquy about murdering
Duncan. This acknowledges the charisma of a kingship—its religions aura
for Macduffe (TLN 819–22, 1935–6)—which audiences nonetheless see
being maintained by pragmatic means:

> Besides, this *Duncane*
> Hath borne his Faculties so meeke; hath bin
> So cleere in his great Office, that his Vertues
> Will pleade like Angels, Trumpet-tongu'd against
> The deepe damnation of his taking-off: ...   (I.vii. TLN 490–4)

Yet this apprehensive, eloquent tribute holds back from the idea of kingship
as a God-given endowment; it is an *office* not a mystery. The term is rarely
used of kingship in Shakespeare. It reduces what might be thought sacred to
the level of the king's employees—the grooms, for instance, those 'spungie
Officers' (I.vii. TLN 552) who drink themselves into a stupor—or the
servants of the Macbeths, for we are told that Duncan, pleased with the
hospitality, 'sent forth great Largesse to your Offices' (i.e. officers) as well
as a diamond to the lady of the house (II.i. TLN 588). 'Office' is the term
used by the Second Murderer to dignify his role (III.iii. TLN 1221).

Once Macbeth is made king, however, he becomes, like many another
poacher turned gamekeeper, a strict advocate of order. This comes out with
crushing irony at the start of the banquet scene, where the regicide greets
his lairds with the hierarchical salutation 'You know your owne degrees, sit
downe: | At first and last, the hearty welcome' (III.iv. TLN 1256–7). Here,

'first and last' underlines the motif of order, of degree, while idiomatically apologizing for the necessary contraction of an appropriate welcome. When Hecate enters with the witches in the following scene (they have acquired a leader, and with that a devilish sense of rank),[63] the question of order will be given further, ironic turns. In the banquet scene itself, however, greeting and welcoming are more conspicuous. Macbeth prompts his wife to greet the lairds ('in best time | We will require her welcome') while she, with accomplished courtliness, declares that he is her mouthpiece: 'Pronounce it for me Sir, to all our Friends, | For my heart speakes they are welcome' (III.iv. TLN 1261–4). When Macbeth becomes distracted by the appearance of Banquo's ghost, it is the value of welcome that she stresses in a vain attempt to stir him: 'the Feast is sold | That is not often vouch'd while 'tis a making: | 'Tis giuen, with welcome' (III.iv. TLN 1294–6).

This motif is so richly articulated that it could be pursued through the rest of the play, most complexly, perhaps, in the English scene (IV.iii), where the idea and practice of welcome help characterize Scotland's estrangement from Malcolme as well as Macbeth—rivals almost fused in Macduffe's elliptical judgement 'The Title, is affear'd'.[64] Among the 'welcome, and unwelcom things at once' (TLN 1966) that make up the fabric of this scene, there is, for example, the almost laboured sequence in which Macduffe recognizes and cordially greets Rosse ('welcome hither') while Malcolme, who sees that he is 'My Countryman' (presumably by his costume), takes time to 'know' and greet him (TLN 1994–6). Does this mean that England generates division? Apparently not, for between these moments of Scottish difficulty there is a glowing description from the Doctor of the powers of Edward the Confessor, a king who can heal scrofula with his touch and whose 'heauenly guift of Prophesie' is the Godly opposite of the witches' divination. Here, it seems, is a monarch at one with his realm and his people, a figure so idealized that it is hardly surprising that Shakespeare did not bring him on stage.

Bearing in mind both the valency of greeting and welcoming in the play, and the positive depiction of the English polity, what, to return to the crux, are we to make of Macduffe's and the thanes' hailing of Malcolme? Though it facilitates an expression of consent not sought when Duncan made Malcolme heir to the crown he now grasps—a motif which survived from early medieval elected kingship into seventeenth-century coronation rituals—it cannot, given its theatricality, avoid an air (shared with the witches' hailing) of manufactured inevitability. Yet if this is not an election, the scene does include and anticipate events which Holinshed set in a parliament called by Malcolme at the start of his reign:

> We shall not spend a large expence of time,
> Before we reckon with your seuerall loues,
> And make vs euen with you. My Thanes and Kinsmen
> Henceforth be Earles, the first that euer Scotland
> In such an Honor nam'd: ...   (V.viii. TLN 2513–17)

Rather as his father (keen on the language of calculation and debt) said that 'signes of Noblenesse, like Starres shall shine | On all deseruers', so Malcolme seeks to please by turning thanedoms to earldoms. That these are English titles is pointed up by his use of the word 'Scotland', in such a way as to make it impossible to decide whether he means by this the nation or his title as monarch. As Malcolme also points out, there is an historical shift. These are 'the first' earls to be 'named' north of the border. Is this a gesture of convergence with England, a step towards Stuart Britain—the sort of realignment that might be expected from a Prince of Cumberland?

According to Buchanan, Malcolme used the assembly to 'restore to the Children their Father's Estates, who had been put to death by *Mackbeth*'.[65] In Holinshed, more cynically, Malcolme rewards his followers (with lands, livings, fees, and titles). But even this seems generous compared with Malcolme in the play, whose mere translation of titles would seem but an assertion of the king's power to regulate honours, did it not have cultural implications. This also has a source in Holinshed, an inauspicious one. It comes in Harrison's *Description of Scotland* (based on work by the Scot Hector Boece), printed along with the chronicles, where the corruption of ancient Scottish virtue by foreign, mainly English, influence is lamented:

> about the daies of Malcolme Cammor, our maners began greatlie to change and alter. ... the temperance and vertue of our ancestors grew to be iudged worthie of small estimation ... we began to follow also the vaine shadow of the Germane honor and titles of nobilitie, and boasting of the same after the English maner, ... now he would be taken most glorious that went loaden with most titles, wherof it came to passe, that some were named dukes, some earles, some lords, some barons, in which vaine puffes they fixed all their felicitie.[66]

From this perspective—and nothing stops its adoption—titles at the end of *Macbeth* are significant chiefly in the vanity which they share with the elaborate welcomes which so often incorporate them.

There are, however, complications. That Macbeth is never shown promoting his followers is strange, since, however committed he might be to degree, a regicide monarch would be even more likely than an untroubled inheritor to stir up support by being generous. This indeed is what Holinshed reports: 'Mackbeth ... used great liberalitie towards the nobles of the realme, thereby to win their fauour'. It may be that King James's own liberality, amounting to extravagance, encouraged Shakespeare to associate abstemiousness on this score with vice. Yet how far does Malcolme fill the void complained of by the anonymous Scottish Lord, who hopes that 'we may againe | Giue to our Tables meate, sleepe to our Nights ... | Do faithfull Homage, and receiue free Honors, | All which we pine for now' (III.vi. TLN 1506–10)? Those earldoms may be freely given, but only to Malcolme's supporters, as a consolidation of royal authority, and for some Scots as a token of decline. We are back, then, with the archipelagic question, of what a London audience, and a British court, would have made of the change in titles.

One thing to say immediately is that, if the pacification of the Western Isles and the rejection of Scandinavian claims to the north were issues for James as a Scottish king, both before and after 1603, as they had been for Duncan and Malcolme, they not only remained so for him as a British monarch who finally had the resources to bring order to Kintyre and to annexe Orkney and Shetland but they merged into the broader problem of managing troublesome lordships around the edges of the multiple monarchy,[67] notably Ireland. This is a second, archipelagic reason why Shakespeare made such a point of Malcolme's granting of earldoms. When he replaces the indigenous, locally derived title of thane with the English title of earl he alludes in telescoped form to the process of 'surrender and regrant' by which Irish lords who had customary but insecure title to lands held under a system of tanistry rather than primogeniture gave them up to the crown and received them back with an earldom bound into feudal service and the payment of rent to the sovereign.[68] This Elizabethan policy (which had analogies with James's own techniques for subduing Scottish Gaeldom, before and after 1603),[69] was being revived as *Macbeth* was written, in the wake of the defeat of the Ulster 'rebel' Hugh O'Neill—often known, because of an earlier surrender and regrant, as Earl of Tyrone.[70]

All this supports the conclusion that, if Macbeth represents in some measure the forces in Scotland (and, indirectly, England)[71] that were hostile to British union,[72] Malcolme is an Anglicizer. Lacking the Gaelic addition he has in Holinshed (Cammore, 'large-headed'), he stands apart in this from his brother Donaldbain (*bán* means 'fair'), from both the Mac-s in the play, and from such lairds as Rosse and Angus whose titles link them with Scottish places. His dependent alliance with Edward anticipates the sort of union which historians like the Master of the Revels, Sir George Buc, argued for in *Daphnis Polystephanos* (1605), a text which folds Malcolme into an overwhelmingly Saxon genealogy of the Kings of England (Fig. 2).[73] James constantly reassured his new English subjects that he would not favour Scottish interests, and he would later, notoriously, insist that his intention had always been to unite Scotland to England, not the other way round.[74] So, even if *Macbeth* did emerge as Anglocentric, in ratifying, however sceptically, the accession of Malcolme, it would not necessarily displease the king (who understood the need to present Anglo-Scottish convergence as doing no harm to the English). Yet if peaceful, stable England saves threatened, factional Scotland in *Macbeth*, the play does not go so far as to show Malcolme submitting to Edward's overlordship (not something James would have been keen to witness), even though this *Valiant Scot* motif was often brought out by English commentators, and may well have figured in the late-Elizabethan lost play *Malcolm Kynge of Scottes*.[75]

Kynge of Scottes. One answer to my question, what were the titles of King James?, would run: King of Scots to his subjects until 1603–4, King of Scotland more often, across the archipelago, thereafter, by virtue of, and in the style of, his being King of England and King of Ireland.[76] The traditional title 'of Scots' had sometimes been Anglicized south of the border; once James became an English king, King 'of Scotland' was more generally and officially current. The title that James aspired to, and claimed by proclamation in 1604, King of Great Britain, would not be secured for British monarchs until the 1707 Treaty. Some time before that, however, the formula 'of Scots' disappeared from the royal title.[77] So the acclamation 'Haile King of Scotland', uttered by Macduffe and repeated by the thanes, is not just a routine example of the avoidance of Scottish locutions in *Macbeth*. It is a gesture of acquiescence in three-kingdom state-formation, centred on the king in Whitehall. There are reasons to believe that James would have been sensitive to a nuance with such potent implications.

Much depends on how far one is prepared to extrapolate. Would Shakespeare's audience (at least at court) have known, as modern audiences

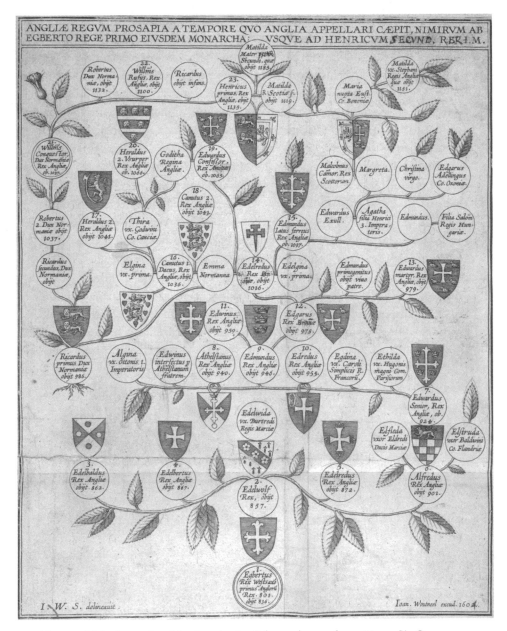

Fig. 2. Malcolme takes his place in English royal genealogy. From Sir George Buc, *Daphnis Polystephanos* (London, 1605).

do not, that the historical Malcolme—whose Anglicizing impulses were limited[78]—would later wage war against England (an England that would plunge into division and the Norman Conquest after the death of Edward the Confessor)?[79] That his place in royal genealogy, whatever men like Buc might believe, gave the crown of Scotland, contrary to English medieval assertions of suzerainty, a claim to the throne of England which James could finally act on.[80] That he was succeeded by Donaldbain—whose period of asylum among the kerns of the Western Isles reinforced his anti-English, Gaelic tendencies—after a bloody dynastic struggle (so much for the resolution of Scottish instability by the introduction of patrilineage). Within the play, and going beyond it, one last thing is clear: while actors may be right never to refer to *Macbeth* by its Folio title, since it brings down broken limbs, empty houses, and other misfortunes, their superstitious sobriquet 'The Scottish Play'[81] is geopolitically hopeless. What do I propose instead? 'The British Play' would be anachronistic, 'The Anglo-Scottish Play' too narrow. The title I seem to have arrived at, the last title I shall mention in this chapter, is 'The Archipelagic Tragedy'. No doubt it will catch on.

3

The Romans in Britain: Wales
and Jacobean Drama

There was controversy in 1980 when Howard Brenton's *The Romans in Britain* opened at the National Theatre. Set in 54 BC, during Julius Caesar's invasion, and in AD 515, when Anglo-Saxon settlers were displacing the Romanized Britons, the play is punctuated by contemporary scenes—calculated to provoke—that show the British Army in action in Northern Ireland. Brenton does not shrink from displaying the brutality of an archaic society. His play starts with a group of ancient Britons killing an outlaw and abusing a slave. But the Romans, despite their developed social order and technology, are as brutal as those they attack. In a scene that prompted Mrs Whitehouse to take the play's director to court, three Roman soldiers, separated from their unit, murder two British 'wogs' and rape a third after slashing him about the buttocks with a knife.[1]

That scene was the more shocking because it subverted a widely held belief. As Brenton says, his play challenged 'a rooted, popular myth from the British national consciousness. Everyone knows the Romans came to Britain. This is vaguely felt to be "a good thing", because they built straight roads and "brought law"' (vii). Like all popular myths this one has a history, and a key phase of its development lies in the early modern period. Medieval chroniclers had accepted the legendary history of Britain put together in the twelfth century by Geoffrey of Monmouth: the tale of a line of kings reaching back to the fall of Troy, through Arthur and Brut. Once his *Historia regum Britanniae* was exposed to Polydore Vergil's critique in *Anglica historia* (1534),[2] it began to lose plausibility, even as his stories gained in contemporary resonance,[3] and historians looking for reliable testimony about ancient Britain turned to Caesar, Tacitus, and other Latin authors. Geoffrey's version of antiquity looked reassuringly like medieval

England. To read William Camden's *Britannia* (1586) was, by contrast, to learn that our ancestors were half-naked, painted with woad, and suspected of human sacrifice—primitives easily placed in the civility vs barbarity paradigm espoused by early modern colonialism (above, pp. 36–7).[4]

Of course, the situation was not that simple. Patriotic conservatism kept Geoffrey's influence alive even in texts aimed at the classically educated. Drayton's verse chorography *Poly-Olbion* (1612–22), for example, is full of Galfridian matter, and, for reasons that will become apparent, he gives a particularly strong defence of the legends to Welsh and Welsh-border rivers (the Wye, Severn, and Dee). As late as 1633, the Oxford play *Fuimus Troes* was using these resources to bolster native dignity in the face of Julius Caesar's invasion. And the governing elite, schooled in classical humanism, could identify their Britishness with Roman civility and tar the mere Irish and Native Americans with the brush of barbarousness. They could shift from Galfridian imperialism—both the internal imperialism of Brut, who gave suzerainty of Scotland to the kings of England, and the north European empire-building credited to King Arthur—to a colonialism that was inspired by the expansion of classical Rome. In place of Geoffrey's belief that the Britons resembled the Romans because both descended from Troy, they began to embrace the idea that the Roman mission to conquer and civilize had translated westwards and been inherited by Britain.

This idea does not preclude an irony, familiar from later postcolonial societies, that a state which breaks out of the shell of an ageing empire and claims its autonomy—as Henry VIII broke free of the power of Rome, asserting in the Act in Restraint of Appeals (1533) 'this realm of England is an empire'[5]—is likely to be imprinted not just with the ideology but the vices of the apparatus that fostered it.[6] This irony troubled a number of early modern writers, especially as the Tudor imperium extended its dominion into Ireland and the New World. It permeates such poems as Spenser's *Ruines of Time* (1591), which is tolerant of Boadicea's revolt against the Romans, and laments the pride and fall of imperial Rome and its dependant, Verulamium, the Roman forerunner of St Albans, along with the vanities of Lord Burghley's England. Classical humanists like Milton could derive from such sources as Tacitus not just an admiration for Rome's civilizing expansionism but an approval of indigenous simplicity contrasted with Roman decadence.[7]

More largely, feelings about the Romans in Britain were complicated, on the one hand, by the capacity of the legend of Brut to underpin the construction of a pan-British state in 1603, and on the other, relatedly, by the cult of the British martyrs persecuted under Diocletian. A focus of devotion and pilgrimage by the twelfth century, these martyrs survived the Reformation, only lightly revised by John Foxe and other questioners of legendary saints' lives, because they could be used to demonstrate the existence of an ancient, British Christianity pre-existing the influence of the papacy, and because their persecution for refusing to worship the pagan idols of Rome could be seen as prefiguring the martyrdom of Marian Protestants who refused to worship the idols of the Roman church. Here are potent reasons why Jacobean writers inherited a view of the Romans in Britain that could be closer to Howard Brenton than to the Enlightenment and Victorian conviction that they were 'a good thing' who 'brought law'.

The positive qualities of ancient Britain were associated with Wales. Of Caledonia little was known. Were the Picts, as Camden thought, a section of the Britons unassimilated to Rome whose name indicated that their bodies were tattooed with pict-ures, or were they a separate people, new-comers like the Scots who arrived before them from Scythia via Spain and Ireland?[8] Such uncertainties meant that, when a site of authentic Britishness was sought, writers looked to the mountainous country which had resisted Rome and kept out the Saxons. 'The Welshmen', as Holinshed put it, 'are the verie Britains in deed'.[9] That is a leading reason why the Jacobean plays which anticipate Brenton's *The Romans in Britain*—William Rowley's *A Shoo-maker a Gentleman* (c.1608), Shakespeare's *Cymbeline* (c.1610), Fletcher's *Bonduca* (1613), and Robert Armin's (?) *The Valiant Welshman* (1612–14)—give Wales such prominence. But their Welsh-British grounding also allowed them to negotiate, through such topics as rape, invasion, and hybridization, both the archipelagic politics reconstituted by 1603 and the relationship between the new Jacobean state and Europe.

It has been noted (above, p. 42) that Henry VIII's incorporation of Wales had the paradoxical effect of producing, for the first time, a coherent Welsh domain. The joining of the principality in the west with the Marches along the Anglo-Welsh border, the shiring of the whole country, and the imposition of an Erastian Reformation gave Wales a new identity that was potentially more than administrative. Locally controlled by a Council in the Marches based at Ludlow, Wales was also peculiarly subject to the crown, because Henry VIII preserved powers to govern it without legislation passing through the Westminster parliament. Praisers of the Tudors liked to claim that this increased the happiness of the Welsh.

Crucially for the plays which interest me, however—and this is not generally realized—the status and extent of Wales were unfinished business in 1603. When James came to the English throne this was not at first apparent. Except among die-hard papists, willing to stir up Welsh patriotism on behalf of a Spanish claimant,[10] his accession was welcomed. Anglo-Welsh poets discovered in regal union the fulfilment of Merlin's prophecy in Geoffrey of Monmouth, that the Britons would be defeated by the Saxons but one day resume a leading role in Britain,[11] and Welsh MPs were placed on the commission to discuss fuller union with Scotland. Yet the borders of Wales and the Marches, already redrawn in 1536–43, remained an issue, and it is no accident that the Jacobean plays about the Romans in Britain coincide with the Four Shire Controversy of 1604–14, during which border magnates and gentry tried to secure the same exemption from control by the Council in the Marches as had been granted to Cheshire and Bristol in the 1560s.[12]

The Welsh elite, who welcomed the opportunity to bring the border country under local control, resisted this. And James refused to redivide Wales, partly for reasons of good order in an area difficult to administer, but also because he wanted to preserve the privileges of a principality that would be granted to Prince Henry. That raised another issue. From about 1607 the rights and honours attached to Wales became topics of interest in Henry's circle. Prompted by George Owen of Henllys, the Pembrokeshire historian, who argued that the principality had not been abolished under the Acts of Union, the case was made that Wales was uniquely attached to the crown and could be separately governed. Yet although this direct connection between the monarch and Wales was gratifying to loyal subjects, it could also be disturbing given a king with absolutist pretentions. The anomaly was patched up in 1610 when James—although he refused to change the Act of 1543—promised not to use his power in Wales arbitrarily.[13]

It is often said that *Cymbeline* was written to celebrate the investiture in 1610 of Prince Henry as Prince of Wales (and of Britain—above, p. 19). Whatever the truth of that, *Cymbeline* reflects contemporary debate, like *A Shoo-maker a Gentleman* and *The Valiant Welshman*, by presenting ancient Wales as a separate entity. There is no developed sense of an independent authority in Shakespeare's Cambria, and Cymbeline is called King of Britain, yet when the Roman envoy, Lucius, is denied tribute in London and sets out for Milford Haven, he is given an escort only as far as the Severn.[14] In *The Valiant Welshman*—which was performed by an acting company called the Prince of Wales's Men—Caradoc, prince of ancient Powys (and thus of a realm which encroached on the early modern border shires) marries the daughter of the King of North Wales, consolidating a Welsh polity; when Guiderius appeals to him for help against the Romans, it is as the King of Britain appealing to a Welsh monarch. In these works Wales is picked out as a retrospective guarantor of the legitimacy of the new British state, a taproot into Galfridian antiquity, but also as a distinct dominion in the manner of Wales in Jacobean debate.

The arguments around the four shires and Jacobean royal authority would not have been so vigorous were Wales the placidly incorporated principality that historians sometimes write of. It is clear even from their writings in or translated into English that the Welsh literati were not lacking in pride and resentment. In his preface to *The Historie of Cambria* (1584), for example, David Powel complains that the Welsh have been condemned as rebellious without their circumstances being understood. Pointing out that Edward I placed the people under English officers who were 'thought oftentimes to be ouer-severe and rigorous for their owne profit and commoditie',[15] he laments the oppression of the country by Henry IV, after Owain Glyn Dŵr's rising.[16] Welsh intellectuals had particularly tense relations with the Scots. It was resented that Hector Boece, for instance, had argued that Caractacus and Boadicea were Caledonian leaders.[17] Denying that the Scots had saved Britain from Julius Caesar's invasion, Humphrey Llwyd noted that 'the most cruell, and sauage nations the *Readshankes* and *Scottes*' had—like their medieval descendants—attacked their Romanized neighbour while its young men were fighting in France.[18]

The accession of James to the English throne gave these relations a further twist, as Welsh writers (like some of the Irish)[19] claimed the king as one of their blood[20]—an understandable reaction given the eagerness of English antiquaries to view him as a Saxon.[21] The Welsh now tailored their patriotism to the pluralities of multiple monarchy. In 'Cambria' (1603), for instance, John Davies of Hereford says that, as a descendant of Camber and Owen Tudor, Prince Henry should come to Wales and govern it. Yet Welsh particularism remained strong. Looking forward to the reconstruction of Roman cities under James, Davies wanted them 'faire as before, | That *Scots*, and *Brittaines* may mixt liue therein'.[22] In a poem designed to welcome an Anglo-Scottish prince to his Welsh inheritance, this is quietly provocative, because it denies Scots the name of Britons. It was a prickliness which the court had reason to respect, because, as advisers warned during the Four Shire Controversy, a balance had to be struck. Union was desirable, but too much of it—removing the border counties from the jurisdiction of the Council in the Marches—would endanger other elements of regional government in Britain and destabilize the Anglo-Welsh precedent for Anglo-Scottish union.[23] It would also risk igniting rebellion.[24]

While the regal union of 1603 encouraged a certain expansiveness in the Welsh intelligentsia by making them feel central to the political mythology of Britishness,[25] English views of Wales combined an acceptance of its symbolic importance with mistrust and condescension. Armin points out in his preface to *The Valiant Welshman* that the English are grudging in their recognition of Welsh achievements. When fears of Spanish invasion rose, Wales was looked upon as a likely point of entry. The idea that the Welsh elite remained potentially troublesome gained credibility from its participation in the Earl of Essex's Rebellion. As late as 1634, when Milton was writing *Comus*, the land west of the Severn was associated with riot, rapes, and robberies.[26] In the English imagination, even more than in reality, Wales was poor, infertile, linguistically alien, and run by a down-at-heel gentry that was, as Humphrey Llwyd admitted, given to 'ouermuch boastying of the Nobilitie of their stocke'.[27]

Much of this comes through in the Jacobean plays about the Romans in Britain. Most obviously, the wars against Rome which dominate all four texts reflect a Welsh history of rebellion. We are shown an impoverished but noble life in *Bonduca* and *Cymbeline*, in the rocky places where Fletcher's Caratach hides with the young prince Hengo, and in the mountains of Pembrokeshire where Shakespeare's Belarius, Guiderius, and Arviragus live by hunting and grubbing up roots. Above all, Wales is a site of magic and romance, not just because the miraculous is inextricable from the Galfridian history that still shaped perceptions of Wales, but because North Wales and the former Marches were associated with superstitious recusancy. This gives rise to the border-country witchcraft of *The Valiant Welshman*, where Caradoc, like the Elder Brother in Milton's *Maske*, who uses a sprig of haemony against Comus, has to see off a monstrous serpent with a sprig of moly. And it contributes to *A Shoo-maker a Gentleman*, where Rowley exploits another paradox that I must now bring into focus: the association of Wales with ancient, primitive Christianity yet also with unreformed religion. Both the origin of British Protestantism and its threatening, recusant opposite, Jacobean Wales could stand for what it was not.

★ ★ ★

Many people resisted Polydore Vergil's historical revisionism lest it damage the case for Britain having received Christianity without the mediation of Rome. Again, the Welsh gave a lead. In the widely read *Epistol at y Cembru* ('Address to the Welsh Nation') which prefaced the Welsh version of the New Testament (1567), the cleric Richard Davies followed Geoffrey of Monmouth in saying that Christianity came to Britain with Joseph of Arimathea, and was established before King Lles the son of Coel corresponded with the Bishop of Rome in the second century. After the invasion of the Saxons, paganism pushed the faith back into Cambria, and when St Augustine came from the pope to convert the Saxons he brought with him a debased, formal religion. For a time the Britons maintained the purity of their faith, but eventually they were drawn in by the tentacles of Rome.

Davies highlights the irony that an anciently believing nation should have sunk into recusancy; playing on the Welsh sense of political inferiority, he urges his countrymen to recover the 'one excellent virtue' which gave them 'a privilege and a pre-eminence, namely, undefiled religion'.[28] After Augustine's mission, he says, the Welsh bishops (anticipating Henry VIII) refused to accept the pope's authority. In the same vein, he finds proto-Protestanism in the British bard Taliesin, who lived in the time of King Arthur and wrote: 'Woe to the worldly priest who does not rebuke evil passion, and who does not preach. Woe to him who does not protect his fold and being a shepherd does not watch. Woe to him who does not protect with his pastoral staff his sheep from the Roman wolves.'[29] Lamenting the destruction of Welsh books during the centuries of war with the English, Davies uses the evidence of proverbs to show that his people had the scripture in their own tongue of old.

English Protestants might seem excluded by this, but they could affiliate themselves with Davies's story through the Henrician union and its associated Reformation, and they were stirred by his complaints about the unreformed darkness of Wales. Spenser, for example, represents Davies in *The Shepheardes Calender* (1579) as Diggon Davie, the pastor who pursued his ministry in 'a farre countrye' and found its church asset-stripped by noblemen, and its flocks infiltrated by Roman wolves.[30] Davies's account of the primitive church made Wales, which helped underpin Tudor legitimacy, the guarantor also of ecclesiastical independence from the pope.[31] As a result, he was consulted by such English divines as Matthew Parker, who had an interest in the Saxon church.[32] And his message did not become less potent when Britain acquired a single defender of the faith in 1603.

Common ground was nowhere clearer than in Davies's account of the Romans in Britain. Medieval collections of saints' lives had not neglected the martyrdom of Christians by Diocletian and his underlings in Britain. But these deaths were peculiarly important to Davies's generation, who had witnessed Queen Mary's execution of Protestants in the 1550s—some of them in Wales. Since the blood of ancient British martyrs ran in their veins, Davies believed, the Welsh should embrace the faith that had been bought for them 'perfect and uncorrupt'.[33] English reformers like Foxe could not claim a blood link but they too saw the sufferings of the Diocletian saints at the hands of pagan Rome as foreshadowing the martyrdom of reformers by an idol-worshipping Roman church. After 1603, the martyrs were well placed to articulate new infra-British confluences and demarcations, and their potential was realized in Rowley's *A Shoo-maker a Gentleman*—a rich historical fantasia, staged for popular audiences at the Red Bull theatre.

The star of this show is Winifred, who makes her first entry wearing a black veil. One does not expect the heroine of a Red Bull play to be a crypto-nun, a version of the St Winifred who, to the consternation of reformers, continued to attract thousands to the holy well in Flintshire which reputedly did miraculous cures.[34] In Caxton's version of *The Golden Legend*, the source-at-one-remove of Rowley's play, the martyr's story is told. She was a Welsh maiden decapitated by a lustful Welsh prince who demanded her virginity. A spring of fresh water welled up where her head fell to the ground. Revived by a holy man, she lived as an abbess, with only a fine scar round her neck to show where she had been decapitated. Much remains in the play's treatment of post-Apostolic miracles that a hot Protestant such as Foxe would disapprove of. At one point, the Roman persecutor Lutio loses and regains his sight through the power of Winifred's well. Yet Rowley follows his immediate source, Deloney's *The Gentle Craft* (1597?), in replacing the tale of virginity and rape—a topic which I shall return to—with a Protestant debate about whether Winifred should live a single, holy life or marry her suitor Sir Hugh, and both authors introduce her well with a miracle which is more like the vision of the Britanno-Roman emperor Constantine (acceptable to mainstream Protestants) than it is to recusant legend. An angel rises from the water, with a crucifix, to urge belief.

Like some other texts, the play never quite seals in its account of Winifred a distinction between the ancient fidelity and modern superstitiousness of Wales.[35] This helps Rowley map, however, both the doctrinal diversity and the geopolitical range of British Protestantism, because the crypto-Catholic ardour of Winifred, and what he sees at her well, spurs the 'Cambrian sectarist' Amphiabell (a puritan sort of description) to go from Wales to Verulamium to convert the agent of Roman rule, Albon.[36] Neither Amphiabell nor Albon appears in *The Gentle Craft*; they come into the drama from Rowley's own reading of *The Golden Legend*, and also, probably, of Foxe. Moreover, in the legend Amphiabell does not meet Winifred, and he does not go to Wales until *after* he has converted Albon. So the play, unlike its sources, reinforces the Welsh-British idea that the origin of pure religion lay in the Wales that now needed reform.

The British idea in this case did not diminish England. For it is an equivocally integrationist feature of Jacobean plays about ancient Britain that they are keen to issue reminders of later, Saxon history—as though the impending formation of a British state created a backflow of English pride towards previously undervalued Saxon origins. In *King Lear*, the British-Galfridian royal house shares the action with the Saxon-named Edgar and Edmund. In *Bonduca*, the child-prince Hengo has a name which hints at Hengist, the leader of the Kentish Saxons at the much later time when the British were being displaced. And in *A Shoo-maker a Gentleman* the romantic leads are young British princes who somehow turn out to be Offa and Eldred. Nothing in his sources would have led Rowley to believe that King Offa was alive during the reign of Diocletian. We are dealing with historical telescoping rather like that found in Howard Brenton. There may be nothing as explicitly topical in *A Shoo-Maker a Gentleman* as Brenton's introduction of the Northern Irish troubles into *The Romans in Britain*, but the marks of recent archipelagic history on the martyrs are just as clear.

Thus Rowley puts the ancient Briton Albon into a Reformation context. Early in the play, he promises: '*Albon* shall still as substitute to *Rome* | Observe, and keepe her high imperiall Doome' (B3v). After his conversion, he says that he cannot persecute Christians because, like Henry VIII in 1534, he is an Englishman free of Rome. Similarly, when the

Romans find Amphiabell and Winifred together in Wales, they use words that elide the Diocletian and the Marian persecutions: 'turne unto *Rome*, and worship give unto | Our Golden *gods*' (E4r). When the pair resist, they are taken to Verulamium to see Albon martyred. Three victims become four, as the Welsh prince Sir Hugh, who has become a shoemaker to avoid persecution, is so appalled to see his mistress a prisoner that he 'rusht in amongst them … rail'd on the *Roman* gods … and swore he would dye if she did' (H2v). The Christians are then tortured and executed—popular scenes, no doubt, the flavour of which can be gathered from the gory woodcut depicting the persecutions of the early church that was tipped into later editions of Foxe's *Actes and Monuments*, and often printed separately. One corner of this sheet is reproduced as Fig. 3; it shows the elision of early Christians with Protestants in their refusal to worship pagan Roman and Roman Catholic idols.

Meanwhile, Offa and Eldred take up careers as shoemakers alongside Sir Hugh, apprenticed to the same merry master and bustling wife. One shows his mettle when the emperor's daughter falls in love with him. There is a charming comedy of shoe-fitting and foot-fondling, as Leodice fights with her feelings and her prejudice against his lowly status. The other enlists in the Roman army and fights the Goths and the Vandals, twice saving Diocletian's life. This display of British valour elicits a favour which seals the stay-at-home brother's marriage with Leodice. It is not the only permission granted. At the end of the general rejoicing, after the Romans have divided Britain to be governed north and south by Eldred and Offa, the latter says

> A Church then, and a beauteous Monastery
> On *Holmhurst*-Hill, where *Albon* lost his head,
> *Offa* shall build; which Ile St. *Albons* name,
> In honour of our first English Martyrs fame. …

and his Roman father-in-law replies: 'Build what Religious Monuments you please, | Be true to *Rome*, none shall disturbe your peace' (L1v–2r). As though the horrors of execution can be instantly forgotten, the play shifts modes, and Rome shuffles off its identity by name and analogy with the Counter-Reformation church. But 'our first English Martyrs fame' is equally striking. Offa finally erases Albon's British identity.

It is tempting to conclude that *A Shoo-maker* is flatly Anglocentric as well as opportunistic about the meanings of Rome. By the end of it, the Welsh

Fig. 3. Early Christians, proto-Protestants, beaten for refusing to worship an idol. From 'A Table of the X. first Persecutions of the Primitiue Church vnder the Heathen Tyrannes of Rome', in John Foxe, *Actes and Monuments*, rev. edn (London, 1583).

characters are dead and the scene has shifted to St Albans. The island has been divided north and south, no-one (*pace* King James) urging union. And the protomartyr of Albion has been reclassified as English, with a Saxon proposing his memorial. Yet Rowley has changed his sources to emphasize the Welshness of the British saints, and thus how much Protestant England owes to the principality. Winifred's well and the Cambrian martyrdoms create the most lasting stage images. So although the play touches down in the patriotism of its London audience, making the Saxons the inheritors (in a way Archbishop Parker would appreciate) of the virtues of the primitive British church, it avoids xenophobia, and within the limits of the theatrical vocabulary available at the Red Bull, it celebrates the hybrid and devolved make-up of British religion. It shows popular theatre reaching an accommodation with the politics of 1603.

★   ★   ★

I began with the scene in *The Romans in Britain* in which three Roman soldiers kill a couple of ancient Britons on a riverbank and cut up and rape a third. It was this episode which landed the play's director in court. Yet although the scene is extreme, it is not untypical of works that deal with imperialism. Rape can be a symptom of, but also symbolize, the penetration of one culture by another: the violence of the rapist rendered reckless by a sense of cultural superiority, the trauma of a victim who is not just personally violated but carries within him or herself the pain of a wounded social order. For the damaging power of rape depends on the physical act having psycho-social implications. In Brenton it is the initiate Druid Marban who is raped, and who then at Caesar's hands has an image of Venus hung about his neck before he is sent back to his people. We later see Marban killing himself because through his degradation he understands that the Romans will displace the British gods and destroy the value systems of his society.

   Among the Jacobean plays that deal with the Romans in Britain, rape—virtual, attempted, and actual—recurs. One reason for this is that, historically, the best-documented British uprising against Rome, that of the Iceni led by Boudica (i.e., Boadicea, Bonduca, Voada), was sparked off by an incident in which she was whipped and her daughters raped by Romans.[37] John Fletcher's *Bonduca* deals with that rebellion, although, in line with the stress on Wales in these plays, it merges the queen's revolt with that of Caradoc, Caratacus, or Caratach—generally thought of as a leader of Welsh or border-country tribes, though in reality the son of Cunobellinus, Shakespeare's Cymbeline. In Armin's *The Valiant Welshman*, a Roman tries to rape Voada herself, who is translated from the territory of the Iceni in what is now East Anglia to being a princess of the Welsh border country. And in *Cymbeline*, the earliest and most influential of these plays, a virtual rape by voyeurism triggers the heroine's journey into Wales and her cooperation with the enemy, Rome. In all three works, conflict between Rome and Britain is articulated through sexual violence in situations shaped by the politics of Jacobean union.

The persistent importance of rape in *Bonduca* can be gauged from the queen and her daughters' last stand in a stronghold that the Romans assail with battering rams. In keeping with the sexualized scenario, a bowl of poison and two swords are produced as instruments of suicide. The second daughter imagines an afterlife 'where no Wars come, | Nor lustful slaves to ravish us', and before the elder daughter stabs herself, she cries out to the besiegers:

> your great Saint *Lucrece*
> Di'd not for honour; *Tarquin* topt her well,
> And mad she could not hold him, bled.[38]

These (tonally volatile) suicides are not, though, the end of the play. With more than an act to go, *Bonduca* concentrates on Caratach who is retreating with the boy prince Hengo to what he calls 'my Countrey' (IV.ii.85). The importance of Wales was a given in Fletcher's material because in Holinshed Voadicia's rebellion broke out during the absence of Roman troops in Anglesey. But Fletcher gives the country greater prominence, not just merging but reversing the order of Caradoc's and Bonduca's campaigns, so that the action devolves towards Wales. Indeed, Caratach and Hengo find a resting place in a precipitous, stony height—some sort of onstage structure—that resembles the stronghold of Caractacus placed by Holinshed in the Welsh borders.[39]

When the Romans attack Holinshed's Caractacus his men retreat to the hilltops. In *Cymbeline*, as the invading Romans advance, Belarius says to the princes: 'Sonnes, | Wee'l higher to the Mountaines, there secure v[s]' (IV.iv. TLN 2801—2). The last act of *Bonduca* starts in the same Cambro-British way, with Caratach musing over Hengo, 'Thus we afflicted Britains climb for safeties' (V.i.1). On this elevation, his defiance and love of liberty reach their zenith. In the absence of Bonduca and her daughters, however, a family romance, not unlike that centred on Shakespeare's orphaned Posthumus, begins to join Britons and Romans. When the cortege of a Roman called Penyus goes by, Caratach tells Hengo, who lost his father before he was born, that 'This worthy Romane | Was such another piece of endlesse honour' (V.i.70—1). Caratach himself is talked into a noble surrender, and his question or prediction to Swetonius, 'I am for *Rome*?' (V.iii.194) is tellingly ambiguous. As I shall show, the resemblance to Rowley's play in this rapprochement with Rome is not accidental.

The Welshness of Fletcher's Caratach is rarely more than tacit, and, strictly considered, nothing in *Bonduca* takes place in Wales. From some angles this might look like English appropriation of a Cambro-British hero. A play about ancient Britain could not exist for post-1603 audiences, however, in a purely English perspective. It is symptomatic that, when George Powell revised *Bonduca* in the late seventeenth century, he introduced a Pict by the name of Macquaire who is as lasciviously attentive to Bonduca's daughter, Claudia, as any Roman.[40] That Powell's satirical eye was directed at Scotland is as secondary as the fact that his Caratach does not speak discernibly Welsh lines. He educed the geopolitics around the play—the pan-British context it brought in train—in ways that are if anything more recognizable for this displacement.

Certainly, the working out of Welsh material in *The Valiant Welshman* and *Cymbeline* involved the introduction of Scottish elements, as though the modelling of Anglo-Scottish on Anglo-Welsh union after 1603 created a dynamic whereby the more Welsh an English writer tried to be the more Scottish matter made itself felt. Reinventing himself as an English monarch, King James apologized to the Welsh-descended Robert Cecil for the 'very rude Scottish spelling' in one of his published works by saying that transcribers had corrupted it into 'good Britaine language or rather Welsh'.[41] Ambitious Scots now joined the Welsh in claiming to be 'British' in order to gain admission to the English-based power structure that controlled the three kingdoms. Out of this overlap between the two peoples (most readily perceived by Englishmen, who categorized them both as not-English) came the possibility of substitution. Anthony Munday's London pageant, *Sidero-Thriambos* (1618), thus brings an 'ancient *Brittish Bard*' out of his grave to address the crowd not in Welsh or Welsh English but Scots.[42]

On the face of it such dislocations are irrelevant to *The Valiant Welshman*. The '*ancient Bardh*' raised from the grave to introduce this play is a firmly '*Welsh poet*',[43] and the action is centred in Cambria. Son of the Earl of March, Caradoc helps Octavian, King of North Wales, fight and defeat a would-be usurper, and marries Octavian's daughter. He is then summoned by Gederus, King of Britain, to help resist the Roman demand for tribute. Undermined in Gederus' eyes by a message that says he is a traitor, he fights the Romans disguised as a common soldier and is given a golden lion by the emperor Claudius as a token for sparing his life. Boudica has already put in an appearance as Caradoc's sister, Voada; she is now saved from being raped by the Roman, Marcus Gallicus. Caradoc, visiting York to persuade

Venusius to fight against Rome, is betrayed and taken to the imperial city. While British forces defeat the Roman army on home ground, he enjoys the moral victory of showing Claudius the golden lion.

Heroic stuff, but the ridicule of Welshness is also represented. Just as *Cymbeline* simultaneously includes classical Romans and the Renaissance Italian Iachimo, so Armin's play combines noble ancient Britons, who speak conventional English, with a Stuart Welshman (ostensibly an ancient Earl of Anglesey) who swears 'By the pones of Saint *Tauy*' (A1v–2r). Yet if this is a doubly Welsh play, it is also, as I have hinted, part-Scottish. For Armin, like Fletcher, combines Caradoc and Voadicia in a single plot, by drawing on some version of Hector Boece's account of ancient Caledonia, most likely via Holinshed's *Historie of Scotland*. In this tradition, Voada, the sister of Caratake, King of Scotland, is put aside by her husband, King Arviragus of Britain, in favour of a Roman wife. Released from prison by her British subjects, she escapes to Wales. Advised by a lord called Comus (possibly remembered by Milton), the Welsh ask Caratake to help her get revenge, and assisted by Picts and Scots they fight the Romans and Arvirgagus to a draw. Eventually defeated, Voada takes her own life, and one of her daughters marries a Roman called Marius who had previously deflowered her.[44]

I have mentioned the quarrel between Welsh and Scottish historians over Boece's location of Boadicea and Caratacus. He moved these figures north because they were valuable cultural capital. If Voada and Caratake were Alban, they could backdate Scottish independence while making it clear that the Picts and Scots had long been willing to lead British resistance to continental invaders. To the English, who had political dominance within Britain, the siting of these stories mattered less. Thus, in William Warner's predominantly Anglocentric[45] *Albions England*, the Scottish version of Voada is adopted despite the Latin evidence and the patriotic gratification that might flow from claiming her for East Anglia.[46] The Scottish account is more selectively followed by Armin because his aim was not to exclude England and Wales as bases for Boadicea but to place them, in a post-1603 spirit, within a British scheme.[47]

The attempted rape in *The Valiant Welshman* fits these composite geopolitics because Voada is not removed from the orbit of the Scottish story by the recasting of Holinshed's Marius into Marcus Gallicus, yet her being Caradoc's sister draws her into a Welsh narrative. Meanwhile the rapist's lust is firmly related to Rome. We are asked to behold how Marcus Gallicus comes 'like bloudy *Tarquin*' into Voada's bedroom, while she, in the style of Lucrece, cries: 'For shame forbeare, and cleare a Romans name, | From the suspition of so foule a sinne'. The episode (H3v–4v) ends in farce, yet it begins to turn the British tide against the Roman invaders. It was patriotic of Armin to contradict his sources and give Voada and her allies victory; but he does not end his play on a xenophobic note. Instead, he inspects the behaviour of Caradoc in Rome.

When the besieged Bonduca is asked to submit in Fletcher, she asks 'If *Rome* be earthly, why should any knee | With bending adoration worship her?' (IV.iv.15–16). The same pattern recurs when Caradoc refuses to kowtow to Claudius:

> I was not borne to kneele, but to the Gods,
> Nor basely bow vnto a lumpe of clay,
> In adoration of a clod of earth. ...   (I3v)

In *A Shoo-maker a Gentleman*, Rome could not so persuasively represent idolatrous Catholicism were it not associated with the idea of earthly power becoming an impious object of admiration, centre of an emperor cult, even (as in *The Ruines of Time*) an emblem of the world's vanities. This protestantized anti-imperialism reinforces the British defiance of Rome in *Bonduca* and *The Valiant Welshman*—defiance that will have carried a topical accent for early audiences, anxious about King James's Caesarian aspirations, his Scottish liking for Roman law rather than common law, and so on. But there is also the pattern that runs through these plays and extends to *Cymbeline*, by which Britons put conflict behind them and unite with Rome; for in *The Valiant Welshman*, Caradoc compromises with Claudius.

To understand that larger conformity it is worth looking back through the telescoped account of early modern history rehearsed by Armin's play. When Caradoc brings his border forces to the aid of the King of North Wales, then marries his daughter and, in the course of helping Gederus, King of Britain, against the Romans, becomes King of Wales, he unifies an enlarged Cambria (including his ancestral Marches) within a version of Tudor union. The next phase of the action is more Jacobean in resonance, since it involves a league between Caradoc and the northern powers of Venusius. Finally, like King James ending the Elizabethan wars against continental Catholicism, Caradoc agrees to live in peace with Rome without losing his freedom. 'We freely giue you all your liberties', Claudius announces, 'And honourably will returne you home | With euerlasting peace and vnity' (I4v). The play that I shall finish with, *Cymbeline*, is far more peculiar and sophisticated, but it probes related issues.

★ ★ ★

Brenton's *The Romans in Britain* would be less adequate to its subject if the psycho-social effect of the rape were simply to anticipate the destruction of Celtic culture by colonialism. After he is assaulted Marban surprises the audience as well as the Roman soldiers by defying them in Latin (37). Told about this, Caesar is unruffled: 'We know Druids on the mainland speak Greek. Even write it. It's no surprise to find a little Druid in Britain, talking Latin' (49). It was a matter of pride among early modern antiquarians that the ancients attributed a knowledge of Greek to the Druids, and said that the Gauls came to Britain to develop their learning. But the real issue, as Brenton knows, is that colonial encounters rarely happen—especially around trading empires—without a pre-history of interaction. A country drawn into tribute-paying will absorb in advance some of the culture of its stronger neighbour, and may even possess knowledge that the empire considers arcane.

Each of the plays I have looked at somewhat Romanizes ancient Britain, though it is often hard to decide how this is meant to be registered by audiences. The references to Pluto, Cerberus, and other classical figures by Caradoc and his fellows in *The Valiant Welshman* might be the dramatist's shorthand way of suggesting a pre-Christian milieu. And the illegality of stage blasphemy after 1606 might also explain the tendency of the Britons to swear by Roman gods.[48] Yet Shakespeare turned these conventions and constraints to dramatic advantage, using classical references to seam British with Roman culture and to prepare for the appearance of Jupiter himself in Posthumus's dream. The play instals a Roman deity—rather than Adraste, as in Act III of *Bonduca*—as divine governor of the isle. The growth of imperial hegemony may be at an early stage, but it is set to merge Britons and Romans into what Camden calls 'one stocke and nation'.[49]

The pull of Rome is clear at the most basic level of plot. Posthumus is drawn there when banished from court for marrying Imogen. His father and two brothers fought the empire, but his royal father-in-law was knighted by Augustus Caesar and gained honour in his service. Cymbeline makes the Roman Lucius 'welcome' despite his declaration of war, and wishes him 'Happines' on departure (III.v. TLN 1912). The wicked Queen and her son are more defiant; but their deserved deaths make possible the play's romance ending, and with them goes the chauvinism that stands between Britain and Rome. The smuggling of Cymbeline's sons to Pembrokeshire by Belarius, another soldier who fought the Romans, reinforces the significance of Wales as a redoubt of resistance. Yet the princes cherish the memory of his wife, their supposed mother, Euriphile (more 'Europhile' than 'Eurosceptic'). So it makes sense that their reunion with Cymbeline, after they turn the tide of battle in favour of Britain, should give him the confidence to overrule his subjects and voluntarily pay tribute to Caesar.

All this makes it less surprising that Imogen's virtual rape, like the assault on Brenton's Marban, should reveal the proleptic penetration of Britain by Latin and by Roman culture. Classicized guilt impels Iachimo to compare himself to 'Our *Tarquine*' as he creeps towards Imogen's bed (II. i; TLN 919), but when he gets there he discovers that the princess has been reading Ovid—the tale of Tereus's rape of Philomel, ironically appropriate to her predicament, if not indicative of a subconscious fear, but significant also in illustrating the domestication of Roman myth. The princess's bedtime reading shows her to be more intimate with Roman values than do the jibes of Bonduca's elder daughter when she shouts from the tiring house that Lucrece enjoyed her rape. When Iachimo back in Rome describes the furnishings of what must have been an almost bare stage, he fills out the details of a classicized bedchamber (while making us believe in things that we did not see, with such ease, that Posthumus' credulity about Imogen's seduction in that chamber should seem more understandable). Hangings of silk and silver showed Cleopatra, he says, meeting Mark Antony on the River Cydnus: a colonial queen welcoming her future Roman lover. The goddess Diana bathing was carved on the chimney piece. The fire irons were 'two winking Cupids'. Posthumus reacts to the account with a Roman oath: 'Ioue'. And when Philario doubts the seduction, Iachimo's swearing 'By Iupiter' adds to the proof of Imogen's infidelity for Posthumus (II. iv. TLN 1226–304).

In emphasizing these ties with Rome I am far from wanting to diminish the importance of archipelagic politics. As Leah Marcus has shown with almost excessive ingenuity, the composition of *Cymbeline* was influenced by the Jacobean union debate.[50] The Anglo-Welsh axis is obvious, and the character of Posthumus carries hints of Scoto-Britishness.[51] It is significant, however, that *Cymbeline* was written after 1607 when the king's plans for legislative union were rejected by the House of Commons. By working in the aftermath of a many-faceted initiative, Shakespeare could play across disparate motifs, assuming a saturated, even insouciant, familiarity in the audience. To cite just one example, the prominence given to Milford Haven as the site of Roman invasion and defeat and of the reunion of the royal family is in line with crown propaganda about British state formation;[52] but where Samuel Daniel's masque for the investiture of the Prince of Wales, *Tethys Festival*, dutifully describes Henry VII's landing at 'Milford... The happy Port of Vnion' as foreshadowing the conception of Prince Henry,[53] Imogen's delight at the prospect of meeting Posthumus there edges the happiness of the place into knowing and punning (haven/heaven) satire. 'Say', she commands Pisanio,

> how farre it is
> To this same blessed Milford. And by' th' way
> Tell me how Wales was made so happy, as
> T'inherite such a Hauen. ...   (III.ii. TLN 1524–9)

So although *Cymbeline* will have been written to please the patron of Shakespeare's acting company, the King, not to mention his Welsh patron, the Earl of Pembroke,[54] and (as will become clear) a potential Scottish patron, Sir James Hay, its dramaturgy is not instrumental. Shakespeare responded to the culturally opportunistic artificiality of the union project, to the mélange of myths and invented traditions which accompanied James's attempts to achieve full political union in Britain, by modulating from tragedy (*King Lear* and *Macbeth*) into the knowing, consciously syncretic genre of tragicomedy, in which artifice is of the essence. If any function were to be ascribed to *Cymbeline*, it would be that of compensating for the *failure* of union through a pan-British family romance in which a pair of Welsh-bred brothers are reunited with their London-British father and a sister who recovers her somewhat-Scottish husband. And any account along those lines would have to acknowledge that the play does not engage in easy wish-fulfilment; it does not slot Wales into Britain, or bring the outsider Posthumus into accord with his princess, without confusion and distress. Its interest in the Romans in Britain, and thus in the relationship between natives and strangers, is part of a scenario that deals with alienation within Britain itself.[55] As late as the 1620s Scotsmen appear in the lists of aliens drawn up in London.[56]

These issues impinge on the virtual rape of Imogen because Iachimo's visit to Britain (and it is neither his first nor his last) is prompted by the competitive patriotism of men of different nationalities gathered in Rome—a city, in the Iachimo scenes, contemporary with and as cosmopolitan as Jacobean London. Feminist critics have rightly pointed out that Posthumus fetishes Imogen's sexuality and uses her as negotiable property in his wager with Iachimo. The analysis is incomplete, however, if we overlook the driving force of patriotic rivalry, and Posthumus's vulnerability as a 'Stranger' (I.iv. TLN 344, 416). Even before he arrives, at least one Italian, a Frenchman, a Dutchman, and a Spaniard have used their mistresses as counters in a dispute about national superiority. That the Frenchman who recalls their quarrel also describes an earlier argument involving Posthumus in Gaul reinforces the point that such competition is a recurrent source of conflict: 'It was much like an argument that fell out last night, where each of vs fell in praise of our Country-Mistresses. This Gentleman, at that time vouching (and vpon warrant of bloody affirmation) his to be more Faire, Vertuous, Wise, Chaste, Constant, Qualified, and lesse attemptible then any, the rarest of our Ladies in Fraunce' (I.iv. TLN 369–75). By the time he gets to Rome, 'the Britaine' (I.iv. TLN 342) is a more seasoned traveller, who only maintains that Imogen is *as* excellent as any woman in Italy. His insecurity as a visitor from the reputedly barbarous island beyond the empire is, however, easily played on by Iachimo.

Although it would be futile to mount a defence of Posthumus, it is worth adding that Imogen's assertion that her husband is astonishingly superior to Cloten—an insult which triggers his vow to rape her[57]—provides an ironic parallel to the men's dispute about which of them has the best mistress. What makes her even more like Posthumus is that insecurity about foreigners obscures her view of him. She regrets she has had no time to make him 'sweare, | The Shees of Italy should not betray | Mine Interest, and his Honour' (I. iv. TLN 297–9). When Iachimo arrives, she is quickly persuaded that Posthumus has found a Roman mistress. Despite learning from this encounter that Iachimo is at least mendacious, when Pisanio tells her that Posthumus wants her murdered she denies that Iachimo was false and concludes that her husband has fallen for 'Some Iay of Italy | (Whose mother was her painting)' (III.iv. TLN 1720). She is still going on about this imaginary 'Roman Curtezan' ninety lines later.

Anti-Italian/Roman prejudice is shared by other virtuous Britons, including Pisanio. It is at its strongest, however, in the plot about paying tribute. Cymbeline's refusal to pay Lucius (unnamed in Shakespeare's sources) no doubt reminded many of King Arthur's defiance of another Roman Lucius who demanded tribute from Britain.[58] But the Queen and Cloten strike a peculiarly insular note. Ironically, however, their speeches resonate strongly with Latin. Early audiences would have heard behind Cloten's outburst,

> Britaine's a world
> By it selfe, and we will nothing pay
> For wearing our owne Noses. ...   (III.i. TLN 1390–2)

the famous description of Britain in Virgil's *Eclogues* that we have already come across in Jonson's *Masque of Blacknesse* (above, p. 50): 'et penitus toto diuisos orbe Britannos'.[59] The Queen adds

> Remember Sir, my Liege,
> The Kings your Ancestors, together with
> The naturall brauery of your Isle, which stands
> As Neptunes Parke, ribb'd, and pal'd in
> With Oakes vnskaleable, and roaring Waters,
> With Sands that will not beare your Enemies Boates,
> But sucke them vp to'th' Top-mast. A kinde of Conquest
> *Caesar* made heere, but made not heere his bragge
> Of Came, and Saw, and Ouer-came: ...   (TLN 1395–402)

Beyond the familiar tag, 'Veni, vidi, vici', this recalls a body of classical poetry, well-known in Renaissance England, describing the ocean-girdled defensibleness of Britain. The Queen might almost be engaging with the Latin lines reprinted and translated in Camden, about

> Britain, I say, far set apart, and by vast sea di[s]join'd,
> Wall'd with inaccessible banks and craggy clifts behind;
> Which father Nereus fensed had with billowes most invincible
> And Ocean likewise compassed with ebs and flowes as fallible. ...

—lines that boast of Julius Caesar's ability to undo the island's apartness: 'What heretofore was world and world is now conjoind in one.'[60]

When Armin echoed this scene in King Octavian's refusal to pay the Romans tribute (C3v), he removed the intertextuality with Latin, wanting no complication of the idea that resisting Rome was right. With its recurrent, often very subtle, implication in Latinity, the balance of *Cymbeline* is different. Plays about the Romans in Britain had a problem with sources once Geoffrey of Monmouth's stock fell. If they wanted to use ancient testimony, dramatists had to rely on Latin, leaving their plays open to the objection that has been levelled even against Howard Brenton,[61] that any more-or-less postcolonial impulse to represent ancient Britain as the victim of empire was compromised by the materials they inherited from the colonizing power. Shakespeare capitalizes on this difficulty, making it part of the drama that the independence asserted by the Queen should be qualified by the formulations she uses.

The aftershock of Imogen's ordeal at the hands of Iachimo continues when she travels to Wales because Cloten pursues her promising to rape her on Posthumus' corpse. There is another way, however, in which the virtual rape reverberates into later acts of the play. Here is the story that Belarius tells the young princes, Guiderius and Arviragus, when they come out of their cave (the upstage 'discovery space') in Act III. '*Cymbeline* lou'd me', he recalls,

> But in one night,
> A Storme, or Robbery (call it what you will)
> Shooke downe my mellow hangings: nay my Leaues,
> And left me bare to weather. ...
> My fault being nothing (as I haue told you oft)
> But that two Villaines, whose false Oathes preuayl'd
> Before my perfect Honor, swore to *Cymbeline*,
> I was Confederate with the Romanes: ...   (III.iii. TLN 1616–27)

Like Imogen, Belarius was betrayed in one night's storm or robbery (or call it what you will). Both suffered at the hands of villains who swore against and dishonoured them: swore that Belarius was too intimate with the Romans, and that Imogen was sexually confederate with the Roman Iachimo.

Belarius goes on to explain how, dogged by royal displeasure—again like Imogen—he left the court for Wales, and spent twenty years in exile. He now has his 'Rocke', the redoubt of a Briton, yet also what he grandly calls his 'Demesnes', where he enjoys the high status privilege of hunting deer (TLN 1627–34). The Welsh scenes present a utopian combination of equality with aristocratic order, a locus free of the conflict created at court when Imogen marries a worthy commoner rather than the base prince Cloten. In Cambria Shakespeare found a setting perfectly adapted to his exploration of the great romance theme of DNA, because the Welsh, as we have seen, were by their own admission given to 'ouermuch boastying of the Nobilitie of their stocke'. Into this world comes Imogen, testing

Belarius's belief in the excellence of the youths only he knows to be royal, and hers in the unique properties of Posthumus.

At this point it is worth forgetting the levelling associations of Welsh Methodism and Trade Unionism. In the early seventeenth century, this drastically unequal society combined an old kin structure, celebrated by the bards, with a tradition of *cymortha*, or armed retaining, that edged into lawlessness.[62] As Richard Davies complained in his preface to the New Testament, Welsh noblemen fostered brigandage.[63] Shakespeare's princes are outlaws, in danger of being pursued into the mountains. Like the Welshmen described by Humphrey Llwyd, they avoid physical labour, and are naturally attuned to ceremony.[64] In fact, they represent what is parodied in stage Welshmen like the beggarly Caradock of Thomas Randolph's *Hey for Honesty, Down with Knavery* (1651), who thinks even his lice descended from Acncas: a glittering pedigree mired in poverty, indigent high status. They also believe in fairies, and occasionally play the harp. Within limits that I shall get to, they have plenty of Welshness about them.[65]

Yet the Pembrokeshire setting of these scenes, in addition to being a compliment to Shakespeare's patron, the Earl thereof, is an ethnically complicating factor, because, although it contained many Welsh speakers, especially in upland areas, the county had English (and Flemish) settlements around Milford, not to mention the more recent Irish immigrants who had set up in the region.[66] The commonplace that Pembrokeshire was a 'little England beyond Wales' might seem irrelevant given the Welsh traits of the princes. Yet they have been reared as Cambro-Britons at a time in British history when Welshness did not exist, and as Cymbeline's children they were born in what would become England. Come to that, with the possible exception of the beggars who give Imogen directions, or misdirections, towards Milford, and who do not appear on stage, the play has no *bona fide* Cambrians. So the fact that Wales forms a unit which is distinct yet not separable from Cymbeline's Britain makes Pembrokeshire an apt focus for the Welsh scenes because it was removed in the Jacobean period from England but also part of it—a piece of the West Country, as it were, that had crossed the Severn and formed a Pale around Milford. In so far as it is part of greater England, it is not less a synecdoche of Wales as a whole, which was from some angles invisible (even nameless) within the 1536–43 union,[67] exemplary of the new British state not just in its ethnic diversities.

When the Jacobean Britishness of the princes appears through their Welshness, their retreat begins to resemble such other wild places as the

Anglo-Scottish borders or the Peak District. Just as, in *The Winter's Tale*, Sicily and the sea-coast of Bohemia matter less as locations because they figure a contrast between the overheated sophistication of Leontes' court and the pastoral world of Perdita, so the intricacy, politicking, and oddly advanced science of Cymbeline's court (where the Queen experiments with poisons) contrast with the simple, bonded, male world of the princes. To put it another way, Belarius has a harp but no leeks, goats, or cheese; the salient properties of his life are not entirely ethnic.

Yet the characteristic Welsh theme of pedigree remains a focus. The princes possess what Belarius calls 'Honor vntaught, | Ciuility not seene from othcr' (IV.ii. TLN 2472–3); their innate quality is gratified when Imogen puts sauce on their meat and cuts their vegetables into letter-shapes. But the notion that virtues are proportionate to breeding is challenged by Imogen's love for her social inferior Posthumus, and by the well-born grossness of Cloten, who arrives in Posthumus' clothes and makes the mistake of insulting Guiderius. Like the fiercest of the Britons depicted in John Speed's *History of Great Britaine* (Fig. 4), the rustic prince does what ancient Britons were notorious for: he chops off Cloten's head. Arranging a funeral, Belarius reduces his belief in inherited excellence to something like Imogen's declaration to Arviragus that all human dust is alike and dignity a social attribute.[68] As for the princess, when she awakes from a drugged sleep, next to the headless Cloten in Posthumus' clothes, her belief that she married a nonpareil does not prevent her from assuming that the body is her husband's. The confusions she endures in Wales encourage her to mean what she perhaps only said to Arviragus about man as clay.

She also has a speech about the princes' merit which carries a larger significance.

> These are kinde Creatures.
> Gods, what lyes I haue heard:
> Our Courtiers say, all's sauage, but at Court;
> Experience, oh thou disproou'st Report.
> Th'emperious Seas breeds Monsters; for the Dish,
> Poor Tributary Riuers, as sweet Fish. ...   (IV.ii. TLN 2284–9)

This has its touch of automatic anti-Roman hostility ('Th'emperious Seas breeds Monsters'), but it matters that Imogen calls the small streams 'Tributary' because that can mean paying tribute. It is another straw in the

Fig. 4. From 'The portraitures and paintings of the ancient Britaines', in John Speed, *The History of Great Britaine* (London, 1611).

wind that Cymbeline, though triumphant in war, will, at the end of the play, rediscover his attachment to Rome and pay tribute to the empire.

I suspect that Shakespeare remembered the rout of Boadicea's army when, near the end of the play, the flight of Cymbeline's Britons, 'all flying | Through a strait Lane', is reported.[69] But the battle had another source, which scholars have long recognized but been unable to make much of. Shakespeare turned from Holinshed's *Historie of England* to his *Historie of Scotland*, and drew on a passage which relates how a farming ancestor of Sir James Hay, one of King James's Scottish favourites, called his sons from their work into 'a long lane fensed ... with ditches and walles made of turfe' where they reversed the fortunes of King Kenneth in a battle against the Danes.[70] The likely occasion for this borrowing was the admission of Sir James as a Knight of the Bath at the 1610 investiture of the Prince of Wales—the probable context, as I have said, for the first performance of *Cymbeline*. But the effect for informed audiences was to make Guiderius and Arviragus (like Prince Henry) Scottish Welsh princes; and the larger pattern once again is of a work about Anglo-Welsh Britain turning Scottish at a decisive moment. Interestingly, the play was revived at Whitehall (and 'Well likt by the kinge') in 1634,[71] on Charles I's return from his Scottish coronation.

In a Jacobean performance, these features would have gratified or consoled those who believed that Anglo-Welsh union remained a precedent for Anglo-Scottish union on the grounds that without Scottish heroism Britain could not defend itself. That raises the question, however, of why *Cymbeline* should diverge from its sources and share the consensus of the other plays in reconciling Britain to Rome. It was not, I believe, because these authors were concerned (as Shakespeare possibly was) to compliment a king whose ambitions for European peace made him irenic towards Spain[72] and even accommodating with the pope,[73] nor just because *translatio imperii* made it possible to interpret submission as the price of an imperial destiny (V.v. TLN 3798–808), but because no rational interest in British politics could now stop at Milford. Recent as well as ancient history showed that the state established in 1603 would only be secure if its relations with the continental empires (active in Scotland and Ireland) were stabilized.

4

William Drummond
and the British Problem

When James VI left Scotland to assume the English throne in 1603, he promised to return to his native land every three years. In the event, it was not until 1617 that time, inclination, and money (most of it borrowed) made a visit possible. For the Scots this was an important event. The honour of the country required a display of hospitality that would persuade the often patronizing English in the entourage that Scotland offered more than 'fowle linen, fowle dishes and potts'.[1] It is also evident, however, that honour required an assertion of national self-esteem which did not comfortably fit the policy of British unity that the king had promoted in England. James was hardly across the border before he was reminded in a Latin oration that the Scots had never been conquered, by the Britons, Saxons, Picts, Danes, Normans, or Romans. In Edinburgh, he was praised for appointing responsible officers to act in his absence. But at Paisley he was welcomed to the home parish of the patriot William Wallace, 'that worthie warrier, to whome, under God, wee owe that you ar ours, and Britanne yours', and treated to an Ovidian fable which cast him as a sun god who had abandoned his first love, Clytia or Scotland, in favour of Leucothoe, England. Though the orator conceded that this triangle could be resolved by the two ladies becoming wholly one, he ended his speech with an image of the rejected Clytia gazing after Phoebus' chariot until she turned into a heliotrope.[2]

The finest literary work produced for this visit, William Drummond's long poem *Forth Feasting*, is less aggressively ambivalent about the union. Even so, as soon as the king began to read the copy presented to him,[3] he will have noticed problems:

> What blustring Noise now interrupts my Sleepe?
> What echoing Shouts thus cleaue my chrystal Deep?
> And call mee hence from out my watrie Court?
> What Melodie, what Sounds of Ioy and Sport,
> Bee these heere hurl'd from eu'rie neighbour Spring?[4]

Ideologically the River Forth is perfectly attuned to the visit. She has a court not a parliament, and raises no puritanical objections to the pleasures of sport. After fourteen years of neglect, however, she finds it hard to recognize the king's 'glittring' train (line 9). Once she realizes that a progress is afoot, the Forth summons the rivers of Scotland. But regret at James's absence looms larger than the occasion requires. While he was away, we are told, the fields were cursed with frost and the kingdom became as dull as a portrait stripped of colours. To point the contrast, Drummond recalls the years before 1603 when James ruled only in Scotland. Praising his abilities as huntsman, philosopher-king, and poet, he mounts a celebration of the Scottish Renaissance of the 1580s and 1590s that qualifies the panegyric which follows on James's pacification of Britain as a whole.

When Ben Jonson paid his celebrated visit to Drummond at Hawthorn-den, his country house just south of Edinburgh, a few months after James's progress, he said 'that he wished to please the King, that piece of Forth-Feasting had been his owne'.[5] Like other remarks in the 'Conversations with Drummond', this is potentially misleading. We know from the draft of a letter preserved in the Hawthornden Manuscripts that the poem did not entirely 'please the King'. Objecting to the Forth's declaration, 'No Guard so sure as Loue vnto a Crowne' (line 246) James 'argued that it is better to gouerne a people by feare than by loue'. This has been interpreted as a passing disagreement about a maxim,[6] but the king surely recognized that in context Drummond's line stirred the thought that a monarch hardly known to his people could not easily be loved and was the less secure. When *Forth Feasting* heightens the value of the king by emphasizing Scotland's grief at his absence, it makes that absence seem unfortunate; and the more it compensates by extrapolating James's success as a Scottish king into his achievements after 1603, the more his northern kingdom seems to be lost in a British polity.

In his *Schort Treatise, Conteining Some Reulis and Cautelis to be Obseruit and Eschewit in Scottis Poesie* (1584), James had advised the poets of his

---

Ruelis and Cautelis: rules and cautions   *eschewit*: eschewed, avoided

circle to 'be warre with composing ony thing in the same maner as hes bene ower oft vsit of before'.[7] In this respect at least, *Forth Feasting* should have pleased him, because it diverges so sharply from the conventions of welcome-poetry.[8] It was traditional to give some account of the sufferings of the welcomer during the absence of the arrivee. Drummond so emphasizes the cost of union, however, that his panegyric edges into elegy.[9] As innovative are the turns that come when the Forth urges James to remain in Scotland. At first, the attractions of the country are partly attributed to the king, whose presence is said to make the woods and silver brooks more alluring. But the verse then shifts uneasily between the suggestion that, secure in its liberty behind high mountains, the country does not need the king to protect it, and the hope that, because it is so full of attractions (especially animals for hunting), it can entice him to stay.

In a self-consciously climactic passage, Drummond describes what sea-going Scots and the poet himself can provide by way of enticement:

> The *Tritons*, Heards-men of the glassie Field,
> Shall giue Thee what farre-distant Shores can yeeld,
> The *Serean* Fleeces, *Erythrean* Gemmes,
> Vaste *Platas* Siluer, Gold of *Peru* Streames,
> Antarticke Parrots, *Aethiopian* Plumes,
> *Sabaean* Odours, Myrrhe, and sweet Perfumes:
> And I my selfe, wrapt in a watchet Gowne,
> Of Reedes and Lillies on mine Head a Crowne,
> Shall Incense to Thee burne, greene Altars raise,
> And yearly sing due *Paeans* to Thy Praise.   (lines 373–82)

Those unlikely sounding 'Antarticke Parrots' are ornithologically correct because the adjective (as in Latin *antarcticus*) can mean 'southern' as well as 'south polar',[10] but the choiceness of the epithet adds to an impression of misplaced indulgence. The king who warned against the use of trisyllables at the start of verse lines[11] could only be discomfited to find 'Antarticke Parrots' followed by '*Sabaean* Odours'. Not just the Forth but the poet runs to excess in his desire to get James to stay; the verse escalates from persuasion to the promise of lavish bribes.

It is a measure of Drummond's sophistication that he should build into the passage an ebbing sense of conviction. The accumulating polysyllables ring emptily with an awareness that Scotland can offer no gifts that will work, and the imagined revival in Scottish poetry is circumscribed by

The
High and mighty
Prince. IAMES
KING of great
Britane Fraunce
and Ireland . &c

Fig. 5. The Scottish monarch in London. From the Edinburgh University Library
copy of William Drummond, *Forth Feasting* (Edinburgh, 1617).

isolation. The poem finally abandons the conventions of *prosphonetikon*
when it moves from arguing against departure to accepting its inevitability.
For early readers whose copy of *Forth Feasting* included the equestrian
frontispiece (Fig. 5), in which James rears up against the background of
London's churches, theatres, commercial districts, and heavy river traffic,

this outcome was implicit from the start. The Thames has more wealth to offer the king than the Forth, and all the poet can plead is that James should

> Loathe not to thinke on Thy much-louing FORTH:
> O loue these Bounds, whereof Thy royall Stemme
> More then an hundreth wore a Diademe.   (lines 398–400)

It is indeed a strange welcome. When the Forth roused the rivers of Scotland, she included the '*Tweed* which no more our Kingdomes shall deuide' (line 60). Now the bounds are reinstated, and the Forth fears that the king will be reluctant even to remember her, despite a line of Scottish ancestors running back (in the traditional genealogy) to Fergus I.

These tensions are typical of Drummond, whose work was conditioned by the relative isolation of Scotland within a culturally conflicted regal union. At first, those circumstances attracted him to *otium* and *contemptus mundi*, and his work showed the often felicitous self-involvement of an art practised in solitude. During the 1630s and 1640s, however, as his country was swept into the political and military crises that afflicted all three Stuart kingdoms,[12] he became more engaged and polemical, galvanized by what historians call the British problem (above, pp. 21–3). It is true that his verse has recently found prestigious admirers capable of looking beyond the timeless, lyrical poet constructed by Palgrave's *Golden Treasury*,[13] but his oeuvre remains neglected on the one hand because its British traits can make it appear too 'English' to satisfy nationalistic depictions of Scottish literature[14] and on the other because our still Anglocentric maps of cultural history can make it seem peripheral and anachronistic. His early poetry has been misconstrued as a hangover from Elizabethan Petrarchism, and his later, often pungent verse satires and prose tracts remain obscure to readers who lack the necessary grounding in Scottish and more largely three-kingdoms history. It is the contention of this chapter that, once his British contexts are understood, Drummond emerges as a more complex and pressured figure than has been realized, and a grossly undervalued writer.

★   ★   ★

When James went south with his court, he did not leave a kingdom devoid of institutions and cultural activity. Scotland kept its own legal system, reformed church, and universities as well as its own parliament and privy council. The nobility sustained a network of country houses, and exercised considerable patronage.[15] In any case, Drummond's estrangement from the royal milieu was qualified. His uncle, the poet William Fowler, secretary to Queen Anne, went to London, with other Scots, in 1603, and Drummond apparently stayed with him three years later, when he witnessed the celebrations that surrounded the visit by the King of Denmark already mentioned in relation to *Macbeth* (above p. 101). His first published poem, an elegy on the death of Prince Henry, appeared or was reprinted in the pan-British and Irish collection *Mausoleum* (1613). He may not have been employed at court, but he corresponded with and entertained such Scottish writers as Sir Robert Kerr of Ancram, who enjoyed a post in King James's Bedchamber, and Sir William Alexander of Menstrie, who rose through the households of Prince Henry and Charles I, and who helped Drummond network with English poets. The lists of 'Bookes red be me' that survive among his papers, and the contents of his extensive library, show that his literary world was at least as full as that of any courtier;[16] and a patent from 1627, which allowed him to develop ingenious weapons of war, not to mention a machine for creating perpetual motion,[17] indicates that, like royalist gentlemen elsewhere in Britain, he was curious about science, and wanted to be a virtuoso.

This is not to say that his culture was homogenized to a new British ideal. Jonson told him that his verses 'were not after the Fancie of ye tyme'[18] because his literary tastes (including his passion for the sonnet) appeared out-of-date to a Jacobean Londoner; but Drummond's grounding in the Scottish Renaissance[19] led him to look to continental Europe for models—advancing beyond Ronsard and Du Bartas to the fashionable Guarini and Marino.[20] In this as in other respects, the polyglot, often highly imitative Drummond[21] can be seen as the beneficiary of the internationalism of earlier Scottish poetry.[22] When he writes,

> Slide soft faire FORTH, and make a christall Plaine,
> Cut your white Lockes, and on your foamie Face
> Let not a Wrinckle bee, when you embrace
> The Boat that *Earths Perfections* doth containe. ... [23]

readers are meant to remember Sidney's Stella on the Thames, and Tasso's mistress on the River Po, placing the Forth among the centres of European literature.

So the localism of Drummond, who was described by his contemporaries as a swan singing on the banks of the Esk, a Grampian shepherd,[24] was by no means naively provincial. Like his correspondent Drayton he relished writing about places unexplored in verse, and he composed commendatory poems and epitaphs for Scots unknown beyond their country.[25] But when he announces in a sonnet, 'Thrise happie hee, who by some shadie Groue, | Farre from the clamarous World doth liue his owne' and says that rustic birdsong is sweeter than 'smoothe Whisp'rings neare a Princes Throne', the lines are loosely translated from the latest Italian poetry,[26] they have classical roots in Horace, and they are sustained by familiarity with the courtly life they reject. They are engaged in a dialogue that becomes explicit when Kerr of Ancram sends Drummond his own '*Sonnet in praise of a Solitary Life*' written from that storm centre of the politics of regal union, '*the very Bed-chamber* [of King James], *where I could not Sleep*'.[27]

It is clear, however, that Drummond's highly sophisticated acceptance of obscurity[28] was mixed with real frustration at life in a country that was distant from the heartlands of European humanism (Paris to Venice, Florence, and Rome) and so small that it encouraged envy among its inhabitants at those who achieved excellence. With the neglect of the Scottish humanist, George Buchanan, in mind, he writes 'Alas! ... What can we perform in this remote part of the earth ... Many noble pieces of our countrymen are drowned in oblivion *per* σκοτιαν *Scotorum*.'[29] In some of his strongest poems, the possibility of retirement as a rewarding alternative to court fails to alleviate isolation. The poet is not a wild bird warbling in the forest[30] but a voice crying in the wilderness—as in his sonnet on St John the Baptist:

> The last and greatest Herauld of Heauens King,
> Girt with rough Skinnes, hyes to the Desarts wilde,
> Among that sauage brood the Woods foorth bring,
> Which hee than Man more harmlesse found and milde:
> His food was Blossomes, and what yong doth spring,
> With Honey that from virgine Hiues distil'd;
> Parcht Bodie, hollow Eyes, some vncouth thing
> Made him appeare, long since from Earth exilde.
> There burst hee foorth; All yee whose Hopes relye
> On GOD, with mee amidst these Desarts mourne,
> Repent, repent, and from olde errours turne.
> Who listned to his voyce, obey'd his crye?

> Onelie the Ecchoes which hee made relent,
> Rung from their Marble Caues, repent, repent.[31]

In this finely wrought poem, almost Miltonic in the intensity it contrives from syntactical foldings and suspensions, flight from society brings suffering, and the saint gets no response to his virtuous message, except that wrung (the pun is expressive) from stones, from the marble of caves that mockingly empty the keyword of the sonnet into echoes.

The relationship between these feelings of provincial isolation and national sentiment in a British context can be tracked through Drummond's dealings with English poets. Alert to their interest in their own country, he was sensitive to possible slights to his own. His very first note on Jonson's table-talk, for instance, says 'that he had ane intention to perfect ane Epick Poeme intitled Heroologia of the Worthies of his [or this] Country, rowsed by fame, and was to dedicate it to his Country'—which by its 'his/this' variant alone educes the British problem[32]—and he recorded his dislike of the way his visitor 'thinketh nothing well bot what either he himself, or some of his friends and Countrymen hath said or done'.[33] His approval of *Poly-Olbion* was heightened by Drayton's plan to extend its range beyond England and Wales, and when Drayton died he asked Alexander to acquire 'those fragmentes... of his Worke which concerne Scotland' so as to 'endevour to put them in this country to the presse... with the best remembrances his love to this countrey did deserve'.[34] But even Drayton could stir resentment: 'I find in him, which is in most part of my Compatriots, too great an Admiration of their Country; on the History of which, whilst they muse, as wondering, they forget sometimes to be good Poets.'[35] In other words, Drayton's chauvinism led him to forget his Aristotle and to weaken poetry by elevating history. But 'my Compatriots' is at odds with 'their Country'. Was Drayton a fellow-Briton or an alien Englishman?

For English writers the trappings of a British identity could be acquired by, for instance, claiming Scottish ancestry, as Jonson did shortly after 1603, and by walking to Scotland to gather materials for a poem about the country and a piscatory or pastoral play set in Loch Lomond—schemes which Jonson was careful to outline to King James on his return to London.[36] The situation was rather different for Scottish poets at Whitehall: not just Kerr of Ancram and Sir William Alexander but Sir Robert Ayton, who succeeded Fowler as private secretary to the queen, Sir David Murray, and others. They were entering a country large and powerful enough to dictate the terms of union, at a time when English national sentiment (already practised in Scotophobia) was stirred by threats from Counter-Reformation Europe. Later history has also been against them, since any refashioning of their Scottishness designed to cope with the new situation has been interpreted as a culpable dilution of identity at a moment when Scotland (with hindsight) began to relinquish its independence.

Scottish nationalists might think it the more deplorable that the court poets who went south anticipated the long-term loss that Scotland would suffer. Writing in that mood in 1603, Ayton asked the Tweed to carry James's 'last farewell' to his native kingdom 'To that Religious place whose stately walls | Does keepe the heart which all our hearts inthralls'—that is, to Melrose Abbey, where the heart of Robert Bruce was buried.[37] Yet it is possible to read this elegiac sonnet as signalling, in its obscure-to-outsiders allusion, Ayton's attachment to an identity that he would preserve. For the careers of the court poets do fit the general picture that Keith M. Brown has established for the early seventeenth-century Scottish nobility. Although they sometimes married English wives, and became involved in the British dimension of Stewart politics, the court-based elite continued to visit Scotland, used their income to buy or improve Scottish estates, and remained Scottish in their cultural assumptions.[38] Kerr of Ancram became a member of the English privy council, but his correspondence 'reveals a sustained interest in his home locality'.[39] Sir William Alexander, the acclaimed author of love sonnets, political closet dramas, and the encyclopaedic *Doomes-day* (1614), was even more successful, acquiring mining rights in Scotland, land in Ulster, and the Governorship of Nova Scotia. Yet he published books in Edinburgh, built a new house in Stirling, and was not just made an Earl by Charles I but became chief of the MacAlexander Clan.

To descend from this big picture to the finer grain of literature is to find clearer signs of hybridity. From a sonnet apparently composed in 1604 or later we know that King James discouraged Alexander from writing 'harshe vearses after the Inglische fasone'. Reminding Alexander that he had been 'bath'd ... in Castalias fountaine cleare', the king objected to him adopting the irregularities of a Sidneian or metaphysical style:

> Although your neighbours haue conspir'd to spill
> That art which did the Laurel crowne obtaine
> And borowing from the raven there ragged quill

> Bewray there harsh hard trotting tumbling wayne
> Such hamring hard the mettalls hard require
> Our songs ar fil'd with smoothly flowing fire[40]

That Alexander responded obediently is clear from a letter that he wrote to Drummond in 1616 to keep him in touch with poetic debate. At Newmarket, he explains, while bad weather delayed hunting, he and the king discussed how the same syllables could function in one place as long and in another as short—a doctrine in happy conformity with what James had said in his *Reulis and Cautelis* (215–16). It is probably significant that the poem Alexander wrote on this occasion, 'When *Britain's* Monarch, in true Greatness great', follows the recommendation of the *Reulis* in using the sonnet form for panegryic (223). Flattering the king's mastery of smooth, Castalian numbers,[41] it implies that this accomplishment contributes to his excellence as a monarch of the union.[42]

The survival of a Castalian bias in elite conceptions of British poetry might seem thinly 'Scottish' beside the vigorous Scots of such Jacobean-period Lowland ballads as 'The Laird of Logie' and 'The Lads of Wamphray' (not to mention the vitality of Gaelic poetry as it evolved beyond bardic conventions). But that raises the question of why Drummond and his contemporaries anglicized their verse. The manuscripts show Ayton writing Scots in the 1580s, being associated with 'a peculiar Scoto-English orthography' after 1603, and subsequently being circulated in 'polished and anglicised' texts.[43] King James, even before the union, arranged for his works to be anglicized. And the presence of more Scots in Drummond's manuscript drafts than in his printed texts[44] again points to a desire to project a public voice closer to southern English than was idiomatic for the writer.

What the poets said about this situation could be insecure. Introducing his first tragedy, *Darius*, in the Edinburgh edition of 1603, Alexander wrote:

> The language of this Poeme is (as thou seest) mixt of the English and Scottish Dialects; which perhaps may be un-pleasant and irksome to some readers of both nations. But I hope the gentle and Judicious Englishe reader will beare with me, if I retaine some badge of mine owne countrie, by using sometimes words that are peculiar thereunto, especiallie when I finde them propre, and significant. As for my owne country-men, they may not justly finde fault with me, if for the more parte I vse the English phrase, as worthie to be preferred before our owne for the elegance and perfection thereof. Yea I am perswaded that both countrie-men will take in good part the mixture of their Dialects, the rather for that the bountiful providence of God doth

invite them both to a straiter union and conjunction as well in language, as
in other respects.[45]

In its edgy and uneven way—insinuating to the English and a touch defiant
on the home front—this proposes a merger of tongues as the concomitant
of union. It advances an ideal of synthesis, comforting to the Scots, though
not invariably advocated by Scoto-British unionists,[46] that ran on at least
until Alexander Hume's treatise *Of the Orthographie and Congruitie of the
Britan Tonge* (c.1619). Yet the unpatriotic assertion that southern English is
superior in elegance and perfection makes Alexander's further reduction of
Scots in the 1604 (London) and later editions of *Darius*, as well as in other
plays and poems,[47] seem less a compromise than a retreat.

If Alexander's appeal to the union was to some extent an opportunistic
rationalization, however, it does not follow that his anglicizing was the
product of cultural cringe. His primary motive was almost certainly the
pragmatic one of not alienating his potentially large English readership,
and he will have been encouraged in his policy by the drift to anglicization which began in Scottish printing long before 1603.[48] This process
has a pre-history, but it is usually related to the mid-sixteenth-century
introduction into Scotland of the Geneva Bible and other Protestant
texts in English. So, if there was an element of British identity formation in Alexander's practice, its roots should be sought in the hopes of
Kirk reformers that they would be strengthened by an alliance with the
Godly in the south.[49] What we call anglicization was easier to accept
because writers could see themselves as shifting not between languages
but between what Alexander calls 'Dialects'. Drummond and his contemporaries knew that their speech was close to that spoken in northern
England, and they regarded themselves as speaking the same 'Inglis' as their
fellow-Britons.[50]

In any case, the Scottish elite was competent in several tongues, including
Latin for educational purposes, French at court, Gaelic in some regions,
Scots for dealing with Lowland tenants and for many official documents;
and just as Scotland's architectural idiom was distinctively mixed, so its
linguistic character was defined by the nature of its eclecticism.[51] Southern
English could be added to this repertoire, as the *lingua franca* of the
king's new British state, without it seeming a betrayal. Here it should be
remembered that, although some of the texts circulating in Scots during
Drummond's lifetime—such as Blind Harry's *Wallace*—were nationalistic,

it was not until the early eighteenth century that publication in Scots *per se* took on a patriotic colouring, and not until much later, and then but patchily, that Scots became privileged, with Gaelic, as an authenticator of national identity.[52] In the early modern period, pride in Scottish culture was if anything more naturally displayed in Latin, because that language could raise the country's profile throughout educated Europe. That is one reason why so many of the poems and speeches welcoming James in 1617 are in Latin, and were published in John Adamson's erudite Τα των μουσων εισοδια, *The Muses Welcome* (1618), and why the anthology *Delitiae poetarum Scotorum* (1637), partly assembled by Drummond's friend Scot of Scotstarvit, is such a landmark.

In short, while the Scottish court poets employed some British motifs, there is little more evidence among them of regal union encouraging cultural synthesis than there is among their English contemporaries. Like the more distantly removed Drummond, they could be associated with Whitehall without compromising their Scottishness—at least until the late 1630s, when political breakdown led them (and especially Alexander) to be viewed as anglicized drones. When the travel-writer William Lithgow wrote about King James's 1617 visit, in a poem about his own departure from Scotland, he declared:

> Amongst these long Goodnightes, farewell yee *Poets* deare,
> Graue *Menstrie* true *Castalian* fire, quicke *Drummond* in his spheare.
> Braue *Murray* ah is dead, *Aiton* supplies his place,
> And *Alens* high *Pernassian* veine, rare Poems doth embrace.[53]

No discrimination is made between Scottish poets north and south of the border. All belong to Scotland; and if Lithgow partly wrote (as seems likely) in the hope of attracting their patronage, that makes the more significant the cultural map he expected these poets to favour.

★　★　★

The problems of regal union galvanized socio-economic discontent in Scotland. A sense that the country was 'maymed' without its monarch[54] grew, if anything, after 1617; it found a focus in the rise of Buckingham (subject of at least one scornful epigram by Drummond),[55] and it was exacerbated, after the death of James, by the failure of his successor not only to be crowned initially in Scotland, the country of his birth, but to avoid coming north for eight years after his accession. When Charles did finally travel to Edinburgh for a coronation, in 1633, his arrival was even more extravagantly celebrated than the progress of 1617. But the visit also prompted petitioning about grievances real and anticipated, and it was handled so badly by the court that it escalated the distrust of England and its episcopacy that would light the touchpaper of war when the Scottish Presbyterians signed their national Covenant in 1638.

The commonplace William Lithgow is once again helpful. We should be careful not to read the crises of 1638–42 straight back into earlier events, but when he says, in *Scotlands Welcome to her Natiue Sonne*, that Charles has not come 'with sterne bloody collours flying', like a Turkish prince seeking to subdue, one wonders why the idea should have been raised only to be denied. And when Lithgow points out that the Scots have great military strength, not least in Ireland, why does his obedience sound minatory? 'Then slight mee not (Dread Sir) since I, and Myne, | Still vow, to serue *Thee*'.[56] By the end of the decade, Charles would indeed come like a Turkish prince, to fight (and lose) two Bishops' Wars, and the Scots would develop their presence in Ireland, arming the Ulster Presbyterians and, in due course, reinforcing them in a multi-angled conflict that required them to take on the Irish Catholics who sometimes fought in support of the king.[57]

Meanwhile, Lithgow grumbles, the Scottish nobility and gentry go to London to squander money exacted from their tenants that should support merchants at home. The courts and privy council are being undermined because people take their complaints to Whitehall. Berwick, as a frontier town, is full of 'Slaughter, Adultry, Incest'.[58] Youngsters are slipping to England to marry without parental consent. The English are buying up Scottish cattle, sheep, and horses. Scotsmen are being infected with southern effeminacy and smoking tobacco. Folk sit in alehouses, telling disaffected stories about Robin Hood and Wallace. They are slow to pay their bills, and because of a shortage of Scottish copper coin little is given to charity. Overall, the country is decaying. Fortifications and ports are neglected. Bridges are not being built. And Sunday is not properly observed. Many of these complaints can be paralleled in English satire, but they do not cluster there around the disadvantages of union. The problems of multiple monarchy provided a magnet for feelings that, south of the border, took on a different inflection.

If the magnificent pageant that Drummond wrote to welcome the king to Edinburgh— *The Entertainment of the High and Mighty Monarch Charles*—is read with Lithgow in mind, it looks even less likely to 'please' than the 1617 *Forth Feasting*. As he rode into the city, Charles met actors playing the parts of Religion and Superstition, Justice and Oppression, Caledonia and Nova Scotia—innocuous sounding pairs, but, as we shall see, provocative. After hearing a speech from his never-conquered Caledonia, Charles then advanced to an arch decorated with the devices of war and peace and the iconography of Great Britain. This might have been the climax of the day. As the king approached, however, a theatre disclosed Mercury 'with an hundred and seven Scottish Kings, which hee had brought from the Elisian fields' and '*Fergus* the first had a speech in Latine'.[59] We know that, of the huge amount of money spent, a large proportion was lavished on these pictures of the Scottish kings. A manuscript quoted in David M. Bergeron's *English Civic Pageantry* suggests that the king's inspection of the portraits, and Fergus's now-lost speech, were time-consuming affairs,[60] though, because they hardly figure in the printed text,[61] Bergeron fails to make the obvious deduction. Together, they made up the core of a pageant that was 'civic' but by no means 'English'—which is why the king was next shown a display of the 'ancient Worthies of Scotland', before being introduced by Endymion to the seven planets, each of which made a speech about the future of the northern kingdom. The Dunfermline-born but English-bred king was being given a crash course in Scottishness.

Awkward issues were raised by each of Drummond's initial tableaux. Religion had created difficulties in 1617, when King James had insisted on the public use of church ornaments and organs and had pressed the General Assembly of the Kirk to accept a number of what might be called Anglican measures.[62] Worse was expected in 1633, because of Charles's known determination to push Laudian policies through the Scottish parliament, and because the coronation service (with its surplices, altar, and crucifix)[63] was a planned affront to Presbyterian sensibilities. Drummond was no Kirk radical, but he shared the wariness of many Episcopalians[64] towards the authority of Canterbury, and was proud of the primitive independence of the Scottish church from Rome.[65] In the *Entertainment* he signalled his preference for simplicity over Laudian-papistical antiquated ceremony by presenting Religion as a maiden in white taffeta trampling Superstition, 'a woman blind, in old and worne garments' (114–15). Later, Caledonia warns the king that '*Faith* (milke-white *Faith*) of old belov'd so well, | Yet in this corner of the World doth dwell | With her pure Sisters, *Truth, Simplicitie*' (119).

When it comes to Justice and Oppression, the *Entertainment* boldly addresses abuses of royal power. More firmly than the London lawyers who a few months earlier had funded Shirley's *Triumph of Peace*, Drummond points out that a good prince 'first subjects himselfe to his owne law' (120). Charles, according to Jove, will relieve '*Iustice* kept low by grants, and wrongs', avoid promoting favourites like Buckingham, and find ways of funding good causes:

> Thou shalt no Paranymph raise to high place,
> For frizl'd locks, quaint pace, or painted face;
> On gorgeous rayments, womanising toyes,
> The workes of wormes, and what a Moth destroyes,
> The Maze of fooles, thou shalt no treasure spend,
> Thy charge to immortality shall tend,
> Raise *Pallaces*, and *Temples* vaulted high,
> Rivers ore arch, of hospitality,
> Of Sciences the ruin'd Innes restore,
> With walls and ports incircle *Neptunes* shore ...   (129–30)

This is strikingly close to Lithgow's round-up of grievances, regarding English effeminacy and the lack of proper expenditure on bridges, ports, fortifications, and colleges. In the *Entertainment*, as in *Forth Feasting*, Drummond says that a king should be loved rather than feared. As Jove ringingly puts it: 'Thou fear'd of none, shalt not thy people feare, | Thy peoples love thy greatnesse shall up-reare' (130). But how could subjects love a king who sought to fund colleges and hospitals by a contentious Revocation[66] and to build 'walls and ports' along the Firth of Forth by imposing new duties on coal and salt?[67] The tax burden, already high in Edinburgh, was doubled during the king's visit, and abrasive methods of collection were applied.[68] When Jove speaks of this, prediction modulates into injunction: 'New and vast taxes thou shalt not extort, | Load heavy those thy bounty should support' (130).

The other topic announced in Drummond's opening tableaux, that of empire, was even more delicate. In one sense the appearance of a woman clad in 'divers coloured feathers, which shew her to bee an *American*, and to represent new *Scotland*' is not surprising. New World iconography was familiar enough in pageants and masques;[69] and Lithgow emphasized Scotland's pride in the possession of Nova Scotia near the end of *Scotlands Welcome* (G2v). Drummond, as a friend of Alexander, the Governor, had particular reason to celebrate a colony that he had already, in *Forth Feasting*, praised as a Scottish achievement (lines 319–34), and to do so in terms reminiscent of those used to describe that wet and in the winter all too bleak part of Canada—'Lands which passe *Arabian* fields | In fragrant Wood and Muske' (*Entertainment*, 130)—in Alexander's *Encouragement to Colonies* (1624) and *The Mapp and Description of New-England* (1630).[70]

Nova Scotia was peopled by English Dissenters as well as Highlanders and Lowland Scots: it had a British aspect. But the colony was primarily Scottish, bound up with patriotic emotion, and its prominence in the *Entertainment* confirms what David Armitage has argued, that the growth of the British Empire needs to be understood in relation to interaction between the three kingdoms, because it was fragmented, during the seventeenth century, by the ambitions of the Scots and English within a political structure that did not always serve them equally.[71] And if Nova Scotia was topical in 1629, when Drummond first wrote his *Entertainment*, in expectation of the king's long-awaited arrival,[72] by 1633 it was politically explosive, because the colony had been ceded to France in 1631 in order to release Henrietta Maria's dowry to her husband.[73] It was by no means the last time that the interests of an absentee king would damage Scottish enterprise overseas, but it was a peculiarly stark example of the drawbacks of regal union, and however Drummond might have claimed to be taking his cue from the king's specious insistence that he had not finally sacrificed Scotland's claims to its American namesake, an Edinburgh audience could only have reacted sardonically to the idea that Charles

> rising high
> To grace this throne makes *Scotlands* name to flie
> On *Halcyons* wings (her glory which restores)
> Beyond the Ocean to *Columbus* shores, ...   (120)

Charles had been warned, but he did little to charm the Scots, who found him stiff and aloof, in the manner of the English elite, and pettily resentful towards those who opposed him.[74] He forced his Laudian reforms and his tax increases through a reluctant parliament, and estranged much of the Scottish nobility. As a result, support was patchy when, in the following year, 1634, he sought to prosecute the Presbyterian Lord Balmerino for possessing a document that challenged his policy on the Kirk. At this point turning to prose, Drummond sent an *Apologetical Letter* about the case to Kerr of Ancram, with the intention of reaching if not the king then at least those closest to him. Noting that poverty makes people rebellious, he accused the king's officers of not so much fleecing as skinning the Scots, and concluded: 'it were not evil for a Prince to read *Jan Marianai* [Juan de Mariana] and *George Buchanans* piece *de jure Regni apud Scotos*, for his own private and the publick good'.[75] Given Buchanan's notorious preference for limiting royal power, this is startling advice to have from a writer who has often been regarded—since the 1711 edition of his *Works* (which omitted this *Letter*)—as 'a great Cavalier, and much addicted to the King's Party'.[76]

Poetry hampered the efforts of Alexander, now Earl of Stirling and Secretary of State for Scotland, to defuse the mistrust created by the Balmerino affair. As early as 1620, he had corresponded with Drummond about King James's translation of the Psalms, and the impossibility of correcting the royal efforts with propriety.[77] On James's death, Alexander was encouraged by Charles to revise and consolidate the translation,[78] and granted the privilege of printing it. The first, 1631 edition, appeared at a time when Alexander was trying to make good his fortunes after the collapse of the Nova Scotia colony. But Charles's efforts to have the familiar, sixteenth-century version of the psalms replaced in his three kingdoms met with a mixed reaction, and in Scotland with concerted hostility. Only too aware that Alexander shared the king's desire to advance Laudianism, the General Assembly of the Kirk resisted his psalms on doctrinal but also poetic grounds. They objected to the 'heathenish libertie and poeticall conceats in this new metaphrase', and said that its 'French, Latine, and hard Englisch tearmes' baffled the common people.[79]

The king was not greatly moved. He forbad further publication in Scotland of the old version of the psalms; then a second edition of 'Menstrie's psalms' was published, and bound together with a new Scottish prayerbook. This was the infamous volume (above, pp. 77–8) that started the slide into war, when, on 23 July 1637, its use triggered a riot in St Giles's Cathedral, Edinburgh. That Alexander was busy at the time preparing his *Recreations with the Muses* (1637) for publication gave ammunition to those who complained that his poetical ambitions were distracting him from affairs of state, and adding to the troubles of the union. Plainly out of touch, he was excluded from the negotiations which Charles undertook to stem the tide of Presbyterian feeling, and he died with his standing almost as low at Westminster as it was in Scotland, where Drummond only mourned him in draft[80] and others were scathing about his misuse of his literary talents (despoiling the psalter), his farming and milling of revenues, and his monopoly of copper coin:

> Hier layes a fermer and a millar,
> A poet and a psalme book spillar,
> A purchessour by hooke and crooke,
> A forger of the service booke,
> A coppersmithe quho did much evill,
> A friend to bischopes and ye devill,
> A waine ambitious flattering thing,
> Late secretary for a kinge;
> Soum tragedies in verse he pen'd,
> At last he made a tragicke end.[81]

★ ★ ★

This anonymous mock-epitaph is a reminder that topical satire and verse abuse (flyting) had sturdy roots in Scotland. Its social, vigorous manner seems far removed from the Drummond who figures in literary history as a 'fastidious', 'somewhat prim' straight-man to the exuberant Jonson of the 'Conversations'.[82] Yet the Hawthornden Manuscripts are not short of rough jokes and bawdy satires, composed as well as gathered by Drummond—like the one about the equestrian girl who, when she got to puberty, thought she was growing horsehair between her thighs.[83] He wrote prefatory verse for an edition of *The Flyting betwixt Montgomery and Polwart*,[84] and was by repute the author of a poem in Scots and pidgin Latin about a scatological battle between the folk of Scotstarvit and Newbarns.[85] Sharp, ribald poetry was provoked in him by political upheavals; his verse became harsher, and closer to popular genres—as in 'A Prouerbe', his response to the prayerbook riots:

> God neuer had a Church but there, Men say,
> The Diuell a chapell hath raised by some wyles.
> I doubted of this saw, till on a day
> I Westward spied great Edinbroughs Saint Gyles.[86]

It is typical that this attack on the Presbyterians should leave scope for disapproval of the bishops for bringing disorder into the Kirk.[87] Though Drummond never sided with the radical reformers,[88] he could be animated, as a poet, by their anger. An early example would seem to be 'Drummonds

Lines One the Bischopes: 14 Appryll 1638', which assumes with Swiftian savagery an anti-Episcopalian voice:

> Naye, pray you Heauens, once lend me bot your thunder,
> Ile crusch and teare thesse sordid slaues assunder,
> And leuell with the dust ther Altars horne,
> With the lascivious organs, pieties scorne;
> Or lett me be as king, then of their skine
> Ile causse dresse lether and fyne Marikin,
> To couer coatches (quher they wount to ryde)
> And valk in bootes and shoes made of ther hyde,
> Vhipe them at neighbour princes courts to show,
> That No Nouations Scotts zeall can allow.[89]

The speaker says that the bishops' pride makes 'poore Brittane smart, | Confound the church, the stait, and all the nation' (lines 46–7). This slyly suggests that the Presbyterians who opposed the pan-British ambitions of the Laudians had enlarged plans of their own; and it is true that, even though their first step was to sign a national Covenant in Scotland, they exported Scots-language and anglicized pamphlets to bring round English puritans.[90] They recognized that if the Kirk was to be safe, a British settlement would be needed.[91]

Elaborating on this in *Irene*, a manuscript treatise far-sighted enough to be a candidate for printing seven years later, Drummond argued that 'If thus, the Protestants of this Isle of Great-*Britain*, who are now united in Religion, and All of one Mind with their King, shall inconsiderately, without his Consent, make a League, they cannot but divide.' Some will go with Charles, others with the Covenanters, and this division, he points out, will simply advantage Rome, and make Britain 'a Bait for Strangers to feed upon'. Having discouraged the Covenanters, he finishes with a section in which Scotia apologizes to the King for the disloyalty of her people but also advises him to 'vanquish and subdue them by Mercy. The impregnable fortress of a Prince', Scotia reflects—in the vein of *Forth Feasting* and the *Entertainment*—'is the Love of his Subjects, which doth only arise from the Height of his Clemency'. Reassuring, or warning, Charles that 'It was not Religion alone which did occasion these Troubles', Drummond repeats the socio-economic complaints of 1633–4, that the Scots were clipped too close, and that poverty was 'the principal Ground of Novations and Alterations'.[92]

Marikin: goatskin leather, as produced in Morocco

It was a time of duress. Scotsmen in London were compelled to disown the Covenant, and Wentworth rigorously enforced the same test on the Scots in Ireland. On the other side, Montrose (not yet a royalist hero) forced the reluctant academics of Aberdeen University to sign it. Drummond, under pressure to subscribe, gave vent to his frustration in a poem which attacked the king's supporters almost as keenly as his opponents. Greed, ambition, and resentment, in his view, drove the Covenanters, but Charles's supporters in the Kirk were equally self-interested in their loyalty:

> Against the king, sir, now why would yee fight?
> Forsooth because hee made mee not a knight.
> And yee my lordes, why arme yee against Charles?
> Because of lordes hee would not make us Earles.
> Earles, why lead you forth these angrye bandes?
> Because wee will not quite the churches landes.
> Most hollye church-Men, what is your intent?
> The king our stipendes largelie did augment.
> Commones, to tumult thus how are yee driuen?
> Our priestes say fighting is the way to Heauen.
> Are these iust cause of Warre, good Bretheren, grante?
> Him Plunder! hee nere swore our couenant.[93]

The conventions of early Drummond are carried over here into a new, indignant idiom, for the passage brilliantly combines an old Petrarchan scheme of escalation (each couplet picking up a keyword or a topic from that which precedes it) with the epigrammatic energy of strongly rhymed interrogation. The movement of the verse reflects a dangerous social dynamic of closed minds and motives spiralling into crisis.

As for the poet, he was caught between the incompetence of the royalist party and the 'rage and malice' which the Covenanters turn against those who resist them. In a passage which runs on from the lines just quoted in the 1711 *Works* but which stands separately in the Hawthornden Manuscripts, Drummond's anxiety about signing the Covenant issues in conflicted virulence:

> Giue me a thousand couenants, I'll subscriue
> Them all, and more, if more yee can contriue
> Of rage and malice; and let eurye one
> Blake treason beare, not bare Rebellione.
> I'll not be mockt, hist, plunder'd, banisht hence
> For more yeeres standing for a ... prince.

> The castells all are taken, and his crown,
> The sword and sceptre, ensignes of Renown,
> With the lieutenant fame did so extoll,
> And all led captiues to the Capitoll;
> I'll not die Martire for any mortall thing,
> It's enough to be confessour for a king.
> Will this you giue contentment, honest Men?
> I haue written Rebelles, pox vpon the pen![94]

The immediate reference is to the surrender of Dalkeith Palace on 22 March 1639 by the Earl of Traquair, the king's chief minister in Scotland, to a company of a thousand Covenanters led by a group of noblemen, including Balmerino. The rebels—whom the poet must learn to call honest men—carried off Charles's Scottish regalia ('his crown, | The sword and sceptre') to Edinburgh Castle ('the Capitoll'). Whatever bisyllabic adjective is implied by the ellipsis before 'prince', it is clearly not complimentary. With royal power so comprehensively stood down, with the king no longer God's representative on earth, but a mere mortal, and with mockery, scorn, and dispossession being the lot of stiff-necked royalists, what alternative was there, Drummond seems to say, to subscribing—an honest man writing himself a rebel. We know that Drummond was, in practice, pushed into signing the Covenant, probably at about this date. Certainly the verse reads like the script of a man troubled about writing one thing and meaning another.

In the tense period between the prayerbook riots and the First Bishops' War (May-June 1639), Scottish royalists like Drummond were at a disadvantage because militant Covenanters could play the patriotic card and denounce them as slaves of the English. One way of countering this was to discount Scottish-English difference by saying that the points of dispute were more verbal than substantive. Epigrammatic poetry was well adapted to advance this claim because traditionally hospitable to quibbling. Yet the style of superiority associated with such wit could look like frivolous disdain and make enemies on both sides—a risk taken by the following, in which differences between the English church and Scottish Presbyterianism are reduced to a trivial quarrel about whether Greek ch- or k- should begin the collective name of the faithful:

> The scottish kirke the English church doe name,
> The english church the Scotes a kirke doe call;
> Kirke and not church, church and not kirke, O shame!

> Your kappa turne in chi, or perishe all:
> Assemblies meet, post Bishopes to the court;
> If these two Nationes fight, its strangeres sport.[95]

This argument against the nations fighting went particularly well into an epigram because it could stop short at 'sport' (the English and the Scots would become the laughing stocks of Europe), making its impact on the reader without inflating into the claim made in *Irene*—which was implausible at least in the short term—that war would expose the Scots and English to the depredations of Spain and France. It was a point that, nonetheless, Drummond continued to press in prose. With the king preparing to launch the First Bishops' War, he asked in *Queries of State* 'Whether this war may renew the old National Quarrels between *Scotland* and *England*, and divide this Island in it self, to be a Prey to Foreign Conquest?'[96] It is a sign of the contradictory priorities set up within royalism by multiple monarchy that a process feared by him was welcomed by the king: faced with a Covenanting movement too united to be broken from within, Charles came to hope that inherited antagonisms would allow him to use the English against the Scots.

In *A Speech ... to the Noblemen ... who have Leagu'd themselves for the Defence of the Religion and Liberties of Scotland*, dated 2 May 1639, Drummond declared that, if war came, the Scots would lose because the king had enough resources to survive short-term defeats, whereas the Scots only had to lose one battle, as at Pinkie and Flodden, to finish their campaign for good.[97] He could not have been more wrong. Once the Scots set out their forces at Duns Law, Charles—unsure of his strength, and ambivalent about accepting Irish Catholic reinforcements[98]—moved to a negotiated settlement. He cravenly yet temporizingly yielded to the substance of the rebels' demands, and a General Assembly of the Kirk persuaded the Scottish Privy Council to pass an act requiring all Scots to sign the Covenant.

Drummond, who had reluctantly sent men to fight the English, and asked the king in verse to send them back in pieces,[99] satirized this act[100] and the protracted parliament that capitalized on the Scottish victory. Lashing out with another epigram—

> The parlament lordes haue sitten twice fiue weekes,
> Yet will not leaue their stooles, knit vp their breekes;

turne in: turn to   *breekes*: breeches

> Winter is come, dysenteryes preuaile:
> Rise, fooles, and with this paper wype your taile.[101]

—he proposed fifty-nine mock measures for the parliament to pass. That the provost of Edinburgh should pray in St Giles's Cathedral to the sound of pistol shots rather than organs. That Buchanan's *De jure regni* (no longer just a book for a prince) should be bound into copies of the Bible. Poetry would play its part: 'That the Books of *Wallace* and King *Robert* the *Bruce* be printed over again, against our old Enemies of *England*, and Pensions be given to some learned Rhimers, to write XII. Books of our Expedition and Victory at *Dunslaw*, or *DUNSLAIDOS Libri* 12.'[102]

If Drummond found it galling that the Covenanters claimed an epic victory without enduring the heat of battle, the events of 1640 would change that. When the king brought his forces north to fight a second Bishops' War, the Scots marched into England, defeated the royal forces at Newburn and took over Newcastle. In three-kingdom terms it was a significant victory because, as Conrad Russell says, with only some exaggeration, it determined that Scotland would not be anglicized in religion and implied that any Act of Union that came would have to allow for diversity. Given the revived threat to use Irish troops to support the crown, it probably also contributed to a long-term Scottish ambition to protestantize Ireland.[103] Above all, in the immediate crisis, victory meant that when the king, pressurized by the Long Parliament, came north to woo the Scots in 1641, it was on terms highly advantageous to the Covenanters.

Drummond's reaction can be gauged from the *Speech for Edinburgh to the King* that was published in the 1711 *Works* but was most unlikely to have been spoken in 1641 because it absolved the king from so much.[104] Pointing out that religious and political conflicts racked much of Europe, Drummond reassured Charles that there were bound to be tremors in Scotland. Against the background of Covenanter moves to establish 'a perfect amity' between England and Scotland,[105] he also struck a chord that became familiar in Scottish royalism—one that was compatible with *Forth Feasting* and the 1633 *Entertainment*, though it tended to erode the integrity of the regal union—that Scotland would be loyal to its monarch regardless of the rest of Great Britain. Writing as, by now, the author of an ongoing *History of Scotland* from James I to James V, in which he was covertly analysing elements of the contemporary crisis,[106] Drummond cites as precedents how

Edinburgh stood by James II, James III, and Mary Queen of Scots. The displaced King of England was being reconstructed as a Scottish monarch.

Charles was forcibly reminded, however, that his Scottish crown was unsafe without control of his other kingdoms, when, in October 1641, news reached him of the Irish Rebellion, and he had to return to England to gather resources to suppress it. To pacify Scotland on his departure, he freed a number of royalists who had allegedly plotted to murder leading Covenanters, but he also placated and promoted his most prominent opponents. Trying to react incisively to the mixed news, Drummond drafted an epigram:

> Behold (O Scots!) the reueryes of your King;
> Those hee makes Lordes who should on gibbetes hing.[107]

The Scots rhyme of 'King' with 'hing' makes it clear where the piece is written from, yet the replacement in manuscript of 'Behold (O Scots!) ... ' by 'Britannes, admire the extravagancyes of your King... '[108] shows how hard it was to disentangle Scottish from British politics (Fig. 6). Try as Drummond might to cast Charles as the king of an ancient, independent Scotland, his future clearly depended on his fortunes south of the border.

Those quickly unravelled after Charles raised his standard at Nottingham, on 22 August 1642, and he was defeated at Edgehill. Disagreement in Scotland over how to resolve or exploit the situation led Drummond to compose, in January 1643, a tract called *Skiamachia* ('fighting with shadows') that was hot in support of the crown. On the British problem, however, it took a step into paradox, arguing that because Scotland was physically conjoined to England it could not maintain its religious distinctiveness if it got involved in English affairs.[109] Drummond feared that the Scots would do a deal to help the English parliament against the king, which is, in fact, what happened, when, on 25 October 1643, a Solemn League and Covenant was sealed, 'to bring the Churches of God in the three kingdoms to the nearest conjunction and uniformity in religion'.[110] In due course Drummond was proved partly right, in that the agreement did contribute to the undoing of Scotland by the English Republic when Independents or sectarians south of the border turned against Presbyterianism.

Now the Scots made their second major incursion into England, intervening militarily on the side of parliament. It had an acute effect on English opinion. Symptomatic is John Cleveland's 'The Rebell Scot', which asks 'What? shall our Nation be in bondage thus | Unto a Land

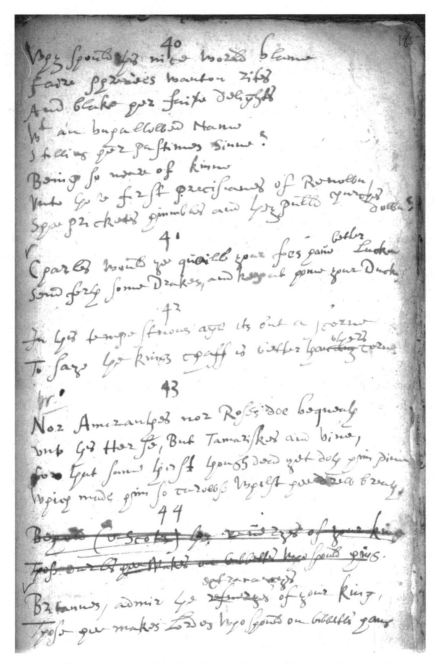

Fig. 6. William Drummond, in the throes of composition, caught up in the British problem. Hawthornden MSS; National Library of Scotland MS 2062, 185r.

that truckles under us?'[111] The Scotophobia curbed in royalists by their respect for the principle of regal union was unleashed,[112] and Cleveland satirized the Covenanters as sub-human ('A *Scot* within a beast is no disguise'). Because Scottish planters were now in Ulster, he quipped, Ireland had lost its claim to be a nation free of snakes. It is ironic that this tirade should so resemble that of Milton at the end of the decade, in his *Observations on the Articles of Peace* (1649), where he excoriates the Presbyterians of Belfast, and Scottish opinion more largely, for renewed royalism after Charles I's execution (below, pp. 231–2). Only in Cleveland's approval of '*Montrose* and *Crawfords* loyall Band' is there any liking for the Scots.

Both distinct and interactive, each Stuart kingdom was also subdivided by regional allegiances which, in some areas, extended into transnational ethnic units. Although the old continuity between Scottish and Irish Gaeldom had been disrupted by the Jacobean plantation in Ulster (above, pp. 99–100), the turbulent mid-1640s revived the prospect of a royalist alliance between the mere Irish and Scottish Gaels. The dashing Earl of Montrose, fine poet as well as brilliant general (below, pp. 220–1), in 1644 joined forces with Alasdair Mac Colla, an expropriated gentleman of the Clandonald South, who had led a couple of thousand Irishmen (mostly MacDonnells) and Islesmen from Wexford to Atholl, whence they marched through central and eastern Scotland, winning a string of victories.[113] For many of those involved, as the Gaelic poetry shows, these battles were part of a clan feud, or a local quarrel with kale-eating Lowlanders.[114] But larger alliances were formed, and members of Drummond's own family were drawn into an army whose leadership understood the three-kingdom predicament of the king.

What the poet thought of Mac Colla's men is not clear. In the *Entertainment* he had generalized the martial prowess of the Scots—as patriotic Lowlanders often did, because the Dalriadic north had never been defeated[115]—from the Highland-bred resilience of those who 'Runne over panting Mountaines crown'd with Ice' (120), and among the measures that he drafted to mock the 1639 parliament was a proposal 'That School-Masters be placed in the remotest High-Lands to instruct Youth in Civility and the *English* Language.'[116] Such scraps of evidence suggest a sympathy with aspects of Gaeldom that began to harden into approval when the long-standing royal mission to civilize and anglicize clan leaders was trans-lated into a parliamentary, evangelizing design to bring them within the pale of the Covenant. At all events there is no doubt that Drummond supported Montrose's campaign. He offered him *Irene* for publication and received his military protection;[117] he wrote a dialogue-epigram relishing the discomfiture of the Covenanters at his success.[118]

It is thus a measure both of how badly things turned out for Scottish royalism, and of how tangled political interests became when the war between the crown and its enemies was cut across by different national dynamics and dispositions of loyalty, that, only two years later, Drummond was seeking approval from the English for the fact that Montrose had been defeated by a Scottish Covenanting army. The event which changed his tack was the king's surrender of himself to the Scots on English soil, in May 1646, rather than fall into the clutches of the New Model Army. The Covenanters then had to decide whether to deal with Charles themselves in his role as King of Scotland, or to hand him over to the English parliament. Drummond's *Objections against the Scots Answer'd* was written to assert the independence of the Scots while insisting that they were no threat to the English in defending their king. To hand him over, he says, would not just go against their homage and fidelity as subjects, but would break the terms of the national Covenant of 1638. As for the objection that the Scottish army in England had not earned its pay from London, part of it did, he says, march north to defeat Montrose, without which 'the State of the Affairs of *England*, had fallen to as low an Ebb as now they swell in a high Tide'.[119]

These unscrupulous arguments did not persuade the Scottish Presbyterians—and they were only tactically addressed to the English—to protect the king. Defeated in June 1646 by the Catholic Irish at Benburb, County Tyrone, and ineffective elsewhere, the Covenanters had lost their ability to produce a favourable outcome to events; so, in January 1647, they pulled out of Newcastle, leaving Charles I to the English parliament. This was not even in the short term the end of Scottish royalism because the rise of Covenanting conservatism led to the signing of a secret engagement with the imprisoned king during the winter of 1647-8. But the Duke of Hamilton's attempt to lead a Scottish force to victory in the Second Civil War—supported by Drummond in his *Vindication of the Hamiltons*—failed because appetite for war was flagging even in royalist Gaeldom, while a Godly rising in south-west Scotland underlined the impossibility of converting the nation as a whole into supporters of cavalier royalism. After Hamilton's defeat at Preston, on 17–19 August 1648, Cromwell came to Edinburgh, where a diehard regime of Covenanters was installed. The British union of crowns was dying, and what promised to replace it was the worst option that Drummond could imagine: the reduction of Scotland to a province under the control of the English parliament.

The 'Life' that introduces the 1711 *Works* says that Drummond 'was so overwhelmed with extreme Grief and Anguish' at the execution of Charles I 'that he Died' (x). Since the poet passed away on 4 December 1649, about ten months after the king, the story is medically implausible, but it is also politically unlikely. It was perhaps a freak of fate that his poems should have been edited in 1656 by a nephew (and amanuensis) of the regicide Milton.[120] But he would not have relished the fact that his prose works were first brought out in the same year by the anti-royalist Englishman John Hall. The appearance of that collection mostly highlights the difference between the British kingdoms which meant that, while Drummond could attack Presbyterian intolerance in Scotland without thinking he would give succour to Independency (which hardly existed north of the border), at least parts of his work could find such English admirers as Cromwell whose anti-Presbyterianism was far from royalist.[121] It is also instructive, however, that Hall's choice of texts was only somewhat more selective than that of the Tory editors of the 1711 works, who sought to project a very different image.

As a three-kingdom perspective brings out, and partly explains, Drummond was a far more multifaceted figure than has been recognized, and the rapidly changing and personally dangerous circumstances of his final decade did nothing to simplify his work. What did remain constant, despite the anglicization of his language, was an identification with Scotland, its ancient monarchy, and the distinctive culture of its elite. This infused him, as a young writer, with an internationalist localism that finds an echo in such modern Scottish poets as his admirer Edwin Morgan.[122] In his later work, the eventualities which spur him into frustrated pragmatism and even savagery are those of a Scotland that has advanced from the almost harmless neglect complained of in *Forth Feasting* into the labyrinth of the British problem.

5
Religion and the Drama
of Caroline Ireland

When Sir Thomas Wentworth, the newly appointed Lord Deputy, went to Ireland in 1633, he found a country outwardly at peace. Though plots by dispossessed Catholics had intermittently troubled Ulster,[1] rebellion had been avoided since the defeats of Hugh O'Neill and Sir Cahir O'Doherty three decades before.[2] Yet the seismograph of literature was telling another story. Texts from Caroline Ireland reveal a mass of unresolved tensions around land ownership, social mores, and the extent of the power of the crown in matters of religion. Since drama is by its nature well adapted to express conflict, it is not surprising that it should so sharply register the issues that would break out into violence during the rising of 1641. The surprise lies in just how much dramatic writing survives, how resourcefully it explores the interactions between family, sex, and marriage on the one hand and religion, faction, and archipelagic politics on the other—concatenations rather different from those of English drama at the time—and how deeply it can carry us into the underexplored world of Irish Catholicism.

Signs of what Wentworth had to deal with can be found in all four corners of the kingdom. To the south, in County Cork, a group of masquers disguised as kerns burst into the Earl of Barrymore's house during the Christmas festivities of 1632.[3] They were only prevented from molesting the white-robed figure of Peace when Mars appeared and forced them to join in a traditional sword dance. Even in long-planted Munster, trouble was just under the surface, and an Old English (Catholic-related) Protestant landowner felt obliged to put on show his willingness to curb his mere Irish neighbours.[4] At the other end of the island one finds the playwright Robert Davenport dedicating his 'Dialogue betweene Pollicy and Piety' (c.1634) to Wentworth's favourite cleric, John Bramhall, Bishop of Derry. In this dramatic poem, Hibernia, clad in a green-fringed mantle, calls the banns for a marriage between economic and religious reform.[5] It was a message congenial to Bramhall who worked for Piety not just by pushing (as an Anglican) for Laudian changes to the Church of Ireland but by recovering lands and fees that had been taken from it by laymen.

As it happens, Wentworth's attempt, abetted by the bishop, who acquired an estate near Omagh, to develop the Londonderry Plantation while creaming off revenues for the crown, rapidly encountered resistance. And so, looking west, did his grand scheme to plant Connacht. Wentworth's own account of how the city of Limerick greeted him, in 1637, with a pageant in which 'all the seauen Plannetts … vtter[ed] in harmony seuerall verses in our praise, telling vs thereby vpon my knowledge, rather what wee ought to be, then what wee were', shows that the Old English Catholics who dominated the Corporation were willing to criticize him publicly.[6] More personally revealing is his gibe that 'the son the King of Planetts … did instead of his indulgent heate benignly squirtt of his sweet waters vpon vs forth of a Seringe, my hopes being all the whilst the instrument was new, and had not been vsed before.' Wentworth's mock anxiety that the syringe had previously been used to sluice out someone's bodily orifices (standard medical practice) shows the abrasiveness that would weaken his government, as Catholic potential allies were driven into an unlikely alliance with his enemies among the Irish Protestants.

It is however, from the east, from Dublin, that most Caroline drama hails. And it is there, with James Shirley's *St Patrick for Ireland*, staged in 1639–40 at the recently opened Werburgh Street playhouse, that I want to begin. Given that the Londoner Shirley had been ordained in the Church of England, and, despite rumours of a conversion to Rome, left the life-records of a Protestant,[7] that he went to Dublin with Wentworth's encouragement, or at least that of his circle,[8] it might not seem a useful starting point. Is the play not condemned to see Ireland from an Anglo-Protestant point of view? The suspicion might seem confirmed when, near the start of the action, the pagan Irish priest Archimagus recites this prophecy:

> *A man shall come into this Land,*
> *With shaven Crowne, and in his hand*
> *A crooked Staffe, he shall command,*

> *And in the East his table stand;*
> *From his warme lips a streame shall flow,*
> *To make rockes melt, and Churches grow,*
> *Where while he sings, our gods shall bow,*
> *And all our kings his law allow.*[9]

Patrick may have a tonsure, but his 'table', which is not an 'altar', does sound Protestant, and its eastward orientation Laudian.[10] With his crozier, and his law (rather Erastianly) allowed by royal authority, he could be a medieval version of Bishop Bramhall. He tells the King of Ireland, Leogarius, 'We are of Britaine, Sir' (B2r)—the Brittany of the saints' lives contracted to imply another country.[11] And he declares that he is legate not, as traditionally, of the Pope, but of God (B2r).

That distinction derives from the researches of James Ussher, Old English Protestant Archbishop of Armagh,[12] who stripped the story of Patrick of medieval accretions to show how closely the beliefs of the early Celtic church resembled (in his view) those of the Church of Ireland after its belated Jacobean Reformation.[13] He thus established for Irish Protestantism the sort of Rome-free origins that the Church of England had earlier derived from the ancient British church (above, pp. 121–2). There are good reasons, however, for not fully equating Shirley's Patrick with Ussher's proto-Calvinist saint. The latter represented the independence of the Irish church from Canterbury as well as Rome, while Patrick in the play seeks to bring pagan Ireland into congruity with the church in 'Britaine'.[14] Shirley's Patrick is an active missionary, who converts Leogarius's queen, his younger son, and others, whereas the commitment of Ussher's church to converting the Irish can be doubted. (The attractiveness to the New English of expropriation and plantation—stripping land from troublesome Catholics—encouraged them to subscribe to the Calvinistic belief that the stubborn ignorance of the Irish proved them not of the elect and therefore unconvertible.[15]) And Patrick, in any case, has an ecclesiastical style at odds with official Calvinism. When he comes on stage, he is accompanied by an angel carrying a banner marked with a cross followed by a procession of '*other Priests*' singing a Latin hymn (B1v). Just acceptable in Bramhall's Derry, this would go down badly in Ussher's Armagh.

How would the pagan Ireland represented in the play strike the religiously mixed audience in the Werburgh Street theatre? For New English Protestants, at least, Archimagus, whose very name recalls the papistical sorcerer in Book I of *The Faerie Queene* (Archimago), would call to mind stereotypically negative features of Romanist priestcraft. He conjures up devilish spirits, is devious, greedy, has King Leogarius under his thumb, and does nothing to civilize the kerns. The opening phase of the play turns on contrasting miracles. A nobleman who threatens Patrick is frozen rigid by God, and brought numbly back to life by the saint. Archimagus matches this by persuading a couple of young men to disguise themselves as statues of Jove and Mars on a candlelit altar. When, in a rudimentary or parodic version of the mass, staged before the royal family, these idols are offered incense, sung and prayed to, they unbend, instruct the king to act against Patrick, and generally deceive those present—including, initially, the theatre audience, who have not been warned that the actors are impersonating more than statues. A ribald follower of Archimagus calls this 'precious jugling' (D1v), a term used by hot Protestants to denounce the mass and the fake miracles (weeping statues of the Virgin and so on) used to stir devotion in Catholic Ireland.

What *sort* of Catholicism would Archimagus evoke for Shirley's audience? To some extent that depends on how the actors exploited the resources of the relatively advanced Werburgh Street playhouse. If the 'jugling' scene could remind viewers how much superstitious paganism had gone into the pre-Reformation Catholicism that persisted in many parts of Caroline Ireland, its use of solemn ritual in the presence of royal worshippers could equally well evoke the sort of noble Counter-Reformation chapel that Shirley would have found in the house of his patron, and Charles I's queen, Henrietta Maria. In any case, though this chapter will pursue some distinctions, and bring them to bear on a series of plays written by Irish Catholics—Henry Burnell's *Landgartha*, Henry Burkhead's *Cola's Furie*, and the anonymous, Jesuit *Titus*—it is often hard to disentangle the survivalist from the post-Tridentine in a country where the Counter Reformation was probably not ascendant until the mid-seventeeth century.[16] The success of Catholic reformers in penetrating not just the Old English areas of the Pale, but also, as we are increasingly aware, Gaelic Ireland,[17] was in some measure a product of its willingness to absorb long-standing, often local attachments to shrines, holy wells, and the like.

One element in Archimagus' character that connects him with negative depictions of priestcraft is his appetite for plotting. This view of the Catholic clergy ran deep in Protestant prejudice on both sides of the Irish sea;[18] it was reinforced by the secrecy with which persecuted Franciscans and Jesuits had to conduct themselves; and it found an answering paranoia in Irish Catholic imputations of conspiracy among Protestants in all three kingdoms. Plotting in this sense can be charged in plays because it instantiates the narrative, character-manipulating drives which create drama in the first place, and it became so self-reinforcingly conspicuous on the Irish stage during the late 1630s and 1640s that it will thread through the remainder of my account. In *St Patrick*, where Leogarius assumes that the saint is pursuing a 'bold designe' (B1v), there is a 'plot' to poison Patrick with a goblet of wine. Since he is, even as he drinks, asking Leogarius for permission 'To build a little chappell in this place', it is not surprising that he proves invulnerable (D4v-E1r). At the climax of the play, Shirley stages the best known of Patrick's miracles. Archimagus schemes, and unleashes against the saint a wriggling, masque-like tableau of 'serpents, vipers, and what ere | Doth carrie killing poyson' (I2v). Fortunately, Patrick is protected by his guardian angel Victor, and the false priest is dragged down to hell.

At this point it might seem tempting to revert to an English Protestant vs Irish Catholic polarity and conclude that Shirley was determined to damn Catholicism by whatever means. That would be to underrate, however, not just the commercial and ideological pressures that, as I shall show, encouraged him to produce a multi-purposive play—a work too conflicted and compromised to be fully coherent as drama, and open to contradictory interpretations[19]—but the paradoxes of survivalism. For as Wentworth and Laud recognized, with distaste and a certain relish, one locus of old Catholicism was the Church of Ireland itself, whose reformation had been so recent that its purgation was incomplete. From an Anglican point of view, it combined the doctrinal offence of Calvinism with recusant irregularity. In a letter to Laud, dated 31 January 1634,[20] Wentworth set out the problems. The church's buildings were in decay, funds were being diverted to keep 'Popish School-Masters' employed, while the family lives of many ministers ('whose Wives and Children are Recusants') suggested that they were only outwardly conforming. From this perspective, Shirley's Patrick resembles Bramhall because he comes to reform not so much Catholic/pagan Ireland as a state church—Archimagus works closely with his king—which is corrupt, steeped in superstition, short of properly built places of worship, and failing in its duty to instruct ordinary Protestants (who were drawn, like their papist neighbours, to holy wells, everyday miracles, and portents).[21] It would not be too contrary to reverse the *prima facie* interpretation and view Shirley's Patrick as a (Laudian) Catholic coming to reform Protestant Ireland.

Such a reading can be taken further—to the point, perhaps, of identifying *St Patrick for Ireland* as one source of Shirley's seventeenth-century reputation for being a Romanist convert. For the play relies heavily on the Irish Franciscan Robert Rochford's *Life of the Glorious Bishop S. Patricke*, a Counter-Reformation version of a medieval Latin *vita* by the Anglo-Norman Jocelyn of Furness.[22] This *Life*, prefaced by an epistle denying that Patrick was any sort of Protestant,[23] circulated widely in Ireland and is heard of in the hands of rebels after 1641.[24] Shirley does not merely replicate elements of the Catholicism of his source, making Patrick a miracle-worker, taking from the *Life* that Protestant-sounding 'table' in the East,[25] and having the saint utter the prediction of a glorious future for Ireland that Rochford had put into his epistle.[26] The Patrick of the play is several times called a 'pale man', the pun on Palesman identifying him with the Old English Catholics who lived in and around Dublin.[27] And the role ends with a sudden, ardent declaration of Counter-Reformation missionary zeal: 'The Blood of Martyrs is the Churches seed'.[28]

All this is consistent with the prominence among Shirley's admirers of such men as Richard Bellings[29] who would become Secretary of the Council of the Confederate Catholics of Kilkenny once the rising of 1641 gave way to civil war. If the Old English gentry warmed to Patrick, however, what did they make of Archimagus? They cannot have relished a play which made it so easy for Protestants to view Catholicism as superstitious. Yet they could hardly object to Shirley giving a dark account of pagan Ireland, since this showed up the light of the faith that Patrick brought to the country and that Catholics claimed still to live by. The saint's mission from Britain could anticipate (as it did for Jocelyn) the twelfth-century invasion of Ireland by the Anglo-Normans. Much as their ancestors, authorized by Adrian IV, supposedly rooted out evil manners and brought papal Catholicism into the country (above, p. 53), so the Old English now imported the Counter-Reformation. To that extent, the play flattered their long-standing self-image as culturally superior to their Gaelic neighbours.

Why would Shirley be friendly to aspects of the Counter-Reformation while feeding hostility towards a superstitious, Gaelic Ireland, represented not just by Archimagus but the treacherous Leogarius, an indulgently treated Bard, and a pair of decidedly contemporary, basely motivated kerns? His leading motive was no doubt commercial. Just as *St Patrick* mixes saint's life, romantic intrigue, masque-like spectacle, and chronicle history in a vain attempt (as it turned out) to please all tastes and put a stop to the dramatist's run of failures at the Werburgh Street theatre,[30] so it tries to square the circle of appealing to both New English Protestants and Old English Catholics (the Gaelic-speaking Old Irish were not part of the potential market).[31] But Shirley was also responding to the opportunities for religious accommodation generated by a moment in which programmes of doctrinal purification, social regulation, and ecclesiastical consolidation around episcopacy in Counter-Reformation Catholicism paralleled similar trends within a Laudianizing Church of Ireland. It seems clear, moreover, that he did so within the pragmatics of patronage. For Wentworth and his circle recognized that anti-Catholic propaganda was of limited value. It must have seemed more promising to support a playwright rumoured to be a Romanist who might draw Old English catholics towards the Laudian policy of the Castle (and away from their Gaelic cousins). The unlikelihood of such a tactic succeeding, especially in the face of developments within Irish Catholicism designed to defuse ethnic difference and consolidate a single community,[32] does not make the attempt implausible. The play would be compatible with the Lord Deputy's strategy of dividing and ruling, and coming down hard, when necessary, on the Castle's natural supporters.

Shirley's ingenuity failed him. The epilogue to *St Patrick* promised a sequel if the play were liked. It was not, and Shirley soon returned to England. Nor did Wentworth's stratagems long survive the signing of the Covenant in Scotland in 1638 and the spread of unrest to Ulster. Religion was his undoing.[33] If it were not for the dominance of Laudianism in England, and Wentworth's dutiful attempt to foster this in the Church of Ireland, his position would have been bolstered by an alliance among Irish Protestants. As it was, his reputation for manoeuvering counted against him in 1640, when Old English Catholics, aggrieved by his plantation policy and his failure to extend religious toleration, were joined by hostile Protestants in framing a Remonstrance. This led directly to his attainder and execution in England and made the outbreak of the civil wars if not inevitable then a great deal more likely. This is the broader, archipelagic context in which Patrick's 'We are of Britaine' should be understood—and it can be opened up by turning to Henry Burnell's *Landgartha*.

★ ★ ★

In his letter to Archbishop Laud about the persistence of pre-Reformation practices within the Church of Ireland, Wentworth goes on to denounce

'Polygamies, Incests and Adulteries'.[34] This reflects an English habit of 'othering' the Irish by regarding them as sexually lax[35]—a prejudice luridly apparent in the subplot of *St Patrick for Ireland*, where Emeria is raped by the brother of her fiancé, disguised as the pagan god, then threatened with further assault by a couple of uncivil kerns. But it also has some basis in the survival into early modern Ireland of medieval or older customs governing cohabitation, illegitimacy, fostering, and the sort of negotiable divorce that could be thought bigamous—conventions attractive enough to tempt the settler English into 'degeneracy'.[36] Dipping his insinuating pen into the acid of his inkpot, Wentworth suggested to Laud that marriage in Caroline Ireland was often little more than post-prandial fornication:

> They are accustomed here to have all their Christnings and Marriages in their private Houses, and which is odd they never marry till after Supper and so to Bed. This breeds a great Mischief in the Commonwealth, which is seen in this, that because these Rites of the Church are not solemnized in the publick and open Assemblies, there is nothing so common as for a Man to deny his Wife and Children, abandon the former and betake himself to a new Task; I conceive it were fit, these Particulars should be reduced to the Custom of *England*, which is not only much better for the Publick, but the more civil and comely. (I, 188)

Legislation against bigamy had failed in the troublesome Irish parliament of 1613–15, though steps were taken within the Dublin and Armagh dioceses of the Catholic church to regulate marriage in accordance with the Council of Trent.[37] Now, in 1634, Wentworth put another bill before parliament—hence the topicality of Davenport's allusion in his 'Dialogue' to the calling of the banns of marriage between Policy and Piety (marriage should not be clandestine). He was, however, frustrated. Though resistance to his reforms came from both sides of the religious divide,[38] the Lord Deputy blamed the Catholic clergy for preferring the authority of Rome to that of the crown in sealing up marriages:

> the Friars and Jesuits fearing that these Laws would conform them here to the Manners of *England*, and in Time be a Means to lead them on to a Conformity in Religion and Faith also, they catholickly oppose and fence up every Path leading to so good a Purpose: And indeed I see plainly, that so long as this Kingdom continues Popish, they are not a People for the Crown of *England* to be confident of. Whereas if they were not still distempered by the Infusion of these Friars and Jesuits, I am of Belief, they would be as good and loyal to their King, as any other Subjects.[39]

Here is the comforting message that Protestants could derive from Shirley: get rid of Archimagus, and Catholic Ireland will be governable. But it is not surprising, given the background, that, when measures to curb bigamy came back to a new parliament, in 1640, they were again resisted. This renewed rejection has been seen as merely tactical, designed to embarrass the Lord Deputy, but it is hard to believe that Catholic MPs were unaware of his Anglicizing agenda. Perhaps there was some advantage for Wentworth in losing this battle. He was almost inciting papists to defend the customs which their hierarchy was rejecting along Counter-Reformation lines.

Landgartha was first performed on St Patrick's Day 1640, in the Werbugh Street theatre, shortly after the opening of the parliament. Much about the play suggests that it was written to appeal to MPs gathered for the session, and, given its sexual politics, and dedicatory address to women, to their wives and daughters. If the Master of the Revels, John Ogilby,[40] took the play's hostility to bigamy as a sign of support for Wentworth's larger position, however, he made a serious mistake when he licensed the play.[41] An Old English Catholic, who joined Wentworth's 'New Army' in Ireland—the force whose inclusion of papists made English parliamentarians so apprehensive about the king's intentions—but who then fought for the Confederate Catholics and is last heard of being transplanted to Connacht, Burnell made few concessions to the Lord Deputy in his play even while he underlined the traditional loyalty of his community to the crown.

Like *Hamlet, Landgartha* reflects on the problems of multiple monarchy by using material derived from Saxo Grammaticus' *Historia Danica* via Belleforest's *Histoires tragiques*.[42] In Burnell's case, however, the Anglo-Scoto/Danish-Scandinavian issues that go into *Hamlet* (above, pp. 15–16) are applied to all three Stuart kingdoms. The play begins with the godless Swede Frollo, who has invaded and occupied Norway, treating a woman abusively. This sets in train the work's interlocked accounts of religious, sexual, and political issues. Frollo is opposed by the Amazon Landgartha, 'with a mighty troope of women, | Gatherd to her from all the parts of Norway'.[43] Reyner, king of Denmark, who has a better claim to Norway than Frollo, brings in his forces, and, although Landgartha is less interested in his rights than in female (even feminist) virtue, she does fight Frollo to his advantage. Reyner, Hubba, and other Danes come on stage just as she is defeating the Swedish tyrant in single combat. Reyner is smitten, though Landgartha feels obliged to listen to his suit only out of duty and her desire for the public good. When Reyner plays on his status as monarch, she says that, while she is willing to love him, he ought to consider carefully what marriage with her would mean since the infamy of breaking up would be grave.

Between the wooing and the predictable betrayal comes a long wedding celebration, a 'semi-masque' which, in a metadramatic gesture, is said to be underprovided 'For want of fitting Actors here at Court; | The Warre and want of Money' (E2r)—Wentworth was, at this date, equipping his army to fight the Scots. This restages, or at least recites, with no encouragement from Belleforest, the horrors of the Trojan War and the medieval story of British descent. But an Irish perspective creeps in as Reyner is told that the British will conquer and be conquered by their 'neighbour Nations' (F2r). At length, there will arise

> a Prince (one way descended
> Of *Troian* race: I'th'other side extended
> Vp by the Royall bloud of *Danes*, unto
> A warlike King call'd *Reyner*, that shall wooe
> And wed a Lady Amazonian,
> *Landgartha* nam'd) ...   (F2v)

—in other words, Charles I, descended on the one hand from Brut, and on the other, through Anne of Denmark, from Reyner and Landgartha. So long as 'sad dissentions' are kept within bounds, this prince, we are assured, will not just enjoy his own government but conquer and re-build Troy and, invading Greece, 'there restrayne | Th'impieties of wicked men' (F2v). The prediction is as unlikely as any to be found in ro-mance, that a valiant Charles I would defeat the Turks on their own ground.[44]

Reyner does not proceed wisely to bring this prophecy about. By Act IV, he is regretting his marriage to 'A poore gentlewoman, an ordinary | Noble mans daughter' (F3r-v). This reversal is characteristic of tragicomic plotting, but audiences could hardly miss, in the wake of the semi-masque, its political application. Since it is already obvious that Reyner is shot through with elements of Charles I's conduct that were unattractive to Irish Catholics, while Landgartha represents the Old English gentry, it will not give too much away if I gloss the king's description of his poor but noble wife as implying that the badly treated Old English are virtuous, gallant, and strategically valuable to the Stuarts, however lacking in resources compared with the magnates of Britain. Despite the urging of a prudent counsellor, Reyner prepares to go back to Denmark leaving Landgartha pregnant in Norway. This is not just immoral, it is politically imprudent. 'She'll be reveng'd at full for her dishonour', he is warned, 'And snatch the Crownes you weare from of your trech'rous | Temples' (F4r). How could she overthrow her husband? Pym, as it were, and his fellow MPs in London might join her, much as they helped Old English Catholics and Irish Protestants make their case against Wentworth. We are now told about a faction of Danes, led by one Harold, who wants to oust Reyner.

So virtuous is Landgartha, however, that, when she hears that Reyner is threatened, she musters her Amazons, and, to his astonishment, saves him from Harold and the rebels. It is worth remembering that Catholic as well as Protestant Old and New Englishmen were arming to protect Charles I against the puritans and their Scottish allies—Burnell, as we have seen, being one of them. *Landgartha* plays out the hope that Old English Catholics, denied religious toleration and threatened by plantation, would rescue Charles I and earn political favours. It would not, though, be easy to draw them into the royalist camp. In a calculatedly awkward, half-comic sequence, Reyner tries to woo Landgartha back to be his queen, while she confronts and denounces his hapless new partner, Vraca, daughter of Frollo. That the women wrangle about the 'lawfulnesse' of the king's second li-aison using technical vocabulary ('clayme ... Possession ... intrusion ... due') connects the sequence the more firmly with the 1640 parliamentary debates about bigamy (I3r). In the end Landgartha will only agree to be a faithful wife to Reyner to the extent of preserving her chastity; she will not live with him, at least not yet.

That Burnell experienced the instabilities of 1639–40 as a crisis of multiple monarchy is clear. More ingenious is the way he turned to advantage the topic of bigamy. The play does not just aim to please Old English MPs and their women in the Werburgh Street audience by saying that their community is best depicted as a noble Amazon faithful to her marriage vows, it repels the charge of laxity by saying that the English are the bigamous ones and proves it at the level of politics. Charles's (Reyner's) relations with the Sweden of Vraca (Scotland)[45] and Landgartha's Norway (Ireland) are scandalously two-timing. When Reyner finds Landgartha victorious against Frollo (i.e. when Old English Catholics have kept down the Covenanters in Ulster), he grants the Norwegians power to legislate for themselves—a claim in line with the arguments of such Old English lawyers as Patrick Darcy[46]—and he endorses their long-established right to give the crown counsel. Landgartha later reminds Reyner that she could have married Frollo but chose not to. The Old English do not rely on England's power but are independent agents, with options. They could—at least in playland—find another sovereign (Catholic views about this would harden).

It is worth pausing over the Amazon who represents Gaelic and/or Gaelicized Ireland. Not found in Belleforest, she derives her name from an Asian warrior-queen in Ariosto's *Orlando furioso*: '*Marfisa in an Irish Gowne tuck'd up to mid-legge, with a broad basket-hilt Sword on, hanging in a great Belt, Broags on her feet, her hayre dishevell'd, and a payre of long neck'd big-rowll'd Spurs on her heels*' (E3r). This costume was questionably legal in the eyes of Protestant authority,[47] and potentially subversive. There had been a reversion to Irish dress during Tyrone's rebellion and the same thing would happen in some areas during the 1640s.[48] Burnell is being playful when he has Hubba assert that this costume came to Norway from Denmark but originated in Ireland, because Norway, in the allegory, *is* Ireland. Equally striking, however, is the appeal to the applause of the audience when Marfisa says that, whatever its origins, 'a handsome woman | Lookes as well in't, as any dresse, or habit | Whatsoever' (E3v).

That this slightly defensive assertion is endorsed by the admiring Hubba makes for a complex theatrical moment, one which overall counters the Old English condescension towards the Gaelic Irish that Shirley apparently hoped to exploit. Yet the groups remain distinct. After the semi-masque, Hubba and Marfisa '*Dance the whip of Donboyne merrily*'. This popular romp[49] is followed by '*the grand Dance in foure Couple*'—a more formal, courtly affair, for the Danish and Norwegian nobility, that leaves out Marfisa and her partner (F2v-3r). The contrast is partly a cultural one between traditional, country Irishness and those (e.g. the nobility of the Pale) equipped with courtly refinement, but the ethnic inheritance is such that there is an implication that the Old Irish and their associates are not integral to the ruling elite, though they are loyal to Landgartha's party. With the 1640 Parliament in session, the play tacitly proposes that the Old English Catholics can deliver their Irish cousins[50] to Charles I so long as he keeps to the terms of their political marriage. And Landgartha does bring Marfisa to fight the rebel Harold. Again, though, the Irish Amazon remains distinct within the royalist ranks, and has a subsidiary role in the fighting.

In Old English fantasy, only months before the 1641 rising flared up in Gaelic Ulster, the Old Irish are colourful, brave, and subordinate.

The play's ending is challengingly open. Not content with refusing a potentially bigamous cohabitation, Landgartha leaves Reyner in Denmark and returns to Norway. After giving the king counsel, on the great Irish theme of plotting ('Be just and vertuous, and you neede not | Feare poyson, poynards, or conspiracie'), she adds that '*Norway* shall be preserv'd for your young sonne' (I4r). This is a loyal-sounding way of announcing that the government of her country will not be in Danish hands; the Old English will look after Ireland. Can Reyner extract nothing more? When urged to follow Landgartha, the king seems eager to cooperate, but the future remains uncertain. In an afterword to the printed text, Burnell reports: 'Some (but not of best judgements) were offended at the Conclusion of this Play, in regard *Landgartha* tooke not then, what she was persuaded to by so many, the Kings kind night-imbraces.' His reply makes much of genre: 'To which kind of people (that know not what they say) I answer (omitting all other reasons:) that a Tragie-Comedy sho'd neither end Comically or Tragically, but betwixt both: which *Decorum* I did my best to observe' (K1v). It may be that Burnell really did encounter the sort of ignorance that Shirley took to complaining of in his prologues and epilogues. But Catholics were also divided about what demands should be made of Charles I and 'all other reasons' must have included, at least for Burnell, political doubts. All that would become explicit seventeen months later when Landgartha joined Marfisa in rebellion.

★ ★ ★

Historians have been scouring the archives to establish the causes and dynamics of the 1641 rising.[51] There was a plot by the Old Irish in Ulster—encouraged by the success of the Scots in resisting the Laudian prayerbook—to relieve the pressure on Catholicism and recover land lost to British planters. A move by Old English Palesmen to seize Dublin Castle (a scheme which possibly enjoyed some backing by the crown) was abandoned before the rising began, but it did not take long for the Catholics of Leinster to join the rebels once a harsh reaction from the government cut down their options. Both groups feared that they were merely countering a conspiracy among puritans in Britain and Ireland to destroy the king's power and suppress Catholicism in all three kingdoms. Economic and

cultural factors contributed, as did slow-burning resentment against the
Ulster Plantation, but religious commitment impelled the rebellion and
shaped its violence.

Certainly, if one looks for Landgartha and her Amazons in 1641, they
can be found among the 'lewd viragoes', led by an Old Englishwoman,
who reportedly abused the bodies of Protestants in Kilkenny. As the
rebels warmed to their task, they took the head of a minister called
Bingham, gagged it, 'and laying the leaf of a bible before him bade him
preach, saying his mouth was open wide enough'.[52] It was a common
belief among Protestants that Catholic priests stirred up rebellion (Fig. 7).
Yet the Roman church brought some order out of turmoil by encouraging the organization of the Confederation.[53] Clergy administered the
Oath of Association which bound Old English and Old Irish leaders
together, and helped them mobilize armies. Without the church's incitement, Marfisa might not have gone to war—as we know she did.
After the battle of Ballintober (County Roscommon), in 1642, when the
helmet was pulled from the head of one of the Irish soldiers, 'there fell
down long Tresses of flaxen hair, who being further search'd, was found a
Woman'.[54]

The early history of the Confederation went into a play published,
and conceivably performed, in Kilkenny, a town whose theatrical traditions, almost as strong as those of Dublin,[55] would burgeon under the
Confederation as diplomatic and military missions called for displays and
entertainments.[56] Probably composed in the second half of 1645, and published the following year, Henry Burkhead's *Cola's Furie* gives an Old
English Catholic account of events between the rising (almost obscured,
for apologetic reasons) and the truce between the Catholic and the royalist,
Protestant forces of 1643.[57] Individuals are identifiable (Cola is the ruthless
Governor of Dublin, Sir Charles Coote), but the play has a persuasive
grasp of the collective order of events. Plots, real and imputed, are thus
flagged from the outset,[58] and this shapes Burkhead's dramaturgy, in which
scenes of deliberation—the participant's view of a conspiracy—alternate
with sudden shocks as the unforeseen designs of an unscrupulous enemy
are put into effect. The play, also from the start, gives a significant role to
religion. While Protestants fear that 'A few of Romish Recusants | Thinke
to subvert the true reformed Gospell',[59] the Catholics fight a 'pious warre'
to 'stop | The current of their puritan designe | Intended for our totall ruine'
(5–6).

The Preestes & Iesuites anointe the Rebells with there Sacrament of vnction before they goe to murther & robe assuringe them that for there meritorious Seruice, if they be killed he shall escape Purgatory & go to heauen im:mediatly

They do usually mangell there dead Car:cases laying wagers who shall cut deepest into there dead flesh with there Skenns,

they destroy our English Sheepe in detesta:tion of us, although one is better then 4 of theirs. they haue vowed to roote out the name of the English

Fig. 7. Priestcraft excusing rebellion. From James Cranford, *The Teares of Ireland* (London, 1642).

War is always fought with words (fortunately for the early modern theatre, which was better at representing speeches than the mass physicality of battle). This was particularly so in Ireland where a defining grievance for Catholics—who formally joined the confederacy by swearing their Oath of Association—was itself the swearing of oaths. The Stuarts had repeatedly sought to split and coerce Irish Catholics by requiring them to commit themselves to oaths of supremacy and allegiance.[60] (The Oath of Allegiance even bound them to counter the sorts of conspiracy that were typically bound by oaths.)[61] The visibility of this issue helps explain why Burnell used marriage to figure archipelagic ties. The vows which should hold lovers and spouses together in *Landgartha* are interpersonal versions of the oaths that regulated relations between leading subjects of the three kingdoms and their monarch. The Confederation offered Catholics the chance of swearing an oath to support the king (as well as their religion and their *patria*) in terms they had chosen for themselves. It created an open conspiracy that demanded to be seen as the opposite of a plot.

Oaths were widely used in mid-seventeenth-century Britain to consolidate alliances, and the contradictions they gave rise to, between such undertakings as the Solemn League and Covenant and the Engagement, generated a corpus of Protestant casuistry.[62] In Ireland, there were distinctive complications. Compared with the Scottish national Covenant, which historians, rightly, regard as a precedent, the Oath of Association is much less legalistic and preoccupied with the errors of other religions.[63] The emphasis is on loyalty to crown, parliament, law and 'the general cause'. It may be that, as the enemies of the Confederation contended, Counter-Reformation thinking about equivocation and the acceptability of breaking faith with heretics made Catholic promises susceptible to casuistry. Yet oaths in Confederate Ireland retained something of their medieval sacralism because they could underpin the religion that supposedly underpinned them. Because my religion is truer than yours I keep my vow more faithfully; that I keep my vow when you break yours proves that you are a heretic. This is one of the ways in which oaths figure in *Cola's Furie*, where Protestants are repeatedly false. But this cannot quite conceal what the later history of the Confederation bears out, that oaths are metaphysical only to be instrumental, and that the existence of the Oath of Association—made much of in the play—was not entirely a sign of strength. The Confederation brought together men who were not inevitably united but who buried their differences in a speech act.[64]

Micheál Ó Siochrú has recently argued that the Old Irish and Old English leaders had more in common than is usually thought. In his view, a joint Catholic identity had been forged in the decades before 1641. When splits developed in the Confederation they were less along ethnic lines than between a royalist faction keen to reach agreement with the Old

English Protestant leader, Ormond, a pro-clerical party, which came to rally around the papal legate Rinuccini, in Ireland from 1645, and a middle group which held the balance.[65] While Ó Siochrú is persuasive in stressing how social status and economic interest affected behaviour (notably, how much landowners stood to gain or lose by staying out as rebels), his playing down of ethnic difference seems more questionable if one arrives at *Cola's Furie* after Shirley and Burnell. The play primarily celebrates the Old English leadership. It does make the Ulster Gaelic general, Owen Roe O'Neill, a conspicuous and valiant figure. It is Theodoric (O'Neill), for instance, who saves the lovely Elleonara from molestation by English soldiers, then almost too promptly marries her—a Catholic Irishman's reply to negative stereotypes of rapacious kerns. Yet Theodoric is a willing implement of the Old-English-dominated Council; his role is much less heroic than the one attributed to O'Neill in the weightiest, pro-clerical account of the period, *An Aphorismical Discovery of Treasonable Faction* (c.1652–9).

The care with which the play manages such rivalries reveals what is concealed by that aspect of it which most strongly appears to confirm Ó Siochrú's thesis. In its thinly disguised geopolitical setting, *Cola's Furie* recognizes only Lirendeans (Irish) and Angoleans (English). Just as Irish Protestantism is elided into Englishness (a procedure which leaves no room for a Protestant Gaelic leader such as Inchiquin), so the play avers that all Catholics in Ireland are Irish. A member of the clerical faction with an aptitude for literary criticism might have responded with the observation that if religion were the only true good in this play, it would not be seen so actively to determine membership of a political alliance and be so constitutive of an emergent national identity. Characters are preoccupied with land ownership, social status, and fear of extermination; religion emerges as a force contingent upon those other factors, though also, undoubtedly, invested with them. And while the play makes it clear how loyalty to Catholicism drove men to fight, it also helps one see that the potency with which religion joined up the confederacy gave it the capacity to create division. Disputes about what sort of church should be defended or developed would shatter the alliance that Catholicism helped hold together.

The Angoleans, as I have said, show their baseness by breaking their promises. Announcing a pardon for rebels who give themselves up, they betray this with torture and execution. Their leaders offer quarter, then turn a blind eye to massacre. When Cola's lieutenant, Tibernus, instructs his soldiers in such a course, one of them sardonically remarks: 'He speaks like a true zealous Protestant' (23). That Catholics would be capable of breaking a promise is on one level so unthinkable as not to be ruled out—inauspiciously, given the disputes about oath-breaking later in Confederate history. When Athenio rallies the leadership he reminds them that 'our quarrell is | Religious, in maintenance whereof we | Are already sworne without equivocation' (19). The very ambiguity of 'religious' (the quarrel concerns religion, maintaining it is a sacred duty) shows that words are slippery, and 'equivocation' part of their nature. When the moderate wing of the Confederation agreed to truces with the Protestant royalists, in the two Ormond Peaces of 1646–8, the clerical party accused them of taking just such advantage of words. According to the *Aphorismical Discovery*, they evaded the Oath of Association 'by equivocations and mentall reservations, makinge like a Gipsies knott, faste or loose, at theire pleasure'.[66]

Cola himself is more given to passion than equivocation.[67] Since Cola is not just a contraction of Carola, Coote's Christian name in Latin, but a pun on *choler*, the title of the play comes to mean *Anger's Fury*, as Cola is driven, like a Fury in Seneca, up the escalator of his own rage. Yet his downfall is not entirely self-generated, and how it comes about exposes another blind spot in the play. For Burkhead, hating Coote, did not choose to recognize how dishonourable was the plot by Mineus, one of the Catholic leaders, to assassinate Cola—announced with a religious oath:

> Then name of God,
> This night we will advance our forces where
> The besotted tyrant now remaines, if
> We but kill his centrie then, we may more
> Boldly enter and surprise him napping
> In his bed asleepe ...   (45–6)

Athenio blithely concurs, and this plot becomes the plot of the play.

On the night of his death, Cola is visited, like Shakespeare's Richard III the night before the Battle of Bosworth, by the ghosts of those he has killed. Predictably, he dismisses the vision as 'a plot of some conjuring Papist' (47). Yet for all the machinery of foreboding, Coote is disposed of briskly. In the *Aphorismical Discovery*, his death is tied to the controversy regarding the power of icons, disparaged by Protestants as idols, and to the domesticated survival of Irish Catholicism after the Reformation—topics

I shall return to. We are told that Coote's son caused 'a great ancient portraiture, or image of Our Blessed Lady engraven in wood, kept with great veneration in the same house since the supression of holy churche in Henry the 8 his time' to be chopped up to make a fire for his father. The moment Coote sat down to warm himself, the Irish launched an attack and he was providentially struck down (I, 32). In keeping with the play's more pragmatic sense of religion, there is no divine framework and no mystery about the agency of death. Cola is merely shot with degrading, anonymous abruptness: '*One meets him and dischargeth a pistoll wherat he falls downe dead*' (48).

Cola's nocturnal visions are not the only ones in the play. The Catholic general Abner (Thomas Preston) is haunted in the Low Countries by a group of classical figures who recall him to Ireland. And Caspilona (Castlehaven), in prison, is told by an angel that he will miraculously escape. It is the closing scene, however, which colours the play's politics most strongly with Catholicism in this way. An angel enters to solemn music, and calls on Victory (rather optimistically, given the circumstances of the 1643 cessation) to 'Grace this nation with a Crowne, | Of perpetuall renowne' (61). The singleness of 'this nation' is in keeping with the play's confessional definition of Irishness, but this more radically and no doubt unconsciously allows the line-ending to raise the thought that sovereignty inheres in the Irish people not the Stuart line. There had been talk of Irish separatism in exile circles in earlier decades, but it is symptomatic that, at just this moment, the Lisbon-based, County Cork Jesuit Conor O'Mahony published a *Disputatio apologetica* (1645) which argued that Irish Catholics should shake off their heretic king and find another ruler.[68]

Too bold for the Confederate leadership, O'Mahony's tract was burned by the common hangman, and preached against in Kilkenny castle; but it reflected, despite its continental formation, the mix of triumphalism and insecurity that characterized Catholic Ireland at this juncture.[69] By dedicating the published text of *Cola's Furie* to the king's envoy to Ireland, the Catholic Earl of Glamorgan,[70] Burkhead was signalling his Old English allegiance to the crown. He was allying himself with the Ormondists who would welcome the marquis to Kilkenny in 1646.[71] Yet the terms in which he couches his royalism have an almost Hobbesian, absolute air: ''Tis a principle of Nature, that Creatures of weake condition, aiming at security, doe direct their course for shelter, to the wings of the more potent, so Principalities and states of inferior note, doe manifest their sollicitude, to gaine the patronage of some Royall Majestie.' The vagueness of 'some' is remarkable. It says, no doubt more clearly than Burkhead himself could hear, that while a nation needed a sovereign there was more than one place in which it could find it.

★   ★   ★

These issues can be pursued into something like a conclusion by turning to *Titus: Or, The Palme of Christian Courage*, a play performed by students of the Jesuit school in Kilkenny. The original may have been in Latin. What survives is a three-page summary, entirely lacking dialogue (the whole artefact is now a *plot*), published in English, in 1644. There is some evidence that it was the custom in Jesuit theatre to distribute a summary of this sort in advance of a performance to advertise the show and help the audience like a crib;[72] but the publication of this résumé by Thomas Bourke of Waterford—printer to the Confederation[73]—makes it natural to assume that the sponsors of *Titus* wanted its story to reach a larger audience than would be gathered in Kilkenny.[74] The Jesuit stamp of the play is clear from such scenes as the one in which St Francis Xavier appears to the protagonist and his family in a vision. More subtle is the way the dominance of the Old English elite among Irish Jesuits[75] informs the work's priorities.

As Fig. 8 shows, Bourke's little pamphlet sets out the 'Argument' of *Titus* on its title page:

> *Titus* a noble Gentleman more illustrious for his Christian courage, then parentage: was sollicited by the King of *Bungo*, to desert his Religion by severall, most artificious infernall plots, all which he sleighted and dashed with his invincible courage, and generous Christian resolution, whereat the King amazed, restored him to his liberty, wife and children, and granted him the freedome of his Religion, with all his lands and possessions of which before he was bereaved as traitor to the Crowne.[76]

Like *St Patrick, Landgartha*, and (if it was performed) *Cola's Furie, Titus* was clearly a play with much to offer audiences in the way of intrigue, high morality, and tragicomic reassurance. Since Bourke's summary as a whole shows that the story of Titus was framed by tableaux that depicted in allegorical splendour Divine Love, Faith and Fortitude, and the church both militant and triumphant, yet was punctuated by comic interludes, the drama must have provided a diverse, at times spectacular entertainment for the troubled, wartime audiences who saw it in performance.

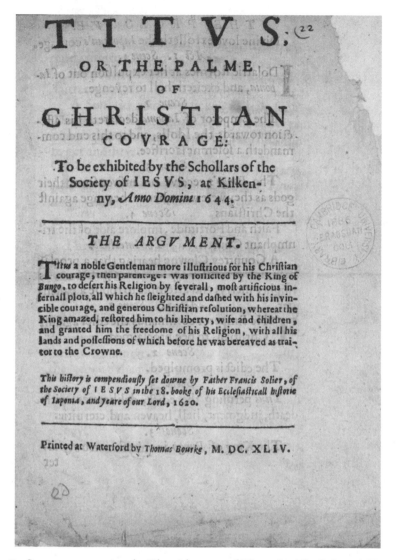

TITVS; [22]
OR THE PALME
OF
CHRISTIAN
COVRAGE:

.To be exhibited by the Schollars of the
Society of I E S V S , at Kilkenny, *Anno Domini* 1 6 4 4.

THE ARGVMENT.

Titus a noble Gentleman more illuftrious for his Chriftian courage, then parentage : was follicited by the King of *Bungo*, to defert his Religion by feverall, moft artificious infernall plots, all which he fleighted and dafhed with his invincible courage, and generous Chriftian refolution, whereat the King amazed, reftored him to his liberty, wife and children, and granted him the freedome of his Religion, with all his lands and poffeffions of which before he was bereaved as traitor to the Crowne.

This *biftory is compendiously fet downe by Father Francis Solier, of the Society of I E S V S in the* 18. *booke of his Ecclefiafticall biftorie of Iaponia, and yeare of our Lord,* 1620.

Printed at Waterford by *Thomas Bourke*, M. DC. XLIV.

Fig. 8. Summary propaganda. The title page of *Titus: Or, The Palme of Christian Courage* (Waterford, 1644).

But their troubles were also addressed. Certainly, the Argument's emphasis on 'most artificiall infernall plots' is striking. Against all the British Protestant charges of popish plotting, the play must have intimated to its public that Charles I (the King of Bungo) was a heretic/pagan who had intrigued against Catholic Ireland.[77] That Titus is not high-born, yet is *generosus* (noble) on religious grounds, is consistent with the tendency of Jesuit drama to replace socially elevated Aristotelian protagonists with exemplary Christian believers.[78] This, however, makes it the more telling that the modestly derived protagonist has 'lands and possessions' to be restored. The implicit hope is that Charles will relinquish his claim to estates put in jeopardy by the 1641 rebellion, if not those lost in Ulster after the flight of the Earls in 1607.[79] The play, in other words, may have accommodated the claims of Gaelic, northern militancy, yet the constitutional language of the summary—'liberty ... the freedome of his Religion ... traitor'—is a clue to its Old English origins.

According to Bourke's title page: '*This history is compendiously set downe by Father Francis Solier, of the Society of* Iesus *in the* 18. *booke of his Ecclesiasticall historie of Iaponia, and yeare of our Lord,* 1620.' The history of the Jesuit mission to Japan[80] does provide the context for *Titus*, but the protagonist and his story cannot be found in Solier.[81] I have discovered the play's source in Morejon Pedro's *A Briefe Relation of the Persecution Lately Made against the Catholike Christians, in the Kingdome of Iaponia* (1619).[82] In its basic design *Titus* followed this text closely. To read beyond Bourke's title page, however, into the larger summary which follows, is to notice some telling differences. *Titus*, for example, gave prominence to a topic that was routine in accounts of the Jesuit mission but not included in the relevant episode of the *Relation*: '*Act* I. *Scene* I. Idolatrie stormes at her expulsion out of *Iaponia*, and exciteth hell to revenge. *Scene* 2. The Emperor of *Iaponia* declareth his affection towards the Idolls, and to this end commandeth a solemne sacrifice. *Scene* 3. The *Bongo's* receive no answer from their gods as they were wont, hence they rage against the Christians.' Idols figure in continental Jesuit as well as English drama.[83] The obvious comparison, though, is with *St Patrick for Ireland*. Much as *Landgartha* rebuts the charge that Irish Catholics are bigamists by showing that, on the contrary, this is the vice of the King of England, so *Titus* reverses the claim that Catholics are idol-worshippers by imputing that sin to the Japanese. The Irish milieu is crucial; in an English Protestant play, the same scenes would be saying that Charles I's Laudian tendencies were turning him into a papist.

Though Titus opposes idols he is not an iconoclast. At one point, '*Titus his wife and familie voweth loyaltie to God before the Crucifix*'. The focus of the scene distinguishes the true beliefs of Titus and his family from a British/Irish puritanism which was as hostile to the crucifix as the Japanese authorities notoriously were. The audience could not have experienced this merely as a representation of events in Japan; the symbolic power of the cross would have drawn them into an involvement more like participation. And it is a measure of the Catholicism of *Titus* that images are potent for good or ill, and not inherently vain. The Japanese idols have been effective in the past, though they prove impotent in the face of Christianity. *Titus* is the product of a culture that refuses to classify its revered icons as idols. While sailing to Ireland from Brittany—the natural route for someone who regarded himself as the new St Patrick[84]—Rinuccini, chased by a Protestant privateer, threw holy water and a picture of St Nicholas into the sea for protection.[85] It worked; he escaped the pirates.

The 1644 summary shows that *Titus* was diversified by three interludes, designed, it seems, to stage low-life versions of the expropriation that in the main plot deprives the protagonist of his estates. A country clown, hearing that an edict would be issued against Christians—like those against the Catholics of Ireland—attempts to rob a passer-by. Soldiers try to pick a doctor's pocket and to force a boy to show them where his mother's purse is hidden. The core of the play, however, is more spiritually engaged. Using threats, deceptions, and torture (another feature of the play that would resonate for Irish Catholics),[86] the King of Bungo seeks to coerce Titus to abandon his religion—so theatrically, at one point, that this *Titus* might be *Titus Andronicus*, or at least *The Dutchesse of Malfy*:

> The King of *Bungo* menaceth death to *Titus* his youngest sonne, if the father abjure not his faith. ... *Martina* the daughter, biddeth adieu, with mother and brother, assuring them of her constancy. ... Tidings are brought to *Titus* of his daughters execution, *Martina* the mother of *Simon* is summoned. ... By the King both are sollicited to desert their faith, *Simon* scourged. ... *Titus* is sent for by the King, in whose view supposed heads of wife and children are produced. ... They are lead from prison before him and a superficiall command given to kill them in his presence, if he persists in his constant resolution. ... The King amazed at this constancie dismisseth them, freedome of Religion granted with their lives and estates.

The king's amazement was surely infectious. *Titus* gave the young scholars who performed it plenty of opportunity to elicit the *admiratio* which neoclassical commentators prized in drama. For the audience in Kilkenny, the protagonist would have been more exemplary than representative in his endurance. By 1644, Irish Catholics, despite discrimination, torture, and war, had not yet suffered as much as their co-religionists in Japan. If one asks the question, however, to what is Titus constant?, the answer the summary gives back has a recognizably Irish accent. For although the play's representation of St Francis Xavier, Faith and Fortitude, not to mention the church both militant and triumphant, connects it with the ethos of the Counter-Reformation,[87] a full-blown post-Tridentine agenda is avoided. The main action deals with a hard-pressed, underground, domestic variety of Catholicism, closer to an Irish survivalist tradition of covert, homely, even (as Rinuccini would see it) slovenly worship—mass celebrated on the dinner table, and so on[88]—than the splendours of a continental-style, state-sponsored Catholicism. *Titus* does not present the church as an institution that transmits grace through the sacraments. There is nothing, anywhere in the summary, about catechesis, the parish system, even the role of priests, yet all these were pillars of the Counter-Reformation in Ireland.

In the absence of a full text, one should avoid speculatively exaggerating differences between the framing scenes and the ethos of the Titus narrative. After a century of stage and screen naturalism, we are likely to underestimate the impact for early audiences of personification allegory (Faith, Fortitude, and the rest) and their capacity to translate what is personified across into Titus's experience. The play should not be taken as a drama about individual suffering superficially ornamented with Tridentine pageantry. Historically, too, it should be remembered that, in Kilkenny, as in other Irish cities, the Counter-Reformation church (locally advanced by Bishop David Rothe) had in practice been sustained by priests accommodated in the houses of Catholic merchants and gentry, who celebrated mass in homely settings but made clear their attachment to Rome and the international church. Yet Titus's mode of fidelity does connect with the long-tested, even indurated belief, pre-dating Trent and reinforced by persecution in Ireland, that Catholicism flourishes in kin-based, custom-led communities, where priests (who might be relatives) distribute the eucharist domestically and eschew public ceremony. It upholds a practice of religion which meshes with the habitus of the Irish family, in its richly interconnected, even rather bigamous, localism.[89]

This version of the old faith was tenacious and it would prove organizationally resilient under the heel of the Cromwellians and the eighteenth-century penal laws.[90] As Rinuccini recognized, however, it was also politically convenient for the elite, especially the Old English gentry, because by pressing only for toleration of discreet Catholic worship it was less threatening to Charles I (with his need to placate British Protestants) than was the clerical party's insistence on full public recognition. That such light demands are represented even while *Titus* encourages audiences to think of Charles I as a pagan tyrant is not the product of Jesuitical sophistry but a showing through of interests that would become explicit in the collapse of the Confederation so warily guarded against by the construction of *Cola's Furie*. The idea of Titus' estates being returned by the crown—a motif not found in *A Briefe Relation*—reflects an Old-English willingness to trust even a heretic King of England to give Irish Catholics back their own, as contrasted with a clerical-party desire to take property back from the planters by main force. But it also evades an issue that would bedevil the imminent peace mission of the Earl of Glamorgan: the question of where reinstatement should stop. For the clerical party argued that, as part of any peace settlement, estates taken from Rome during the Henrician Reformation in Ireland which had found their way into the pockets of the Old-English gentry should be returned to the church.[91] Consciously or not, by focussing on a form of reinstatement that all could agree on, *Titus* preserved Catholic unity while anticipating how the majority of Jesuits would side with the royalist-leaning Supreme Council of the Confederation when Rinuccini split the Catholics by his uncompromising demands in 1648.[92]

So we are back with the clutch of issues inaccurately known as the British problem. The insularity of Ireland that is accented even by Davenport, who followed Wentworth in wanting the country to be economically self-sufficient, that is celebrated crypto-nationally in *St Patrick*,[93] and that emerges more assertively in *Landgartha* and *Cola's Furie*, is plainly a feature of *Titus*. From one perspective it has unity of place; all its actions happen in Ireland/Japan. From another, if Titus is Irish and the King of Bungo is Charles I, then two islands, and three kingdoms, must be involved.[94] This makes sense of the fact that, on the face of it, Titus is an implausible Irishman because he is surrounded by a population of pagans, not by fellow-Catholics.[95] At this date, some Irish Catholics were oppressed by Protestants in their own communities, especially in such cities as Dublin and Cork, where Jesuits went undercover. That is unlikely, however, to have been a pressing concern for the audience of the play gathered in Kilkenny. They felt beleaguered for reasons that would be borne out just a few years later when Cromwell invaded Ireland. Like *Landgartha, Titus* assumes the machinations of English and Scottish puritanism, and feels the threat closing in. Even this most insular-global play, which, looking beyond the archipelago, engaged with the claims of Rome and the missionary reach of the Counter-Reformation, was unable to break free of the forces that tied the Stuart kingdoms into an unholy knot.

6

God in Wales: Morgan Llwyd, Henry Vaughan, Katherine Philips

K atherine Philips' *Poems* (1664) opens with a set of couplets 'Upon the Double Murther of K. Charles I in Answer to a Libellous Copy of Rimes Made by Vavasor Powell'.[1] Powell was one of a group of Welsh puritans—including Walter Cradock, William Erbery, and the bilingual poet Morgan Llwyd—who, during the 1640s and 1650s, evangelized their native land, and who were encouraged, by the turbulence of their mission, to commit to extreme beliefs. The activities of these men have rightly been seen as both rousing to mystical exaltation and scarring with outbursts of contempt the rapt, devotional poetry that Vaughan wrote in Brecknockshire (where Powell was particularly active),[2] but I want to argue in this chapter that they also stimulated the more temperately royalist Philips into advanced religious thought. Given that seventeenth-century manuscript collections of her work put poems about friendship, rather than affairs of state, first,[3] it is appropriate that she should have been retrieved from relative obscurity in the last couple of decades as a poet of female (even lesbian) amity. But her contemporaries made much of her piety, and what is most striking, though now neglected, is the reasoned power of her religious verse.

The indifference of modern criticism to Philips's theological adventurousness is symptomatic of a larger blindness to the simple, striking fact, which I also want to highlight, that, during the middle decades of the century, when Milton was writing prose, it was Wales, among the countries of the archipelago, that produced the most lastingly valuable body of religious verse. If the crucial generative factor was the impact of millenarian puritanism[4] on a dominion in which Anglicanism was tenacious, and Catholicism still entrenched ('The Devill', as Cradock put it, 'hath a *great* Kingdome in *Wales*'),[5] the poetry also shows how interpenetrating ethnicities could be culturally productive even when dissonant. Certainly, Philips's response to Powell's 'Libellous … Rimes' would not have been so vigorous had he and his followers not been influential in West Wales. The poet had migrated from London to this relatively underdeveloped, strongly Welsh-speaking region in about 1646, and she settled there in 1649, the year of Charles I's execution, by marrying the Cardiganshire Colonel, James Philips. It was the position of her husband, as a moderate Cromwellian associate of the radical Powell, that encouraged her to exploit a difference between the two men by writing 'Upon the Double Mur-ther'—a manoeuvre which was hazardous at the time but which after the Restoration usefully testified to long-standing loyalty to the Stuarts in the Philips household.

The poem by Vavasor Powell that Philips answered[6] complains that Charles Stuart systematically broke the Ten Commandments. Married to an idolatrous Catholic, the late king swore, abused the sabbath, and so forth. 'Of all Kings I am for Christ alone', Powell concludes: 'For he is King to us though Charles be gone.' With its echo of the Fifth Monarchists' slogan 'No King but Jesus', this places Powell among those who believed that the fourth great empire of the ancient world—that of Rome, usurped by the papacy—was coming to an end, and that Christ's thousand-year rule of the saints on earth (promised by the Book of Revelation) would soon begin. 'Christ will be King', Philips orthodoxly agrees, but she does not say when, never mind how, He will claim his throne; and anyway,

> I ne're understood
> His Subjects built his Kingdom up with bloud,
> Except their own; or that he would dispence
> With his commands, though for his own defence.
> Oh! to what height of horrour are they come
> Who dare pull down a Crown, tear up a Tomb!

The regicides were murderers unwilling to be martyrs, and the violent, armed Fifth Monarchists follow them, rather than Charles I, in despising such commandments as 'Thou shalt not kill'.[7] In a turn which is typical of Philips, who has such a charged sense of language not least because it circulates the 'honour' that she prizes as a mark of virtue, she accuses the

militants of killing the king twice over by libelling the man they have
murdered.

Since historians agree that the civil wars were in large measure fought
over religion, Wales might appear, in this respect, merely a subset of the
general picture. Yet the acerbity of the conflict between radical puritanism
and the established church in the dominion was exacerbated by cultural
and linguistic factors. When Powell fled from Brecknockshire, just before
the outbreak of the civil wars, after being charged with 'drawing away
the Kings Subjects' and 'speaking against the Book of Common-Prayer',
he took himself to London, and developed there a powerbase which he
preserved for the rest of his career.[8] Elegists would emphasize his Welshness,
but they also cried '*England* with Sackcloth gird thy self'.[9] This double
orientation was typical. Though Welsh preachers and soldiers had a role
in driving reform across all the three kingdoms (from Fifth Monarchist
MPs in London to Colonel John Jones in Ireland), puritanism moved
into Wales through the medium of English from the border counties and
trading communities in Glamorganshire and Pembrokeshire. It was the
triumph of parliamentary arms in England (against such Welsh royalist
soldiers as Henry Vaughan)[10] that created an opening for puritanism west of
the Severn; and, when it burst into the dominion, it upset the indigenous
power structure. The Welsh gentry, long dominated by the English, but
accommodated after 1536-43 to the Tudor state and its religion (above,
pp. 42-3), were now subjected to a less acceptable Reformation by
interloping social inferiors.

The resulting ethnic takeover triggered the sort of hostility that finds
expression in Vaughan's 'To his Retired Friend, an Invitation to Brecknock'
(*c*.1645?)—a sweeping attack on the Anglo-puritan regime that came to
dominate the town:

> Abominable face of things! here's noise
> Of bang'd Mortars, blew Aprons, and Boyes,
> Pigs, Dogs, and Drums, with the hoarse hellish notes
> Of politickly-deafe Usurers throats,
> With new fine *Worships*, and the old cast *teame*
> Of Justices vext with the *Cough*, and *flegme*.
> Midst these the *Crosse* looks sad, and in the *Shire-*
> *Hall furs* of an old *Saxon Fox* appear,
> With brotherly Ruffs and Beards, and a strange sight
> Of high Monumentall Hats t'ane at the fight

> Of *Eighty eight*; while ev'ry *Burgesse* foots
> The mortall *Pavement* in eternall boots.[11]

Vaughan's satire is so heated that it overrides the measure of his couplets (most extravagantly at '*Shire-/Hall*'). There might be personal animus against a particular Saxon fox, the editors tell us—one Eltonhead, a Lancashire man, who replaced the poet's employer, Sir Marmaduke Lloyd, as Chief Justice of the Brecon Circuit. But Vaughan comprehensively despises the town's upstart governors, with their vulgar ethos of industry, their unscrupulous money-making, and their ruffs, beards, hats, and boots as datedly Protestant-patriotic as the Armada victory of 1588. Meanwhile the market cross, sign of ancient Catholic values, stands bereft.

The sense of grievance among royalists was intensified when the Act for the Propagation of the Gospel in Wales was passed by the Rump Parliament in 1650.[12] Though a few ministers of the established church had been turned out of their livings from 1646, it was as a result of this Act that large numbers were dispossessed (including Vaughan's twin brother, Thomas, who lost the family parish, Llansantffraed). The Propagation has been called 'the nearest thing Wales ever acquired to Home Rule', because it treated the dominion separately and as a whole,[13] but the shortage of Welshmen to enforce the Act makes the analogy implausible. For Alexander Griffith, the ousted North-Wales cleric who wrote *Mercurius Cambro-Britannicus* (1652), so many Saxon foxes were coming into Wales that the native gentry were 'ready to sell the remnant of their estates to come and inhabit in *England*'.[14]

As 'To his Retired Friend...' and *Mercurius* demonstrate, resistance, politically frustrated, took a literary form. The leading target of the royalists, as in Philips's refutation of Powell, was puritan millenarianism. Griffith's *Strena Vavasoriensis* (1654)—'a new year's gift for Vavasor'—thus reproduces a hymn by Powell that opens with a Fifth Monarchist address, '*To* Christ *our* King, *let us* praise *sing*', then parodies it stanza by stanza: 'The *Devil's* your *King*, his *praise* you sing...'.[15] Powell had told parliament that the Act for the Propagation would usher in the Second Coming by bringing down Babylon in Wales.[16] *Strena* ends with 'A True *Description* of Mr *Vavasor Powells*, and his *Itinerants Propagation* in *Wales*' that presents the puritan mission as itself the evil described in Revelation: Apollyon, a flaming Dragon, the bitter star called Wormwood.[17] Anglicans mocked the puritans for bringing the return of Christ into the mundane present.

Strena accused Powell of announcing in Llandetty (close to Vaughan's home parish) '*That Christ was already come in the flesh the second time*', and reported that one of his followers had farcically explained to the people '*That Christ Iesus was such another man as old* Rice Williams *of* Newport, one of the Commissioners for the *Propagation*, and that he had a *large grey beard*' (6).

Satire also battened on those reliable themes: money and sex. With the propagators entitled to use the tithes of ejected ministers for Godly purposes, the charge of misappropriation was inevitable. In the preface to *Mercurius Cambro-Britannicus*, one P. P. wrote:

> These *Saints* have a certain pious *Wawle* in the *Pulpit*, but out of it they are all *Clutch* and *Claw*; ... he who had scarce *Frize* for his *breech*, struts it now in *Holy lace* and *Scarlet*. ... I have no more to trouble thee withall at present, unlesse thou art a *Britan*, if so, make true *Use* and *Application* of the two lines under-written,
>
> > Da iw'r Kelwydd trâ i Koylîr
> > Pen elir ym-hell gwell iw'r Gwîr.   (2–3)

Swaggering about in luxurious lace—if that is what they did—the ill-bred Saints who had ousted gentlemen clerics attracted the charge of lubricity. *A Welsh Narrative* said that Powell had 'adulterers and buggerers' in his entourage,[18] while *Strena* claimed he had excused 'a *Sister*, that had *slipped*' by 'call[ing] God to witnesse, He *never saw a Saint Occupie or F——a Saint*, which he explained thus in the Welch tongue, *Yr ywf yn Galow Duw yn dîst, ni welais i yr'ioed Sainct yn myned ar Sainctes*'.[19]

The use of Welsh is striking. Though their primary audience was anglophone, both P. P. and Griffith take sly advantage of bilingualism. If this shows the importance of winning support in England (some of it Welsh-speaking—there was a substantial community in London), it also points to a linguistically complex situation within Wales. Powell's bilingualism enabled him to translate Godly books out of English 'for my dear and soule-hungring Countrey-men',[20] but it also weakened a charge that was gleefully levelled by Anglicans and defensively fought off by Welsh puritans,[21] that a lack of English among the Saints was evidence of low birth and poor education. Uncertainty among puritans as to whether Welsh was

---

Da iw'r Kelwydd trâ i Koylîr ... Gwîr. The lie is good while it is believed; when one goes further [literally 'far'] the truth is better. (tr. Oliver Padel)

a dignified language (the tongue of primitive British Christianity) or a sign of backwardness and enemy to Godliness was matched by opportunism among their critics. Henry Nicchols, a minister in South Wales, attacked William Erbery for not knowing Welsh—though this was a mercy to poor Wales—yet also for demeaning his tract *The Welsh Curate* (1652) by using 'Welsh' in the title.[22]

The question of cultural confidence is illuminated by a stranger claim made by Erbery and satirized by Nicchols: the notion that the Welsh were 'descended from the *Iews*'.[23] As the Propagation made inroads, the Saints began to think that the Second Coming might be imminent because the Welsh were a chosen people, seventeenth-century Israelites,[24] whose conversion resembled that of the Jews in foreshadowing (according to scripture) Christ's thousand-year rule on earth. Erbery announced that St Paul was 'a *Welshman born*; for *Tarsus* was a Sea Towne, so is *Cardiffe in Wales*'. He had the universalizing message of the Bible to back this up ('If *Paul was all*, why not a *Welshman?*'), but it was driven by a patriotism which unravels even his attempt to present his theory as even-handed. 'Why *Paul* should be call'd a Welshman', he insists, 'is no disparagement to the English, though the Welsh be the better Gentlemen, being pure *Britaines*, but the English are of kin to the Dutch, that dull and muddy people, designed to destruction or subjection, as *Esau* was to his younger brother.'[25]

Erbery saw England as the fount of liberty, but Wales as the country where freedom would be realized and the chosen saved. Citing the Old Testament he proves that a redeeming whirlwind will come out of the north because 'these Northern Isles were the first that acknowledged Christ; here the first King and Kingdom was.'[26] This invokes the legend—embraced by Protestants of every stripe, but particularly popular among the Welsh, who were proud of their descent from the ancient British—that Christianity came early to Britain, brought by Joseph of Arimathea (above, pp. 121–2); but Erbery gives the legend a twist by saying that, 'as Christ, so Antichrist first appeared with power in *Wales*: for when Kings and Kingdoms became Christian, then Antichrist began to be great.'[27] Within a couple of centuries after Christ, Wales—his synecdoche for Britain—had turned into Babylon. As then, so now: the revolution appears secure, yet the spread of Presbyterianism and the wicked acceptance of tithes by puritan ministers makes Wales a haven of Antichrist and prime site for a Second Coming. The key to this chiliastic geography is once again provided by scripture, this time Psalm 48, which places '*Mount Sion on the sides of the North*'. '*England* is part of the Northern British Isle', Erbery concedes, 'but Wales is the *sides of the North*, being just the wing of great *Britain*... where will be the City of the great King.'

★   ★   ★

Morgan Llwyd's bilingualism carried him more profoundly than Erbery into Anglo-Welsh entanglements. On the one hand, he was, in the words of a contemporary, 'the deepest truest Welsh-man and the most absolute British orator [i.e. preacher in Welsh], perhaps that ever was in the Ministerial Function'.[28] His *Llyfr y tri aderyn* (1653) is not just—even when read in translation[29]—a remarkable account of the religious choices that afflicted interregnum Britain, it is also, by all accounts, a landmark in the development of Welsh prose. On the other hand, his English was richly idiomatic enough to absorb the influence of Welsh without sounding like Fluellen. In the early modern period, English influence typically fed into the vocabulary and prosody of Welsh poetry. In Llwyd, Welsh means and matter permeate a body of anglophone verse that is grounded in English tradition.

This is nowhere clearer than in his millenarian sequence '1648'. Though the bulk of this magnificent cycle is written in common metre (the rhythm of popular ballads, yet also of Sternhold and Hopkins's Psalms), it starts with lines which are neither metrically nor formally quite idiomatic in English but which recall Llwyd's use elsewhere (in both languages) of the four-line, single-stanza folk poem known as *penillion*:

> A spring in spring
> Poore birds now sing
> Our head is high
> Our sumer nigh.[30]

As often in *penillion*, lines simple in language are dense with implication. The immediate referent of 'A spring' (the season) does not deaden the metaphorical ('spring' as uplift) because of its indefinite article. Real birds cannot be 'Poore', so who are the creatures that sing? Both impoverished and poor in spirit (Matthew 5: 3),[31] the Welsh are now in good heart, because their gathered churches can rise—led not by a pope or bishop but by the plural-singular 'Our head'. Do the birds sing the last two lines of the lyric, or do these lines set out the conditions which inspire song? The ambiguity is subtly effective, as a change in the possibilities of belief is inextricable from acts of witness.

Summer may be in prospect, but it is not the spiritual zenith. The sequence works on a longer cycle of winter (retrospective), spring (present hope), summer (rule of Christ on earth) and harvest (the Last Judgement). It insists on a British context,[32] but also a European one. Opening his historical account with 'The Winter', Llwyd surveys a general chaos:

> A thousand dayes great Beelzebub and Pope his son and foole
> made christendome their slaughterhouse, the church their dancing shcoole
>
> And Hell breaks loose, the smoke comes up, the hounds gods people trace
> The sons of God whom Jesus bought, they hang before his face.
>
> Their puffs blew downe the christian trees, five thousand every day.
> They crye. Their blood upon us bee. Away with them Away.
>
> Brave Hug[ino]ts, stiffe Mordecais, stout lollards you stood fast
> a glana iw'r gelynen wyrdd that scornd the Romish blast   (19–20)

The dancing school and the slaughterhouse evoke the Laudian-papistical church of the 1630s, the Thirty Years War on the continent, and the civil wars in Britain. The martyrs include the Huguenots persecuted by Louis XIV, the stiff-necked believers who, like Mordecai in the Book of Esther, resisted the Hamans of, presumably, the Caroline church, and the 'stout Lollards' who are the English proto-Protestants. The shifts of tone are extraordinary, as Llwyd moves from scriptural echo to nursery-rhyme informality ('Their puffs blew downe the christian trees'), and, at a climactic moment, slips between tongues[33] and most likely quotes a *penillion*[34] to praise the Welsh Saints for their evergreen faith: '[and purest is the green holly tree] that scorned the Romish blast'.

'Spring' and 'Summer' focus on the triumph of common believers, and, with prosaic visionary assurance, on the Second Coming:

> fifty goes big, or fifty sixe
> or sixty five some say
> But within mans age, hope to see
> all old things flung away.   ('The Spring', 22)

The lines have been derided for misplaced confidence, but in the tempestuous late 1640s, when everything seemed possible, they must have lifted the spirits of the oppressed. For all their literalness, they do not pin down the return of Christ: Llywd's indeterminacy, which anticipates his later, mystical internalization of the millenarian process,[35] shows that calendrical numbers matter much less than 'hope'. Yet how, he wonders, can Christ be looked for when there are so many quarrels among the Saints? Like Milton in *Areopagitica*, Llwyd is confident at this stage that truth will survive the blasts of error. In any case, God will guide the elect, whatever ordeals they are put through, and song is the best response:

> Sing on a brittle sea of glasse
> Sing in a furne of fire
> In flames wee leap for joy and find
> a cave a singing quire.   ('The Summer', 24)

Though Llwyd's perspective is broad he never loses sight of Wales. In 'The Summer' a list of troubled nations spirals in from the continent through Ireland, Scotland, and Albion to the beautiful younger sister:[36]

> O Wales, poore Rachel, thou shalt beare
> sad Hannah now rejoyce
> The last is first, the summer comes
> to heare the turtles voice.   (28)

Wales is an unvalued place, a poor place, which now, in the last days, will be made first. Scriptural allusions invoke the Second Coming: 'The last is first' echoes the New Testament on the Last Judgement,[37] 'the turtles voice' the Song of Solomon—a major resource for Llwyd, as for Vaughan and other contemporaries, in linking lyric with apocalyptic.[38] Yet the self-consciously afflicted Saints, last of the last who will soon be first, are not above criticism. If unionist-minded Presbyterians, who worshipped at the shrine of the Solemn League and Covenant, and sought to impose by means of it restrictive doctrines and church government on their British brethren, were as 'bitter' as their name suggests ('The letter of our covenaunt— | Bitterians Idolize'), the Godly associated with Llwyd himself can also be judgemental and 'sowre'. The spirit of Christian soldiery and harmony should prevail: 'Bee listed in some regiment | and go not still astray' (29).

The final section of '1648' is so beautifully strange and various that I want to quote it whole. It is as though *Piers Plowman*, Blake, Welsh nature poetry, and at moments Emily Dickinson (whose own verse grew out of Protestant hymns) come together, in writing freed up by the turmoil and heterodoxy of the war years. Events of profound significance lie in the future, Llwyd announces, but they are concealed from man who has no affinity with depth because he is thin all round, a mere husk. So help us, Lord, and unlock the cabinets of scripture, especially the prophetic passages; otherwise no one can be sure what you have in mind for us. ... Llwyd says it much more powerfully.

The Harvest

A depth. A depth in things to come!
man is a shallow shell.
The scripture closetts lord unlocke,
else, none thy mind can tell.

Christ's coming, and end of the world
are two distinctive times
This busy harvest makes short worke
with doctrines, tares and crimes.

The field is large, the barne at hand
the reapers quicke and wise
The stubble flames, and sinfull soules
lye downe and never rise.

In summer Christ is all in all
as Pope in winter was.
But after harvest God is all
Then, never turne our glasse.

In Gog and Magog hell shall spew
that last and filthy fome
and before winter comes againe
wee shall bee all at home.

No eye hath seene, no eare hath heard
no man can well conceave
How God will angells Christ and saincts
into himselfe receave.

Now I have given a sparing hint
for wise men to enlarge
lett fooles sleepe on, and Atheists laugh
yee saincts, Advance and charge.

I tyre thee friend, I make an end
But see thou bend thy line

> and heart to sing in this thy spring
> of Christ thy king and mine.   (30–1)

All is hardly clear even after the opening stanza, though the obscurity can be tempered by reading Revelation, where Gog, Magog, and the reapers are found (20: 14). Llwyd's appetite for the cryptic ('man is a shallow shell') may have been fostered by his reading in Hermeticism and Jacob Boehme but it is inextricable from the bilingualism of a mission which had to force its way on the ground through incomprehension and inexpressibility. The experience of spreading the Word Llwyd generalized into the perception that 'neither do the Welsh, any more than others, understand themselves, nor is there scarcely a person who understands all his own words to his neighbour, much less what the heart has to tell day and night'.[39] The paradoxes of such opacity were enabling for Llwyd as a poet, which is why, in '1648', he moves from St Paul on obscurity ('No eye hath seene ... ')[40] into the deep balladry of 'I tyre thee friend, I make an end'. By this ending point of a poem about eschatological endings, to 'make an end' cannot simply be a turn of phrase, just as the instruction to shape a line of song to usher in the spring is no formulaic valediction but a mystical incitement to bring about the return of Christ through utterance.

★   ★   ★

Where '1648' invokes the seasons to make millenarian claims, Vaughan employs them, in his prose work *The Mount of Olives* (1652), to more traditional *contemptus mundi* effect. An extract from Fig. 9:

> The *Spring* comes constantly once a yeere, and *flowers*, when the *frosts* are past, keep *house* no longer under *ground*, but feel the *Sun*, and come *abroad*. The *leaves* come again to *whisper* over our heads, and are as *green* and as *gay* as ever, *but man dieth and wasteth away, yea man giveth up the ghost, and where is he?* In these sad contemplations was the *Brittish Bard*, when he broke out into this Eloquent complaint
>
> > Mis mawrddh [marw] rhyddhig Adar,
> > Pob peth y ddhaw trwr ddhayar,
> > Ond y marw maur [ei] garchar.
> >
> > *In March birds couple, a new birth*
> > *Of herbs and flowers breaks through the earth,*
> > *But in the grave none stirs his head;*
> > *Long is th' Impris'ment of the dead.*[41]

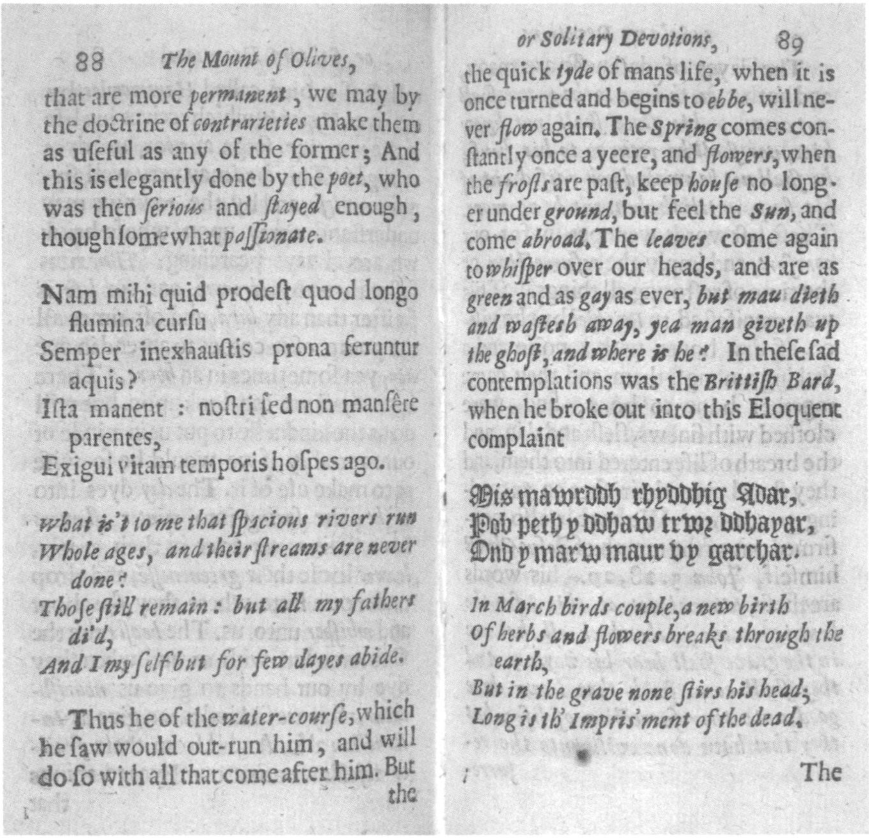

88   *The Mount of Olives,*

that are more *permanent*, we may by the doctrine of *contrarieties* make them as useful as any of the former; And this is elegantly done by the *poet*, who was then *serious* and *stayed* enough, though somewhat *passionate*.

Nam mihi quid prodest quod longo
    flumina cursu
Semper inexhaustis prona feruntur
    aquis?
Ista manent : nostri sed non mansêre
    parentes,
Exigui vitam temporis hospes ago.

*what is't to me that spacious rivers run
Whole ages, and their streams are never
    done?
Those still remain: but all my fathers
    di'd,
And I my self but for few dayes abide.*

Thus he of the *water-course*, which he saw would out-run him, and will do so with all that come after him. But the

or Solitary Devotions,   89

the quick *tyde* of mans life, when it is once turned and begins to *ebbe*, will never *flow* again. The *Spring* comes constantly once a yeere, and *flowers*, when the *frosts* are past, keep *house* no longer under *ground*, but feel the *Sun*, and come *abroad*. The *leaves* come again to *whisper* over our heads, and are as *green* and as *gay* as ever, *but man dieth and wasteth away, yea man giveth up the ghost, and where is he?* In these sad contemplations was the *Brittish Bard*, when he broke out into this Eloquent complaint

𝕯𝖎𝖘 𝖒𝖆𝖜𝖗𝖉𝖉𝖍 𝖗𝖍𝖞𝖉𝖉𝖍𝖎𝖌 𝕬𝖔𝖆𝖗,
𝕻𝖔𝖍 𝖕𝖊𝖙𝖍 𝖞 𝖉𝖉𝖍𝖆𝖜 𝖙𝖗𝖜𝖗 𝖉𝖉𝖍𝖆𝖞𝖆𝖗,
𝕺𝖓𝖉 𝖞 𝖒𝖆𝖗𝖜 𝖒𝖆𝖚𝖗 𝖇𝖞 𝖌𝖆𝖗𝖙𝖍𝖆𝖗.

*In March birds couple, a new birth
Of herbs and flowers breaks through the
    earth,
But in the grave none stirs his head,
Long is th' Impris'ment of the dead.*

The

Fig. 9. The languages of Henry Vaughan, Silurist and British Bard: Latin, English, Welsh. From *The Mount of Olives: Or, Solitary Devotions* (London, 1652).

It has been claimed by Roland Mathias, the poet and deep student of Anglo-Welsh culture, that Vaughan 'never translated from the Welsh', and that this helps prove him an Englishman at heart. Evidently the assertion is false and the conclusion partial.[42] The knowingness of Vaughan's reference to 'the *Brittish Bard*' (i.e. Aneirin),[43] the accuracy of his rendition,[44] and the signs that he knows the whole eight-line poem from which he quotes,[45] show him to be an assured translator of the language he spoke from childhood.[46]

Progress can be made by recognizing that Mathias's conception of Anglo-Welshness has been conditioned by modern nationalism, and that, in seventeenth-century Wales, identity and affiliation were localized. This is why Vaughan describes himself on title pages as 'Silurist'. The Silures, a tribe of ancient Britons whose lands ran into areas contained by early modern Brycheiniog/Brecknockshire,[47] attracted him because of the valour with which they resisted the Romans and then the Saxons—forerunners of the puritans who also encroached from the east. Vaughan spoke Welsh and English as the languages of a district that he scarcely left during a long lifetime. Though he could declare 'CAMBRIA *me genuit*' ('Wales gave me birth'), his knowledge of the country was patchy, especially along the north-south axis which remains to this day relatively hard to travel. When his cousin John Aubrey asked him about notable gentlemen in North Wales, Vaughan had to confess that he and his neighbours were ignorant of them.[48] Nor did his religion encourage him to develop an apprehension of the Welsh people as a whole, as Erbery and Llwyd did in seeing them as the new Israelites. For puritans the church was the manifestation of a living Godly community, an entity with some relation to the inclusiveness of a nation, but for Vaughan it was an 'ancient way' of custom and hierarchy that reached back to the Old Testament patriarchs.[49]

What did Vaughan understand by a '*Brittish Bard*'? In the correspondence with Aubrey, he describes 'the antient Bards' as 'a very learned societie' who communicated their knowledge by tradition:

> As to the later Bards, who were no such men, butt had a societie & some rules & orders among themselves: & several sorts of measures & a kind of Lyric poetrie: wch are all sett down exactly In the learned John David Rhees, or Rhesus hys welch, or British grammer: you shall have there (in the later end of his book) a most curious Account of them. This vein of poetrie they called Awen, which in their language signifies as much as Raptus, or a poetic furor; & (in truth) as many of them as I have conversed with are (as I may say) gifted or inspired with it.[50]

Vaughan apparently had a reliable source in front of him; he had taken a copy of Rees's grammar from the library of Jesus College, Oxford decades earlier, when an undergraduate, and failed to return it.[51] But his authority is not simply that of the scholar: as a child he had absorbed 'The visions of our black, but brightest Bard', Merlin;[52] and when he writes to Aubrey of raptures and fury, he says that all the bards he knows ('as many' implies at least a few) are inspired. The encomiast N. W., probably himself a Welshman, was responding to something when he said of Vaughan's *Thalia Rediviva* (1678), 'Where Reverend Bards of old have sate | And sung the pleasant enterludes of Fate, | Thou takest the hereditary shade',[53] for it is clear from *The Mount of Olives* that Vaughan would be glad to think of himself as belonging to an 'hereditary' line that ran from Aneirin to certain Welsh–British contemporaries.

Vaughan's sense of a live connection between British bards ancient and modern[54] registers potently a few pages later in *The Mount of Olives* when George Herbert (a poet of Anglo-Welsh stock) and Aneirin participate in the same discourse of fragility, a discourse that connects British Anglican thought with medieval Catholicism as it invokes the seasons to resist rather than to forward the millenarian impulse:

> We have had many blessed Patterns of a holy life in the *Brittish Church*, though now trodden under foot, and branded with the title of *Antichristian*. I shall propose but one to you, the most obedient *Son* that ever his *Mother* had, and yet a most glorious true *Saint* and a *Seer*. Heark how like a *busie Bee* he *hymns* it to the *flowers*, while in a handful of *blossomes* gather'd by himself, he foresees his own *dissolution*. ...   (186)

This is Herbert in Vaughan's bardic image: a 'Seer' and, in a marginal note, the author of 'prophetick Poems' about the church,[55] a 'true *Saint*' not one of the puritan Saints with their predictions of an imminent Fifth Monarchy. After quoting Herbert's lyric 'Life' ('I made a Posie while the day ran by ... '), Vaughan reminds us how close it comes to replicating Aneirin on the seasons:

> As often therefore as thou seest the *full* and *ripe corne*, to succeed the *tender* and *flowery Spring*, the *Autumne* again to succeed the *Summer*, and the *cold* and *snowie Winter* to succeed the *Autumne*, say with thy self, *These seasons passe away, but will returne againe: but when I go, I shall returne no more.*   (187)

That Vaughan was a follower of Herbert is a commonplace of scholarship; that he did so as a British bard has not been noticed. Yet the evidence is clear from a lyric such as 'The Brittish Church' (composed shortly after Vaughan turned, in 1647, to Herbert). In Herbert's poem of the same title, the established church sits in a landscape which is a moral diagram, between the overdressed, Roman Catholic 'She on the hills', and the puritan 'She in the valley'.[56] In Vaughan the hills and mists, the fleeces and flocks, of Brecknockshire are drenched in scripture and British history:

> Ah! he is fled!
> And while these here their *mists*, and *shadows* hatch,
> My glorious head
> Doth on those hills of Mirrhe, and Incense watch.
> Haste, hast my dear,

The Souldiers here
Cast in their lots again,
That seamlesse coat
The Jews touch'd not,
These dare divide, and stain.

2.

O get thee wings!
Or if as yet (until these clouds depart,
And the day springs,)
Thou think'st it good to tarry where thou art,
Write in thy bookes
My ravish'd looks
Slain flock, and pillag'd fleeces,
And haste thee so
As a young Roe
Upon the mounts of spices.

*O Rosa Campi! O lilium Convallium! quomodò nunc facta es
pabulum Aprorum!*[57]

'Ah! he is fled!' is urgently unclear, like a cry heard in turmoil (the royalists
routed in battle?); Christ emerges as the primary referent, yet the rhyme
with 'head' adds an allusion to Charles I (head of the British church)
that is sharpened by the contrast with the Welsh puritans who 'here'
(in this corner of Brecknockshire, as well as in this mortal world) brood
over spiritual bad weather and obscurity. (Given the decapitation of the
king between the composition of the poem and its publication in 1650,
Vaughan's strong metonymy, detaching 'My glorious head' and setting it
on high as though already gone to heaven, to look down on the fate of the
church, makes him indeed a 'Seer' and his poem uncannily 'Prophetick'.)
This royal, sacred head—a cliché of Anglican loyalism—could hardly less
resemble the collective 'Our head is high' in Llwyd's 'Spring'. Meanwhile,
'seamlesse coat' brings out the latent pun in Herbert's title 'Church Rents
and Schisms'. Vavasor Powell and his followers were armed, and with their
Propagation were rending up the wealth of the church, worse even than
the soldiers who diced for Christ's cloak after the crucifixion.[58]

Walter Cradock celebrated the success of the puritan mission at this date
with a touch of homely ferocity: 'the *Gospel* is run over the *Mountaines*
between *Brecknockshire*, and *Monmouthshire*, as the fire in the *thatch*'.[59] The
words of Vaughan's church are equally alive to the harsh facts of life in

the homesteads of the border counties, where theft and pillage had been exacerbated by civil war ('My ravish'd looks | Slain flock, and pillag'd fleeces'). The church urges Christ to return, or at least to keep a record of the injuries done to the faithful against the Day of Judgement; yet, resembling some of Llwyd's poetry in this, Vaughan's apocalypticism is softened by the sensuality of the Song of Solomon—a text evoked by the rose and lily of the Latin motto, the bounding roe, and those hills of myrrh and mounts of spice[60] which are visionary transformations of the border landscape described by Cradock. The effect is typical of Vaughan, whose manifesto-poem 'Religion' makes groves and fountains near the River Usk sites for encountering angels and Old Testament prophets.[61]

Vaughan's commitment to the subject of the last days was unusual among Anglican poets. Like the later Morgan Llwyd, he was encouraged to imagine the end by his despair about the present. There was for both men in the 1650s an element of compensation. Do not trouble your spirits about Cromwell becoming a tyrant, Llwyd tells the Saints, for Christ will very soon be the only king that matters.[62] 'O come! refine us with thy fire!', Vaughan cries in the final stanza of 'White Sunday', that fine, angry poem about the impact of the Welsh puritans. 'Refine us!', he repeats, as though indeed at a loss, 'we are at a loss'.[63] Significantly, however, Llwyd emphasizes the return of Christ, Vaughan the Last Judgement.[64] Even at his most Llwyd-like, in his common-metre paraphrase of Revelation, 'Day of Judgement', Vaughan blurs the scriptural evidence that, in the words of '1648', 'Christ's coming, and end of the world | are two distinctive times', for he will not encourage the thought that the Lord might return to Wales to govern the puritan Saints for a thousand years.

As instructive is the divergence between Llwyd's early, active millenari-anism and the troubled patience of Vaughan. In Llwyd the created world is an elemental bare platform on which the events of Revelation will be played out. Like other Welsh royalists, Vaughan was driven by defeat into a solitude where the intricate fullness of the natural world could ameliorate disempowerment.[65] In such poems as 'The Seed Growing Secretly' the vision of nature set out in *The Mount of Olives* returns; the self is again a 'seed'; but it now survives seasonal change by hiding in viridian darkness and awaiting a chance to flourish, if only in the last days:

> Then bless thy secret growth, nor catch
> At noise, but thrive unseen and dumb;

> Keep clean, bear fruit, earn life and watch,
> Till the white winged Reapers come![66]

The consoling power of an approaching apocalypse is caught up in the quiet intensity of this self-counsel. For a Welsh royalist in the early 1650s the only hope was to go underground politically, to be faithful, do good by stealth, and resist the blandishments which tempted others to work for the Commonwealth.[67] In this lovely poem, the theme of retirement fuses into that of spiritual vigilance. It is a nexus that one also finds, with a rather different outcome, in the poetry of Katherine Philips.

★ ★ ★

Her attack on Vavasor Powell (in the poem which opened this chapter) created a stir in Wales. An influential supporter of Powell—probably Jenkin Jones of Llandetty, a radical given authority under the Propagation, a neighbour and college contemporary of Vaughan's—read 'Upon the Double Murther' and circulated a dangerous reply.[68] Writing to her friend Anne Owen about this, Philips asserts 'the Privilege of a native Spark, | To shed a constant Splendour in the dark', and presents the condition of 'retreat' as a defence against dishonour; but she can hardly conceal the paradoxes that surround such open seclusion. Until her poems were published, apparently against her wishes, in 1664, manuscript circulation gave Philips some control over the disposition of her readership: we can track likely networks between London, West Wales, and, after a Restoration visit to Ireland, Dublin. The content of her poetry reflects this, especially its Cardiganshire base (elegies on the deaths of neighbours, letters and verse epistles to friends about being in Wales); but the connections were always permeable and subject to shifting alliances within Welsh politics.

The paradoxes of retirement mean that Philips's situatedness can be most salient when least overt, as in

> A Retir'd Friendship, To Ardelia
>
> Come, my *Ardelia*, to this Bower,
> Where kindly mingling Souls awhile
> Let's innocently spend an hour,
> And at all serious follies smile.
>
> 2.
> Here is no quarrelling for Crowns,
> Nor fear of changes in our Fate;

No trembling at the great ones frowns,
Nor any slavery of State.

3.
Here's no disguise nor treachery,
Nor any deep conceal'd design;
From Bloud and Plots this Place is free,
And calm as are those looks of thine.

4.
Here let us sit and bless our Stars,
Who did such happy quiet give,
As that remov'd from noise of Wars
In one anothers hearts we live.

5.
Why should we entertain a fear?
Love cares not how the World is turn'd:
If crouds of dangers should appear,
Yet Friendship can be unconcern'd. ...

An authoritative manuscript of this poem is dated 23 August 1651,[69] which places it in the wake of a royalist rebellion in Cardiganshire (Ceredigion to its Welsh speakers) which James Philips was appointed to help clear up.[70] So the text resists to the point of denial quarrels and plots which did not just crowd about Philips's bower but pushed into her domestic life and—given her royalist sympathies—quite possibly troubled her marriage.

This was not a rebellion of merely local significance. The Welsh Saints were in arms to defend a pan-British revolution; Cradocke, Powell, Llwyd and their followers had gone north with English roundheads to counter Charles II as he came south and west (in the hope of rousing Welsh support) with a largely Scottish army.[71] When he was defeated at Worcester, Philips wrote a poem of subdued regret.[72] So the unrest in Ceredigion was part of an archipelagic picture, yet 'A Retir'd Friendship' denies all this in order to construct a virtual retreat. Philips would be a lesser poet, certainly a less interesting one, if the process of occlusion were complete. When she suggests that fear is an emotion that we can 'entertain' or not at will, that 'Love' need not care about the state of the world, and that Friendship 'can' be indifferent to dangers (with what consequences she does not say), the propositions are wishful.

The paradoxes of retirement were intensified by the fact that bleak, impoverished Wales had not yet acquired the reputation for virtuous simplicity of life and mountainous sublimity that it would gain during the Romantic period.[73] When Daniel Kendrick praised Aphra Behn's works in 1688, he said that Philips's were, in comparison, 'uncouth, like her countrys soyle ... Mean as its Pesants, as its Mountains bare.'[74] Philips, the incomer from London, identified herself with West Wales even while she acknowledged its rudeness.[75] She writes of the region's 'obscurity' and of being 'in my Rocks confin'd'.[76] But she informs her supporter at court, Sir Charles Cotterell, that she is both ashamed of Cardiganshire and sees herself as *born* there (born as a writer?): 'born and bred in so rude and dark a Retreat'.[77] It is not the least of the paradoxes that the value of a dark retreat[78] depends on an awareness of its distance from the bright lights, and Philips's identification with Wales seems to have been heightened by her familiarity with London and Dublin. She became a Welsh poet through having an archipelagic sense of her situation.

How consciously, though, did Philips produce herself as Welsh, rather than an English poet in far-flung retirement? Was Cowley merely being gallant when he said in complimentary verses that her achievement had been prophesied by Merlin?[79] Why did Sir Edward Dering call her 'the wise & learned Druyde of Cardigan'. [80] That she was interested in Welsh Britishness and the Bards is clear from lines in her elegy on Sir Walter Lloyd of Llanfair Clydogau[81] and from her poem 'On the Welch Language'. It has been rightly said that the latter's 'equation of the "great remains" of the "Brittish Language" [the works of Aneirin and the like] with those of Greek and Latin literature is unexpected and possibly unique in a seventeenth century author with an English background'.[82] Even so, doubts may stir:

> And as the *Roman* and the *Grecian* State,
> The *British* fell, the spoil of Time and Fate.
> But though the Language hath the beauty lost,
> Yet she has still some great Remains to boast.
> For 'twas in that, the sacred Bards of old,
> In deathless Numbers did their thoughts unfold.
> In Groves, by Rivers, and on fertile Plains,
> They civiliz'd and taught the list'ning Swains;
> Whilst with high raptures, and as great success,
> Virtue they cloath'd in Musick's charming dress.[83]

It is unlikely that Philips had more than 'kitchen Welsh' (the smattering that the English wives of Welsh gentlemen acquired for dealing with servants), and her knowledge of ancient Brythonic was surely nil, making the claim that 'the Language hath the beauty lost' derivative if not merely, and uncharacteristically, clumsy.[84] Meanwhile 'deathless Numbers', 'high raptures', and 'charming dress' do more to make the Bards suitable for salon society than bring the grandeur of antiquity alive.

Like Vaughan celebrating Herbert, and writing to Aubrey about inspiration, Philips makes the Bards over into her own image. Associating her with Welsh ground, the same move lays claim to a rhapsodic register that was becoming fashionable among such English poets as the Pindaric Cowley (his poem in praise of Philips is an ode). Philips's identification with the Bards makes it the more telling that she should stress their sacredness, their mission to civilize and inculcate virtue. It was a role that Vaughan imputed to Philips even before she came to Wales, when he declared, in *Olor Iscanus* (1647), that her poems are devoted to 'thoughts as Innocent, and high | As *Angels* have, or *Saints* that dye'.[85] 'The Matchless Orinda' was congratulated on her virtue and piety even more fulsomely than was usual for women poets at the hands of their defenders. Cotterell declared in his Preface to the second, posthumous, 1667 edition of *Poems*, that, 'for her Vertues, they as much surpass'd those of *Sappho* as the Theological do the Moral, (wherein yet *Orinda* was not her inferiour) or as the fading immortality of an earthly Lawrel, which the justice of men cannot deny to her excellent Poetry, is transcended by that incorruptible and eternal Crown of Glory, wherewith the Mercy of God hath undoubtedly rewarded her more eminent Piety.'

The pressure of religious conflict in Wales threw up moral issues—to redeploy Cotterell's terms—that rapidly became theological for Philips. From such texts as 'Upon the Double Murther', in which questions of political morality are inextricable from doctrine, it is not far to 'The World', 'The Soul', and 'Death'—texts that draw *Poems* (1664) to a conclusion—in which Philips sets out latitudinarian and platonic beliefs that are as unorthodox in their way as was the mysticism of Morgan Llwyd. Like her correspondent Jeremy Taylor, then based in Carmarthenshire,[86] Philips was a tolerationist whose tolerance was severely tested by puritan claims to election. She believed in general salvation, and the only poem of hers that explicitly starts from the Bible (its title is '2 Cor. 5. 19.')—in part because scripture was the cause of so much dissension—is on that point anti-Calvinist. Philips manages to be at once charitable and minatory as she warns the likes of Vavasor Powell, 'Be silent then, ye narrow Souls, take heed | Lest you restrain the Mercy you will need.'[87] If the millenarianism of the Saints drove Philips even further than Vaughan away from apocalyptic discourse, she must have felt confirmed in this by her reading in the advanced religious work of the Great Tew circle;[88] and she responded both quickly and for the most part positively to the rational theology developed out of Descartes by Henry More and the Cambridge Platonists. The classical, slightly abstracted Orinda that greets the reader of the 1667 *Poems* (Fig. 10) is a visible projection of Philips's deliberated reaction to turbulence. Her cultivated, innovative moderation is more significant in its time, and owes far more to its place, than we are likely to assume if we view it through later, Augustan neo-classicism.

The prominence of reason in Philips's theology means that the devil gets to work by sowing ignorance and untruth. 'On Controversies in Religion' recounts how

<blockquote>
that great Enemy of Souls perceiv'd,
The notion of a Deity was weav'd
</blockquote>

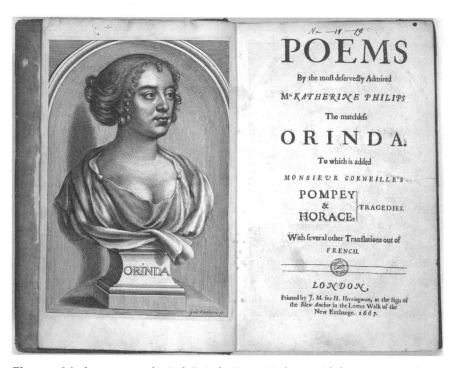

Fig. 10. Moderate, neo-classical Orinda. From Katherine Philips, *Poems*, 2nd edn (London, 1667).

> So closely in Man's Soul; to ruine that,
> He must at once the World depopulate.[89]

A reference to the religious ferment that drove the civil wars is unmistakable (the roots of her theology are again circumstantial). Platonic acclamations of Reason are often short on argument, and as the poem unfolds Philips does not entirely avoid an impression of easy transcendence. Yet the conflict she seeks to soar above makes itself felt in metaphor, and formidable syntactical control builds intellectual excitement. The final section of 'On Controversies', nearly thirty lines in more or less a single sentence, involvingly mimes the progress of the soul as it seeks to join the Divine—a quest that is, for Philips, a form of anti-apocalyptic: abstract and individualistic beside Llwyd's often devastatingly concrete account of the way God's will bears down on mankind, rationalistic beside Vaughan's commitment to the 'ancient way' of the church, yet equally a reaction against millenarian enthusiasm in Wales.

Her rationalism is peculiarly apparent in the address to the Divine that *Poems* (1667) calls 'A Prayer'. In manuscript, under the title 'God', and in the collection of 1664, where it becomes 'out of Mr. More's *C[u]p. Conf.*', this assured, philosophical text is headed by lines from Henry More's *Cupid's Conflict* (1646). Philips's prompt engagement with this early piece of Cambridge Platonism will seem surprising until one recalls that Thomas Vaughan, the poet's brother, was in contention with More from 1650. New ideas could spread rapidly from the universities into Wales.[90] There are old ideas in More too. His belief that man should not seek bodily pleasure but rise to higher things is older than Christianity, and Philips happily echoes it—though she characteristically ignores his apocalyptic claim that 'A three-branch'd Flame will soon sweep clean the stage | Of this old dirty drosse and all wex young.'[91] Addressing God as 'Eternal Reason', she represents all created excellence as a dim reflection of the Divine. The world is like the shadows produced by moonbeams in streams, yet God is innate in all human beings. Philips wants to break the clogs of sensuality and fancy so that she can hear the Divine speak within her. It all sounds admirably pure, yet hearkening to the spirit within curiously resembles the enthusiasm of her opponents, the Quakers and Ranters. Provoked by her unorthodoxy, one early reader rejected with misogynistic contempt the doctrine that 'those who yield to what their Souls convince, | Shall never need another Law.'[92]

The quest of the soul to fuse with the Divine might seem to have no specific connection with the site of Philips's retirement. Yet the epigraph she takes from More comes from a passage about the poetic career. Concerned with honour and libel, as in her reply to Vavasor Powell, but also with the difference between (in Cotterell's terms) an earthly laurel and a heavenly crown, Philips quotes: 'Thrice happy he whose name is writ above, | And doeth good though gaining infamie' (8). Divided about fame, because it conflicts with the ethos of retirement, she does not quote the lines in which More says that (feminine-sounding) authors who 'by nice needle-work ... seek a name' are in 'the retinue of proud Lucifer' (8–9). Her ambivalence around this topic was further roused when *Poems* (1664) appeared without her approval. In a letter to Cotterell she wrote, 'But is there no retreat from the malice of this World? I thought a Rock and a Mountain might have hidden me, and that it had been free for all to spend their Solitude in what *Resveries* [sic] they please, and that our Rivers (though they are babbling) would not have betray'd the follies of impertinent thoughts upon their Banks.'[93] It is conventional for rivers to babble, and often enough to figure in that a socially destructive garrulity; but why do they babble here, blurring a contrast between the metropolitan world and the poet's rural retreat? Philips concedes a murmur even in the 'Remoteness' which she enjoyed, or manufactured, before her poems were printed (the babble, as it were, of the Powell controversy). And this insecurity has, as we saw from the poem to Ardelia, a basis in the restlessness of the West Wales she wrote in, and the values that were put in question by the upsurge in puritanism, not just in the lot of being a gentlewoman writer exposed to the indignity of print.

The late poem 'To his Grace Gilbert Lord Arch-Bishop of Canterbury, July 10. 1664', is revealingly close to the letter I have just quoted. From the modesty of retirement, Philips finds herself rudely thrust into the public arena:

> That private shade, wherein my Muse was bred,
> She alwaies hop'd might hide her humble head;
> Believing the retirement she had chose
> Might yield her, if not pardon, yet repose;
> Nor other repetitions did expect,
> Than what our Ecchoes from the Rocks reflect.
> But hurry'd from her Cave with wild affright,
> And dragg'd maliciously into the Light

> (Which makes her like the Hebrew Virgin mourn
> When from her face her Vail was rudely torn)
> To you (my Lord) she now for succour calls,
> And at your feet, with just Confusion falls.[94]

Brought up a Presbyterian, then, in the 1650s, lacking an established church to join, Philips now records in the most fulsome terms her submission to Restoration Anglicanism. The temptation to interpret this as a fawning accommodation with the ruling powers should be resisted by recalling the Great Tew formation of the Archbishop, Gilbert Sheldon, and by noticing his links with Welsh Anglicanism during the interregnum.[95] That a mesh of friendship, patronage, and doctrine connected Sheldon with the Welsh gentry and, closely, with the poet[96] must have encouraged her to believe that gaining his protection and being 'retir'd' anew under his 'wing' could make up for the violation of her Welsh retreat by the appearance of her poetry in print. That is why the Archbishop attracts such glowing praise:

> The Piety of the Apostles Times,
> And Courage to resist this Ages Crimes,
> Majestick sweetness, temper'd and refin'd,
> In a Polite, and Comprehensive Mind,
> Were all requir'd her Ruines to repair,
> And all united in her Primate are.

Whatever need (actual or occasional) drove Philips to turn to Sheldon, we are unlikely to agree with her claim that she has been driven by her subject into bardic 'Raptures' and 'Fury'. There is a dispiriting contrast between the elevation of such texts as 'A Prayer' and the decorous flattery of this passage. Philips believed that verse was strengthened by the coincidence of syntax with couplet units,[97] but she sacrifices word order at this point to enforce such a coherence ('And all united in *her Primate are*'). Even in this, no doubt, she was responding to her moment. An ethos of polite conformity, of imposed regularity, became the mode of the Anglo-Welsh gentry. Fear that the 'Ages Crimes' would flare up again through puritan unrest reinforced the urge towards hierarchy and order.[98] So although 'The Piety of the Apostles Times' lacks the patriotic extravagance of Erbery's account of St Paul as a Welshman, or the dispossessed Anglican ardour of Vaughan's vision of patriarchs and angels among the woods beside the River Usk ('Religion'), it shows Philips alive to the realities of the British church. Her desire to creep under the episcopal wing has behind it the experiences of West Wales during the 1650s, but she operates, even here, with an acute sense of the relationship between the rocky echoes of her home ground and the larger British and Irish worlds in which her poems increasingly circulated.

7
The Archipelago Enlarged:
Milton and Marvell to 1660

The execution of Charles I in January 1649 appalled his followers in the three kingdoms and alienated much continental opinion, but nowhere was its impact greater than among the royalist exiles—many of them Scots—who had gathered in The Hague around the Prince of Wales. When the battle-hardened Earl of Montrose (a leading figure in the entourage) heard the news, he fainted clean away,[1] then wrote a poem promising revenge: 'I'le sing thy Obsequies, with Trumpet sounds, | And write thy Epitaph with *Bloud* and *Wounds*.'[2] Montrose's campaign may be said to have begun in May 1649 with the assassination, apparently by the Earl's men, of the Dutch-born Cambridge scholar, Isaac Dorislaus, who had returned to the United Provinces to represent the English Commonwealth. This murder heightened tension, but it was only one example of the wars of the three kingdoms reaching into the Netherlands. Entangled with English politics since at least the 1580s, when Elizabeth I backed the Dutch against their Spanish rulers (the Earl of Leicester became their Governor-General), and within a few decades integrated the more firmly into archipelagic affairs when the Stadholder Willem van Oranje took the crown from James II and VII, the United Provinces were a crucible of the military and literary conflicts that troubled mid-seventeenth-century Britain and Ireland.

Montrose's plan to take arms and men from the Netherlands to Scotland was compromised from the start. Though he had been one of the earliest signatories of the Scottish national Covenant, he had defied the Kirk by opposing the abolition of episcopacy in England, and his 1644–6 campaign in Scotland with Alasdair Mac Colla and his Irish Catholic troops (above, pp. 166–7) further estranged him from the Kirk party. When their commissioners reached The Hague to negotiate with Prince Charles, they refused to be in the same room as Montrose.[3] Like his father inclined to back competing factions as a form of insurance, Charles encouraged both sides, so that Montrose reached Scotland in 1650 knowing that many royalists would now turn caution into a principle and not rise until the Kirk backed the Stewarts. After a short but gallant campaign, he was captured, brought to Edinburgh, and tried.

The horror of his sentence is captured in a poem which he supposedly wrote with the point of a diamond on the window of his cell:

> On Himself, upon hearing what was his Sentence
>
> Let them bestow on ev'ry Airth a Limb;
> Open all my Veins, that I may swim
> To Thee my Saviour, in that Crimson Lake;
> Then place my purboil'd Head upon a Stake;
> Scatter my Ashes, throw them in the Air:
> Lord (Since Thou know'st where all these Atoms are)
>   I'm hopeful, once Thou'lt recollect my Dust,
>   And confident Thou'lt raise me with the Just.[4]

These grisly lines are not quite gruesome enough. Montrose was ignobly hanged, and after being hacked into pieces, so that several 'airths' or regions could put his limbs on display, his trunk was buried in unconsecrated ground. For Iain Lom of the Macdonalds, who regarded Montrose as a traditional Highland warrior-leader, the spoiling of his body—

> Bu ro mhath rudhadh gruaidhe
>   'N am tarrainn suas gu trod;
>
> Deud chailc bu ro mhath dlùthadh
>   Fo mhala chaoil gun mhùgaich ...[5]

—was particularly vile. But the fate of Montrose's corpse, and most conspicuously his parboiled head, which spent a decade grinning from a spike on the Edinburgh tolbooth, was widely deplored.

It even found its way into the correspondence of John Milton. In a letter dated 15 January 1653,[6] the Scottish royalist Andrew Sandelands, who had been at university with Milton,[7] advised him, as Secretary for Foreign Tongues of the English Republic, how the regime could secure

---

Bu ro mhath rudhadh gruaidhe ... mhùgaich: splendid was the flushing of his cheek when drawing up to fight. Teeth of chalk, regularly set, below slender eyebrows without frown (tr. in Davidson (ed.))

the timber and tar that it needed to equip its navy, which was fighting the first of the three wars that racked Anglo-Dutch relations in the seventeenth century (1652–4, 1665–7, and 1672–4).[8] Warning, or, as a royalist, boasting, that no Scot would agree to log the Caledonian forests 'because it is reputed a disservice to ye king and Country', Sandelands outlines a plan by which 'ye State undertaking ye worke ym selves may have abundance of tarre for nothing and timber which will not only defray all charges but pay yor garriesons in ye Highlands & North of Scotland.' In return, he seeks 'ye gift of yt weatherbeaten scull of my Noble and truly honoble. patron' Montrose. This is an extraordinary appeal; but a shared hatred (by this date) of 'Jac Presbyter' was a strong enough motive for the ultra-royalist to woo the republican; Sandelands wants the head 'that it remaine noe longer a Contemptuous object & ludibrium Presbyterorum Scotorum [laughing stock of the Scottish Presbyterians], who ar thee bassest of men.'[9]

Montrose's head interests me because his campaign and Sandelands's letter both foreground an Anglo-Scoto-Dutch triangle that has been insufficiently explored by historians[10] and hardly noticed by literary scholars. As a result, few seem to be aware that, while the Commonwealth was tightening its grip on Ireland and Scotland, in the wake of the victories celebrated by Marvell's 'Horatian Ode' and Milton's sonnet to Cromwell, it sought union with the United Provinces—a project which collapsed into the First Anglo-Dutch War, and precipitated Milton's sonnet to Sir Henry Vane and Marvell's 'Character of Holland'. Indeed, that ebullient satire was probably written to demonstrate Marvell's employability just when Sandelands was lobbying Milton, because a letter dated 21 February 1653 from Milton to the President of the Council of State indicates Marvell's knowledge of the United Provinces (which he had visited in the early–mid 1640s) and of the Dutch language and recommends that he be made his assistant as Secretary for Foreign Tongues.[11]

The triangular matrix highlighted here was multibraided and full of conflicts. There were regional contacts (e.g. East Anglia and Holland) and differences—between the west and (Episcopalian) east of Scotland, for instance, or between such Protestant cities as Leiden and the royalist-Catholic areas of the Dutch Republic that shaded southwards into the Spanish Netherlands (where, in Ostend and Bruges, Irish merchants, dispossessed during the 1640s and 1650s, relocated with success). National identities were bolstered by war propaganda, but in every part of the jigsaw there were potent dissenting minorities, eager to cross-collaborate. And elites could invoke ethnic stereotypes (as Milton and Marvell both did) without regarding them as comprehensively valid. That the matrix incorporated variables, however, did not make its interactions any less intense. One reason why the Dutch connection makes for a richer triangulation with Britain than can be found between, say, Britain and France at this date, is precisely that the links included so much contention as well as so much that was compatible.

The vitality of the Anglo-Scottish axis should not be underrated. Though the English, after a flurry of panegyric and satire around the regal union of 1603, preferred to ignore the frigid north, they were rudely awoken to Scottish affairs by the signing of the Covenant. Thereafter, friction between sections of the English and the Scots led to violence in 1639–40, 1644, 1648, and 1650–1, while union was in varying degrees a feature of the Solemn League and Covenant between the Scots Estates and the English parliament (1643), the Scottish Engagement with Charles I (1647), the coronation of his son as King of Great Britain at Scone (1651), and a short-term achievement of the Protectorate (1654–60).[12] To judge from poems and pamphlets, however, while the Cromwellians incorporated Scotland largely to complete the defeat of royalism and bolster the security of the Commonwealth, and were encouraged in this by antipathy, they positively sought union with the Netherlands because of perceived affinity and historical involvement, and were driven into hostility by Dutch reluctance.

To the south, there was more contact than is often realized. The English looked to Dutch models in painting, architecture, and such practical arts as fen drainage. The reclamation of large parts of East Anglia with Dutch help can only have made more evident what the marking of dykes, sandbanks, and sea-lanes on maps was imparting,[13] that the British archipelago extended physically into the Netherlands—that patchwork of canals and polders derided as a 'quagmire isle'.[14] Through the medium of newsbooks, both peoples were kept informed about their neighbours across the water. When the Orangeist prince, Willem II, died in 1650, a satirical Dutch epitaph was reprinted, with a translation, in the English government newsletter, *Mercurius Politicus* (Fig. 11), and throughout the 1650s this widely read journal published letters from Leiden, Amsterdam, and The Hague, made ventriloquistic comedy out of Dutch reactions to English success,[15] and summarized Dutch publications.[16] Owen Felltham's spirited, mocking, and sympathetically imaginative *Brief Character of the*

Low-Countries under the States (1628? pub. 1648/51) was only the most celebrated of a number of such accounts. Though the Dutch were not the object of as much abuse as the Scots, they could be accused of the same greed and duplicity. When Felltham's *Brief Character* was republished as *Batavia: Or, The Hollander Displayed* (1672), it was printed along with Sir Antony Weldon's contemptuous 'Perfect Description of the People and Country of Scotland'.

It is not necessary to labour the point that, from the mid-sixteenth century onwards, the Scottish and the Dutch were drawn together by trade, higher education, Latin literacy, and religious affinity.[17] On a continent where English/Inglis of any kind was hardly ever spoken, parts of the United Provinces thus became relatively anglophone (much as parishes in East Anglia and London picked up some Dutch). Many Scots and

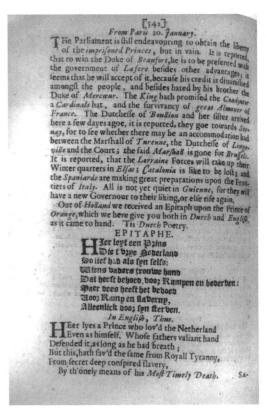

Fig. 11. Satirical Dutch epitaph on Willem II, with English translation. From *Mercurius Politicus*, 33 (16–23 January 1651).

English texts, including James VI and I's *Basilikon Doron* and Milton's *Doctrine and Discipline of Divorce*, were published in Dutch translation;[18] but anglophone books also circulated (as did English theatre companies) and found their way into libraries, in part because Dutch printers turned out enormous numbers of English-language texts for shipping or smuggling into London and the Scottish ports.[19] Ships carried exported goods to the Low Countries and returned from Veere, Rotterdam, or Middelburg with books by such Presbyterian authors as George Gillespie and Robert Baillie.[20] The trade was so large that works produced in England sometimes purported to have been published in the United Provinces to avoid censorship or other difficulties. Marvell's *Account of the Growth of Popery, and Arbitrary Government* (1677) has 'Amsterdam' on its title page for that reason.

For such poets as Milton and Marvell—well travelled, widely read, and informed—but also for the likes of George Wither (puritan, prolific, and broadly pro-Dutch), what happened in Britain was part of European Politics. The projected Anglo-Dutch union was international in its design to strengthen North European Protestantism against the Counter-Reformation. This European reach was integral to English insularity, given the way England (then, as now) defined itself in relation to what the channel both divides and connects. Union would have re-established the footprint on the continent that had been part of England's self-image since the middle ages—an image of imperial prowess that had been dented by the loss of Calais a century earlier and that would be temporarily gratified when Cromwell took Dunkirk from the Spanish. Although Anglo-Dutch union failed to materialize, it is not surprising (though it is bizarre) to find Marvell, as late as 1677, attributing a common border to both countries when he says that 'the *Spanish Nether-land* ... had alwayes been considered as the natural Frontier of *England*.'[21]

This bears on the paradoxical way in which the moves to unite England with the Netherlands (inspired by classical-republican but also Dutch models of state construction)[22] were complicated by national sentiment. Even Milton's well-known appeals to Englishness have a way of proving, under scrutiny, to be tactical in purpose, socially stratified (the common people lapse from a native love of liberty into deluded royalism) and seamed with disappointment. The pamphlet literature shows, however, that ethnic as well as religious values could be tapped and reinforced during the mid-century crisis.[23] And certainly, from the eloquent passage in *Areopagitica* (1645) that imagines England as 'a noble and puissant Nation rousing herself like a strong man after sleep'[24] to the crying-up of the Republic's victories around the archipelago in *Defensio secunda* (1654),[25] Milton projects a patriotism that did not easily square with the Protestant internationalism that encouraged the 1651 union.[26] Infusions of patriotic feeling with the politics of liberty were, if anything, stronger in the United Provinces, which had only finally shaken off Spanish rule in 1648. A number of the English statesmen who supported union were nourished by currents of Dutch thought that argued for a people's right to self-determination.[27] The social group that fostered the development of the word 'patriot' in the 1650s[28] was imprinted by ideas from a country with which it sought a union that would dilute the integrity of the nation.

The Dutch intellectual Constantijn Huygens is one product of this interface: frequent visitor to England and assiduous reader of its poetry, translator into Dutch of nineteen poems by Donne—texts which Marvell may have had a hand in circulating[29]—as well as of many verses by James VI and I's jester Archie Armstrong.[30] Huygens had the sort of interlingual facility which led him to start one poem in English then modulate into Dutch,[31] and to exploit the language of the enemy during periods of conflict. Hence his playful, belated epitaph for the Scotsman William Welwood (fl. 1577–1622), author of works that asserted first Scottish Jacobean and then British sovereignty over coastal waters that the Dutch claimed the right to navigate and fish:

> Well wood I Welwood lived and saw himself undone,
>   Even after he is gone.
> Well wood he, by mij troth I know not, weepe or laugh,
>   At such an Epitaphe.[32]

Dutch naval success refutes Welwood so patly that even he would find it hard not to laugh at the burial of his arguments. Dated 1 February 1653, this contribution to ultra-archipelagic English takes us back to the moment of Sandelands's correspondence with Milton about Montrose, of Milton's recommendation of Marvell to Secretary Bradshaw, and of the younger poet's 'Character of Holland'. It gives us a Dutch angle on a phase of Anglo-Dutch conflict when things were going well for the

Well wood I: I very much wish

United Provinces, and foregrounds once again the triangulating presence of Scottish issues.

★ ★ ★

Having established the significance of the Anglo-Scoto-Dutch triangle, I now want to suggest how Milton and Marvell figure in the enlarged design. To do so is to help dispel the residually Whig view of both writers as narrowly English patriots, rather than archipelagic in outlook. Scholarship has begun to correct the inherited account. 'Lycidas' has been returned to North Wales and the Irish sea,[33] the *Mask Presented at Ludlow-Castle, 1634*—still widely known as *Comus*—to the Welsh Marches;[34] Milton's hostile account of Catholic Ireland in his *Observations on the Articles of Peace* has generated debate,[35] while Satan's revolt in *Paradise Lost* has been linked to Charles I's incitement (according to Milton and others) of the Irish Rebellion of 1641.[36] Some have even noticed, beyond Marvell's 'Horatian Ode', that his 'Loyall Scot' advocates British union, and that he shows a great deal of sympathy for Presbyterians north of the border during the 1670s (see Chapter 9). Yet the devolution of analysis remains woefully incomplete. This is particularly surprising in the case of Milton, given that he owed so much to the thinking of 'Jac Presbyter' about church and state.

He absorbed the ethos early. Between the ages of ten and twelve he was taught by the Scottish Presbyterian Thomas Young, and at eighteen he addressed a Latin elegy to him while Young was a chaplain in Hamburg[37]—getting a taste of the European wars of religion that the Presbyterians would bring to Britain. When Charles I resisted the Covenant, Milton was himself abroad, but on his return to England he gave polemical support to the Scots, no doubt stirred by the propaganda that was reaching England from printers in the United Provinces as well as Scotland.[38] *Of Reformation* (1641) zealously exhorts: 'Goe on both hand in hand O NATIONS never to be disunited...joyn your invicible might to doe worthy, and Godlike deeds, and then he that seeks to break your union, a cleaving curse be his inheritance to all generations.'[39] In *The Reason of Church-Government* (1642), Milton's scope enlarges to take in the Irish Rebellion. He shows no searching interest, however, in the dislocations and injustices of Ireland, but uses the rising to fuel a pro-Scottish attack on prelates. The bishops are responsible for the 'cruelties [of] these murdrous Irish', because they have failed to bring the Reformation to Ireland and thus denied the people spiritual sustenance.[40]

Although it is doubtful that Milton was ever a Presbyterian,[41] he supported the group of Scottish and English Presbyters known as Smectymnuus (one of whom was Young) and in 1643 signed the Solemn League and Covenant. The usual explanation for his change of heart—that Presbyterian attacks on his divorce tracts persuaded him that a remodelling of the church along Kirk lines would replicate old abuses—is no doubt substantially true; but Milton, already tolerant of sectarianism in *Church-Government*, was also troubled by the readiness with which Presbyterians could follow Montrose's path from Covenanter to Cavalier. In the sonnet 'A Book was writ' (1647?), he thus adds the name of George Gillespie, one of the Scots who spoke for the Kirk in the body designed to reform the English church (the Westminster Assembly),[42] to a list of Montrose's soldiers in the campaign of 1644–6. Compared with such hard names, he asks, is the title of his divorce tract, *Tetrachordon*, so difficult?

> Cries the stall-reader, bless us! what a word on
>   A title page is this! And some in file
>   Stand spelling fals, while one might walk to Mile-
>   End Green. Why is it harder Sirs then Gordon,
> Colkitto, or Macdonnel, or Galasp?
>   Those rugged names to our like mouths grow sleek
>   That would have made *Quintilian* stare and gasp.
> Thy age, like ours, O Soul of Sir *John Cheek*,
>   Hated not Learning wors than Toad or Asp;
>   When thou taught's *Cambridge*, and King *Edward* Greek.

Some of these names are so 'barbarous' (the manuscript reading for 'rugged') that even the Scots cannot get their mouths around them: Colkitto is a Lowlands simplification of 'Coll Keitach', the patronym sometimes applied to Montrose's lieutenant, Alasdair Mac Colla. 'Galasp' shows the English struggling with the more familiar—though also Gaelic-derived—Gillespie.[43] Yet the ludicrous ease with which this contraction rhymes with 'gasp' shows how readily a Scottish accent can creep into English mouths, making names as 'rugged' as the Cairngorms seem fitting ('sleek') to the culturally invaded. Milton views the Westminster Assembly as entrenching the power of the Scots; still occupying the four northern counties of England in the wake of the Bishops' Wars,[44] they now threaten to corrupt the reform of the church, replacing rule by bishops with the repressive greed of Presbyters. As a good Renaissance humanist, Milton represents cultural encroachment as linguistic pollution. Much turns on 'our like mouths', which makes most sense as ' "rugged" also'. This is John Carey's gloss, and he also points out that 'In his discussion of "barbarisms" *Quintilian* I v 8 includes the use of foreign words, and cites examples.'[45] Abandoning the rhetoric of 1641, Milton casts the Scots as 'foreign' infiltrators who are endangering English identity.

Hostility of this sort grew,[46] especially in the New Model Army, because, after handing Charles I to the London parliament for money in 1647—only for half the back pay promised them by the English, but the episode reinforced the stereotype of the impoverished, grasping Jockie, whose true religion was avarice—the Scots muddied parliament's negotiations with the king by secretly agreeing with him the pro-Presbyterian Engagement that helped trigger, in April-May 1648, a second civil war. The Scottish reputation for greed was now compounded with evidence of duplicity. Milton's reaction can be found in his translations of Psalms 80–88, which lament the invasion of Israel/England by rampaging outsiders ('Why hast thou laid her Hedges low | And brok'n down her Fence'),[47] but also, more explicitly, in the heroic sonnet 'On the Lord General Fairfax', written between 8 July and 17 August. By this date, parliamentarians needed reassurance not just because the Scots had invaded England but because the fleet, having defected to Prince Charles in Holland, was blockading the Thames. 'Thy firm unshak'n vertue', Milton reassures, 'ever brings | Victory home'. There is no attempt now to present Britain as a shared Protestant realm (Scotland must be other, for England to be 'home'), even in this panegyric to a pro-Presbyterian general:

> though new rebellions raise
> Thir Hydra heads, & the fals North displaies
> Her brok'n league, to impe her serpent wings,
> O yet a nobler task awaites thy hand;
> For what can Warrs but endless War still breed,
> Till Truth, & Right from Violence be freed,
> And Public Faith cleard from the shamefull brand
> Of Public Fraud. In vain doth Valour bleed
> While Avarice, & Rapine share the land.

Paradise Lost was not yet written, but we know that Milton was preparing the ground and there are surely pre-echoes here. Recalling Isaiah

14[48] but also the proverbial falseness of the north, restated in republican propaganda,[49] Milton, in the epic, gives 'the Quarters of the North... the spacious North' to Satan (V. 689, 726). Raphael locates Lucifer's palace not just in 'the limits of the North' but in the celestial Highlands, 'High on a Hill... as a Mount | Raised on a Mount' (V. 755–60), and the good angels sight the bad before war breaks out in heaven as armed ranks bristling across a specifically northern horizon (VI. 78–86). The 'brok'n league' of the sonnet is the Solemn League and Covenant, troubling to the Independents because of its arguable implication that Presbyterian government should be adopted in the English church, but for them voided by the influx of Scottish troops in the renewed war that Fairfax was now fighting. Everything 'fals' descends from Eve and Adam's sin, but earlier from the fall of Lucifer and the rebel angels who were created glorious but turned into serpents; here that lapse is recapitulated in the 'serpent wings' of the once-heroic (c.1641) Scots.

Meanwhile the epic resonance of the sonnet's rhetorical question, 'what can Warrs but endless War still breed', situates the England of fraud, avarice, and rapine in Chaos, the elemental sphere 'Of endless Warrs', that Sin shows to Satan in *Paradise Lost* (II. 897). It also anticipates the military deadlock that God describes in the war in heaven:

> in perpetual fight they needs must last
> Endless, and no solution will be found:
> Warr wearied hath perform'd what Warr can do ...   (VI. 693–5)

Fairfax has no fiery chariot, but like Christ at least in this he must break the cycle of 'endless War' and stem the tide of sin by the exercise of moral authority. His victory cannot be merely military: success in battle is assured (in the encomiastic idiom of the poem, as in the War in Heaven); that is the easy part. The shape of Milton's thinking here recurs in *Paradise Lost*. If the Irish Rebellion left its mark on the epic, by showing Charles, in league with the rebels, to resemble Satan and the fallen angels, so, rather more obviously, did the corrupted militancy of the Scots.

The stubbornness of their royalism—the blindness to God's decision that drove Montrose and his followers into exile, and allowed the Kirk to compact with the Prince of Wales—remained a threat, and the work that Milton wrote, in January 1649, to justify Charles I's trial, *The Tenure of Kings and Magistrates*, sets a pattern for the other prose works of this momentous year by turning against the Presbyterians the weapons he had picked up

from them in his anti-episcopal pamphlets. A key section of the treatise
relates how the Scottish Protestants opposed Mary of Lorraine, mother of
Mary Queen of Scots, to preserve their religion. Milton invokes Buchanan.
In support of his contention that kings derive authority from the people he
quotes a number of continental thinkers, but adds: 'Of the Scotch Divines
I need not mention others then the famousest among them, *Knox*, & his
fellow Labourers in the reformation of *Scotland*; whose large Treatises on
this subject, defend the same Opinion. To cite them sufficiently, were to
insert thir whole Books, writt'n purposely on this argument.'[50]

The now infamous *Observations on the Articles of Peace* is also best
understood in an Anglo-Scottish context, despite the occasion of the treatise
being the refutation of texts from Ireland.[51] Of the four publications which
Milton reviewed it was not the three involving the Ormondists and the
pro-parliamentarian forces in Leinster that detained him,[52] but the *Necessary
Representation* in which the Belfast Presbytery denounced the execution
of Charles I. Scholars have rightly been troubled that, with Cromwell's
punitive invasion imminent, Milton should have made atrocities against
Irish Catholics more likely by regurgitating impossibly large statistics for the
massacre of Protestants in the 1641 Rebellion, and by calling such native
customs as roasting oats in straw 'absurd and savage'.[53] For reasons that
quickly become apparent, however, Milton lavishes much more space and
forensic energy on the Ulster-Scots elders of Belfast. Though they write
from a 'barbarous nook of *Ireland*' (327), their statement is, by their own
admission, 'a *Scotch* Protestation, usherd in by a *Scotch* interest' (330), and a
troubling indication of how too many Scots would tend. By denouncing
the Belfast Presbytery, Milton was able to attack a 'fals North' that it would
have been premature and undiplomatic to have taken on directly.

As it happens, the Belfast Presbytery had discouraged its members from
joining the royalist Engagers in Scotland and fighting in England in 1648,
and even as he wrote (though Milton may not have realized this) a body of
Ulster Covenanters was resisting the *Necessary Representation*;[54] but Milton
feared—with the Kirk's commissioners already in The Hague—that the
Scots were in danger of forgetting the lessons of history: 'these blockish
Presbyters of *Clandeboy* know not that *John Knox*, who was the first founder
of Presbytery in *Scotland*, taught professedly the doctrine of deposing, and
of killing Kings. And thus while they deny that any such rule can be found,
the rule is found in their own Country' (329)—that country not being
the one that they inhabit. Milton exploits the overdetermined position of

Ulster, as a seat both of the 1641 Rebellion by Irish Catholics and of Scottish encroachment (yet again) into a kingdom under English sovereignty, to shift the political agenda from a country (Ireland) that he regards as merely troublesome towards one that in his view poses a threat to the revolution.[55] He secures this by blurring the distinction that has so often been made between the Scots and mere Irish in the province. Noting their support around Derry for the Gaelic leader Owen Roe O'Neill, he denounces the Belfast Presbyterians as 'a generation of High-land theevs and Red-shanks' (those mercenary soldiers from the Western Isles). They are as Gaelic—and some of them were—as their uncivil Irish neighbours (333).

Milton is sharply antagonistic towards the Scots in the *Observations*, yet the arguments drawn out of him show that he was not motivated by obtuse xenophobia (however willing he was to exploit such sentiment in his readers) but by a practical, disabused mistrust of the impulse of Scottish Presbyterians to protect their interests by seeking alliance, influence, and advantage outside the borders of 'their own Country', even if that meant challenging the power of the Godly English to dominate the archipelago. The informed, pragmatic astuteness of Milton's animosity put him ahead of most English opinion in fearing that an improbable alliance between Ulster-Scots Presbyterians and mere Irish would extend across the North Channel; but once the erstwhile leader of pan-Gaelic royalism, the Earl of Montrose, landed in Scotland, in March 1650, it became a common belief that the Scots would seek to join 'with the Rebels of *Ireland*, for the common cause of his *clouted Majesty*, and to compleat the work of *Reformation*, that the *Teigs* and *Presbyters* may both become one Body (as they desire) *According to the Covenant*.'[56]

★   ★   ★

When the '*clouted*' Prince of Wales (so young he should be in nappies) arrived in Edinburgh, some three months later, he found 'for his better entertainment', as *Mercurius Politicus* wickedly put it, '*Montrose's* head of the *Kirks* own dressing, provided for his *Break-fast*, and mounted on the *Town-house*, on purpose to bid him welcome.'[57] Charles was prepared to stomach this repast not just for the sake of the Scottish crown but to secure the more ambitious title, required by the ongoing unionism of the Solemn League and Covenant, 'King of Great Britain and Ireland'.[58] The

Commonwealth and its apologists could not ignore this claim to authority south of the border, and a run of anti-Scottish pamphlets followed, with such titles as *The Changeable Covenant* and *The False Brother*.[59]

Marvell's 'Horatian Ode' (May-July 1650) has points of contact with this literature, though it has traditionally been read as a diptych contrasting the mixed virtues of Oliver Cromwell with those of Charles I, and it has tended in recent scholarship, like Milton's *Observations*, to be thought about in relation to Ireland. This is justified by its full title, 'An Horatian Ode upon Cromwel's Return from Ireland',[60] as well as by its inclusion of a twelve-line passage in which the Irish are said to have confessed how good Cromwell is, and how just—ignoring the atrocities of Drogheda and Wexford; but the rhetorical energies of the poem turn on the Lord General's preparations to invade Scotland. The *occasio* of the ode is signalled in its second line ('The forward Youth that would appear | Must now forsake his *Muses* dear'), and this 'now' returns when attention shifts from Ireland, and what is vaguely threatened to unfree states on the continent, to Scotland as an immediate objective: 'The *Pict* no shelter now shall find | Within his party-colour'd mind' (lines 105–6).

If we can be guided by what Marvell wrote a few years later, the Pict represents the Scots at their most primitively uncivil.[61] His mind is 'party-colour'd' because factious and conspiratorial—twin implications of 'party' at this date—and because he thinks, as he dresses, like a clown, in tartan motley (lurking in the heather, he hides under 'the Plad').[62] This places him beyond the Highland line, among the followers of Montrose. Even if he is taken as standing in for the Scots as a whole, his presence deflects hostility from Lowland Presbyterians. Only months before, the poet had been employed by Fairfax, who, despite the bloodshed forced on him by Scottish participation in the second civil war, had some sympathy with the Kirk, and who refused to invade Scotland, leaving that task to Cromwell. How far should we look in the 'Horatian Ode' for hints of the pan-British outlook that figure in 'The Loyall Scot'? Given the climate of 1650, not very far perhaps, though it may show an impulse to inclusiveness, rather than Anglo-centric complacency, that Marvell should write, just before the lines about the Pict, of the potentially glorious future of 'our *Isle*' under Cromwell.

However this passage is interpreted, it draws into its shifting fields reminders that there was much for the English Republic to resolve within Britain, without looking for trouble on the continent. That contemporary manuscripts read 'kingdoms' where the text printed (then rescinded) in 1681 says that Cromwell 'cast the Kingdome old | Into another Mold' is further evidence that, whatever Marvell's intentions at that point, the poem's reception caught it up in archipelagic pluralities. Yet one cannot read far in the anti-Scottish literature of 1650–1 without finding a Dutch dimension. Even those English readers who were unaware of the two-way print-flow between Amsterdam and Edinburgh at the time would have found on the London bookstalls such works as *Anglia Liberata: Or, The Rights of the People of England, Maintained against the Pretences of the Scotish King*—a pamphlet which reproduces, supposedly from a Dutch source, an English quarrel with the pro-Stewart Scottish ambassador in the Netherlands, the reply of 'an ingenious *Dutch-man*' to the ambassador's case, and a further reply from an English author who, like Milton, refutes the Scots with their own precedents.[63]

This was the setting for the attempts, in 1651, to negotiate a union between the English Republic and the United Provinces. The Dutch resisted the overtures on Anglo-Scottish grounds, at first because of uncertainty about the outcome of the renewed civil wars, but then, once that doubt was removed by Cromwell's victory against the Scots at Worcester (September 1651),[64] because they did not want to lose their independence as they saw the Scots losing theirs. Union might mean domination. The political and religious similarities between royalist Presbyterians in Britain and the union-resistant Orangeists damaged that section of the Dutch in the eyes of Independents like Milton. It was now that English pamphlets began to dovetail stereotypes of the Scots and the Dutch, saying that both were false, self-serving, and only interested in money. With this grew a feeling among republicans that the Dutch should either accept union or suffer the same coercion as had been used against the Scots, a sentiment that spurred the output of Anglophobic publications in the Netherlands. It has been plausibly argued by Steven Pincus that 'War between England and the United Provinces broke out not because of their irreconcilable economic differences, but because popular images had been created on each side of the North Sea which made it impossible to negotiate a peaceful settlement.'[65]

Like Marvell later, Milton was involved in diplomacy with the Netherlands. He translated documents for the Council of State, learned some Dutch, and developed a respectful relationship with the ambassador Adrian Pauw.[66] One of his earliest tasks was to deal with letters from the United

Provinces regretting the murder of Dorislaus. The claims of the state affected his representation of the Dutch (*and* the Scots) as directly as they did the writings of Marvell, who pressed his case for patronage by composing a Latin poem to celebrate Oliver St John's mission to The Hague.[67] Milton had urged the merits of an alliance with the Dutch as early as *Of Reformation*,[68] but that context presses more urgently on the two *Defences of the English People*, which, published in 1651 and 1654, frame the war of 1652–4. Those controverted in the *Defences*, Salmasius and Morus, were professors in the United Provinces (though Salmasius had moved on), and both sought, according to Milton, to seduce Dutch youth from the path of liberty. English ambassadors went to the Netherlands armed with the *Defensio prima*; twenty-five copies were ordered on behalf of the Dutch government. There were Dutch translations of this treatise, and of John Rowland's reply, by the end of 1651.[69] Yet while *Defensio prima* engages with the Dutch, it keeps referring (this being Milton) to the wretched example of the Scots.

Addressing an anglophone audience in *Eikonoklastes* (1649), Milton had cast the Dunfermline-born Charles I as a duplicitious Scot. Even though his Presbyterian countrymen had been 'robustious' with the bishops, Charles had gone to Edinburgh (in 1641), and when defeated by the English in 1646 had handed himself over to the Scottish Army, 'which argues... that to *England* he continu'd still, as he was indeed, a stranger, ... to the Scots onely a native King'. Moreover, Charles proved willing to give the Scots (and the Irish) the ecclesiastical reforms they requested ('*preferring, as some thought, the desires of Scotland before his own interest and Honour*'), but not to satisfy the English. In short, he dealt with the archipelago as David did the multiple polity of the Hebrews: '*Ireland* was as *Ephraim*, the strength of his head, *Scotland*, as *Iudah*, was his Law-giver; but over *England* as over *Edom* he meant to cast his Shoo'.[70] The idea that Charles was primarily a Scottish monarch continues in the *Defensio prima*, where Milton repeats the charge that he sought to bribe the Scots by promising that they could annex the four northern counties of England that they occupied after the Bishops' Wars.[71] But he now somewhat perversely insists that the Scots had no right to stop the English trying and executing the king.[72]

The impact of the *Defensio prima* was so great that the Dutch tried to head off its successor, though it was exported to the Netherlands in quantities and reprinted there. We hear in June and July 1654 of the Dutch ambassador, Willem Nieupoort, trying to persuade Milton not to publish the *Defensio secunda*, by asking John Thurloe, Secretary of the Council, to intervene with Cromwell, and by sending two mutual friends to visit the poet. Though Milton refused to be diverted, he undertook to say nothing to the prejudice of the United Provinces. In practice, he seized the opportunity to criticize the now-humbled Netherlands for trying to save Charles I from execution and for paltering in 1651;[73] and his admiration for the Dutch in defeat does not prevent him from once more pressing for the union that had precipitated the war. Milton characterizes his attack on his intellectual enemies as a contribution to the war effort.[74] Meanwhile he keeps Scottish issues in view, not just in relation to the execution of Charles I but in the climactic encomium on Cromwell and his victories (641–3, 670).

If one turns to the small amount of poetry that Milton completed during these years, similar concerns emerge. Take the sonnet

To the Lord Generall Cromwell May 1652
On the proposalls of certaine ministers at ye Comm[it]tee for Propagation of the Gospell

> Cromwell, our cheif of men, who through a cloud
>   Not of warr onely, but detractions rude,
>   Guided by faith & matchless Fortitude
>   To peace & truth thy glorious way hast plough'd,
> And on the neck of crowned Fortune proud
>   Hast reard Gods Trophies & his work pursu'd,
>   While Darwen stream with blood of Scotts imbru'd,
>   And Dunbarr feild resounds thy praises loud,
> And Worcesters laureat wreath; yet much remaines
>   To conquer still; peace hath her victories
>   No less renownd then warr, new foes aries
> Threatning to bind our souls with secular chaines:
>   Helpe us to save free Conscience from the paw
>   Of hireling wolves whose Gospell is their maw.

It has been pointed out that the words 'peace & truth' appear on a coin minted to celebrate Cromwell's victories;[75] but since they had earlier been used to epitomize the aims of the Solemn League and Covenant they figure ironically in a sonnet which deals with a union by conquest, on terms welcome to English Independents. Milton's list of battles is not random: as any contemporary would recognize, he selects victories won against the Scots—at Preston (1648), Dunbar (1650), and then, at a structurally loaded juncture, as Cromwell's triumphs sweep beyond the octave and reach the volta at a caesura, Worcester (1651). The phrase 'Worcesters laureat wreath' replaced the manuscript reading 'twenty battles more' because this was, indeed, the single triumph that sealed the success of the Republic, and made the United Provinces acknowledge its power.

In that context the date of the sonnet is significant, not just because May 1652 was when the Committee for the Propagation of the Gospel seemed in danger of constructing a quasi-Presbyterian church (an English Kirk) in which the clergy would be paid through tithes, but because tension between England and the Netherlands was at this stage so high that a discourtesy in the channel started the Battle of the Downs (19 May). The Dutch were provocatively flying the colours of the House of Orange, and were earlier said to have flaunted those of the King of Scots.[76] Though the sonnet is about winning the peace,[77] it would not make military prowess such a syntactically unrelenting force were the Republic externally secure. Designed to stir Cromwell into protecting the right of all free souls to determine their own forms of worship, it broadcasts a larger message concerning the power of the Godly nation.

Many of the same personnel were involved in Anglo-Scottish and Anglo-Dutch conflict: Cromwell himself, Oliver St John, and also Sir Henry Vane, subject of a second sonnet written between Milton's *Defences*. Dated July 1652, this poem comes after a worsening diplomatic situation had led to the departure of the Dutch ambassadors, and it more or less coincides with the publication of the Republic's *Declaration against the Dutch*—in effect, a declaration of war—which Milton translated into Latin. In 'To Sir Henry Vane the Younger', the addressee is wise in giving counsel:

> Whether to settle peace or to unfold
>   The drift of hollow states hard to be spelld,
>   Then to advise how warr may best, upheld,
>   Move by her two maine nerves, Iron & Gold
> In all her equipage; besides to know
>   Both spirituall powre & civill, what each meanes,
>   What severs each thou 'hast learnt, which few have don
> The bounds of either sword to thee we ow.
>   Therfore on thy firme hand religion leanes
>   In peace, and reck'ns thee her eldest son.

As in the Cromwell sonnet the final appeal is to the case for freedom of worship. But the politics of that are now explicitly tied into diplomacy and war.

Scottish and Dutch affairs flow together in the phrase 'Whether to settle peace'—as they did in Vane's state business during spring and summer 1652, when, as a key member of parliament's Irish and Scottish Committee, he had a leading role in the pacification of Scotland while he negotiated with the Dutch.[78] 'To settle peace', in other words, means to make the peace in Scotland stable but also to strike a deal with the Netherlands. Compound in another way is 'The drift of hollow states', which puns on *States of Holland* (the formal title of the most powerful of the seven provinces in the Netherlands), the *Low* Countries—low in morals as well as in relation to sea-level (a routine wordplay in anti-Dutch writing)—and *hollow* in geology (built on a morass, not solid rock) as well as in deceit (full of *hollow* promises) and in making lots of noise (empty vessels make most sound, as the proverb has it). 'Hard to be spelld' indicates the obscure tenor of Dutch politicians in the first half of 1652 but perhaps also in the period after their ambassadors left (in June) and Vane was put in charge of correspondence with the United Provinces[79]—at which point his job was literally to 'unfold' and 'spell'. Dutch deviousness on and off paper was much remarked on, by Marvell in his poem to St John among others. But 'Hard to be spelld' also cues the reader to unpack the meanings hidden in the phrase 'drift of hollow states', and shows Milton, if only subconsciously, recalling the anti-Scottish sentiment of that earlier sonnet against Presbyterianism, 'A Book was writ of late', where the words '*spelling fals*' and 'Why is it *harder* Sirs then Gordon, | Colkitto, or Macdonnel, or Galasp?' first came together.

★ ★ ★

St John, Cromwell, and Vane were among the most pro-Dutch members of the new regime. The war of 1652–4 was prosecuted by those who sought union not destruction. This paradox is reflected in Marvell's 'The Character of Holland', which strikes me (*pace* some eminent readers)[80] as relatively tolerant of the enemy—more mockingly abusive, even admiringly derisive, than hostile, and disinclined to describe bloodshed (the sea laughs at the Dutch who seem to fire butter and cheese at the English). This is compatible with Marvell's post-Restoration attachment to the Netherlands (see Chapter 9), but it may also point to the circumstances of composition. In the background, undergirding all, was a desire for union. And when Marvell was actually writing, most likely in February-March 1653, the

Holland of his title (the most potent of the seven United Provinces) was suing for peace.[81] Though Marvell's debt to anti-Dutch satire is often mentioned, his poem owes more to the witty-fantastical idiom of Felltham's pre-war *Brief Character* than to such ugly products of the conflict as *The Dutch-mens Pedigree: Or, A Relation, shewing how they were first Bred, and Descended from a Horse-turd, which was enclosed in a Butter-box* (1653).

Even so, Marvell's opening line is—like Milton's pun on 'hollow states'—unflattering:

> *Holland*, that scarce deserves the name of *Land*,
> As but th'Off-scouring of the *Brittish Sand*;
> And so much Earth as was contributed
> By *English Pilots* when they heav'd the Lead; ...
> This indigested vomit of the Sea
> Fell to the *Dutch* by just Propriety.   (lines 1–8)

Holland can hardly be called land because it is a mass of mud and water. More literally and phonetically, take '*Land*' away from '*Holland*' and you are left with a 'hole', a dark, menial dwelling. What follows is no more complimentary, yet there is a unionist subtext to 'Off-scouring of the *Brittish Sand*', because it makes the landforms consubstantial. The idea was not unique. In Huygens's 'De uijtlandighe herder', for instance, which was quite likely known to Marvell, an exiled shepherd is placed

> Aende blancke Britter stranden,
> Daer de Son ten Zuijden blaeckt,
> Daer de vlacke Vlaender-landen
> Eertijds laghen aengehaeckt,
> (Kan de ghissing over weghen
> Vande leeper letter-liên ...)[82]

While 'Off-scouring' ties Holland into a union with the chalk-white strand across the channel, '*Brittish*' points further north, and is a telling word-choice given the contrast with '*English Pilots*'. Marvell tacitly reassures us that the prevarication of the 'hollow states' is vain, now that the Republic has conquered Scotland. That Sandelands was at this time advising Milton on how to pay for garrisons in the Highlands is a reminder that '*Brittish*' is more an assertion than an assurance. Bulletins in *Mercurius Politicus* show

---

Aende blancke Britter stranden ... letter-liên: On the chalk-white strand of Britain, | Where the sun to southwards burns, | To which shores our Flemish lowlands | Were connected, long ago | (If we may believe the theories | Of deep scholars of our days) (tr. Davidson and van der Weel)

that the level of threat among the parti-coloured Scots waxed and waned with Dutch success.[83] As for 'just Propriety', it rebuts the likes of Huygens's epigram on Welwood, written at this time. *Pace* Grotius's *Mare liberum*, the most formidable contribution to the Dutch side of the argument, gibed at later in the poem, the reality of naval power confirmed the rightness of British dominion, leaving the Hollanders entitled only to the mud puked up by the sea.

While never sacrificing satire, Marvell deftly traces threads of interconnectedness that make Dutch attempts to fight their neighbours absurd as well as vain. Is their drainage system not governed by an English commission (line 52)? Even their proffered treaties (in 1651) were designed to invade by stealth, not to oppose from across the water (117–18). A similar tactic governs the bristling paronomasia of the poem, which is, like Milton's sonnets, interested in 'hard' words.[84] When the sea invades the polders, there are 'Whole sholes of *Dutch* serv'd up for *Cabillau* ... For pickled *Herring*, pickled *Heeren* chang'd' (lines 32–4). Yet Dutch *kabeljauw* (codfish) is about as hard as it gets. Marvell gives his poem a Dutch flavour by using terms that were familiar from newsbooks and satires, such as *Heeren*, terms which, often enough, so shadow English as to sound like a form of pidgin. The formula *Hoog-mogenden* ('high and mighty'), for example, often used in accounts of Dutch affairs, is evoked in the punning little beast fable: 'How fit a Title clothes their *Governours*, | Themselves the *Hogs* as all their subjects *Bores*!' (lines 79–80). It was, and is, routine to make fun of foreigners by giving them words which have inappropriate meanings when heard as English. 'The Character of Holland' does a bit of that (Herring/*Heeren*), but it favours words whose Dutch meanings are close to English ones—most 'boers' were rustics, hence 'boors' as well as 'boars'. This makes the Netherlanders seem more like comic dialect speakers than aliens (the polders are as British as Shropshire).

The high-profile placing of Dutch words that were current (however briefly) in English—e.g. the '*Dyke-grave*' who maintains sea-walls, '*Hans-in-Kelder*' (i.e., Hans in the cellar, 'child in the womb')[85]—reinforces this convergence. And Marvell exploits the point, which Felltham had made with philological gravitas, that 'still among us all our old words are *Dutch*':[86]

> Or what a Spectacle the *Skipper gross*,
> *A Water-Hercules Butter-Coloss*,

> *Tunn'd* up with all their sev'ral *Towns of Beer*;
> When Stagg'ring upon some Land, *Snick and Sneer,*
> They try, like Statuaries, if they can,
> Cut out each others *Athos* to a Man:[87]
> And carve in their large Bodies, where they please,
> The Armes of the *United Provinces.*   (lines 93–100)

'*Skipper*' and '*Snick and Sneer*' ('thrust and cut') are Dutch imports into English of this period. Their presence alerts the reader to the common fabric of both tongues: the shared Germanic roots of 'gross' and 'land' ('*some* Land' nicely mocks the marshiness of the provinces); the Latin borrowing 'colossus' truncated to match Dutch *koloss*; and the fact that *Bier* can mean 'beer'—appropriate to tuns—as well as introduce town-names, in both languages. The Dutch are split into 'sev'ral *Towns*' (whereas Britain is putatively whole); their mode of interaction is, to put it mildly, divisive, all about cutting up, carving each other with quarrelsome weapons; but they do have a living connection with English and thus with the English.

It is a sign of continuity in the politics of the extended archipelago that Marvell's poem (originally circulated only in manuscript) was printed up to this point in 1665 and 1672, during the Second and Third Anglo-Dutch Wars. These texts have a non-authorial conclusion in praise of Restoration naval commanders. Why do they not also reproduce the fifty-plus remaining lines of the 1653 text? Partly because union—less of an issue in the later wars—is so pronounced a theme in them. 'But when such Amity at home is show'd; | What then are their confederacies abroad?' (lines 101–2). Given that the Dutch enjoy drunken brawling, why should we be surprised that they are so bad at uniting with the English? What makes their behaviour the more fatuous is that alliance, indeed dependency, is an historical fact, though the Dutch (as at the Battle of the Downs) refuse to signal this:

> all ancient Rights and Leagues must vail,
> Rather then to the *English* strike their sail;
> To whom their weather-beaten *Province* ows
> It self, when as some greater Vessel tows
> A Cock-boat tost with the same wind and fate;
> We buoy'd so often up their *sinking State.*   (lines 107–12)

The singular form '*Province*' is presumably a hyper-correct reference to the Holland of Marvell's title, just one of the United Provinces; yet if the term is primarily selective, it simultaneously allows the insinuation that part if

not all of the Netherlands constitutes a province of England—the larger
vessel towing behind it a puny unstable boat, a state that threatens to swamp
with water as the dykes are beaten by the sea.

Given all this emphasis on continuity, linguistic overlap, and common
history, it is not surprising to learn that in 1653 'At least some English
politicians were looking forward to an Anglo-Dutch alliance with the same
enthusiasm which lay behind the 1651 mission',[88] nor that when, in April
1654, the conflict was resolved—within a week of an Act uniting Ireland
and Scotland with England—it was represented in some quarters not as a
crushing victory but a joining together with the Dutch.[89] In the years which
followed, the Protectorate would turn its aggression towards Spain. But as
late as 1659, in the context of the recall of the Rump, moves were being
made by Vane and others who shared his outlook to combine England
with its errant '*Province*', only for the dynamics of 1651–2 to recur, and for
talk of 'nearest union'[90] to turn within months to threats of war.

Let me end with Milton, for these late moves by the Rump are the proper
context for understanding his celebrated, last-ditch attempt to resist the
Restoration. In *A Readie and Easie Way* (1660), he declares that the return
of the Stuarts will 'redound the more to our shame, if we but look on our
neighbours the United Provinces, to us inferiour in all outward advantages:
who notwithstanding, in the midst of greater difficulties, couragiously,
wisely, constantly went through with the same work, and are settl'd in all
the happie injoiments of a potent and flourishing Republick to this day.'[91]
Modern scholars have failed to evaluate Milton's repeated references to
the Dutch in this pamphlet; contemporaries instantly noted his pro-Rump
attraction to the Netherlands. William Colline asked of his plans for a
governing assembly, 'Whether *I.M.* his readie and easie way... be not
borrowed in copy from the States of *Holland*';[92] and in his full-scale reply to
Milton, *The Dignity of Kingship Asserted* (1660), George Starkey goes out of
his way to rebut his adversary regarding the make-up of the Netherlands (it
is a hotch-potch, not a commonwealth), and recycles familiar slights about
Dutch boorishness and money-grubbing.

That Starkey's treatise was reprinted after the Restoration as *Monarchy
Triumphing over Traiterous Republicans* (1661) is suggestive. The Dutch would
continue to figure as objects of abuse and admiration both because of what
they could be made to represent culturally and constitutionally and because
of what they could provide, in the way of arms and supplies for rebellion;
but whereas, during the interregnum, the Low Countries attracted hard-up

cavaliers like Thomas Killigrew (as well as a few republicans who could not be reconciled to the Protectorate), they later became a hotbed of dissent. While the Anglo-Scoto-Dutch triangle was, if anything, reinforced by the emergence of a Williamite solution to the challenge of Stuart absolutism, the alliances around it shifted; Presbyterians learned to co-operate again with English radicals (even Milton, by the late 1660s, was softening towards Jack the Presbyter). As I shall show in Chapter 9, the archipelago remained in this sense an extended, enlarged phenomenon, with Scottish writers like James Stewart and William Cleland making common cause in the Netherlands with such English radicals as John Locke.

8

Orrery's Ireland

I n 1669, the Earl of Orrery's *Guzman* was performed at the Theatre
Royal, Lincoln's Inn Fields. This charming, lightweight comedy—very
different from the rhymed heroic dramas which made the Earl's reputation
earlier in the decade—concerns a young gentleman of decayed fortune
who pretends to be a magician in order to fleece the rich and advance the
marriage prospects of his siblings. Francisco's skills are most apparent when
the anti-hero, Guzman, who is obliged to fight a duel, visits the supposed
sorcerer to purchase a charm against death. The scene is set with '*flashes
of Fire*' and much dancing around by boys '*in hideous Dresses, making great
Noises and Hums*'. Does Guzman require protection against sword-thrust
or gun-shot?, Francisco asks. And shouldn't the charm be tested? Claiming
that he has used the magic on himself, Francisco hands over a pistol which
is charged with powder but not loaded. In the words of the stage direction:
'Guzm[an] *Shoots, and* Fran[cisco] *lets fall a Bullet at his own Feet, which he
hastily takes up and shews to* Guzm[an] *who is amaz'd at the Shot.*'[1]

What suggested this trick to Orrery? His editor, William Smith Clark,
scoured Spanish as well as English literature to find sources for the plot of
Guzman, only to conclude that the author probably 'invented the whole
flimsy structure'.[2] Clark overlooked, however, an episode in Ireton's
Irish campaign which Orrery—then Lord Broghill—participated in, and
promptly reported to the English public in *A Letter from the Lord Broghill
to the Honourable William Lenthall Esq.* (1651). It seems that, after a bloody
encounter with Catholic forces in North Cork, Broghill found, on the
corpses of the defeated Irish, charms against death by sword-thrust and
musket-shot which had been distributed by the priests who sprinkled
the troops with holy water as they went to fight. In his *Letter* Broghill

transcribes one of these charms, and remarks: 'Certainly they are a people strangely given over to destruction, who though otherwise understanding enough, let themselves be still deluded by rediculous things, and by more rediculous persons; Had I been one of the charmed, I would have first tryed mine on the Priest which gave it.'[3]

Much could be said about Protestant attitudes to the Catholic Irishry's weakness for hocus pocus.[4] What interests me more immediately is the effect on the received picture of Orrery of this link between 'rediculous things' on a Munster battlefield and a gulling plot on the London stage, nearly two decades later. That literary scholars have underestimated the importance of Orrery's experiences of conflict and government in the peripheries of the archipelago is the more surprising given that the leading facts of his life—which was always centred on Ireland—were set out by Kathleen M. Lynch as long ago as 1965.[5] The best accounts of his prose romance, *Parthenissa*, by Paul Salzman and Nigel Smith, both see it as reflecting 'the pervasive political concerns of England in the Interregnum',[6] while the fullest, essay-length discussions of his plays, by Mita Choudhury and Nancy Klein Maguire,[7] are innocent of Irish data. As a result, scholars have failed to understand why his early plays were so successful with audiences attuned to the politics of the three kingdoms and their relationship with the United Provinces, Spain, and France. They have also neglected how his political and literary activities were both animated and compromised by the stresses, fractures, and volatile coalitions which emerged in the multiple monarchy—complications that were at their most intricate and bloody (as Chapter 5 has begun to show) in Ireland.

It is true that Broghill's career was tied into specifically English politics in 1649 when, *en route* to join the exiled court on the continent, he was (the story goes)[8] intercepted in London by Cromwell and offered a choice between working for parliament and languishing in the Tower. But he won Cromwell's trust by campaigning with him in Munster, and governing for him in Scotland, and he renewed his influence at Whitehall by advising Charles II on advantageous ways of satisfying the Protestant interest in Ireland. So his moves from royalism through co-operation with the Lord Protector into support for a Stuart Restoration only superficially resemble the gyrations of such English politician-writers as Edmund Waller. His shifts of allegiance were typical of those born into the New English families that had established themselves in Munster in the wake of the Tudor reconquest, and who had stayed true to the Church of Ireland—those known by the mid-seventeenth century as Old Protestants—for whom the contest between king and parliament was compounded by religious war and conflict over land ownership after the Irish Rebellion of 1641.

It would be a mistake, however, to view Broghill as merely representative, not just because he was unique in his mixture of piety, opportunism, physical courage, erudition, low avarice, and high imagination, but because his Protestant community was heterogenous even before the arrival of the dissenting Independents who followed Cromwell. It included such leaders as Murrough O'Brien, Earl of Inchiquin, whose switches of loyalty and faith (often conflicting with those of Broghill) were encouraged by his Gaelic background, his Catholic relatives and clients.[9] By 1641, morever, the interests of the New English were patchily interwoven with those of the traditionally Catholic Old English and mere Irish. When Broghill's father, Richard Boyle, 1st Earl of Cork was brought news of the rising, this unscrupulous Elizabethan adminstrator turned magnate, who was, in many respects, the quintessence of exploitative, New English invasiveness,[10] was dining, in a neighbourly way, in the house of his Old English son-in-law the Earl of Barrymore, with the Old Irish landowner, Viscount Muskerry, who was later a leading rebel. Such relationships did nothing to simplify the political choices which faced Old Protestants in the 1640s, and they adopted a variety of positions between the devoted royalism of Broghill's brother, Viscount Shannon (who went into exile with Charles II and remained loyal even when cuckolded by the king), and the intellectual republicanism of his sister, Lady Ranelagh.

The range of literary culture caught up in these social intricacies can be quickly gauged by triangulating an Old English soldier, a Gaelic poet, and John Milton, around the deaths of two Boyle family members shortly after the outbreak of the Rebellion. In September 1642, Broghill and other Protestant royalists recaptured a castle at Liscarrol from a group of Catholic rebels commanded by Gerat Barry—a professional soldier in the Spanish service, who had published, in Brussels, in 1634 (with the strikingly ethnic assertion 'Composed by Captaine GERAT BARRY Irish' on the title page) one of the most sophisticated military treatises to appear in English before Orrery's own *Treatise of the Art of War* (1677). It must have added to the bitterness of the fray that, in dedicating his *Discourse of Military Discipline* to the head of his family, Barry had honoured one of the men who now opposed him: the same Earl of Barrymore that had married Broghill's sister, Alice,[11] and hosted Clavell's *Introduction to the Sword Dance* in 1632 (above, p. 169). The rebellious kerns of that entertainment caught up with Barrymore now; he was killed by Barry's men, along with Broghill's brother, Kinelmeaky. Writing about this battle years later, the poet Dáibhí Ó Bruadair ignored the Protestant convert Barrymore and praised the Catholic *seanghaill* who took Kinelmeaky's life.[12] Earlier, though, he had lamented the death of Alice Boyle's second husband—surprisingly enough, a Catholic, Sir John Barry—and wished success to Barrymore's eldest son,[13] who went with his mother to England in 1645 and became, at Lady Ranelagh's prompting, a pupil of Milton.[14] So the literary contexts of Liscarrol link Barry and Ó Bruadair with the greatest puritan poet of the day, a poet whose life may have been saved at the Restoration by the mediation of Orrery at the instigation of Lady Ranelagh.[15]

Broghill's own literary connections were in one respect more circumscribed than those I have just sketched. Though he possibly learned some Gaelic in childhood,[16] he seems, as an adult, neither to have read the language nor to have understood the culture which the Cromwellians assaulted. It is unlikely that he knew the lines in which the poet Piarais Feiritéir, a tenant of the Boyles, praised his father as 'Iarla calma Corcaighe' ('the brave Earl of Cork'), and there is no sign of his responding to the innovative body of work in which Feiritéir registers the breakdown in relations between neighbours, and the fierceness of the Cromwellian 'gang from Dover'.[17] Feiritéir was caught up in the troubles which he lamented: initially on good terms with the planters he was given arms to oppose the rebels, but he joined the rising, and, after several years holding Tralee Castle, he was treacherously executed. That Broghill knew something about him is clear from his complaints to parliament about Inchiquin's dealings with Catholics, but he there mentions favours done to Feiritéir as a rebel with no reference to his being a poet.[18]

Despite his indifference to the fact that some of the finest verse of the age was being composed on the Boyle estates—an undervaluation of Irish that he shared with most of his Protestant contemporaries—Broghill's acquaintance with poets was extensive, and archipelagic. Did his appreciation of drama begin when he was five and six years old and visiting players (probably English) performed at his father's castle at Lismore?[19] As a young man at the Caroline court, he befriended Suckling and possibly Davenant. The former wrote him a marriage poem,[20] while the latter subsequently praised him as 'A great new World', lauded his cruelties in Munster—when he made the Lee run red with blood, and hanged a Catholic bishop[21]—and helped him, after the Restoration, get his plays staged in London. During the interregnum, Broghill exchanged poems with Cowley.[22] Irish politics linked him with Roscommon, and encouraged his correspondence with Denham. After the Restoration, he was admired by such younger writers as Dryden for pioneering rhymed heroic drama.[23] The origins of this mode have been disputed, but however the laurels are divided between Orrery and Katherine Philips, its emergence had an Irish dimension.

The London-born Philips was more a Welsh than an Irish writer (see Chapter 6). Yet because her marriage portion was partly paid in Irish land that had been confiscated after the 1641 Rebellion,[24] she went to Dublin in 1662–3, when appeals against expropriation were being heard, to secure her husband's claim. It was then that Orrery was shown her translation of the third act of Corneille's *La Mort de Pompée*. He was no doubt attracted by the local topicality of a work which deals with the rights and wrongs of clemency after a civil war[25] in the context of conspiracies that threaten a victorious Caesar at the Egyptian edge of empire—resembling the plots against the Lord Lieutenant which stirred among radical Dissenters in Ireland (above, p. 79). Orrery encouraged Philips to complete her translation, and advanced a hundred pounds to buy costumes for its production at the Smock Alley theatre. He tendered her this help shortly before the public première of his own *Altemera*, the heroic play which took London by storm as *The Generall*.[26] Much remains obscure about Orrery's support for Philips,[27] but the Cromwellian sympathies which persist in this royalist poet's translation (married as she was to a parliamentarian colonel) will not have made him less interested in seeing her work performed.

Philips's political connectivity in 1662–3 is just one reminder of how Orrery's sizeable output—which includes not just romances, plays, and the *Art of War*, but religious poetry, state letters, and controversial pamphlets—was sustained by social networks that discouraged fixed positions, even after the concentrating shock of the 1641 Rebellion and the consolidation of Protestant fortunes which followed Charles II's sponsorship of the Act of Explanation (written by Orrery to justify the Restoration land settlement in Ireland). In the 1660s the newly promoted Broghill had to get along with Irish Catholics who had rebelled in the 1640s and gone into exile with the king, and who now returned to court and to their lands in Munster—much as his father had found it necessary to deal with Old Irish and English landowners.[28] His contacts within Ireland may never have been as eclectic as those of, say, Ormond, the Old English leader of Protestant royalism, but his tentacles reached further. Unlike Ormond, he inherited an estate in England, which he used for periods of retirement when politics became too hot, and which was well-placed, in Somerset, for keeping an eye on supply lines between the West Country and Cork. More unusually, he construed his position archipelagically because of his dealings in Scotland.

Like many royalist gentlemen, Broghill initially encountered the Scots in the débacle of the First Bishops' War. But he returned north in 1655–6, as President of the Council in Edinburgh, when his task was to strengthen union by adapting the Scottish legal system to English practice, to extend the Protectorate's support-base by manipulating disagreements between the Remonstrant and Resolutioner factions within Presbyterianism (a strategy which, it was hoped, would control Ulster too), and to root out royalist conspiracy.[29] The task was made easier for him by blood and marriage ties that linked Munster to Scotland,[30] but it still required political tact. Broghill's relationship with George Monck was probably cemented in 1647, during Monck's third visit to Ireland, when both sided with parliament's Lord Lieutenant, Viscount Lisle, against the volatile Inchiquin. It was in Scotland, however, as servants of Cromwell, that the two future agents of Charles II really worked together. In Edinburgh, Broghill developed his skills as a spymaster, and he was alerted to the seditious traffic between the West of Scotland and Ireland which preoccupied him beyond the change of régime.[31] It was all excellent preparation for the greatest crisis of his life—the Restoration—when he exploited his Presbyterian contacts, and his knowledge of underground royalism, to plot with Monck and conspire to snatch Dublin castle from the Army's commissioners. These are the circumstances which precipitated his first popular success, *The Generall*, a play which loses much when thought about Anglocentrically.

★   ★   ★

Before turning to that drama, however, I want to show how Orrery's Ireland illuminates an earlier work: the huge, narratively convoluted but continuously readable *Parthenissa*, which began to be published in Waterford, in the year of the *Letter* to Lenthall, 1651, and which broke off with a London instalment in 1669, the year of *Guzman*.[32] This text is less *à clef* than some other romances of the period, such as Sir William

Sales's *Theophania* (1655), Richard Brathwaite's *Panthalia* (1659), and Sir George Mackenzie's thinly veiled account, in Book III of *Aretina* (1660), of Anglo-Scottish politics from 1603 to the Restoration (see Chapter 9). But it starts from a rebellion in Armenia, at the edge of an expansionist Roman Empire, against the background of the Social War (91–87 BC) between Rome and its dependent neighbours on the Italic peninsula. J. G. A. Pocock has argued that the war of the three kingdoms is difficult to analyse because it combined three different kinds of conflict: civil war in several spheres; imperialistic expansion by the English; and a *bellum sociale* resembling that fought between Rome and its neighbours, over citizenship rights and the like.[33] On the showing of *Parthenissa*, Broghill would agree with Pocock: in his partly topical romance, these modes of conflict are all present, compounded, and concatenated in ways that allow the reader to investigate the processes which generate crisis.

That *Parthenissa* has an Irish aspect is suggested by a letter to Broghill from his brother, the scientist Robert Boyle, in December 1649: 'I am not a little satisfied, to find,' he writes,

> that since you were reduced to leave your *Parthenissa*, your successes have so happily emulated or continued the story of *Artabanes*; and that you have now given romances as well credit as reputation. Nor am I moderately pleased, to see you as good at reducing towns in *Munster*, as *Assyria*; and to find your eloquence as prevalent with masters of garrisons, as mistresses of hearts.[34]

This compliment turns on a comparison between the campaigns of a hero in the romance and those of Broghill, with Cromwell, in Ireland. And although *Parthenissa* draws from its sources—which include Polybius and Raleigh's *History of the World*[35]—a number of un-Irish set-piece battles fought with enormous armies, it also describes the long sieges, savage reprisals, piracy or privateering by sea, switches of allegiance, and confusing pacts which characterized war in the Irish theatre.

The rebellion in Armenia, for instance, quickly mounts to a siege which the hero of this part of the narrative, Artavasdes, resists. In describing his success, Broghill is far more attentive to logistics and tactics than is usual in romance—as one might expect from the defender of Lismore against the Irish in 1642 and Youghal against Castlehaven's Confederate troops in 1645. Like those rebels, Artavasdes's opponents have influence at court. More immediately (to isolate a source for this episode), like the Protestants of Cork, who learned from experience in 1644 to secure their garrison by expelling papists, the royalists in Artaxata are betrayed from within the siege.[36] 'That which brought us so often into hazard', Artavasdes says, 'was, That *Artaxata* was twice set on fire, by the treachery of those within, which requiring many hands to quench it, robb'd us of so many hands for our defence' (52). Once the traitors have been identified, Broghill relishes their execution, then reveals how, like the papists, their leader abuses his contacts: 'There was also one of the Prisoners that being upon the point of death, and repenting his Rebellion, sent to me, and to discharge his Conscience, assur'd me, that *Celindus* had a friend in the Kings Council, who gave him a constant intelligence of our proceedings...' (ibid.). This 'friend', Crassolis, resembles such courtiers as the Earl of Glamorgan (above, p. 187), a counsellor trusted by Charles who, in Old Protestant eyes, put the interests of the Irish Catholics before those of the crown.

It was an uncomfortable fact for Broghill that, whatever the disloyalty of the Confederate Catholics, it was the besieged Old Protestants who broke the truce called by the king in 1643 so that he could boost his strength in England with Irish troops. At the time they made their case in declarations that Broghill recorded in his letter book—telling the Ulster Scots, for example, that they had been forced to accept the treaty by 'unsupportable sufferings', and explaining that they now end it because 'the Irish are like to obtaine an advantagious Peace, from his Ma[jes]tie by their insinuatinge, and by the wicked Counsell about him'.[37] In the romance, a similar matter is handled more obliquely:

> *Celindus*, who perceiv'd that force was unsuccesful, and that two assaults had cost him neere 7000 Men, lost all hopes of taking *Artaxata* by Storm, and therefore began to make his Approaches, and endeavor to possess himself of that by industry and time, which valour had deny'd him; but not wholly to rely upon the blind events of War, he design'd to attempt something by Treaty...   (ibid.)

Working with Crassolis at court, Celindus puts terms to the king that are calculated to secure an advantageous peace, and to render his opponents 'surprizable' by making them drop their guard. As a gloss on Confederate motives[38] this could hardly be more jaundiced, but Broghill's account of the debates that went on around Charles I regarding the legitimacy of treating with rebels is absorbingly cogent.

Never less than refracted, Irish history in *Parthenissa* becomes virtual. The King of Armenia, Artabazus, escapes the rebellion in his own realm by fleeing to a neighbouring province, where the loyal governor, Phanasder, provides enough men from his overstretched forces to rescue the Princess Altezeera from Artaxata. The troops sent to England by Inchiquin during the cessation did Charles, in practice, little good, and when the truce was broken the Munster Protestants followed him in looking to parliament. It is perhaps not surprising that this betrayal should be justified in the narrative by accusation. In the romance, King Artabazus so ungratefully seizes power from Phanasder in his province that Artavasdes turns against the monarch he had previously protected from rebels. Such changes of allegiance are common in *Parthenissa*, and they are never more Irish than when associated with Broghill's excuse that he was defending Charles's interests by joining his opponents. As Surena puts it: '*If I have been so unfortunate, as seemingly to take up Arms against my King; yet I am so happy as to be satisfied they are really for him*' (527). Inconveniently for Broghill, this was also the justification which Confederates used for the 1641 rising.

What raises *Parthenissa* from apologia to literature, however, is precisely its willingness to seek out and develop such points of difficulty. Artavasdes may be right to oppose Artabazus for being ungrateful, but the rebel Surena's motives prove more ambiguous: justified in protecting Parthenissa against the oppressive suit of his king, he allows noble resistance to rationalize personal ambition and misuses his growing power to harass the heroine himself. As events unfold it becomes harder to categorize causes as good or bad. The combination of local crisis management and expedient royal policy which made it impossible for Old Protestants to be consistent created a writing-climate for Broghill in which scepticism and suppleness could flourish. Even when his virtuous characters do not change sides, they find their natural equals—courageous, courteous, and ardent in love—in those ranged against them, sparing them as strangers because of their acts of valour, or pulling off a helmet to reveal a friend in the ranks of the enemy. This mode of romance proved lastingly attractive,[39] but it was peculiarly consoling to Broghill's contemporaries in Ireland who knew what it was to fight against those who had been allies, and who wanted to believe, despite or because of the acrimony of Irish conflict, that, once the wars were over, the amity of such characters as Artabbanes and Artavasdes, who met when fighting one other, could be viable.

In the sections of *Parthenissa* published in 1669, Orrery is less interested in the reduction of towns in Assyria and Munster than in such Protectorate and Restoration topics as the spectacle of war at sea. The romance continues to be troubled, however, by the fear of neighbourly betrayal which no doubt did afflict Old Protestants traumatized by the 1641 Rebellion but which they also played up whenever the Dublin government seemed likely to deal tolerantly with Catholics. Even after the Restoration, when Ireland had been at peace for a decade, there is a pressurizing vigilance in Orrery's letters to Ormond about conspiracies, and the same anxiety dictates the tone of the treatise which he addressed to the Lord Lieutenant in 1662, *The Irish Colours Displayed*. There Orrery resists the royal counsels of reconciliation, describing the Irish as inveterate enemies of the English, and giving climactic emphasis to 'the late unparallel'd Massacres'.[40] The best way to avoid a repetition of the rising, he insists in his letters, is to have a Protestant militia ready for instant use.

Near the end of *Parthenissa* these views come through in the account of unrest in Nicomedia. As its name suggests, this city falls within the historical territory of Nicomedes of Bithynia, but it is held by an elite governing on behalf of Mithridates of Persia. Like Dublin or the Munster garrison towns, the place is divided. Numbers of the inhabitants are loyal to the wrong monarch, much as the 'Vulgar *Irish*', according to *The Irish Colours Displayed*, believe 'that the Kingdome of *Ireland* lawfully belongs to the Crown of *Spain*' (5). In the romance, 'a rich *Nicomedian*' (for which read an Old English Catholic), who is entertaining the Princess of Persia at his house, abducts her on behalf of a 'Conspirator's party' while 'the ancient Inhabitants of the place' (the Gaelic Irish) take up arms against the government. Fortunately 'the then Chief Magistrate of *Nicomedia*', being a wiser lieutenant than Ormond, has anticipated the unrest, and the hero of this section, Callimachus (who might here be Orrery), can 'the more hastily put the *Pontick* Militia of *Nicomedia* in Arms' (719–20).

Those equations are speculative and circumstantial because the topicality of *Parthenissa* is not determinate. Its procedures owe much to the seventeenth-century belief—summarized by John M. Wallace—that

> to moralize about contemporary affairs and yet to write a piece of literature [an author should] see in the local incidents the general rules that they typified. Then he had to find his fable, usually in history books, although no source was barred and a pure invention was quite permissible; and finally ... work up his fable with all the expertise at his command. The reader ... would reverse the process, going from particulars to generals to particulars again.[41]

This catches well the work of analysis, extrapolation, and analogy construction that has gone into *Parthenissa*. Broghill makes it impossible to read the romance as ancient history by mixing figures from different periods—Hannibal, Sulla, Pompey—and introducing pieces of 'pure invention' inspired by French romance (oracles, arduous quests, recovery from apparent death, erotic intrigues). Relevance to warfare in the three kingdoms is local and fleeting, or elusively paradigmatic, or it lies in the strands of resemblance which make a hero such as Artabbanes suggest now one contemporary figure and now another.

Artabbanes is certainly prismatic. While Robert Boyle was right to see Broghill in his make-up, he also smacks of Cromwell.[42] In Book III of Part I, he turns into the historical figure of Spartacus, leading a slave revolt and showing great military acumen. Because we are accustomed to the Spartacus of Hollywood and Soviet ballet, it is easy to overlook how unusual Broghill's positive account of him is. Elsewhere in early modern anglophone literature and political theory he seems to be ignored or glancingly vilified. In his Preface, Broghill recommends Spartacus as more admirable even than Masaniello, the Neapolitan fisherman who led a 'Revolt…from the King of Spayne in the Present' (A2v). The Europe-wide cult of Masaniello which followed the rising of 1647 awaits its historian,[43] but medals pairing him with Cromwell were definitely struck.[44] In the case of Artabbanes it looks as though war in Ireland led Broghill to compound his royalist liking for princely heroes with a devotion to Protestant liberty under a low-born leader.

★   ★   ★

To read *The Generall* after *Parthenissa* is to be made to think harder about the King of Spain. Although, as events would show, Spain posed less of a threat to the stability of post-Restoration Ireland than did Louis XIV's France, Old Protestants remembered how Catholic soldiers recruited by Gerat Barry and others for service in Spain's own *bellum sociale*, between Castile, Catalonia, and Portugal had stayed in Ireland in 1640–1 and been deployed in the Rebellion.[45] Once the Cromwellian invasion took hold, and Catholic landowners began to be dispossessed and sent into Connacht or the West Indies, Spain was the country to which defeated rebels went. The belief, reported by Orrery, that the King of Spain was properly the ruler of Ireland (above, p. 253), was widely current among the 'Vulgar *Irish*' throughout the period.

Nor was the Spanish threat perceived solely as coming from the Catholics. Shortly after the première of *The Generall*, in 1663, Orrery informed the king that republicans were working for an invasion of Ireland by Spain.[46] Clark (Orrery's editor) may be right to say that the setting of *The Generall* in Sicily is not significant, but when he backs this up by pointing out that Mora, the base of those rebelling in the play, is actually in Spain, not Sicily, one is inclined to wonder. For Masaniello's revolt in Naples was linked to a rising in the Spanish dominion of Sicily,[47] a place of strategic importance which interested Orrery enough for a 'map of Scicily' to be prominent in his library.[48] By choosing the locale he did, Orrery was able to correlate unrest in one island that was breaking its links with Spain (i.e. Sicily) with the troubles in another (i.e. Ireland) that accompanied the Restoration—an event that Orrery wanted to construct as freeing Munster from the threat of Catholic hegemony long associated with Spanish power.

Like a number of heroic dramas written in the 1660s—for which it provided the pattern—*The Generall* is about the overthrow of an usurper. Having seized power in Sicily, put the legitimate heir (Melizer) in prison, and sent his general, and rival for the heroine Altemera, into banishment, the play's unnamed usurper-king finds himself confronted by rebels and uncertainly supported by an army that wants its general back. This general, Clorimun, is another of Orrery's prismatic characters: primarily a version of Monck, he has touches of Broghill himself (who was General of the Horse in Ireland for parliament and Major-General of the Army in 1662), and like both men he is drawn into events reluctantly, expressing a preference for retirement. Once involved, his contribution is decisive. The jealousy of the usurper and the pleas of Altemera ignite his loyalty to Melizer, and he helps effect a Restoration in the course of which he is reconciled to Lucidor, the leading rebel and Altemera's lover.

As a dramatist Orrery has been seen by Choudhury as a propagandist for Charles II, and by Maguire as a troubled ex-Cromwellian who is driven by guilty repetition-compulsion to return to the same clutch of issues. My own view is very different. In his plays, as in *Parthenissa*, Orrery strikes me as calculating: both critical of Carolean policy and cannily defensive. The latter was particularly necessary when he wrote *The Generall* because his role in the run-up to the Restoration had been more duplicitious than he retrospectively claimed.[49] Apart from anything else, he had compromised the position of the Church of Ireland by networking with the 'Presbyterian knot'.[50] When he plotted in this way from Munster, Broghill was only partly smoothing the way for Monck in Scotland and England. He was also preparing, as some recognized at the time, to set hard conditions for the king—resisting the Restoration which did occur for the sake of another (more advantageous to Old Protestants) which did not. Despite his part in the conspiracy to seize Dublin castle and other garrisons in 1659, he was not an unconditional royalist, and he expressed surprise at the swift liberality of the invitation issued to Charles by the London parliament.[51] He was slow to make the advances which his royalist relatives expected, and careful to write critically to Thurloe about 'odd plots here concerning the King'.[52]

In *The Generall* these awkward facts are finessed, while open resistance to the Cromwells is subtly discredited. Thrasolin, an officer working for the usurper, as Broghill did for the Protectorate, proves more useful to Melizer (i.e. Charles II) than those who are frankly rebellious because he can orchestrate unrest in the army, and persuade the usurper to recall the general. Since the seeds of conflict are already sown between Clorimun and the usurper, it is then only a matter of time before Melizer's Restoration is secured. Who, though, are the rebels, in their Irish-sounding stronghold, Mora? (Moira, up in Ulster, was a flashpoint in more than one seventeenth-century campaign.) Since they are not fighting in support of Melizer[53]—though their leader is reconciled with Clorimun, who, by that stage, is—they can hardly put us in mind of, say, the English royalists of Booth's rebellion. A 1660s audience would have pricked up its ears at 'Rebels' and 'Confederacy' when Thrasolin describes the usurper's mistrust of his own men: 'Sometimes hee thinkes, the Rebells being nigh, | That wee and they are in Confederacy' (I.[i.]86–7). *The Generall* is hardly more *à clef* than *Parthenissa*, but these rebels sound very like Catholic Confederates: justly opposed by the usurper and his general—until he treats with them—they can as properly be turned to royalist ends by the right sort of well-intentioned collaborator.

If *The Generall* were simply an apology for Monck, this section of the plot might be taken as rendering more palatable the truce which he made with the Spanish-trained mere Irish leader, Owen Roe O'Neill, in 1649[54]—that year of shifting alliances which provoked Milton in his *Observations on the Articles of Peace* to denounce the Belfast presbytery for its similarly dangerous accommodation with Catholic rebels (above, pp. 231–2). Yet the denouement of the play, in which the darkly named Lucidor is given the hand of Altemera by Melizer, would more pressingly have put contemporaries in mind of the post–1660 situation of Catholic moderates. From the grudging point of view of Orrery, the Ormondist-fringe Confederates were the great winners in the Restoration game—the chief beneficiaries of the restored king's mercy—because many had rebelled in 1641, yet, due to their later seeming fidelity,[55] they were granted lands and favour.

Certainly, the passive royalism of the rebels in Act V—

> To their true sovereigne gladly they submitt.
> Against the usurpers pow'r they made defence,
> But they to you are all obedience. (V.[i.]402–4)

—most naturally evokes the dutifulness of loyal Catholics, while not excluding the thought that hard-line followers of O'Neill were being indulged by Melizer/Charles II, who responds to the submission by saying:

> My mercies still shall be to those more great,
> Which to it trust, and for it doe not treat.
> Past faults I'le never to Remembrance bring… (409–11)

Any suggestion of laxity is qualified, however, by Melizer's wisdom in giving Clorimun, the character who most resembles Monck and Broghill, the authority and military means to protect Sicily/Ireland against invasion from Catholic Europe (Puglia was at this date under Spanish control): 'Now, *Clorimun*', he declares, 'The *Apulian* king on *Sicily* does fall, | And of this Warr I make you Generall' (417–18).

It is worth recalling the circumstances in which *The Generall* was performed. Before its public première, the play (or a version of it) was privately staged in Dublin in front of the Lord Lieutenant, Ormond, under the title *Altemera*. In London, in 1664, it opened to an audience which included Charles II. Both occasions gave Orrery the chance to set up for admiration the royal policy of oblivion, while avoiding (through the impersonality of drama) full endorsement of the king's tolerance, and pressing for power in Dublin to be exercised by his own faction. Once that is noticed, the play's willingness superficially to harmonize with official policy itself seems calculated, and the tenor of the work can be squared with Orrery's more aggressive *Irish Colours Displayed* and its elaborately documented partner, *An Answer of a Person of Quality to a*

Scandalous Letter—both published in 1662, the year of *The Generall*'s Irish performances, in reply to Peter Walsh's *Letter Desiring a Just and Mercifull Regard of the Roman Catholicks of Ireland* (1662?). Brought out anonymously not least to conceal the author's involvement with those he now called 'the late horrid Usurpers',[56] these pamphlets whitewash the erratic record of Old Protestant royalism and condemn the conduct of Irish Catholics into the period covered by *The Generall*. Whatever Walsh may claim, Orrery scoffs, 'not the Birds nor the Flies contributed lesse to [the Restoration] then the *Roman* Catholique *Irish*'.[57]

The Old English Franciscan Walsh, an opponent of the Jesuit militant Conor O'Mahony during the crises of the Confederation (above, p. 187), is an interesting target for Orrery to have selected because he was execrated by such firm Romanists as Ó Bruadair for his willingness to obey the king rather than the pope in spiritual matters.[58] As so often in Irish politics, the compromiser was perceived by all sides as especially threatening. In his *Letter* to Ormond, Walsh admits that wrongs had been done by Catholics, but says that they have been punished by the scourge of war, and that Protestants have behaved badly too. The Lord Lieutenant should even-handedly 'preserve the ... people of so many different Nations of the Brittish Monarchy'.[59] Orrery responded to this by warning against the adoption of measures which might strengthen Catholic rebels. A powerfully built passage in *The Irish Colours Displayed* predicts endless contention in Ireland given the long history of animosity, the differences of habit and language, and the 'enmity' which naturally holds between a 'subjected people' and 'their Conquerors'. Orrery must have written this with a copy of Spenser's *View of the State of Ireland* in hand, because he ends up refuting the Latin tag with which Sir James Ware, in his 1633 preface,[60] had rebuked the poet's pessimism: 'When all these thoughts ... run thorough my head, I cannot hope to live so long as to hear *Iam cuncti gens una sumus* [now we are one whole people] plaid by the *Irish* Harp, though I know it was sung by some *English* in their discourses about the beginning of the late Kings Reign' (4–7). Orrery prefers to cite Spenser on the savagery of Irish funerals (5), and to recommend his policy towards papists. As he puts it in the *Answer*: 'the BEAST if *pamper'd*, will *Kick*, if kept *low*, OBEY' (82).

Walsh lacks Orrery's forensic skill, but he qualifies his divisive pessimism, in *The Irish Colours Folded* (1662), by invoking other multiple monarchies and cultural genealogies. Comparing the 1641 Rebellion with the rising in Catalonia, he points out that the Spanish now sit amicably with 'the

Catalonians, who ... transferred the Dominion over them to a Foreign Prince, [and] murdered ... all the *Spaniards* that came in their way' (4). Pursuing a line that reflects the relatively integrationist experience of the Old English, he says that the Irish are as capable of getting on with their conquerors as their conquerers were with theirs: 'The *Brittains*, the *Danes*, the *Saxons*, and the *Normans* are now so incorporated in *England*, as the memory of all distinction is lost amongst them' (3). Orrery had categorized Ormond as culturally English;[61] Walsh prefers to stress his Anglo-Norman ancestors, and how they kept their lands. If Ormond adopts the mercy and justice of his forebears, he predicts, peace will break out and 'the posteri[t]y of those that proclaim lowdly the English interest, must within an age, admit themselves to be called Irish as well as the Descendants from the first Colony of English planted in *Ireland*' (11).

Three and half centuries later it is still too early to say whether Walsh was right. It took the Old Protestants decades to feel secure enough in their Irishness and hostile enough to England to generate what has been called colonial nationalism, and to this day, in Ulster, the Presbyterian pieces of the jigsaw do not fit. Yet Ulster also complicated Orrery's perception of the three kingdoms, as can be seen from his typically Irish Protestant, unresolved use of the word 'British'.[62] Early in *The Irish Colours Displayed* he sweepingly describes his theme as 'The contention lying ... between His Majesties *British* Protestant Subjects, and His *Irish* Romane Catholique in the Kingdome of *Ireland*' (2). Later, though, he applies 'British' exclusively to the Ulster Scots and writes instead about the 'English'—itself an ambiguous term, which sometimes includes the Anglo-Normans who remained Catholic, and sometimes more restrictively the Old Protestants and Cromwellians. His less than frank assertion that Charles II could rely on 'His Protestant Subjects in *Ireland*, whom I look upon all as one body'[63] would crumble in 1666 when the Covenanters revolted in Scotland. 'I consider Ireland as consisting of three sorts of people', he then told Ormond: 'the protestants, the Scotch presbyters and other sectaries, and the papists.'[64]

Orrery's self-presentation as not Irish, not fully British, and not yet Anglo-Irish, but as—in a peculiar sense—one of 'the English in Ireland', was shaped by his London life as a young man, and by periods in Somerset. It was, however, focussed by the conflicts of the 1640s and 1650s, when the Old Protestants were caught between Scottish complications in Ulster and rebellious Gaelic Irish, and by their vulnerability after the Restoration—a vulnerability which hindsight tends to underestimate, compounded as it was by archipelagic interconnections and a changing international scene that brought war with France and the United Provinces close to the shores of Munster. Those are the springs of Orrery's fear, in 1666, that unrest in Scotland would spread to Presbyterian Ulster and incite Catholics to plot a rising with help from the continent. In his letter to Ormond about the 'three sorts of people' in Ireland, Orrery predicts that Louis XIV will send arms, encouraged by the presence in France of 'the desperatest sort of Irish'. What made the dangers worse, as he pointed out, was that the London parliament (which had already refused to countenance an Act of Union on commercial grounds)[65] was damaging the revenue on which the defence of Ireland depended by legislating against the import of Irish cattle.[66]

★   ★   ★

All this explains why Orrery, whose *Parthenissa* and *The Generall* are so rooted in Irish conditions, and who was so staunch in defending the interests of Munster Protestants against England,[67] should have gone on to write plays that are unique on the early Restoration stage in dealing with English history (and should have added, in 1676, a romance about Henry VIII called *English Adventures*). *Henry the Fifth* and *The Black Prince* do not represent the full spread of his drama, even in the 1660s: *Mustapha*, for instance, a tragedy about false counsellors, is set in Hungary among the Turks, and his most searching usurper play *Tryphon* revisits the cruces of *The Generall* in a setting vaguely drawn from Josephus' history of the Maccabees. They are the clearest symptoms, however, of an Englishness which was the more assertive and anxious for being Irish, and threatened by the power of France—a preoccupation not just in the history plays but in the long poem called 'A Vision' that Orrery wrote in 1675, and in his *Art of War*.

The constructed Englishness of *Henry the Fifth* is apparent in the homogeneity of its dramatis personae. In giving Owen Tudor a large (and unhistorical) role as Henry's confidant, Orrery erased his Welsh descent: nothing in the play recalls the fractious exchanges between MacMorris, Fluellen, Pistol, and Jamy in Shakespeare. Orrery's English characters are, inevitably, virtuous, courageous, and faithful, though their sharing a code of love and honour with the French nobility does smooth Henry's path to achieving his territorial rights and the hand of the Princess Katherine.

This code is richly capable of generating dramatic tension. Owen Tudor, for instance, feels obliged to woo the Princess on the king's behalf when requested, even though he loves her himself. It is significant that his predicament should be counterpointed with an intrigue in which the Duke of Burgundy breaks a treaty with the English king, because although it is only in a limited sense political it transposes the dilemmas which Broghill and others faced when choosing between obedience to the crown and self-interest in the 1650s.

No doubt the huge success enjoyed by *Henry the Fifth* when it opened in London in 1664 partly stems from this ability to tent the wounds of both loyalty and betrayal. The French accept Henry as their monarch, for example, not just because of his victories but because they are persuaded that 'since *Charles the Fair* | Our Kings insensibly Usurpers were'.[68] This translates into the thought that, since the demise of Charles I, the three kingdoms had almost inadvertently been governed by usurpers—from Oliver Cromwell through his sons Richard and (in Ireland) Henry. Now, as King Henry puts it, '*English* and *French* ... but one people are: | And both shall have my equal love and care' (V.[vii.]551–2). What makes this different from other Restoration appeals for reconciliation between former enemies is its multinational setting. The king asserts a unity which (as at the end of *The Generall*) would join Irish Catholics to the English—a reconciliation somewhat speciously conjured up by a language of 'one people' used by the English in Ireland not about the mere Irish but about the English of England,[69] especially when hoping for an Act of Union or relaxation of customs dues.

Does that mean that Orrery's *Henry the Fifth* can, like Shakespeare's,[70] be read as shadowing a suppression of rebellion in Ireland—as putting on stage the reconquest which Broghill joined Cromwell to achieve but which he now wished to think of as always a royal cause? Here is what the Archbishop of Canterbury says to the French about the conflict among the barons and the Peasants Revolt that marred the reign of Richard II:

> Civil Wars our Isle destroy'd:
> Our Swords against our selves were long imploy'd.
> Whilst sick with Civil War, Prides worst disease,
> We bled in *France*, and lost three Provinces.
> But, now when those Intestine Wars are done,
> We come here to receive, or take our own.   (IV.[i.]53–8)

This so transparently and plausibly blames the loss of most of Ireland on the first English Civil War that alert spectators would have interpreted *Henry the Fifth* as saying *inter alia* that the crown should now receive or take its own in Ireland and not succumb to a show of peace from the Catholics. As Orrery put it in his *Answer* to Walsh, 'The Crown hath often lost by Credulity what it hath got by Valour; it hath lost by pretence of Peace what it had gain'd in open War: The Kings interest in *France* was thus lost, the GOD of peace prevent the like in *Ireland*.'[71]

These intimations are not surprising in a play which was completed in Dublin, in 1662, when Orrery was preoccupied with the Walsh controversy, and which opened in 1664 when he was in London working on the Act of Settlement.[72] Yet the work's potency as political fantasy depends on the France it presents suggesting not just contemporary Ireland but the France of Louis XIV that threatened it. It revels in the idea that Charles II could maintain by force the medieval title 'King of France' that the Stuart monarchs clung to and that Louis XIV was challenging at the time, and indulges the equally unlikely notion that the policy of 'closer union' that both crowns entertained could be clinched on terms advantageous to England by an ill-equipped Royal Navy and underfunded army.[73] A truer measure of the relative power of the two states emerged in the very month that *Henry the Fifth* was licensed (November 1663), when the king's last piece of France, Dunkirk, taken from Spain by Cromwell, was not exactly lost by credulity in pretence of peace but sold to Louis to help Charles pay his bills.

Orrery was not alone in feeling, by 1662, that the greatest threat to the three kingdoms was no longer posed by the Protectorate enemies, Spain and the United Provinces. Anti-French sentiment ran so high in 1661 that there was rioting in London. He was more alert to the danger than many at court, however, because of his Munster perspective. When Charles II was drawn into war with the United Provinces, in March 1665, Orrery could believe that the Dutch were plotting an insurrection with Ludlow and other recidivists;[74] but his fear of Irish Catholicism made him more nervous of France—rightly, as it proved, not just because Louis XIV did go to war against the three kingdoms in January 1666 but because he later sent troops to Ireland in support of James II. And if Orrery was ahead of much highly placed thinking in 1662, by the time *Henry the Fifth* was performed it was so acceptable that the king allowed his court to be projected into its fantasy. In his role as Owen Tudor, Betterton wore Charles II's coronation robe,

Harris, as Henry, that of the Duke of York, and Smith, as the Duke of Burgundy, the robe of the Earl of Oxford. When Orrery began his second dramatic celebration of English arms in France, later in 1664, it was at the king's command.

Even more than *Henry the Fifth*, *The Black Prince* rewrites history as romance. Bluntly warlike in its prologue (which predicts a coronation of Charles II in Paris), it revels in the paradoxes of duty and devotion that are thrown up by rivalry between Edward III, his son the Black Prince, Lord Delaware, and the captive King of France, as they seek the favours of the same woman, the bright Plantagenet. This drama of English nobility and French defeat was just one of Orrery's contributions to the war effort during a year (1666) in which he raised a militia in Munster, made plans to rebuild the fort at Kinsale, and kept Ormond informed about the landing of priests, public masses, and a visit by French ships to Kerry. He even gave him a résumé of a play put on by a Jesuit schoolmaster about a pastor who, with the help of his scholars, destroyed the wolves (i.e. the Protestants) that had ravaged his flock—evidence that Irish Catholics could be as topical as Orrery in their drama.[75] Anxiety was widespread in the three kingdoms, but the apprehensiveness in County Cork was such that Orrery was unable to write a letter recommending *The Black Prince* without discussing the likelihood of French arms reaching the Irish.[76] In some ways appropriately, because the play is set in the aftermath of war, *The Black Prince* was not staged until October 1667, by which time a treaty had been ratified with France and her allies. It is a sign of the problematic position of Munster within the British entity, however, that Orrery had to seek guidance from Ormond as to whether the waters around the province were excluded from the peace declared in 'the British seas'.[77]

No doubt this continuing sense of exposure contributed to the treatment of a merchant called Lynch, who had the misfortune to raise Orrery's suspicions in October 1667—as *The Black Prince* was being premièred—with a letter that he was carrying in French about procuring items from Ireland. Explaining to Ormond that he 'looked upon the cerf, mouton, and poules des Indes as being false names...for ammunition, horse, foot, &c.', Orrery said that he had only menaced, not injured, Lynch by tying lighted gunpowder matches to his fingers.[78] What would have happened to Lynch had he not managed to placate his tormenter can be deduced from the fate of Guillaume Preudhomme who was similarly treated in 1669 (the year of *Guzman*) and, according to a doctor, 'burned to the very sinews, which was a naughty thing'.[79] For a man of Orrery's make-up—refined, but inured to atrocities—the risk of another 1641 licensed ruthlessness. It would have confirmed rather than challenged his belief that little had changed to have known that, while he was torturing Preudhomme, Charles II and his inner circle—including Sir Richard Bellings, son of the author and Confederate leader—were negotiating with Louis XIV the secret Treaty of Dover. The deceiving counsellor Crassolis, who misled King Artabanus in *Parthenissa*, was active again at court.

Orrery discovered as much when his enemies, and some former allies, weakened his influence in 1672 and deprived him of his powers in the Lord President's court of Munster.[80] The sense that history was regressing to the condition of 1641 can only have been enhanced for him by the recruitment, in Ireland, of troops for Louis XIV's armies. Under pressure from the House of Commons in 1675, Charles recalled a brigade of soldiers—many of them Irish—from the French service, but he then committed the blunder of leaving them together in Ireland under Catholic officers.[81] A similar build-up of Irish forces had been unacceptable to parliament forty years earlier under Wentworth, and it was not pleasing now. When the House voted against granting the king any supply, Orrery responded by writing his 'Vision', in which the headless ghost of Charles I appears to his sleeping son and urges him to respect law and property while the Genius of France, laden with guns and money bags, tempts him with popery, absolutism, and French gold. This poem about 'poore Englands Fate' nowhere mentions Ireland, but, as surely as *Henry the Fifth*, it was generated by Irish circumstances.[82]

For wealthy Protestants, Restoration Munster was a place of increasing affluence; its big houses filled up with fine carpets, silver dishes, expensive looking-glasses, and oriental porcelain.[83] Yet fears of another 1641 grew during the 1670s, fed by London editions—publication was banned in Dublin—of Sir John Temple's *History of the Irish Rebellion* (1646). Orrery had always regarded the revolt as an archipelagic phenomenon because he saw how the Irish Catholics had been emboldened by the Scottish covenant into pressing Charles I for concessions; so the Covenanter rising of 1666 left him with anxieties which the king's toleration towards the Catholics (which might have pulled Old Protestants and Ulster Presbyterians together) did nothing to allay. Repeatedly after 1674, signs of unrest in Scotland prompted the Dublin government to send troops to Ulster, and there was continuous vigilance regarding contacts between Presbyterians across the

North Channel. From the composition of 'A Vision' in 1675 to the letters which he wrote shortly before his death, in 1679, harassing Ormond about the Popish Plot, Orrery was busy with security: rousing the militia, and, despite his gout, supervising from a sedan chair the reconstruction of the fort at Kinsale.

The regressive political psychology of this decade helps explain why, when reading Orrery's last major work, the *Treatise of the Art of War* (1677), one is so often reminded of *Parthenissa* and *The Generall*. Though the urge to warn Charles II (Fig. 12) about the French threat encourages him to illustrate his text with examples from Louis XIV's campaigns against the Spanish, he keeps adverting to the Irish Rebellion, and, when discussing foreign policy, to the ongoing revolts in Sicily which the French now fed with supplies. When he writes about treachery within garrisons, and about how to deal with fires during sieges, it is the Protestant towns of Munster in the 1640s that he has in mind, just as he had when writing about the siege of Artaxata in *Parthenissa*.[84] And when he urges the usefulness of pikes, or the prudence of having passwords, he invokes encounters like the one described in his 1651 *Letter to Lenthall*—triumphs he was revisiting as he prepared his unfinished and now lost history of the Confederate Wars.

So the opening boast of the *Art of War*, that 'no one Nation in the World, hath acquir'd more Glory by Arms, than the *English*', and the disquisition which follows on why English soldiers are as courageous as the Greeks and Romans, follows *Henry the Fifth* in celebrating an Englishness constructed by Ireland—a position which verges on paradox when Orrery, who is elsewhere happy to call Ireland 'my Countrey',[85] and who now lived permanently in Munster, calls the English 'my Countreymen'.[86] What the comparison with classical soldiery also brings into focus, however, is Orrery's relative reluctance to institute any categorization that would support a contrast between English civility and Irish barbarousness. When discussing Caesar's wars, for instance, he praises the Celtic leader Vercingetorix as 'a Person worthy to command a National Army', and he is sarcastic about the Greek and Roman habit of referring to their opponents as 'barbarous Nations (as they were pleas'd to term them)' (168, 130). Even in *Parthenissa*, where Hannibal's 'barbarous Affricans' and the Parthians who carry their enemies' heads on spears, 'according to their barbarous custome', resemble the savage, Moorish-tainted Irish of Spenser's *View*,[87] Orrery had made it clear that the leaders of these forces, though sometimes (like Hannibal

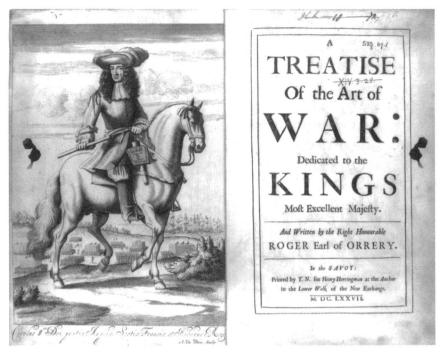

Fig. 12. The Stuart monarch as warrior (contrast James VI and I in Fig. 5). Charles II against a backdrop of troops in close formation, with the British navy offshore, from Orrery, *A Treatise of the Art of War* (London, 1677).

himself) gripped by primitive passions, were capable of noble behaviour. While he was happy in his controversy with Peter Walsh to echo the charge of barbarism levelled against the Irish by earlier propagandists and still heard after the Restoration,[88] his slights were primarily tactical.

The implications of this are various, but one point worth bringing out, given the way postcolonial theory and new historicism—with its New World interests—have assimilated early modern Ireland to an anachronistic account of empire (which is not to deny the reality of colonialism in English exploitation of the country) is how Orrery's prejudices were shaped and directed by the contingencies of three-kingdom interaction. That Irish Protestants compared Gaelic Catholics with Native Americans is indisputable;[89] but the works of Orrery show that such a construction was far from automatic. Because he could not afford to underestimate his opponents by taking their inferiority for granted, he was more pragmatic than programmatic in contrasting English with Irish mores (the more salient contrast, for him, as for the Confederate leaders whom he opposed in battle, was between landowners and poorer social groups).

It would thus be misleading to elide his attitudes with those developed in the more systematically colonialist Elizabethan and early seventeenth-century treatises, even though he was a hard-line advocate of expropriation, who bent his energies to redistributing Catholic-owned estates and to entrenching the big house, landed society that would develop, after the victories of William of Orange, into the Ascendancy. His intelligence was mobilized by unpredictable conflict and messy accommodation with competing groups across the Atlantic islands, including a sizeable Catholic elite within Munster. *Parthenissa* is evidently a product of those factors, but the polished eloquence of the heroic plays—which can be misread as complacent—is just as fraught with the strain of maintaining, or manufacturing, a display of loyalty. In Orrery we see history and place fostering an archipelagic sensibility that is more than Irish or English, and not yet Anglo-Irish.

9

Our Scotland: Marvell, Mackenzie, Cleland

The Restoration of Charles II was accompanied by widespread rejoicing but also by acts of revenge.[1] Regicides were executed in London; Cromwell's corpse was dug up and his head impaled on Westminster Hall. In Edinburgh scores were settled with similar brutality. Though Andrew Sandelands had been unable to persuade Milton to save Montrose's head from display by the Presbyterians in 1653 (above, pp. 221–2), he got his way in 1661, when, in a solemn ceremony, Mungo Graham of Gorthie lifted the mouldering skull from its spike on the tolbooth and placed upon it the coronet of a marquis. Celebrating Charles's coronation, which took place a few days later, Iain Lom looked forward to the execution of Montrose's enemy, the Covenanter leader, Argyll.[2] In his unctuous, opinionated, and compulsively readable *History of My Own Time*, the Scottish bishop of Salisbury Gilbert Burnet reports that 'It was designed [Argyll] should be hanged, as Montrose had been: it was carried that he should be beheaded, and that his head should be set up where Montrose's had been set.'[3]

Although the reception of the king north and south of the border was equally enthusiastic, there were differences. For one thing, there was no purely cavalier party in Scotland, where almost all the elite over the age of forty had, like Montrose himself, been at some stage at odds with the Stewarts. This was a point exploited by the gifted littérateur and lawyer George Mackenzie when he defended Argyll in court. In complying with Cromwell's regime, he observed, Argyll had done no more than most.[4] These Scottish complications, stemming from controversies within the Kirk and not always fully appreciated in England, were reinforced by constitutional distinctions which resurfaced once the Cromwellian union of the three nations ended and the Solemn League and Covenant was burned in London by the hangman. Though Charles toyed with the idea of Anglo-Scottish union in 1669, partly as a distraction from other, even more contentious approaches to France, but also in the hope of bringing to Westminster a group of biddable Scottish MPs,[5] his instinct, encouraged by his Scottish minister, Lauderdale, was to keep the countries separate so as to maximize his power.[6] The crown was more absolute in Scotland, and to unite that country with England would be to subject its affairs to an often uncooperative House of Commons.

In that sense the English viewed Scotland as belonging both to the past and to a possible future. It was a more primitive polity, governed by a clique of noblemen, with limited rights for subjects (no habeas corpus, for example); but it was also a model of what England would become if Charles II and, even more threateningly, his brother the Duke of York—from 1685 James VII and II—were allowed to inflate the royal prerogative. This is a leading reason why the English governing elite, including Andrew Marvell, MP (from 1659) for Hull, circulated information about Scotland, wrote satires about Scottish issues, and read poems and pamphlets written north of the border.[7] It has rightly been said that 'The archipelagic dimension of later Stuart history arose less from the degree of interaction between the component nations and kingdoms than from the unnatural degree of isolation of each from the others.'[8] As this chapter will demonstrate, this did not prevent England and Scotland from being mutually aware, interpreting each other as warnings of where the Stuarts and their parliaments were taking the two kingdoms.

In any case, the determination of English bishops to restrict the worship of Scottish Presbyterians, and the threat posed to archipelagic security by the rebellious Covenanters in the west of Scotland, guaranteed cross-border conflict. The reality of 'isolation' may have exacerbated apprehensiveness about 'interaction', fuelled in England by the recollection among royalists that Scottish Covenanters had started the civil wars by invading England, and by the knowledge, among those hostile to the court, that the 'fals North' had 'impe[d] her serpent wings' and marched south to save Charles I in 1648.[9] That is why Lauderdale's ambition for Charles II to have a Scottish militia at his disposal to keep the English in order, which was confirmed by Bishop Burnet to the House of Commons in 1675, was such a red rag to English opinion, including Marvell. As for the Scots, they could hardly forget that their religious divisions and feuds (Iain Lom was a MacDonald, Argyll a Campbell) had been exacerbated when they were played out in the arena of pan-British politics, where the strength and wealth of England increased the level of destruction and dictated outcomes.

Thus, in Book III of Mackenzie's first publication, *Aretina: Or, The Serious Romance* (1660), there is a thinly veiled account of seventeenth-century Scottish history (including an elaborate scaffold speech by Oranthus, a version of Montrose), yet the affairs of so-called Athens are shown to be contingent on the troubles of its neighbour, Lacedemon.[10] Mackenzie was something of an Athenian patriot in the 1660s, opposing Lauderdale and the crown, not least in their scheme for Anglo-Scottish incorporation; and when, in 1676, he threw in his lot with the court, he remained attached to Scottish tradition, citing the antiquity of the Stewart line as part of his case for absolutism.[11] Yet the literary qualities of *Aretina*, as well as its pan-British vision, are far from narrowly Scottish. In the 'Apologie for Romances' which begins it, Mackenzie aligns himself with Sidney and Broghill. And throughout the 1660s, although his books were published in Edinburgh, he followed English fashion, and corresponded with writers in London. Sir Thomas Browne is the inspiration behind his *Religio Stoici* (1663),[12] while his *Moral Essay, Preferring Solitude to Publick Employment* (1666) elicited a reply from John Evelyn.[13] Among the sources of his estate poem, *Caelia's Country-House and Closet* (1667?), which circulated in London, are the works of Waller and Denham, which he recommended to Dryden, probably in 1678–9, as mines of 'Beautiful Turns of Words and Thoughts'. Dryden would later claim that his style had been enriched by following the advice of 'that Noble Wit of Scotland'.[14] The tribute is more complimentary than persuasive, but it attests not only to the standing of the now almost forgotten Mackenzie but to the British cultural mix that informed his ultimately Scottish absolutist position.

While the young Mackenzie got into dialogue with English literary forms, radical Covenanters were developing the mode of Godly complaint advanced by John Brown's *An Apologeticall Relation of the Particular Sufferings of the Faithful Ministers and Professours of the Church of Scotland, since August, 1660* (1665). After the suppression of a rising in Galloway which spread to the Pentland Hills, south of Edinburgh, in 1666, and the execution of its leaders—despite an attempt by Mackenzie to defend them in court—there was much to complain about. The harshness of the government's clamp-down is understandable. The rising came at a time when England was for a second time at war with the Dutch (1665–7), and a spy network in the United Provinces (which included the adventurous Aphra Behn) detected many contacts with Scottish radicals.[15] The Dutch were glad to have Charles II believe that they could destabilize Scotland,[16] and at least one modern historian maintains that the Pentland Rising took place in response to their promises of support.[17] More likely it arose spontaneously from the ill-treatment of Covenanters in St John's Town of Dalry. The Whigs, as radical Covenanters were called before the term became an English party label,[18] tramped the countryside, held prayer-meetings or conventicles,[19] and renewed the national Covenant, before marching towards Edinburgh, where they were scattered by troops led by Dalyell of Binns.

Accounts of their defeat do not suggest a well-organized conspiracy. Bishop Burnet, no friend of the radicals, called them 'a poor harmless company of men, become mad by oppression',[20] while a catalogue poem of the period accumulates pathos as it stacks up satire:

The Covenanter's Army, 28 November 1666

It was in Januar or December,
Or else the end of cauld November,
When I did see the outlaw Whigs
Lye scattered up and down the riggs,
Some had hoggars, some straw boots,
Some uncovered legs and coots,
Some had halbards, some had durks,
Some had crooked swords like Turks,
Some had slings, and some had flails,
Knit with eel and oxen tails,
Some had spears, some had pikes,
Some had spades which delvit dykes,
Some had guns with rusti[e] ratches,
Some had fierie peats for matches,
Some had bows, but wanted arrows,
Some had pistols without marrows,
Some the coulter of a plough,
Some had syths, men and horse to hough,
And some with a Lochaber axe
Resolved to gie Dalziel his paiks.[21]

riggs: strips of farmland, fields   hoggars: coarse stockings without feet, gaiters
coots: ankles   ratches: barrels   marrows: matching pairs (single pistols, not braces)
Lochaber axe: long-handled battle-axe with single elongated blade (originating in the Highland district of Lochaber)   Dalziel: Dalyell (Dalzell)   paiks: well-deserved thrashing

The longer this goes on, the more the rising seems a triumph of faith over circumstance. Though categorized by their weapons, the men are not reduced to a mass; we seem to glimpse individuals who have brought their working lives onto the battlefield. The disarray, the points of bathos clinched with strong Scots rhymes, create comic effects that are not hostile to the rebels, while such lines as 'Some had syths, men and horse to hough' and 'Resolved to gie Dalziel his paiks' are darkly even-handed.

South of the border there was less sympathy for the rebels. English radicals found it as hard to ally with Scottish Covenanters as Milton had during the late 1640s, because they threatened freedom of worship. And the response of Andrew Marvell, who had many Presbyterian contacts and who represented a constituency with an extended franchise[22] and a high proportion of Dissenters,[23] is revealing. To the Mayor of Hull he wrote, 'For the Scotch businesse truly I hope this nights news is certain of their totall rout.'[24] Marvell's sensibility was oblique; his beliefs are notoriously difficult to divine from his poems, and, because mail was not secure, he sometimes put in his letters almost the opposite of what he meant; yet what he wrote to Hull connects, in his indirect way, with his 'Last Instructions to a Painter' (1667)—a poem which satirizes the way Peter Pett, a Nonconformist, was being made a scapegoat for a Dutch victory in the Medway, because Marvell's impulse (and that of most English Nonconformists)[25] at this difficult moment for Dissent was to stress the loyalty of Presbyterians to the crown.

For Scottish Covenanters, the rising and its aftermath constituted the first of a series of tribulations that would climax in the 'killing times' of 1684–7. Many who escaped execution slipped across the channel to Ulster, or, capitalizing on the Scoto-Dutch axis described in Chapter 7, went to the Netherlands, where they continued their sedition in print.[26] One of their most vigorous productions was *Naphtali* (1667), probably written by the attorney James Stewart and the minister James Stirling. This made available the last testaments of Argyll and the executed Galloway rebels, it rehearsed the case against Erastianism, and it reprinted such Presbyterian agreements as the 1560 Confession of Faith and the Solemn League and Covenant. In some respects a Scottish supplement to Foxe's *Actes and Monuments* (which merely gestured, on its 1563 title page, towards Scotland),[27] *Naphtali* has a national agenda. It was 'for Loving of our Nation and building of our Synagogue' that Argyll and others 'were led like Innocent sheep to the

Slaughter'.[28] The Godlessness of England comes out in the testimony of Ralph Shields, an Englishman who was executed for joining the rebels:

> O that it were the happiness of my Nation of *England*, once to subiect themselves unto the sweet yoke of Christs Reformed Government, under which this Nation of *Scotland* hath enjoyed so much of the Power and life of the Gospel, by a faithful Ministry according to the Covenant sworn by them both. (255)

'O Backsliden *Scotland!*', Stewart and Stirling conclude, '*remember from whence thow art fallen, Repent and Do the First works*' (306).

The Scottish Council ordered *Naphtali* to be burned by the hangman, and fined those found with copies. A less effective rebuttal came from Andrew Honeyman, Bishop of Orkney, who published *A Survey of the Insolent and Infamous Libel, Entituled, Naphtali* in 1668. Responding to the charge that the king's forces had mounted a 'plain *Hostile Invasion*' of Galloway,[29] he appealed to an idea of the nation as indivisible:

> Now it is left to the arbitrement and lust of every party, even lesser party of the people, to break off the old union with the Nation, to erect themselves into new Societies and Combinations, as being now as free as if they had not been members of this Nation; they are relapsed into their primaeve liberty, and now every Paroch in *Galloway* is allowed to cantonize themselves into a free Re-publick, or to become a little Kingdom of *Ivetot*, or make Combinations, and Heads of these Combinations, as they see fit...[30]

Stewart's refutation of Honeyman, in his heavyweight *Jus Populi Vindicatum* (1669), was comprehensive, but he reserved particular scorn (in a book accused of 'scurrilous raillery')[31] for this geopolitical claim.

Making a move that looks very modern, but which is rooted in Calvinist thought, Stewart argues that there is nothing God-given about political geography:

> The time was when all the World was under one head, and after they were multiplied, they became distinct Republicks without any sinful or seditious secession. ... The time was when *Scotland*, *England*, and *Irland*, were distinct Kingdomes, and under distinct Soveraigne Magistrates, and what repugnancy were it either to the Law of God or Nature, to say they might be so againe? So were there once Seven Kings in *England* at once; and moe then one King in *Scotland* at once: and by no reason can he prove that it should always be, as it is at present, but by the same reason his adversaries could prove him guilty of treason...[32]

This is a telling affront to the Erastian claim to Scotland. The Bible does not support, Stewart notes, the belief that states should be of unchanging extent; nor did the early church oppose the break-up of the Roman Empire. This does not mean that he is against 'preserving the immemorially setled frame of this Nation, and the union of all his Majesties Dominions, to all generations'. The king should keep the Covenant that he swore in Scotland (not an oath that Charles liked to be reminded of), and religion would then heal division: 'what bonde more strong to unite and keep together his Majestie's Dominions can the wit of Man imagine?' (376–7). At a time when the unity of Scotland, and its difference from England, was coming under scrutiny thanks to Charles II's interest in Anglo-Scottish union, this was a provocative intervention. It might even have sat on Marvell's desk as he wrote 'The Loyall Scot'.

★   ★   ★

That poem is textually and contextually one of the most challenging in the Marvell canon. A composite work, variant between manuscripts, it probably evolved over time (1669–73?), it may have been patched with extra Marvell material by other hands (above, p. 79), and some would say, though on weak grounds, that it includes non-authorial elements.[33] Its peculiar etiology quickly becomes apparent. After a frame-passage in which the ghost of the poet John Cleveland is required, by shades in Elysium, to make good his abuse of the Scots in 'The Rebell Scot' by praising one Captain Douglas, who died in the Dutch raid on the Medway when he refused to abandon his burning ship, the poem recycles a description of Douglas's death already included in 'Last Instructions':

> Not so brave Douglass, on whose Lovely Chin
> The Early down but newly did begin,
> And modest beauty yet his sex did vail,
> Whilst Envious virgins hope he is a Male.
> His shady locks Curl back themselves to seek
> Nor other Courtship knew but to his Cheek.
> Oft as hee in Chill Eske or Seyne by night
> Hardned and Cool'd those Limbs soe soft, soe white,
> Among the Reeds to bee espy'd by him
> The Nymphs would Rustle, hee would forward swim ... [34]

Douglas is an Ovidian hero, part-statue, part-Narcissus. As the passage unfolds, other tonalities emerge, but there remains an air of extravagance, of almost cavalier excess. The captain's bravery, more admired than approved (though both), is shown not in fighting—he only fires the occasional shot at the Dutch—but in his self-consciously observed embrace of death:

> That pretious life hee yet disdaines to save
> Or with known art to try the Gentle Wave.
> Much him the glories of his Antient Race
> Inspire, nor cold hee his own Deeds deface;
> And secrett Joy in his own soul doth Rise
> That Monk lookes on to see how Douglass dies.
> Like a glad lover the fierce Flames hee meets
> And tries his first Imbraces in their sheets.   (lines 37–44)

In a deeply researched essay Martin Dzelzainis has shown that Archibald Douglas was, in all likelihood, a Catholic, and known to be such, and he argues that the reason for using in 'Last Instructions' a Scot who had been in France and is not reported as having set foot on English soil ('extraterritoriality personified') is that this allows Marvell to praise resistance to the Dutch without giving any credit to the court's running of the campaign.[35] This is highly persuasive, but not easy to reconcile with the hostility in anti-court satire (to which 'Last Instructions' belongs) to Charles II's habit of surrounding himself with Scotsmen, Irish Catholics, and Frenchmen.[36] A stronger reason for the highlighting of Douglas may be that, by the date of the poem's composition, in June–November 1667, the French, who had treated with Charles, had been exposed as leagued with the Dutch; the brave captain shows that even Francophile Britons, co-religionists with Louis XIV (and Douglas had led a company of Scots in the service of Louis),[37] will fight for England given the perfidiousness of France.

Whatever intentions drove this passage in 1667, they were adjusted in 1669–73 when Marvell recycled it in 'The Loyall Scot'. Douglas must still have had an anti-French function, because, in 1670, Charles signed a Treaty of Dover with Louis XIV that, even without knowledge of its secret clauses, perturbed many Protestant Englishmen, and because, from 1672–4, England was allied with France (to Marvell's distress) in the Third Anglo-Dutch War. But 'The Loyall Scot' also celebrates an apparently Catholic Scot at a time when Charles II was oscillating between persecuting Dissenters (as in the Clanking Act of 1670, which Marvell called 'the Quintessence of arbitrary Malice')[38] and extending toleration towards both papists and Presbyterians.[39] That the latter policy, which the king preferred, was resisted by English and Scottish bishops gave Marvell an opportunity to attack them, and their allies in the old cavalier party, while siding with the king.[40] If an anti-prelatical poet can praise a Catholic Scot, Marvell implies, why cannot bishops tolerate Presbyterian fellow-Protestants?

Here, as in *The Rehearsal Transpros'd* (1672), Marvell's aim was to use anti-prelatical drollery to drive a wedge between the king (who hugely enjoyed the prose work) and his more stridently Episcopalian supporters. The poet was able to exploit the separateness of Scotland to this end both because the king's power, which was meant to be stronger north of the border, was compromised by the bishops, to his evident frustration, when he sought to try out (for future transfer to England?) a policy of toleration and of accommodation within the Kirk for moderate Dissenters, and because of Charles's ostensible pursuit of a second scheme which perturbed many Anglicans: that of uniting more closely largely Presbyterian Scotland with England. How close this plan was to Marvell's heart it is difficult to say, though his familiarity with the argument that union would not threaten the dominance of England[41] may have made it easier for him to side with Lauderdale and the court party in Scotland in supporting a measure that was resisted by a range of opposition opinion in the north from Mackenzie to the disciples of James Stewart.[42] At all events, the hostility of the bishops to union goes far towards explaining why this anti-prelatical poem argues in favour of the policy. And here again Douglas has an important role in a text to which he might seem merely prefatory: he counters the stereotypes of unreliability and greed built up over decades of English royalist and republican antagonism towards the Scots,[43] and does this, even more importantly, as the scion of a family of border magnates.

The name Douglas was prestigious. One rhyme popular in Scotland, according to David Hume of Godscroft, ran: 'So many, so good, as of the *Douglasses* have been, Of one sirname were ne're in Scotland seen.'[44] For Hume, in his *History of the Houses of Douglas and Angus* (1633),[45] reprinted in both Edinburgh and London, the antiquity, nobility, greatness, and valour of the Douglases put them on a par with the leading families of classical Rome. They could trace their lineage back to the near-mythical beginnings of early medieval Scotland, and they had distinguished themselves over generations in the Anglo-Scottish warfare that almost inevitably embroiled them because they held so much land near the border.[46] From their role in such battles as Otterburn came their prominence in the border ballads—including *Chevy Chase*, which Marvell alludes to in 'The Loyall Scot'. That 'the hunttis of cheuet', as it was also called (*The Hunting of Cheviot*), was familiar north of the border is shown by an approving mention in Robert Wedderburn's patriotic *Complaynt of Scotland* (1550), published at a time when 'the rough wooing' of the infant Mary Queen of Scots on behalf of Edward Prince of Wales was trying to force a union of the crowns. But *Chevy Chase* had a large and appreciative audience in England too, including Philip Sidney and Ben Jonson as well as a vulgar readership,[47] because it dealt with events that elicited divided sympathies.

The ballad, in its variant forms, tells of a hunting party led by Percy, Earl of Northumberland, across the border into Scotland. Earl Douglas views the incursion as hostile, and counters it with force. Many are killed, and the two Earls engage in single combat. Percy is worsted, and almost forced to yield, but Douglas is then shot through the heart by an English arrow. The scene is not historical, but it is crudely affecting. As the text current in England from the 1620s puts it:

> Then leaving life, Earle Piercy tooke,
> the dead man by the hand,
> And said, Earle Dowglas for thy life,
> would I had lost my Land.[48]

It should by now be clear why Marvell, in lines 69–70 of 'The Loyall Scot', urges, 'Noe more discourse of Scotch or English Race | Nor Chaunt the fabulous hunt of Chivy Chase' (lines 69–70). The ballad keeps alive the traditions of Anglo-Scottish conflict, though in Percy's hard-won respect for Douglas it also anticipates the possibility of resolution which Charles II's union proposals advance. We should stop rehearsing the tribal, ethnic, even legendary antagonisms celebrated by the ballad, and build on the opportunities for healing provided by Scottish valour. Captain Douglas, by virtue of his name and lineage, and his death on behalf of Anglo-Britain, shows how an historical Scottish (and Franco-Scottish) threat to England can become a source of strength if the riven borders which the Douglases almost incarnate are allowed to knit into scar tissue and unify the island.

   The border associations of Douglas have been neglected by modern
scholars but for Marvell's early readers the point would have been obvious
enough. Yet if the appearance of one of this name at the start of a poem
about Anglo-Scottish union is apt, the description of the captain's death
also feels curiously preliminary because stylistically so different from what
follows. Marvell does nothing to downplay the change in idiom, marking
the break with a sudden imperative: 'Skip Sadles: Pegasus thou needst not
Bragg, | Sometimes the Gall'way Proves the better Nagg' (lines 63−4). A
Galloway horse is a sturdy sort of beast that makes up in stamina what it lacks
in grace, and the verse does become less sinuous and syntactically ambitious
from this point; but 'Gall'way' also glances with approval at the Covenanter
heartland. As the manner of the writing shifts from cavalier indulgence to
Presbyterian-sympathetic plainness, Marvell fixes in the reader's mind both
extremes of the religious spectrum in Scotland and turns to the British
question. After alluding to *Chevy Chase*, he declares that the border has no
basis in nature: 'Prick down the point whoever has the Art | Where Nature
Scotland doth from England part' (lines 75−6).
   Redrawing this border had been a live issue during the mid-century. It
was not just that Charles and parliament accused one another of inviting
the Scots to annex the northern counties of England (above, p. 43) but that
when Cromwell marched into Scotland both the logic of incorporating
invasion and the imperatives of royalist retrenchment[49] made it look as
though the fertile, orderly, more typically Presbyterian southern Lowlands
were ripe for absorption into a greater England. In early, though all of them
posthumous, editions of 'The Loyall Scot', the mobility of the border down
the centuries, from Roman times to the Middle Ages, provides a pleasant
diversion ('Why draw you not as well the thrifty Line | From *Thames*, from
Humber, or at least the *Tine*?'),[50] but the key point is that there is nothing
special about the Tweed, no line that Nature has inscribed there, though
there is an island just south of Berwick that can stand for what does divide:

>   'Tis Holy Island parts us not the Tweed.
>   Nothing but Clergie cold us two seclude:
>   Noe Scotch was ever like a Bishops feud.
>   All Letanies in this have wanted faith:
>   Theres noe 'deliver us from a Bishops Wrath'.
>   Never shall Calvin Pardoned bee for Sales,
>   Never for Burnetts sake the Lauderdales,
>   For Becketts sake Kent alwayes shall have tails.   (lines 88−95)

How mischievous prelates have been: the bishop of Geneva, St François de Sales, abusing the reformer, Calvin; the Restoration Archbishop of Glasgow, Alexander Burnet, refusing to forgive Lauderdale for a venture into toleration; and Thomas a Beckett, resister of royal authority, using black magic to fasten tails onto his opponents. The deviousness of the poem is apparent in Marvell's so positioning himself that he can ostensibly speak well of Lauderdale, whom he at best distrusted by 1670 (he remarks in a letter about the union that many thought his Lordship deserved hanging),[51] in order to heighten tension between the king's inner circle and the bishops. Overall the wit of the poem is driven by couplets that syntactically and in their rhyming play out division and unity—technique as an engine of attack. The list of bishops, however, uniquely in this poem employs triple rhyme, to create a climax that stresses their responsibility for breaking up Protestantism. As Marvell punningly puts it: 'What the Ocean binds, is by the Bishops rent, | The[ir] Sees make Islands in our Continent.'[52] They turn Britain itself into an archipelago.

By this late stage in the poem, the theme of division might seem exhausted, but Marvell reinvigorates it with a cartoon-like account of a 'scotch Twin headed man' (line 186). This unfortunate freak of nature, displayed at the court of the Scottish king James IV, is simultaneously an emblem of the mutual isolation of Scotland and England and of the unholy threat posed to Charles's power by the bishops. Even if Britain becomes single, either the king or the bishops must go if there is to be unity in the state. In any case—and this is a canny move in a poem calculated to work on the king—bishops do not just threaten Charles's authority, they make him look absurd:

> Nature in Living Embleme there Exprest
> What Brittain was, betwixt two Kings distrest.
> But now, when one Head doeth both Realmes controule,
> The Bishops Nodle Perks up cheek by Jowle.
> They, tho' noe poets, on Parnassus dream,[53]
> And in their Causes think themselves supream.
> Kings head saith this, But Bishops head that doe.
> Doth Charles the second rain or Charles the two?   (lines 190–7)

Having used this startling conceit[54] to exacerbate the division he purports to deplore, Marvell presses his advantage by denying that nations are essentially different. This has been read as an apology for the witty xenophobia of 'The Character of Holland',[55] but the earlier poem's satire is relatively indulgent, and its bias towards Anglo-Dutch convergence (above, pp. 238–42) makes the unionism of 'The Loyall Scot' less of a contrast. The latter poem, in fact, avoids setting out even for rebuttal the supposed characteristics of the Scots. The discussion of difference serves a more immediate, instrumental purpose. By arguing that the world is divided into only two nations, the good and the bad, 'and those mixt every where', Marvell works to weaken the position of the cavalier party. 'Nation is all but name as Shibboleth' (line 246): the causes of ethnic conflict are nominalist, and distrust will dissolve, even for disloyal ex-cavaliers, if we subject ourselves to the king. The poem's accumulated dialectic of singularities and doubleness is flatteringly resolved into the wisdom of Charles himself, and thus into his bishop-resisted policy of making division 'one':

> Charles our great soul this onely Understands:
> Hee our Affection both and will Comands,
> And, where twin Simpathies cannot atone,
> Knowes the last secret how to make them one.   (lines 262–5)

★ ★ ★

The years in which 'The Loyall Scot' took shape were those in which Lauderdale became overweening in Scotland. A Covenanter who turned into an instrument of the crown, prepared, at the king's behest, to extend toleration or crack down on conventicles, he was maximally placed to be unpopular.[56] He developed the reputation of being more interested in political survival than in any religious principles. This bulky, choleric man was not good with people close up either. Gilbert Burnet, who fell out with him, reports: 'his hair was red, hanging oddly about him; his tongue was too big for his mouth, which made him bedew all that he talked to: and his whole manner was rough and boisterous'.[57] What Burnet does not add, though he fell foul of the same prejudices himself,[58] is that being a Scot in England automatically earned Lauderdale opprobrium, even as being a Scot with influence at Westminster attracted blame north of the border when policies went against one or other faction. Marvell's distrust of him would have been stoked by such poems about the king's ministers as *A Dream of the Cabal* (1672), which plays up Lauderdale's Scottishness:

> Then Lord of northern tone,
> In gall and guile a second unto none,
> Enraged rose, and, chol'ric, thus began:
> 'Dread Majesty, male beam of fame, a son
> Of th' hundred-and-tenth monarch of the nore, ...
> De'il hoop his lugs that loves a parliament! ...
> Ten thousand plagues light on his crag that 'gin
> To make you be but third part of a king.
> De'il take my saul, I'll ne'er the matter mince,
> I'd rather subject be than sike a prince.
> To hang and burn and slay and draw and kill
> And measure aw things by my own guid will
> Is gay dominion; a checkmate I hate
> Of men or laws, it looks so like a state.'[59]

Conventicling was not confined to Scotland. In 1670 Dissenters disrupted Marvell's home town, Hull, abetted, it was claimed, by the Mayor; 'great disturbances' were reported in the garrison. Though unrest continued in the city,[60] the temperature flared up highest in Scotland, where the authorities, fearing a re-run of the Pentland Rising now that England was again at war with the Dutch, deployed troops in the south-west of the country. By 1674, Marvell was fearful that the government wanted 'to put the Scotch upon rebellion and make another good Old Cause of it' (i.e., to restart the civil wars), but the 'unnatural degree of isolation' between the kingdoms of Charles II (above, p. 269) meant that, as he confessed to his correspondent, information was hard to come by.[61] His suspicions appeared confirmed when Gilbert Burnet testified to the House of Commons that Lauderdale had hoped that the Covenanters would rise during the 1672–4 Anglo-Dutch War because 'He would then hire the Irish Papists to come ouer and cut their throats'—a plot which Marvell linked with Burnet's other claim that Lauderdale was preparing a Scottish army to fall upon England in support of the royal prerogative.[62] (This anxiety was in a manner fulfilled a few years later when James VII and II moved most of his Scottish forces south of the border in anticipation of an invasion by William of Orange.) Though there were attempts at rapprochement with the Covenanters, in a state whose security apparatus was so basic there was often no middle way between conciliation and brute force, and the crown pursued a general policy of repression from 1675. Marvell would not have been surprised to learn from modern

---

nore: north   *De'il hoop his lugs*: may the devil box his ears   *crag*: neck

historians that this policy was not triggered by a rise in conventicling: the king became willing to countenance force as the result of a realignment in English politics that brought him closer to the Anglican bishops.[63]

One instance of severity that Marvell took up in verse concerned the Covenanter James Mitchell. A Pentlands rebel in 1666, Mitchell sought two years later in Edinburgh to assassinate James Sharp (the prelate who was believed to have betrayed the Kirk to episcopacy at the Restoration), but instead he wounded Bishop Honeyman, the author of *A Survey of the Insolent and Infamous Libel, Entituled, Naphtali*. As Gilbert Burnet describes it:

> he intended to shoot through his cloak at Sharp ... but the bullets stuck in the bishop of Orkney's arm, and shattered it so, that, though he lived some years after that, they were forced to open it every year for a new exfoliation. Sharp was so universally hated, that, though this was done in full daylight, and on the high street, yet nobody offered to seize on the assassin. So he walked off, and went home, and shifted himself of an odd wig, which he was not accustomed to wear, and came out, and walked on the streets immediately.[64]

Mitchell spent five years in Holland, England, and Ireland before returning to Edinburgh, allegedly planning to make another attempt on Sharp. Arrested in 1673, and interrogated the following year, he was at first the beneficiary of Lauderdale's fading attempts to conciliate the Covenanters. He was promised his life if he confessed, which he did, but then, after an escape attempt, in the harsher climate of 1676–7 he was required to confess again, under torture, without promise this time of his life, and he resisted. His eventual trial was a travesty. Though he gained only limited public sympathy when he 'defended that it was lawfull to kill such [as Sharp] and endeavour'd by wrested places of scripture to defend himself and gain proselytes thereby',[65] Sir George Mackenzie's newly assumed role as advocate for the crown was compromised by the production of evidence that Lauderdale, Sharp, and others perjured themselves when they swore that no promise of life had been made. Once prosecution was secured, Lauderdale quipped, 'Let Mitchell glorify God in the Grass Market', the place where he was duly hanged.[66]

The execution of Mitchell produced a rush of poems which 'flew abroad like hornets in great swarmes'.[67] George Hickes's treatise *Ravillac Redivivus* reports that verses were 'put up in several *places*' in Edinburgh, while *Ravillac* itself, published in London (then Dublin) and subtitled *In a Letter from a Scottish to an English Gentleman*, set examples before English readers.[68]

Though it included a Latin 'Deploratio Mortis Jacobi Mitchel', it took more pleasure in reproducing 'a severe Satyr in *Scottish*':[69]

> O-y-e-s O-y-e-s Covenanters
> Filthy, Cruel, lying Ranters
> Come here, and see your murdering Martyr
> Sent to Hell i'th' Hangmans Garter...   (57)

According to this poet, backed by Hickes, conventicles are not Godly gatherings (yet the prayers are interminable) but occasions of sexual anarchy and incitements to sedition:

> For at, and after your long prayers,
> You lye together pairs by pairs,
> And every private Meeting-place,
> Is [made] a Bawdy-house of Grace; ...
> He that Whores best, and Murders most,
> Of him the Sect shall always boast.
> And put him, as they've put Mas *James*
> Among their Saints, and Martyrs Names.   (57–8)

Given the unscrupulousness of the authorities in the way they contrived Mitchell's death, it is tempting to read 'O-y-e-s O-y-e-s Covenanters' as guiltily strident. It was almost impossible to defend the conduct of Lauderdale and Sharp, though Mackenzie sought to justify the prosecution in the eyes of educated Europe by publishing his case against Mitchell in Latin.[70] Popular opinion was swayed by often libellous hearsay, while debate within the Kirk was influenced by a new run of pamphlets written by the exiled Covenanters in Holland.[71] Ministers like John Brown, who had protested against the bishops in the 1660s, vehemently attacked the policy of the crown.[72] Even those who disapproved of Mitchell's attempt on Sharp could be shocked by the ruthlessness of his accusers, and their willingness to risk, or desire to provoke, rebellion. 'Mitchell that Designed to Murder Dr Sharp, Archbishop of St Andrews, his Ghost, 1678', a poem not included in *Ravillac Redivivus* but widely circulated, catches well a mood shared by many. In it, Mackenzie, who acquired a limp in middle age, is compared to the lame god Vulcan, and blamed for blowing up the flames of unrest then retreating to his Highland estates:

> That crooked Vulcan will the bellows blow
> Till he'll set all on fire, and then he'll goe
> A packing to his Highland hills to hide him,

And loves not Mars, for Venus' sake, beside him,
Because through ways unworthy and unjust,
Betrayes the just, and murders under trust. ...
Of witnesses, assizers, and of judges,
For swearing, w——g, and base subterfuges,
Of such ane hellish crew let Mitchell rest,
Of all the pack (bad as he was) the best.[73]

If anyone had a limp, it was the unfortunate Mitchell, who had been tortured with a wooden 'boot' into which wedges were driven. His ordeal was widely reported, gloated over, and deplored after his trial and execution made him a *cause célèbre*, and it still has power to compel.[74] As his account of the death of Douglas shows, Marvell was peculiarly stirred by physical suffering. But his attraction to the topic of Mitchell's torture owed much to the contention of this chapter that, for all their mutual 'isolation', the English and the Scots saw in each other's country warnings about the direction in which the Stuarts and their parliaments were going. For torture, which had never been allowed in England to produce evidence admissable in court, and which was, in effect, illegal, had been legally revived in Scotland, where the different, Roman law tradition offered fewer safeguards.[75] The chances of torture being introduced south of the border were in practice slight, but it was an easy topic on which to scaremonger, and the sufferings of Mitchell in any case showed what Stuart absolutism naturally ran to.

That Marvell seems to have written 'Scaevola Scoto-Brittannus' even before its subject was put on trial shows how alert he was to these issues. His vigilance was no doubt heightened by the presence of Sharp in London, as Lauderdale's assistant, in 1674–5,[76] and focussed by the opportunity that the case of Mitchell provided to limit the Duke's power at Westminster by highlighting his tyranny in Scotland. The very title of his poem suggests that although the unionism of 'The Loyall Scot' was tactically convenient it was based on a belief that what happened in the country that the Latin poem calls our Scotland, 'Scotia nostra', was hyphenated into the condition of Britain as a whole:[77]

Sharpius exercet dum saevas perfidus iras,
    Et proprii Pastor fit Lupus ipse gregis,
Lenta videbatur coeli vindicta Michello,
    Et fas in talem creditit omne Nefas.
Peccat in insonti sed Praesule missile Plumbum

(Insons si Praesul quilibet esse potest)
Culpa par, at dispar sequitur fortuna Jacobos:
  Ocrea torquet idem, mitra beatque scelus. (lines 1–8)[78]

Mitchell's mettle is shown by the courage with which he accepts, indeed exacerbates, his suffering. Like Douglas he embraces (because he is observed) more damage than is required. When the torturer makes to set the boot on his left leg, he instructs that his more useful 'right leg should atone for the fault of the right hand'.[79] There might be an allusion here to the threat made to Mitchell that he would have a hand chopped off if he refused to confess. There is certainly a reference to Gaius Mucius Scaevola, a hero of the early Roman Republic, who, attempting to assassinate Lars Porsena, king of the Etruscans, then blockading Rome, killed Porsena's secretary who was standing beside him. When arrested, Gaius Mucius put his right hand into an altar flame to show his own courage and that of the Roman people—three hundred of whom, he warned, had sworn to kill the king.[80] Marvell, often shy of political directness, and divided in his view of Mitchell, nonetheless underlines his opposition to Stuart absolutism by celebrating a republican in his own (Latin) tongue. More immediately, when Mitchell 'sits as a spectator at his own shin, unmoved, though pitied by the crowd',[81] he shows the determination of Scottish resistance to the bishops:

> Scaevola si Thuscum potuit terrere Tyrannum,
> Fortius hoc specimen Scotia nostra dedit.
> Numina quam temnas, homines ne spernito Sharpi,
> Hic è tercentum Mutius unus erat.

> Explosa nequiit quem sternere glande Michellus,
> Explodet saevum Scotia Pontificem.

Sharpius exercet dum saevas perfidus iras, … mitra beatque scelus: While perfidious Sharp was practising his cruel rage and the shepherd himself became the very wolf of his own flock, the vengeance of heaven seemed slow to Mitchell, and he believed any sin was justified against such a person. But his bullet miscarried upon an innocent bishop (if any bishop can be innocent). Equal guilt but unequal fortune attends the two Jameses. The boot punishes and a mitre blesses the same crime. (tr. Nigel Smith)
Scaevolo si Thuscum potuit terrere Tyrannum, … quod est: If ever Scaevola was able to frighten the Etruscan tyrant, our own Scotland has afforded in this an even more impressive example. Sharp, though you despise gods, despise not men. This was one Mucius from three hundred. The cruel bishop whom Mitchell could not quell with his exploded bullet, Scotland herself will lay waste. What is the difference between a bishop and a murderer? The difference between a Lucifer and a gallows-rogue. (tr. Smith)

Inter Pontificem quid distat Carnificemque?
Inter Luciferum Furciferumque quod est.   (lines 29–36)

It was subversive enough to write of the 'equal guilt' of assassin and bishop, but now this bishop is a devil masquerading as an angel of light. Given that Sharp would be murdered in 1679, as Scotland plunged again into rebellion, the lines 'Explosa ... Scotia Pontificem' are chillingly prophetic.

What escalated the situation was the decision of Lauderdale to order a body of soldiers known as the Highland Host into the west of Scotland. In a defence of this policy that was referred to by one opponent as *Aretina*, Part II, because he regarded it as so fanciful, Mackenzie argued that the course of the Pentland Rising had shown that conventicles needed to be suppressed.[82] Others countered that Lauderdale wanted to stir up a rebellion that would line his pockets and those of his friends with fines and confiscations.[83] That troops were billeted on tenants of his Whig-inclined opponent, Hamilton, probably was a bonus for Lauderdale. But there was another, Anglo-British motive for the policy: to bolster the Duke's standing in the eyes of the English bishops.[84] That, combined with the simultaneous alerting of English and Irish troops, which led to a suspicion that Lauderdale was aiming to promote absolutism throughout the archipelago, would have sufficiently alarmed Marvell. In a letter to Sir Edward Harley (7 August 1677), he shows himself well informed about the Highland Host and sympathetic to the Covenanters. This was in sharp contrast to his declared position in 1666. The increasing threat of tyranny made him and others more ready to find common cause with dissident Presbyterians in the north:

The Field Conventicles in Scotland are very rife, more then ever. And the proceedings against them as violent. Even poore herd-boys are fined shillings and sixpences. They quarter Troopers all where they heare Conventicles haue bin kept. One Gentleman fined 500li sterlin & imprisond because he will not take the Oath to answer all their questions & tell the Nonconf[ormist]s name that baptized his child. At a Nonc[onformist] Ministers childs buriall at Glasgow there came from seuen miles about neare 3000 people to spight the Bishop of Argyle who is also Parson of Glasgow who would not suffer the Bellman to publish the buriall after the usuall manner Child to such an one Minister of the Gospell at Maidlan but somtimes Minister wherfore they imployd not the Bellman at all but a Woman seeing the Bishop peep out cryed aloud Ha Theefe thou wilt never haue so many at thy buriall except thou be hanged.[85]

The British reach of Lauderdale's policy became more apparent in April–June 1678 when rival Scottish factions came to London to lobby and quarrel. While Mackenzie talked to Dryden about verse style, Hamilton and his party complained to the king about the Highland Host, and briefed members of the House of Commons against Lauderdale.[86] Marvell must have met them, though he continued to have intelligence sent from Scotland. As he wrote to his nephew, William Popple, on 10 June:

> The Patience of the *Scots*, under their Oppressions, is not to be paralelled in any History. They still continue their extraordinary and numerous, but peaceable, Field Conventicles. One Mr. *Welsh* is their Archminister, and the last Letter I saw tells, People were going forty Miles to hear Him. There came out, about Christmass last, here a large Book concerning *the Growth of Popery and Arbitrary Government*. There have been great Rewards offered in private, and considerable in the Gazette, to any who could inform of the Author or Printer, but not yet discovered. Three or four printed Books since have described, as near as it was proper to go, the Man being a Member of Parliament, Mr. *Marvell* to have been the Author; but if he had, surely he should not have escaped being questioned in Parliament, or some other Place.[87]

The juxtaposition of the Scottish unrest with Marvell's anti-government treatise of 1677 could hardly be more expressive. The oppression of the conventiclers is a prime example to him of the growth of arbitrary government. The torture of Mitchell, the suppression of Covenanters with Highland troops, are indications of how badly the English may be treated if Lauderdale's grip on the king is not broken.

Shortly after writing this letter Marvell died (16 August 1678). Where his views were leading historically can be deduced, however, from the way the opposition played the Scottish card in 1679–80, when attempts were made to exclude the Catholic Duke of York from succession to the throne. It may be that Shaftesbury and his anti-court supporters had been cooperating (as George Hickes would later complain) with Lauderdale's opponents in Scotland since the mid–1670s.[88] If so, given Marvell's association with Shaftesbury, his 'Scaevolo Scoto-Brittannus' has a context in Anglo-Scottish, proto-Whig networking. Certainly, just months after the poet's death, Shaftesbury declared in the House of Lords that, whereas other northern countries in Europe protected liberty and property by law, Scotland had 'outdone all the eastern and southern countries' by having their 'lives, liberties and estates sequestered to the will and pleasure of those that govern'. He arranged for forty printed copies of this speech to be sent to Edinburgh, where it was received as 'a Trumpet Signal' by disaffected Scotsmen, because it gave them 'cause to think there was a Party in Parliament, already formed to assist and sustain them'.[89] The court party countered by arguing that, since the Scots were loyal to the Duke of York, any change in the succession would encourage Scotland to separate from England and whip up another round in the wars of the three kingdoms.[90]

Had Lauderdale simply been attacked at Westminster,[91] he might have survived in office, but events got out of hand in Scotland, when, on 3 May 1679, a group of Covenanters murdered Archbishop Sharp in front of his daughter and his servants. For contemporaries in all three kingdoms, the principles espoused by *Naphtali* and James Mitchell ran their course in this assassination. As one pamphlet informed Irish readers, James Stewart had declared in *Jus Populi* 'That there could be no greater Gift made to *JESUS CHRIST*, then the sending the Archbishop of St *Andrews*'s Head in a silver box to the *KING*: Which Doctrine prevailed with Mr *James Mitchell*... to attempt the Killing of the said Lord Archbishop.'[92] When the murderers caught up with Sharp's coach, they 'reproached him with Mr *James Mitchell*'s death', while shooting and stabbing him.

> And though he put them in mind that he was a Minister, and pulling off his Cap, shewed them his Gray Hairs intreating, *That if they would not spare his Life, they would at least allow him some little time for Prayer*; they returned him no other answer, but *That God would not hear so base a Dog as he was*; ... Notwithstanding of all which, and of a Shot that pierced his Body above his Right Pap, and of other Stroaks which cut his Hands, whilst he was holding them up to Heaven in Prayer, he raised himself upon his Knees, and uttered only these words, *God Forgive you all*. After which, by many stroaks that cut his skull to pieces, he fell down dead. (5)

For embattled English churchmen, this was what their whiggish opponents had in mind for Anglican bishops. It was even claimed that Shaftesbury's speech about the sufferings of the Scots (his trumpet-blast in the Lords) had directly whipped up the murderers.[93] 'Explosa nequiit quem sternere glande Michellus, | Explodet saevum Scotia Pontificem', 'The cruel bishop whom Mitchell could not quell with his exploded bullet, Scotland herself will lay waste': Marvell's dark prediction, in 'Scaevola Scoto-Brittannus', now reads like a *threat*.

The Covenanter rising which followed Sharp's murder, celebrated in such ballads as 'The Battle of Loudon Hill'—'Weel prosper a' the gospel-lads | That are into the west countrie'[94]—was only successful in the short term. As Sir Walter Scott brings out in *Old Mortality*, dissension in the Presbyterian ranks, which seemed manageable in 1666, was too great for them to sustain a campaign.[95] And Charles was now thoroughly alert to the pan-British scale of the threat to his authority; he swiftly moved an English army, under the crypto-whiggish Duke of Monmouth, to defeat the rebels at Bothwell Brig on 22 June 1679. The ballad 'Bothwell Bridge' is probably the finest of all poems on the Covenanter uprisings because its division of sympathy responds to the complexity of the event. The Covenanters are magnificently defiant—

> Out then spak a Lennox lad,
>   And waly, but he spoke bonnily!
> 'I winna yield my weapons up,
>   To you nor nae man that I see.'

—but unprepared for battle—

> They stelld their cannons on the height,
>   And showrd their shot down in the how,
> An beat our Scots lads even down;
>   Thick they lay slain on every know.[96]

And the government forces are split between ruthless cavaliers and the humane Duke of Monmouth (' "O hold your hand... Gie quarters to yon men for me" '). At the end of the ballad, the Duke is executed, about five years ahead of history, in London, as a result of false witness borne against him by the ultra-royalist Claverhouse, who refuses mercy to the enemy.[97]

One effect of this rebellion was to erode the dominance of Lauderdale, who resigned as Secretary of State. As the Exclusion Crisis took hold, Charles sent the Duke of York to Edinburgh for almost three years, to enhance royal authority but also to create a power-base for his brother. York revived a court culture that had been missing from Scotland for eighty years. Plays by Dryden and by Lee were performed;[98] medical, cartographic, and legal studies flourished under Sir Robert Sibbald and Mackenzie; the

---

waly: alas   *stelld*: placed, set up   *how*: hollow in the ground   *know*: knoll, hillock

Advocates' Library was founded; and in 1683 Charles II commissioned Jacob de Wet to paint a series of 111 portraits of the kings of Scotland in Holyrood House[99]—an artistic statement in line with the post-Restoration policy of keeping the kingdoms distinct. As for the defeated radicals, they fled, as after the Pentland Rising, to Ulster and to Holland. This time, however, relations with English radicals in exile were so much warmer that the Anglo-Scoto-Dutch triangle explored in Chapter 7 was reactivated as a breeding-ground for such intrigues as the Rye House conspiracy of 1683, which threatened the lives of Charles II and the Duke of York, and the risings led by Monmouth (in the English West Country) and Argyll (in the west of Scotland) in 1685.

★   ★   ★

The extent and import of Marvell's involvement with the Dutch after the Restoration is one of the most tantalizing obscurities of his career. In the United Provinces for several months in 1662–3—for what purpose we do not know—he encountered obstructive Dutch merchants in Muscovy and disrespectful, indeed hostile, Dutch shipping during his embassy with the Earl of Carlisle to Russia, Sweden, and Denmark in 1663–4.[100] To judge from such poems as 'Last Instructions', those experiences did not prejudice him. In the early 1670s, when Charles II was steering a pro-French and anti-Dutch course, Marvell seems to have worked as a Dutch agent in London. We can deduce from 'The Loyall Scot' and his letters that events in Britain as a whole encouraged him to join the 'fifth column' associated with Peter du Moulin, one of Willem van Oranje's diplomats in London,[101] whose *England's Appeal* (1673) was a stimulus to Marvell's *Account of the Growth of Popery, and Arbitrary Government*—a work which, as we have seen, gives 'Amsterdam' as its place of publication. In the *Account* he argues that Charles II is sacrificing the Dutch to French and short-term English interests, and insists that the House of Commons favours 'a *League Offensive and Defensive with the Dutch*'.[102] Apparently in correspondence with Dutch contacts over this period, it is likely that Marvell returned to the United Provinces in person in 1674.

Scholars have often failed to notice the depth and persistence of the poet's interest in Anglo-Dutch relations, and effectively ignored how often he triangulated the Netherlands with Scotland (e.g. in the appearance of Douglas in 'Last Instructions to a Painter'), but contemporaries were more alert. One of the sprightliest accounts of his literary and political character fastens on just this matrix. Written by a pro-government satirist, *A Letter from Amsterdam, to a Friend in England* (1678) assumes the voice of an English radical on a secret visit to The Hague, where he dines with a Dutchman and a Scot and conspires to subvert the Stuarts:

> We were last night no less than *Three Nations* together at Supper; but all of a *Knot*: nothing can untie us but want of Money. My *Scots Fugitive* was so sharp and quick upon sight of Flesh-meat, that he laid aside his long Grace, and without blessing God, or cursing the Duke of *L[auderdale]* he fell to, and fed like a Farmer, whilst I, snapping a bit now and then, fell to tunning up *Old Hock* in Min Heer the Burgomaster; for our Companion is of such a humour, that till he be top-full, he never vents his Oracles against the house of *Orange,* and Court of *England.*[103]

Though it can be found in other contexts, '*Three Nations*' was used by parliamentarians during the interregnum to substitute for the royalist-tainted phrase 'the three kingdoms'. Here, though, it describes another, more subversive geopolitical structure. The passage plays on stereotypes of the starved and voracious Scot, the boorish, boozy Dutchman, and the spare and calculating English puritan. 'What a sight 'tis to see our Friends in *England, Holland,* and *Scotland,* so well twisted!', the persona observes: 'This *Three-fold Cord* is strong enough to hang, or hamper all our Adversaries' (3).

What advice does this conspirator have for his friend in England? He should flatter the king but tell him that his counsellors are bad, or weak, banging home any peg to create division—exactly the procedure of *The Rehearsal Transpros'd* and 'The Loyall Scot'. And then (in case there is any doubt as to who has piqued the satirist), 'Bring on *new Accounts of [the] Growth of Popery and Arbitrary Government*' (4). Another rebuke to Marvell, *An Account of the Growth of Knavery* (1678), is subtitled *A Parallel betwixt the Reformers of 1677, and those of 1641, in their Methods, and Designs.*[104] The *Letter* takes up this theme in a British register: "Tis fine, to see our *Scottish Friends* trace the old Method of 1640. ... They, and we have walkt hand in hand like Brethren ever since. What have we to do next, but to revive and rake that *Phoenix* the COVENANT, out of its Ashes?' (4). Though false about the relationship between English radicals and Scottish Covenanters from the mid–1640s to the late 1660s, this betrays the anxiety of a regime that recognized the danger posed by the reconstitution of a subversive cross-border alliance. The very choice of words turns the clock back to 1641, when Milton urged the Covenanting Scots and the restless English,

'Goe on both hand in hand O NATIONS never to be disunited' (above, p. 227). Then comes the acute mock-tribute to Marvell:

> make sure of *Andrew*. Hee's a shrewd man against *Popery*, though for his Religion you may place him, as *Pasquin* at *Rome* placed *Henry* the *Eighth*, betwixt *Moses*, the *Messiah*, and *Mahomet*, with this *Motto* in his Mouth, *quò me vertam nescio*. 'Tis well he is now *Transprosed* into Politicks: they say he had much ado to live upon Poetry. What a blunt tool the people's become! No mutiny? However, let him whet on till they take an Edge, and be sure that you and the rest of our Comrades whet him. (5)

Thanks to Richard L. Greaves, Richard Ashcraft, and Ginny Gardner we now have a much fuller picture of the Anglo-Scoto-Dutch network which sharpened the blade of Marvell's wit.[105] Among the exiles were writers from both sides of the border, from the philosophically polemical John Locke to the satirically trenchant William Cleland. The latter joined the restless Covenanters in his native west of Scotland after leaving the University of St Andrews in 1677; he led troops at Loudon Hill (Drumclog Moor) and Bothwell Brig, and fled to the United Provinces where he published a *Disputatio juridica de probationibus*. Like the Scot in the anonymous *Letter*, and like the author of *Jus Populi*, James Stewart, who became active in the Netherlands, Cleland twisted a threefold cord. In 1685 he helped plot the Argyll/Monmouth rebellion from Amsterdam, and prepared the ground for it in Scotland. After the failure of those risings, he returned to Holland and intrigued with William of Orange. During the oppression of the Covenanters that followed the Argyll Rebellion, he sided with those who sought to persuade William to oust his father-in-law, James VII and II. Back in Scotland in 1688, he encouraged the Covenanters to support William (they split over the issue), and died in a bloody skirmish with Jacobite Highlanders in 1689.

One of his earliest poems is about those Highlanders, and their cultural difference from the Covenanters. In his long 'Mock Poem, upon the Expedition of the Highland-Host: Who Came to Destroy the Western Shires, in Winter 1678' he draws on the techniques of the anti-Presbyterian *Hudibras* to satirize the enemies of Presbyterianism—as when he describes the 'Redshank-Squires' who lead their men into the west:

---

quò me vertam nescio: I do not know which way to turn (Cicero)   *pirnie Standarts*: variegated (tartan-like) flags

> But those who were their chief Commanders,
> As such who bore the pirnie Standarts;
> Who led the Van, and drove the Rear:
> Were right well mounted of their Gear:
> With Brogues, Trues, and pirnie Plaides,
> With good blew Bonnets on their Heads:
> Which on the one side had a flipe,
> Adorn'd with a Tobacco pipe,
> With Durk, and Snap-work, and Snuff-mill,
> A bagg which they with Onions fill,
> And as their strick Observers say,
> A Tupe Horn fill'd with *Usquebay.*
> A flasht out Coat beneath her plaides,
> A Targe of timber, nails and hides;
> With a long two handed Sword,
> As good's the Countrey can affoord ... [106]

Weatherproofed, like their sheep, by daubings of tar, these men are free of honesty and religion, and skilled in nothing 'Except in Bag-pipe, and in Harpe'. They are, however, unswervingly hostile to the Covenanters and the writings which sustain their cause. Their leader reports that, although *Naphtali* has been 'refuted' by the hangman,

> Yet I'm afraid for all our pains,
> That their Seditious Seed remains,
> With other Pamphlets stuff'd with Lies,
> Like *Mitchels* Ghosts and Tragedies,
> And Answers to *Oyas* Covenanters, ...   (20).

These are texts we have heard of already. Across the ideological spectrum in Scotland it was recognized that poems and pamphlets sustained a radical tradition.

If Cleland's brio is at odds with the stereotype of dour Presbyterianism, so is the flexibility with which, throughout his output, he adopts different voices. This is at its most blatant when he brings out the cavalier brutality of the government troops who put down the Monmouth and Argyll risings in his ballad 'Now Down with the Confounded Whiggs'. In 'A Mock-Poem', the voice of the Highland squire, and the sometimes literary-classical, more

---

Trues: trews, trousers   *flipe* (emending *stipe*): flap, fold of a garment   *Durk*: dirk, dagger
Snap-work: firing mechanism   *Snuff-mill*: snuff-box   *strick*: strict   *Tupe Horn*:
ram's horn   *Usquebay*: whisky   *her*: their

often demotic, narrator, gives way to that of a suavely turned-out western nobleman who complains to the authorities about the excesses of the Host:

> They durk our Tennents, shames our Wives,
> And we're in hazard of our Lives,
> They plunder horse, and them they loaden,
> With Coverings, Blankets, sheets and Plaidin, ...
> They ripe for Arms; but all they find,
> Is arms with them, leaves nought behind,
> Is't not a strange mistake in that,
> Our tankerds, and our Chamber Pot,
> And stool-pans, should be thought Granads
> They take our Sadles and our Pades,
> They stripe our Lecquies, ripes their Pouches,
> They leave us neither Beds nor Couches,
> Yea to be short they leave us nought,
> That can from place to place be brought, ...
> As if they could not Doe eneugh,
> They fall on poor men at the pleugh,
> Because they doe not understand,
> Their Language they'll cut off their hand ... [107]

As we have seen, *Naphtali* called the oppression of Galloway in 1666 a 'plain *Hostile Invasion*' (above, p. 273); similar terms could be used to describe this onslaught by the Highland Host. The nastiness of the ethnic violence is a reminder that regional conflicts could be more polarized than those between the diffusely constituted nations of the archipelago (e.g. the Bishops' Wars). Near-contemporary historians attest to the extent of the pillaging. Kirkton describes how, as the last contingents of the occupying force (not strictly, in this case, Highlanders) pulled back across Stirling Bridge, 'every man drew his sword to shew the world they hade returned conquerors from their enemies land, but they might as well have showen the pots, pans, girdles, shoes taken off countrey men's feet, and other bodily and household furniture with which they were loadened.'[108]

It was this abuse of property which made Lauderdale and his faction vulnerable to royal disapproval, and when the Duke of York took over in Edinburgh he set about calming the situation. His moderation did

---

durk: stab with a dagger   *Plaidin*: plaid cloth   *ripe*: search, ransack   *Granads*: grenades   *Pades*: straw pads (to go under saddles)   *Lecquies*: lackeys, servants

not last, however, and in 1680 he exploited the militancy of the most
zealous Covenanters—followers of Richard Cameron (1648–80)—known
as Cameronians (among whom Cleland could be found), to reimpose the
law. Meanwhile pressure for orthodoxy in England once again impacted on
Scotland, when the 1681 Test Act, designed to exclude papists from public
office, divided Presbyterians over the issue of state-control of religion, and
threw into relief the Catholicism of York, who was granted exemption
from swearing the oath required by the Act. Cleland, in the United
Provinces, rose to the occasion by penning another burlesque, 'Effigies
Clericorum: Or, a Mock Poem on the Clergie when they met to Consult
about Taking the Test in the Year 1681'. It is an assembly poem that plays to
Cleland's ventriloquizing gifts, and his ability swiftly to conjure up vibrant
characters—the red-nosed, irascible cavalier-cleric, for instance, who speaks
for the government, and the solid, conforming minister who does not look
for trouble but resents the Catholicism of the Duke of York and the
discharge of English ecclesiastical controversy into the affairs of the Kirk:

> Should we receive the Noxious Humors,
> That raised Gangrens, Pox, and Tumors:
> And at the length by strong Purgation,
> Evacuat by the *English* Nation?
> A hout upon us a Disgrace,
> Let's fling their Dirt back on their Face:
> I had said —— had not my senses
> Been clogg'd with Pestsome Effluences,
> Of thir *Chymerick* Naughty Talkers, ... [109]

It would be wrong to imply that all the vitality was on the Covenanting
side. Mackenzie's efforts to build a defence of absolutism out of the materials
of early seventeenth-century royalism, in a series of treatises, including the
magisterial *Jus Regium: Or, The Just and Solid Foundations of Monarchy* (1684),
were ponderable at the time, and attracted later commentary. The attention
to Scottish kingship in *Jus Regium* (Fig. 13) is linked to a larger belief in
national distinctiveness. Although Mackenzie had imitated English literary
forms in the 1660s, after about 1672 he

> turned to writing on legal subjects and his literary ambitions grew closer to his
> professional practice. He sought a distinctive Scots cultural identity in clas-
> sicism and style. The legal profession could contribute to both of these, and

---

hout: exclamation expressing dissent or impatience   —— : shit/arse

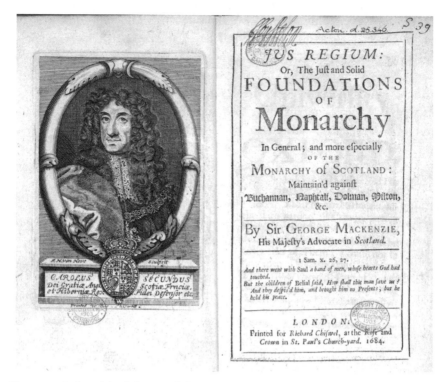

Fig. 13. A Scottish defence of the Stewarts against opponents from both sides of the border. Portrait of Charles II and title page of Sir George Mackenzie, *Jus Regium* (London, 1684).

increasing confidence allowed its members to imitate the 'Virtuoso' intellectual who should display them. Classical public virtue and a Scots forensic style 'like ourselves, fiery, abrupt, sprightly and bold', could adorn 'the ingenious and learned men of our Profession' and through them Scotland itself.[110]

Because the ideal of the royalist virtuoso was also cultivated in London, Mackenzie's belief that he was accenting something particularly Scottish needs to be approached with caution. But his desire to find that accent is important in itself, not least because, in his political writing, he often shows an awareness as resentful as that of Cleland's conforming minister of how hard it was to insulate Scotland from England.

Thus, in *A Vindication of His Majesties Government, and Judicatures, in Scotland* (1683), he defends the attachment of the Scottish nobility to the Duke of York during the Exclusion Crisis by saying: 'no honest man, will think we in *Scotland* have owned his *Royal Highness*, because *England* had an aversion for him'. Yet what starts as an irritated assertion that the English should not believe that the Scots like to differ out of contrariness tilts into a happy declaration of how the Scots do prefer to be unlike their neighbours, how wise they are in this, and how much stronger 'an Union in Principles' is 'then that of the Kingdoms'.[111] Even Covenanters now tempted to walk hand in hand with English radicals should remember that 'interaction' is worse than 'isolation', and go in fear of genocide in the guise of union:

> Open then your Eyes, my dear Countrey-men, and let not your own *Fanaticism*, nor their Cheats perswade you, that such as endeavour to lessen and asperse the Monarchy in our Neighbour-Nation, will be ever Faithful to you, who are sworn, even in your *Covenant*, to maintain it in this, to you who opposed them in the last War, in their grand Designs for a Common-wealth, and the Extirpation of the *Scottish* Race, to you who think that Presbytery *jure divino*, which they laugh at, and never use it as an useful Government in the Church, ... (6)

That the controversies of the 1660s were still potent during the reign of James II and VII is apparent from the banning in Scotland, in 1688, of such radical Presbyterian works as *Jus Populi, Naphtali*, and Stewart's reply to Honeyman's *Survey of ... Naphtali*. The fall of the Catholic king did not curtail the retrospective tendency of the disputes around toleration, and Mackenzie—who had resigned from high office in 1686 in reaction to James's papistical policies, and even defended some conventiclers in court—responded to the Whig triumphalism which followed the Glorious Revolution by publishing, in 1691, the year of his death, *A Vindication of the Government in Scotland during the Reign of King Charles II*. This revives the claim that the Covenanters of the 1670s resembled those of the 1630s in threatening chaos in the state; it defends the use of torture, and seeks again to justify the prosecution of James Mitchell. That these arguments were familiar encouraged those who opposed them to recycle, for instance, Mitchell's ordeal and testimony in a new, post-Revolution edition of *Naphtali*[112]—which is why the last word in this chapter can be given to the ghost of Marvell, or at least to a poem called 'Marvell's Ghost', which appeared in 1691, though it purports to be 'a True Copy of a Letter sent to the Archbishop of Canterbury upon his Sudden Sickness at the Prince of Orange's First Arrival into London, 1688/9'.[113]

Archbishop Sancroft had suffered from a diplomatic illness when William entered the English capital because he was faithful if not to James II and VII himself then to his oath of loyalty to the king. 'Marvell's Ghost' uses the non-juring sympathies of the bishops to denounce them as a class. Like 'The Loyall Scot', the poem grumbles that bishops luxuriate in fine linen, frolic in their wealth, and are too dull or feeble to preach. They 'Foment divisions', and break up Britain with their sees: 'The land they canton, and divide the spoil, | And drain the moisture of our wealthy isle' (lines 10, 87–8). More connects the poems than derivativeness, or continuity in anti-prelatical complaint. The moments of inception of Marvell's poem and that of his ghost were similar enough politically to mean that they could share a phase of reception: though current earlier in manuscript, 'The Loyall Scot' only got into print in the mid-1690s.[114] It became newly topical because William II and III was trying to create an ecclesiastical policy that suited the differing make-up of his two British kingdoms. The ghost of Marvell presses for a Presbyterian solution across the whole of the island:

> Good God! forbid thy church should e'er be swayed
> By those again, that have thy truth betrayed, …
> Should it be thus, how would our isle complain, …   (lines 97–102)

It was only north of the border, however, that episcopacy was disestablished,[115] leaving the kingdoms, ecclesiastically speaking, quite as 'isolated' as Mackenzie would have wished (to return to the terms I started from), yet not in the terms he favoured, and still paradoxically 'interactive' because of the apprehensiveness they felt about each other.

10

The Derry School of Drama

One of the strongest texts thrown up by the Williamite wars is John Mitchelbourne's two-part drama, *Ireland Preserv'd: Or, The Siege of London-Derry. Together with The Troubles of the North* (1705). Written by a Protestant Englishman who commanded the garrison in Derry[1] and became joint-governor of the city during the siege of 1689, it has the partial, compelling authority of an eye-witness account. From Tyrconnell's promotion of Catholics in Ireland, through the northward advance of James II's Irish army, to the eventual relief of Derry by a flotilla, it deals in lively detail with the bravery, bad faith, and ruthlessness of the campaign. The dramaturgy is crudely efficient: scenes alternate between opposing camps, combining high politics and low comedy, a great variety of tongues (Irish, French, Scots, Hiberno- and mainstream English), and much interethnic brutality. The whole thing is so confidently executed that Mitchelbourne's biographer says it must have been ghostwritten by George Farquhar, who was brought up in Derry, and may well have lived through the siege.[2] The attribution is implausible, but the plays command respect.

Mitchelbourne makes much of the deprivations of the besieged. At a dinner party held in the lodgings of Granade (Mitchelbourne's name in the drama), a female soldier called Amazon and two other ladies sit down to eat tallow thickened with oatmeal and 'what we call in *French Ragout de Chien*, in *English* a *Ragoo*, of the Haunch of my Dog *Towzer*'.[3] A few scenes later, Granade orders horseblood to be fed to starving children. He agrees to act as the father of an orphaned little boy. And he then becomes reflective:

(Takes his Purse out, and puts a Guinea in his Mouth, and chews it.)

There is no relish or comfort in it, no more than a Stone, a piece of Leather has more Sustenance. And this is what the World admires, and by which the World is govern'd.

(Takes the Purse of Guineas and throws it against the Wall.)

Go thy ways, if I had ten times as much.
  It is no cure to an hungry famish'd Soul,
  But otherwise, it does the World controle.   (Siege, 135)

These are routine sentiments, but they carry weight in a work that was written to support Mitchelbourne's appeals to the crown for back-pay. Although some had profited from the siege—most conspicuously Mitchelbourne's co-governor, George Walker, who published *A True Account of the Siege of London-derry* in 1689 then went on a triumphal tour of Britain—the garrison was unpaid and ordinary citizens were not recompensed for their losses. In 1698 a committee of the House of Commons reported that Mitchelbourne was owed £ 15,941 18s 6d, but as late as 1710–11 he was languishing in the Fleet prison because of debts contracted while he was pursuing his case, and payment only eventually came in part. So Granade's pious contempt for money is driven by Mitchelbourne's needy hatred of what he was forced to beg for, but also calculated to demonstrate that he deserved his pay precisely because the siege had taught him not to value it—that he did not hold out against the Jacobite forces for anything so base as money.

The expressiveness of Granade's gesture owes something to the fact that the usual reason for putting a guinea into your mouth and chewing it is to test whether the coin is true (gold is relatively soft). William III's wars against James II and Louis XIV, which began, within the archipelago, in the siege of Derry, produced turmoil in the currency: clipping and debasement were rife, and in 1695–7 there had to be a comprehensive reminting. This turmoil was most dramatic in Ireland, where the effects of war were immediate. While foreign specie streamed into the country, James dealt with a shortage of gold and silver by coining in brass. By selecting a prestigious guinea to chew, Mitchelbourne tests the currency at its most stable point of value (but see below, p. 316) and does not find any comfort.

The pots and pans, church bells, and cannon that were melted into the coinage of Jacobite Ireland represent in extreme form the fungibility of property in an economy racked by war, pillage, and the purchase and resale of land by adventurers and disbanded soldiers. You could hardly say that capitalism was invented in early modern Ireland, but the liquidization of traditional landholding, and the large fortunes made and lost when estates changed hands commercially, induced premature modernization.

Derry was an epicentre of this process because the plantation of 1609, on land escheated to the crown from the rebel Hugh O'Neill, Earl of Tyrone and his followers, inserted a London mercantile ethos into a part of Ireland that had been defiantly Gaelic. As Mitchelbourne puts it in his preface: 'this City and County of *Derry*, was by Grant given by King *James* the First to the *Londoners*: A Country that was always before accounted a Nest of Rebels, ... inhabited by the *O-Neiles*, *O-Ca'ha[n]s*, and the *Macdewles*; and not in subjection till an *English* Colony was Planted there; and to forward that work, which was of so great Consequence, the *Londoners* spared no Cost, sent over Masons, Carpenters, Smiths, and other Artizans, to build that City, and gave it the name of *London-derry*' (d1v).

Mitchelbourne goes on to explain how County Londonderry was divided into twelve proportions, allotted to such investors as 'the *Mercers, Grocers, Drapers, Fishmongers, Goldsmiths*' (d1v). The principles of metropolitan business were imposed on a quite different economic base, and a variety of settlers from Britain was brought in to dilute if not displace the mere Irish. Similar shocks were administered to other regions of Ireland during the 1650s and 1660s, and again after the Williamite wars. Part of the scandal, for Mitchelbourne, of going without his pay, was seeing confiscated Irish estates being granted to royal favourites, including Elizabeth Villiers, William III's mistress (who acquired more than ninety-five thousand acres), rather than to those who had fought for the king. The House of Commons resolved that the bulk of these grants should be revoked and the land put up for auction; the wrangling and speculation that followed did nothing to change the atmosphere of volatility.[4]

Literature was shaped by this. In *Hic et Ubique: Or, The Humors of Dublin* (1663)—a comedy by the Ulster-born Richard Head, who had himself returned to Ireland to escape debts contracted in England—London adventurers come to Ireland to avoid their creditors and pursue get-rich-quick schemes. They are told that 'The generality of *Dublin's* Inhabitants may justly boast of as great a measure of civility as the greatest pretenders thereunto elsewhere; only their losses and crosses has so refin'd their wits, that they are become the best oeconomick Polititians.'[5] The life-skills of such locals as Thrivewell are formidable, but Colonel Kiltory, who spent the war years 'scouring the Mountains and skipping the Boggs, not sparing the very spawn of rebellion' (7), is less able to manage the post-Restoration peace. Desperate for a wife, he is tricked into making over his estate to

Mrs Hopewell, one of the blow-ins, only to learn that she is already married, and he has to pay £200 to get his property back. Wealth taken from the Catholic Irish (represented in the play by Kiltory's servant, Patrick) to pay Cromwellian officers is starting to recirculate.

The same energies are evident in the slightly later drama that I shall investigate in this chapter. My focus will be on plays connected—sometimes exiguously—with Derry, starting from John Wilson's *Belphegor* (1677–8) and Mitchelbourne's two-part drama (both *The Siege* and *The Troubles of the North*), but going on to Farquhar's first comedy (staged in London), *Love and a Bottle* (1698) and the Dublin drama *St Stephen's Green* (1700) by William Philips—son of the George Philips who is still remembered in Derry because he encouraged the Apprentice Boys to shut the gates against the Jacobites. My claim will not be that these authors constitute, in any conventional sense, a literary school, but that they were all schooled in the conflicts of Derry and its hinterland. (The work of Charles Hopkins, another Derry-connected dramatist,[6] relates more tangentially to the matter of this chapter, and he goes undiscussed, though his liking for storylines that involve siege warfare, usurpation, and empire, and his strain of Protestant Jacobitism,[7] chime with Wilson and Philips.) Character types and motifs recur in all their plays: 'oeconomick Polititians' are conspicuous, warfare is never far away, while narratives turn on fortune-hunting by disbanded officers and competition for estates. What also emerges is a sense of the drama inherent in Anglo-Irish relations. These plays belong to a period in which the rights of Irish Protestants to challenge the economic and political dominance of England were being acted out by such controversialists as Bishop William King in Derry and William Molyneux in Dublin.

A larger context is provided by the advanced state of Anglo-Irish writing about political economy.[8] When George Philips left Derry for England in 1689, he rallied support for the city by publishing *The Interest of England in the Preservation of Ireland*. Though his treatise touches on the importance of shared Protestantism and ties of blood, it concentrates on commercial issues. The value of Irish wool, tallow, harbours, pilchards, linen, rabbit skins, and so on, is exhaustively set forth. Partly because the conquest of Ireland in the 1650s had presented the country to the English as an opportunity for enrichment, a discourse of schemes and projects came readily to such Anglo-Irish writers as Richard Lawrence and William Temple. Not all the projects put forward were as mad as those of Contriver in *Hic et Ubique*, who plans to improve Irish agriculture by filling the bogs with earth from the mountains, and to make trade easier with England by empty-ing St George's Channel of seawater, but some now seem implausible. Sir William Petty, for instance, proposed that most of the population of Ireland should be transferred wholesale to England and the country be turned over to grazing.[9] Yet Petty was a serious social scientist, regarded by Marx as the founding figure of political economy, whose *Political Anatomy of Ireland* (1672/91) gives a thorough statistical survey of the island.

Historians have reacted against Whig accounts of the Glorious Revolu-tion by insisting on the importance of confessional allegiances and political theologies. This rebalancing of the picture is salient for Ireland, where 1688–9 saw not constitutional reform but a resurgence of religious warfare. To highlight religion is also to become more accurately aware of the divi-sions between Irish Protestants—especially between Scottish Presbyterians and Church of Ireland conformists in Ulster—that later history has tended to conceal. Yet the productions of the Derry school reassert the impor-tance of the socio-economic matrix that I am highlighting in this chapter, by showing that religious motives were entwined with the old Adam of acquisitiveness, from the plundering undertaken by soldiers, through the gains in pilfered estates made by prudent marriages, to the distribution of spoils by William III himself—all contributing to a pattern of life in which wealth was made and could be lost quickly, and where property often did not have deep roots in the social order. The drama places these issues, moreover, within a geopolitically multiple framework. It demonstrates what can be deduced from other, more conventionally historical materials, that, whatever the importance of interactions between England and Ireland, the British-Irish problematic was intricately triangulated and contingent on a Scottish dimension that is to this day unignorable in Ulster.

★   ★   ★

As he muses on hunger in Derry, the inedibility of money, and the consolations of heaven, Granade is interrupted by a Beggar, who cries: 'For the Lord's sake, worthy Gantleman, hand your Charity tu'l a peaur awd Man, fourscore and saxteen years; ean Farthing or Haupeny tu'l a peaur aw'd *Scotch-man*.' Scots could hardly be broader, but Granade recognizes the beggar as a spy called 'Honest Darby', and Darby slips from an English as acquired, we come to realize, as his name (an anglicized version of Diarmuid) into an Irish brogue, as he explains how he infiltrated the

Jacobite army: 'I was last Night hopping about the Camp, begging Alms. It was some Shaints Day, and upon de next Guard to your Shelf in de Trenches, dere all de Officers be Drunk' (*Siege*, 138–9). By the time Granade's men reach those trenches, the Irish are thoroughly hungover, after a night gambling with French gold and brass money, and it is easy for the raiding party to make off with a sack of bread. Once they are back in Derry, the laws of supply and demand push the price of this delicacy up to five guineas a loaf. Granade blithely calls this 'A very good price,—give me two of them', and distributes slices to his men (*Siege*, 143). Guineas have food value after all.

The sequence offers a lesson in political economy, but also in archipelagic identities. Mitchelbourne repeatedly emphasizes the strategic significance of Derry. If it were not for the staunchness of the garrison, he points out (well over a dozen times), James II would have taken his Irish forces into Scotland and so marched into England. Derry was, in that sense, pivotal.[10] What the shifts in Darby's disguise bring out is that Derry was also a site of archipelagic plurality. Though the development of the city was directed from London by an organization called the Irish Society, the plantation drew (chiefly Lowland) Scottish as well as English settlers into an area from which the Gaelic Irish were incompletely expelled. Relations between the Irish and the incomers could be highly charged. An ugly episode in *The Troubles of the North* shows Irish women stripping clothes from a pair of Ulster Scots women and a child, backed up by two rapparees who threaten to ravish the '*Scotch* Bitches' (109–11). Yet although these ethnic differences, violently exacerbated during the 1640s, were still raw in 1689, individuals became adaptive, and could shift between camps. At one point Granade employs an Ulster Scots spy who understands Irish. Another spy reports saying to a sergeant in the Irish army, 'Sir, I have ean four-pence, ken you where is awny of my Country Swats, Ise give you a Drink', and a marginal note explains Swats as 'Small Scotch Ale' (*Siege*, 164).

The prominence of the Scots in those examples reflects their growing importance in Derry and its hinterland. Many arrived in the 1650s and late 1670s, and numbers swelled again in the final decade of the century. Contacts with Scotland remained close, both in trade and religion. Such Presbyterian radicals as John Crookshanks (reputedly the translator of George Buchanan's *De jure regni apud Scotos*) moved back and forth across the North Channel. The emergencies of 1663 (Blood's plot against Dublin Castle, in which Crookshanks was implicated), 1666

(the Pentland Rising), and so on to 1685 (Argyll's Rising) all encouraged
the authorities to keep an eye on traffic between Ulster and Scotland.
One extreme Scottish Covenanter, David Houston, who spent much of
his life in Ulster, appears with his followers in Mitchelbourne's *Troubles*,
mouthing such Godly-predictable slogans that the bystanders '*all fetch a
Yawn*' (104).[11]

An acute moment of crisis came with the assassination of James Sharp,
Archbishop of St Andrews, in 1679 (above, p. 288). This ostensibly
Scottish event prompted the English Privy Council to monitor movement
between Scotland and Ireland, and to order the Lord Lieutenant to
prohibit inflammatory conventicles in Ulster. In his capacity as Recorder of
Londonderry, John Wilson intervened at this point to pass on information
picked up in the city gaol to the Archbishop of Armagh. He reports
how a prisoner called Osborne said 'that whosoever killed the Archbishop
of St Andrews in Scotland did God good service'. On learning of this,
Wilson adds, 'I consulted with myselfe, what was fitt for me to doe in
it, and considering there was some difference between the citty and me,
I thought it prudent to lett it sleepe'. He has now, however, decided to
contact Archbishop Boyle because further intelligence informs him 'what
the Presbyterians say heere, namely, that their brethren in Scotland are too
hasty with the Covenant, since it was comeing about of itselfe'.[12]

The multi-talented Wilson—poet, translator, lawyer, political commentator, and dramatist—gives us an entrée into the archipelagic factionalism
of Protestant Derry. He became Recorder, thanks to the Duke of Ormond,
against local resistance, in 1666, and within two years was having to defend
himself against a report made to the Irish Society by the Lord Mayor
that he favoured the Scottish over the English interest. Wilson denied this
to Ormond,[13] and there is nothing in his English, high royalist past (and
Jacobite future) to suggest that he would side with the Ulster Scots. The
accusation points to a determination by the Mayor to use any pretext to
explode Wilson in the minefield of patronage and commerce. Certainly
his later problems pitched him against the Scots, who were developing a
stranglehold on trade. (This was also the period in which the Ulster Scots
textually consolidated their trajectory as a community, collecting during
the 1670s materials for the history which Patrick Adair would write.)[14]
The minute books of the Corporation, which survive from 1673, show
Wilson regularly present at meetings in Derry, with tensions becoming un-
sustainable by 1677–8. Hence the phrase in his letter to Boyle about 'some

difference between the citty and me', and the implication that he would get into trouble if he reported the subversive views of local Presbyterians (which he nonetheless did). Writing to Ormond slightly later, from Derry, Wilson mocked his enemies by saying, in Scots, that he was not one of their brood of chickens: 'It is my original sin (as to this citty) that I am not (to use their owne phrase) of ther eane clucking; and it is my actual transgression, that I can neither lead, nor drive, with a faction'.[15]

Staged at the Smock Alley Theatre, Dublin, probably during the 1677–8 season,[16] *Belphegor* suggests how hellish Wilson's life had become. The tragicomedy is about a devil who comes to earth and finds it more acquisitive and tormentingly duplicitous than hell itself. People are 'so exquisitely practis'd in Cheating one another, that the best of us is a meer Novice to 'em'.[17] The devil of the title, Belphegor, takes on human form and marries a wife called Imperia, who ruins him with her extravagance: an onomantic allegory of a life wedded to politics. Wilson was outmanoeuvred in Derry and lost his Recordership in 1679–80, though not the support of Ormond. Perhaps he sensed the imminence of defeat, because he wrote into his play, which takes its substance from Machiavelli or Straparola, a plot about a deposed public servant, who announces:

> He's a Beast that serves
> A Commonwealth; for when he has spent his Blood,
> And sunk his Fortune, to support the Pride
> And Luxury of those few that Cheat the rest,
> He streight becoms the Object of their Scorn
> Or Jealousie.   (8)

Montalto is a prodigy of virtue; when Belphegor offers him a bribe from a foreign ruler who might attack his native Italy, he indignantly refuses, and he is then tactfully subsidized with funds by a nobleman called Grimaldi.

This plot is easy to read as an appeal for support from Ormond, whether consciously pitched or not. What makes it more unusual, more strangely proleptic, is its capacity to develop new meanings when the notably Jacobite Wilson arranged for *Belphegor* to be restaged in London in 1690. Now when the devil tests Montalto, the analogy is with James II, dethroned by William III and fled for safety to France:

Rod[erigo]. [= Belphegor] ... There is a Prince, whose Name must be as yet conceal'd, is so sensible of your Merit, and this Republick's Ingratitude, that he

has order'd ye Ten thousand Pistoles, as a small Pledge of his future Favour;—and I'll advance the Money.
[Mont[alto] *starts*
Mon. Ten Thousand Pistols!—and from a Prince unknown!—and what must I do for all this?
Rod. Kings have their Reasons to themselves, too deep for private Men to fathom.—Who knows, but he may have a design upon *Italy.*—This—or some other place;—and, which is further in my Instructions,—has pitcht on you, as General for the Expedition. ...
[*Mon.*] I lend a Hand to Slave my Country!—No;
That won't *Montalt'*; the disoblig'd *Montalt'*;
Vertue forbid the Thought.—Tho' she may've lost
Th'affection of a Mother, she's my Mother ... (15)

Louis XIV is split into threatening and benign aspects here. The Williamite view that he wants James Stuart to invade England for the good of France is rejected. James would never accept subsidy on those terms. It is, however, satisfactory for Montalto to be paid by Grimaldi, a friend and fellow-nobleman, acting anonymously—Louis XIV in purified guise.

Wilson published a poem *To His Excellence Richard Earle of Arran &c. Lord Deputy of Ireland* in Dublin in 1682. To judge from a letter of recommendation that Arran wrote to Ormond at the end of that year,[18] he then returned to England: there is no evidence to support the nineteenth-century belief that he was in Ireland in 1687–90 as secretary to Tyrconnell and, for a second time, Recorder of Londonderry. Even so, his treatise in favour of the royal prerogative, *A Discourse of Monarchy* (1684), is full of Irish matters, from the planting of English laws by King John to the way Charles I's parliamentary opponents 'hired *Owen Roe O Neal*, to raise the Siege at *London-Derry* in *Ireland*, then Beleaguer'd by his Majesties Forces'.[19] It was an example of Commonwealth hypocrisy that Wilson liked to savour; he recycles it word-for-word in his reply to a reprint of Milton's *Eikonoklastes* published in 1692.[20] Perhaps the instance was too good to forget. As likely, Derry was in his mind as a place more recently besieged, and a city he knew something about.

★ ★ ★

Wilson's Stuart loyalism was far from unique in Derry. Even among those who resisted King James there was dissension, both during the siege and afterwards, as Episcopalians such as George Walker and Presbyterians, including John Mackenzie, published a stream of pamphlets claiming credit for saving the city. The effects of this can be seen in the anonymous *Royal Voyage: Or, The Irish Expedition* (1690), a virulently Williamite play about the events of 1689–90. In texts about war, individuals are more often identified on one's own side than that of the enemy. *The Royal Voyage*, by contrast, shows us such Irish leaders as Tyrconnell, Mac-Carty, and Nugent, and soldiers with the stock names Mac-Shane, O Donnel, and Teigue, yet the protestants are called Governor of Derry, English Captain, and so forth. ''Tis out of choice that I have named no Persons', the author explains in a preface, 'unless of the Enemics side.—As all shared in the Danger, so let 'em all in the Glory,—whatever parties there might then be, or are since, there shall be none in this Play, but *English* and *Irish*.'[21]

There were other attempts to celebrate the collective effort of Protestants. Joseph Aickin's *Londerias* (1699), for example, is an epic, in abysmal couplets, that begins as it means to go on: 'I Sing the Men, who *Dery* did *restore* | To the condition, as it was before.'[22] Aickin's inclusive approach required him to gloss over conflict between Church of Ireland and Kirk factions, while the influence of the classics ('I Sing the Men'), and especially of the *Iliad* as siege narrative, encouraged him to respect the gallantry of Catholic leaders—to make them worthy opponents, as Greeks and Trojans had been. It cannot be pretended that *Londerias* becomes great literature as a result, but Aickin is involvingly alert to a range of local and familial contacts, and he repeatedly brings out the ethnic basis of institutions. As when he discusses Tyrconnell's purging of the Scottish-packed but theoretically English Corporation (and shows that John Wilson was not Recorder of Londonderry at the time):

> The Learn'd *Rochfort* Recorder of the Town,
> Opposed the same to his great Renown;
> Yet in spight of Reason and the English Laws,
> *Talbot* the Charter from the City draws:
> Turn'd out the English Corporation,
> And chose all Popish Members of his own.   (26)

That Mitchelbourne's two-part drama was a product of this infighting shows in its anti-Presbyterian touches. It is, however, relatively tolerant of the Catholic Irish. In *The Royal Voyage*, written during the heat of the Williamite war, they brag about burning a hundred Protestants in a house and tossing a baby on a pike (B4v). Their idea of preparing steak is to dance around a fat English ox, singing an Irish song, then to chop slices out of the live animal and roast them in hot coals (C1r). Mitchelbourne is obtusely contemptuous (his bog Irish are sexually loose, predatory, and under the thumb of the priest), but he avoids such lurid extremes. Nor are his peasants, though ignorant and short-sighted, as fatuous as those depicted in, for example, *The Irish Hudibras* (1689).[23] In their cabins beside the bog, Mitchelbourne's Taigs count up the gains of looting. But theft is the rule on all sides, from the Governor (Lundy) who drinks away William of Orange's gold, rather than use it to fight the Jacobites, to the soldiers who return to Derry with jackboots, a fine-laced saddle, and other luxuries seized from the Catholics. The Irish capacity for mischief is limited by lack of ambition. A looted amber necklace is sold for sixpence to buy a bottle of *usquebagh*. When they abuse their betters, they reassuringly mimic them rather than destroy the social order.[24]

In a ponderously comic way, it even becomes a question how different the Irish are from the English whom they disposssess. One scene has Mitchelbourne (here known as 'Major') release two Irish prisoners because he is amused by their insinuation of common kinship. Teigue Burn assures the Sussex-born Major that '*Michelburn*, is de same ting, as *Michal Burn, Michal Mac-Burn*, or *Burn-Mac-Michel*; fen de *Burn*, come behind or before, dey are still de Blood of de *Burn*, and de *Burn* be de Clan, or de great Shentlemans of the County of *Wicklow*' (*Troubles*, 115). A scion of one of the most notoriously rebellious families in Ireland here turns to advantage the claim of Spenser and Sir John Temple that the Burns were of British stock.[25] There may be an autobiographical in-joke—Mitchelbourne moved to Wicklow as a child, and became a -bourne growing up among the Byrnes[26]—but for most early readers Teigue's plea would have represented the flip-side of an assertion often made by Irish Protestants in the late seventeenth century, especially when looking for sympathy from England, that most of the population of Ireland was of English blood.[27] It points to a degree of indulgence in Mitchelbourne towards his former enemies—but then, it was easier to forgive those he had defeated in battle than the people, on his own side, who had profited from his unpaid valour. The effect is heightened when his soldier, Franc, orders the prisoners to give him their coats as his fee (the impulse to pilfer again), and the Major overrules him.

Having been given quarter, Teigue and Dermot must be allowed their clothes.

Acquisitiveness and quarter are issues within the city. Early in the siege we hear that people are wavering, tempted by a bribe from Tyrconnell, and abandoned by affluent neighbours who have run off to Scotland. Eventually the Militia of Derry is down to only two Aldermen, Captain Buff and Captain Step-stately, who, as their names suggest, are not the bravest of soldiers. They resolve to contact 'one *George H——* that keeps Correspondence with the [Jacobite] Lieut. General, and sells Protections privatly, and gets half a Guinea apiece for them' (*Siege*, 46). How will a protection save them in an onslaught? Step-stately has barricaded his door with his wife's kneading trough, and ties a scarf about his leg as a bandage to make himself look disabled. Buff's wife is not so pliable. She demands that he show courage, and, when he will not, ties her apron around him, puts on his sword and dubs him, with a stroke on the crown, 'Sir Knight of the Order of the *White Apron*' (*Siege*, 47). Later, Buff and Step-stately contend to be mayor of the city. Despite his record of cowardice, the latter wins the election, then makes a speech claiming Mitchelbourne's feats as his own.

These thinly disguised characters are two of the enemies in Mitchelbourne's own ranks. That the Derry Militia was so disloyal and depleted is unlikely. Aickin commends 'all the Aldermen' for the part they played in the siege.[28] What seems to have happened is that, like John Wilson, Mitchelbourne fell foul of the politics of the Corporation, and settled his scores in drama. In 1690, he stood for mayor and got only one vote from the Aldermen (his own?). In 1698, an eventful year, he was accused of publishing in London *The Case of the Governor, Officers and Soldiers actually concerned in the Defence of London-Derry*—a document which slights the city's contribution to its own defence in order to press the claims of the garrison. When he refused to answer the charge, Mitchelbourne was expelled from the Corporation, and began a legal action that proved so intractable that the city had to ask the Recorder of Londonderry not to charge legal fees on top of his salary.

Though Mitchelbourne's dramaturgy is simple, its engagement with history is compound. He deals with 1688–9 through the filter of 1698, and his subsequent petitions for payment,[29] while the 1705 edition of his double drama, which incorporates maps and diagrams (including the prospect reproduced as Fig. 14), is bracketed with preliminary and

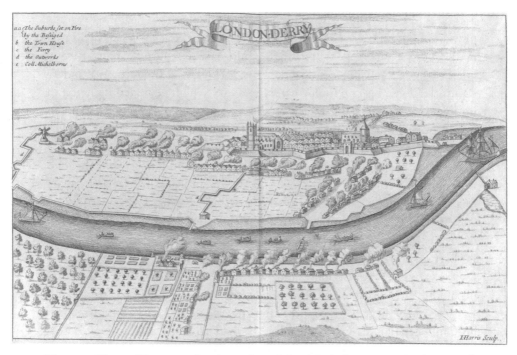

a a The Suburbs set on Fire
   by the Besieged
b the Town House
c the Ferry
d the Outworks
e Coll. Michelborne

LONDON-DERRY

J.Harris Sculp.

Fig. 14. View of Derry under siege, from John Mitchelbourne, *Ireland Preserv'd: Or, The Siege of London-Derry. Together with The Troubles of the North* (London, 1705).

back-matter that has a Queen Anne flavour. These paratexts use the word 'British', for example, not (as occasionally in the plays) to signify an *ad hoc* alliance of English and Scottish Protestants in Ulster but inhabitants of the other island, moving towards union. Indeed there is a copy of this edition in the Bodleian, with its publication date altered by pen to 1707, probably by the author, that contains a begging letter from Mitchelbourne to Robert Harley—one of the architects (as the next chapter will show) of the British union secured in that year. Taken as a whole, the 1705–7 volume shifts from the archipelagic geopolitics of 1689, according to which, in Mitchelbourne's view, the Protestant resisters of Derry prevented Irish troops from landing in Scotland and marching south with their allies into England, to the commercial occasion of the Anglo-Scottish Treaty. If Louis XIV had taken control of Ireland and its harbours, the preface points out, that would have been 'Inconvenient to the Trade of *England*. But *DERRY*, the last Stake, restor'd the *British* Losses' (C1r).

The audiences were also multiple. Though the 1705 edition was addressed to a London readership, a manuscript draft of *The Siege* is dedicated to the Lord Lieutenant of Ireland,[30] while Mitchelbourne's desire to win Ulster readers, and mock his opponents in Derry, is obvious and understandable, given his continuing career in a city which he ended up living in until his death (1721). In fact *The Siege* is a good example of a work that was lost to Eng. Lit. because its subject ceased to matter to metropolitan readers but whose devolved influence was so potent as to have had more than a local effect. Reprinted only a couple of times in London, it went through dozens of editions in eighteenth- and nineteenth-century Ireland, many of them in Dublin but others in such northern towns as Belfast, Newry, and Strabane.[31] In his autobiography the Tyrone writer William Carleton (1794–1869) says that, during his childhood, Mitchelbourne's *Siege*, and Robert Ashton's play about the Williamite war, *The Battle of Aughrim* (1728),[32] 'were school-books', and 'were acted in barns and waste houses night after night, ... attended by multitudes, both Catholic and Protestant'. Because of the heated atmosphere after the 1798 rising, these performances became sectarian flashpoints; audiences had to intervene to stop actors hacking one another with their swords.[33] *The Siege* helped keep alive in Ulster—and wherever the Irish went[34]—the historical resentments whose consequences still haunt the British state.

★   ★   ★

At this point it would be rewarding to probe other texts from Derry associated with the siege. One might, for instance, contrast the geopolitical vision of the sermons preached to the garrison by the Church of Ireland George Walker on Judges 7: 20 ('The Sword of the Lord, and of Gideon') and the Presbyterian Seth Whittle, who chose Jeremiah 1: 18–19 ('For behold, I have made thee this day a defenced City, and an Iron Pillar, and Brazen Walls against the whole Land ...'). Despite his Scottish origins, Walker emphasized the English stem of Ulster protestantism, going back to the Henrician Reformation, while for Whittle Derry was an isolated Jerusalem that put no trust in princes. Both sermons typify aspects of the English-Scots divide in the city, and both reached archipelagic audiences.[35] Equally, one might investigate later, literary representations of the siege, noticing how they were inflected by changes across the archipelago (Catholic emancipation, commitment to the British Empire, and the like) as much as by the local peculiarities of Derry.[36] The readiest way to pursue my socio-economic theme, however, is to move to plays by Mitchelbourne's younger contemporaries, George Farquhar and William Philips.

Early records tell us that Farquhar's father was 'an Eminent Divine of the Church of England' (i.e. Ireland), living near Derry, who, during the Williamite war, 'was plundred and burnt out of all that he had, and not long after dy'd with greif'.[37] That Farquhar was in the city during the siege is probable, though he seems too young (b.1677–8) to have fought, as some claim, in the Battle of the Boyne (1690). He did, however, write an ode 'On the Death of General *Schomberg* kill'd at the *Boyn*', which, considering his brilliant future, reads disconcertingly like the work of Aickin:

(2.)

The *Brittish* Lyon roars
Along the fatal Shores;
The *Hibernian* Harp in mournful Strains,
Mixt with the *Eccho* of the Floud, complains. ...[38]

After schooling in Derry, Farquhar went to Trinity College, Dublin and had a brief career on the stage with the Smock Alley company. The great Irish actor Robert Wilks, who afterwards starred in his most successful play, *The Constant Couple* (1699), is said to have encouraged him to take his first script, *Love and a Bottle*, to England. By 1698 Farquhar was in London; yet he maintained his Irish connections, and returned to Dublin as a soldier in 1704. The 1711 edition of his works shows Ben Jonson, crowned with laurel, presenting Farquhar to Apollo and the Muses. Farquhar holds an Irish harp.

It cannot be supposed that Farquhar was unaffected by his experiences in Derry, and his plays incorporate hostile and patronizing views of Irish Catholics. There is Macahone, the absurd fortune-hunter in *The Stage-Coach* (1701), the comic servant Teague in *The Twin-Rivals* (1702), and the priest Foigard in *The Beaux' Stratagem* (1707), who is caught in the double trap of English hegemony and Irish speech-habits:

Aimwell. ... (*Takes* Foigard *by the Shoulder*.) Sir, I arrest you as a Traytor against the Government; you're a Subject of *England*, and this Morning shew'd me a Commission, by which you serv'd as Chaplain in the *French* Army: This is Death by our Law, and your Reverence must hang for't.

Foigard. Upon my Shoul, Noble Friend, dis is strange News you tell me, Fader *Foigard* a Subject of *England*, de Son of a *Burgomaster* of *Brussels*, a Subject of *England*! Ubooboo — (IV.ii.52–9)

That these are familiar types might seem to make it less likely that Farquhar's life and times impacted on his depiction of the Irish. But Macahone, for one, is not particularly derivative: the eighteenth-century line of (often military) stage Irishmen, who try to make up for their poverty by catching rich wives in England, starts with George Roebuck in *Love and a Bottle*. It is as though the structure of Farquhar's situation, seeking his own fortune in London,[39] compelled him to invent a type: one that could reflect the disadvantages of the Irish gentry and its dependency on England. For to call Roebuck autobiographical is to diminish the interest of the case: he does not so much echo as anticipate what Farquhar would do in 1703, when he married Margaret Pemell, a widow with two children, in the belief that she was wealthy. She was, in fact, poor, and Farquhar's life became a struggle to support his new family.

Mitchelbourne would have warmed to *Love and a Bottle* if, as is entirely possible, he saw it in 1698 (the year when his claims for back-pay were being investigated by a committee of the Commons), because its opening shows how the disbanding of regiments in 1697, after the signing of a treaty with Louis XIV, had left even more officers in poverty. Roebuck begins the play with a quotation from Dryden:

Thus far our Arms have with Success been Crown'd. — Heroically spoken, faith, of a fellow that has not one farthing in his Pocket. If I have one Penny to buy a Halter withal in my present necessity, may I be hang'd; ... But hold—Can't I rob honourably, by turning Soldier?

Enter a Cripple begging.

Cripple. One farthing to the poor old Soldier, for the Lord's sake. ... Our greatest Benefactors, the brave Officers are all disbanded, and must now turn Beggars like my self... (I.i.1–9, 29–30)

To join the army was the usual recourse for an indigent Irish gentleman—a rich English wife might then follow. That route is blocked for Roebuck, and he must find alternative ways of supporting himself in London. Not having lost a leg, he cannot even beg in the streets, and can only be a soldier by declaring 'open War' on Fortune (I.i.59–60) and stabbing the next person worth robbing who comes on stage.

That person proves to be Lucinda, the beloved (though Roebuck does not yet know this) of his English-based, Irish-landowning friend, Lovewell. Roebuck does not quite stab her, but accosts her as 'An *Irish*-man, Madam, at your Service.' 'Oh horrible!', Lucinda replies, 'an *Irish*-man! a meer Wolf-Dog, I protest' (I.i.148–50). Her response is extravagant, but provoked by an unusual self-description. Those with names like George Roebuck (neither a Mac- nor an O') did not call themselves Irishmen at the time, but the Protestants of Ireland, or the English of Ireland. (Later, Roebuck flings himself into a sword-fight with the words 'Have at thee—St *George* for *England*', a piquant battle-cry when spoken in an Irish accent: ''Tis I be gad' (I.i.202–6).) By 'Irish' the Protestants of Ireland meant Gaelic Irish, or, commonly after the Williamite wars, any member of the Catholic population. It was not until the 1720s, for the economic and political reasons which I am tracking, that the New English would start to call themselves Irish.[40] So this is one of those archipelagic interactions in which being in England makes someone aware of the limits of his Englishness. Given Farquhar's description of Roebuck in the dramatis personae as 'An *Irish* Gentleman, of a wild roving temper', we can go further and say that England was making the dramatist aware of his Irishness.

Lucinda's teasing now looks less extreme. If this is an Irishman, then he will have the uncouth qualities associated for the English with the 'wild' or (a word she employs) 'meer' Irish. Nor are her doubts misplaced: Roebuck does paw and nuzzle her like a wolfhound, stealing a kiss and trying to drag her off-stage. In flight from Ireland to avoid marrying a woman he has impregnated and does not love, penniless, and desperate, Roebuck displays the attributed behaviour which Farquhar's London audience, caring little for the ethnic nuances, often generalized from the 'wild' Irish to all the inhabitants of a country that they regarded as uncivilized. Farquhar capitalizes on this, however, to make Wildean jokes in which Ireland functions as a screen on which to project English faults. When Lucinda quips, for example—again from anti-Catholic propaganda—that 'the people wear Horns and Hoofs' in Ireland, Roebuck replies: 'Yes, faith, a great many wear Horns [i.e. they are cuckolds]: but we had that among other laudable fashions, from *London*' (I.i.156–9).

The nub of the play is money. In his first exchange with Roebuck, Lovewell jokes about the merchants' wives that his friend ought to 'trade with', then enquires about the state of his purse. Once again, Farquhar seizes a chance to point up the inequalities of Anglo-Irish relations. 'You have brought Bills?', Lovewell asks: 'No, faith. Exchange of Money from *Dublin* hither is so unreasonable high' (I.i.277, 290–2). Money values were not the same on both sides of St George's Channel. The guinea bitten in Mitchelbourne's *Siege*, for example, declined in value in England from thirty shillings to twenty-two in 1695, yet was worth twenty-six in Ireland.[41] This would make a purseful of gold, or bills, expensive to take to London in 1698, but, of course, Roebuck is simply broke. Fortunately, his friend is generous, and Roebuck can later exclaim: 'I have got about twenty Guinea's in my Pocket; and whilst they last, the Devil take *George* if he thinks of Futurity. I'll go hand in hand with Fortune' (III.ii.359–62).

This rakish, wastrel disposition was less attractive to audiences in 1698 than it had been two or three decades earlier. Jeremy Collier's *Short View of the Immorality, and Profaneness of the English Stage*, published in that year, was a sign of the times. Traits that would jar in the moderate protagonists of Steele or even the later Congreve are licensed in Roebuck, however, by his Irishness: he carries into the play his country's reputation for improvidence and laxity. Money and sexuality are also tied into ethnicity in the triangle of women who gather around him. From Ireland comes Mistress Trudge, clutching her baby boy, and wanting the marriage she was promised. As first imagined she may have been, like Roebuck, one of the English of Ireland. She has no brogue marked in the dialogue, and Roebuck's father is keen for him to make her an honest woman. Yet she has a song, not published with the play (and not incontrovertibly by Farquhar) but performed in its first season,[42] that begins '*On Sunday after Mass, | Dormett and his Lass, | To the Green wood did pass*', and its Catholic Irishness is heightened by Hiberno-English and Gaelic vocabulary.[43] Poor, needy, loose, Trudge is the female equivalent of Roebuck, and like him acquires 'wild' characteristics, but, because of the play's double standards, she is even less assimilable to Anglicized civility, and she has to be grateful to be paid off with money tricked from a fool.

Roebuck's flight from Trudge means leaving the desirable Leanthe, Lovewell's sister, on her brother's estate in Ireland. Then there is the English heiress, Lucinda, with whom he intrigues, but does not in fact seduce. What he fails to realize is that Leanthe has followed him and is now employed as Lucinda's page. In a fifth act assignation, Leanthe substitutes for Lucinda, and is duly married to Roebuck. All this might suggest a tangling together of Anglo-Irish experiences, but in practice the play seems alert to an emerging alienation between England and its neighbour. There is a hierarchy of virtue, in which wealth and a degree of chastity meet at an apex which is Englishness. Yet the dynamic element in the drama is provided by Roebuck and Leanthe, whose appetitive life is integral to their Irish background. At their wedding they are treated to '*An* Irish *Entertainment of three Men and three Women, dress'd after the Fingallion fashion*'. This rustic-Hibernian show[44] was originally promised (or, as Lucinda tellingly jests, 'threatned') by Lovell for performance at the English couple's marriage (V.iii.213, 217–18), but it now resolvingly slips to the Irish side of the action. Meanwhile, Roebuck is given Lovewell's Irish land. Marriage binds friends and families across St George's Channel, but there is a clarification of identities, with Irish connections being shaken off by Lovewell and Lucinda, and the power to bestow wealth being shown to lie in England—a pattern that recurs even in William Philips's more patriotically Irish comedy, *St Stephen's Green*.

Philips's background resembles Farquhar's. No doubt he was brought up on the family estate at Limavady, a few miles from Derry; his father George was ruined by the fighting of 1689–90 and sold his lands a few years later. George remained active in the area, however, writing to the new Bishop of Derry, William King, about a legal case in 1691,[45] and he was re-elected MP for County Londonderry in 1695. A couple of years later we first hear about his son, Captain William Philips, who became Burgess of Limavady when his father died. Mitchelbourne, Farquhar, Philips (to whom one could add the Dublin-born Thomas Southerne): the gravitation of Anglo-Irish dramatists to the military life is striking. The extent of Philips's fighting activity is not clear, though it is possible that he was in arms under the Irish Lord Ikerrin between 1702 and 1706,[46] and engaged in the Spanish campaign that Farquhar (then garrisoned in Dublin) celebrated in his heroic, unsatisfactory poem in six cantos, *Barcellona* (1710). In outline, Philips's career sounds standard for an Ulster Protestant gentleman, whose early years accustomed him to war. But he seems to have developed Jacobite connections, and he produced in *Hibernia Freed* (1722) a drama sympathetic to Gaelic Ireland—using MacCurtin's 1717 adaptation of Seathrún Céitinn's *Foras feasa ar Éirinn*[47] as a source.[48]

There are signs of Jacobitism even in his first play, *The Revengeful Queen* (1698). This centres on a brave but bad king of the Lombards, who makes his queen drink from a goblet made out of her father's skull, then announces that he killed the father in battle. Understandably vexed, she arranges for her husband's murder. Philips took the situation from Machiavelli's *History of Florence*, but the Gothick appeal of the story meant that he was not the first to dramatize it: he followed, unwittingly it seems,[49] in Davenant's footsteps. But the interest of the plot was enhanced in 1698 by its ability to comment on the relationship between James II, his daughter Queen Mary (*d.*1694), and son-in-law William III. James's defeat by William in Ireland notoriously troubled his daughter, who found herself married to a man widely regarded, if not quite as a regicide (though often compared with Cromwell), then as a usurper—indeed, a fortune-hunter, whose marriage was but a step towards acquiring the wealth of the three kingdoms. At least as significant, given Philips's Derry background, are two revisions made to Machiavelli: the addition of a siege, as a frame around the action, and much emphasis on questions of honour in the soldiers who are called upon to defend their city but have divided feelings about their monarch.

Philips's second play, *St Stephen's Green*, however, clarifies more sharply the issues I am pursuing. Like *Love and a Bottle* it deals with four young people who turn into couples: Freelove and Aemilia (both of whom have money but disguise this, so as to be chosen for love), and Bellmine and Marina. The Englishman Freelove needs some introduction to Dublin—a city full of disbanded officers,[50] in which landed wealth is essential for status but its possession suspect. As Marina exclaims: "tis as Difficult to be thought [a Fine Gentleman] here, without an Estate; as it is to be thought Honest and Get one' (2–3). In this hard-edged, adventurist country, the problems of dependency on England keep forcing their way into dialogue. When Bellmour speaks of fearing marriage, for instance, he says 'I dread it as much as our Farmers do the Wool-Bill' (5)—a bill passed by the English House of Commons in 1699 to protect West-country farmers against Irish competition.

In the preface to his *Case of Ireland's Being Bound by Acts of Parliament* (1698)—a hugely influential treatise, which fuelled Irish Protestant nationalism and American separatism in the late eighteenth century—William Molyneux insisted that 'I have not any Concern in *Wooll*, or the *Wooll-Trade*. I am no wise Interested in the *Forfeitures*, or *Grants* [the distribution of confiscated Jacobite land]. I am not at all Solicitous, whether the *Bishop*, or *Society* of *Derry* Recover the Land they Contest about' (A6v). That he had, in fact, strong views about these issues can be seen not just from later references in the text but from manuscript evidence that shows him helping Bishop King of Derry prepare his 1698 case against the London-based Irish

Society regarding fishing and other property rights[51]—yet another Derry controversy that sprang from the growing strength of Scottish Presbyterians on the Corporation.[52] The point about this landmark case is that, when King won an appeal to the Irish House of Lords, the Society took the matter to the English House of Lords, which, notwithstanding contested jurisdiction, found in the Society's favour. When this was followed by the Wool Bill, Irish Protestant anger mounted, stirred up from Derry; and Molyneux argued in his *Case* that, since England and Ireland were distinct kingdoms, and since Ireland had never been conquered, because Henry II had been invited into the country (in contrast to William the Conqueror who fought his way into England), and since the English of Ireland had assuredly not been conquered but had repeatedly suppressed Irish rebellions, the English parliament had no right to bind Irish Protestants with laws made in its own favour. Following Locke, he asserted that taxation without consent (the predicament of his community) was a form of theft.

Molyneux's *Case* outraged English MPs and consequently alarmed the Irish elite, including King, but it is clear from *St Stephen's Green* that Dublin audiences found aspects of their subordination irksome. When Bellmine tries to impress Marina by talking about his visit to England (9), she is pointedly unimpressed. Later, the dim-witted Vainly tells Freelove and Bellmine that he is 'forced to go to *England* once a year, to refine my understanding', boasts that his coat has been sent express from London, because 'I cannot bear any thing but what comes from thence', and condescends to the hospitality, climate, and soil of Ireland. After a few dozen lines of this even Sir Francis Faignyouth, who loves squandering his money on fashionable trifles, can bear it no longer and cries: 'Why thou little worthless Contemptible Wretch! Do you entertain Strangers with your aversion for your Country, without being able to give one Reason for liking it' (42–3). It is one of several black marks against the villainess, Lady Volant, that she longs to 'leave this hideous Country for ever' (75).

Volant is the lynchpin of a fortune-hunting plot which shows that the greedy deceptions of *Hic et Ubique* were still operative in Williamite Ireland. An incomer to Dublin, she has been putting it about, with the help of her servant (and intimate) Timothy Tellpenny, that she is rich, in order to catch the wealthy Faignyouth in marriage. Her situation is complicated by the arrival of Timothy's old acquaintance, Trickwell, who, glad to see that

Timothy is doing well in Ireland, sardonically adds 'I suppose you Despise it'. Philips has contrived another opportunity to play on the resentment of a patriotic audience: 'for I have observ'd that none Despise *Ireland* so much as those who thrive best in it. ... I have known many of 'em, when they come first to London, think there is no way so ready to purchase the Title of a Wit, as to Ridicule their own Country' (52). What of Trickwell himself? After a military career in Flanders, he 'pretended to an Estate ... and so went a Fortune hunting' in London, 'met with a Lady who was on the same scent; and we Believ'd, Cheated, and Marry'd each other.' Timothy, who might have Farquhar's marriage in mind, says, 'The common Fate of Fortune-hunters. But what is become of your Spouse?' (54). She is, of course, the woman who now calls herself Lady Volant.

All the machinery is in place to tie Faignyouth into a fraudulent marriage and, at a price, to get him out: the same drives and denouement entangle him as they did Colonel Kiltory. With a satirical dig at the likes of Elizabeth Villiers (above, p. 301), the old man laments: 'had [Volant] been a Miss to some Favorite, and beg'd an Estate of Forfeited Lands, that had been some Comfort. But to be a Strumpet, and a poor Strumpet!' (76–7). Much more romantically reconciled are the lovers who pretend to have no money but will marry in any case. Even here, however, Ireland is economically subordinated. Freeman can afford to look for love because he has 'an estate in *England* of Three thousand Pounds a Year', while Aemilia reveals that she has twenty thousand pounds from an English uncle, a sum which she concealed to avoid being 'pester'd by Fortune-hunters' (79–80). Philips could perfectly well have made this lump sum a parcel of Irish land. But here, as in *Love and a Bottle*, England is the owner and distributor of wealth, while Ireland, in its shadow, must shift as best it can.

The Bishop of Derry's case was the first of several controversies that drove a wedge between Irish Protestants and England. A celebrated contest, *Annesley vs Sherlock*, which ran from 1709 to 1718, ended with the British Lords again claiming authority over the Irish courts. In 1720, the 'sixth of George I' or Declaratory Act rejected the appellate powers of the Irish House of Lords and insisted on the right of Westminster to 'make laws ... to bind the kingdom and people of Ireland'.[53] Both the Annesley case and the Act prompted the appearance of new editions of Molyneux's treatise; but it was the economic front that saw the sharpest conflict. The Dublin parliament rejected, for instance, proposals for an Irish bank modelled on the Bank of England. Debate was joined around themes which equally divided British opinion, regarding the reliability of money as against land as the basis for prosperity,[54] but the wrangling was inevitably caught up in mutual Anglo-Irish suspicion. With an eye to the Vainlys of Dublin, Jonathan Swift maintained that the Irish should set about 'burning *every Thing that came from* England, *except their* People *and their* Coals', and opposed the '*Thing* they call a *Bank*'.[55] With mass deprivation being caused (as Swift pointed out) by absentee English landlords like Lovewell grinding the faces of the poor,[56] the scene was set for a showdown over money. It came in the most literal way when a Wolverhampton ironmaster, William Wood, was granted a patent to coin Irish halfpence, thanks to an enormous bribe paid to George I's mistress. William King of Derry (now Archbishop of Dublin) protested that this insufficiently regulated coinage—reminiscent of Jacobite brass money—would drain gold and silver from the system, while Swift excoriated the scheme, and with it the stranglehold of England over Irish land and trade, in *The Drapier's Letters* (1724–5).

That Molyneux rejected the claim 'That *Ireland* is to be look'd upon only as a *Colony* from *England*',[57] on grounds of both reason and history, does not mean that the country was not treated as such by the English. As I indicated in my introduction, and echoed in Chapters 5 and 8, it would be as wrong to ignore the process of plantation and expropriation in Ireland as it would be to reduce the pattern of British intervention to a single paradigm. And if Protestant Ireland lost its raw, colonizing energy in the early eighteenth century, and developed an estate-based affluence reminiscent of other *ancien régime* elites,[58] it is also the case that, as competition mounted among trading nations, and the great age of imperialism began, Ireland looked less and less like one of three kingdoms and increasingly like a colonial dependency. Yet the evidence of the literature is that any discussion of this thorny issue cannot be restricted to Anglo-Irish relations, because the union of Scotland with England in 1707 contributed to the asymmetry. Molyneux's notable, glancing remark that union with England was 'an Happiness we can hardly hope for'[59] was only one of a number of unionist gestures, some of them more assertive.[60] That the Scots were politically incorporated into a British state rubbed salt into Irish Protestant wounds by highlighting their own satellite, inferior status.[61] To anticipate my epilogue: Swift echoed a widespread disappointment in his *Story of the Injured Lady* (1707, published in 1746), which has the lady (Ireland) complain at her rejection by a lover who had enjoyed her (England) in favour of a sluttish rival (Scotland)—though, perhaps because he had spent early, difficult years running a Church of Ireland parish in a part of Ulster dominated by Presbyterians, Swift is unusually bitter towards the Scots.[62]

The impact of these changes can be seen in the high patriotism of the play I shall end this chapter with: Philips's *Hibernia Freed*. In his dedicatory epistle to the Earl of Thomond, the author says that love of his country induced him to set a play in Ireland. As much might be said of *St Stephen's Green*, but *Hibernia Freed* celebrates ancient, Gaelic Ireland, not Protestant Dublin, and laments the condition it has been reduced to by invasion. As the high king, O Brien (putative ancestor of Philips's dedicatee) cries:

> Fertile *Hibernia*! Hospitable Land!
> Is not allow'd to feed her Native Sons,
> In vain they toil, and a-mid Plenty starve.
> The lazy *Dane* grows wanton with our Stores,
> Urges our Labour, and derides our Wants.
> *Hibernia*! Seat of Learning! School of Science!
> How waste! How wild dost thou already seem!
> Thy Houses, Schools, thy Cities ransack'd, burnt![63]

This extraordinary speech is closer to eighteenth-century Gaelic poetry than to Mitchelbourne or Farquhar. Jacobitism and the ecphonetic energy of complaint draw out of Philips a passage that (whatever his conscious design) resonates with regret for the destruction of traditional culture—elided with the achievements of Ireland's medieval, scholarly elite—and the devastation of cities like Athlone, as well as Protestant-owned great houses, in the Williamite wars. Unlike Vainly, O Brien is proud of the fertility of Ireland, he denies that its hospitality is improvident, and he mounts a social critique that recalls Swift on the exploitation of the poor by landlords. The Danes represent the English. The Irish noblewoman Agnes says that they were welcomed into the country (like Henry II, according to Molyneux), but then encroached and became tyrannical. William III's army in Ireland, we remember, included Danish guards.

How militantly Jacobite is Philips's patriotism? The biographical record is patchy, but we know that, after a period as MP for Doneraile, he went to Paris, in 1713, where he apparently said that 'he wod dey to serve' the Old Pretender.[64] There is a correlation between the mailed-fist beliefs of Turgesius, the Danish king, when he tries to coerce the love of O Brien's daughter, Sabina ('And what like Conquest gives a Right' (27)), and the values imputed to William by his enemies. Moreover, when bullying fails, Turgesius proposes that, if Sabina gives him love, she can (like

Queen Mary—who, constitutionally speaking, inherited James II's crown, not William) 'Reign in thy Father's stead, receive his Crown, | And be thy self the Mistress of this Isle'. It is a Jacobite view of the succession that could be extended to the reign of Mary's sister, Anne, since both took the throne at the expense of their brother the Old Pretender. 'What!', Sabina indignantly replies, 'snatch the Crown from him who gave me life, | Deprive my Brother of his native Right' (35–6).

Resisting the Danes is difficult because the Irish are so factious. One leader, however, emerges, from William Philips's backyard: O Neill, King of Ulster. He pushes the Danes from the north, then—taking a leaf out of William III's book—marches south to the Boyne, where he is united with O Brien and his promised wife, Sabina. At this point a decisive battle might be expected, but O Neill uses disguise and intrigue to defeat the bloodthirsty Danes. It is a hint that policy can achieve much in the face of Williamite or Hanoverian force. As he is led away to execution, Turgesius utters a prophecy which underscores the anti-English strain in the play:

> But e'er I part, remember I foretell,
> Another Nation shall revenge my Death,
> And with successful Arms invade this Realm.
> And if Hereafter be, and Souls can know,
> And taste the Pains which Mortals undergo;
> Mine shall rejoyce to see thy Land subdu'd,
> And Peasants Hands with Royal Blood embru'd; ...   (57)

When we find it said, of an early (London) performance of *Hibernia Freed*, 'I never knew a Play so Clapped ... till a Friend put me in Mind that half the Audience were *Wild Irish*',[65] it is natural to assume that speeches such as this one, critical of English brutality, stirred the crowd's enthusiasm. But does the observer mean that half the audience members were Gaelic Irish, or, more plausibly, that they were English Irish people like 'wild' Roebuck? What would he applaud in the play?

It is an index of the complexity of Irish Protestant patriotism that Turgesius' prophecy is followed by a second, from the bard Eugenius:

> Another Nation shall indeed succeed,
> But different far in Manners from the *Dane*.
> (So Heav'n inspires and urges me to speak)
> Another Nation, famous through the World,
> For martial Deeds, for Strength and Skill in Arms,

Belov'd and blest for their Humanity,
Where Wealth abounds, and Liberty resides,
Where Learning ever shall maintain her Seat,
And Arts and Sciences shall flourish ever.
Of gen'rous Minds and honourable Blood;
Goodly the Men, the Women heav'nly fair,
The happy Parents of a happy Race,
They shall succeed, invited to our Aid,
And mix their Blood with ours; one People grow,
Polish our Manners, and improve our Minds.   (57)

Given the drift of the play as a whole, it is hard to know what to make of Eugenius' praise of the English. Philips's best interpreter is tempted to hear the lines as 'tongue in cheek'.[66] They are more plausibly taken as complementary to Turgesius' speech in proposing an uncertain outcome (which is how O Brien rounds off the play: 'Whatever Changes are decreed by Fate, | Bear we with Patience ...'). For Philips, Anglo-Irish relations are at a critical point: the country could be ruined by the Williamites/Hanoverians, or the Gaels could mix their blood with the best traits of the English of Ireland to produce a new Irish people.

This brings out the dynamic ambiguity of patriot drama. Historians have stressed that Irish Protestants could at this date be robust in their anti-English views without wanting to break the link which secured their position in an overwhelmingly Catholic Ireland. The split between Turgesius and Eugenius allows Philips to express hostility towards selfish, commercial England while holding on to the English connection. Whatever the extent of his cultural patriotism, his interest in antiquities should not be confused with the folkloric Protestant nationalism of such later intellectuals as Lady Gregory and W. B. Yeats. Far from identifying Irishness—as they did—with a peasantry supposedly faithful to an ancient way of life, Philips omits the lower orders from his play and seeks to consolidate the growth of an ethnically mixed but Protestant-dominated landowning class by associating it with a vision of noble, archaic Hibernia. Ideologically, this formation resembles the aristocratic and gentry patriotisms that emerged at about the same time in France, in Magyar Hungary, and among the Polish oligarchs who found themselves Sarmatian roots.[67] An interest in the Gaelic past came readily to men like Molyneux, who valued historical precedent, even when it faded into legend,[68] without them being in favour of anything so threatening as Catholic emancipation.

Looking back, what is most striking is the scale of cultural as well as economic change. Only thirty years earlier, in the wake of the siege of Derry, it would have been inconceivable for an Ulster Protestant to have written a play in which an O Neill, ancestor of the Hugh O'Neill whose rebellion brought about the Ulster plantation, was a virtuous protagonist. Yet relations with the English court, with the City of London and the agricultural interest at Whitehall, were as difficult for Irish Protestants during the decades of peace as they had been during the Williamite wars, when at least they could appeal to a common, embattled religion, shared with their allies in Britain. The indignities suffered by Roebuck and Bellmine, not to mention the contempt for Ireland shown by the likes of Lady Volant, register a significant resentment. By 1722, the Anglo-Irish connection, given a further, painful wrench by Anglo-Scottish union, had deteriorated to such an extent that George Philips, incidental hero (for Ulster Protestants) of the siege of 1689, must have tossed and turned in his grave not knowing which was more deplorable, the ingratitude of England or the plot of his son's play, *Hibernia Freed*. What had not changed was the importance of Derry and its hinterland to archipelagic events and literature.

11

Defoe, Scotland, and Union

Defoe is usually thought of as a London Dissenter, most at home in the
City and the streets around Newgate prison, though his imagination
famously ranged as far as the South Seas. His geopolitical views and some
of his leading traits as a writer were formed, however, by his travels in
Europe, during the years of exile that apparently followed his involvement
in Monmouth's Rebellion against James VII and II (1685), and by those
journeys into the English regions, Wales, and Scotland that inform his
Tour Thro' the Whole Island of Great Britain (1724–7). His association with
Scotland was particularly strong. Troubled by the pro-French, Jacobite
influence that persisted north of the border, he was also attracted to a
country in which his fellow-Presbyterians were not oppressed but were
members of an established church. Once the 1707 Treaty of Union was in
prospect, he looked to Scotland as a place where liberty could flourish, a
Protestant succession be secured, and the bases of empire develop.

The extent of Defoe's early acquaintance with Scotland remains unclear,
but he seems to have visited the Highlands as an agent of William II and
III,[1] and when he went to Edinburgh in the secret employment of Queen
Anne's secretary of state, Robert Harley, in 1706, he dared not use an
assumed name because he was so well known by sight.[2] Various scholars
have touched on Defoe's presence in Edinburgh during the session of the
Scottish parliament that agreed to the union,[3] but the significance of his
stay has been drastically underrated. Defoe went north as a bankrupt and
ex-convict, a man of conspicuous ability who was denied most forms of
advancement, and who had alienated many supporters by his too subtly
ironic impersonation of extreme Tory views in *The Shortest-Way with
the Dissenters* (1702). The mission to Scotland allowed him to use his
talents in the service of the crown, and to recover in large measure his

social and financial standing. His visit was protracted, and he began to go native. In Edinburgh from September 1706 through most of 1707, he returned to Scotland after the abortive Jacobite invasion of March 1708 and remained there on and off until 1712, developing his commercial interests, extending his range as a writer, and—it seems to me—accumulating skills and materials that would go into the major novels that he wrote a decade later.

At first, his main task was to gather intelligence for Harley. Given that the union was 'contrary to the inclinations of at least three-fourths' of the Scottish people, this was a risky undertaking. The Scottish commissioner for the union who recorded that statistic, Sir John Clerk of Penicuik,[4] later said that Defoe was 'a Spy amongst us, but not known to be such, otherways the Mob of Edin[burgh] had pulled him to pieces'.[5] The dangers that he faced encouraged Defoe to deny in print that he was a spy,[6] but he so liked to cut a dash in coffee-houses that he couldn't resist hinting at his role. A contemporary pamphlet mocks him for flaunting a foppish blue cloak, an iron-bound hat, a long tasselled wig, and a diamond ring, while 'endeavouring to perswade the *Northern Britains*, that you were sent thither by *Somebody*; which would bring the greatest Scandal in the World upon that Person, if any such, did you discover his Name and Post.'[7]

The idea of the novelist as a spy who probes the social world looking for hidden motives has often been applied to writers of omniscient narrative, but it chimes even more closely with Defoe, whose novels tend to be written from the point of view of protagonists who are vigilant because they have something to hide. They need, as Roxana does, to monitor the intentions of a daughter who could unmask her as a whore, or, like Colonel Jack—the character who most interests me in a Scottish connection—they eavesdrop on old acquaintances who might expose their Jacobite past. Briefly an outlaw after the proscription of *The Shortest-Way*, Defoe had already lived an undercover life, but his mission to Scotland licensed him in deceptions that he clearly found congenial. As he told his master a couple of months after arriving in Edinburgh:

I am Perfectly Unsuspectd as Corresponding with anybody in England. I Converse with Presbyterian, Episcopall-Dissenter, papist and Non Juror, and I hope with Equall Circumspection. ...I have faithfull Emissaries in Every Company And I Talk to Everybody in Their Own way. To the Merchants I am about to Settle here in Trade, Building ships &c. With the Lawyers I Want to purchase a House and Land to bring my family & live Upon it (God knows where the Money is to pay for it). To day I am Goeing into Partnership with a Membr of parliamt in a Glass house, to morrow with Another in a Salt work. With the Glasgow Mutineers I am to be a fish Merchant, with the Aberdeen Men a woollen and with the Perth and western men a Linen Manufacturer, and still at the End of all Discourse the Union is the Essentiall and I am all to Every one that I may Gain some.[8]

Buoyed up by his virtuosity, the author of *The Shortest-Way* risks joking with the Anglican Harley about Episcopalians being Dissenters in Scotland, the bankrupt salves his shame by making a jest out of his need for cash, and the pious Presbyterian is playful about St Paul's advice to be all things to all men (1 Corinthians 19–22). This was a text that Defoe had already recommended to Harley as permitting 'Dissimulation' and even 'Hyprocrise' in a politician,[9] but it is hard not to read it here as justifying to the author's puritan conscience the pleasures of impersonation that he would live out most intensively and extensively in his novels. 'I Talk to Everybody in Their Own way' is especially revealing, because Defoe wrote fiction partly out of a penchant for adopting the language of others that not even Newgate could cure. After rashly impersonating a Tory in *The Shortest-Way*, he was prosecuted in 1713 for pamphlets that reproduce with insufficiently sustained irony the thinking of resolute Jacobites. These are only the most conspicuous instances of a ventriloquism that runs so persistently through his work that it is impossible to know how many of the hundreds of items that have been claimed for him are from his pen.[10]

Even if Defoe's account of himself in the letter to Harley shows the inventiveness of a novelist in the making, his ability to adapt to Scottish mores is not in doubt. After the Treaty came into effect, Defoe built a career on the contacts he had ambiguously constructed.[11] He became a horse trader, shipped ale and wine to Scotland, and probably invested in salt. In an almost symbolic act, he took advantage of the favourable terms which the union created for the Scottish linen industry to commission a weaver to produce tablecloths decorated with the new arms of Great Britain. There were indications, around this date, that Defoe would settle in Scotland. A solidly respectable citizen, he sent his son Benjamin to the University of Edinburgh and joined a branch of the Society for the Reformation of Manners. Members patrolled the streets rooting out lewd and criminal behaviour—just the sort of grounding in low life that the future author of *Moll Flanders* needed.

Defoe was so busy networking that it is hard to think of him having any time left to write, yet he wrote so much in Scotland that it is impossible to think of him doing anything but sit at his desk. While producing three issues of *The Review* a week (seventy of them devoted to the union), he wrote a clutch of pamphlets about Scottish religious affairs.[12] To the pair of *Essays at Removing National Prejudices against a Union* published in London, he added four for a Scottish audience.[13] He rushed into verse to satirize an anti-union speech by Lord Belhaven[14] and laboured over *Caledonia, &c. A Poem in Honour of Scotland, and the Scots Nation* (1706). Behind the scenes he wrote letters that were calculated to discredit the anti-union Jacobites[15] and scripted speeches and position papers for unionist politicians. Penetrating the corridors of power, he testified to a parliamentary committee on the taxation of salt, and made himself so indispensable that (as he later boasted) his proposals on taxing beer 'stand in the Treaty of Union in his very Words'.[16] He thus became part-author of the history that he recorded in his climactic Scottish production, *The History of the Union of Great Britain* (published 1709–10). That work may have started, as he told Harley, as a front for spying ('Undr pretence of writeing my hystory I have Every Thing told me'),[17] but it ripened into a book which influenced generations of historians and helped Defoe achieve the style of eyewitness immediacy that would be the hallmark of his novels.

★ ★ ★

Few historians now believe that the union of 1707 was inevitable.[18] When Defoe went to Scotland for Harley the two kingdoms were so estranged that there was even talk of war. As we saw in Chapters 1 and 7, there had been a long tradition of unionist advocacy north of the border, of which the Solemn League and Covenant (1643) was the most spectacular outcome. In 1688, Scottish exiles in the Low Countries—many of them still active in the controversies of 1706–7—encouraged William of Orange to establish 'ane entire and perpetuall union betwixt the two kingdoms' as a bulwark against Jacobitism and Catholicism.[19] Against these tendencies, however, a downward spiral began in 1698–1700, when the English supported Spanish suppression of a Scottish colony in Darien, Central America.[20] They then passed an Act of Settlement that handed the crown after Queen Anne's death to the Hanoverians, without consulting the Scottish parliament. The Scots responded with an Act of Security (1704) that committed them to offering the throne of Scotland to a successor different from the one chosen by the English if inequalities in trade were not corrected. Defoe was partly right when he said, in his ambitious poem *Jure Divino* (1706), that the Scots wanted to jolt the two countries into harmony.[21] But the political climate was not improved when the English passed an Alien Act (1705) which threatened to limit the rights of Scots living south of the border.

To explain how union came about in such inauspicious circumstances, historians have returned to Burns's complaint, 'We're bought and sold for English gold',[22] and confirmed (what Defoe denied)[23] that the London government used the payment of arrears and promises of office to change minds in the Scottish parliament. Graft was almost always a factor in eighteenth-century politics, but it flies in the face of the vitality of the union debate to deny the importance of ideological commitment. Certainly, the leading analyst of the mechanics of corruption, P. W. J. Riley, is wrong to say that Defoe got involved in the union controversy 'as merely another job, in the hope of immediate reward and a lucrative future in the Scottish customs'.[24] Even before Harley planned his mission, Defoe was troubled by the vulnerability of Queen Anne's multiple polity. In *The Dyet of Poland* (1705), he parallels British politics with those of the notoriously unstable federation of Poland-Lithuania;[25] by alluding to a recent Jacobite scandal called 'the Scotch plot' as 'a deep *Livonian* Plot'[26] he compares the semi-detached northern neighbour of Poland-Lithuania, encroached on by the Swedes, with Scotland, ripe for French subversion. Riley is right to say that Defoe is locally inaccurate and opportunistic in his writings about union, but his attachment to the principles of the 1688 Revolution is almost counter-productively consistent. It is as though his concern with large issues—the superiority of Protestantism, the balance of power in Europe—justified, to his mind, being less than scrupulous about details. This seriousness about big questions fits Defoe readily into the picture that is now being advanced by intellectual historians, for whom the early eighteenth-century explosion of writing around the union[27] is more than the rationalization of cupidity.[28]

Defoe intervened across the whole field of the union debate, and its dimensions can be more or less reconstructed from his work. To judge by the time he spent reasoning with clerics as well as writing, the most important topic for many was religion. In Scotland it was feared that union threatened the Kirk because the Church of England would bolster the position of the Episcopalians. This encouraged Presbyterians (especially the intransigent Cameronians in the West) to oppose the Treaty, despite their commitment to the religious unionism enshrined in the Solemn League and Covenant agreed with the English parliament in 1643. Because of his Dissenting background Defoe was well placed to reassure the bulk of the Scots, and he apparently made some converts,[29] though Presbyterian opinion if anything hardened after the Treaty came into effect.

These 'Refractory, Scrupulous and Positive People'[30] could aggravate Defoe. His mixed feelings show even in the panegyrical *Caledonia*, where he signals the Kirk's reluctance to be overwhelmed by his arguments:

> Grave in Behaviour, in Discourse *sedate*,
> And apter *to believe* than to *debate*;
> And if they can exceed in doing Well,
> 'Tis in *a little* little TOO MUCH ZEAL.[31]

But his respect for the basic soundness of the Kirk leaves its mark on *Robinson Crusoe*, where the rekindling of the castaway's faith on reading the Bible owes much to the Scottish Presbyterian upbringing of Defoe's part-model for Crusoe, Alexander Selkirk;[32] and it is explicit in *Colonel Jack*, where the protagonist looks back on the changes wrought in his life when he left off thieving in London and went north: 'I had been bred indeed to nothing of either religious, or moral Knowledge; what I gain'd of either, was first by the little time of civil Life, which I liv'd in *Scotland*, where ... some sober religious Company I fell into, first gave me some Knowledge of Good and Evil, and shew'd me the Beauty of a sober religious Life.'[33]

Defoe often emphasized that he wanted a union between equals. This was his way of respecting Scottish sensitivities about the antiquity and independence of their kingdom. Anti-incorporationists like James Hodges (Defoe's most conspicuous opponent) were scornful of those who revived the English medieval claim to suzerainty, insisting that '*Scotland* had an Independent Sovereignty long before, either the *English Normans, Danes, Saxons, Heptarchy,* or *Romans,* had a Sovereignty in *England*'.[34] Hodges was skating on thin ice, however, when he reminded his readers that England was a composite state, stitched together from a Saxon Heptarchy, because unionists could reply that Scotland had itself been formed out of an incorporation of Dalridian and Pictish realms.[35] It was easy for Defoe and others to present Anglo-Scottish union as the logical next step.[36]

Hodges asserts 'the Independency of the *Scots* Nation'[37] without characterizing that nation, or its sense of nationhood. The gesture is typical of anti-incorporationists, who wanted to rally support without heightening internal divisions. Though English stereotyping posited a common culture north of the Tweed (based on poverty, lice, ignorance, and pride), Highland/Lowland contrasts in family structure, language, and economic interest, and ongoing friction between Catholics, Episcopalians, and rival strands of Presbyterianism, confounded homogeneity. Yet the Scottish historian William Ferguson has a point when he finds 'a strong sense of "Mazzinian" nationalism' in the anti-unionist belief that 'the rights of the nation transcend the claims of the state',[38] because even a committed incorporationist such as the First Earl of Cromarty sought a union of states not nations, and soothingly asked: 'Doth the Change of Governments, or Form of Constitutions of Government, annihilate the People or the Nation?'[39] In the context of a debate which so stirred up national sentiment on both sides of the border that only limited incorporation could be envisaged,[40] Defoe was unusually bold. As the Treaty took effect, he announced 'We are now one Nation' and proposed 'that we shall ... become one Nation, one Kingdom, one People'.[41]

Incorporationists highlighted trade. After the poor harvests of the 1690s and the Darien disaster, Scotland was hungry for commerce that would mobilize the larger economy.[42] When he wound up the final issue of *The Review*, Defoe confessed that 'Writing upon Trade was the Whore I really doted upon',[43] and his interventions in the debate constantly harp on this theme. In his third *Essay at Removing National Prejudices* he even claimed that the anti-unionists avoided the issue because they knew it was clinching (34). When it came to the topic of trade, Defoe was formidably well informed,[44] as well as rhetorically resourceful. Potent arguments were, however, put about by his opponents, who contended (apparently wrongly) that the Scottish economy had steadily declined since the union of the crowns in 1603 because the court and leading landowners had taken their riches south, and predicted that this effect would deepen after 1707.

The most penetrating exponent of this view, Andrew Fletcher of Saltoun, argued along neo-Harringtonian lines that metropolitan centres always drain wealth and opportunity from provincial markets. Look around the archipelago, he counsels, and 'consider that Wales, the only country that ever had united with England, lying at a less distance from London, and consequently more commodiously to participate in the circulation of a great trade than we do, after three or four hundred years, is still the only place of that kingdom, which has no considerable commerce, though possessed of one of the best ports in the whole island; a sufficient demonstration that trade is not a necessary consequence of an union with England.'[45] Pro-unionists might cite the protection of Welsh interests at Westminster to reassure the Scots that English MPs would not combine to oppress them after the union,[46] but they could do little to counter the feeling that the English patronized the Welsh for being poor, and indulged them only because they were powerless.

For Fletcher and his associates, who construed the position of Scotland in a fully three-kingdom setting, the predicament of Ireland was even more troubling. Scottish Presbyterians saw their brethren in Ulster (whose labours enriched a country subject to the English crown)[47] discriminated against by a Sacramental Test (1704) which excluded them from public office, and watched Irish manufacturers having their woollen goods legislated out of English markets. We have seen how such policies encouraged the Dublin Protestant William Molyneux to argue in *The Case of Ireland ... Stated* (1698) that it was wrong to treat the English of Ireland as if they were conquered subjects (above, p. 319). In a classically negative round of archipelagic concatenation, the anger provoked in England by Molyneux's treatise heightened anxiety in Scotland. When William Atwood, who had attacked *The Case of Ireland ... Stated* in 1698, published his *Superiority and Direct Dominion of the Imperial Crown of England over the Crown and Kingdom of Scotland* (1704), it was burned by the hangman in Edinburgh at parliament's command.[48]

Like the London government, which arranged for troops to be stationed in Ulster while the Edinburgh parliament debated the union,[49] Defoe understood that, if England bullied Scotland into war, the Ulster Presbyterians would side with the Scots, and perhaps even, as Hodges warned, ally themselves for long enough with Irish Catholics ('whom the Scots own to be of one Original Stock and Blood with them')[50] to pressure the disaffected Anglo-Irish into joining a full-scale rebellion against England. He followed other unionists, however, in trying to ignore the agenda taken by Fletcher and others from Molyneux. He did not explore the suggestion of his Scottish friend William Paterson that the incorporation of England with Scotland could facilitate the Anglo-Irish union that Molyneux thought 'an Happinesse we can hardly hope for'.[51] Instead, he dealt with Ireland selectively and cynically, reassuring the Scots that they could import Irish wool after the union, that the Irish linen industry would lose ground to their own, and that the Test Act 'foisted upon the Dissenters in *Ireland*' was no practical threat to them.[52]

Because the position of Ireland was an embarrassment, unionists preferred to extract political blueprints from classical and continental models. Cromarty, Defoe, and others pointed to the rights gained by the Italic peoples when they were incorporated with Rome.[53] Defoe shared the enthusiasm of federalists for the United Provinces and Switzerland because they showed that unions could hold between communities divided by religion,[54] but he joined incorporationists in doubting the long-term stability of federal states, arguing that the Scots might win short-term benefits from such an arrangement and then split away,[55] as Portugal had from Spain, and Sweden from Denmark.[56] Cromarty contrasted 'the short duration of the Union 'twixt *Hungary* and *Pole*' with the solid 'Union of the *English* Heptarchy, and thereafter of *Wales*, and of the Town of *Berwick*'[57]—that little bit of Scotland united with England in the fifteenth century.

Scottish patriots sought to avoid the embrace of the auld enemy by projecting union with the Dutch or the French. Defoe and other incorporationists urged the impracticality of such plans,[58] and switched attention to the strategic advantages that union would bring to the whole island. Together, Seton of Pitmedden argued, the British could weaken the Dutch fishing industry, and stem the power of France—a country so opposed to the union that it was not beyond hiring 'some Mercenary *English* Poet or Historian, to represent *Scotland*, with all the Rancour that ill Nature and Ignorance can inspire in them'.[59] Defoe showed that a mercenary writer could avoid ill nature by generously comparing the herring grounds with the pearl fisheries of the orient and silver mines of America; he trumped the patriots by saying that, by allowing Scotland to exploit this wealth, the union would '*Caledonia* to her self restore'.[60] As for curbing France, it was rarely far from his mind. How much better it is for the Scots to fight in British armies against Louis XIV than to cut each other's throats in the service of foreign princes.[61]

Europe, however, was not the horizon of the union debate. By opening up the English colonies in America, and permitting what Seton called 'Trade over the whole World',[62] union, it was argued, would allow Scotland to revive the imperial ambitions lost to France in Novia Scotia and Spain in Darien.[63] It is thus consistent with the Anglo-Scottish rationale of *Colonel Jack* that, after leaving London, the protagonist abandons Edinburgh for the Virginia plantations, and ultimately points towards Darien by trading with Spanish merchants in Central America. Before turning to the novel, however, I want to look at how the difficulty of advocating union to a divided audience developed Defoe as a writer and prepared him for the challenge of prose fiction.

★   ★   ★

Even when sympathetic to the Scots, Defoe's approach to British politics prior to his residence in Edinburgh was decidedly Anglocentric. What he says in *Jure Divino* about Edward I ('In *Caledonian* Triumph see him come, | And yielding Nations shout the Hero Home' (232)), was not calculated to appease admirers of Barbour's *Bruce* and Blind Harry's *Wallace*, whose patriotic liking for Scots verse and books on Scottish antiquities was stirred up by the union debate.[64] Once in Scotland Defoe changed his tone, at first pragmatically and then because he became in some measure acculturated. Yet he never found it easy to manage the compound readership that he developed in Edinburgh. He encountered, in fact, a literary variant of the British problem, with readers north and south proving as troublesome to couple as they were to keep apart.

The problem quickly became daunting. In the pair of *Essays at Removing National Prejudices* published in London, Defoe proposed that 'these two Twin Nations may become one United *English* Empire', and assured the English that their woollen industry would be safe because the Scots could never 'outwork or undersell ours'.[65] Not surprisingly, these pro-union texts were circulated in Scotland as anti-union propaganda. In the third *Essay*, published in Edinburgh, Defoe was obliged to explain himself, and the weakness of his apologia was not just a product of the awkwardness of making a public climbdown, nor of his probable sense that his initial point was correct (years later, in the *Tour*, he would admit that the Scottish woollen industry had suffered through union).[66] Defoe knew that he could not change his analysis convincingly without this getting back to London and damaging the union case at home.

There were, initially, advantages in having a divided audience. When he began to send copy for the *Review* from Edinburgh to London, Defoe could exploit English ignorance of Scottish affairs. 'Since I am chiefly speaking to the *English*, I shall principally argue on our own side', he wrote: 'not that I think the *Scots* do not want a Union; for every body will own fast enough they want it'.⁶⁷ It seems apt that an issue of the *Review* which so smoothly glosses over popular hostility in the interests of the court should end with an advertisement for an unction called 'THE *Royal Chymical Cosmetick*'. But while Defoe could hope to get away with being all things to all men in conversation, print has a way of standing on the record and circulating beyond the writer's control, and his duplicity about unrest made him enemies in Scotland⁶⁸ as copies of his journal came back north—a market which he rationalized in 1709 by arranging for the *Review* to be published in Edinburgh as well as London, for circulation to subscribers in Scotland and the northern parts of Ireland and England.⁶⁹

The increasing spread of his readership encouraged Defoe to develop a rhetoric of plain-dealing (syntactically straightforward and non-figurative) which could appeal to all moderate men. Yet he varied his pitch in *The Review* with jokes, lists, anecdotes, minutely scrupulous refutations, high-flown odes, and quasi-dramatic dialogues between a Jacobite and a Cameronian. His forte was paradox. Both nations will gain by union, he argues; in a war both would lose by winning.⁷⁰ Opposition creates strange alliances: 'In *Scotland*, the *Jacobite* and *Prelatist* take care of the *Presbyterian*; in *England*, the *Occasional-Conformist* [i.e., the compromising Dissenter] ventures his Life for the *Church*'.⁷¹ And the union is the greatest paradox, 'bringing Contraries, not only to illustrate, but to support and subsist one another'.⁷² Writing at the very moment, on 1 May 1707, when the Treaty came into effect, Defoe finds it:

> impossible to put the lively Sound of the Cannon just now firing, into any other Note to my Ear, than the articulate Expression of UNION, UNION.
>   Strange power of Imagination, strange ... that it makes even the Thunder of warlike Engines cry Peace; and what is made to divide and destroy, speaks out the Language of this Glorious Conjunction?⁷³

Defoe found it easy to dismiss the patriotism of the lairds. When Lord Belhaven, in a celebrated speech, told the Scottish parliament, 'I think I see *our Ancient Mother* CALEDONIA, like *Caesar* sitting in the midst of our Senate, Rufully looking round about her, Covering her self with her Royal Garment, attending the Fatal Blow, and breathing out her last with a[n] *Et tu quoque mi fili*',⁷⁴ Defoe asked how many Scots would understand Mother Caledonia's Hebrew. Writing so quickly that copies of *The Vision* were on the streets the morning after Belhaven delivered his speech, Defoe reduced the hero of the moment to a dismal prophet full of noise. It sealed his triumph that, in his reply, Belhaven was misled by Scotticisms in *The Vision* into taking it as the joint work of Scottish and English authors;[75] by his opponent's baffled admission, Defoe had produced a hybrid comedy to match the new politics of union.

Street-level hostility to the Treaty posed a more serious problem because Defoe was associated with such radical expressions of popular will as the Kentish Petition of 1700. One anti-unionist tract, *The Scotch Echo to the English Legion* (1707), consisted of extracts from Defoe and other English Whig writers arguing that parliament should represent the views and interests of the people—a principle which they refused to extend to Scotland.[76] Though Defoe initially dealt with this challenge by playing down popular unrest, and by denying the representativeness of anti-union petitions,[77] later, the strength of resistance was so widely reported, even in England, that denial and obfuscation would not serve. At which point he was driven to find new ways of discrediting his opponents, which he did in *The History of the Union* by describing their riots with an immediacy that broke new ground in documentary reportage. These passages show Defoe experimenting with prose realism a decade before he wrote his novels.

It is understandable that students of the novel should have overlooked the role of the union debate in Defoe's technical development because the *History* includes such an admixture of bald annals, reprinted documents, and details of parliamentary debates. At the time all these materials would have interested educated readers. Now the only passages that leap off the page are those dealing with popular protest. To bolster the legitimacy of the Treaty, Defoe imputed savagery to the rabble with a narrative energy and concreteness unprecedented in his work and unparalleled in other accounts. There is a powerful story-telling drive, yet the unrest proves episodic, and thus seems merely disruptive, while high drama is grounded (as it would be in the novels) in everyday, even banal, detail—as when we are told how the Provost of Glasgow, chased by a mob into a tenement, escaped being murdered by hiding in a fold-up bed.

From the start of his career, Defoe had been alert to the value of significant detail when quoting opponents and educing facts. An empirical attention to discrete materials had been encouraged by his education. By 1704, in the preface to *The Storm*, he was elevating respect for the empirically unadorned into a principle: "'Tis the Duty of an Historian to set every thing in its own Light, and to convey matter of fact upon its legitimate Authority, and no other'.[78] *The Storm* showed its fidelity to this principle, however, not just by avoiding empty flourishes and the story-telling seductions of romance but by largely eschewing the subjective force of authorial testimony. It validated its account of a recent natural disaster by gathering a mass of letters, statistics, and other reports, with Defoe acting as compiler and occasional commentator. So although it anticipates by a few years the documentary procedures of the *History*, *The Storm* also highlights how innovative the *History* is in its use of narrative, and points up how surprising if not (by his own standards) coercive is Defoe's developed use of personal testimony in the later work.

The innovations in technique are local but cumulative. Take the occasion in October 1706 when the Edinburgh crowds attacked the house of Sir Patrick Johnston, one of the negotiators of the Treaty:

> His Lady, in the utmost Despair with this Fright, comes to the Window, with two Candles in her Hand, that she might be known; and cryed out, *for GODs Sake*, to call the Guards: An Honest Apothecary in the Town, who knew her Voice, and saw the Distress she was in, and to whom the Family, under GOD, is obliged, for their Deliverance, ran immediately down to the Town Guard; but they would not stir, without the Lord Provosts Order;—but that being soon obtain'd, one Captain *Richardson*, who Commanded, taking about thirty Men with him, March'd bravely up to them; and making his way with great Resolution thro' the Croud, they Flying, but Throwing Stones, and Hallowing at him, and his Men, he seized the Foot of the Stair Case; and then boldly went up, clear'd the Stair, and took six of the Rabble in the very Act; and so delivered the Gentleman and his Family.—[79]

In his essay on Defoe's fiction Sir Walter Scott notes that he gives 'an appearance of REALITY to the incidents which he narrates' by seeming 'a man of plain sense', and by including 'some point which ascertains the eyewitness, and some expression which would seem to have only occurred to an individual who had heard and seen the facts to which he speaks'.[80] In the assault on Johnston's house, credence is won by the *two* candles in the lady's hands, the flicker of direct speech that merges back into report at '*for GODs Sake*, to call the Guards', the immediate 'and...but' syntax, which seems to eschew invention, the combination of honest-sounding approximation ('about thirty Men') with persuasive exactness ('six of the Rabble in the very Act'), and the way the passage is underwritten by Defoe's location as an observer: 'the Author of this had one great Stone thrown at him, for but looking out of a Window; for they suffered no

Body to look out, especially with any Lights, lest they should know Faces, and Inform against them afterwards'.[81] Drive and particularity convince the reader that Defoe knows enough to sustain his charge that the people were a rabble led astray by Jacobites, yet the construction of the scene recalls the mélées in *Moll Flanders*. The motive is propagandist, but the fruit is a breakthrough in realism.

★ ★ ★

As a unionist by conviction, committed to the growth of Anglo-Scottish ties and the development of a British identity, it was natural for Defoe to be perturbed by the popular unrest, which did not stop in 1707. It was true, as he pointed out in the preface to his *History*, that the thwarted Jacobite invasion of Scotland in 1708 did not prompt a rebellion against union. But he also says that only Providence saved the day, because, if the Pretender had landed, the rabble would have risen in Edinburgh and been recruited along with Highlanders to French regiments under Irish officers. Beyond the immediate backlash recorded by Iain Lom,[82] there was a growing disillusionment with the way the union affected Scotland. Defoe was sympathetic. Having concentrated on persuading the Scots to accept the Treaty, he now tried to convince the English to make it work. As an Edinburgh businessman, a Londoner turning into a North Briton, Defoe experienced the difficulties first-hand. Already in 1707 capable of writing on his neighbours' behalf, 'To stop and Seize Our Goods who are scots Men is highly Injurious to us',[83] he continued to protest about the negative consequences of the Treaty.[84] Even his distribution of those iconic tablecloths bearing the British coat of arms was damaged by the archipelagic exigencies of union, when, in 1711, tariffs protecting the Scottish linen industry were removed in response to lobbying from Anglo-Irish MPs and peers.[85]

Defoe's defence of the union in *The Review* on the eve of a Commons debate that almost dissolved the Treaty (1713) was far from his only intervention: in addition to issues of *The Mercator* devoted to Anglo-Scottish trade, he wrote *The Scots Nation and Union Vindicated* (1714), *Memoirs of the Church of Scotland* (1717), and several other works.[86] And despite the failure of the 1708 invasion he remained preoccupied with the Jacobite threat to union. He anatomized the 1715 rising in *A View of the Scots Rebellion* and *A Trumpet Blown in the North* (both 1715),[87] while his journal, or that of someone very like-minded, *Mercurius Politicus*, followed the fortunes of the captured rebels and defended the legality of their being transported to England for trial.[88] After the attempted invasion from Spain in 1719, he was still reflecting in *The Commentator* on the Jacobite mentality. But his thoughts were by then feeding into the novels *Memoirs of a Cavalier* (1720), which uses the civil wars of the 1640s to warn against supporting the Stuarts, and *Colonel Jack* (1722).

Like *The Dyet of Poland*, *Memoirs of a Cavalier* is archipelagically self-conscious because written by someone alert to the regionally heterogenous and perplexed situation of England, exposed to a Scottish army during the Bishops' Wars, pushed into conflict by Charles I's ability to raise Welsh recruits, and fearful of his Irish Catholic troops. *Colonel Jack* is more deliberate in its retrospective account of Jacobitism in a British context. Yet even the best-informed Defoe scholars overlook this, because their mindset is Anglocentric. Here, for instance, is Paula Backscheider's summary of the novel:

> The child, we are led to believe, of some of the many immoral gentility in Restoration England, Jack is left on his own by the death of his nurse. In the course of his long life, Jack is an errand boy and thief (thereby learning about goldsmiths' bills and Jews' diamonds), a soldier in northern England, a kidnapped bondservant, a plantation owner and colonial trader, a gentleman traveler, a soldier in France and Italy on the side of France and Spain, a Jacobite who witnesses the battle at Preston (and, thereby, becomes a rebel), a captive of privateers, and a smuggler.[89]

This catches much of the action, but it leaves out Jack's sobering trip to Scotland (above, p. 331), where he joins the Scottish army. That taste of military adventure prepares him to serve in Dillon's Irish Regiment (which, as Defoe points out, was full of Scots),[90] the 1708 expedition, and the 1715 battle at Preston, where he joins Scottish soldiers moving south. It is, in fact, the Scottish connection that explains why the novel usually called *Colonel Jack* has on its title page *Colonel Jacque*. Writing about the Edinburgh mob, Defoe says in *The Vision*: 'Protesters appear | And the *Jacques* they adhere'.[91] A Jacques was a French-sympathizing Jacobite, a type not hard to find along the network that ran between Scotland and the Pretender's court at St Germains. So Backscheider's conclusion that 'Jack has absorbed English history, and his "memoirs" ... explain what and why a nation was' (151) is debatable all the way from the spelling of 'Jack' through 'English history' to the singularity of 'a nation'.

Jack's wretched childhood in Restoration London, sleeping in ashpits and picking pockets, might seem to have nothing to do with the union, but Defoe supported the Treaty not just for reasons of security but because he thought it would strengthen social and religious reform by bringing the better elements of Scotland and England together. When James Hodges warned the Scots not to incorporate with their neighbours because they were immoral, Defoe pointed out that English branches of the Society for the Reformation of Manners (the charity he supported in Edinburgh) had 'erected Schools, and caused Numbers of vagrant and poor Children, who have been left to the Streets and to all Manner of Vice, and perhaps some to the Gallows, to be taught better Manners and Religion', and said that it was precisely during periods of such reformation (as under Edward VI and William II and III) that England proposed union with the Scots.[92] Brought up in the laxer reign of Charles II, Jack graduates from a deprived infancy in the shadow of the gallows into feckless manhood, ripe for corruption by popery and Jacobitism. Despite his native intelligence, it takes him years to find the opportunity to learn to read and thus reflect on life, and longer still to overcome the desire for social status (manifested in his childhood nickname, 'Colonel') that provides him with a substitute for virtue—not that he is not very likely the illegitimate son of a gentleman, but that real worth, for Defoe, consists in being socially productive and achieving a proper level of religious understanding.

The correlation between crime and Anglo-Scottish division before 1707 is made palpable when Colonel Jack flees to Scotland with his boyhood companion Captain Jack, who has fallen foul of the law. To help them on their way the Captain steals a horse, and he is pursued by a hue and cry across the Tweed near Kelso:

> It was true, that he was before upon *Scots* Ground, *as they call'd it*, and consequently they had no power to have carried him off, if any Body had oppos'd them; yet as they were in a full Chase after him, could they have come up with him, they would have run the Risque of the rest, ... ; however, as he got over the *Tweed*, and was landed safe, they could neither follow him, the Water being too High at the usual Place of going over, nor could they have attempted to have brought him away, if they had taken him ... (97)

The border encourages crime because its divided jurisdiction as well as its physical obstacles allows the thief to escape justice. More precisely, it creates a zone where law is unreliable, dependent on local customs and permissions. Defoe is not just fetishizing the border because it symbolizes Anglo-Scottish disunity but reflecting the conditions of a territory that had long been difficult to administer (above, pp. 34–5). With their debatable lands (north of Carlisle), where for centuries no king's writ ran, and their Marches (which extended from Berwick through Kelso, westwards), the borders had traditionally been a region apart. Their ambiguities are still inscribed in late seventeenth- and early eighteenth-century maps, which seem unsure how close to Kelso the border ran, what areas were comprised by 'Mers', 'Marcia' or 'The Merches', and whether Berwick was in England or Scotland (Figs. 15–17). The passing of Acts for the Better Execution of Justice in 1610–12 had gone some way towards strengthening law in the border counties, but, as Defoe lamented in 1706, 'The Country lies barren to this Day, which ... has only been plow'd with the Sword'. Along this belt of country, the English and the Scots are divided by 'Hatred'.[93]

That Defoe was consciously interested in legal differences and border abuses can be seen from a succession of events. In Edinburgh the Captain

Fig. 15. Where is Kelso? where are the Marches? Detail from Richard Blome, *A Mapp of the Kingdome of Scotland*, in Blome's *Britannia* (London, 1673).

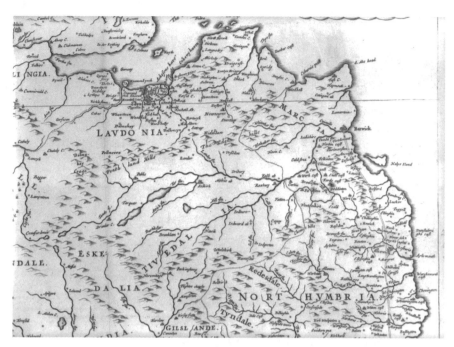

Fig. 16. The shifting Scottish border. Detail from Wenceslaus Hollar, *The North-Part of England and the South-Part of Scotland*, in John Garrett, *The Kingdome of England, and Principality of Wales* (London, 1676).

and Colonel are told that two men being whipped through the streets are receiving the punishment reserved for English pickpockets, 'and that they were afterwards to be sent away, over the Border' (101). When the Colonel's Scottish employer, a Customs Officer, is 'Charged with some Mis-applications', he 'take[s] Shelter in *England*', and leaves his men unpaid with impunity (103). The Captain, who has meanwhile 'got over to *Ireland*, wander'd about there, turn'd Raparee ... escap'd from *London-Derry*, over to the *Highlands*' and joined 'a Body of Recruits rais'd in the North', persuades the Colonel to enlist in Douglas's regiment (a Scottish contingent). Deciding, not long after, to desert, they make for the border, because 'when we are on the other side of the *Tweed*, they can't take us up' (103–4, 106).

If Defoe were simply highlighting the deficiencies of British justice before 1707, *Colonel Jack* would be less engaged. Like other committed unionists, he looked for a 'more perfect' incorporation. Before the passing of the Treaty he had reassured the Scots that they would keep their own

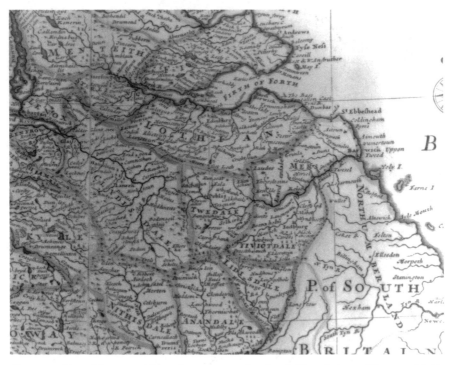

Fig. 17. Berwick-upon-Tweed reverts to Scotland. Detail from Herman Moll, *The North-Part of Great Britain called Scotland*, 1714 (London, 1714–1726).

legal system, and that accused persons would be tried locally.[94] Yet his justification in *Mercurius Politicus* of the trial of the 1715 rebels in Carlisle was consistent with his hankering after 'one Nation, one Kingdom, one People'. From the start he had hoped that good legal practice on one side of the Anglo-Scottish border would be followed on the other,[95] and had mused with tactful vagueness: 'Who knows... what this first union may be an Introduction to, when all agree to a general Reformation both in Principle and Practice.'[96] His hopes for closer union were shared by English politicians around the time of *Colonel Jack*, who put the Customs of both countries under a single commission and curbed the power of Scottish magnates by appointing English Secretaries to manage North Britain's affairs.[97]

In keeping with its account of the circumstances of a union that ultimately came about (from a Scottish perspective) to make the English empire British, *Colonel Jack* pays two visits to Virginia, before and after

1707. In the first of them, the protagonist, along with some Scottish fellow-deserters, is kidnapped and sold into service. After working his way up from slave to plantation owner, he makes enough money to return to England—the core of the empire at this point. On the way, he is captured by a privateer, and gets a French passport to go into the Spanish Netherlands, where he sees something of the Nine Years War. The poor impression that he forms of the English troops leads him, back in London, to call himself Jacques, to talk French, and employ a French servant. These are the beginnings of Defoe's anatomy in the novel of the Jacobite as not so much the opposite as the inverse of a true-born Englishman. In the popular poem of that title (1701), Defoe had pointed out that his countrymen had always been hybrids, compounded not just of Saxons, Danes, and Normans but of ancient pan-British union:

> Thus from a Mixture of all Kinds began,
> That Het'rogeneous Thing, *An Englishman*:
> In eager Rapes, and furious Lust begot,
> Betwixt a Painted *Britton* and a *Scot* ... [98]

If the Englishman is a mongrel, *Colonel Jack* shows us the Jacobite putting on and off identities (as Jack will do yet again when he disguises himself as a Spaniard), as though his nature were contingent on the customs of the countries visited by the Pretender's entourage in pursuit of elusive support. The Jacobite, Defoe said in *The Review*, is afflicted by 'a Confusion of Nations form'd in their own Imaginations'.[99]

When he expatiated on Jacobitism in *The Commentator*, not long before writing *Colonel Jack*, Defoe characterized its adherents as broken traders, despairing bachelors, hen-pecked husbands, and other losers.[100] Before he accepts the embrace of the Hanoverian British empire, Jack conforms to this type. It is after he has been betrayed by his first wife that he goes to Dunkirk and joins Dillon's Irish regiment. Disloyal in fighting for the French in what becomes the War of the Spanish Succession, he compounds his treachery by offering to raise recruits from England, then seeks a way out of the war by taking 'the *Chevalier*'s [i.e. the Pretender's] Brevet for a Colonel' (222) and joining the 1708 expedition to Scotland. It is a nice stroke that the consummation of his ambitions, which translates his nickname into an actual rank, should be an empty Jacobite title. Perhaps an empty title is all he deserves, not merely because the Jacobite claim is, in

Defoe's eyes, nugatory (all its titles are as empty as that of the Pretender), but because his attachment to the Stuarts can seem weak.

How weak it was, or how varyingly strong, is a question which runs like a vein of unease, though also of complacent comedy—Jack's perspective not being that of the author—through the novel. Jack presumably did enough for the Pretender to justify being promoted to colonel. Yet he declares at this point in the narrative, 'I had no particular attachment to [the Chevalier's] Person, or to his Cause, nor indeed did I much consider the Cause' (223). Is this honesty, disingenuousness, or denial? Much of the novel's interest for the reader turns upon the making of such judgements, because although, whatever the answer, the protagonist's commitment turns out to have been shifting, there is quite some difference between a life of susceptible opportunism (the story Jack wants us to hear) and a career of militant Jacobitism that is obfuscated in the telling because the Hanoverians have come out on top. There are too many pointed slippages between event and explanation, between stated motives and reported behaviour, for uncertainty about Jack's place on this spectrum not to be part of Defoe's design. Doubts both sly and generous are in this way seamlessly generated from gaps and rationalizations in the otherwise fluent drive of the unreliable narrator's story—qualities in Defoe himself ('all to Every one') turned into characteristics of his creation. He challenges and amuses by inviting us to gauge whether Jack became a Jacobite because he was feckless and unprincipled, or whether Jacobitism fostered in him an ability to deceive himself and others.

Jack's unreliability does not, however, prevent us from believing in the next emotional disaster that he outlines. What he describes is too humiliating to doubt, and it jibes with the ethos of deception in which his story now seems dipped, that, when he gets home to Paris, he should find his second wife in bed with another man. Even when he returns to Britain, he fails to learn his lesson. The solid ground of England does not improve his values; it fails to rouse his patriotism, never mind stirring him to a recognition of the benefits of union. Jack has plenty of excuses. Pestered, he says, by the Romish priest who married him to his new wife Moggy, he decides to ignore her entreaties and join the Scottish Jacobite army when it reaches Lancashire in 1715. Already, he admits, fired up, yet, he would have us believe, lukewarm, he slips between ardour and inconsequentiality into 'The Invasion of the Scots' (250). At Preston he encounters Scotsmen that he had known when in Dillon's Regiment, and disguised almost despite himself (a symptom of his Jacobitism), in that he is taken for a French officer, he offers them tactical advice. When they ignore this, he concludes (or claims he did) that the rebels are doomed,[101] and he only just manages to get back to Moggy (so how late did he reach that conclusion?) without being captured or discovered.

Now the imperial reach of the union catches up with him, because, when he returns to Virginia after Moggy's death, some of the Scottish rebels 'sent to *Virginia*, and other *British* Colonies, to be sold after the usual manner of condemn'd Criminals' arrive on his estate (266), and Jack, afraid that he will be recognized and denounced, becomes a prisoner in his own house. The miseries of plantation life, the cruelty of the masters, and Jack's desire to institute a more humane regime—all matters explored during his first stay in Virginia—are given no scope this time, because Defoe is narrowing his focus onto the theme of empire for union. Virginia is now a place in which the Scottishness of the convicts is more worryingly distinctive, and as instantly recognizable, as the blackness of the negro girl who tends the fire in Jack's closet. Only when he hears that George I has granted a general pardon do the narrator's fears resolve, and he then declares at such reasoned yet slavish length his devotion to the crown (276) that his conversion seems to owe more to relief than conviction. The unease created by the passage is consistent with Defoe's clear-sighted concentration on how to neutralize the Jacobite enemy, not to improve his character (which may be beyond redemption). The persuasive effect of the pardon is spelled out in order to endorse the Hanoverian policy of making the empire British (and thus strengthening the union) by transporting Jacobites to the colonies rather than executing them for treason.

As the duplicities and divagations unfold, it becomes the more apparent that *Colonel Jack* is not simply an exemplary fable of Jacobite folly and the merits of union. Like other novels by Defoe, it complicates the reader's experience by generating sympathy for its protagonist—a sentiment that creeps over us despite Jack's own efforts to earn it by pushing his hard-luck story about a deprived, misleading childhood, his ill-treatment by women, and so forth. In the course of writing this novel, as in the pamphlets that got him into trouble in 1713, Defoe so empathized with what he opposed that what might have been Hanoverian propaganda incorporated convincingly Jacobite thought-processes—webs of evasion and denial that were, from his perspective, integral to the Jacobite mentality, but also indispensable to the art of fiction. The same issue can be approached more externally. If one is looking for reasons why Defoe would project this sort of character when creating a Jacobite persona, it is hard to ignore the overlaps between Jack and the well-travelled author who was accused of stealing a horse on one journey to Scotland,[102] who supplemented his birth name, Daniel Foe, with a French-sounding 'de' in 1695, and who aspirationally connected himself with the Norman family 'De Beau-foe'.[103] When Jack resolves 'to settle … where I might know every Body, and no Body know me' by passing himself off as M. Charmot among the English and Mr. Charnock among the French (233-4) one can sense a closeness to the Defoe who wrote to Harley from Edinburgh under the soubriquet 'Claude Guilot' as well as 'Alexander Goldsmith'. Though undoubtedly a true-born Englishman—i.e. descended from Flemish immigrants—Defoe was as practised as Jack in putting on and off identities. In Scotland he was engaged in what have been called 'the Jacobite spy wars',[104] and a good spy understands the importance of adopting the psychology of the enemy.

What should be clear in any case is that to think about Defoe and Scotland is to go beyond his stay in Edinburgh and his part in the union controversy. That period in his life has an undeniable fascination, because no other literary figure has been as concretely involved in the production of the constitutional machinery of the British state. But the minor debate which has grown up about the effectiveness of his propaganda in 1706[105] should not distract from the importance of his long-running interest in Anglo-Scottish difficulties, nor from the value of what Scotland gave him as a novelist. Lifting him out of disgrace, it introduced him to new cultural formations, not just in the slightly alien social hierarchy of Edinburgh but between the Lowlands and the Jacobite Highlands, between Scotland and the Presbyterians of Ulster, and overseas to the colonies. The complexity of identities within those contexts encouraged Defoe as an agent to develop the powers of empathy and analysis that later informed his fiction, including, palpably, *Colonel Jack*.

More largely, his engagement with Scotland moves this book towards an ending, not just because Defoe was a major writer actively engaged with geopolitical questions that were important during his lifetime and that are once again current but because the texts he produced around and about the union highlight the difficulty of stabilizing, never mind resolving, the interactions of the archipelago. Even after the union of 1707, Defoe kept arguing, interpreting, inciting, and pushing for integration. His fertility underlines, moreover, the creative potential of the British-Irish problematic, its capacity to spur inventiveness beyond political pamphleteering. While Defoe involved himself in the most literal sense in changing archipelagic geopolitics (scribbling his way into the constitutional instruments, helping draft the Treaty of Union), he also shows the current flowing back into literary innovation. The poetry, drama, and prose fiction that was written in archipelagic English during the period 1603–1707 contributed to the creation of a state system that contributed to the state of our literature.

12

Epilogue: 1707 and All That

(i) Scott, the Scots, and 1707

When the young Edward Waverley, protagonist of Scott's great novel, leaves the English estate on which he was brought up and goes to Scotland with his regiment—loyal to King George and the union—just before the rising of 1745, he finds himself in a social landscape little changed since the seventeenth century. From Dundee, where he is quartered, he travels to Tully-Veolan in Perthshire, at the outer edge of the Lowlands, where his uncle's old Jacobite comrade, the Baron of Bradwardine, holds fast to feudal principles on a manor which his family has enjoyed 'since the days of the gracious King Duncan'.[1] Tracking stolen cattle into the Highlands, Waverley encounters the brigand Donald Bean Lean and his protector Fergus Mac-Ivor (presiding over a traditional feast, entertained by a *bhaird*). We are shown a clan system under economic pressure but unchanged in its essentials from the one which troubled the English Commonwealth during the 1650s and which fought against William Cleland and his Dutch allies in 1689 (see above, Chapters 7 and 9). Scott has been accused of exaggerating the connection between Jacobitism and the Highlands,[2] but Bradwardine is as ready as Fergus to support the Chevalier when the call to arms is heard. On the other hand, as he moves back into the Lowlands, Waverley does encounter a different Scotland: more urban, Protestant, and Hanoverian. Even the dissenting Cameronians, who had risen with the Jacobites against the union in 1715, are now on the government side. What has not changed is their adhesion to seventeenth-century events and issues. Their leader, Gifted Gilfillan, carries 'a broad-sword and pistols, which ... might have seen the rout of Pentland, or Bothwell Brigg', and he holds forth—as though he had been reading *Archipelagic English*—about

'the Book of Sports and the Covenant, and the Engagers, and the
Protestors, and the Whiggamores' Raid, and the Assembly of Divines
at Westminster ... and the slaughter of Archbishop Sharpe', not to mention
'the case of Mas James Mitchell' (172–6).

Waverley: Or, 'Tis Sixty Years Since, published anonymously in Edinburgh
in 1814, is a formidably innovative work, unprecedented in the scale and
depth of its depiction of a society in crisis. In Scott's long, anonymous
review of the *Culloden Papers*, which came out just after the novel,[3] the '45 is
presented as the culmination of the series of archipelagic conflicts involving
the Highlanders and Western Islemen that has punctuated this book—from
the Jacobean skirmishes in Kintyre (above, Chapter 2), through Montrose's
victories with Irish support (Chapter 7), the descent of the Highland Host
on the West (Chapter 9), to the risings of 1708 and 1715 (Chapter 11).
Compared with even this review, *Waverley* is saturated in the prehistory
of Culloden. As a novel it is inaugurative not just in showing how deeply
individual character is informed by the collective past but in recognizing
how far that process is interpretative. Different groups and individuals in it
affiliate with different histories—the *bhaird*'s genealogies, Gilfillan's account
of the oppressions inflicted on the Godly, the Jacobite treatise written by
Waverley's tutor, and so on.

   If the sociological, comparative, and historicist cast of this novel demonstrates how much Scott learned from the philosophical historiography of
the Scottish Enlightenment—from the writings of such men as Adam
Smith, David Hume, and Adam Ferguson[4]—he is equally with them in
believing that the pivotal change in Scotland came not in 1707 but after
Culloden. This is the burden of the celebrated passage in which the narrator of *Waverley* compares the course of history to that of a river, which
imperceptibly moves us forward, and declares: 'There is no European
nation which, within the course of half a century, or little more, has
undergone so complete a change as this kingdom of Scotland. The effects
of the insurrection of 1745,—the destruction of the patriarchal power of
the Highland chiefs,—the abolition of the heritable jurisdictions of the
Lowland nobility and barons,—the total eradication of the Jacobite party,
which, averse to intermingle with the English, or adopt their customs, long
continued to pride themselves upon maintaining ancient Scottish manners
and customs,—commenced this innovation' (340).

   The title of this chapter echoes W. C. Sellar and R. J. Yeatman's *1066
and All That: A Memorable History of England* because that minor classic

reminds us that looking back historically is always a form of travesty.[5] Like 1066, 1707 has been variously construed and constructed. Its current status as the date when the Scottish people were bought and sold—as Burns put it—for English gold has early origins. The union was resisted by rioters in Edinburgh and Glasgow (above, pp. 337–9), and, as Scott's *The Heart of Midlothian* (1818) brings out, it would be blamed over the years for increases in taxes and customs. Recent scholarship has emphasized, however, that, as the decades went by, 1707 was thought about in Scotland less in terms of Anglo-Scottish relations and more as providing leverage for the suppression within North Britain of archaic social features—what *Waverley* calls 'the patriarchal power of the Highland chiefs' and 'the heritable jurisdictions'.

Yet educated Scots, looking back through the period covered by this book, did not regard 1603 as straightforwardly a step towards 1707, and thus to the legislative measures which followed the '45. James VI and Charles I may have hoped to curb the clans and abolish heritable jurisdictions (above, pp. 95–6, 99, 111), but the regal union was thought to have been bad for Scotland because it removed royal control from the magnates. After 1603, it was said, they were left alone to exploit their inferiors while money and initiative went to London.[6] Cromwell was praised for quashing the more pernicious jurisdictions, a measure reversed at the Restoration. (The brief assault on them by Charles II in 1681 had always been seen as limited and self-serving.)[7] For Scottish Whigs, who simplified what reform entailed,[8] the abolition of the jurisdictions did not just make it harder for Jacobites to bring 'out' their followers, it amounted to the end of feudalism.

Given that, how appropriate is it to end this book with 1707? Would 1747–8 not make more sense? How long did the conflicts of the seventeenth century continue to be active in Scotland (like Gilfillan's weaponry and rhetoric)? When, in practice, and when in perception, did the effects of union take hold? That the case for regarding 1707 as a watershed—cultural as much as political—can be heard more eloquently in Scotland after the '45 than in the decades following the union[9] might simply demonstrate that it takes time for the historical significance of some major events to be shown and understood. It could also, however, reinforce the claim—for which there is literary evidence—that Culloden and its aftermath brought about the real shift in perspective. If the latter is the case, what were the equivalents of the post-Culloden measures in England/Wales or Ireland, and was this reflected in literary production? Would it not be more appropriate to look to 1801 for a terminus, when Ireland was drawn into the United Kingdom with 1707 as a hotly debated precedent? Or 1829, the year of Catholic emancipation, when Scott returned to *Waverley* and gave a fresh account—marked by that moment—of what the novel was aiming to achieve? To answer these questions requires some ranging forward, but also much retrospection. Throughout *Archipelagic English*, history and literature have been thought about together. In this chapter, the two prove inextricable, as I examine how people looked back on 1603–1707, and what they thought about the terminal-inaugurative status of Anglo-Scottish union.

A preliminary matter first. If 1707 was initially so unpopular in Scotland, why did the Treaty stick? One answer is that it scarcely did—hence the closeness of the vote to maintain it in 1713 (above, p. 339), and the freedom with which the English bent its provisions (even the reforms after Culloden broke guarantees in the Treaty). It was part of Bonnie Prince Charlie's appeal to many Scots that he promised to dissolve the union. But a second answer is that those features of the union which struck Defoe and others as paradoxical (above, p. 336) were sources of strength. As Jim Smyth puts it: 'The mostly episcopalian Scottish Jacobites were ecclesiastical "unionists" and political, or more precisely, dynastic, "nationalists". Presbyterians were ecclesiastical nationalists and, after the union guaranteed the status of the Kirk, political unionists.'[10] Eighteenth-century Scots were not as likely as modern nationalists to cry up the autonomy of the Kirk and the Scottish legal system as life-support systems of identity, but the ability to separate Scottish Presbyterianism (which had its own difficulties with Episcopalianism) from the heated, English conflict between Anglicanism and Dissent was undoubtedly a factor in maintaining the peace.

In the second half of the century, as Scott claims in *Waverley*, union probably helped Scotland economically. But the human cost of 'improvement', particularly in the Highlands, where Culloden was followed by slaughter, despoliation, and depopulation, was large. What of the literary 'improvement' often associated with commercial prosperity by Scottish commentators? For most Whigs in North Britain, the spread of polite letters, the dawning of Enlightenment, was another consequence if not of 1707 then of an associated symbiosis with England and the British legacy of the 'Glorious Revolution'. This is not a contention that need be taken at face value.[11] The Scottish Enlightenment had Jacobite as well as Presbyterian roots; by the time Scott's Bradwardine was spouting the Latin tags which make him such an object of affectionate comedy, the classical-patriotic ethos had sunk into pedantry, but it can be traced back through such writers as Sir George Mackenzie to the Restoration.

To push the origins of the Scottish Enlightenment back to 1660 is to make a more than chronological point. Periodization is always conceptually loaded. So it is with 1707. If we start from 1660, the Treaty of Union can be seen as completing the negotiations that broke down in 1669–70 (above, p. 276) and as representing—at a stretch—the fulfilment of James VI and I's aspirations under the last Stuart monarch, Queen Anne; if we see it as owing more to 1688–9, it represents the pragmatic consolidation of a Protestant, fiscal-military alliance (the Williamite Leviathan) against Jacobitism and Louis XIV. Both constructions-by-period look different if told from English/Welsh as against Scottish perspectives—not to mention Irish. And, indeed, to look back through the timelines followed by this book is to be struck by how out-of-phase many of the period-dividing dates are between the three kingdoms. Within Scotland, most would highlight 1623 (famine), 1638 (national Covenant), 1643 (Solemn League and Covenant), 1666 (the Pentland Rising), the near-civil war of 1690–1, and King William's 'ill years', 1695–9—none of them dates to conjure with in England, Wales, or Ireland. Literary chronologies are even less likely to respond to pressures felt across all three kingdoms: what correlates, in Scotland, with the stand-out years 1616 or 1645 in England? An archipelagic account of *Literature, History, and Politics* has to respect what is distinct as well as what is connected about the processes that plait their way through each of the kingdoms, neither exaggerating the importance of those transitions which caught up the entire archipelago (e.g. 1603, 1660) nor imagining that they signified in the same way for writers around the islands. If 1707 mattered in Scotland, then mattered differently after 1745, it counted for less in England, Wales, and less again in Ireland—though not, as we shall see, for the infuriated Jonathan Swift—where the penal laws passed against Catholics in 1703–4 and 1709 were of far greater moment.

Even when literary, political, and historical events share dates, it is often hard to be sure about the extent or mode of connection. It is still debated, for instance, whether the Treaty of 1707 accelerated the anglicization of Lowland Scotland. 'The appearance of *Tatlers, Spectators* and *Guardians* in the reign of Queen Anne', which, according to John Ramsay of Ochtertyre, 'prepared the minds of our countrymen for the study of the best English authors, without a competent knowledge of which no man was accounted a polite scholar'[12] probably owed less to union than to the effectiveness of the book market and postal network after 1695 which was widening the distribution of journals through provincial England and Wales.[13] On the other hand, the surge of interest around 1707 in old writing in Scots does seem to have been partly a reaction to union.[14] It was possible for Scott to identify and attribute to Bradwardine a recognizably patriotic-Jacobite diet of reading as late as 1745: 'As for literature, he read the classic poets, to be sure, and the Epithalamium of Georgius Buchanan, and Arthur Johnstoun's Psalms, of a Sunday; and the Deliciae Poetarum, and Sir David Lindsay's Works, and Barbour's Bruce, and Blind Harry's Wallace, and the Gentle Shepherd, and the Cherry and the Slae' (57). This list is largely made up of material read in 1603–1707, but it is not entirely antiquated. It includes Allan Ramsay's 1725 play in Scots, The Gentle Shepherd.

Ramsay's career shows that the orientation of writers could be as perplexed after 1707 as during the century of regal union. The author of Tartana: Or, The Plaid (1718) and editor of The Ever Green, being a Collection of Scots Poems (1724) was according to some accounts the son of a Derbyshire mother, and his popular books of song, The Tea-Table Miscellany (1724–37) were aimed at English as well as Scottish audiences. Ramsay was identified as a Jacobite, but, during the '45, he prudently left Edinburgh to visit Sir John Clerk of Penicuik (that pro-union negotiator of the 1707 Treaty) and was detained by an indisposition. At the other cultural pole, James Thomson, author of 'Rule Britannia'—first performed in his co-authored masque about the English king Alfred[15] —and the epitome of Lowland whiggery, wrote his 'Elegy Upon James Therburn, in Chatto' in an idiom thickened with Scots.[16] To claim Thomson for Scottish tradition, intertextually connected with Gaelic poetry though he may be,[17] would be too restrictive,[18] but his diction—repeatedly cited as non-standard in Johnson's Dictionary[19]—was not strictly English. His elaborate lucidity shows the labour of a Scot writing as a Briton. The Seasons often reads like a translation of Milton.

The historically specific complexes out of which such poets wrote —Thomson's different from Ramsay's, Burns's and Fergusson's different again—should not be reduced to anything as formulaic as 'the divided self' (that cliché of Scottish literary historiography).[20] Susan Manning has persuasively suggested that we should, almost on the contrary, 'regard the condition of Britishness as offering Scottish writers a range of rhetorical resources with which to explore the implications of "being modern" in the post-Union period'.[21] Having said that, conflicts of identity are still legible, and audible. They are writ large, for example, in the way Thomson's collaborator on *Alfred*, born and bred David Malloch in Scotland, changed his name to the less alien-sounding Mallet when he came to London. The vigilance which men like David Hume kept up to prevent Scotticisms slipping into their work[22]—while their conversation remained robustly Scots—must have limited spontaneity, even while it incited (at least in Hume's case) clarity, sceptical detachment, and other valued features of Enlightenment prose.

Thomson gives us the essential, immediately *post hoc* Scottish defence of the union. In *Spring* (1728), he describes a shepherd sitting on a mountain brow, somewhere in the Borders—where the poet had been brought up—surrounded by frolicking sheep:

> And now the Race
> Invites them forth; when swift, the Signal given,
> They start away, and sweep the circly Mound
> That runs around the Hill; the Rampart once
> Of Iron War, in antient barbarous Times,
> When disunited *Britain* ever bled,
> Lost in eternal Broil; ere yet she grew
> To this deep-laid, indissoluble State,
> Where *Wealth* and *Commerce* lift their golden Head;
> And, o'er our Labours, *Liberty* and *Law*
> Illustrious watch, the Wonder of a World![23]

The economic incentives to union which won over so many Scots (above, pp. 332–3) are triumphantly re-stated here, as though the first two decades of incorporation had delivered what had been promised. With less risk of challenge, Thomson also acclaims, like the pious Whig he was, Liberty and Law. All these benefits have been made possible by Anglo-Scottish peace. This argument for union goes back at least a century, to the preoccupations and literary propaganda of James VI and I. When he describes the buried fort, however, Thomson is not blandly reminding us that Anglo-Scottish war is an antiquated, medieval phenomenon but glossing or grassing over recent English threats of force against Scotland, during the 1690s and early 1700s—threats, centred on the Protestant succession, that were the more alarming given the Cromwellian (and later) record of invasion and coercion. The passage resonates with the contention, often aired in eighteenth-century Scotland, that the Treaty of 1707 had brought the cycle of civil wars to an end.[24] English poetry about 1707 sometimes makes the same claim, but because Scotland had not for decades posed a plausible military challenge to England, the security issue more often to the fore was the way union could consolidate Protestant resistance to France (that traditional ally of Scotland).

One effect of the '45—in the short term, at least—was to make it harder to justify union in this way. That Lowlanders, as well as many of the Highland clans, came out in support of Charles Edward encouraged the ill-disposed in England to interpret the rising and the march south (which got as far as Derby) as another treacherous assault on their country by the Scots. During the rising, Tobias Smollet was was forced to hide down an alleyway from an anti-Scottish London mob. It is a measure of the vigour of his unionism, as well as of his recognition that the '45 had indeed been substantially a Scottish civil war, that in his poem 'The Tears of Scotland', written shortly after Culloden, no direct reference is made to the victorious Duke of Cumberland and his English troops. Smollett serves both his patriotism and his desire not to disturb the legacy of 1707 by lamenting that Scotland, never conquered by 'foreign arms' (ignoring, in one reading of 'foreign', Cromwell as well as Cumberland), has now fallen to 'civil rage, and rancour'.[25] By stressing the cost of division—son against father, parent killing child (lines 35–6)—Smollett can mourn the wounds that Scotland has inflicted on itself while tacitly advocating union, the principle of being *united*.

That the '45 cast doubt on the belief that 1707 had ended the cycle of British wars did not mean that the defence of the union as fostering peace was discredited. Once the shock of the rising and its suppression had been absorbed, the viability of 1707 as a topic in Scottish writing was revived because the violence of 1745–6 demonstrated even more clearly the desirability of ongoing union. Put more psychologically, to celebrate union in texts about Anglo-Scottish warfare could alleviate the trauma of the rising and its aftermath. In Home's *Douglas: A Tragedy* (performed in 1756), for instance, Lady Randolph's passionate speech against war between 'kindred arms' is—as Goldsmith noted in an early review—'an oblique panegyric on the Union'.[26] And in Robert Colvill's *The Field of Flowdon* (1771), a long poem about the defeat of the Scots by the English in 1513, the atrocities of Culloden are projected back into the field of 'horrid FLOWDON! stain'd with kindred gore'[27]—disunion as intrafamilial strife again, here even more obviously Anglo-Scottish. Taking a long, visionary look at Scottish history from an epigraph out of Ossian to the country's late eighteenth-century imperial expansiveness, Colvill sees the union of 1707 under Queen Anne as a turning point:

> Like Concord thron'd, see sov'reign Anne restrain
> Two jealous realms, she calms their ancient hate,
> She binds them strong in one compacted state,
> Bids Freedom's banner wave, extends firm Union's golden chain.
> No more two sister-nations wage
> Detested war, with barb'rous civil rage:
> The sword of parricide is stain'd no more,
> And their descending faulchions blush with only foreign gore.
>
> (16–17)

By the end of the century, the clans had proved their loyalty to Hanover and the union by serving with ferocious success in the British army. The brutality indulged at Culloden, and in the devastation of the Highlands which followed, was exported to the empire, where the swords of former Jacobites joined in shedding 'foreign gore' for the crown.[28] Tartan, proscribed after the rising, became required dress for all Scottish regiments, even those from the Lowlands with no tradition of wearing the plaid. In 1795, the American-born, meta-Caledonian Anne Grant wrote in praise of the customs and the long-sustained Jacobitism of *The Highlanders* without arguing against the union. Her gathering-up of Highland superstitions was a more anthropological than political activity.[29] In *Eighteen Hundred and Thirteen*, published in the year of *Waverley*, she expects readers to remember Scottish battles against the English with sorrow and pride yet be grateful for 1707:

> When mournful memory wakes sad Flodden's tale,
> Still the heart throbs and still the cheek grows pale;
> And still we feel our ancient pride return,
> When Scottish muses sing of Bannockburn;
> Yet grateful hail the reign of peace begun,
> The day that joined two hostile realms in one.[30]

Less florid ways of dealing with 'mournful memory' and 'ancient pride' were worked out in eighteenth-century Scotland. The literary and historical interdisciplinarity that goes into *Archipelagic English* owes something to the success with which intellectuals of Hume's generation created a comparative, socio-cultural account of the British and Irish past. Stimulated as much by Montesquieu as by English historiography, they were sceptical of the seventeenth-century English Whig tenet—still current after 1707—that English (or, in some accounts, British) liberties derived from an ancient constitution. They preferred the 'modern Whig' thesis, promulgated by supporters of Walpole, that liberty had been defended by parliament against the Stuart kings of England, and secured in the Revolution of 1688–9 (in which Scotsmen had participated). But they did accept, in grandly enlarged terms, the progressive impetus of Whig thought. Lord Kames, Adam Smith, and others espoused a stadial theory according to which human societies inexorably pass through four stages, from hunting, through pastoralism and agriculture, into the age of commerce. Theirs was not necessarily a crude celebration of progress; in Adam Ferguson, for instance—who came from a Gaelic background—there was a sense of what had been lost when the older, heroic order was ousted by modernity. Overall, however, these thinkers provided the historical rationale for 'improvement'. Their findings were calculated to encourage Scotland to catch up with advanced, commercial England. It was a perspective at once distinctively Scottish—not least in its debt to the French Enlightenment—and unionist. Just as the Edinburgh intellectuals looked to London and its language for advancement (selling books, advancing careers), so should Scotland as a whole.

If polite Edinburgh wanted evidence of how Scottish society had looked at an earlier stage of development, it need only turn—so the argument went—to the impoverished clans of the Highlands. As Scott noted without much irony, in his review of the *Culloden Papers*: 'it must have been matter of astonishment to the subjects of the complicated and combined constitution of Great Britain, to find they were living at the next door to tribes whose government and manners were simply and purely patriarchal, and who, in the structure of their social system, much more resembled the inhabitants of the mountains of India than those of the plains of England' (288). Though Scott avoids the terms 'civilized' and 'barbarous'—and he was, like Ferguson, conscious of the benefits as well as the drawbacks of the clan system[31]—his contrast draws on seventeenth-century polarities,[32] which had strengthened as much because of the literary advocacy associated with James VI and I's reform of the Highlands and Western Isles and the hostility of the English Republic to the royalism of the clans as because of economic changes in the Lowlands. Arguably in Scott, and indisputably among many of his contemporaries, the contrast would become racialized.[33] It assisted the Victorian construction of 'Eng. Lit.' as the patrimony of the

British, imperial state—a version of the past which had room for William Drummond and Burns and Scott and which was inculcated on both sides of the border by indomitable Scotch professors (above, p. 3)—that anglophone Lowlanders should be thought of as Saxon/Teutonic/Gothic and Gaelic Highlanders as unruly Celts.[34]

In such works as Hume's *History of England* the progressive historicism of the Enlightenment was tempered by all manner of qualifications and subtleties. Published in 1754–62, this *History* went through fifty-five editions by the early nineteenth century, and its influence reached even further. At the time it created controversy because it avoided partisanship, being, as Hume famously put it, Whig as to measures and Tory as to men. Welcoming the growth of liberty, within sceptically determined limits, it was also sympathetic to such Whig hate-figures as Laud. What is less often noticed is its Anglo-Scottish (though not systematically archipelagic) inclusiveness. When the first two volumes were published, covering 1603–88, they were called *The History of Britain*. It was only as Hume wrote his way backwards to the Roman invasion (of *Britannia* ...) that he put *England* into the title. John Morrill has said of Hume's account of the mid-seventeenth century: 'Never before or since have the histories of England and Scotland been so tightly or cogently woven together.'[35] And it is true that, compared with Clarendon, or the Whig histories of England which precede and follow Hume, he is alert to interactivity. He reminded his readers that seventeenth-century literature as well as politics and history had a British-Irish framework. But this does not prevent him writing what Murray Pittock calls a 'new Anglocentric history',[36] pulling actions and events into line with English values. And although his account stopped short of 1707, culminating, almost whiggishly, in the Revolution of 1688 in England, he promoted union in the *History*—as when writing about James VI and I[37]—much as he did (according to such contemporaries as Boswell) in conversation.

The old patriotic history of Scotland, with its line of shadowy kings going back to Fergus I, proved surprisingly persistent during the seventeenth century (above, pp. 154, 290), but it did not long survive 1707.[38] By bringing Scotland to an end as an independent kingdom, the Treaty made it possible, unusually enough, to put history into the past. Once there, the auld legends could be subjected to critical scrutiny, often enough by those who, like Hume, were philosophically sceptical and committed to union. (For Hume the two so closely ran together as to constitute—it has been proposed—an intellectual pathology.)³⁹ Like his contemporary William Robertson, whose *History of Scotland* warmly endorsed 1707,⁴⁰ Hume was prepared to see his forefathers as caught up in social structures less civilized and progressive than those of the English. He contributed to the cultural-ethnic splitting of Scotland which union had tended to exacerbate by distinguishing too sharply between early modern Lowlanders and Highlanders, whom he continued to refer to as Irish. As for the mere Irish themselves, he called them 'barbarous savages', 'wanton', and 'cruel', recycling the language of the New English propagandists.⁴¹ His account of 1641 owed far too much to Sir John Temple's lurid and sectarian *The Irish Rebellion* (1646). (That Hume's distaste for religious extremism, such as he found among the Irish catholics, also made him hostile to English and Scottish puritanism does not excuse his lack of balance.) Nor is it always the case that he gives English events a British dimension. By narrowing his conclusion to Westminster in 1688, for example, he avoided the tangled branches of the Revolution in Scotland and Ireland.

It is not generally realized that Hume's *History* incorporates cultural, and specifically literary, analysis. In this, he was true to the principles of Scottish Enlightenment historiography—to the inclusiveness of such works as Kames's *Sketches of the History of Man* (1774). As it happens, his judgements are superficial, striking only because so narrowly of their time. Shakespeare shows 'a total ignorance of all theatrical art and conduct'; Jonson was 'A servile copyist of the antients, [who] translated into bad English the beautiful passages of the Greek and Roman authors'; in *Paradise Lost*, 'there are very long passages, amounting to near a third of the work, almost wholly devoid of harmony and elegance, nay of all vigour of imagination'; 'Waller was the first refiner of English poetry'; 'Otway had a genius finely tu[n]ed to the pathetic; but he neither observes strictly the rules of the drama, nor the rules, still more essential, of propriety and decorum'.⁴² Hived off into their own sections, these 'disquisitions' are not well integrated with the overall account. But this is not entirely a weakness if one is looking to Hume for the beginnings of *literary* history—anticipating by several years Warton's *History of English Poetry* (1774–81), which breaks off, in any case, in the early seventeenth century. Hume's 1603–88 volumes provide the first literary overview of the period dealt with by this book, and they do so in modestly British though not Irish terms.

The prominence of literary material not just in the historiography, but in the development in Edinburgh and Glasgow—first by Adam Smith, and then by Hugh Blair—of the extra-mural and then university-based study of vernacular poetry and prose under the heading of 'Rhetoric and Belles Lettres',[43] has encouraged Robert Crawford to write of 'the Scottish Invention of English Literature'.[44] Several qualifications are called for: first, that the corpus of 'Eng. Lit.' had been under construction (however crudely) in England from the late sixteenth century in conduct books, 'Sessions of the Poets', biographical compendia, occasional essays by Addison, and so on; second, that, although Latin and Greek remained the focus of study in English grammar schools and universities into the nineteenth century, there were other institutions, including the Dissenting Academies—such as the one attended by Defoe between 1676 and 1681—in which vernacular literature was taught; third, that for all his anglicizing drive, Blair was an admirer of Ramsay who encouraged Burns to write in Scots, an advocate of the poems of Ossian who was committed, in his own way, to Scottish as well as Anglo-British culture; and fourth, that 'Rhetoric and Belles Lettres' was more concerned with utility, eloquence, composition, and the cultivation of taste as a social virtue than with the historical, moral, and philological issues which characterized English studies during their later, Victorian development. Yet those caveats[45] are not as damaging as they might sound. Thomas Warton would soon *re*invent 'Eng. Lit.' at Oxford, but we should accept the thesis—an archipelagically gratifying one—that the advanced study of English was begun in Scotland. That said, the discipline of 'Rhetoric and Belles Lettres' remained static during Blair's long career, and did not evolve thereafter.[46] It could have been otherwise. On the death of Blair in 1800, Walter Scott was offered but refused his professorial chair at Edinburgh. It is an intriguing might-have-been. As it is, to get some sense of what Scott might have said about 1603–1707 if he had followed Blair to the lectern, we must turn to his edition of Swift.

(ii) Swift and the patriots

This edition, which overlapped in its preparation with the composition of *Waverley*, and which was published in 1814, the same year as the novel, is the best resource to consult for Scott's view of 1707 at the time when he was starting his fictional exploration of Scottish history. It was clearly a topic which preoccupied him. Swift's antagonism towards Anglo-Scottish union looms large in the biographical essay which introduces the edition, and his inaccuracy about seventeenth-century union policies in *The Public Spirit of the Whigs* (1714) prompts Scott, rather tangentially, to compare Scotland with Jephthah's daughter. We are back with the narrator of *Waverley*, but with a surprisingly negative undertow:

> It was not until the generation was utterly extinguished, that remembered the independence of Scotland, and framed their views and schemes upon principles which preceded the Union; it was not until a new race had arisen, who hardly remembered the distinction between English and Scottish, that my countrymen were enabled to avail themselves of the incalculable resources which the Union had placed in their power. It seemed as if Scotland bewailed, in her wilderness, the loss of her monarchy, as Jephthah's daughter did her virginity, for a certain term of years, and then, with energy, opened her eyes to the brighter prospects acquired by that sacrifice of imaginary independence.[47]

In Judges, Jephthah's daughter is allowed to wander in the mountains for two months to 'bewail her virginity' before she is sacrificed as a burnt offering in fulfilment of a rash vow made by her father to Jehovah. To compare her fate with what happened to Scotland in the later eighteenth century, as the effects of union took hold, is hardly celebratory. 'The brighter prospects' won by 1707 were a kind of death.

What the Scots felt around and about 1707 itself would be explored by Walter Scott in such novels as *The Black Dwarf* (1816)—which is set just after the Treaty—and *Rob Roy* (1817), which deals with the rising of 1715. For a summary, however, one can turn to the headnote that Scott attached to Swift's poem 'On the Union': 'Swift's hatred to the Scottish nation led him to look upon the Union with great resentment, as a measure degrading to England. The Scottish themselves hardly detested the idea more than he did; and that is saying as much as possible' (XIV, 69–70). As it happens, the textual history of 'On the Union' spans exactly the period during which Jephthah's daughter was wandering in the wilderness. Published a few months after Swift's death in September 1745—he lived just long enough to witness (had he been sane) what he had long predicted, the Jacobite unreliability of the Scots—the poem was evidently written in the immediate heat of the Treaty:

Verses Said to be Written on the Union

The Queen has lately lost a Part
Of her entirely-*English* Heart,

For want of which by way of Botch,
She piec'd it up again with *Scotch*.
Blest Revolution, which creates
Divided Hearts, united States.
See how the double Nation lies;
Like a rich Coat with Skirts of Frize:
As if a Man in making Posies
Should bundle Thistles up with Roses.
Whoever yet a Union saw
Of Kingdoms, without Faith or Law.
Henceforward let no Statesman dare,
A Kingdom to a Ship compare;
Lest he should call our Commonweal,
A Vessel with a double Keel:
Which just like ours, new rigg'd and man'd,
And got about a League from Land,
By Change of Wind to Leeward Side
The Pilot knew not how to guide.
So tossing Faction will o'erwhelm
Our crazy double-bottom'd Realm.[48]

Queen Anne reassured her subjects that, despite being a Stuart, her heart was entirely English. For Swift, she had lost a piece of this organ, the repository of her people's affections, by countenancing the alienation of the English of Ireland. 'Probably', as Pat Rogers suggests, he had in mind 'the rejection of proposals for a Union by the Irish parliament in 1703'.[49] That we cannot be sure exactly what loss the lines refer to does not so much weaken the poem as remind later readers that the Irish Protestants had a long list of complaints regarding their treatment since 1691. They had fought on Irish soil England's war against James II and Louis XIV—an archipelagic service which Swift felt keenly[50] —and they believed that they had deserved better than the Woollen Act, the pocketing of confiscated Catholic estates by William's favourites, and so on (above, pp. 318–21). Now, in 1707, the hearts of the English people are both divided by the Irish sea and by Anglo-Scottish union. England and Scotland have become a 'double Nation' as freakish as a bouquet of roses and spiky thistles—those contrasting, appropriate emblems (as one would expect at this date, no Welsh leek is mentioned). Whether or not they wanted union with England, Irish Protestants now felt excluded.

Swift's poem combines levity with rancour. Thus the couplet 'Whoever yet a Union saw | Of Kingdoms, without Faith or Law?' seizes on the

fact that the Kirk and Scottish legal system were preserved by the Treaty
to imply that the union is dishonest (not just incomplete but 'faithless')
as well as lawless—an insinuation anticipated by 'the double Nation *lies*'.
The phrase 'our Commonweal' is as slippery, and, one assumes, less
under control. No doubt Swift was thinking of the Commonwealth of
England, to which the English of Ireland felt attached—still essentially
singular because Scotland has been incorporated rather than federated
(the plurality of 'united States' is threatening because it questions whether
England has managed to digest its troublesome neighbour). Yet the eager
possessiveness of '*our* Commonweal' betrays the weakness of the English
of Ireland, barely consulted about Anglo-Scottish union and unrepresented
in the Westminster Parliament before and after its passage yet dragged
into its consequences because of their subordination. The reader could
even be forgiven for taking 'double Keel' as referring, against Swift's likely
intentions, to Britain and Ireland rather than England and Scotland with
Ireland on the side.

Busy with many tasks, Scott edited Swift in a cursory, even plagiaris-
tic, fashion,[51] and he does not say what is alluded to in 'A Vessel with
a double Keel'. It refers to a catamaran designed several decades earlier by Sir William Petty, the English projector and political economist
whose assessment of Irish resources after the Cromwellian invasion has
been highlighted in Chapter 10. The failed trial of his 'double Keel'
in Dublin had been the subject of much amusement.[52] Like Petty's
boat, Swift is saying—and he may yet be proven right—Anglo-Scottish
union is doomed to fail. The allusion helps make Ireland part of the
poem's implicit field of reference ('just like *ours*') because projectors
were a conspicuous product of Irish conditions. This was a country in
which bright ideas, often brought in by Englishmen, could be thrown
at deep-seated problems, without taking account of what the country
really needed, and without being blocked, as they would have been
across the water, by moderating layers of law, custom, and education.
Such schemes infuriated not just the intellectually impatient like Swift
but others in his community who thought that they had the right to
live quietly like Englishmen on their estates and not be treated as the
inhabitants of a testing ground for madcap plans. Projectors are a feature
of anglophone Irish writing from Richard Head's *Hic et Ubique* (above,
pp. 301–3)—where Phantastick and Contriver talk about draining St
George's Channel, and getting 'a Patent for the sole transportation of Boggs

and Loughs of Irish growth into forreign parts'[53]—to the persona of Swift's
Modest Proposal, who very reasonably maintains that the children of the
Irish poor should be sold for eating at table.

Early readers of Swift's poem would have associated Petty with another
bright idea: Anglo-Irish union.[54] Given that Swift tended, like other Irish
Protestants, to regard union as an either/or choice for England between
what *The Injured Lady* depicts as faithful, abused Ireland and scrawny,
awkward Scotland (above, pp. 321–2), the allusion to Petty might seem
to weaken the thrust of his satire; for, if Anglo-Scottish union absurdly
mixes roses with thistles, the Anglo-Irish alternative is the sort of crazy
scheme that the inventor of a catamaran would come up with. But this
is to anticipate the question of how serious the English of Ireland were
about seeking union *c.*1707. All that the poem asks us to recognize is that
Petty's boat was unseaworthy and that Anglo-Scottish union is no better.
Meanwhile, it is significant that brooding over 1707 should have pushed
Swift to look back to the union schemes of the mid-seventeenth century.
We do not usually think of him as an historian, but like all early modern
polemicists he recognized the persuasiveness of precedent, and he was
impressed enough by classical historiography to nurture his own ambitions.
Scott was dismissive of his efforts—'As an historian Swift is entitled to little
notice' (I, 492)—because he did no primary research, and was politically
partisan. But this is to judge his *History of England* and his *Account of the
Four Last Years of the Queen* by the standards of the Scottish Enlightenment
and Romantic-period antiquarianism, not those of the early eighteenth
century. To read Swift's verse and prose with an eye to his views about
union is to find that a vigorous account of 1603–1707 runs through his
Story of the Injured Lady, that the sifting of faded statutes takes up much
of *The Drapier's Letters*, and that his 'Verses Occasioned by the Sudden
Drying up of St Patrick's Well near Trinity College, Dublin' are satirically
mock-antiquarian in their debt to legendary history.

The background of *The Injured Lady* goes back into the 1690s, where
Swift can be found sniping at the Scots in his early poetry, written in praise
of William III,[55] but the anti-Presbysterian animus that was sharpened by the
experience of running a Church of Ireland parish in County Antrim (above,
pp. 321–2) was not alleviated when he moved to Dublin and saw how
English policies were favouring Nonconformists in Ireland. The matter
was archipelagic not just because of the live connection between the West
of Scotland and Ulster (a flood of hungry immigrants came across the

North Channel during King William's 'ill years'), but because the English parliament threatened the position of the Church of Ireland when its passing of the Woollen Act bolstered the Ulster linen industry and then again when it proposed to abolish the 1704 Sacramental Test in Ireland. Swift's defence of the Test, which was not, in the event, repealed until the more tolerant climate of 1780, can be most expansively found in *A Letter from a Member of the House of Commons in Ireland to a Member of the House of Commons in England* (1709)—notorious for its attack on 'the Fellow that was *pilloryed*, I have forgot his Name...so grave, sententious, dogmatical a Rogue, that there is no enduring him'.[56] Defoe—for it was he—was a threat because he had been spilling so much ink to convince the Kirk that 1707 would strengthen Presbyterianism. An enlarged, post-union Westminster parliament, filling up with allies of the Kirk, could only leave the Church of Ireland more exposed. Yet English statesmen, Swift complained, were in favour of dropping the Test not on grounds of principle but of convenience and party advantage.

The tone of this *Letter* suggests that Swift's protectiveness towards the Church of Ireland was the shell within which his more extensive, later Irish patriotism grew. In Ulster, he testifies, Presbyterians push good English Protestants out of their neighbourhoods; their intolerance is perverse, hating the Church of Ireland even more than Roman Catholicism. They will not tolerate fellow-Protestants in the way they are themselves tolerated (and it is true that, in Scotland, there had been much 'rabbling' of Episcopalian ministers). They are dishonest when they claim to be allies, and anyway their help is not needed in keeping Ireland orderly because the Catholics have been reduced by the penal laws to hewers of wood and drawers of water (a notorious passage this, deeply offensive to later Catholic nationalism, but tactically placed by Swift to bring round Protestant readers). He finishes the *Letter* by pointing again to the excesses of Presbyterians in a place that he just calls 'the *North*'. Ulster might as well be Scotland to Ireland's England.

With the vehemence of the *Letter* in mind we can return to *The Injured Lady*, which is, like 'On the Union', a work of *c*.1707 that was not published until after Swift's death, probably because he was courting the very Whigs who were pushing for Anglo-Scottish union. In its figuring of different national groups in a love triangle, the fable has been seen as anticipating the structure of colonial romance in Owenson, Edgeworth, and Maturin.[57] Though priority might be given to *Landgartha* (above, p. 177–81), Swift's tale does anticipate novels such as *Waverley* in which plots about courtship figure the politics of union (Edward eventually marries not the Highland Jacobite Flora, but the milder, Lowland daughter of Bradwardine, who has the English-emblematic name Rose). Swift's own starting point was a tradition of satire in which political exploitation is represented as sexual abuse,[58] a parallel invoked by others to attack the Treaty.[59] Yet *The Story of the Injured Lady* is unusual, and anticipates *Waverley* the more keenly, in the prominence that it gives to looking back historically.

'A Gentleman in the Neighbourhood had two Mistresses, another and myself', the narrative begins, 'and he pretended honourable Love to us both. Our three Houses stood pretty near one another; his was parted from mine by a River, and from my Rival's by an old broken Wall'—a witty way of shrinking the Irish sea to something like the size of Hadrian's wall.[60] According to the lady, Scotland's hostility towards England, although of very long standing, became intolerable in the seventeenth century: 'Once, attended with a Crew of Raggamuffins, she broke into his House, turned all Things topsy-turvy, and then set it on Fire. At the same Time she told so many Lies among his Servants, that it set them all by the Ears, and his poor Steward was knocked on the Head; for which I think, and so doth all the Country, that she ought to be answerable' (4). This is a cleverly unscrupulous way of blaming the Scots for the decapitation of Charles Stewart (though mild compared with Swift's comments on the same period of history in his copy of a 1707 edition of Clarendon's *History of the Rebellion*: 'Scottish scoundrels', 'Scotch Dogs', 'cursed Hellish Scots for ever', 'Greedy Scotch Rebellious Dogs!', 'Deceitfull Scots', 'most damnable Scots', 'Rank Scotch Thieves' and so on).[61] During and after the interregnum, the Scots not unreasonably thought the English answerable for the execution of a King of Scotland about which they had not been consulted.

The ill-treated lady describes how waves of English settlers came across to Ireland, and were won over by her charms (earlier Protestant writers would have denounced this as 'degeneration'). She gave them her best land (i.e., it was expropriated from Catholics), 'and treated them all so kindly, that they began to love me as well as their Master. ... When my Lover observed this, he began to alter his Language; and, to those who enquired about me, he would answer, that I was an old Dependent upon his Family, whom he had placed on some Concerns of his own; and he began to use me accordingly, neglecting by Degrees all common Civility in his Behaviour' (5–6). In this manner, we are led to believe, the relative independence of Ireland as a lordship and a kingdom was eroded, and the country was rendered subordinate. Bitterly recalling the trade restrictions of the 1690s, Swift imputes to the English something of the neurotic fastidiousness that would make Gulliver so wary of dealing with the Yahoos (those versions of the mere Irish, confused, by indifferent Englishmen, with their Anglo-Irish rulers): 'because we were a nasty Sort of People, and that he could not endure to touch any Thing we had a Hand in, … we must send all our Goods to his Market just in their Naturals; the Milk immediately from the Cow without making it into Cheese or Butter; the Corn in the Ear; the Grass as it is mowed; the Wool as it cometh from the Sheeps Back…' (6).

At the climax of the fable, Swift gives an exaggeratedly archipelagic account of the lead-up to 1707. The Irish Protestant sense of having been ill-used is both validated and compensated for by an overinflated description of Ireland's importance to England after the Scottish Act of Security (1704) and the associated threats of alliance between the Scots and the Irish that we found (above, p. 333) in James Hodges' *War Betwixt the Two British Kingdoms Consider'd* (1705):

> Matters being in this Posture between me and my Lover; I received Intelligence that he had been for some Time making very pressing Overtures of Marriage to my Rival, until there happened some Misunderstandings between them; she gave him ill Words, and threatened to break off all Commerce with him. He, on the other Side, having either acquired Courage by his Triumphs over me, or supposing her as tame a Fool as I, thought at first to carry it with an high Hand; but hearing at the same Time, that she had Thoughts of making some private Proposals to join with me against him, and doubting with very good Reason that I would readily accept them, he seemd very much disconcerted. This I thought was a proper Occasion to shew some great Example of Generosity and Love; and so, without further Consideration, I sent him Word, that hearing there was like to be a Quarrel between him and my Rival; notwithstanding all that had passed, and without binding him to any Conditions in my own Favour, I would stand by him against her and all the World, while I had a Penny in my Purse, or a Petticoat to pawn. This message was subscribed by all my chief Tenants; and proved so powerful, that my Rival immediately grew more tractable upon it. The Result of which was, that there is now a Treaty of Marriage concluded between them, … I cannot but have some Pity for this deluded Man, to cast himself away on an infamous Creature, who, whatever she pretendeth, I can prove, would at this very Minute rather be a Whore to a certain Great Man, that shall be nameless, if she might have her Will. (7–8)

Swift's romantic drollery omits the role of English military power, and money, and access to the Atlantic trade, in persuading the Scots into union. It is true that troops were rushed to Ulster in the run-up to the Scottish debates of 1706 to encourage compliance, or at least to guard against unrest spilling across the North Channel, but any indications of support from Protestant Ireland made little difference. Yet the lady's pity for England comes from more than sour grapes. The rising of 1708 would show that Swift was right to believe that many in Scotland would rather be in bed with the Pretender than with Queen Anne.

In *The Injured Lady* it is merely a passing insult that England should call Ireland 'an old Dependent upon his Family' (5). As one would expect, however, the idea of being thought dependent got under Swift's skin. The grandest rebuttal of the insult comes in the fourth *Drapier's Letter* (1724), provoked by the scandal of Wood's halfpence (above, p. 321), and often, understandably, regarded as the zenith of Swift's patriotic output. Here again, he plays the historian:

> And this gives me an Opportunity of explaining, to those who are ignorant, another Point, which hath often *swelled in my Breast*. Those who come over hither to us from *England*, and some *weak* People among ourselves, whenever, in Discourse, we make mention of *Liberty* and *Property*, shake their Heads, and tell us, that *Ireland* is a *depending Kingdom*; as if they would seem, by this Phrase, to intend, that the People of *Ireland* is in some State of Slavery or Dependance, different from those of *England* whereas, a *depending Kingdom* is a *modern Term of Art*; unknown, as I have heard, to all antient *Civilians*, and *Writers upon Government*; and *Ireland* is, on the contrary, called in some Statutes an *Imperial Crown*, as held only from God; which is as high a Style, as any Kingdom is capable of receiving. Therefore by this Expression, a *depending Kingdom*, there is no more understood, than that by a Statute made here, in the 33d Year of *Henry* VIII, *The King and his Successors, are to be Kings Imperial of this Realm, as united and knit to the Imperial Crown of* England. I have looked over all the *English* and *Irish* Statutes, without finding any Law that makes *Ireland depend* upon *England*; any more than *England* doth upon *Ireland*. We have, indeed, obliged ourselves to have *the same King with them*; and consequently they are obliged to have *the same King with us*. For the Law was made by *our own Parliament*; and our Ancestors then were not such *Fools* (*whatever they were in the preceding Reign*) to bring themselves under I know not what *Dependance*, which is now talked of, without any Ground of *Law, Reason,* or *common Sense*.[62]

The bulk and detail of this long march down the avenues of constitutional history pioneeringly laid out by Molyneux is calculated to create an impression of propriety, but the citing of precedent is highly selective and pragmatic. In his long trawl through the statues Swift has strangely overlooked the 1720 Declaratory Act (above, p. 320), which he and others loathed because it made Ireland so explicitly 'dependent'. His jibe about the folly of the Old English in the reign of Henry VII—when they accepted Poynings' Law, 1494—is evidence of a partisanship that is only just under the surface. And the way that he overbalances 'We have ... obliged ourselves to have *the same King with them*' with 'and consequently they are obliged to have *the same King with us*' carries the revolutionary, satirical implication that if the Irish political nation (essentially, the landed Protestants) choose a monarch for themselves then the English ought to accept him, or at least that the Protestant Irish have a veto over an English choice.

This makes it the less surprising that Swift should declare in the very next paragraph that he would be willing to breach the statute that he only too plainly appeals to, and would resist a Jacobite monarch: 'For I declare, next under God, I *depend* only on the King my Sovereign, and on the Laws of my own Country, And I am so far from *depending* upon the People of *England*, that, if they should ever *rebel* against my Sovereign, (which GOD forbid) I would be ready at the first Command from his Majesty to take Arms against them; as some of *my* Countrymen did against *theirs* at *Preston*. And, if such a Rebellion should prove so successful as to fix the *Pretender* on the Throne of *England*; I would venture to transgress that *Statute* so far, as to lose every Drop of my Blood, to hinder him from being *King* of *Ireland*.' Swift would later 'apologize' for writing so subversively, drawing on his considerable resources of irony, in a *Letter* addressed to the leading Irish Whig, and vocal advocate of Commonwealth politics, Viscount Molesworth. His excuse is that he had been reading Locke, Molyneux, Algernon Sidney, 'and other dangerous Authors, who talk of *Liberty as a Blessing, to which the whole Race of Mankind hath an Original Title; whereof nothing but unlawful Force can divest them*.'[63] We can blunt the irony a little by asking the ghost of Swift whether Catholics were entitled to liberty. Most likely they were not members of the whole race of mankind.

According to Yeats, the fourth *Drapier's Letter* articulated its patriotic doctrine with 'such astringent eloquence that it passed from the talk of study and parlour to that of road and market, and created the political nationality of Ireland'.[64] This claims too much. When Swift addressed his letter 'To the Whole People of Ireland', those he sought to enlist were Protestants of middling rank. The Gaelic-speaking peasantry would not have been able to read him, and their sense of 'political nationality' had different, Catholic sources. On the other hand, to describe Swift as having 'evidently, a feudal outlook'[65] is too reductive, and unhistorical. His sympathies were mobile, his paternalism troubled. As a member of the Protestant elite, he wanted the Church of Ireland to preserve its privileges intact, Catholicism kept in check, rents and tithes paid, but 'dependency' taught him something of what it was to be oppressed, and if there is an element of mock-pastoral in his description of his friend Sheridan's country house as a 'rotten Cabbin, dropping Rain'[66] it also shows a degree of identification with the Irish poor.

Among the many anecdotes told of Swift is one recorded in Scott's edition, that, when the printer of *The Drapier's Letters* was in jail, 'Swift actually visited him in the disguise of an Irish country clown, or *spalpeen*' (I, 299). How far such evidence can link with him the Gaelic world is debatable.[67] In *An Answer to Several Letters* (1729) he proposes the extirpation of Irish, but in the idiom of a projector patently condemned to failure.[68] His translation of the Irish poem 'O'Rourk's Feast'—incomplete, but finished by Scott[69]—suggests a curiosity about Gaelic culture, as does his friendship with the harper Carolan (who set the Irish text of 'O'Rourk's Feast' to music)[70] and his conspicuous habit of consorting with 'Teagues'.[71] That the English regarded Irish Protestant gentlemen such as Farquhar's Roebuck as alien, uncouth, and 'wild' (above, pp. 315, 323) can only have reinforced Swift's self-doubting, indignant identification with what he pitied and feared in the bog Irish. Related anxieties fed his obsession with propriety in English usage,[72] laying down the law for the Anglo-English, asserting in his style an Englishness that could not be gainsaid, and becoming for such men as Adam Smith and Hugh Blair a model of the anglicized discourse that they recommended in 'Rhetoric and Belles Lettres'.[73] It is peculiarly archipelagic that Swift's Scotophobic dislike of Scotticisms in the English of the planters[74] should have contributed to making him an exemplar for Scotsmen seeking to become British.

1707 and all that. How far Swift wanted Anglo-Irish union, as against *not* wanting Anglo-Scottish union, is unclear—as is the level of commitment in other Irish Protestants who advocated union with England, or Britain, before and after the Treaty.[75] Arguments for it would resurface in the middle of the century. Lord Hillsborough's 1751 treatise, *A Proposal for Uniting the Kingdoms of Great Britain and Ireland* is often cited, though its refusal to argue historically—unusual at that time, and certainly in that place—and its concentration instead on economics and governance, looks like a tacit admission of the weakness of the appeal.[76] It was instantly confuted by an *Answer* which anticipated controversies to come by pointing out that the name, liberty, and fortune of Scotland had been sacrificed in 1707, that the habits of its 'common natives' had not been improved by union (so why expect this of the Irish peasantry?), and that—with the blood scarcely dry at Culloden—the Hanoverian dynasty had not been secured by union, 'since every Attempt against his Majesty's Crown takes its Rise from [Scotland], and may, probably, be owing in a good Degree to the Union itself.'[77]

The volatility of Charles Lucas's arguments about union—in favour, then violently against—is symptomatic of the difficulty which even the most independent Irish Protestant opinion had with the proposal. The case for union would not flourish until a revival of sectarianism and fear of Revolutionary France divided the patriot alliance which brought leading Catholics and Protestants together in the late 1770s and early 1780s. That was all in the future, but Swift would be constantly invoked and re-read during those phases of controversy.[78] Back in the 1720s, his sense of grievance exacerbated by the Declaratory Act, he had himself moved decisively against English involvement in Irish affairs. He presumably recognized—though he does not seem to state this directly—that the dependency of Ireland would not be alleviated by union, because, as would be shown after 1801, a small group of Irish MPs in Westminster could hope only intermittently to influence government policy. Already the country was subject to a warped form of union. In Book III of *Gulliver's Travels* (1726), the cities of Lagado and Lindalino, equivalents of London and Dublin, are situated on a *single* island, Balnibarbi, which the flying island of Laputa (occupied by the court) menacingly traverses. The adventures recorded in this book are fictionally dated '1707'.[79]

Swift's determination in the fourth *Drapier's Letter* to believe that, because the three kingdoms are ruled by one monarch, the Irish can appeal to the crown over the authority of the Westminster parliament, is one of the most 1603–1707 things about him. Like Irish patriots later in the century, he was following principles worked out by constitutional royalists in seventeenth-century England/Wales and Scotland. This view of how sovereignty operated, however, was already anachronistic, and would become dangerously so. Power now lay in the hands of ministers, and their authority was underpinned by 'the sovereignty of parliament'.[80] The resonances of this were transatlantic. Irish Protestant patriotism or what can still be called colonial nationalism is a plural and disputed phenomenon,[81] but pathways lead from Swift's account of Ireland as a distinct realm under the crown to the secession of the American colonies.

When Molyneux asked whether Ireland was not constitutionally different from '*Virginia, New-England*, or *Mary-Land*?' (above, p. 57), he did so with an emphasis which anticipated English indifference or scepticism. Swift's complaint in 1720, that 'some *Ministers*' had been inclined 'to look *down* upon this Kingdom, as if it had been one of their *Colonies* of *Out-casts* in *America*',[82] is riddled with an acrimony which is not merely temperamental but a sign that colonial relegation was becoming a reality for the English of Ireland. Because the grievance of such men—even for instinctively Tory, Church of Ireland loyalists such as Swift—was both coloured by the ideas of Locke and Sidney and sustained by readings of the statutes along the lines of Swift's of 'the 33d year of Henry VIII', Irish patriotism could evolve from resentment at quasi-colonial 'dependency' in the direction set (as in America) by the Revolution of 1688. The afterlife of Molyneux's *Case of Ireland . . . Stated*, reprinted in America after decades of relative neglect in Ireland,[83] then reissued in Ireland, in the heady year for patriotism of 1782, with its solitary, positive reference to union deleted (above, pp. 321, 323), is a product of this genealogy.[84] That Grattan did not actually declare, in the parliament of 1782: 'Spirit of Swift—spirit of Molyneux—Your genius has prevailed—Ireland is now a nation',[85] does not negate the historical significance of his later attributing these words to himself.

One way in which the English of Ireland could deal with the sense of exclusion thrust upon them by 1707 was to refuse to dwindle retrospectively into the condition of a colony, whose history had only begun with the arrival of the Anglo-Normans, and to follow Ussher, Ware, and other seventeenth-century antiquarians in exploring the insular origins of Hiberno-British antiquity. This had the double benefit of asserting the venerable dignity of the Kingdom of Ireland while appropriating for the children of planters all sorts of legends and precedents which in earlier generations had been claimed by Gaelic Catholics. We have touched on this phenomenon while discussing William Philips's *Hibernia Freed* (above, pp. 322–5). A related instance, as traditional in its sources as it is rejecting in its conclusion, is Swift's 'Verses Occasioned by the Sudden Drying up of St Patrick's Well near Trinity College, Dublin' (*c.*1729). This is another posthumously published work, and its appearance in 1762 can only have enhanced the growing profile of Swift as an Irish patriot. Walter Scott printed it without comment, perhaps because it so fully endorses his dismal view of Swift the historian. In some respects, it was outmoded even when Swift put pen to paper; in its knowing way, it might have been written a century earlier, as part of the Ussher/O'Sullivan Beare controversy about the life of St Patrick. It is thickly encrusted with notes from such old-fashioned sources as Giraldus Cambrensis on the topography of Ireland, plus Fordon, Boece, Buchanan, 'and all the *Scotch* Historians' on how their founding monarch, Fergus I, was the son of a King of Ireland.[86]

This gives Swift yet another opportunity to air his Scotophobia and resentment about 1707. Patrick, as speaker of the poem, points out that the Scots' own patriotic history makes them an Irish conquest and colony:

> Thee, happy Island, *Pallas* call'd her own,
> When haughty *Britain* was a Land unknown.
> From thee, with Pride, the *Caledonians* trace
> The glorious Founder of their kingly Race:
> Thy martial Sons, whom now they dare despise,
> Did once their Land subdue and civilize:
> Their Dress, their Language, and the *Scottish* Name,
> Confess the Soil from whence the Victors came.
> Well may they boast that antient Blood, which runs
> Within their Veins, who are thy younger Sons,
> A Conquest and a Colony from thee,
> The Mother-Kingdom left her Children free ...   (lines 9–20)

That this is largely about compensating for Ireland's post-1707 demotion is evident in the casting of Scotland in the colonial role. At first glance, 'haughty *Britain*' refers to classical *Britannia*, but the adjective drags the noun forwards and associates it with the 'double Nation' (so arrogant in its treatment of Ireland) officially given this title at the union. The 1707 context is relevant to Swift's negotiation of that most tricky point for Protestant followers of Molyneux, whether Ireland was originally conquered by the Anglo-Normans (backed up, worryingly, by a papal bull) or was, more conveniently, drawn into some sort of agreement that was subsequently betrayed. According to the sources, Patrick notes, the Scots were not treated as slaves of the Irish in their northern colony. How differently did (and does) Britain treat the Irish:

> From thee no Mark of Slavery they felt,
> Not so with thee thy base Invaders dealt;

> Invited here to 'vengeful *Morrough*'s Aid,
> Those whom they could not conquer, they betray'd.
> *Britain*, by thee we fell, ungrateful Isle!
> Not by thy Valour, but superior Guile: ...   (lines 21–6)

Britain, Patrick declares, was converted to Christianity by the Irish. Yet now the flow is reversed, as rapacious English-born clerics strip the country of its assets and drive it into vice. Swift was always too loyal to the Williamite Revolution, and too wary of Catholic Ireland, to become a Jacobite, but he lashes out against the Hanoverians ('See, where the new-devouring Vermin runs, | Sent in my Anger from the Land of *Huns*' (lines 59–60)). The best estates have been seized, the sources of learning are drying up (like the spring which occasions the poem), the students of Trinity College have no incentive to excel. They are condemned to a life of country dullness, or must flatter 'foreign Prelates', read legal tomes rather than the gentlemanly classics, and work in customs and excise (lines 69–78). As the catalogue builds, Swift characteristically turns in rage and despair against Ireland itself, even though he has identified the root of its corruption in Britain. Patrick would so much rather be the patron saint of some other country that he even praises the Scots: they at least would have fought off the English. The Irish will soon be slaves, their currency 'Shells and Leather'—worse than Wood's debased copper; absentee landlords will eat out the vitals of the country and carry its wealth to England. Patrick has had enough: 'I scorn thy spurious and degenerate Line, | And from this Hour my Patronage resign' (lines 79–102).

1745 and all that. If we look on the past as 'memorable history' we travesty it by missing the importance of what did not happen. Certainly what did not happen in Ireland in 1745—when Scotland was in turmoil—changed how historians at the time looked back.[87] That Catholics, despite their devotion to the Jacobite cause,[88] chose not to rebel made new interpretations and alignments possible. Having proven, at least for a time, that 1641 would not come again, they could join Dissenters excluded from public office by the Test in appealing to the Williamite Revolution as a charter for toleration. In a development that Swift would have appreciated, the ancient history of Ireland was recast along Whig lines reminiscent of English, and even

---

Morrough: Dermot MacMurrough, i.e. Diarmait Mac Murchada (*d.*1171), the king of Leinster whose invitation to Henry II to help him regain his throne is conventionally regarded as initiating English domination in Ireland.

Scottish, harking-back to an immemorial constitution. (The Welsh, as we shall see, had quite different claims to make about antiquity.) This, if ever, was the moment when an Irish Enlightenment historiography could have broken through sectarian hostilities. As Jacqueline Hill puts it: 'Round about 1750 ... there appeared to be substantial areas of agreement among the patriots, the Gaelic enthusiasts and the "enlightened" Catholics. They all accepted the Williamite revolution, the Protestant establishment and close relations between England and Ireland. They all condemned arbitrary monarchy and acknowledged the importance of parliamentary institutions.'[89]

A further incitement to unity came in a series of challenges issued by Scottish historians. There was, first, the Enlightenment scepticism about remote origins, especially civilized ones, which, for thinkers such as Hume, threw Ireland back upon the imputation of a barbarous past. Secondly, and more troublingly, there was the success of Macpherson's Ossianic poems, which claimed priority for Scotland in the creation of the legends of Fionn Mac Cumhaill and Oisín. Irish antiquarians argued that the Ossian poems were forgeries, a view which would become predominant though it is probably too simplistic.[90] In the paratexts published with *Fingal* (1762) and *Temora* (1763), however, Macpherson advanced a broader thesis, unfolded in his *Introduction to the History of Great Britain and Ireland* (1771), which was harder to refute. He rejected the traditional account, reasserted by Swift's St Patrick in the poem first published at just this date, that the Dalriadic kingdom of Scotland had originated in an Irish invasion. Macpherson regarded the Highlanders as descendants of the original Britons, pushed to the north of the island by incomers from the continent. (This thesis had the merit, for a Highlander such as Macpherson, of reclaiming the clans for the Britishness which many of them had challenged in 1745.) At some point, Macpherson argued, Ireland had been settled by contingents of these ancient Britons, moving in from Scotland. Resisting this thesis put Irish antiquarians on their mettle, and required their outlook to be archipelagic.

Yet neither the uneasy calm of 1745 nor the need to contest Scottish challenges could overcome the insularity and divisiveness of Irish looking back. The competition between Catholics and Protestants for ownership of the past rendered 1707 incidental: it was far less contentious than 1641, 1691, or indeed the nature of Milesian antiquity. The question of how much liberty should be given to Catholics was, as Clare O'Halloran puts it, 'a critical subtext for almost all Irish antiquarian writing. Works which supported the claim of a great pre-colonial golden age were understood as signalling a pro-Catholic stance, whereas sceptics of the claims were taken as opponents of the relaxation of the penal laws.'[91] And divisions were kept alive as much by what the historians said about the seventeenth century as they were by rural unrest or doctrinal difference. If one looks at library lists and sales catalogues, the weight of books about the period between Tyrone's Rebellion and the Treaty of Limerick overwhelms even the growing output of accounts of ancient Ireland.

It did not help the cause of reconciliation that so many of these texts had been written and first published in the troubled and historiographically acrimonious seventeenth century itself.[92] Sir John Davies' *Discouerie of the True Causes why Ireland was Neuer Entirely Subdued* (1612), Sir James Ware's *Historie of Ireland* (1633), and Cox's *Hibernia Anglicana* (1689) are typical post-1707 reprints, associated with new editions of letters and memoirs by Ormonde, Orrery, Clanricarde, and Castlehaven. The 1640s, always a controversial decade, had left a divisive legacy in print.[93] Landed Protestants would read (or own iconic copies of, and/or show their convictions by subscribing to) one of the numerous, unrest-related reprints of Sir John Temple's *The Irish Rebellion* (1646) or William King's *The State of the Protestants of Ireland under the Late King James's Government* (1691),[94] though they could also consult the more moderate, Ormondist *History of the Rebellion and Civil Wars in Ireland* (1719–20), which was attributed, dubiously, to Clarendon. Popular attitudes were fed by two widely distributed chapbooks, also products of the earlier period: Hugh Reilly's *Impartial History*, first published in Paris or Louvain as *Ireland's Case Briefly Stated* (1695), which emphasized the loyalty of Catholics to the crown even during the supposed rebellions of the 1590s and 1640s,[95] and Nathaniel Crouch's firmly Protestant *History of the Kingdom of Ireland*, which appeared in London in 1693.[96]

Given the dominance of embattled and self-interested Protestant accounts it was difficult to change perceptions of what had happened during the seventeenth century. Reassessments of 1641 were particularly liable to be read as Catholic apologetics, aimed at undermining the penal laws. For it was the propensity of papists to commit atrocities against peaceful Protestants which justified the legislation.[97] Both John Curry and Charles O'Conor, the leading Catholic historians of the mid-century, put on Protestant personae—to avoid the charge of merely pushing the aspirations of their community—when arguing over the past.[98] They took the line that penal laws had been a cause of the 1641 Rebellion and would not prevent further troubles. Repeatedly drawn back to the decades covered by this book (even though O'Conor's specialism was ancient Ireland), both sought to promulgate a more balanced version of 1641 than was available from Protestant historians.[99] They urged Hume to revise his biased, unresearched account, and fed information to Thomas Leland, Librarian of Trinity College, Dublin, who was regarded as the likeliest author of an enlightened history. In the event, although (and because) Leland's *History of Ireland from the Invasion of Henry II* (1773) lightly adjusted the received account, it pleased few.

The reappraisal of ancient Ireland contributed to the patriotic revival which took off in the 1760s, encouraged by the efforts of O'Conor, Curry, and others associated with the Catholic Committee.[100] This literary, historiographical, and cultural-revivalist movement, which had parallels in Wales and England, helped create an environment in which Catholic intellectuals could join with liberal Protestants to clear away the penal laws. From Charles Lucas to Grattan, not without turbulence along the way, patriots sided with the reforms which culminated in the Catholic Relief Acts (1774–93) and the constitutional upheavals of 1779–82, when Poynings' Law and the Declaratory Act, attacked decades earlier by Swift, were respectively neutered and repealed. O'Halloran has shown that antiquarianism remained a significant, equable factor even in the more divided later decades of the century; but sectarian divisions persisted in the study as in the street, and the ghosts of 1641 still haunted the historiography. It is true that some Protestant patriots—Church of Ireland as well as Dissenters—remained committed to separation. They would fight and die alongside Catholics as members of the Society of United Irishmen. For most, however, 1782 set the limit of nationalism. To have pressed for independence from Britain would have left Irish Protestants exposed to the Catholic majority, resentful however quiescent. And after the outbreak of revolution in France, even that quiescence was in doubt, thanks to Wolfe Tone, the Defenders (Catholic secret societies), and the United Irish. This is what put 1707 back onto the agenda.

Arguments in favour of union had begun to shape historical discourse. Thomas Campbell's 'Historical Sketch, of the Constitution, and Government of Ireland' (published 1789) is the most striking instance.[101] But it was revolutionary ferment in Ireland, combined with a British need for security in the face of French aggression—as in 1707—which set the scene. Once again, patriotic verse (in Ireland, now, as well as Britain) invoked 'heavenly union' as a charm against 'the Gallic vulture'.[102] Internally, the flashpoint was the rising of 1798, which Protestants came to regard as a recurrence of 1641,[103] though nationalists have often represented it as provoked by the authorities to make union more attainable. From the point of view of English ministers, enlargement of the United Kingdom to include Ireland as well as Great Britain offered the prospect of enfranchising property-owning Catholics without endangering Protestant Ascendancy because Catholics, though a potential majority in the Dublin Parliament, would be only a minority at Westminster. And consolidation of the inner 'empire' was felt to be essential to secure Britain's western flank against the French—who did, in fact, land in County Mayo in 1798.[104]

Irish Protestants liked to proclaim that Britain and Ireland had effectively been united in 1688–91, when King Billy's victories with their support brought liberty and security to all three kingdoms. William Hamilton Drummond's *The Giant's Causeway* (1811) gives a nicely overblown account: 'From east to west see equal rights prevail, ... One king, one sceptre rules the sister isles, | In Union's flowery wreaths blithe Erin smiles'.[105] In the late 1790s, however, in the run-up to the Act of Union, 1707 was the template, both in discussions within government, and in the public debate which, as in Scotland a century earlier, burst out in Dublin.[106] The official line that looking forward meant looking back to 1707 was set out by the Poet Laureate, Henry James Pye:

> O! as the era past saw Anna join
> Each warrior nation of Britannia's line,
> So may the auspicious hours that now ascend,
> The sister isles in ceaseless Union blend—— ...[107]

Defoe's *History of the Union* (above, pp. 336–9) was widely read. It was extracted in a package of material assembled by the Home Office to advise ministers in 1798, and published in Dublin the following year.[108] Two 'updated versions' of Swift's *Injured Lady* were published in the satirical newspaper, *The Anti-Union* (1798–9).[109] In the controversy that exploded before the passing of the Act of Union, on the second attempt, in 1800 (taking effect, 1 January 1801)—with Scottish levels of intrigue, reluctance, and buying of votes—the success of 1707 was constantly disputed.[110] English failures to honour the Treaty, their condescension towards the Scots, and the possibility that Edinburgh would have flourished even without union were cited. On the whole, however, the line taken by Scott in *Waverley* was accepted, that, while it had been greeted with reluctance, the union had brought prosperity to Scotland in the second half of the century. That did not mean, however, that the union of 1707 could simply be extended to Ireland.

(iii) Anglo-Scoto-Cambro

The Irish novelist Maria Edgeworth had been one of the first readers of *Waverley* to write to Scott applauding him as the only possible author of the anonymous work. When he returned to the novel, more than a decade later, Scott, who had in the meantime stayed with the Edgeworths in Ireland (1825), repaid the compliment. In the 'General Preface' (1829), he says that he was encouraged to complete *Waverley* by

> the extended and well-merited fame of Miss Edgeworth, whose Irish characters have gone so far to make the English familiar with the character of their gay and kind-hearted neighbours of Ireland, that she may be truly said to have done more towards completing the Union, than perhaps all the legislative enactments by which it has been followed up.
>
> Without being so presumptuous as to hope to emulate the rich humour, pathetic tenderness, and admirable tact, which pervade the works of my accomplished friend, I felt that something might be attempted for my own country, of the same kind with that which Miss Edgeworth so fortunately achieved for Ireland—something which might introduce her natives to those of the sister kingdom, in a more favourable light than they had been placed hitherto, and tend to procure sympathy for their virtues and indulgence for their foibles.[111]

This is the sort of writing that gets Scott a bad name among nationalists. 'Indulgence for their foibles ...' is patently ironic, but it remains defensive, even apologetic. In its calculatedly unthreatening way, it resembles Scott's manner as master of ceremonies during George IV's visit to Edinburgh in 1822—an occasion now routinely mocked as a tartan pageant (even the portly Hanoverian wore a kilt). Yet there are ways of regarding Scott's contribution to that visit as patriotically constructive,[112] and there is no reason to believe that his ambivalence about Hanover and the union, aired during the composition of *Waverley*,[113] had changed. In 1826, he showed what he had learned as a patriot from Swift in his *Letters from Malachi Malagrowther.*

The Drapier's Letters resisted the imposition of Wood's halfpence on Ireland. In *Letters from Malachi*, Scott opposes a bill presented to the Westminster parliament that sought to restrict the right of Scottish banks to issue notes for small sums. The existing arrangements are, he argues, well-adapted to local conditions, but there is also a question of national self-determination. 'When I look back,' Malachi laments, 'I think I see my native country of Scotland, if it is yet to be called by a title so discriminative, falling, so far as its national, or rather, perhaps, I ought now to say its *provincial,* interests are concerned, daily into more absolute contempt.'[114] The tough patriotism of the *Letters* puts into a different light Scott's comments in the 'General Preface'. Whether hard-line or soft, he is saying that the problems of union lie with the English, who fail to respect their neighbours. Giving an aggressive twist to the historical theses proposed in *Waverley* and the Swift edition, Malachi declares that, before 1745, the English would not have dared take such liberties with the Scots ('some thought claymores had edges'), and that, after the suppression of the rising, it was not the 'incalculable resources' generated by union—as he had put it in the passage about Jephthah's daughter (above, p. 363)—but *neglect* which had enabled the country to grow economically five times faster than England: 'Scotland... was left from the year 1750 under the guardianship of her own institutions, to win her silent way to national wealth and consequence' (274).

The situation has been changed by the enlargement of the United Kingdom. Steps taken to curb revenue abuses in Ireland—where 'Pat, poor fellow, had been playing the loon' (that good Scots word)[115]—have been imposed on Scotland to prevent the Irish feeling persecuted into taking up 'the pike and shilelah' (278–9). For the Scots to be treated in this way is unjust, but they should not threaten physical force.[116] Scott did not want a 1798, another '45, in Scotland, and that restricts Malachi's nationalism (though his aggravation is evident when he envisages a status for Scotland *below* that of an English county): 'We had better remain in union with England, even at the risk of becoming a subordinate species of Northumberland, as far as national consequence is concerned, than remedy ourselves by even hinting the possibility of a rupture.' Yet there is another option: 'there is no harm in wishing Scotland to have just so much ill-nature, according to her own proverb, as may keep her good-nature from being abused; so much national spirit as may determine her to stand by her own rights, conducting her assertion of them with every feeling of respect and amity towards England' (280).

The problem with 1707 once it was compounded by 1801 was that so far from enhancing a consciousness of diversity it tempted English ministers to work for *uniformity*. This is the core of Malachi's complaint, that uniformity does not affect the parts of the union uniformly, and is in some instances grotesquely inequitable. To impose a single banking system on Britain is like passing 'a law that the Scotsman, for uniformity's sake, should not eat oatmeal, because it is found to give Englishmen the heart-burn. ... The nation which cannot raise wheat, must be allowed to eat oat-bread' (291). In any case, the proposal is contrary to the Treaty:

> This levelling system, not equitable in itself, is infinitely unjust, if a story, often told by my poor old grandfather, was true, which I own I am inclined to doubt. The old man, sir, had learned in his youth, or dreamed in his dotage, that Scotland had become an integral part of England,—not in right of conquest, or rendition, or through any right of inheritance,—but in virtue of a solemn Treaty of Union. Nay, so distinct an idea had he of this supposed Treaty, that he used to recite one of its articles to this effect: — 'That the laws in use within the kingdom of Scotland, do, after the Union, remain in the same force as before, but alterable by the Parliament of Great Britain, with this difference between the laws concerning public right, policy, and civil government, and those which concern private right, that the former may be made the same through the whole United Kingdom; but that no alteration be made on laws which concern private right, *excepting for the evident utility of the subjects within Scotland.*' When the old gentleman came to the passage, which you will mark in italics, he always clenched his fist, and exclaimed, 'Nemo me impune lacesset!' which I presume, are words belonging to the black art, since there is no one in the Modern Athens [i.e. Edinburgh] conjuror enough to understand their meaning, or least to comprehend the spirit of the sentiment which my grandfather thought they conveyed. (297)

Malachi proposes that the old Treaty should be searched for, and either respected or, if voted obsolete, be preserved in the Museum of the Antiquaries. The method of the satire is Swiftian, even if its severity is softened by Scott's Tory-philosophical sense that so much that is worthwhile recedes into desuetude, and that the Museum of the Antiquaries is not such a bad

---

Nemo me impune lacesset: No one provokes me with impunity; the motto traditionally employed by the Scottish monarchs

resting place to have. That Swift was on his mind is shown by a reference, at this point in the *Letters*, to the trouble the Dean got into when he 'passed some sarcasms on the Scottish nation, as a poor and fierce people' (301). And Swift is there too in Malachi's development of the point that uniformity smacks of system, theory, and abstract principles—the French Revolutionary curse according to men like Burke, Coleridge, and Scott:

> The philosophical tailors of Laputa, who wrought by mathematical calcula-
> tion, had, no doubt, a supreme contempt for those humble fashioners who
> went to work by measuring the person of their customer; but Gulliver tells us,
> that the worst clothes he ever wore were constructed upon abstract principles;
> and truly I think we have seen some laws, and may see more, not much better
> adapted to existing circumstances, than the captain's philosophical uniform
> to his actual person. (306)

Anyone who replaces abstract principles with historically informed knowl-edge will realize that a policy of uniformity, whether deliberate or unthinking, creates trouble in Anglo-Scottish relations. The measures in hand resemble the attempted imposition of Episcopalianism in the 1670s and 1680s (see Chapter 9 above): 'Can you tell me, sir, if this *uniformity* of civil institutions, which calls for such sacrifices, be at all descended from, or related to, a doctrine nearly of the same name, called Conformity in reli-gious doctrine, very fashionable about 150 years since, which undertook to unite the jarring creeds of the United Kingdom to one common standard, and excited a universal strife by the vain attempt' (308).

Malachi is not done yet. Advancing an old Scottish argument, raised against regal union after 1603 and elaborated by Fletcher of Saltoun (above, pp. 140, 332–3), he expatiates on the dangers of giving too much power to London. Because authority had been centralized in Paris, all France was exposed to the Revolution once the capital had fallen. The United Kingdom will be stronger if the separateness of its parts is maintained, like a rope twined out of three strands which is tougher than a rope with just one. 'For God's sake, sir, let us remain as Nature made us, Englishmen, Irishmen, and Scotchmen, with something like the impress of our several countries upon each!' (373)—a cry which would be merely exclamatory, forgetting culture in the appeal to Nature, were it not also symptomatic of the enhanced role of race in early nineteenth-century views of the archipelago. There is no advantage in everyone becoming similar, like so many shillings rubbed smooth by use. By the law of Nature, 1707 and

1801 should allow for diversity in union: 'The degree of national diversity between different countries, is but an instance of that general variety which Nature seems to have adopted as a principle through all her works, as anxious, apparently, to avoid, as modern statesmen to enforce, any thing like an approach to absolute "uniformity" ' (374).

Scotland can be saved from declining into a province, by using its votes at Westminster but also by taking advantage of Irish representation. That the forty-five MPs granted the country after 1707 carry less weight in a post-1801 parliament as a result of the inclusion of Ireland does not mean that Scotland cannot increase its pressure on the English. Pat, the Irishman, can be persuaded that any breach of the 1707 Treaty sets a bad precedent for that of 1800. More positively, the Scots should appeal to the honour and goodwill of English MPs. For times have changed since the virulent 1760s—of which more in a moment. Now Scotsmen coming south are if anything overvalued. That the English are unsympathetic to the national interest of Scotland does not prevent them from being generous on a one-to-one basis. John Bull is a willing giver though hard when driving a bargain. He needs to be educated out of selfishness and lazy uniformity.

What, in practice, was the view in England? In 1707, while the Scots were rioting, the mood in London was buoyant because union was seen as enhancing security against France.[117] It safeguarded the established church and a Protestant succession to the British crowns. Smollett would later assert that 'the majority of both nations believed that the treaty would produce violent convulsions',[118] but this was an exaggeration calculated to bring out the union's subsequent success. Yet a willingness to incorporate Scotland was not the same as liking the Scots. As surely as their seventeenth-century predecessors, Hanoverian Englishmen were suspicious of Scottish politics, religion, and poverty. The ambitious lads o' pairts who streamed south to London (a more socially mixed influx than the courtiers, soldiers, and divines who made the same journey after regal union) were taking advantage of what the negotiators of the Treaty foresaw would be a beneficial effect of incorporation—that the Scots would have access to opportunities in England without an equivalent counter-flow, given the relative wealth of the countries and the paucity of government posts in North Britain (notwithstanding the occasionally expressed wish of Scotsmen such as Boswell that more Englishmen should hold office in Scotland).[119]

Despite allusions to the Treaty in English literary and historical works in the opening and closing decades of the century, there were no annual celebrations to keep the event alive in public consciousness, as there were on 5 November, the anniversary of the Gunpowder Plot (or as there were in Protestant Ireland, on 23 October, to mark the outbreak of the 1641 Rebellion).[120] The union was not given and did not win a place in what the Scot W. C. Sellar and the Englishman R. J. Yeatman call the *Memorable History of England*; and it is telling, to jump forward a couple of centuries, that, although Scottish events figure selectively in *1066 and All That*, 1707 does not. Why then, does the *Oxford English Dictionary*, that magisterial product of Scottish lexicography, define *union* (n 4b) as an event in 'Eng. Hist.' but not 'Scot. Hist.'? That the experience of union was more challenging for eighteenth-century Scots—even for those who did not travel south—than it was for their neighbours does not entirely discredit the dictionary, because it was largely the failure of the English to appreciate the significance of the union that made its historical consequences difficult for them.

England incorporated Scotland without the constitutional fundamentals changing. The imperial conception of the realm established by the 1533 Act in Restraint of Appeals (above, p. 49) was merely enlarged, as it had been in 1536–43 with the shiring of Wales. English statesmen, conscious of their military and economic strength, saw no reason to adapt, and continued not to reflect—as their predecessors had done, briefly, under the Republic and Protectorate—on how the imperium should expand. This stored up problems for church as well as state, as in the long-drawn-out crisis over Catholic emancipation, and it would put intolerable pressure on relations with the American colonies. As J. G. A. Pocock puts it: 'The English of 1707' lacked political vision, 'and it was their indifference and introversion, rather than their vaulting ambition, which ensured that the Union would be one of incorporation rather than confederation. They acquired empire, in this case at least, not in the lapidary "fit of absence of mind", but out of unwillingness to consider their relations with others in any conceptual form, with the result that these could take no other form than that of an extension of the system to which they were accustomed.'[121]

Of course, we should not attribute everything to 'indifference and introversion', for there was a degree of calculation in the unwillingness of English MPs. 'The Scots were inclined to a foederal union', Smollett notes, 'like that of the United Provinces: but the English were bent upon an incorporation, so as that no Scottish parliament should ever have power to repeal the articles of the treaty.'[122] Why create a union which could be undone at will by the Scots—a weapon which they could constantly threaten to use—if the English could require a veto? Whatever the motives of the English, however, the logic of incorporation left Great Britain with no confederative precedents to fall back on in 1776, when the American colonies sought to enhance their status.[123] We should contrast the paucity of theorizing about 1707 in England with what went on in Scotland, where the classical and European scope of debate about union (see Chapter 10) laid foundations for the comparative method of Scottish Enlightenment thought.[124]

Pocock, the great archipelagist, argues that the historical phase begun by Henry VIII's Act in Restraint of Appeals extended not to 1707 or 1801 but 1829 because that was when the 'national apostasy' of the Tractarians within the Church of England began breaking up the Erastian settlement.[125] This date also mattered outside England. For 1829 was the year of Catholic emancipation, the year in which the penal laws that were passed while Swift was complaining about the union of 1707 were finally laid to rest. It was to the abolition of these laws that Scott was primarily referring when, in his 1829 'General Preface', he wrote of Edgeworth's novels doing more to complete the union between Britain and Ireland than 'perhaps all the legislative enactments' which had 'followed up' the Act of 1801. The granting of emancipation finally made good an inducement which had been offered to Irish Catholics in the run-up to that Act, an inducement whose denial (supposedly at George III's instigation) had provoked the sort of unrest in Ireland which, in Scott's rather inventive account, Edgeworth's novels were designed to exculpate.

When younger, Scott had been hostile to Catholicism. By 1829 he was merely contemptuous. His visit to Ireland had apparently 'moderated' his views about emancipation. He still believed that there had been a strong case for not relaxing the penal laws in the late eighteenth century. Now that liberalization had begun, however, he felt it was pointless to deny fuller rights. As he confided to his Journal for 1829:

> I cannot get myself to feel at all anxious about the Catholic Question. I cannot see the use of fighting about the platter, when you have let them snatch the meat of[f] it. I hold popery to be such a mean and depriving superstition that I am not clear I could have found myself liberal enough for voting the repeal of the penal laws as they existed before 1780. They must and would in course of time have smotherd popery and I confess I should have see[n] the old Lady of Babylon's mouth stop'd with pleasure. But now you have taken the plaister off her mouth and given her free respiration I cannot see the sense of keeping up the irritation about their right to sit in Parliament.[126]

Gifted Gilfillan is half-absurd in *Waverley* because he identifies so obsessively with seventeenth-century Protestantism. Scott handles the comedy
of his own beliefs more urbanely, but his prejudice against the old Lady of
Babylon—which he shared with the average John Bull—still registers in
what he feels about the Irish. It is a reminder of how potently within Britain
as well as Ireland the problems of union and the repercussions of difference remained tied to the Reformation.[127] Though Pocock's 1533–1829
periodization has an English weighting, it better reflects the confessional
nature of the incompatibilities which continued from 1603–1707 into the
eighteenth century and shaped its political landscape than the other, more
Whig-constitutional terminus which also attracts him: 1832, the year of the
Great Reform Act.[128]

After 1707, more Scots than English people saw themselves, or chose to
describe themselves, as British. (The same could not be said for the Irish
after 1801.) Yet English panegyrics on the union were initially quite thick on
the ground. A flock of loyal poets, including Nahum Tate, Charles Darby,
Mary Pix, Elkanah Settle, Lewis Theobald, and Edward Vernon recycled
the familiar topics of seventeenth-century union literature—the Tweed
no longer divides but joins, Britain is a world apart, Protestantism will
triumph, military greatness is assured—and threw into the mix celebrations
of commercial opportunity and lofty denunciations of the French.[129] (When
taken in this context, Swift's 'On the Union' reads like a satire on a minor
verse genre as much as a satire on the new state.) Camden's *Britannia*
reaffirmed its claim to represent official history by including, from 1722,
a section on 'The Union' which discussed Tudor and Stuart attempts
to build Anglo-Scottish union and reprinted documents associated with
the Treaty of 1707. In the corpus of 'patriotic poetry' which bulked
so large in eighteenth-century England,[130] the terms Britain/England and
British/English are used freely and almost interchangeably, though this is
double-edged evidence for anyone seeking to argue that British cultural
identities took hold during the period. More often, the usage looks like early
evidence of the English willingness to regard 'Britain' as England writ large,
or at least as standing for England in its royal and imperial manifestations.

A stronger sense of Great Britain as a composite state, yoked to Ireland, and building a global empire, while fighting its battles on the
continent—evident in the poems written immediately after 1707—returns
during the Napoleonic wars. This suggests that it was not just the novelty of
the state system created in 1707 that made English writing about the union

initially so alive to the heterogeneity of the United Kingdom, but also a desire to stress that disparate parts of the archipelago had been unified against France. Fear that Louis XIV was intent on 'universal monarchy', explicit in a long run of texts from Marvell to Elijah Fenton's 'Verses on the Union' (collected in 1717),[131] gives way in such later poems as Ann Yearsley's 'The Genius of England' (1796), and, at a popular level, Charles Dibdin's 'The Four Saints' (1807), to anxiety about the Jacobins and Napoleon.[132] But the cumulative message is strong, that the threat of French expansionism is an argument for uniting the kingdoms, including, by the end of the period, Ireland. As one example among many, take Thomas Park's description, in *Cupid Turned Volunteer* (1804), of the Jacobean union flag, enhanced after 1801 by the saltire cross of St Patrick:

> the standard Britons show,
> To mark the sister-union which combines
> England and Scotia, while Ierne twines
>   Her verdant shamrock in the royal field,
> Where from the same stem grows
> The purple thistle with the crimson rose,
>   And, all conjoining, scorn to yield,
> To the drear nightshade of delirious France ...[133]

That a single phase of state formation ran from 1533 to 1829 remains a bold, even tendentious, claim, but it incidentally chimes with the inclusion of 'The Song of Union. By a Cambrian Bard' in the fourth edition of Joseph Cottle's *Malvern Hills, with Minor Poems* (1829). Cottle was a Bristol publisher, friend (in the 1790s) of Coleridge and Southey, whose rendering of Welsh topics[134] had an English inflection. Asserting the potency of union against French aggression, his 'Song' is effectively an answer to Thomas Gray's 'The Bard'. Where Gray's defiant bard—his lines informed by Welsh patriotic scholarship—cries out against Edward I's invasion of Wales, Cottle's sees in this campaign the beginnings of Anglo-Welsh union and the triumph of Great Britain after 1707. The Welsh leader, Llwellyn and his comrades did not die in vain, the bard prophetically declares, but in the 'noble cause' of the future. In line with the old Galfridian legends, Cambria provides the heroic bases of a resurgent British state, strong enough to take on France:

> England bold, and Cambria fair!
> Now are join'd, a happy pair!

Whilst their progeny shall rise,
Great, as good, and brave, as wise!
Far off I gaze! as years advance,
Gallia wields the bloody lance!
The base she raises to renown,
Or tramples thrones, and sceptres, down.
I see her, in her rebel pride,
O'er plains of waste, and carnage, stride!
With one, her lord, deform'd with crimes,
(The Attila of after times)
Dealing, wide, his treacherous smile,
Who, ere he stabs, his victim blinds!
While, in this wave-sequester'd isle,
Affrighted Freedom refuge finds.[135]

It is remarkable how much English writing about union, from Tate's *Triumph of the Union* in 1707 to Cottle's 'Song of Union' in 1829, involves long-range looking back. That this is presented as, on the contrary, a looking *forward*, by means of prophetic figures such as the Cambrian bard, is not surprising. Historical narrative usually proceeds chronologically, though its vantage point is hindsight. The anticipatory, even visionary impulse both cohered with the ideology of progress which informed Whig advocacy of union and made sense of the resulting heterogeneity. To justify the creation of a polity that incorporated peoples as diverse as the Welsh, the English, the Scots (both Lowland and Highland) and after 1801 the Irish (Catholic and Protestant), it was desirable to tell the story in stages—few would propose creating a state like the United Kingdom from scratch—and to attribute what seemed unlikely in its make-up to providential guidance.

The 'memorable history' projected into the Anglo-British past by union tended to consist—even for strident Whigs—of a stately succession of monarchs. When Tate, for example, calls upon Britain's ancient bards and old Saturn to 'cast | A backward look on glorious Ages past', in his proto-union poem 'On the Assembling of the New Parliament' (1701), this is how he urges a coming-together of the Scots and English. Like so many later patriotic poets, he summons up Edward III, 'our FIFTH Harry', and 'Phoenix-ELIZA, ANNA of That Age!' as 'British' monarchs who resisted the French.[136] (The disagreeable habit of the Scots of siding with France against embattled England—stressed in earlier English accounts of all three monarchs—is forgotten.) Scottish unionists addressing English audiences adopted a similar strategy. In Thomson and Mallet's *Alfred*, for

instance, the Saxon king and lawgiver Alfred, in retreat from the invading
Danes, is confined to 'the little isle of Athelney in Somersetshire' (5).
The island sanctuary represents Britain in miniature, and though Alfred is
repeatedly characterized as 'English', he is protected by a countryman who
calls himself British and addressed by a Hermit who prophetically discloses
his succession through Edward III ('Beneath his standard, Britain shall
go forth'—neglecting Scottish antagonism again) and the Black Prince,
Elizabeth, then William III and the Hanoverians (30–6).

How did English people explicitly writing histories adapt to the new
priorities established by 1707? Around the date of the Treaty we find
antiquarians producing such texts as *The Queen an Empress, and Her Three
Kingdoms One Empire* (1706), which argues that the enclosing seas had kept
the inhabitants of Britain largely free of foreign blood. The Romans, Saxons,
Danes, and Normans were 'never perhaps more than a Tenth to the Natives
of the whole Island among whom they settled.'[137] Even those who denied
racial continuity to the British asserted a political tradition. Throughout the
eighteenth century, and especially before the divisiveness of 1745, patriots
who were primarily English in their identification harked back to (largely
imaginary) institutions associated as much with ancient Britain as with the
Saxon *witenagemots*. This habit of mind had seventeenth-century sources,
though 1707 gave it new salience. Yet an awareness of 'the Gothic bequest',
an appreciation of 'Saxon liberties', which was even more distinctively a
product of seventeenth-century English thought,[138] would become more
pronounced as the century wore on. At this stage, as Colin Kidd notes,
'Saxonist historiography was not primarily a celebration of ethnicity.
It focused principally on institutions—political, legal and ecclesiastical.
Customs, manners and culture were subordinate considerations, though
the Tacitean inheritance meant that they were always a component part
of the Gothicist package.'[139] Racialized Teutonism would come later; it
was a largely Victorian indulgence.[140] What mattered between 1707 and
1801 was the extent to which, regardless of union, Saxonism provided the
constitutional back-story to the Whig version of history.

English (and some Scottish) Whig historians looked back to Magna
Carta, and beyond that to the Saxon forests, for the origins of a native
liberty which, in their view, continental nations, such as the French, did
not enjoy; but they were more immediately galvanized—'old' as well as
'modern' Whigs—by the seventeenth-century victories of parliament over
the crown. Their accounts of the period were at least as Anglocentric as

Fig. 18. A hundred years since. The prayerbook riots in Edinburgh, 1637. From the 1737 reprint of Robert Burton [= Nathaniel Crouch], *The Wars in England, Scotland, and Ireland* (first published 1681).

that of the Earl of Clarendon, who had his own reasons for discouraging the exiled Charles II (his most important, intended reader) from getting too interested in Irish royalism or relying on Scottish support.[141] This is not to say that only David Hume stood between eighteenth-century readers and ignorance. Nathaniel Crouch, for instance, whom we encountered a few pages back as a chapbook historian of Ireland, published in 1681 *The Wars in England, Scotland and Ireland, ... From the Beginning of the Reign of King Charles I in 1625, to His Majesties happy Restauration, 1660.* This highly successful epitome went through half a dozen editions by the end of the century, and it was reprinted as late as 1737. Illustrations were part of its appeal: Fig. 18 shows how it depicted the prayerbook riots in Scotland. Such eruptions as the 1715 rising recalled English minds to the unfinished business of archipelagic pacification. At such moments, readers would have been receptive to the inclusiveness of works like Edward Ward's *History of the Grand Rebellion* (1713—reprinted in 1715).[142]

That Anglocentric Whig historiography was not unqualified is even more apparent in the writings of Viscount Bolingbroke, the one-time

Jacobite, country-oppositional, philosopher patriot. In his *Letter on the Spirit of Patriotism* and his *Idea of a Patriot King* there is an easy slippage between 'England' and 'Britain' which at first sight seems to promise the occlusion of Scotland and Wales. And it is true that Bolingbroke uses the word 'union' far more often as the opposite of 'faction' than he does to signify state formation. In his *Remarks on the History of England*, published pseudonymously in 1730, however, he is peculiarly thoughtful about British-English issues. His alertness, for instance, to the difficulties that Elizabeth I overcame in her management of Anglo-Scottish relations is heightened by a perception that she faced on British soil the sorts of problems that continental states with common borders were having to deal with in the age of Walpole and that England was being spared by virtue of the union. It is as though looking back to 1707 made Bolingbroke more, not less, analytical about the tessellation of the island. His shrewd, admiring account of the statecraft of Queen Elizabeth ushers in a celebration of 1707 which it is not usual to find in England between the first flush of union panegyric and the Napoleonic wars: 'It is impossible to make these reflections, and not to reflect, at the same time, on that happy change which the union of the two kingdoms has brought about. We are now one nation under one government; and must, therefore, always have one common interest; the same friends, the same foes, the same principles of security, and of danger.'[143]

Bolingbroke's understanding of the importance of 1707, and no doubt his familiarity with the Jacobite networks which ran between France, Scotland, and Ireland,[144] encouraged him to anticipate Hume in foregrounding the British dimension of seventeenth-century English history. The evidence that Bolingbroke draws on was familiar, but he is newly emphatic in arguing that the civil wars arose from a mismanagement of Scottish affairs. At times he reads like a modern historian giving a précis of 'the British problem'. Of the period around the time of Charles I's visit to Edinburgh in 1633 (above, pp. 153–6), he observes: 'Jealousies about religion and liberty were now at their height. The former, as far as they affected the king and his Protestant ministers, were ill-founded; but for that very reason, it would have been easy to cure them; and if they had been cured in time, as we think, on my lord Clarendon's authority, that nothing could have led the Scotch nation into rebellion, so are we persuaded that a great motive and spur to the rebellion in England would have been taken away' (445). As for the imposition of the prayerbook: 'Whilst things were in this situation here, king Charles lighted up another fire in Scotland, by resuming the project of modelling that church, which king James had begun. Archbishop Laud, who had neither temper nor knowledge of the world enough to be intrusted with the government of a private college, conducted this enterprise, and precipitated the public ruin. The puritans of England soon united in a common cause with the puritans of Scotland; and the army, which the latter had raised, marched into England' (446).

Yet Bolingbroke remains, in this as in other ways, something of an exception. English Whig historiography, which shuffled off its revolutionary, martyrological origins and sold widely to the respectable public after 1707[145] remained essentially indifferent to North British and Irish dimensions. To read John Hughes and White Kennett's *A Complete History of England* (1706), Laurence Echard's *The History of England* (1707–18) and *The History of the Revolution, and the Establishment of England, in the Year, 1688* (1725), or John Oldmixon's rather more devolved 1603-George I *History of England* (1730–5)[146] is to find minimal attention even to the 1641 Rising or the Williamite wars in Scotland and Ireland. Proportionately, there is little more in the multi-volume, respected *Histoire de l'Angleterre* (1723–5) written by the Huguenot Paul de Rapin de Thoryas and quickly translated and extended by Nicholas Tindal, even though Rapin had fought in William III's Irish campaign. In all of these works, 1688 rather than 1707 provides the watershed or culmination. The same is true of Catharine Macaulay's *History of England* (1763–83), though her radical, even republican, eagerness to counter Hume makes her more attentive to Scotland and Ireland than other Anglo-Whig historians (she broadly approves of the Covenanters, but agrees with Hume that the 'native Irish' of the mid-century were 'barbarians'). Her formidable, eight-volume *History* concludes with the Revolution, sparing only a line or two for the debate about Anglo-Scottish Union in 1689,[147] though it does more than Hume to follow through the aftermath in Scotland and Ireland. While the Scottish Whig intelligentsia was thinking in European, comparative terms about an Anglo-British history of liberty and improvement, the English focussed on a national destiny that held in orbit around it victory in continental wars and the acquisition of a global empire. It was not until Lord Macaulay—himself, as we have seen, from a Scottish family—that Whig historiography would match David Hume's archipelagic scope.

If Whig England was reluctant to embrace the pluralities of 1707, what of the Welsh literati, so often keen to represent themselves as the old

Britons during the seventeenth century? Anglicization and assimilation to the Henrician union (1536–43) had been going on for generations before the reign of Queen Anne, and there was talk on both sides of the Severn of the English and the Welsh having merged. 'Since the happy incorporation of the Welsh with the English', declared the Welsh historian William Wynne in 1697, 'the History of both Nations as well as the People is united.'[148] Although 1707 could be seen—in the prophetic, retrospective mode of Nehemiah Griffith's *The Leek* (1717)[149]—as the culmination of the old British history, for most anglophone Welsh poets, especially those of a Whig disposition, the Revolution of 1688 and Hanoverian succession of 1714 were more definitive.[150] This remained the prevalent view, though 1714 would lose much of its charge, and, as we shall see, advanced proto-nationalists finessed or passed over the Henrician union. What *did* come to matter about 1707 was the publication in that year of Edward Lhuyd's *Archaeologia Britannica*. This staggeringly erudite work would underpin Welsh historical and literary endeavour later in the century.[151] It gave substance to the Welsh belief that their claim to Britishness derived from antiquity, and not, as could be said of the Scots, from an Act of Parliament passed in 1707.

The currency of Geoffrey of Monmouth, still respected in seventeenth-century Wales despite the scepticism of English scholars, actually enlarged after 1707. Theophilus Evans's defence of Geoffrey's *Historia*, in *Drych y prif oesoedd* (*A Mirror of the First Ages*) (1716, often reprinted), reached large, popular audiences in bilingual as well as Welsh-speaking areas. Meanwhile, an English-language recycling of Geoffrey's narrative, in John Lewis of Llynwene's *History of Great-Britain*, dedicated to Prince Henry *c*.1610, was belatedly published in 1729, while Wynne's revision of David Powel's *Historie of Cambria* (1584) was printed four times between 1697 and 1812. Though Scottish intellectuals abandoned the old, mythical history of their country after 1707, such patriotic antiquarians as Lewis Morris (1701–65)[152] and Evan Evans—Ieuan Fardd, known as Ieuan Brydydd Hir—(1731–88), who corresponded with Gray and Percy (of the *Reliques*), and whose book of translations *Some Specimens of the Poetry of the Antient Welsh Bards* (1764) won the admiration of such exacting readers as Dr Johnson, endorsed Galfridian history.

What led a scholar like Evans to face down the evidence? His attachment to the old stories was reinforced by 'the ill usage our country has of late years received from English writers'. Dilating on this in the preface to his

Love of Our Country: A Poem, with Historical Notes (1773),[153] he fastens on
the slights against the Welsh perpetrated by Lord Lyttelton in his Life of
Henry II.[154] (It made matters worse that Lyttelton had Welsh ancestors
on his mother's side.) Evans defensively explains that he has written his
poem in English rather than Welsh—even though he prefers the work
of the old British bards above that of the best English poets—so as to
be understood by the learned of both countries. From the start, he shows
his attachment to Cambro-Britonic sources. He calls upon his muse to
be inspired by mistletoe, like the Druids of Anglesey when they plumbed
nature's and God's mysteries and 'taught the social duties to mankind' (9). If
these Druids sound more like eighteenth-century philosophers than ancient
Britons, Evans's universalist account of his poem's major topic is even more
of its period: 'Whatever clime we travel or explore, | To love our Country
still is nature's lore'. All peoples are committed to their piece of 'earth',
their 'spot', their 'Country' (10–11). Evans' title-word 'Country' had, by
the 1770s, attractive associations with patriotic, anti-court integrity. Yet it
is likely that he kept writing 'country' rather than 'nation'—a term which
slips into his preface, in an old-fashioned, genealogical sense—because it
better fitted the counties west of the Severn, internally divided and bound
up with England.

   This is not to deny his incipient nationalism. Evans writes with pugna-
cious enthusiasm about ancient British victories ('Whole troops of Saxons
in the field they mow'd, | And stain'd their lances red with hostile blood'),
and when celebrating Owain Glyn Dŵr ('like timorous deer | The coward
English fled, aghast with fear').[155] About Edward I and his tyranny he is (unlike Cottle) indignant. Yet his most anglophobic statement is prompted not
by bloodshed but by historiographical fury at the neglect of Welsh-British
achievements by the English:

> Let England in her Alfred's high renown
> Boast of a monarch worthy of her crown;
> But let not Cambrian science be forgot,
> How Affer taught, how Alfred learning got.
> Monsters ingrate, how can you barbarous call
> The men that taught the brightest of you all?
> The false Historians of a polish'd age,
> Shew that the Saxon has not lost his rage,
> Tho' tam'd by arts, his rancor still remains,
> Beware of Saxons still, ye Cambrian swains.   (15–19)

In line with this, although Evans alludes to Anglo-Welsh union, he subsumes it in the providential liberation of Wales by the coming-to-power of the Tudors (the fulfilment of Galfridian prophecy).

With the advent of Henry VII, the Welsh were released from English rule and governed by one of their own:

> The day of liberty, by heaven design'd,
> At last arose—benevolent and kind—
> The Tudor race, from ancient heroes sprung,
> Of whom prophetic Bards so long had sung,
> Beyond our warmest hopes, the sceptre bore,
> And brought us blessings never known before,
> The English galling yoke they took away,
> And govern'd Britons with the mildest sway.   (25)

There is no attempt to show union unfolding through 1707 into an eighteenth-century imperial state-system in which the Welsh took their place as progenitors and inheritors of Britishness. On the contrary, the Reformation, the most glorious achievement of the Tudors, has been betrayed in Wales by the appointment of English prelates. The established church is overlooking the needs of the Welsh. 'Mourn Cambria! Mourn, thy wretched state deplore!' (26). *State* means 'status' and 'condition', but context makes it resonate with the 'mode of government, statehood' which has reduced Wales to this servitude. Ordinary folk are denied access to the word of God, while overworked curates like the author of the poem go without proper livings.[156]

And it is true that, despite his prestigious connections, Evans's circumstances were bleaker than those of Percy, comfortable in his church career, or Gray, ensconced at Cambridge. Like other Welsh antiquarians during the eighteenth-century Renaissance, he suffered physical and economic hardship as he tracked down and transcribed mouldering manuscripts, retrieving what he could of the remains of ancient Britain. Ground down by his pastoral duties, frustrated by lack of security, and by the failure of patrons to support his work—to love, as he saw it, their country—he was overtaken by alcoholism and isolation. It would take a Fanon to do justice to the connections between Evans's irascible fractiousness (notorious at the time) and his bilingual self-division, his dependent resentment on the English and intense cultural nostalgia combined with resistance to the established order in Wales. The syndrome was even more painful in the case of his friend and successor as translator of the early bards, Edward

Williams or Iolo Morganwg (1747–1826), whose life as a semi-itinerant stone mason was darkened by bereavement, depression, and volatile relationships with friends and patrons, alleviated by laudanum, forgery (of poems 'by Dafydd ap Gwilym'), hopes of emigrating to America, political radicalism and Unitarian religion, and a fascination with invented tradition including fancy-dress Druidism and a revival of the Eisteddfod.[157]

Williams's *Poems, Lyric and Pastoral* (1794) combine quietly conventional but observant accounts of rural life, often translated from his own Welsh, with ambitious, ode-like versions of early Britonic poetry (including the *Gododdin*) and radical, '*Kingflogging* Notes'.[158] In their miscellaneous way, the *Poems* reconstruct Welsh identity, looking for the origins of the nation in the accounts of ancient Britain given by Aneirin and Taliesin rather than in the legends of Geoffrey's *Historia* (dismissed as fabulous in Williams's notes) and the associated myths of Tudor succession and union. The Acts of 1536–43 and 1707 are passed over, and although England is a constant presence, as a country in which the poet has been obliged to ply his trade as a mason, a site of urban estrangement (London) and source of tyranny (especially Edward I), the pull of the English connection is now countered by that of America and its Revolution. Colonized by the Welsh prince Madoc in the twelfth century—as Williams fashionably claims[159] —America now offers a haven to radicals fleeing the deprivations which afflicted the poet's Vale of Glamorgan and South Wales in general from the mid-eighteenth century to the depression of 1829.

When Williams writes about the seventeenth century he puts the complications of multiple monarchy into this transatlantic context. In his 'Address to the Inhabitants of Wales, Exhorting them to Emigrate, with William Penn, to Pennsylvania', the speaker, a Welsh Nonconformist, laments the laws which oppressed Dissenters after the Restoration despite the loyalty of the principality to the Stuarts during the civil wars:

> O! thou, possess'd of BRITAIN's Crown,
> Is gratitude for ever flown
>   From thy relentless heart?
> Has thou forgot how CAMBRIA bled
> For thee, when at thy trampled head
>   The Rebel flung his dart?[160]

Williams admits in his notes that some of the Welsh—Vavasor Powell and the like—had been 'turbulent', but the people had rallied around

Charles II (sic) at the outbreak of the second civil war in 1648, and it was unfair that 'The lash of intolerant laws' should have fallen later on 'many of the most loyal' (50, 56–8). Welsh people became Nonconformists only because the established church was passing through a Laudian phase ('inspired by the true spirit of *Popery*') and because—echoing Evans—it was abandoning their language: 'This execrable policy, of attempting to force the *English language* on the *Welsh*, first occasioned the dissention amongst them, which, as the original cause does still, in a great measure, exist, will in all probability end in their total defection from the Established Church' (54–5).

So Welsh Dissenters should emigrate rather than drag a chain 'in *Slavery's* realm' (59)—that Pennsylvania had been a slave state, that William Penn owned at least a dozen slaves, is an awkwardness suppressed by Williams as an ardent supporter of Wilberforce. The post-Restoration Welsh, including, by implication, those living a century later, should fly to a colony that had almost been named New Wales, it was so thickly populated by Welsh Dissenters. Where Madoc went before, 'BRITAIN's injur'd race' will live like Old Testament patriarchs. What does this have to do with a Welsh identity rooted in the Britishness of the ancient bards? As Williams explains in a footnote (the very length of which is self-proving), the poem contributes to a tradition of complaint against a Britain which betrays the truly British: 'The *Welsh* still retain a lively sensibility of the numerous injuries that they have, through a long succession of ages, experienced from the *Coritani, Belgians, Scots, Picts, Romans, Saxons, Danes, Normans*, &c. &c. and complaints of this nature are, to this day, the frequent themes of the *Ancient British* Muse' (68).

That the eclectic materials of nationalism were starting to come together in Lewis Morris, Evan Evans, and Iolo Morganwg makes it the less surprising that their work should be marked by paradoxes familiar from later, postcolonial experience. England, the wellspring of 'tyranny'—from Edward I to its eighteenth-century legal system, imposed on hapless Wales, in which poor men get no justice—provides the organizing centre against which 'liberty' is defined, as well as being the polity to which Welsh radicalism owes most. Welsh patriotism flourished in a linguistic, social, and economic medium that was heavily anglicized when not primarily English. The London Welsh, for example—through the Society of Ancient Britons, the Honourable Society of Cymmrodorion ('Aborigines') and its successor the Gwyneddigion ('Men of Gwynedd')—fostered the recovery of the

Cambro-Britonic past by providing financial and intellectual resources, and a physical setting in which literati from all over Wales could meet.

In the principality itself, the aspiring gentry, like the 'titan' landowners who were taking over more and more small estates, did not speak Welsh, and regarded the language as backward ('Why should we use or think in such a poor, anonymous tongue?', they asked Lewis Morris, 'English is the language of this kingdom').[161] And yet, like Evans's patron, Sir Watkin Williams Wynn, they could be persuaded that it was noble to have an ancient British heritage. The publication of Evans's *Specimens* was explicitly a Welsh response to the appearance of Macpherson's *Ossian*; it correlates with Percy's *Reliques* (1765) for England and the Scottish borders and Charlotte Brooke's *Reliques* (1789) for Ireland. Across the archipelago, the recovery of antiquity (real and/or forged) reconfigured ownership of Celtic tradition. Making it available in English had complicated effects, at one extreme laying the bases for union by cataloguing shared origins and long-entwined histories, and at the other reinforcing national sentiment in Scotland, Wales, and Ireland by connecting English speakers in those countries with indigenous heritage and displaying to England the ancient pluralities that its imperiousness threatened.

Wales did still count in the historical mythology of Anglo-Britain—more, certainly, than it had during 1603–1707, when the genealogical link between the Stuart monarchs and Margaret Tudor (who had married James IV) and thus the Welsh Tudors hardly registered in England. Indeed, Wales was peculiarly important to the English intelligentsia at a time when ancient Britain, with its Bards, Druids, and Ossianic virtues was being invoked to aid the construction of identities adequate to England's stake in British commercial and imperial grandeur. After 1707, and especially after the mid-century, with the slow, spreading influence of Edward Lhuyd's scholarship—he had, for instance, enhanced the Welsh components in Camden's *Britannia* from 1695—there was a Celticist element in English poetry that went deeper than fashion. This was the period in which Thomas Gray swooned over the poems of Ossian (despite his doubts regarding their authenticity) and researched, with Evans's help, the early British bards—producing such poems and translations as 'The Death of Hoel', 'Caradoc', 'Conan', 'The Triumphs of Owen', and, most notably, 'The Bard'. (Evans repaid the compliment by quoting 'The Bard' in the last line of his 'Paraphrase of Psalm CXXXVII, alluding to the Captivity and Treatment of the Welsh Bards by King Edward I'). It was also the period, after Culloden, in which Collins wrote his 'Ode on the Popular Superstitions of the Highlands of Scotland'.

Celticism was a ramifying phenomenon, not easily confined to the 1750s and 1760s as the older textbooks would have it but running into many areas of Romantic-period writing.[162] We find some of the beginnings here of the synthesizing of 'Saxon' with 'Celtic' traits that Arnold would influentially claim as the pedigree of English culture in his Oxford lectures *On the Study of Celtic Literature* (1867), but it was inextricable at this date from the reception of Lluyd, Lewis Morris, and Evans, in other words from the 'Cambrian' input into Anglo-British identity formation. I have argued that, in Wales itself, 1707 was not thought of as a turning point, at least as the century went on. When we consider the contribution of Welsh looking back (i.e. to ancient Britain) to the repertoire of Anglo-British identifications, however, we are faced with the question of whether the effects of 1707 were not played out some forty or fifty years later, in England as in Scotland.

I shall pursue that question in a moment. More immediately, it is worth stressing that this mid-century context was the setting in which Thomas Warton produced the first large-scale survey of 'Eng. Lit.', in his *History of English Poetry*.[163] As a young man, Warton edited an anthology called *The Union* (1753). Ostensibly published in Edinburgh, by a certain Archibald Monro and David Murray, but actually produced in Oxford, this was a gathering of work by English and Scottish poets. Though Warton's preface is reticent, *The Union* was presumably published to mark the hundred and fiftieth anniversary of the regal union (its more immediate envelope would be moderate English reaction against the brutal 'pacification' of Scotland, which went on for several years after Culloden). It opens with a lightly anglicized version of Dunbar's 'The Thistle and the Rose', which commended, a hundred years before James VI became James I, the marriage between James IV of Scotland and Margaret Tudor. Though it showcases a number of English poems, including Collins's 'Ode to Evening' and that sounding of deep England, Gray's 'Elegy', it also includes among contemporary works Collins's elegy on Thomson, 'In yonder grave a Druid lies', and Smollett's 'The Tears of Scotland'. Warton even signalled—with donnish indirectness—his liking for Scottish poetry by including two works of his own attributed to 'a late member of the university of Aberdeen, whose modesty would not permit us to print his name'.[164]

Warton's scholarship was not yet equal to the ambitions announced by his preface: '[*The Union*] contains [an] Intermixture of poems both Scotch and English. Nor is this variety less agreeable than useful; as from it, we have an opportunity of forming a comparison and estimate of the taste and genius of the two different nations'. Three of the poems in Scots are drawn from Allan Ramsay's readily available *Ever Green*, and one of them is comically entitled 'The Eagle and Robin Red-breast... by Mr Archibald Scott', a misunderstanding of the ascription in *Ever Green* to 'AR. SCOT.'—i.e., Allan Ramsay, the Scot.[165] On the other hand, *The Union* goes beyond Ramsay's selection to include (pioneeringly for an English anthology) part of Lindsay's 'The Dream',[166] and little scholarly attention had been given to the older Scots poets north of the border, never mind south. Twenty years later, in his *History of English Poetry*, Warton could still lament the lack of an adequately researched account of medieval 'Scotch poetry'. It would not be produced until the mid-Victorian period.[167]

Why would that concern him? When he came to write his *History*, he was almost as reluctant as he had been in 1753 to do without Scottish—and indeed Welsh—perspectives. Like Gray, who bequeathed him his plan (itself derived from Pope) for a systematic English literary history,[168] and who was most engaged with Ossian, Evans's *Specimens*, and Old Norse poetry when preparing to write that history, Warton felt driven to be comparative in his reconstruction of the genealogy of English letters. If he was to be convincingly historical, he could no longer—like his predecessors—construct the English literary past out of catalogues of national worthies, county histories, *Spectator* essays, and the like.[169] In any case, his educated, Tory cultural politics were set against narrow, Whig Englishness.[170] Volume I of the *History* thus starts with an ambitious dissertation on the origins of romance; it gives the Welsh a leading role by arguing that Brittany (Armorica), invaded by the Britons—soon to be Cambrians—after the departure of the Romans, was the route through which Arab romantic motifs made their way into insular literature. Geoffrey of Monmouth, with his dragons in the oriental style and legend of Arthur as a once and future king, is a product of this interface, which makes his account of Britain entirely different from that of the early British bards. (Though Warton is sceptical about Geoffrey, he footnotes Lewis Morris's belief that the *History* is based on a venerable British source, still extant in Welsh.) As for the roots of Eng. Lit., no one should look for those in the Saxon period. A distinctive English poetry emerges only once Saxon culture—succumbing to Norman influence before the conquest—had been fertilized by French.

Scottish writing, equally, cannot be excluded. Warton includes a substantial discussion of Barbour and Blind Harry, and he begins a three-chapter 'Digression' on Dunbar and other late medieval 'Scotch poets' by declaring: 'when I consider the close and national connection between England and Scotland in the progress of manners and literature, I am sensible I should be guilty of a partial and defective representation of the poetry of the former, was I to omit in my series a few Scotch writers, who have adorned the present period, with a degree of sentiment and spirit, a command of phraseology, and a fertility of imagination, not to be found in any English poet since Chaucer and Lydgate.'[171] One can only speculate on how Warton would have dealt with such anglicized Scottish poets as Drummond and Alexander, had he taken his *History*, as his full title promised, *to the Commencement of the Eighteenth Century* (which sounds more like 1707 than 1700—going back, in fact, to the priorities established by *The Union*).[172] What is clear from his monumental study, is that the *English* invention of English literature, had, like the Scottish phase under Adam Smith and Hugh Blair, a British dimension.

(iv) Saxon and North Briton

We have found some reasons for believing that 1707 did not play out in Scotland until after the Battle of Culloden. No such claim could be made for Ireland—1707 did not even arrive in 1801—and in Wales the idea of union had another historical trajectory. (For related reasons, 1745 had little impact west of the Severn. Despite the cultural Jacobitism that was active especially in north-east Wales, the principality remained passive while Bonnie Prince Charlie marched south[173] not least because he could not offer undoing union as the incentive it was in Scotland.) In England the literary evidence points to a reaction against 1707 after the '45—against which the young Warton of *The Union* in turn reacted—though the rising was more often a trigger, and sometimes just a pretext, for anti-Scottish rhetoric than a lasting cause of genuine anxiety. We saw in Chapters 2 and 9 how Scotophobia boiled up in London when James VI's followers arrived there and when Lauderdale was promoted by Charles II. After 1707, the growing visibility of Scotsmen in business, politics, and the arts made

them targets of resentment.[174] Opposition to the government fastened
on the conspicuous Scottishness of courtiers and ministers, and radicals
began to attack the cultural elites by saying that they were pro-Scottish as
well as treacherously Frenchified—an old pairing of prejudices, the more
plausible after 1745 because of the Jacobite connection. As Jim Smyth puts
it: 'English antipathy towards the Scots peaked between the mid-1740s,
when many—quite inaccurately—equated Jacobite rebellion with Scottish
treason, and the 1760s, when the Wilkesite opposition stigmatised the king's
first minister, the Earl of Bute—a Scottish peer who gloried in the surname
of Stuart!—as a conspirator against English liberty.'[175]

The dispute was noisily thrashed out between the government-sponsored
journal, *The Briton*, edited by Smollett, and John Wilkes's and Charles
Churchill's outrageously satirical *North Briton*. The latter repeatedly pushes
its animus back to 1707, the year when the English had made the mistake of
giving the Scots a claim on their affairs. As an imaginary Scotsman explains
in issue number 4:

We found our right to sharing every thing in common with the English on
the *Union*, and we justify our endeavouring to engross every thing to our
own use, on the common principles of prudence, which teaches every man
to do as well for himself as he can. Whatever inequality there might have
been before the *Union* was completed, it afterwards intirely ceased, and we
were all upon a level. Our national weakness and poverty might perhaps
have been well and properly argued to prevent that treaty from taking place;
but after the conclusion of it they can never be given as reasons for our not
turning it as much as possible to our own advantage. The *Union* indeed was
not of our seeking; we opposed it with our whole force, for we considered
it as contrary to the *dignity* and *interest* of our nation. Notwithstanding the
specious pretences on which that treaty was grounded, and the seeming
equity and impartiality with which it was planned and conducted, we could
not persuade ourselves but the weaker nation would in the common course
of things be swallowed up in the stronger, and our *most antient* kingdom by
degrees become a province of England. These were our apprehensions, and
on these we grounded our opposition. If time has proved our error, if things
have taken a quite different turn, if through the great parts of our glorious
countryman [the Earl of Bute], and our own supple behaviour, dissimulation,
and temporizing, we have turned the Union to our own advantage; if we
see ourselves arrived at the height of our wishes, and consider England as a
country intended for our use and refreshment, where we may revel at large,
and scorn to ask the lordly owners leave; if this is the case, the English must
thank themselves for it. They made the *Union*, and can have no right to

complain of the consequences of it; they laid these advantages open to us, and as we have had the address to obtain, I trust we shall have the resolution to preserve them.[176]

This is witty, accomplished propaganda: clever in not seeming too clever, not spinning into self-hatred like Swift; effective in turning to advantage so much that was historically true about Scottish reluctance in 1707, and in avoiding national stereotyping. Granted, the Scots, by the persona's admission, are supple, dissimulating, and temporizing—but who would not willingly be so in pursuit of such sensible ambitions? The English, not the Scots, are made the fools of this anti-Scottish passage.

Wilkes and Churchill could be more scurrilously direct. The latter's mock pastoral, *The Prophecy of Famine* (1763), starts from the same predicates as issue 4 of *The North Briton* but then rounds on the starveling disloyalty of typecast, alien Scots:

> JOCKEY, whose manly high-bon'd cheeks to crown
> With freckles spotted flam'd the golden down,
> With mickle art, could on the bagpipes play,
> E'en from the rising to the setting day;
> SAWNEY as long without remorse could bawl
> HOME'S madrigals, and ditties from FINGAL: ...
>   Far as the eye could reach, no tree was seen,
> Earth, clad in russet, scorn'd the lively green.
> The plague of Locusts they secure defy ...[177]

Scotland is a waste of heather relieved only by 'one white rose'—the stubborn emblem of Jacobitism (15). 1707 was not the end of that, any more than 1745. As Scott's *Redgauntlet* (1824) reminds us, Jacobite disaffection smouldered on in the 1760s. Among works written at the time, Smollett's *Humphrey Clinker* (1771), the most genially pan-British, unionist novel of the century, has the Scottish officer Lismahago argue at cogent, intransigent length against 1707 and its consequences. 'Black be the day that e'er to England's ground | Scotland was eikit by the UNION's bond', wrote Fergusson a couple of years later.[178]

The staunchest English reply to Churchill came in John Langhorne's *Genius and Valour* (1763), a poem which does not just rebut the libels of *The Prophecy of Famine* but reminds its readers of the turbulence created by divisions within Britain in the seventeenth century, and climaxes in a

eikit: added

celebration of 1707 which recycles the topics employed by Thomson as well as those favoured by Tate and Fenton:

> Hail, ANNA, hail! O may each Muse divine
> With Wreaths eternal grace thy holy Shrine.
> Grav'd on thy Tomb this sacred Verse remain,
> This Verse more sweet than Conquest's sounding Strain:
> 'She bade the Rage of hostile Nations cease,
> 'The glorious Arbitress of Europe's Peace.'
> She, thro' whose Bosom roll'd the vital Tide
> Of BRITAIN'S Monarchs in one Stream allied,
> Clos'd the long Jealousies of different Sway,
> And saw united Sister-Realms obey.[179]

Queen Anne was the confluence of Stuart and Williamite legitimacy, but also the summation of British royal history looking back to whenever. On the back of union, Langhorne goes on to remind us, talking like a Scotsman—and his work had its adherents in North Britain[180]—came peace, and with that commerce, industry, and empire (16–17).

English detractors of the Scots, by no means confined to the Wilkesites, could turn these very 'improvements' to prejudicial effect, crediting Scottish progress to the anglicizing effects of 1707. Dr Johnson repeatedly said this, apparently not just to annoy Boswell.[181] When the Great Cham was in this vein (and he could also show respect for the old ways of the Highlands), 'the Union' was not so much an event which had changed Anglo-Scottish relations as a state of affairs which acted as a constant reminder of the socio-economic inferiority that had driven the Scots to accept the Treaty. Such people, Langhorne believes, should acknowledge the merits of Scottish heroes from Wallace to the 3rd Duke of Argyll and Lord Bute. It might be incidental that Langhorne was a Westmoreland poet (as well as eager for noble patronage). More likely, his interest in the Scots was fed by some of the regional factors which went into the building of union.[182] Three kingdom-, or four nation-, approaches should never neglect proximity.

Among the radicals there was a hardening of Saxonism. The patriotic opposition of the 1720s and 1730s had engaged in a moderate revival of seventeenth-century, Harringtonian, 'country' policies.[183] The disaffected now reverted to the hard-line doctrine of 'the Norman Yoke', which had taken hold among Levellers in the 1640s.[184] Wilkesites claimed to be reviving the ancient liberties of the English, quashed by the Norman

Conquest. 1066 and all that. If William had brought in royal and aristocratic abuses from the very country (France) which now stood for popery and wooden shoes, Bute was set on imposing a 'Scottish Yoke'.[185] Despite the willingness of the Wilkesites to exploit an ethnic, proto-racialized, belief in English superiority over their British and Irish neighbours,[186] the reaction to Saxonist rhetoric west of the Severn, where politicians had long stood as 'Freeborn Englishmen', was limited. No Welsh Bute provided a focus for English antagonism. And Evan Lloyd, the Merioneth-born poet who was imprisoned along with Wilkes, claimed that the radical leader had 'a thousand well-wishers among the hills of Wales'.[187] The effect on Anglo-Scottish relations was, however, damaging (especially for Scots living in London) as the Wilkesites waged cultural war. The poems of Ossian, for example, whose appearance in 1760–3 (and subsequent dedication to Bute) coincided with the resurgence of Saxonism, were either denounced as forgeries, typical of the mendacious Scots, or travestied as emblems of the backwardness of the north. Bute and the Tories were polarized against Saxon, populist Englishness.[188]

Are we witnessing here the emergence of a full-blown English nationalism to parallel developments in France and Germany? Was *that* the late, unexpected offspring of 1707? According to Gerald Newman, England is a paradigmatic case of the 'renewal' nationalism that advances by looking back. Radicals reviled the elite as Francophile as well as Caledonian, inheritors of Norman privilege. 'By 1789', he declares, 'the making of English nationalism was over. All its ideological elements were in place, its cultural realization was well under way. The following half-century ... saw the natural unfolding of much of its moral, social, aesthetic, political and intellectual program into the realities of Victorian Britain.'[189] There are problems with Newman's account, from his simplifying insistence that 'the "theory of the Norman Yoke" is *the theory of the English nation!*' (190), through his contention that the idea of English national character derived from the 'literary concept of the "Noble Savage"' and cohered around 'Sincerity' (127),[190] to issues of chronology.[191] Most intractable is his repeated confounding of English with British patriotism. Yet this is almost unavoidable given that 'renewal' nationalism was, as he says, inextricable in the English case from what historians of the subject call 'territorial' nationalism—the geopolitical dominance which led Welsh, Scottish, and to some extent Irish patterns of self-definition to be hyphenated into or modelled upon resurgent Englishness. And beyond that—in theory, a slightly different phenomenon—is the interference generated by the synthesizing growth of Britishness, because, by general (though not universal) consent, the period which Newman identifies as establishing English national identity was also the period in which various modes of Britishness claimed widespread allegiance even in England.

It is not the aim of this epilogue to open another front in the strenuous dispute among historians and literary scholars about how far and by what means British identities were diffused around the islands over the eighteenth century. My focus has been more narrowly on how 1603–1707, and especially 1707, played into and were constructed in the period. A great deal of analysis would be needed to arbitrate between the view of Linda Colley, on the one hand, that a British identity was spreading even at popular levels as an effect of wars against Catholic France[192]—an account which tends to discount divisions within British Protestantism, not to mention the anti-British turn which Protestant patriotism showed in Ireland[193]—and, on the other, that of Murray Pittock, who has emphasized how many people in Britain and Ireland remained outside the established churches, were Gaelic or Welsh speaking, and/or Jacobite, and thus not readily assimilable to the Anglo-British story of state formation that may be latent even in the ostensibly neutral structuring of this chapter around 1707, 1745, 1801, and 1829.[194]

Britishness in the period 1707–1829 is so complicated by the emergence of modern, culturally driven nationalism, through both older archipelagic, and newer imperial and unionist, structures, that it is impossible to generalize about how literature was implicated. Early on, a shift is announced by the pro-union writing of Nahum Tate and James Thomson. At the end of the period, a horizon is set by the poetry of Felicia Hemans, which is patriotically stirred by Wallace, bardic Wales, the stately homes of England, and the sorrows of Erin. The mobility of Hemans's sympathies was encouraged by the shifts in her life between Liverpool, Gwrych, Bronwylfa, and Dublin, but it was underpinned by a liberal nationalism that fed off and against imperial unionism, Catholic emancipation, and nascent arguments for home rule. With that structure we are passing beyond the archipelagic formations of 1603–1707.

Meanwhile, we should remember Wilkes, Churchill, Evans, and Lismahago, and not take the inclusive, tolerant antiquarianism of Gray, Collins, and Warton as representative. Howard Weinbrot's influential account of

Britishness as 'a *concordia discors*' is too dependent on such figures, too unsplit and harmonious:

> Britons define their constitution, drama, and language ... as mixed entities appropriate for a mixed people. This mixing nevertheless preserves roles for component parts that make up the whole. Celtic imagination, Anglo-Saxon liberty, classical Roman constraint, of course together with Christian and Hebrew contexts and spirituality, make their mark and contributions. Poets could pick and choose from a variety of riches to make a yet richer product. Collins' classically regular odes include Celtic rural mythology; Gray's sublime Pindarics include a Welsh heroine; Macpherson's northern epic uses both Hebrew and Greek poetic devices.[195]

This is not all wrong, but it betrays its anachronistic assumptions by adopting a consumerist idiom of mixing, choice, and wealth. The contradictions in Macpherson, Highland MP for a Cornish constituency, cultural-Jacobite unionist and 'primitivist' favourite of Whig, commercial Edinburgh, go deeper than Weinbrot admits—and they help explain why Ossian has still not been assimilated to Eng. Lit.[196] As Evan Evans and Iolo Morganwg equally show, the Anglo-Welsh crossing points within Britishness could be conflicted, full of resistance and resentment.

So the official, top-line narrative that can be taken from the panegyrics on 1707 through the unionism of Smollett's journalism and fiction is only part of the story. It needs to be read against the tensions which run through the work of a writer such as Burns, radical but with Jacobite hankerings, willing to denounce 1707 but respectful, in poems like 'The Solemn League and Covenant', of the patriotic unionism of the seventeenth century. In Ireland, there was a legacy of division—after the 1690s more religious than ethnic—which British identity-building could do little to penetrate,[197] especially in the absence of union. This reinforced insularity and ossification, reflected in the historiography. Only the most radical patriots of the 1780s, such as the Ulster Presbyterian William Drennan, were willing to urge fellow-Protestants to reject 'the refined delusion of history' which told them of their 'relationship with the Saxon *Alfred ... Hampden, ... and Sidney*' when they were in reality 'all *native Irish*, under the controul of an *English pale*'.[198] In his celebrated lyric 'Erin' (1795), an answer to 'Rule Britannia', Drennan, by then a United Irishman, has a feminized Ireland even-handedly denounce the bloodshed of the seventeenth century ('O, sons of green Erin! lament o'er the time | When religion was—war, and our country—a crime') and blame Britain for the divisions which persist:

'Drive the Demon of Bigotry home to his den, | And where Britain made brutes, now let Erin make men!'[199] This is a striking rebuttal of the 'British' identification among Ulster Protestants which ran back to the plantation of 1609 (above, p. 24). Yet in Ireland, even more than elsewhere, union and a sense of Britishness were distinct, though overlapping, phenomena. After 1801 the patriotic Drennan came to accept the union he had opposed in the 1790s.

Even when the exceptions and the counter-flows are given full weight, however, there is plenty of literary and historical evidence that, as compared with 1603–1707, when Britishness (outside the borders of Wales, where it meant something very particular) was largely a royalist or pan-Presbyterian project, imposed and unevenly taken up, the period between 1707 and 1829 saw British identities emerging more strongly. (It might be more accurate to write of British *identifications* being made, associated with old ethnicities, with hallowed, often legendary history, and with aspirations to empire, commerce, and modernity.) These new varieties of Britishness, especially attractive to Lowland Scots, were the product of opportunities created by union as well as inherited assumptions. They were also qualified by nationalisms—at this date, we can legitimately begin to speak of 'the four nations'—which put on the guise of antiquity. Within their diversity they developed at different rates between social groups and institutions (as in the seventeenth century, the Scottish nobility and the British armed forces led the way). It also seems clear, despite recent claims to the contrary, that Britishness had limited purchase in Ireland before 1801, that the psychology of war (against America, as against France) broke down English/British distinctions within England even while it heightened the patriotic appeal of both affiliations, that belief in the advantages of union did not preclude patriotic, even nationalist, sentiment (which returns us to Sir Walter Scott), that regional forcefields of Britishness were encouraged—far more than in the seventeenth century—by commerce (as in the triangulation of Glasgow, Belfast, and the textile towns of Lancashire), and that the extravagant growth of empire transformed Anglo-British as well as Scottish and Irish identities more extensively than we yet understand.

I have set out those conclusions on a scale that runs between factors already active in 1603–1707 and those more characteristic of later decades. Despite the continuities, more than enough points cluster at the latter end of the list to show that it makes sense for *Archipelagic English* to end with 1707—which cannot mean *in* 1707, since the implications of the Treaty, and its lasting importance, were in key respects only realized later, and in different ways around the archipelago. The literary response to Anglo-Scottish union was initially superficial: a flurry of panegyrics in London, a stirring of resentment in Dublin. It did not appear at the time to create a cultural watershed, and, across much of the archipelago, the impact of 1707 would remain limited. The union did, however, have transformative, belated effects on particular zones and sites (Edinburgh being the pre-eminent case), and the literary consequences of that could be immense. It made for vibrant innovation in certain genres and modes of enquiry, catalysing, for example, the historiography of the Scottish Enlightenment, and encouraging the scholars who invented 'Eng. Lit.' both north and south of the border to recognize—what is now even more the case—that the subject can neither be defined, nor anglophone literature be historically understood, along purely national lines.

Notes

CHAPTER I

1. See Tom Nairn's pioneering study, *The Break-Up of Britain: Crisis and Neo-Nationalism* (London: New Left Books, 1977).

2. To review the work that runs from e.g. Peter Hulme, *Colonial Encounters: Europe and the Native Caribbean 1492–1797* (London: Methuen, 1986) through and beyond Jonathan Hart's *Columbus, Shakespeare, and the Interpretation of the New World* (Basingstoke: Palgrave, 2003) would require another book.

3. E.g. David Armitage, 'Literature and Empire', in Nicholas Canny (ed.), *The Origins of Empire: British Overseas Enterprise to the Close of the Seventeenth Century*, Oxford History of the British Empire, 1 (Oxford: Oxford University Press, 1998), 99–123, esp. pp. 102–5.

4. E.g. Willy Maley, *Salvaging Spenser: Colonialism, Culture and Identity* (Basingstoke: Macmillan, 1997); Terence Hawkes, 'Bryn Glas', in Ania Loomba and Martin Orkin (eds.), *Postcolonial Shakespeares* (London: Routledge, 1998), 117–40.

5. But see e.g. Bernard Bailyn, *The Peopling of British North America: An Introduction* (New York: Knopf, 1986); Bernard Bailyn and Philip Morgan (eds.), *Strangers within the Realm: Cultural Margins of the First British Empire* (Chapell Hill, NC: University of North Carolina Press, 1991); and Mark Netzloff, 'Writing Britain from the Margins: Scottish, Irish and Welsh Projects for American Colonization', *Prose Studies*, 25/2 (2002): 1–24.

6. See below, pp. 361–2, 401–3.

7. See e.g. D. J. Palmer, *The Rise of English Studies: An Account of the Study of English Language and Literature from its Origins to the Making of the Oxford English School* (London: Oxford University Press for the University of Hull, 1965); Franklin E. Court, *Institutionalizing English Literature: The Culture and Politics of Literary Study, 1750–1900* (Stanford: Stanford University Press, 1992); also Robert Crawford, *Devolving English Literature* (Oxford: Clarendon, 1992), 41–4; and Cairns Craig, 'The Study of Scottish Literature', in Ian Brown (gen. ed.), *The Edinburgh History of Scottish Literature*, 3 vols. (Edinburgh: Edinburgh University Press, 2006), I, 16–31, pp. 25–30.

8. Masson was an advocate of Burns and Scott, and analyst of Scottish identity. In seventeenth-century scholarship, note his *Life of John Milton: Narrated in*

Connexion with the Political, Ecclesiastical and Literary History of his Time, 6 vols. (London: Macmillan, 1859–94), his edn. of Milton's *Poetical Works*, 2 vols. (London: Macmillan, 1874, [rev. 1882]), *Drummond of Hawthornden: The Story of his Life and Writings* (London: Macmillan, 1873), and the essays on 'King James's Farewell to Holyrood' and the 'Proposed Memorial to Drummond' in his *Edinburgh Sketches and Memories* (London: A. and C. Black, 1892).

9. Robert Chambers (ed.), *Cyclopaedia of English Literature: A History, Critical and Biographical, of British Authors, from the Earliest to the Present Times*, 2 vols. (Edinburgh: William and Robert Chambers, 1844).

10. See James A. Secord, *Victorian Sensation: The Extraordinary Publication, Reception, and Secret Authorship of 'Vestiges of the Natural History of Creation'* (Chicago: University of Chicago Press, 2000).

11. David Patrick, 'Preface', in idem. (ed.), *Chambers's Cyclopaedia of English Literature*, 3 vols., rev. edn. (London and Edinburgh: W. and R. Chambers, 1901–3), I, v–x, pp. viii–ix; cf. 831–2.

12. Gerald Graff, *Professing Literature: An Institutional History* (Chicago: Chicago University Press, 1987), chs. 5–8; Chris Baldick, *The Social Mission of English Criticism, 1848–1932* (Oxford: Clarendon, 1983), chs. 3–4.

13. Among publications by members of the committee note Ernest de Selincourt's *English Poets and the National Ideal: Four Lectures* (Oxford: Clarendon, 1915), with its rousing account of Shakespeare's history plays and Milton's love of liberty, and Sir Arthur Quiller-Couch's wartime lectures on 'Literature and Patriotism', in his *Studies in Literature* (Cambridge: Cambridge University Press, 1918), which contrast statist, autocratic German nationalism with local, rural, irreverent Englishness—and which, with a negligence that is indeed very English, incorporate Irish and Scottish song. Even George Sampson's *English for the English: A Chapter on National Education* (Cambridge: Cambridge University Press, 1921), which is primarily committed to ending Gradgrindish teaching in the elementary schools, makes claims for what English can give the nation, and starts from the pride in native literary achievement expressed by Mulcaster's *Elementarie*. On the Englishing of English at this date, see Balz Engler, 'Englishness and English Studies', in Balz Engler and Renate Haas (eds.), *European English Studies: Contributions Towards the History of a Discipline* (Leicester: English Association for ESSE, 2000), 335–48; more polemically, Brian Doyle, *English and Englishness* (London: Routledge, 1989), esp. ch. 2.

14. Corkery's valuable, though romanticized, account of the survival of Gaelic literature and culture, *The Hidden Ireland: A Study of Gaelic Munster in the Eighteenth Century* (Dublin: Gill, 1925) starts from the period covered by this book. His view of what was acceptably 'Irish' and nationalist in anglophone writing is clearest in *Synge and Anglo-Irish Literature* (Cork: Cork University Press, 1931). For contexts see Colin Graham, 'Literary Historiography,

1890–2000', in Margaret Kelleher and Philip O'Leary (eds.), *The Cambridge History of Irish Literature*, 2 vols. (Cambridge: Cambridge University Press, 2006), II, 562–98.

15. Cf. Peter Mandler, *The English National Character: The History of an Idea from Edmund Burke to Tony Blair* (New Haven, CT: Yale University Press, 2006), 148.

16. See Cairns Craig, 'The Criticism of Scottish Literature: Tradition, Decline and Renovation', in Brown (gen. ed.), *Edinburgh History of Scottish Literature*, III, 42–52.

17. The advanced teaching of Anglo-Welsh literature began with Raymond Garlick at Trinity College Carmarthen during the 1960s, and with Ned Thomas's more international, even postcolonial slant at University of Wales, Aberystwyth. The field was consolidated in the early 1980s with the setting up of the Association for the Study of Welsh Writing in English. AWE has held annual conferences, managed a programme of publications, and seeks to influence the policies of devolved government in Wales. (M. Wynn Thomas, personal communication.)

18. A chair of 'Scottish History and Scottish Literature' was established at Glasgow University in 1912 (pre-dated by a Chair in Celtic at Edinburgh, 1882, and by the study of Celtic literature at Glasgow from 1901), but departments specializing in Scots and Anglo-Scottish texts would not emerge until the 1950s and 1960s.

19. Eliot's review of Herbert Grierson's edn. of *Metaphysical Lyrics and Poems of the Seventeenth Century: Donne to Butler* is reprinted in his *Selected Essays*, 3rd edn. (London: Faber, 1951), along with such related pieces as 'Andrew Marvell' and 'John Dryden'.

20. See e.g. T. S. Eliot, *The Varieties of Metaphysical Poetry: The Clark Lectures at Trinity College, Cambridge, 1926 and the Turnbull Lectures at the Johns Hopkins University, 1933*, ed. Ronald Schuchard (London: Faber, 1993).

21. David Goldie, *A Critical Difference: T. S. Eliot and John Middleton Murry in English Literary Criticism, 1919–1928* (Oxford: Clarendon, 1998), 49–60, cites T. E. Hulme and Yeats, among others. For an earlier, Scottish example see David Masson, *British Novelists and Their Styles* (Cambridge: Macmillan, 1859), 84.

22. For contexts see Steve Ellis, *The English Eliot: Design, Language and Landscape in 'Four Quartets'* (London: Routledge, 1991), chs. 2–3.

23. See e.g. *Notes Towards the Definition of Culture* (London: Faber, 1948) which insists on the 'great advantage for English culture to be constantly influenced from Scotland, Ireland and Wales' (55) under the chapter title 'Unity and Diversity: The Region'.

24. This is the centrepiece essay in F. R. Leavis, *Education and the University: A Sketch for an 'English School'* (London: Chatto and Windus, 1943).

25. Historically discontinuous, linguistically divided, and often religiously pre-occupied, seventeenth-century Scottish literature could hardly be expected to meet Leavisite requirements for maturity, felt life, and organic tradition. (The same holds for anglophone Irish literature, only more so.) The major Leavisite studies—John Speirs, *The Scots Literary Tradition* (1940), 2nd edn. (London: Faber and Faber, 1962) and David Craig's *Scottish Literature and the Scottish People 1680–1831* (London: Chatto and Windus, 1961)—say virtually nothing about the period.

26. See, respectively, Owen Dudley Edwards, *Macaulay* (London: Weidenfeld and Nicolson, 1988), Macaulay's 1828 review essay 'History', and Jane Millgate, *History and Politics: Macaulay and Ireland* (Toronto: University of Toronto Press, 1973).

27. J. W. Burrow, *A Liberal Descent: Victorian Historians and the English Past* (Cambridge: Cambridge University Press, 1981), Timothy Lang, *The Victorians and the Stuart Heritage: Interpretations of a Discordant Past* (Cambridge: Cambridge University Press, 1995).

28. For his use of the term see e.g. 'The Literature of Britain: A Speech Delivered at the Opening of the Edinburgh Philosophical Institution on the 4th of November 1846'.

29. Macaulay made his name with his 1825 essay on Milton in the *Edinburgh Review*; a stream of pieces on Bacon, Dryden, Bunyan, William Temple, and others followed; on India see his notorious 'Minute on Indian Education' (1835) and Guari Viswanathan, *Masks of Conquest: Literary Studies and British Rule in India* (London: Faber, 1990); on the civil service exam, see e.g. Baldick, *Social Mission of English Criticism*, 70–2.

30. *History of the Great Civil War*, 3 vols. (London: Longmans, Green, 1886–91), *The History of the Commonwealth and Protectorate*, 3 vols. (London: Longmans, Green, 1894–1903), brought to completion by C. H. Firth, *The Last Years of the Protectorate, 1656–1568*, 2 vols. (London: Longmans, Green, 1909).

31. John Morrill, 'The War(s) of the Three Kingdoms', in Glen Burgess (ed.), *The New British History: Founding a Modern State 1603–1715* (London: Tauris, 1999), 65–91. Cf. Michael Bentley, *Modernizing England's Past: English Historiography in the Age of Modernism, 1870–1970* (Cambridge: Cambridge University Press, 2005).

32. On these trends towards Anglocentrism see also Alastair MacLachlan, *The Rise and Fall of Revolutionary England: An Essay on the Fabrication of Seventeenth-Century History* (Basingstoke: Macmillan, 1996).

33. See his 'Thinking about the New British History', in David Armitage (ed.), *British Political Thought in Literature, History and Theory* (Cambridge: Cambridge University Press, 2006), 23–46, pp. 33–4, essentially an update of 'War(s) of the Three Kingdoms'.

34. On the limits of Hill's gazetteer see MacLachlan, *Rise and Fall of Revolutionary England*, 72, 125 and on Stone's, Morrill, 'War(s) of the Three Kingdoms', 72.

35. See esp. David Loewenstein and Janel Mueller (eds.), *The Cambridge History of Early Modern English Literature* (Cambridge: Cambridge University Press, 2002).

36. About two-thirds of the population of Britain and Ireland spoke English or Scots in 1500; by 1700, though the proportion able to speak the Celtic tongues remained high, a knowledge of English or Scots was universal among the educated and propertied. Having said that, now four times the size of Wales, Ireland, and Scotland combined, the population of England, even in the early eighteenth century, after destructive wars in Ireland, was only roughly equal to the total of those other countries combined.

37. See esp. Richard Helgerson, *Forms of Nationhood: The Elizabethan Writing of England* (Chicago: University of Chicago Press, 1992); Claire McEachern, *The Poetics of English Nationhood* (Cambridge: Cambridge University Press, 1996); Maley, *Salvaging Spenser*; Andrew Hadfield, *Edmund Spenser's Irish Experience: Wilde Fruit and Salvage Soyl* (Oxford: Clarendon, 1997) and *Shakespeare, Spenser and the Matter of Britain* (Basingstoke: Macmillan, 2004); Christopher Highley, *Shakespeare, Spenser, and the Crisis in Ireland* (Cambridge: Cambridge University Press, 1997); Andrew Murphy, *But the Irish Sea Betwixt Us: Ireland, Colonialism, and Renaissance Literature* (Lexington: University of Kentucky Press, 1999); Tristan Marshall, *Theatre and Empire: Great Britain on the London Stages under James VI and I* (Manchester: Manchester University Press, 2000); Richard A. McCabe, *Spenser's Monstrous Regiment: Elizabethan Ireland and the Poetics of Difference* (Oxford: Oxford University Press, 2002); Joan Fitzpatrick, *Shakespeare, Spenser, and the Contours of Britain: Reshaping the Atlantic Archipelago* (Hatfield: University of Hertfordshire Press, 2004); Philip Schwyzer, *Literature, Nationalism, and Memory in Early Modern England and Wales* (Cambridge: Cambridge University Press, 2004).

38. Peter Davidson (ed.), *Poetry and Revolution: An Anthology of British and Irish Verse 1625–1660* (Oxford: Clarendon, 1998); Jane Stevenson and Peter Davidson (eds.), *Early Modern Women Poets (1520–1700): An Anthology* (Oxford: Oxford University Press, 2001), and Andrew Carpenter (ed.), *Verse in English from Tudor and Stuart Ireland* (Cork: Cork University Press, 2003).

39. Deana Rankin, *Between Spenser and Swift: English Writing in Seventeenth-Century Ireland* (Cambridge: Cambridge University Press, 2005); cf. Anne Fogarty, 'Literature in English, 1550–1690: From the Elizabethan Settlement to the Battle of the Boyne', in Kelleher and O'Leary (eds.), *Cambridge History of Irish Literature*, I, 140–90.

40. David Baker, *Between Nations: Shakespeare, Spenser, Marvell, and the Question of Britain* (Stanford: Stanford University Press, 1997); Willy Maley, *Nation, State and Empire in English Renaissance Literature: Shakespeare to Milton* (London: Palgrave, 2003).

41. See esp. the essays in David Baker and Willy Maley (eds.), *British Identities and English Renaissance Literature* (Cambridge: Cambridge University Press,

2002) and Philip Schwyzer and David Mealor (eds.), *Archipelagic Identities: Literature and Identity in the Atlantic Archipelago, 1550–1800* (Aldershot: Ashgate, 2004).

42. *Silex Scintillans: Sacred Poems and Private Ejaculations*, 2nd edn. (London, 1655), bk II, quoting *The Works of Henry Vaughan*, ed. L. C. Martin, 2nd edn. (Oxford: Clarendon, 1957).

43. E.g. Madeleine Forey, 'Poetry as Apocalypse: Henry Vaughan's *Silex Scintillans*', *Seventeenth Century*, 11 (1996): 161–86, Alan Rudrum, 'Resistance, Collaboration, and Silence: Henry Vaughan and Breconshire Royalism', in Claude J. Summers and Ted-Larry Pebworth (eds.), *The English Civil Wars in the Literary Imagination* (Columbia, Mo: University of Missouri Press, 1999), 102–18.

44. Cf. M. Wynn Thomas, ' "In Occidentem & Tenebras": Putting Henry Vaughan on the Map of Wales', *Scintilla*, 2 (1998): 7–25.

45. 'A New Language, A New Tradition', *Scintilla*, 6 (2002): 161–82. The jointly written introduction to Raymond Garlick and Roland Mathias (eds.), *Anglo-Welsh Poetry 1480–1980* (Bridgend: Poetry Wales Press, 1988)—rpt. in the later, enlarged *Anglo-Welsh Poetry 1480–1990* (Bridgend: Seren Books, 1993)—had been more sympathetic to Vaughan's claims.

46. For a symptomatic placing of this undatable remark see Helen Gardner (ed.), *The Metaphysical Poets*, rev. edn. (Oxford: Oxford University Press, 1961), xix.

47. See the entries for *Inglis* and *Scottis* in the online *Dictionary of the Scots Language*, <http://www.dsl.ac.uk>.

48. For a fine account of the latter, in relation to the construction of Englishness, which inevitably (given the content of witches' cauldrons) touches on the former, see Wendy Wall, *Staging Domesticity: Household Work and English Identity in Early Modern Drama* (Cambridge: Cambridge University Press, 2002).

49. See e.g. the commendatory ode—a chorographical survey of Britain and Ireland—supplied to the Llwyd-born poet, Hugh Holland's, *Pancharis* (London, 1603). Contexts are established by Mark Bland, ' "As far from all Reuolt": Sir John Salusbury, Christ Church MS 184 and Ben Jonson's First Ode', *English Manuscript Studies, 1100–1700*, 8 (2000): 43–78.

50. E.g. David Riggs, *Ben Jonson: A Life* (Cambridge: Harvard University Press, 1989); Ian Donaldson, *Jonson's Magic Houses: Essays in Interpretation* (Oxford: Clarendon, 1997), ch. 4; James Knowles, 'Jonson in Scotland: Jonson's Mid-Jacobean Crisis', in Takashi Kozuka and J. R. Mulryne, *Shakespeare, Marlowe, Jonson: New Directions in Biography* (Aldershot: Ashgate, 2006), 259–77.

51. See e.g. *Hymenaei* (1606), *The Irish Masque at Court* (1613), and *For the Honour of Wales* (1618).

52. On the process of penetration see T. M. Devine, *Scotland's Empire 1600–1815* (London: Allen Lane, 2003).

53. E.g. Arthur H. Williamson, 'Scotland, Antichrist and the Invention of Great Britain', in John Dwyer, Roger A. Mason, and Alexander J. Murdoch (eds.), *New Perspectives on the Politics and Culture of Early Modern Scotland* (Edinburgh, 1982), 34–58; Roger A. Mason, 'Scotching the Brut: Politics, History and National Myth in Sixteenth-Century Britain', in idem (ed.), *Scotland and England 1286–1815* (Edinburgh: Donald, 1987), 60–84, 'Scotland, Elizabethan England and the Idea of Britain', *Transactions of the Royal Historical Society*, 6th ser., 14 (2004): 279–93; Marcus Merriman, *The Rough Wooings: Mary, Queen of Scots, 1542–1551* (East Linton: Tuckwell, 2000). Cf. Jane E. A. Dawson, 'Two Kingdoms or Three? Ireland in Anglo-Scottish Relations in the Middle of the Sixteenth Century', in Mason (ed.) *Scotland and England*, 113–38.

54. For examples by Daniel, John Saville, Jonson, Drayton and others, see John Nichols (ed.), *The Progresses, Processions, and Magnificent Festivities of King James the First*, 4 vols. (London: J. B. Nichols, 1828), vol. I.

55. More than two dozen were written on Anglo-Scottish union in 1603–5; for a representative selection see Bruce Galloway and Brian Levack (eds.), *The Jacobean Union: Six Tracts of 1604* (Edinburgh: Scottish Historical Society, 1985). On the recycling of their arguments, whenever closer union was a possibility, as in the late 1660s, or in the lead-up to 1707, see Brian P. Levack, *The Formation of the British State: England, Scotland, and the Union 1603–1707* (Oxford: Clarendon, 1987), and John Robertson (ed.), *A Union for Empire: Political Thought and the British Union of 1707* (Cambridge: Cambridge University Press, 1995).

56. See Bruce Galloway, *The Union of England and Scotland, 1603–1608* (Edinburgh: John Donald, 1986) and Graham Parry, *The Golden Age Restor'd: The Culture of the Stuart Court, 1603–42* (Manchester: Manchester University Press, 1981), ch. 1.

57. Cf. Martin Butler, 'The Invention of Britain in the Early Stuart Masque', in R. Malcolm Smuts (ed.), *The Stuart Court and Europe* (Cambridge: Cambridge University Press, 1996), 65–85.

58. E.g. William Hubbocke, *An Oration Gratulatory to the High and Mighty Iames ... When his Maiesty Entered the Tower of London* (Oxford, 1604), B2r, Latin on A3r, citing 2 Samuel 19. For a review of sermons on the union, see Charles W. A. Prior, *Defining the Jacobean Church: The Politics of Religious Controversy, 1603–1625* (Cambridge: Cambridge University Press, 2005), 75–9.

59. Graham Parry, *The Trophies of Time: English Antiquarians of the Seventeenth Century* (Oxford: Oxford University Press, 1995).

60. See Derek Hirst, 'Literature and National Identity', in sect. 5 of Loewenstein and Mueller (eds.), *Cambridge History of Early Modern English Literature*, 633–63, p. 641. Across the water, see Edward Evans, *Historical and Bibliographical Account of Almanacks, Directories, etc., etc.: Published in Ireland from the*

Sixteenth Century (Dublin: Office of 'The Irish Builder', 1897); Raymond Gillespie, *Reading Ireland: Print, Reading and Social Change in Early Modern Ireland* (Manchester: Manchester University Press, 2005), 168–70.

61. For a review of the secondary literature see Willy Maley, 'British Ill Done?: Recent Work on Shakespeare and British, English, Irish, Scottish and Welsh Identities', *Literature Compass*, 3 (2006): 487–512.

62. On O'Neill, see Hiram Morgan, *Tyrone's Rebellion: The Outbreak of the Nine Years War in Tudor Ireland* (Woodbridge: Boydell, 1993).

63. E.g. the rebellion of the Percys in *1 and 2 Henry IV* would recall, for London audiences, the 1569 'Rising of the North', led by Thomas Percy, 7th Earl of Northumberland, the last great assertion on English soil of regional, magnate power, and survivalist Catholicism, which Elizabeth brutally suppressed.

64. On Shakespeare's hand in the play see e.g. *Edward III*, ed. Giorgio Melchiori (Cambridge: Cambridge University Press, 1998), 9–17.

65. *The Raigne of King Edward the Third* (London, 1596), B1v.

66. *The Scottish Historie of Iames the Fourth, Slaine at Flodden* (London, 1598). For advocacy see the final speeches of the heroine, English Dorothea, who marries a largely fictional King James IV of Scotland ('these nations if they ioyne, | What Monarch with his leigemen in this world, | Dare but encounter you in open field?' (K3v)), for anti-Scottishness see the representation of James IV throughout, while the anti-Jacobean note struck by the comical, misrule character Bohun is startlingly explicit: 'in the yeare 1520. was in *Scotland*, a king ouerruled with parasites, misled by lust, and many circumstances, too long to trattle on now, much like our court of *Scotland*, this day' (A4v).

67. Quoted by Melchiori, who argues that *Edward III* is 'their play' (ed. cit., 12). It is just as likely that such lost works as the anonymous *Vortigern* (performed by the Admiral's Men from December 1596 to April 1597) or William Rankins's *Mulmutius Dunwallow* (bought up by Henslowe in October 1598)—both of which, to judge by their chronicle sources, had scope for anti-Scottish satire—are referred to, or that an ongoing body of performance (another sense of 'in their play') was being challenged. The players continued to raise awkward questions about the Scots and their Stuart monarchs; on the lost *Robart the second Kinge of Scottes Tragedie* (1599) see James Shapiro, '*The Scot's Tragedy* and the Politics of Popular Drama', *English Literary Renaissance*, 23 (1993): 428–49.

68. *The Life of Henry the Fift* (I.ii. TLN 316), in *The First Folio of Shakespeare: The Norton Facsimile*, ed. Charlton Hinman (London: Paul Hamlyn, 1968).

69. For ways into the critical debate see Andrew Gurr, 'Why Captain Jamy in *Henry V*?', *Archiv für das Studium der neueren Sprachen und Literaturen*, 226 (1989): 365–73; David Baker, *Between Nations*, ch. 1; and Richard Dutton's thought-provoking ' "Methinks the Truth Should Live from Age to Age":

The Dating and Contexts of *Henry V*', *Huntington Library Quarterly*, 68 (2005): 173–204.

70. E.g. Lilian Winstanley, *Hamlet and the Scottish Succession* (Cambridge: Cambridge University Press, 1921), Roland Mushat Frye, *The Renaissance Hamlet: Issues and Responses in 1600* (Princeton: Princeton University Press, 1984), ch. 3; Andrew Hadfield, '*Hamlet*'s Country Matters: The "Scottish Play" within the Play', in Willy Maley and Andrew Murphy (eds.), *Shakespeare and Scotland* (Manchester: Manchester University Press, 2004), 87–103.

71. See the account of Burnell's *Landgartha* in Chapter 5.

72. Stuart M. Kurland, '*Hamlet* and the Scottish Succession?', *Studies in English Literature*, 34 (1994): 279–300.

73. 'One king, one law, one people'. For a deeply informed summary of the king's policy and strategy see the 1603–1610 section of Jenny Wormald, 'James VI and I', *Oxford Dictionary of National Biography*.

74. *Tragedie of King Lear* (I. i; TLN 7), *Historie of King Lear* (London, 1608), B1r.

75. Compare e.g. the Fool's prophecy, number games, and Gloucester and Edgar's interest in astrology with the Scottish preoccupations explored in Arthur H. Williamson, 'Number and National Consciousness: The Edinburgh Mathematicians and Scottish Political Culture at the Union of the Crowns', in Roger A. Mason (ed.), *Scots and Britons: Scottish Political Thought and the Union of 1603* (Cambridge: Cambridge University Press, 1994), 187–212.

76. *Basilikon Doron* (Edinburgh, 1599), 99; (London, 1603), 83. Locrine inherited England, Albanact the lands to the north, and Camber the Celtic West.

77. Cf. e.g. John Doddridge, 'A Breif Consideracion of the Unyon', Sir Henry Spelman, 'Of the Union', and Sir Henry Savile, 'Historicall Collections', in Galloway and Levack (eds.), *Jacobean Union*, 143–60, p. 145, 161–84, pp. 168–70, 185–239, p. 211.

78. Contexts are given in Alex Garganigo, '*Coriolanus*, the Union Controversy, and Access to the Royal Person', *Studies in English Literature*, 42 (2002): 335–59.

79. Michael J. Braddick, *State Formation in Early Modern England c.1550–1700* (Cambridge: Cambridge University Press, 2000).

80. See esp. Paul Brown, ' "This Thing of Darkness I Acknowledge Mine": *The Tempest* and the Discourse of Colonialism', in Jonathan Dollimore and Alan Sinfield (eds.), *Political Shakespeare: Essays in Cultural Materialism* (Manchester: Manchester University Press, 1985), 48–71; Francis Barker and Peter Hulme, 'Nymphs and Reapers Heavily Vanish: The Discursive Con-texts of *The Tempest*', in John Drakakis (ed.), *Alternative Shakespeares* (London: Methuen, 1985), 191–205; David J. Baker, 'Where is Ireland in *The Tempest*?', in Mark Thornton Burnett and Romana Wray (eds.), *Shakespeare and Ireland: History, Politics, Culture* (London: Macmillan, 1997), 68–88; Dympna Callaghan, 'Irish Memories in *The Tempest*', in her *Shakespeare Without Women: Representing Gender and Race on the Renaissance Stage* (London: Routledge, 2000), 97–138.

81. Philip Edwards, 'Shakespeare, Ireland, Dreamland', *Irish University Review*, 28 (1998): 227–39.

82. Christopher Worthen, 'Shakespeare, James I and the Matter of Britain', *English*, 45 (1996): 97–122.

83. From the inadequate critical history see A. E. Hughes, 'Shakespeare and his Welsh Characters', *Transactions of the Honourable Society of Cymmrodorion* (1917–18), 159–89; Joan Rees, 'Shakespeare's Welshmen', in Vincent Newey and Ann Thompson (eds.), *Literature and Nationalism* (Liverpool: Liverpool University Press, 1991), 22–40; Christopher Highley, *Shakespeare, Spenser, and the Crisis in Ireland*, ch. 3; and Lisa Hopkins, 'Welshness in Shakespeare's English Histories', in *Shakespeare's History Plays: Performance, Translation and Adaptation in Britain and Abroad*, ed. Ton Hoenselaars (Cambridge: Cambridge University Press, 2004), 60–74.

84. See the chapter of that title in Terence Hawkes, *Shakespeare in the Present* (London: Routledge, 2002).

85. J. G. A. Pocock, 'British History: A Plea for a New Subject', *New Zealand Historical Journal*, 8 (1974) rpt. in *Journal of Modern History*, 47 (1975): 601–28 and revised in his collection, *The Discovery of Islands: Essays in British History* (Cambridge: Cambridge University Press, 2005), 24–43; quoting here 'The Limits and Divisions of British History: In Search of the Unknown Subject', *American Historical Review*, 87 (1982): 311–36, p. 318.

86. 'Limits and Divisions', 317.

87. More recent anticipations, in different modes, include Richard S. Tompson, *The Atlantic Archipelago: A Political History of the British Isles* (Lewiston, NY: Edwin Mellen Press, 1986); Hugh Kearney, *The British Isles: A History of Four Nations* (Cambridge: Cambridge University Press, 1989); and David Stevenson, *Scottish Covenanters and Irish Confederates: Scottish-Irish Relations in the Mid-Seventeenth Century* (Belfast: Ulster Historical Foundation, 1981).

88. See e.g. the 'Comments' by A. J. P. Taylor, Gordon Donaldson, and Michael Hechter appended to the rpt. of his 'British History' in *Journal of Modern History*, at 622–6.

89. For a recent, distinctive but well-documented account, see Ronald Hutton, *Debates in Stuart History* (London: Palgrave, 2004), chs. 1–3. Outstanding revisionist works, from which I have learned much, include Conrad Russell, *The Causes of the English Civil War* (Oxford: Clarendon, 1990) and Kevin Sharpe, *The Personal Rule of Charles I* (New Haven: Yale University Press, 1992).

90. J. H. Elliott, 'The King and the Catalans, 1621–1640', *Cambridge Historical Journal*, 11 (1953): 253–71 and 'A Europe of Composite Monarchies', *Past and Present*, 137 (1992): 48–71; cf. H. G. Koenigsberger, '*Dominium Regale* or *Dominium Politicum et Regale*: Monarchies and Parliaments in Early Modern Europe', in his *Politicians and Virtuosi: Essays in Early Modern History* (London: Hambledon Press, 1986), 1–25. The topic is revisited by Geoffrey Parker,

'The Crisis of the Spanish and the Stuart Monarchies in the Mid-Seventeenth Century: Local Problems or Global Problems?', in Ciaran Brady and Jane Ohlmeyer (eds.), *British Interventions in Early Modern Ireland* (Cambridge: Cambridge University Press, 2005), 252–79.

91. See the groundbreaking essays by Conrad Russell, 'The British Problem and the English Civil War', *History*, 72 (1987): 395–415 and 'The British Background to the Irish Rebellion of 1641', *Historical Research*, 61 (1988): 166–82.

92. The description is usually credited to J. C. Beckett, *The Making of Modern Ireland 1603–1923* (London: Faber, 1966), ch. 4.

93. See Conrad Russell, *Causes of the English Civil War* and *The Fall of the British Monarchies 1637–1642* (Oxford: Clarendon, 1991), an analysis developed and debated—with new paradigms emerging—in John Morrill (ed.), *The Scottish National Covenant in its British Context* (Edinburgh: Edinburgh University Press, 1990); Alexander Grant and Keith J. Stringer (eds.), *Uniting the Kingdom?: The Making of British History* (London: Routledge, 1995); Steven G. Ellis and Sarah Barber (eds.), *Conquest and Union: Fashioning a British State, 1485–1725* (London: Longman, 1995); Brendan Bradshaw and John Morrill (eds.), *The British Problem, c.1534–1707: State Formation in the Atlantic Archipelago* (Basingstoke: Macmillan, 1996); Martyn Bennett, *The Civil Wars in Britain and Ireland, 1638–1651* (Oxford: Blackwell, 1997); John R. Young, *Celtic Dimensions of the British Civil Wars* (Edinburgh: John Donald, 1997); Brendan Bradshaw and Peter Roberts (eds.), *British Consciousness and Identity: The Making of Britain, 1533–1707* (Cambridge: Cambridge University Press, 1998); Burgess (ed.), *The New British History*; Andrew D. Nicholls, *A Jacobean Union: A Reconsideration of British Civil Policies under the Early Stuarts* (Westport, CT: Greenwood Press, 1999); S. J. Connolly (ed.), *Kingdoms United? Great Britain and Ireland since 1500: Integration and Diversity* (Dublin: Four Courts, 1999); Allan I. Macinnes and Jane H. Ohlmeyer (eds.), *The Stuart Kingdoms in the Seventeenth Century: Awkward Neighbours* (Dublin: Four Courts, 2002); Brady and Ohlmeyer (eds.), *British Interventions in Early Modern Ireland*. The approach now permeates student primers; see e.g. Barry Coward (ed.), *Companion to Stuart Britain* (Oxford: Blackwell, 2001). Much further reading is listed in the above, but note esp. four pieces by Jenny Wormald: 'The Creation of Britain: Multiple Kingdoms or Core and Colonies?', *Transactions of the Royal Historical Society*, 6th ser., 2 (1992): 175–94; 'The Union of 1603', in Mason (ed.), *Scots and Britons*, 17–40; 'Oh Brave New World? The Union of Scotland and England in 1603', in T. C. Smout, ed., *Anglo-Scottish Relations from 1603–1900, Proceedings of the British Academy*, 127 (2005): 13–35; 'The Happier Marriage Partner: The Impact of the Union of the Crowns on Scotland', in Glenn Burgess, Rowland Wymer, and Jason Lawrence (eds.), *The Accession of James I: Historical and Cultural Consequences* (Basingstoke: Palgrave, 2006), 69–87.

94. Clarendon: 'though Scotland blew the first trumpet, it was Ireland that drew the first blood; and if they had not at that time rebelled, and in that manner, it is very probable all the miseries which afterwards befell the King and his dominions had been prevented', *The History of the Rebellion and Civil Wars in England*, ed. W. Dunn Macray, 6 vols. (Oxford: Clarendon, 1888), VI, 2–3.

95. Conrad Russell, 'Composite Monarchies in Early Modern Europe: The British and Irish Example', in Grant and Stringer (eds.), *Uniting the Kingdom?*, 133–46, p. 133.

96. For a long-reaching account, see Norman Davies, *The Isles: A History* (London: Macmillan, 1999).

97. See e.g. David Armitage, *The Ideological Origins of the British Empire* (Cambridge: Cambridge University Press, 2000), 57–8. The pattern of usage was, in practice, variable to the point of paradox; thus English settlers in Ulster usually referred to themselves as English, yet, as Nicholas Canny notes, the Englishmen in Dublin who compiled statements from victims of the Ulster rising of 1641 'described Scottish and Irish (and on a few occasions even Welsh) Protestants by their nationality, and reserved the generic description British ... for those deponents who were of English birth' (*Making Ireland British 1580–1650* (Oxford: Oxford University Press, 2001), 483).

98. For a classic account of the early Stuart situation see Caroline M. Hibbard, *Charles I and the Popish Plot* (Chapel Hill: University of North Carolina Press, 1983). Titus Oates later claimed that Jesuits disguised as Presbyterian ministers would be sent into Scotland to stir those suffering episcopal tyranny to rebel, whip up a Catholic uprising in Ireland, have Charles II assassinated, start another great fire in London, and instruct papists to rise up and massacre Protestants—a rerun of 1637–41 for the period of the Exclusion Crisis, as Tim Harris notes in *Restoration: Charles II and his Kingdoms, 1660–1685* (London: Allen Lane, 2005), 137.

99. See e.g. Gilbert Burnet, a Scot south of the border, on James VI and I's error in seeking too much for his native country in union, and then alienating it, which led to the civil wars and Charles I's execution (*History of My Own Time*, Part I, ed. Osmund Airy, 2 vols. (Oxford: Clarendon, 1897–1900), I, 9–10), or the Old Irishman Charles O'Kelly on Charles I's failure to keep his several kingdoms in balance, *Macariae Excidium: Or, The Destruction of Cyprus*, ed. John Cornelius O'Callaghan (Dublin: Irish Archæological Society, 1850), 44.

100. Michael Hechter, *Internal Colonialism: The Celtic Fringe in British National Development, 1536–1966* (London: Routledge, 1975).

101. See e.g. his essays on 'The Church in England 1643–9', in Morrill (ed.), *Reactions to the English Civil War 1642–1649* (London: Macmillan, 1982), 89–114; 'The Religious Context of the English Civil War', *Transactions of the Royal Historical Society*, 5th ser., 34 (1984): 155–78; 'Introduction: England's

Wars of Religion', in Morrill (ed.), *The Nature of the English Revolution* (London: Longman, 1993), 33–44, opening out in 'The National Covenant in its British Context', in Morrill (ed.), *Scottish National Covenant in its British Context*, 1–30 and 'A British Patriarchy?: Ecclesiastical Imperialism under the Early Stuarts', in Anthony Fletcher and Peter Roberts (eds.), *Religion, Culture and Society in Early Modern Britain: Essays in Honour of Patrick Collinson* (Cambridge: Cambridge University Press, 1994), 209–37.

102. *Discovery of Islands*, 167.

103. Tim Harris, 'In Search of a British History of Political Thought', in David Armitage (ed.), *British Political Thought in History, Literature and Theory, 1500–1800* (Cambridge: Cambridge University Press, 2006), 89–108, p. 90. Cf. Quentin Skinner's judicious endorsement, in his 'Afterword' to the book, 278–85, p. 279.

104. Jane H. Ohlmeyer, *Civil War and Restoration in the Three Stuart Kingdoms: The Career of Randal MacDonnell, Marquis of Antrim, 1609–1638* (Cambridge: Cambridge University Press, 1993); Colin Kidd, *British Identities before Nationalism: Ethnicity and Nationhood in the Atlantic World, 1600–1800* (Cambridge: Cambridge University Press, 1999). Cf. Ohlmeyer's article co-authored with Steven Zwicker, 'John Dryden, the House of Ormond, and the Politics of Anglo-Irish Patronage', *Historical Journal*, 49 (2006): 677–706.

105. Mark Netzloff, *England's Internal Colonies: Class, Capital, and the Literature of Early Modern English Colonialism* (New York: Palgrave Macmillan, 2003).

106. See e.g. her studies *The Causes of the English Civil War*, 2nd edn. (Basingstoke: Macmillan, 1998) and *'Gangraena' and the Struggle for the English Revolution* (Oxford: Oxford University Press, 2004).

107. For studies of Anglo-English literature in this line see e.g. Christopher Hill, *Milton and the English Revolution* (London: Faber, 1977), his *Collected Essays*, vol. I, *Writing and Revolution in Seventeenth-Century England* (Brighton: Harvester, 1985) and *A Turbulent, Seditious and Factious People: John Bunyan and his Church* (Oxford: Clarendon, 1988). Punctuated by Kevin Sharpe's incisively revisionist *Criticism and Compliment: The Politics of Literature in the England of Charles I* (Cambridge: Cambridge University Press, 1987), the tradition is deepened and extended by such major studies as Nigel Smith, *Literature and Revolution in England 1640–1660* (New Haven: Yale University Press, 1994); David Norbrook, *Writing the English Republic: Poetry, Rhetoric and Politics, 1627–1660* (Cambridge: Cambridge University Press, 1998); and David Loewenstein, *Representing Revolution in Milton and his Contemporaries: Religion, Politics, and Polemics in Radical Puritanism* (Cambridge: Cambridge University Press, 2001).

108. The poem, which was presented to the Protestant, royalist leader Ormond between late 1649 and late 1650, can be read in Carpenter (ed.), *Verse in English from Tudor and Stuart Ireland*, 299–309.

109. *Pairlement Chloinne Tomáis*, ed. N. J. A. Williams (Dublin: Dublin Institute for Advanced Studies, 1981).

110. McEachern, *Poetics of English Nationhood*, 29.

111. 'What God hath conjoined then, let no man separate. I am the Husband, and all the whole Isle is my lawfull Wife': 'A Speach, as it was Delivered in the Vpper House of the Parliament… on Munday the XIX. Day of March 1603 [1604]', in James VI and I, *The Workes of the Most High and Mightie Prince, James by the Grace of God, King of Great Britaine, France and Ireland* (London, 1616), 485−97, p. 482.

112. Luke Gernon, 'A Discourse of Ireland, Anno *1620*', in C. Litton Falkiner (ed.), *Illustrations of Irish History and Topography, Mainly of the Seventeenth Century* (London: Longmans, 1904), 348−62.

113. John Taylor, *The Pennyles Pilgrimage: Or, The Money-lesse Perambulation* (London, 1618), F3r-v.

114. Stevenson and Davidson (eds.), *Early Modern Women Poets*, xlvi.

115. 'To William Drummond of Hawthornden', in Drummond's *Poems* (London, 1657), here quoting Stevenson and Davidson (eds.), *Early Modern Women Poets*, 170−1.

116. See e.g. Nicholas P. Canny, 'The Attempted Anglicization of Ireland in the Seventeenth Century: An Exemplar of "British History"' and Keith M. Brown, 'British History: A Sceptical Comment', in Ronald G. Asch (ed.), *Three Nations—a Common History? England, Scotland, Ireland and British History, c.1600−1920* (Bochum: Brockmeyer, 1993), 49−82, 117−27; Canny, 'Irish, Scottish and Welsh Responses to Centralisation', in Grant and Stringer (eds.), *Uniting the Kingdom?*, 147−69.

117. John Adamson, 'The English Context of the British Civil Wars', *History Today*, 48/11 (1998): 23−9.

118. Pocock, *Discovery of Islands*, esp. 53, 289, 295.

119. e.g. Allan I. Macinnes, *The British Revolution, 1629−1660* (Basingstoke: Palgrave, 2005); Jim Smyth, *The Making of the United Kingdom, 1660−1800: State, Religion and Identity in Britain and Ireland* (Harlow: Longman, 2001).

120. Russell, *Causes of the English Revolution*, 27.

121. Fynes Morison, 'The Description of Ireland' (from his *Itinerary*), in Falkiner (ed.), *Illustrations*, 214−32, p. 214.

122. Stan A. E. Mendyk, *Speculum Britanniae: Regional Study, Antiquarianism, and Science in Britain to 1700* (Toronto: University of Toronto Press, 1989); Jan Broadway, *William Dugdale and the Significance of County History in Early Stuart England*, Dugdale Society Occasional Papers, 39 (1999).

123. For a text with discussion of authorship, see *The Dramatic Works of Thomas Dekker*, ed. Fredson Bowers, vol. IV (Cambridge: Cambridge University Press, 1961).

124. Cf. Pocock, *Discovery of Islands*, 32, noting that 'the modern historian S. T. Bindoff dates the final absorption of the Northumbrian marches

into "England" no earlier than the repression of the Northern Rising of 1569'.

125. W. J. Jones, 'Palatine Performance in the Seventeenth Century', in Peter Clark, Alan G. R. Smith, and Nicholas Tyacke (eds.), *The English Commonwealth 1547–1640: Essays in Politics and Society Presented to Joel Hurstfield* (Leicester: Leicester University Press, 1979), 189–204.

126. E.g. John Morrill, *The Revolt of the Provinces: Conservatives and Radicals in the English Civil War, 1630–1650* (1976), rev. as *The Revolt in the Provinces: The People of England and the Tragedies of War, 1630–1648* (London: Longman, 1999); Eveline Cruickshanks, 'The Revolution and the Localities: Examples of Loyalty to James II', in Cruickshanks (ed.), *By Force or Default?: The Revolution of 1688–1689* (Edinburgh: John Donald, 1989), 28–43; Paul D. Halliday, *Dismembering the Body Politic: Partisan Politics in England's Towns, 1650–1730* (Cambridge: Cambridge University Press, 1999).

127. E.g. Clive Holmes, 'The County Community in Stuart Historiography', *Journal of British Studies*, 19 (1980): 54–73, Ann Hughes, 'Local History and the Origins of the Civil War', in Richard Cust and Ann Hughes (eds.), *Conflict in Early Stuart England: Studies in Religion and Politics, 1603–1642* (1989), 224–53.

128. For attempts to identify socio-economic determinants see David Underdown, *Revel, Riot and Rebellion: Popular Politics and Culture in England 1603–1660* (Oxford: Oxford University Press, 1985) and John Morrill, 'The Ecology of Allegiance in the English Revolution', *Journal of British Studies*, 26 (1987): 451–67.

129. 'The Description of Cooke-ham', lines 73–4, in Stevenson and Davidson (eds.), *Early Modern Women Poets*.

130. 'To My Friend G. N. from Wrest', in *The Poems of Thomas Carew with his Masque 'Coelum Britannicum'*, ed. Rhodes Dunlap (Oxford: Clarendon, 1949), lines 7, 109.

131. Richard Davies, *Chesters Triumph in Honor of her Prince* (London, 1610).

132. E.g. David M. Bergeron, *English Civic Pageantry 1558–1642* (London: Edward Arnold, 1971).

133. Peter Clark and David Souden (eds.), *Migration and Society in Early Modern England* (London: Hutchinson, 1987); Ian D. Whyte, 'Population Mobility in Early Modern Scotland', in R. A. Houston and Ian D. Whyte, *Scottish Society, 1500–1800* (Cambridge: Cambridge University Presss, 1987); Ian D. Whyte, 'Scottish and Irish Urbanisation in the Seventeenth and Eighteenth Centuries: A Comparative Perspective', in S. J. Connolly, R. A. Houston and R. J. Morris (eds.), *Conflict, Identity and Economic Development: Ireland and Scotland, 1600–1939* (Preston: Carnegie, 1995), 14–28.

134. E.g. Peter Clark (ed.), *The Cambridge Urban History of Britain*, vol. II, *1540–1840* (Cambridge: Cambridge University Press, 2000), chs. 1–13; Raymond Gillespie, 'Dublin, 1600–1700: A City and its Hinterlands', in Peter Clark and

Bernard Lepetit (eds.), *Capital Cities and their Hinterlands in Early Modern Europe* (Aldershot: Scolar, 1996), 84−101; Peter Clark and Raymond Gillespie (eds.), *Two Capitals: London and Dublin, 1500−1840, Proceedings of the British Academy*, 107 (2001).

135. Lawrence Manley, *Literature and Culture in Early Modern London* (Cambridge: Cambridge University Press, 1995); Cynthia Wall, *The Literary and Cultural Spaces of Restoration London* (Cambridge: Cambridge University Press, 1998); Paul Griffiths and Mark S. R. Jenner (eds.), *Londinopolis: Essays in the Cultural and Social History of Early Modern London* (Manchester: Manchester University Press, 2000); J. F. Merritt (ed.), *Imagining Early Modern London: Perceptions and Portrayals of the City from Stow to Strype, 1598−1720* (Cambridge: Cambridge University Press, 2001).

136. Valerie Pearl, *London and the Outbreak of the Puritan Revolution: City Government and National Politics, 1625−43* (Oxford: Oxford University Press, 1961); Stephen Porter (ed.), *London and the Civil War* (Basingstoke: Macmillan, 1996); Keith Lindley, *Popular Politics and Religion in Civil War London* (Aldershot: Scolar Press, 1997); Pearl, 'London's Counter-Revolution', in G. E. Aylmer (ed.), *The Interregnum: The Quest for Settlement, 1646−1660* (London: Macmillan, 1972), 29−56; Tim Harris, *London Crowds in the Reign of Charles II: Propaganda and Politics from the Restoration until the Exclusion Crisis* (Cambridge: Cambridge University Press, 1987); Gary Stuart de Krey, *London and the Restoration, 1659−1683* (Cambridge: Cambridge University Press, 2005).

137. Sean Kelsey, *Inventing a Republic: The Political Culture of the English Commonwealth, 1649−1653* (Manchester: Manchester University Press, 1997).

138. James Harrington, *The Common-wealth of Oceana* (London, 1656).

139. Christopher Durston, *Cromwell's Major-Generals* (Manchester: Manchester University Press, 2001).

140. E.g. *An Account of a Conversation Concerning a Right Regulation of Governments for the Common Good of Mankind* (Edinburgh, 1704), in *Andrew Fletcher: Political Works*, ed. John Robertson (Cambridge: Cambridge University Press, 1997), 175−215.

141. See Mark Stoyle, *West Britons: Cornish Identities and the Early Modern British State* (Exeter: University of Exeter Press, 2002).

142. Derek Hirst and Steven N. Zwicker, 'High Summer at Nun Appleton, 1651: Andrew Marvell and Lord Fairfax's Occasions', *Historical Journal*, 36 (1993): 247−69.

143. 'Upon Appleton House, To My Lord Fairfax', lines 309−10, in *The Poems and Letters of Andrew Marvell*, ed. H. M. Margoliouth, 3rd edn. rev. Pierre Legouis with E. E. Duncan-Jones, 2 vols. (Oxford: Clarendon, 1971), I.

144. See Sarah Barber, 'The People of Northern England and Attitudes Towards the Scots, 1639−1651: "The Lamb and the Dragon Cannot be Reconciled" ', *Northern History*, 35 (1999): 93−118.

145. Braddick, *State Formation in Early Modern England*, 345.

146. Quoted by Jane H. Ohlmeyer, ' "Civilizinge of those Rude Partes": Colonization within Britain and Ireland, 1580s–1640s', in Canny (ed.), *Origins of Empire*, 124–47, p. 126.

147. See Penry Williams, 'The Welsh Borderland under Queen Elizabeth', *Welsh History Review*, 1 (1960): 19–36, 'The Attack on the Council in the Marches, 1603–42', *Transactions of the Honourable Society of Cymmrodorion* (1961), pt 1, 1–22, and 'The Northern Borderlands under the Stuarts', in H. E. Bell and R. L. Ollard (eds.), *Historical Essays 1600–1750* (London: Adam and Charles Black, 1963), 1–17; Steven G. Ellis, *Tudor Frontiers and Noble Power: The Making of the British State* (Oxford: Clarendon, 1995).

148. *Scottish Historie of Iames the Fourth*, A3r: 'Bohan *a Scot*, attyred like a yidstall man'.

149. E.g. Julian Goodare and Michael Lynch, 'The Scottish State and its Borderlands, 1567–1625', in Goodare and Lynch (eds.), *The Reign of James VI* (East Linton: Tuckwell, 2000), 186–205.

150. Thomas I. Rae, *The Administration of the Scottish Frontier, 1513–1603* (Edinburgh: Edinburgh University Press, 1966), ch. 9.

151. See 'A Proclamation for the better and more peaceable government of the middle Shires of Northumberland, Cumberland, and Westmerland', 23 December 1617, in James F. Larkin and Paul L. Hughes (eds.), *Stuart Royal Proclamations*, vol. I (Oxford: Clarendon, 1973), 374–80.

152. *Pennyles Pilgrimage*, C4r-v.

153. E.g. Allan I. Macinnes, 'Crown, Clans and Fine: The "Civilizing" of Scottish Gaeldom, 1587–1638', *Northern Scotland*, 113 (1993): 31–55; Julian Goodare, 'The Statutes of Iona in Context', *Scottish Historical Review*, 77 (1998): 31–57.

154. ' "Civilizing of those Rude Parts" ', 145.

155. E.g. Milton, above, p. 235. On Charles's Scottish proclivities, which include the appearance of Scots diction in his letters (scribal?), his liking for Scottish attendants, and the fact that it was under him rather than James that the number of Scots in the Privy Council peaked, see e.g. Steve Murdoch, *Britain, Denmark-Norway and the House of Stuart, 1603–1660* (East Linton: Tuckwell, 2000), 4–6, 25.

156. The strongest, at times overstated, account is by Mark Stoyle, *Soldiers and Strangers: An Ethnic History of the English Civil War* (New Haven: Yale University Press, 2005).

157. For one way in to a contentious topic see Steven G. Ellis, 'The Collapse of the Gaelic World, 1450–1650', *Irish Historical Studies*, 31 (1999): 449–69.

158. Margaret T. Hodgen, *Early Anthropology in the Sixteenth and Seventeenth Centuries* (Philadelphia: University of Pennsylvania Press, 1964); Anthony Pagden, *The Fall of Natural Man: The American Indian and the Origins of Comparative Ethnography* (Cambridge: Cambridge University Press, 1986).

159. Kidd, *British Identities*, 185.
160. Kidd, *British Identities*, 196–7. Buchanan's interest in Gaelic origins was not, of course, narrowly linguistic: see e.g. Roger A. Mason, 'Civil Society and the Celts: Hector Boece, George Buchanan and the Ancient Scottish Past', in Edward J. Cowan and Richard J. Finlay (eds.), *Scottish History: The Power of the Past* (Edinburgh: Edinburgh University Press, 2002), 95–119.
161. Macinnes, *British Revolution*, 4, drawing on Simon James, *The Atlantic Celts: Ancient People or Modern Invention?* (London: British Museum Press, 1999). The *OED* gives 1656 as its earliest appearance of 'Celtic' ('*Celtique*, pertaining to the people of Gaul') and *Paradise Lost* (1667) as its first literary use.
162. George Saltern, *Of the Antient Lawes of Great Britaine* (London, 1605), 16, quoted by Kidd, *British Identities*, 62.
163. E.g. Edward Douglas Snyder, 'The Wild Irish: A Study of some English Satires against the Irish, Scots and Welsh', *Modern Philology*, 17 (1920): 687–725; J. O. Bartley, *Teague, Shenkin and Sawney: Being an Historical Study of the Earliest Irish, Welsh and Scottish Characters in English Plays* (Cork: Cork University Press, 1954); David Hayton, 'From Barbarian to Burlesque: English Images of the Irish, c.1660–1750', *Irish Economic and Social History*, 15 (1988): 2–31; Joseph Th. Leerssen, *Mere Irish and Fíor-Ghael: Studies in the Idea of Irish Nationality, its Development and Literary Expression Prior to the Nineteenth Century* (Amsterdam: John Benjamins, 1986); Peter Lord, *Words with Pictures: Welsh Images and Images of Wales in the Popular Press, 1640–1860* (Aberystwyth: Planet, 1995); Mark Stoyle, 'Caricaturing Cymru: Images of the Welsh in the London Press, 1642–6', in Diana Dunn (ed.), *War and Society in Medieval and Early Modern Britain* (Liverpool: Liverpool University Press, 2000), 162–79.
164. Michael Roberts, ' "A Witty Book, but Mostly Feigned": William Richards' *Wallography* and Perceptions of Wales in Later Seventeenth-Century England', in Schwyzer and Mealor (eds.), *Archipelagic Identities*, 153–65.
165. Letter of 20 July (British Library, Harleian MSS 6852), quoted by Stoyle, *Soldiers and Strangers*, 166.
166. 'How the first Helandman of God was Maid of ane Hors Turd in Argylle as is Said', *The Bannatyne Manuscript*, iii, ed. W. Tod Ritchie (Edinburgh: Blackwood, 1928), 84; cf. Cleland's almost equally vigorous comments in Chapter 9.
167. On this highly charged early seventeenth-century dispute, see Mary Ann Lyons, 'Foreign Language Books, 1550–1700', in Raymond Gillespie and Andrew Hadfield (eds.), *The Irish Book in English 1550–1800*, The Oxford History of the Irish Book, 3 (Oxford: Oxford University Press, 2006), 347–67.
168. Geraint H. Jenkins, *The Foundations of Modern Wales: Wales 1642–1780*, History of Wales, 4 (Oxford: Clarendon/University of Wales Press, 1987), 7.

169. Edmund Spenser, *A View of the State of Ireland ... 1596*, in Sir James Ware, *The Historie of Ireland, Collected by Three Learned Authors* (Dublin, 1633), 28; on cultural connections with Africa through Spain see e.g. 31–2, 39–40.

170. Cf. Kim F. Hall, *Things of Darkness: Economies of Race and Gender in Early Modern England* (Ithaca: Cornell University Press, 1995), 7.

171. Kidd, *British Identities*, 170–1.

172. Barbara Fuchs, 'Spanish Lessons: Spenser and the Irish Moriscos', *Studies in English Literature*, 42 (2002): 43–62 quotes a 1609 reference to the O'Moores of Queen's County, who had been transplanted to Munster and Connacht, as 'those white Moores' and Sir John Davies's advice, in 1610, that troublesome Irish be uprooted: 'the Spaniards lately removed all the Moors out of Granada into Barbary, without providing them any new seats there' (50–1). Cf. Paul McGinnis and Arthur H. Williamson, 'Britain, Race, and the Iberian World Empire', in Macinnes and Ohlmeyer (eds.), *Stuart Kingdoms*, 70–93 and Sarah Barber, 'Settlement, Transplantation and Expulsion: A Comparative Study of the Placement of Peoples', in Brady and Ohlmeyer (eds.), *British Interventions in Early Modern Ireland*, 280–98.

173. Cited in Canny, *Making Ireland British*, 497–8.

174. *An Aphorismical Discovery of Treasonable Faction*, in *A Contemporary History of Affairs in Ireland from 1641 to 1652*, ed. J. T. Gilbert, 3 vols. in 6 (Dublin: Irish Archaeological and Celtic Society, 1879–1880), I, 116.

175. *An Aphorismical Discovery of Treasonable Faction*, I, 27.

176. A good introductory overview is Anthony D. Smith, *Nationalism: Theory, Ideology, History* (Cambridge: Polity, 2001).

177. Ernest Gellner, *Nations and Nationalism* (Oxford: Blackwell, 1983).

178. Benedict Anderson, *Imagined Communities: Reflections on the Origins and Spread of Nationalism*, rev. edn. (London: Verso, 1991).

179. E.g. Robert Munter, *The History of the Irish Newspaper, 1685–1760* (Cambridge: Cambridge University Press, 1967); Bob Harris, 'The Press, Newspaper Fiction and Literary Journalism, 1707–1918', in Brown (gen. ed.), *Edinburgh History of Scottish Literature*, II, 308–16.

180. Anderson, *Imagined Communities*, 35.

181. E.g. Liah Greenfeld, *Nationalism: Five Roads to Modernity* (Cambridge, MA: Harvard University Press, 1992).

182. On ethnicity, law, and kingship see the work of Patrick Wormald, e.g. '*Engla Lond*: The Making of an Allegiance', *Journal of Historical Sociology*, 7 (1994): 1–24 and 'Germanic Power Structures: The Early English Experience', in Len Scales and Oliver Zimmer (eds.), *Power and the Nation in European History* (Cambridge: Cambridge University Press, 2005); cf. Sarah Foot, 'The Making of *Angelcynn*: English Identity before the Norman Conquest', *Transactions of the Royal Historical Society*, 6th ser., 6 (1996), 25–49, and, from a literary angle, Janet Thormann, 'The *Anglo-Saxon Chronicle* Poems and the Making of the English Nation', in Allen J. Frantzen and John D. Niles (eds.),

Anglo-Saxonism and the Construction of Social Identity (Gainesville, FL: University Press of Florida, 1997), 60–85. Larger claims for a 'nation state' have been made by James Campbell, from 'The Late Anglo-Saxon State: A Maximum View', *Proceedings of the British Academy*, 87 (1994): 39–65 to *The Anglo-Saxon State* (London: Hambledon, 2000).

183. E.g. M. T. Clanchy, *England and its Rulers 1066–1272: Foreign Lordship and National Identity*, 2nd edn. (Oxford: Blackwell, 1998); Hugh M. Thomas, *The English and the Normans: Ethnic Hostility, Assimilation, and Identity 1066-c.1220* (Oxford: Oxford University Press, 2003).

184. Laura Ashe, *Fiction and History in England, 1066-1200* (Cambridge: Cambridge University Press, 2007).

185. R. R. Davies, *The First English Empire: Power and Identities in the British Isles 1093–1343* (Oxford: Oxford University Press, 2000), 145. From the stack of books around this topic, see John Gillingham, *The English in the Twelfth Century: Imperialism, National Identity and Political Values* (Woodbridge: Boydell, 2000), adding, for later developments, Thorlac Turville-Petre, *England the Nation: Language, Literature, and National Identity, 1290–1340* (Oxford: Clarendon, 1996) and Gerald Harriss, *Shaping the Nation: England 1360–1461* (Oxford: Clarendon, 2005).

186. Patrick Collinson, 'Biblical Rhetoric: The Elect Nation and National Sentiment in the Prophetic Mode', in Claire McEachern and Debora Shuger (eds.), *Religion and Culture in Renaissance England* (Cambridge: Cambridge University Press, 1977), 15–45.

187. Mary Morrissey, 'Elect Nations and Prophetic Preaching: Types and Examples in the Paul's Cross Jeremiad', in Lori Anne Ferrell and Peter McCullough (eds.), *The English Sermon Revised: Religion, Literature and History 1600–1750* (Manchester: Manchester University Press, 2000), 43–58.

188. E.g. J. P. Somerville, *Royalists and Patriots: Politics and Ideology in England, 1603–1640*, 2nd edn. (London: Longman, 1999).

189. Stoyle, *Soldiers and Strangers*, ch. 6.

190. For a classic statement of the case see Hans Kohn, 'The Genesis and Character of English Nationalism', *Journal of the History of Ideas*, 1 (1940): 69–94. Cf. Stoyle, *Soldiers and Strangers*, ch. 10. The best counter-argument is mounted by Krishan Kumar, *The Making of English Identity* (Cambridge: Cambridge University Press, 2003), ch. 6, whose influence is felt in Jason Scott-Warren's sceptical account in *Early Modern English Literature* (Cambridge: Polity, 2005), ch. 6.

191. See the opening chs. of R. R. Davies, *The Age of Conquest: Wales 1063–1415*, rev. edn. (Oxford: Oxford University Press, 2000).

192. E.g. R. R. Davies, 'Colonial Wales', *Past and Present*, 65 (1974): 3–23 and John Davies, *A History of Wales* (London: Allen Lane, 1990), chs. 5–6.

193. The most stimulating overall account is Gwyn A. Williams, *When was Wales?* (London: Black Raven, 1985); for 1603–1707, see Glanmor Williams, *Recovery, Reorientation and Reformation: Wales, c.1415–1642*, History of Wales, 3 (Oxford: Clarendon/University of Wales Press, 1987); J. Gwynthor Jones, *Early Modern Wales, c.1525–1640* (Basingstoke: Macmillan, 1994); G. Dyfnallt Owen, *Wales in the Reign of James I* (Woodbridge: Boydell, for the Royal Historical Society, 1988); and Jenkins, *Foundations of Modern Wales.*

194. Under its sixteenth-century title, *The Vnion of the Two Noble and Illustrate Famelies of Lancastre [and] Yorke beeyng long in Continual Discension for the Croune of this Noble Realme* (London, 1548).

195. Peter Roberts, 'Tudor Wales, National Identity, and the British Inheritance', in Bradshaw and Roberts (eds.), *British Consciousness and Identity*, 8–42.

196. E.g. the young John Milton, suspicious of Welsh recusancy, praising the Earl of Bridgewater: 'A noble Peer of mickle trust, and power | Has in his charge, with temper'd awe to guide | An old, and haughty Nation proud in Arms'; *A Mask Presented at Ludlow-Castle, 1634*, lines 31–3, quoting *The Riverside Milton*, ed. Roy Flannagan (Boston: Houghton Mifflin, 1998).

197. E.g. Peter R. Roberts, 'The Welsh Language, English Law and Tudor Legislation', *Transactions of the Honourable Society of Cymmrodorion* (1989), 19–75; Mark Ellis Jones, ' "An Invidious Attempt to Accelerate the Extinction of our Language": The Abolition of the Court of Great Sessions and the Welsh Language', *Welsh History Review*, 19 (1998): 226–64.

198. Philip Jenkins, 'Seventeenth-Century Wales: Definition and Identity', in Bradshaw and Roberts (eds.), *British Consciousness and Identity*, 213–35, p. 219; for contexts see R. Brinley Jones, *The Old British Tongue: The Vernacular in Wales 1540–1640* (Cardiff: Avalon Books, 1970).

199. For informed circumspection see G. W. S. Barrow (ed.), *The Declaration of Arbroath: History, Significance, Setting* (Edinburgh: Society of Antiquaries, 2003).

200. Beginnings are summarized by Dauvit Broun, 'The Origins of Scottish Identity' and Alexander Grant, 'Aspects of National Consciousness in Medieval Scotland', in Claus Bjørn, Alexander Grant, and Keith J. Stringer (eds.), *Nations, Nationalism and Patriotism in the European Past* (Copenhagen: Academic Press, 1994), 35–55, 68–95.

201. E.g. Julian Goodare, *State and Society in Early Modern Scotland* (Oxford: Oxford University Press, 1999).

202. E.g. Alexander Grant, 'Scotland's "Celtic Fringe" in the Late Middle Ages: The Macdonald Lords of the Isles and the Kingdom of Scotland', in R. R. Davies (ed.), *The British Isles, 1100–1500: Comparisons, Contrasts and Connections* (Edinburgh: John Donald, 1988), 118–41.

203. For the royalist accusation see e.g. Margaret, Duchess of Newcastle, *The Life of William Cavendish Duke of Newcastle*, ed. C. H. Firth, 2nd edn.

(London: Routledge, 1907), xliv: 'the rebellious Parliament, finding themselves overpowered … rather than to be utterly ruined (as was unavoidable),
did call the Scots to their assistance, with a promise to reward so great a
service with the four northern counties of Northumberland, Cumberland,
Westmoreland, and the bishopric of Durham.' On the parliamentarian side,
see e.g. the Milton of *Eikonoklastes* and *Defensio Prima* (above, p. 235). The
charge of seeking to bargain away the north sticks more firmly to Charles than
his opponents; see the apparently judicious account by Gilbert Burnet (well
read in the Duke of Hamilton's papers and able to confer with Lauderdale),
History of My Own Time, pt I, I, 59.

204. For a recent example see Mark Kishlansky, 'Charles I: A Case of Mistaken
Identity', *Past and Present*, 189 (2005): 41–80.

205. E.g. Arthur H. Williamson, *Scottish National Consciousness in the Age of James
VI: The Apocalypse, the Union and the Shaping of Scotland's Public Culture*
(Edinburgh: Donald, 1979); David Stevenson, 'The Early Covenanters and
the Federal Union of Britain', in Mason (ed.), *Scotland and England*, 163–81;
E. J. Cowan, 'The Making of the National Covenant', in Morrill (ed.),
Scottish National Covenant in its British Context, 68–89.

206. E.g. George Buchanan, 'Genethliacon' (celebrating the birth of James VI),
handsomely translated by Fanshawe decades later; Andrew Melville, 'Principis
Scoti-Britannorum natalia' (on the birth of Prince Henry) in *George Buchanan:
The Political Poetry*, ed. and trans. Paul J. McGinnis and Arthur H. Williamson
(Edinburgh: Scottish History Society, 1995); *The British Union: A Critical
Edition and Translation of David Hume of Godscroft's 'De Unione Insulae Britan-
nicae'*, ed. Paul J. McGinnis and Arthur H. Williamson (Aldershot: Ashgate,
2002).

207. See the nuanced discussion in J. H. Burns, *The True Law of Kingship: Concepts
of Monarchy in Early-Modern Scotland* (Oxford: Clarendon, 1996).

208. On James's resemblance to the supposedly British-born Roman emper-
or Constantine, who made Christianity the religion of the empire, see
e.g. John Gordon, *A Panegyrique of Congratulation for the Concord of the
Realmes of Great Britaine in Unitie of Religion, and under One King* (London,
1603).

209. Derek Hirst, 'The English Republic and the Meaning of Britain' (1994), rpt.
in Bradshaw and Morrill (eds.), *The British Problem*, 192–219, p. 211.

210. Contrast the sermons around regal union, where the emphasis is on the role
of David/James VI and I. Williamson, *Scottish National Consciousness*, 14–15;
Edward Vallance, *Revolutionary England and the National Covenant: State Oaths,
Protestantism and the Political Nation, 1553–1682* (Woodbridge: Boydell Press,
2005), 14.

211. Readers needing an overview can still turn with some confidence to T. W.
Moody, F. X. Martin, and F. J. Byrne (eds.), *Early Modern Ireland, 1543–1691*,
New History of Ireland, 3 (Oxford: Clarendon, 1976) and T. W. Moody

and W. E. Vaughan (eds.), *Eighteenth-Century Ireland, 1691–1800*, New History of Ireland, 4 (Oxford: Clarendon, 1986).

212. See e.g. Vincent Carey, '"Neither Good English nor Good Irish": Bi-Lingualism and Identity Formation in Sixteenth-Century Ireland', in Hiram Morgan (ed.), *Political Ideology in Ireland, 1541–1641* (Dublin: Four Courts, 1999), 45–61.

213. The Franciscan Fathers, Dún Mhuire, Killiney (eds.), *Father Luke Wadding: Commemorative Volume* (Dublin: Clonmore and Reynolds, 1957); P. J. Corish, 'Father Luke Wadding and the Irish Nation', *Irish Ecclesiastical Record*, 5th ser., 88 (1957): 377–95.

214. See e.g. Raymond Gillespie, 'The Social Thought of Richard Bellings', in Micheál Ó Siochrú (ed.), *Kingdoms in Crisis: Ireland in the 1640s* (Dublin: Four Courts, 2001), 212–28, and Rankin, *Between Spenser and Swift*, ch. 5.

215. E.g. Marc Caball, *Poets and Politics: Continuity and Reaction in Irish Poetry, 1558–1625* (Cork: Cork University Press, 1998)—*contra* the less convincing picture of sclerosis painted by Michelle O Riordain, *The Gaelic Mind and the Collapse of the Gaelic World* (Cork: Cork University Press, 1990).

216. Hiram Morgan, '"Faith and Fatherland" in Sixteenth-Century Ireland', *History Ireland*, 3/2 (1995): 13–20; Clare Carroll, *Circe's Cup: Cultural Transformations in Early Modern Writing about Ireland* (Cork: Cork University Press, 2001), esp. 104–44; Micheál Mac Craith, 'The Gaelic Reaction to the Reformation', in Ellis and Barber, *Conquest and Union*, 139–61, pp. 144–50; Canny, *Making Ireland British*, 418–32.

217. Breandán Ó Buachalla, 'James our True King: The Ideology of Irish Royalism in the Seventeenth Century', in D. George Boyce, Robert Eccleshall, and Vincent Geoghegan (eds.), *Political Thought in Ireland Since the Seventeenth Century* (London: Routledge, 1993), 7–35, p. 14; Mac Craith, 'Gaelic Reaction', 152.

218. Micheál Ó Siochrú, *Confederate Ireland 1642–1649: A Constitutional and Political Analysis* (Dublin: Four Courts, 1999), 239, citing the work of J. H. Elliott.

219. *A Jacobite Narrative of the War in Ireland 1688–91*, ed. John T. Gilbert, rpt. with an introd. by J. G. Simms (Shannon: Irish University Press, 1971).

220. For O'Mahony's only extant contribution to archipelagic English, 'A kind of a Ballad, briefly expressing the pride of Englishmen in this kingdom' (1642)—if the attribution of the London newsletter can be trusted—see Carpenter (ed.), *Verse in English from Tudor and Stuart Ireland*, 237–41. That the ballad, which to judge from its phrasing was the work of an Irish speaker, seethes with hatred towards the English settlers, is consistent with O'Mahony's authorship, though it describes massacre giving way to remorse ('fainting in heart, we lately repent') and it ends with hesitation: 'But whether to kill them tis doubtful to say, | Or else to ship them and send them away.'

221. Tadhg Ó hAnnracháin, ' "Though Hereticks and Politicians should Misinter-
     pret their Goode Zeal": Political Ideology and Catholicism in Early Modern
     Ireland', in Jane H. Ohlmeyer (ed.), *Political Thought in Seventeenth-Century
     Ireland: Kingdom or Colony* (Cambridge: Cambridge University Press, 2000),
     155−75, pp. 161−3. For contexts see Patricia O'Connell, *The Irish College at
     Lisbon, 1590−1834* (Dublin: Four Courts, 2001).
222. During the hostilities with France in 1627, which centred on the expedition
     to La Rochelle, the French released half the British vessels impounded at
     Bordeaux because they were Scottish (see Macinnes, *British Revolution*, 52,
     who notes comparable discrimination in favour of the Scots and Irish by the
     Spanish after Charles I declared war in 1625). On the limits of the auld alliance
     once the Covenanters fell out with Charles, see Conrad Russell, 'The Anglo-
     Scottish Union 1603−1643: A Success?', in Fletcher and Roberts (eds.),
     Religion, Culture and Society in Early Modern Britain, 238−56, pp. 255−6 and
     Mark Charles Fissel, *The Bishops' Wars: Charles I's Campaigns against Scotland,
     1638−1640* (Cambridge: Cambridge University Press, 1994), 3, 45−6.
223. E.g. Murdoch, *Britain, Denmark-Norway and the House of Stuart*.
224. E.g. Steve Murdoch, 'James VI and the Formation of a Scottish-British
     Military Identity', in Steve Murdoch and A. McKillop, *Fighting for Identity:
     Scottish Military Experiences c.1550−1900* (Leiden: Brill, 2002), 3−31 and
     'Scotland, Scandinavia and the Bishops' Wars, 1638−1640', in Macinnes and
     Ohlmeyer (eds.), *Stuart Kingdoms*, 113−34.
225. Alexia Grosjean and Steve Murdoch (eds.), *Scottish Communities Abroad in the
     Early Modern Period* (Leiden: Brill, 2005) and Steve Murdoch, *Network North:
     Scottish Kin, Commercial and Covert Associations in Northern Europe, 1603−1746*
     (Leiden: Brill, 2006).
226. E.g. Geoffrey Parker and Lesley M. Smith, *The General Crisis of the Seventeenth
     Century*, 2nd edn. (London: Routledge, 1997)—first published in 1978.
227. Philip A. Knachel, *England and the Fronde: The Impact of the English Civil War
     and Revolution on France* (Ithaca, NY: Cornell University Press, 1967).
228. Aidan Clarke, 'Ireland and the General Crisis', *Past and Present*, 48 (1970):
     79−99.
229. For a sweeping version of the argument that European issues and con-
     texts—intellectual, dynastic, military—were so definitive that a three-
     kingdom approach is incomplete, and projects the modern state system
     back onto the seventeenth century, see Jonathan Scott, 'England's Troubles
     1603−1702', in R. Malcolm Smuts (ed.), *The Stuart Court and Europe: Es-
     says in Politics and Political Culture* (Cambridge: Cambridge University Press,
     1996), 20−38, enlarged in his *England's Troubles: Seventeenth-Century English
     Political Instability in European Context* (Cambridge: Cambridge University
     Press, 2000).
230. Pocock, *Discovery of Islands*, 100, but see 107−8; on Willem van Oranje's
     displaced struggle with Louis XIV for supremacy in the Low Countries and

Germany see e.g. Jonathan Israel (ed.), *The Anglo-Dutch Moment: Essays on the Glorious Revolution and its World Impact* (Cambridge: Cambridge University Press, 1991).

231. The most comprehensively (and largely persuasive) archipelagic analysis is by Tim Harris, *Revolution: The Great Crisis of the British Monarchy 1685–1720* (London: Allen Lane, 2006).

232. *A Panegyrick to my Lord Protector* (London, 1655), 6.

233. See e.g. Austin Woolrych, *Britain in Revolution 1625–1660* (Oxford: Oxford University Press, 2002), chs. 18–24. For a telling account of the difference between the Commonwealth's annexation of Ireland and its negotiated incorporation of Scotland, see Macinnes, *British Revolution*, 199–205 (though evidence of enforcement is stressed by Morrill, 'The English, the Scots, and the Dilemmas of Union, 1638–1654', in Smout (ed.), *Anglo-Scottish Relations*, 57–74, pp. 64–5).

234. James Thomson and David Mallet, *Alfred: A Masque. Represented before Their Royal Highnesses the Prince and Princess of Wales, at Cliffden, on the first of August, 1740* (London, 1740), 42.

235. Richard Head, *The Western Wonder: Or, O Brazeel, an Inchanted Island Discovered* (London, 1674).

236. For contexts see Josephine Waters Bennett, 'Britain among the Fortunate Isles', *Studies in Philology*, 3 (1956): 114–40.

237. See below, pp. 226–7, 238–42; Armitage, *Ideological Origins of the British Empire*, ch. 4.

238. 'A Rough Draft of a New Modell at Sea', quoted by Deborah Orr, *Empire on the English Stage 1660–1714* (Cambridge: Cambridge University Press, 2001), 39.

239. 24 Henry VIII c. 12; see e.g. Walter Ullmann, ' "This Realm of England is an Empire" ', *Journal of Ecclesiastical History*, 30 (1979): 175–203 and cf. Roger A. Mason, 'This Realm of Scotland is an Empire? Imperial Ideas and Iconography in early Renaissance Scotland', in Barbara Elizabeth Crawford (ed.), *Church, Chronicle and Learning in Medieval and Early Renaissance Scotland* (Edinburgh: Mercat, 1999), 73–91.

240. E.g. Roger A. Mason, 'The Scottish Reformation and the Origins of Anglo-British Imperialism', in Mason (ed.), *Scots and Britons*, 161–86; Armitage, *Ideological Origins of the British Empire*, 36–45.

241. Bruce Ward Henry, 'John Dee, Humphrey Llwyd, and the Name "British Empire" ', *Huntington Library Quarterly*, 35 (1972): 189–90; Gwyn A. Williams, *Welsh Wizard and British Empire: Dr John Dee and a Welsh Identity* (Cardiff: University College Cardiff Press, 1980).

242. For contexts see Anthony Pagden, *Lords of All the World: Ideologies of Empire in Spain, Britain and France, c.1500–c.1800* (New Haven: Yale University Press, 1995).

243. *The Workes of Beniamin Jonson* (London, 1616), 893–901, p. 895.

244. The italicized words allude to Virgil's celebrated description of Britain, in *Eclogues* I.66: 'et penitus toto diuisos orbe Britannos'.

245 E.g. the reference to James as King of England, Scotland, France, Hibernia, and Ireland in a Russian document of 1617, or Gustav II Adolf of Sweden's request for permission to levy troops in England, Scotland, Ireland, and Great Britain. See Murdoch, *Britain, Denmark-Norway and the House of Stuart*, 15.

246. Armitage, 'Literature and Empire', 106–12.

247. Cf. Blair Worden, 'Marchamont Nedham and the Beginnings of English Republicanism, 1649–1656', in David Wootton (ed.), *Republicanism, Liberty, and Commercial Society, 1649–1776* (Stanford, CA: Stanford University Press, 1994), 45–81, p. 73, who notes that encouragement came from Machiavelli's *Discourses*, II.4.

248. S. A. G. Taylor, *The Western Design: An Account of Cromwell's Expedition to the Caribbean* (1965; London: Solstice Productions, 1969); David Armitage, 'The Cromwellian Protectorate and the Languages of Empire', *Historical Journal*, 35 (1992); 531–55; Orr, *Empire on the English Stage*, 253.

249. Cf. Armitage, *Ideological Origins of the British Empire*, 9–10.

250. Stevenson and Davidson (eds.), *Early Modern Women Poets*, 531–4, p. 531.

251. E.g. Karl S. Bottigheimer, 'Kingdom and Colony: Ireland in the Westward Enterprise 1536–1660', in Kenneth R. Andrews, Nicholas P. Canny, and P. E. H. Hair (eds.), *The Westward Enterprise: English Activities in Ireland, the Atlantic and America, 1480–1650* (Liverpool: Liverpool University Press, 1978), 45–64; Ciaran Brady, *The Chief Governors: The Rise and Fall of Reform Government in Tudor Ireland 1536–1588* (Cambridge: Cambridge University Press, 1995); Nicholas Canny, *The Elizabethan Conquest of Ireland: A Pattern Established 1565–96* (Hassocks: Harvester Press, 1976) and *Kingdom and Colony: Ireland in the Atlantic World 1560–1800* (Baltimore: Johns Hopkins University Press, 1988); Ellis, *Tudor Frontiers and Noble Power* and *Ireland in the Age of the Tudors: English Expansion and the End of Gaelic Rule, 1447–1603* (London: Longman, 1998); Felicity Heal, *Reformation in Britain and Ireland* (Oxford: Oxford University Press, 2003); Rolf Loeber, *The Geography and Practice of English Colonization in Ireland from 1534–1609* (Athlone: Group for the Study of Irish Historic Settlement, 1991).

252. For case studies see Nicholas P. Canny, 'Raleigh's Ireland', in H. G. Jones (ed.), *Raleigh and Quinn: The Explorer and his Boswell* (Chapel Hill, NC: North Caroliniana Society, 1987), 87–101, and *The Upstart Earl: A Study of the Social and Mental World of Richard Boyle First Earl of Cork, 1566–1643* (Cambridge: Cambridge University Press, 1982); a rich account of Jacobean conditions is given by Victor Treadwell, *Buckingham and Ireland, 1616–1628: A Study in Anglo-Irish Politics* (Dublin: Four Courts, 1998).

253. The standard work is Karl S. Bottigheimer, *English Money and Irish Land: The 'Adventurers' in the Cromwellian Settlement of Ireland* (Oxford: Clarendon,

1971). Cf. T. C. Barnard, *Cromwellian Ireland: English Government and Reform in Ireland, 1649–1660* (London: Oxford University Press, 1975). On agriculture and natural history as aspects of plantation at this date, see Gerald Boate, *Irelands Naturall History* (London, 1652), and William Petty, *The History of the Survey of Ireland: Commonly Called the Down Survey, A. C. 1655–6*, ed. Thomas A. Larcom (Dublin: Irish Archaeological Society, 1851), backed by T. C. Barnard, 'The Hartlib Circle and Ireland', *Irish Historical Studies*, 19 (1974): 56–71 and 'Sir William Petty, Irish Landowner', in Hugh Lloyd-Jones, Valerie Pearl, and Blair Worden (eds.), *History and Imagination: Essays in Honour of Hugh Trevor-Roper* (London: Duckworth, 1981), 201–17.

254. Karl S. Bottigheimer, 'The Restoration Land Settlement: A Structural View', *Irish Historical Studies*, 18 (1972–3): 1–21; J. G. Simms, *The Williamite Confiscation in Ireland, 1690–1703* (London: Faber, 1956).

255. E.g. John Morrill, 'Three Kingdoms and One Commonwealth? The Enigma of Mid-Seventeenth-Century Britain and Ireland', in Grant and Stringer (eds.), *Uniting the Kingdom?*, 170–90, pp. 175–6; David Stevenson, 'Cromwell, Scotland and Ireland', in John Morrill (ed.), *Oliver Cromwell and the English Revolution* (London: Longman, 1990), 149–80, pp. 160–3.

256. E.g. Patrick Little, 'The English Parliament and the Irish Constitution, 1641–9', in Ó Siochrú (ed.), *Kingdoms in Crisis*, 106–21.

257. *Pace* the substantial, nationalist scholarship of Eoin MacNeill, *Early Irish Laws and Institutions* (Dublin: Burnes Oates and Washbourne, 1935). See e.g. the corrective J. F. Lydon, *The Lordship of Ireland in the Middle Ages* (Dublin: Gill and Macmillan, 1972) and Marie Therese Flanagan, *Irish Society, Anglo-Norman Settlers, Angevin Kingship* (Oxford: Clarendon, 1989). The best guide to later developments is Katharine Simms, *From Kings to Warlords: The Changing Political Structure of Gaelic Ireland in the Later Middle Ages* (Woodbridge: Boydell, 1987).

258. In 1154, the English-born Pope Adrian IV authorized Henry II to proceed to Ireland 'to check the torrent of wickedness, to reform evil manners, to sow the seeds of virtue'. An opportunity came in 1168 when Diarmait Mac Murchada, King of Leinster, sought Henry's protection. By 1171, Henry, preceded by expeditions led by Fitzgerald and Strongbow (de Clare, Earl of Pembroke), was in Dublin, where he received the submission of almost all the Irish chiefs.

259. R. Dudley Edwards and T. W. Moody, 'The History of Poynings' Law, Part I: 1494–1615', *Irish Historical Studies*, 2 (1941): 415–24; Aidan Clarke, 'The History of Poynings's Law 1615–41', *Irish Historical Studies*, 18 (1972): 207–22. For this paragraph generally, see Brendan Bradshaw, *The Irish Constitutional Revolution of the Sixteenth Century* (Cambridge: Cambridge University Press, 1979).

260. *The Statutes at Large, Passed in the Parliaments held in Ireland … A. D. 1310 to … A. D. 1800*, 21 vols. (Dublin, 1786–1804), I, 176. Again, Irish Catholic

commentators could dissent, arguing, like the Gaelic antiquary Roderic O'Flaherty in *Ogygia* (London, 1685), that it was not until 1603 that Ireland was legitimately subject to a king of England (i.e. descended from ancient Irish kings).

261. On this design—which undoubtedly figured among English views of Ireland, though with fluctuating official support—see Canny, *Making Ireland British*.

262. The classic account of Ireland as the site of a colonial enterprise that led on to North America is David Beers Quinn, *The Elizabethans and the Irish* (Ithaca: Cornell University Press, 1966), ch. 9. For debate see Hiram Morgan, 'Mid-Atlantic Blues', *Irish Review*, 11 (1992): 50–5 and Andrew Hadfield, 'Rocking the Boat: A Response to Hiram Morgan', *Irish Review*, 14 (1993): 15–19. The contentions are reviewed e.g. by Jane H. Ohlmeyer, 'Seventeenth-Century Ireland and the New British and Atlantic Histories', *American Historical Review*, 104 (1999): 446–62, 'A Laboratory for Empire? Early Modern Ireland and English Imperialism', in Kevin Kenny (ed.), *Ireland and the British Empire* (Oxford: Oxford University Press, 2004), 26–60.

263. Certainly, after the Cromwellian period, it was hard to recover the notional, though symbolically significant, belief, officially sponsored in the 1630s, that Ireland could emulate Scotland and plant American colonies of its own. On New Albion, near Virginia, licensed by the Irish crown and serviced from Ireland (though largely peopled by English adventurers), see *The Earl of Strafforde's Letters and Dispatches*, ed. William Knowler, 2 vols. (London, 1739), I, 72–3.

264. The usual estimate is that 400,000 English people emigrated to North America and the Caribbean during the seventeenth century, from a country with a population of about 5 million. See e.g. Ian K. Steele, *The English Atlantic 1675–1740: An Exploration of Communication and Community* (New York: Oxford University Press, 1986); Alison Games, *Migration and the Origins of the English Archipelagic World* (Cambridge, MA: Harvard University Press, 1999).

265. The literature is extensive; see e.g. Philip F. Gura, *A Glimpse of Sion's Glory: Puritan Radicalism in New England, 1620–1660* (Middletown, CT: Wesleyan University Press, 1984).

266. There is a text in Stevenson and Davidson (eds.), *Early Modern Women Poets*. For contexts see Francis J. Bremer, *Puritan Crisis: New England and the English Civil Wars, 1630–1670* (New York: Garland, 1989) and Christopher Ivic, ' "Our British Land": Anne Bradstreet's Atlantic Perspective', in Schwyzer and Mealor (eds.), *Archipelagic Identities*, 195–204.

267. See e.g. Kidd, *British Identities*, ch. 4.

268. Calls for an oceanic enlargement of the new British history have been made by, among others, David Armitage, *Greater Britain, 1516–1776: Essays in Atlantic History* (Aldershot: Ashgate, 2004); Macinnes, *British Revolution*, 2.

269. See the essays by Richard S. Dunn and others in Canny (ed.), *Origins of Empire*.

270. Preface to *Roderick Hudson* [New York Edition] (Harmondsworth: Penguin, 1969), 9.

271. William Molyneux, *The Case of Ireland's being Bound by Acts of Parliament in England, Stated* (Dublin, 1698), 148.

272. Carla Gardina Pestana, *The English Atlantic in an Age of Revolution, 1640−1661* (Cambridge, MA: Harvard University Press, 2004), 9.

273. E.g. David Armitage and Michael J. Braddick (eds.), *The British Atlantic World, 1500−1800* (London: Palgrave, 2002); Carole Shammas and Elizabeth Mancke (eds.), *The Creation of the British Atlantic World* (Baltimore: Johns Hopkins University Press, 2005).

274. Scottish emigration and punitive expulsion from Ireland change the composition of the colonies from 1648 onwards. See T. C. Smout, Ned C. Landsman, and T. M. Devine, 'Scottish Emigration in the Seventeenth and Eighteenth Centuries' and L. M. Cullen, 'The Irish Diaspora of the Seventeenth and Eighteenth Centuries', in Nicholas Canny (ed.), *Europeans on the Move: Studies on European Migration, 1500−1800* (Oxford: Clarendon, 1994), 76−112, 113−49.

275. Donald Harman Akenson, *If the Irish Ran the World: Montserrat, 1630−1730* (Montreal: McGill-Queen's University Press, 1997).

276. See the more convinced discussion by Alison Games, 'Migration', in Armitage and Braddick (eds.), *British Atlantic World*, 31−50, p. 32.

277. E.g. Betty Wood, *The Origins of American Slavery: Freedom and Bondage in the English Colonies* (New York: Hill and Wang, 1996); James Walvin, *Making the Black Atlantic: Britain and the African Diaspora* (London: Cassell, 2000).

278. See e.g. Alan I. Macinnes and Arthur H. Williamson (eds.), *Shaping the Stuart World, 1603−1714: The Atlantic Connection* (Leiden: Brill, 2006).

279. Pestana, *English Atlantic*, 3−4; April Hatfield, *Atlantic Virginia: Intercolonial Relations in the Seventeenth Century* (Philadelphia: University of Pennsylvania Press, 2004).

280. E.g. William Sachse, 'The Migration of New Englanders to England, 1640−1660', *American Historical Review*, 53 (1948): 251−78.

281. Eliga H. Gould, 'Revolution and Counter-Revolution', in Armigate and Braddick, (eds.), *British Atlantic World*, 196−213, pp. 206−7.

282. Carla Gardina Pestana, 'Religion', in Armitage and Braddick (eds.), *British Atlantic World*, 69−89, p. 79.

283. Cf. Nicholas Canny, 'England's New World and the Old, 1480s−1630s'—an account which searches assiduously for signs of tolerance among the colonists—and the grievous record of animosity, exploitation, and violence set out by Peter C. Mancall, 'Native Americans and Europeans in English America, 1500−1700', in Canny (ed.), *Origins of Empire*, 148−69, p. 152, and 328−50.

284. *The Hireling Ministry None of Christs: Or, A Discourse Touching the Propagating the Gospel of Christ Jesus* (London, 1652), quoted by, among others, Christopher Hill, 'Puritans and "the Dark Corners of the Land" ', in his *Change and Continuity in Seventeenth-Century England*, rev. edn. (New Haven: Yale University Press, 1991), 3–47, p. 20.

285. For the picture around the islands see e.g. Ceri Davies, *Latin Writers of the Renaissance* (Cardiff: University of Wales Press, 1981); J. W. Binns, *Intellectual Culture in Elizabethan and Jacobean England: The Latin Writings of the Age* (Leeds: Francis Cairns, 1990); Benignus Millett, 'Irish Literature in Latin, 1550–1700', in Moody, Martin, and Byrne (eds.), *Early Modern Ireland, 1543–1691*, 561–86; Jack MacQueen, 'From Rome to Ruddiman: The Scoto-Latin Tradition', in Brown (gen. ed.), *Edinburgh History of Scottish Literature*, I, 185–208.

286. Patricia Palmer, *Language and Conquest in Early Modern Ireland: English Renaissance Literature and Elizabethan Imperial Expansion* (Cambridge: Cambridge University Press, 2001); Richard A. McCabe, *Spenser's Monstrous Regiment: Elizabethan Ireland and the Poetics of Difference* (Oxford: Oxford University Press, 2005). Cf. Tony Crowley, *Wars of Words: The Politics of Language in Ireland 1537–2004* (Oxford: Oxford University Press, 2005), chs. 2–4.

287. Leerssen, *Mere Irish*, 204–15; Canny, *Making Ireland British*, 573–6.

288. Éamonn mac Donnchadh an Dúna, 'Mo lá leóin go deó go n-éagad', lines 127–36, in Cecile O'Rahilly (ed.), *Five Seventeenth-Century Political Poems* (Dublin: Dublin Institute for Advanced Studies, 1952).

289. *OED Tory* n. 1.a (dating the word from 1646, though note a probable earlier occurrence in *The Welsh Embassador* [1624?], IV.ii.87, where the Clown says to a supposed Irishman 'And I hugg thee sweete Tor<y> for it'). For the likely means of transmission between languages at the mid-century, see Allan Macinnes, 'Gaelic Culture in the Seventeenth Century: Polarization and Assimilation', in Ellis and Barber, *Conquest and Union*, 162–94, pp. 178–9.

290. *OED*. The word is said to derive ultimately from 'whiggam', a term used in Scotland in driving horses, 'whiggamores' being horse-drivers and, in common parlance, men from the West of Scotland where Presbyterianism was particularly radical (see Chapter 9). There was a Whiggamore Raid in 1648, when a contingent of Covenanters marched to Edinburgh against Charles I and the Duke of Hamilton, giving the name 'Whig' to those who opposed the court.

291. E.g. the poet Brigid O'Donnell, defending herself in 1607 against the charge of receiving money from her outlaw husband, claimed that she had scarcely enough Irish to understand their go-between (Stevenson and Davidson (eds.), *Early Modern Women Poets*, 165).

292. Alan Bliss, *Spoken English in Ireland: 1600–1740* (Dublin: Dolmen, 1979), 11–30.

293. See the entries in Derick S. Thomson (ed.), *Companion to Gaelic Scotland* (Oxford: Blackwell, 1983); also Colm Ó Baoill, 'Borrowing between Scots and Gaelic', *Scottish Language* (Aberdeen), 10 (1991): 9–17 and 'The Scots-Gaelic Interface', in Charles Jones (ed.), *The Edinburgh History of the Scots Language* (Edinburgh: Edinburgh University Press, 1997), 551–68.

294. Gerard Murphy, 'David O'Bruadair', *Irish Ecclesiastical Record*, 78 (1952): 340–57; Pádraigín Riggs (ed.), *Dáibhí Ó Bruadair: His Historical and Literary Context* (Dublin: Irish Texts Society, 2001).

295. Palmer, *Language and Conquest*.

296. The depositions made by Protestant survivors of the 1641 Rising indicate that bilingualism was relatively widespread; Canny, *Making Ireland British*, 452–4.

297. For early appreciation see E. S. Shuckburgh (ed.), *Two Biographies of William Bedell* (Cambridge: Cambridge University Press, 1902); Aidan Clarke, 'Bishop William Bedell (1571–1642) and the Irish Reformation', in Ciaran Brady (ed.), *Worsted in the Game: Losers in Irish History* (Dublin: Lilliput Press, 1989), 61–70.

298. On missionary Irish see e.g. Alan Ford, *The Protestant Reformation in Ireland, 1590–1641* (1985; Dublin: Four Courts, 1997); T. C. Barnard, 'Protestants and the Irish Language, c.1675–1725', *Journal of Ecclesiastical History*, 44 (1993): 243–72.

299. The first book to be printed in Welsh, composed by John Price of Brecon, consisted of the Creed, the Lord's Prayer, and the Ten Commandments (1546); the English Prayerbook and the New Testament were translated by William Salesbury (1551 and 1567); the complete Welsh Bible, tr. William Morgan, appeared in 1588. Irish versions of the New Testament (*Tiomna Nuad*) and the Book of Common Prayer followed in 1602 and 1608; William Bedell's translation of the Old Testament, undertaken 1632–40, was published with the support of the scientist Robert Boyle (brother of the Earl of Orrery) in 1685. Movement on Scottish Gaelic was slower: a translation of Calvin's Catechism appeared in 1630; there were versions of the metrical psalms in 1659 and (a full text) 1694; a roman-type edn. of the Irish Bible, published in London in 1690, and the 1608 Book of Common Prayer, had some impact, but it was not until 1767 that the NT was translated afresh (from Greek) into Scottish Gaelic, with the OT appearing in four parts between 1783 and 1801.

300. Carpenter (ed.), *Verse in English from Tudor and Stuart Ireland*, 312.

301. 'A New Song', in *Poems on Affairs of State: Augustan Satirical Verse, 1660–1714*, gen. ed. George DeF. Lord, 7 vols. (New Haven: Yale University Press, 1963–75), IV, 311–12.

302. Paul Muldoon, *To Ireland, I* (Oxford: Oxford University Press, 2000), 114–15.

303. Printed separately (though often enough included with 'A New Song') in *Poems on Affairs of State*, IV, 312–13. In heraldry, the talbot, a variety of

hound, was associated with the family of Richard Talbot, Earl of Tyrconnell, the ass being either King James or Richard's brother, Peter, Roman Catholic archbishop of Dublin.

304. Bodleian Library, MS Rawlinson D. 71, quoted by Bliss, *Spoken English in Ireland*, 27.

305. Ibid., 27–8. Cf. the informative discussion in Carpenter (ed.), *Verse in English from Tudor and Stuart Ireland*, p. 563.

306. Stevenson and Davidson, *Early Modern Women Poets*, xlvi.

307. The pull of Chester and its speech was strong in North Wales, especially along the coast; Shrewsbury was a centre for the Anglo-Welsh gentry of mid-Wales, while those in the south had more contact with Bristol.

308. E.g. F. E. Hutchinson, *Henry Vaughan: A Life and Interpretation* (Oxford: Clarendon, 1947), ch. 12, qualified by Mathias, 'New Language'.

309. Jenkins, *Foundations of Modern Wales*, 221–5.

310. Richard Carew noted how certain Cornishmen 'so affect their own' that they refuse to answer Englishmen in English, saying, 'Meea Navidna Cowza-sawzneck' ('I can speak no Saxonage' or, more firmly, 'I *will* speak no Saxonage')—cited by Stoyle, *West Britons*, 17–18.

311. The best overall account in relation to literary usage is Ronald D. S. Jack, 'The Language of Literary Materials: Origins to 1700', in Jones (ed.), *Edinburgh History of the Scots Language*, 213–63.

312. Quoting the Edinburgh, 1599 edn., 154. Cf. the slightly variant passage in the London, 1603 edn., 149, and 'A Speach, as it was Delivered in the Vpper House of the Parliament... on Munday the XIX. Day of March 1603 [1604]', *Workes*, 485–97, p. 488.

313. George Puttenham, *The Arte of English Poesie* (1589), ed. Gladys Doidge Willcock and Alice Walker (Cambridge: Cambridge University Press, 1936), 145.

314. For a range of theses see Galloway and Levack (eds.), *Jacobean Union*.

315. Alexander Gill, *Logonomia Anglica (1619)*, tr. Robin C. Alston, ed. Bror Danielsson and Arvid Gabrielson (Stockholm: Almqvist and Wiksell, 1972), 86.

316. James Hunt, *These Spiritual Verses of James Hunt, Concerning the Downfall of the Ceremonies* (London, 1642), quoted by the still useful Richard Foster Jones, *The Triumph of the English Language: A Survey of Opinions Concerning the Vernacular from the Introduction of Printing to the Restoration* (Stanford: Stanford University Press, 1953), 321.

317. Thomas Wilson, *The Arte of Rhetorique* (London, 1553), 86r.

318. The following discussion is indebted to Paula Blank, *Broken English: Dialects and the Politics of Language in Renaissance Writings* (London: Routledge, 1996) and Manfred Görlach, 'Regional and Social Variation', in Roger Lass (ed.), *The Cambridge History of the English Language*, vol. III, *1476–1776* (Cambridge: Cambridge University Press, 1999), 459–538.

319. See e.g. Richard Verstegan, *A Restitution of Decayed Intelligence* (Antwerp, 1605): 'wee see that in some seueral partes of *England* it self, both the names of things, and pronountiations of woords are somwhat different, ... as one would say at *London* I would eat more cheese yf I had it, the northern man saith, Ay sud eat mare cheese gin ay hadet, and the westerne man saith: Chud eat more cheese an chad it. Lo heer three different pronountiations in our own countrey in one thing, and heereof many the lyke examples might be alleaged' (195).

320. Richard Carew, 'Excellencie of the English Tongue', printed in William Camden, *Remaines, Concerning Britaine: but Especially England*, rev. edn. (London, 1614), and quoted in Görlach, 'Regional and Social Variation', 496.

321. John Aubrey, *Brief Lives*, ed. Oliver Lawson Dick (London: Secker and Warburg, 1950), 253–60, p. 255.

322. John Ray, *A Collection of English Words Not Generally Used* (London, 1674).

323. Ray, *Collection*, 2nd edn. (London, 1691), A6r.

324. Thomas Heywood, *An Apology for Actors* (London, 1612). F3r.

325. George Meriton, *A Yorkshire Dialogue* (York, 1683), 1.

326. Görlach, 'Regional and Social Variation', 485.

327. See the extract anthologized in Carpenter (ed.), *Verse in English from Tudor and Stuart Ireland*, 411–17.

328. Cf. the similarly annotated *The Irish Rendezvous: Or, A Description of T[yrconne]ll's Army of Tories and Bog-Trotters* (London, 1689).

329. Andrew Carpenter, 'Virgil Travesty in Restoration Ireland: Some Preliminary Notes on an Unexplored Literary Phenomenon', in Michael Kenneally and Rhona Richman Kenneally (eds.), *From 'English Literature' to 'Literatures in English': International Perspectives* (Heidelberg: Universitätsverlag Winter, 2005), 53–65, p. 55.

330. *The Irish Hudibras: Or, The Fingallian Prince* (London, 1689), 15; see 'A Medley of the Nations' above, p. 62.

331. William K. Sessions, *The First Printers in Waterford, Cork and Kilkenny* (York: Ebor Press, 1990).

332. See Mary Pollard, *Dublin's Trade in Books 1550–1800* (Oxford: Clarendon, 1989), esp. chs. 3–5, and, variously, Gillespie and Hadfield (eds.), *Irish Book in English*, plus Gillespie, *Reading Ireland*.

333. E.g. M. J. Walsh, 'The Publishing Policy of the English Press at St Omer, 1608–1759', in Keith Robbins (ed.), *Religion and Humanism* (Oxford: Blackwell, 1981), 239–50.

334. Alastair J. Mann, *The Scottish Book Trade, 1500 to 1720: Print Commerce and Print Control in Early Modern Scotland* (East Linton: Tuckwell, 2000), ch. 3.

335. On circulation (and translation) see Bernadette Cunningham, *The World of Geoffrey Keating: History, Myth and Religion in Seventeenth-Century Ireland* (Dublin: Four Courts, 2000), chs. 10–11.

336. E.g. M. O'N. Walsh, 'Irish Books Printed Abroad 1475–1700: An Interim Checklist', *Irish Book*, 2/1 (1963): 1–36.

337. The array of seventeenth-century material in Eluned Rees, *Libri Walliae: A Catalogue of Welsh Books and Books Printed in Wales, 1546–1820*, 2 vols. (Aberystwyth: National Library of Wales, 1987) is formidable. For discussion see e.g. Charles Parry, 'From Manuscript to Print—II. Printed Books', in *A Guide to Welsh Literature*, vol. III, *c.1530–1700*, ed. R. Geraint Gruffydd (Cardiff: University of Wales Press, 1997), 263–76, and Philip Henry Jones, 'Wales', in John Barnard and D. F. McKenzie (eds.), *The Cambridge History of the Book in Britain*, vol. IV, *1557–1695* (Cambridge: Cambridge University Press, 2002), 719–34.

338. Andrew Murphy, 'Reading Ireland: Print, Nationalism and Cultural Identity', *Irish Review*, 25 (1999–2000): 16–26. For contexts see Robert Welch, 'The Book in Ireland from the Tudor Re-Conquest to the Battle of the Boyne', in Barnard and McKenzie (eds.), *Cambridge History of the Book*, IV, 701–18, and, for an authoritative list, E. R. McC. Dix, *Catalogue of Early Dublin-Printed Books, 1601–1700*, 3 vols. (Dublin, 1898–1912).

339. Harold Love, *Scribal Publication in Seventeenth-Century England* (Oxford: Clarendon, 1993).

340. The London trade dominates Barnard and McKenzie (eds.), *Cambridge History of the Book*, IV, as it does the lists given in the standard, period catalogues: A. W. Pollard and G. R. Redgrave, *A Short-Title Catalogue of Books Printed in England, Scotland, and Ireland and of English Books Printed Abroad, 1475–1640*, 2nd edn., rev. by W. A. Jackson, F. S. Ferguson, and K. F. Pantzer, 3 vols. (London: The Bibliographical Society, 1976–91); Donald Wing, *A Short-Title Catalogue of Books Printed in England, Scotland, Ireland, Wales and British America, and of English Books Printed in other Countries 1641–1700*, 2nd edn., rev. John J. Morrison, Carolyn Nelson, and Timothy Crist, 4 vols. (New York: Modern Language Association of America, 1982–98); and *The Thomason Tracts 1640–1661: An Index* (Ann Arbor: University Microfilm International, 1981).

341. W. G. Stitt Dibden (ed.), *The Post Office, 1635–1720* (Bath: n.p., 1960), 1–15.

342. Joad Raymond, *The Invention of the Newspaper* (Oxford: Clarendon, 1996); James Sutherland, *The Restoration Newspaper and its Development* (Cambridge: Cambridge University Press, 1986).

343. C. H. Firth, 'Thurloe and the Post Office', *English Historical Review*, 13 (1898): 527–33.

344. Stitt Dibden (ed.), *Post Office*, 29–33.

345. Susan E. Whyman, 'Postal Censorship in England 1635–1844', <http://www.psc.gov.uk/postcomm/live/about-the-mail-market>.

346. Karin Bowie, 'Public Opinion, Popular Politics and the Union of 1707', *Scottish Historical Review*, 82 (2003): 226–60.

347. See the many volumes in the University of Toronto Press *Records of Early English Drama*, to which has been added David N. Klausner (ed.), *Wales* (Toronto: University of Toronto Press, 2005), in series but discreetly retitled *Records of Early Drama*, together with Alan J. Fletcher, *Drama and the Performing Arts in Pre-Cromwellian Ireland: A Repertory of Sources and Documents from the Earliest Times until c.1642* (London: Boydell and Brewer, 2001).

348. Since girls often left school after they learned to read but before they learned to write, this test almost certainly leads to an underestimate of female reading ability.

349. My discussion is indebted to Harris, *Restoration*, 17–18.

350. Sources include David Cressy, *Literacy and the Social Order: Reading and Writing in Tudor and Stuart England* (Cambridge: Cambridge University Press, 1980); Adam Fox, *Oral and Literate Culture in England*, esp. introd.; cf. Richard Suggett and Eryn Mant, 'Language, Literacy and Aspects of Identity in Early Modern Wales', in Adam Fox and Daniel R. Woolf (eds.), *The Spoken Word: Oral Culture in Britain, 1500–1850* (Manchester: Manchester University Press, 2002), 42–83.

351. R. A. Houston, *Scottish Literacy and the Scottish Identity: Illiteracy and Society in Scotland and Northern England 1600–1800* (Cambridge: Cambridge University Press, 1985); John Bannerman, 'Literacy in the Highlands', in Ian B. Cowan and Duncan Shaw (eds.), *Renaissance and Reformation in Scotland: Essays in Honour of Gordon Donaldson* (Edinburgh: Scottish Academic Press, 1983), 214–35.

352. E.g. Lord Conway's library at Portmore, Country Antrim (8,000 titles in the 1630s), the Limerick Catholic doctor Thomas Arthur's (293 volumes), and that of his fellow-citizen, the Protestant Christopher Sexton (131 volumes), those of Bishop Jones of Meath (99 titles in 1661), Bishop Samuel Foley of Down and Connor (almost 1,700 titles), and Bishop Ward of Raphoe (over 1,200 titles in the 1680s), and, further down the social hierarchy, Cornet Wilkinson, possibly in Kilkenny (over 100 books)—all noted by Raymond Gillespie, 'Print Culture, 1550–1700', in Gillespie and Hadfield (eds.), *Irish Book in English*, 17–33, pp. 21, 25. Cf. P. J. Corish (ed.), 'Bishop Wadding's Notebook', *Archivium Hibernicum*, 29 (1970): 49–114; Hugh Fenning (ed.), 'The Library of Bishop William Daton of Ossory, 1698', *Collectanea Hibernica*, 20 (1978); 30–57; H. J. Lawlor, 'Primate Ussher's Library before 1641', *Proceedings of the Royal Irish Academy*, 22C (1900): 216–64; Canice Mooney, 'The Library of Archbishop Piers Creagh', *Reportorium Novum*, 1 (pt. 1), 117–39; and Marcus Mac Enery, 'A Seventeenth-Century Anglo-Irish Library', *Irish Book Lover*, 30 (1946–8): 30–4.

353. Raymond Gillespie, *Reading Ireland*, 36–9.

354. Gillespie, *Reading Ireland*, 41. For contexts, and later decades, see Toby Barnard, 'Learning, the Learned and Literacy in Ireland, c.1660–1760', in Toby Barnard, Dáibhí Ó Cróinin, and Katharine Simms (eds.), *'A Miracle*

of Learning': Studies in Manuscripts and Irish Learning: Essays in Honour of William O'Sullivan (Aldershot: Ashgate, 1998), 209−35, pp. 220−1, 'Reading in Eighteenth-Century Ireland: Public and Private Pleasures', in Bernadette Cunningham and Máire Kennedy (eds.), *The Experience of Reading: Irish Historical Perspectives* (Dublin: Rare Books Group of the Library Association of Ireland, 1999), 60−77.

355. Cf. John Barnard and Maureen Bell, 'The English Provinces', in *Cambridge History of the Book*, IV, ed. Barnard and McKenzie, 665−86.

356. Mann, *Scottish Book Trade*, chs. 1−2, 5−6. For a catalogue see Harry G. Aldis, *A List of Books Printed in Scotland before 1700* (Edinburgh: National Library of Scotland, 1970).

357. This paragraph is indebted to Mann, *Scottish Book Trade*, quoting 98, 124.

358. Mann, *Scottish Book Trade*, 38−9, 91, 122−3.

359. Gillespie, *Reading Ireland*, 55.

360. Sessions, *First Printers in Waterford, Cork and Kilkenny*.

361. Gillespie, *Reading Ireland*, 87−90.

362. Gillespie, *Reading Ireland*, 78.

363. See the useful summaries in Tony Sweeney, *Ireland and the Printed Word: A Short Descriptive Catalogue of Early Books, Pamphlets, Newletters and Broadsides Relating to Ireland. Printed: 1475−1700* (Dublin: Éamonn de Búrca, 1997).

364. See selectively in James W. Phillips's 1952 doctoral thesis, pub. as *Printing and Bookselling in Dublin, 1670−1800* (Dublin: Irish Academic Press, 1998); Pollard, *Dublin's Trade in Books*, ch. 2; Gillespie, *Reading Ireland*, 79−93, 114−15, 146−53.

365. State control of the press was probably most concerted, in England but also more widely, during the Cromwellian union; see Jason Peacey, 'Cromwellian England: A Propaganda State?', *History*, 91 (2006): 176−99. English evidence is marshalled by e.g. Cyndia Clegg, *Press Censorship in Jacobean England* (Cambridge: Cambridge University Press, 2001); Sheila Lambert, 'The Printers and the Government, 1604−1637', in Robin Myers and Michael Harris (eds.), *Aspects of Printing from 1600* (Oxford: Oxford Polytechnic Press, 1987), 1−29; Anthony Milton, 'Licensing, Censorship and Religious Orthodoxy in Early Stuart England', *Historical Journal*, 41 (1998): 625−51; Mark Knights, *Representation and Misrepresentation in Later Stuart Britain: Partisanship and Political Culture* (Oxford: Oxford University Press, 2005), ch. 5. Cf. Mann, *Scottish Book Trade*, chs. 5−6; Mary Pollard, *Dublin's Trade in Books 1550−1800*, ch. 1; and Gillespie, *Reading Ireland*, esp. ch. 5.

366. Gillespie, *Reading Ireland*, 76, cites a document in the Public Record Office which indicates that books were being exported from England in the following proportions: 175 hundredweight to Ireland, 131 to Holland, 119 to Scotland, 108 to Virginia.

367. Mann, *Scottish Book Trade*, 124.

368. Welch, 'Book in Ireland', 704. Cf. Gillespie, 'The Book Trade in Southern Ireland, 1590–1640', in Gerard Long (ed.), *Books beyond the Pale: Aspects of the Provincial Book Trade in Ireland before 1850* (Dublin: Library Association of Ireland, 1996), 1–17.

369. Welch, 'Book in Ireland', 705.

370. David A. O'Hara, *English Newsbooks and Irish Rebellion, 1641–1649* (Dublin: Four Courts, 2006).

371. Gillespie, *Reading Ireland*, 59.

372. Ibid, 710.

373. British Library Sloane MS 900.

374. *The Works of Sir Thomas Urquhart of Cromarty*, ed. Thomas Maitland (Edinburgh: Maitland Club, 1834), 189–90, 312, quoted by R. D. S. Jack in the *Oxford DNB* entry on Urquhart.

375. See Mann, *Scottish Book Trade*, 152 on the interrogation and imprisonment of Geills Willamsone for printing the *Declaration* at Campbeltown; also William Sessions, 'Edward Jones: The Travelling Printer with William III in 1690', in his *Further Irish Studies in Early Printing History* (York: Ebor Press, 1994), 24–52.

376. Mann, *Scottish Book Trade*, 39–40.

377. See Gordon Donaldson, *The Making of the Scottish Prayer Book of 1637* (Edinburgh: Edinburgh University Press, 1954).

378. *Poems on Affairs of State*, IV, 313–14.

379. The plot posed a significant challenge, involving up to ten members of the Dublin parliament, one of whom, Alexander Jephson, was executed. For a freshly researched account see Smyth, *Making of the United Kingdom*, 38–40.

380. 'Bludius, ut ruris damnum repararet aviti, | Addicit fisco dum Diadema suo' becomes 'When daring Blood to have his rents regain'd | Upon the English Diadem distrain'd'; 'Bludius et Corona', lines 1–2 and 'The Loyall Scot', lines 178–9, in *Poems and Letters of Marvell*, ed. Margoliouth, I.

381. It was in response to the posthumous publication of a treatise by Bramhall, tricked out with an introduction by Parker, that Marvell—apparently still working on 'The Loyall Scot'—wrote his best-selling prose satire, *The Rehearsal Transprosed* (1672).

382. Chief among my sources are A. W. Moore, *A History of the Isle of Man*, 2 vols. (London: T. Fisher Unwin, 1900), I, bk. II, chs. 2–3; J. R. Dickinson, 'The Earl of Derby and the Isle of Man, 1643–1651', *Transactions of the Historic Society of Lancashire and Cheshire*, 141 (1991): 39–76; and idem., *The Lordship of Man under the Stanleys: Government and Economy in the Isle of Man, 1580–1704* (Manchester: Chetham Society, 1996), introd. and ch. 1.

383. For a list see *The Stanley Papers*, III.2, *Chetham Society*, 67 (1867): cccvii-cccxi.

384. See 'Eubonia's Praise: A Song', 'Prologue to a Play Acted in Castle Rushin, before the Right Honourable Iames Earl of Derby, to Divert his Pensive

Sp*irit* and Deep Concern for the Calamity of his Country—Occasiond by the Grand Rebellion begun Anno 1641', and 'A Threnodia—Or Elegiac Song on the Direfull Effects of the Grand Rebellion'—recorded with contemporaneous Manx versions in Manx Museum Library Moore MS 154A, *Archdeacon Rutter's Song Book*, ed. Roger Dickinson, in David George (ed.), *Lancashire*, Records of Early English Drama (Toronto: University of Toronto Press, 1991), app. 5. Cf. Rutter's ode 'To the Glorious Memory of the Blessed Martyr, James, Earle of Derby, in *Stanley Papers*, III.2, app. 15.

385. George (ed.), *Lancashire*, 273−8. In classically archipelagic fashion, the 'Nation' celebrated in the poem does not entirely coincide with the 'Country' whose fate after 1641, according to its full title (see previous note), had lowered Stanley's mood. The earl's interests in Lancashire tied his 'his Pensive Sp*irit* and Deep Concern into what was happening in Britain.

386. Quoting George (ed.), *Lancashire*, 281. The note, originally made by Thomas Parr, vicar of Malew 1641−91 (d. 1695), continues with a reference to the previous Twelfth Night: 'All the men just with the earle and the wives with the Countesse likewise there was such another feast that day was twelve moneth at night beinge 1643 [i.e. 1644]'.

387. Edward Cowan, 'The Political Ideas of a Covenanting Leader: Archibald Campbell, Marquis of Argyll, 1670−1661', in Mason (ed.), *Scots and Britons*, 241−62.

388. *Discovery of Islands*, 293.

389. Keith Brown, 'A Blessed Union? Anglo-Scottish Relations before the Covenant', in Smout (ed.), *Anglo-Scottish Relations*, 37−55, p. 39.

390. 'The English, the Scots', in Smout (ed.), *Anglo-Scottish Relations*, 70.

391. 'Inscription on a Monument in the Church at Gowran, County Kilkenny', in Carpenter (ed.), *Verse in English from Tudor and Stuart Ireland*, 263.

392. *Common-wealth of Oceana*, B1v−2r.

393. They are discussed in Chapters 8 and 9.

394. 'Panegyrick', 5−7. The title page of the edition by Thomas Newcombe, a printer with strong connections to the Protectoral government, says that the poem (which was published just after the suppression of a series of royalist uprisings) was composed 'by a Gentleman that loves the Peace, Union, and Prosperity of the English Nation'.

395. Cf. the Protector's repeated emphasis on the interests of 'this nation', i.e. England, despite inclusive references to 'the three nations', in his widely read opening speech to the parliament (4 September 1654); *The Writings and Speeches of Oliver Cromwell*, introd. and ed. Wilbur Cortez Abbott, 4 vols. (Oxford: Clarendon, 1937−47), III, 434−43.

396. *OED* union 2. a.

397. *OED* shows the words nationalism/unionism and nationalist/unionist pushing into the language as twinned opposites between about 1798 and the 1880s.

398. Cf. Davies, *Isles*, 689.
399. *OED* union 2. b. *Painting*. Agreement or harmony in respect of colour, design, etc., citing a text from 1704, '*Union* (a Term among Painters) is the mutual Agreeableness and Sympathy of the Colours in a Piece of Painting'. 3. a. *Scots Law*. The uniting into one tenantry of lands or tenements not lying contiguous.
400. Cf. Marie Axton, *The Queen's Two Bodies: Drama and the Elizabethan Succession* (London: Royal Historical Society, 1977), 111–15, Dutton, ' "Methinks the Truth Should Live from Age to Age" ', 185–8.
401. See the evidence summarized in Kurland, '*Hamlet* and the Scottish Succession?'
402. For the data, see Keith J. Lindley, 'The Impact of the 1641 Rebellion upon England and Wales, 1641–5', *Irish Historical Studies*, 19 (1972): 143–76.
403. Cf. Ethan Howard Shagan, 'Constructing Discord: Ideology, Propaganda, and English Responses to the Irish Rebellion of 1641', *Journal of British Studies*, 36 (1997): 4–34.
404. Bacon wrote a discourse in favour of Anglo-Scottish union as early as 1603; his support of the policy in the House of Commons during 1604 and 1606–7 helped advance him to the clerkship in 1608. See 'A Draught of a Proclamation Touching his Majesty's Stile, prepared not used' (1604), 'Certain Articles or Considerations touching the Union of the Kingdoms of England and Scotland' (1604), and 'Certain Considerations Touching the Plantation in Ireland' (1606), in *The Works of Francis Bacon*, ed. James Spedding, Robert Leslie Ellis, and Douglas Denon Heath, 15 vols. (London: Longmans, 1857–74), and, for lively discussion, Maley, *Nation, State and Empire*, ch. 5.
405. Our leading source is her daughter's manuscript *Life*, printed in Heather Wolfe, *Elizabeth Cary, Lady Falkland: Life and Letters* (Cambridge: RTM Publications, 2001), 119–25. For a fuller picture see Deana Rankin, ' "A More Worthy Patronesse": Elizabeth Cary and Ireland', in Heather Wolfe (ed.), *The Literary Career and Legacy of Elizabeth Cary, 1613–1680* (London: Palgrave, 2007), 203–21.
406. In the absence of a modern biography, see the tantalizing leads thrown out in D. R. Woolf's life of Howell in the *Oxford DNB*.
407. Kirk's ms text of 1691 is entitled *The Secret Commonwealth: An Essay off the Nature and actions of the Subterranean (and for the most part) Invisible people heirtofor going under the name of Elves Faunes and Fairies: or the like, among the Low-Countrey Scots, and termed* hubhrísgedh, caiben, lusbartan *and* siotbrudh *among the Tramontaines or Scotish-Irish, as they are described by those who have the Second Sight.* See e.g. Michael Hunter's contextualizing edn., *The Occult Laboratory: Magic, Science and Second Sight in Late Seventeenth-Century Scotland* (Woodbridge: Boydell, 2001); also D. MacLean, 'The Life and Literary

Labours of Rev. Robert Kirk of Aberfoyle', *Transactions of the Gaelic Society of Inverness*, 31 (1922–4): 328–66.

408. His philosophical course can be traced from *Christianity Not Mysterious: Or, A Treatise Shewing, that There is Nothing in the Gospel Contrary to Reason*, published in London in 1696 (dated 1695), through *Adeisidaemon* (1709) and *Nazarenus* (1718), which represent early Celtic society as Whig-egalitarian and religious without superstition, to the even more speculative *Tetradymus* (1720) and *Pantheisticon* (1720). For Irish angles see *John Toland's Christianity Not Mysterious: Text, Associated Works and Critical Essays*, ed. Philip McGuinness, Alan Harrison, and Richard Kearney (Dublin: Lilliput Press, 1997).

409. See e.g. Ole Peter Grell, Jonathan I. Israel, and Nicholas Tyacke (eds.), *From Persecution to Toleration: The Glorious Revolution and Religion in England* (Oxford: Clarendon, 1991).

CHAPTER 2

1. J. W., *The Valiant Scot* (London, 1637), E1v.
2. The poem was available to J. W. in at least six editions published in Edinburgh between 1570 and 1620; ten further editions are recorded during the seventeenth century, from Aberdeen, Edinburgh, and Glasgow—none from south of the border, which is hardly surprising given Harry's repeated, outspoken hostility to the auld enemy.
3. A date of *c*.1626 is hazarded by George E. Byers, in his edition of *The Valiant Scot* (New York: Garland, 1980), 55–64, though I would place it a few years later.
4. *A Second Discovery by the Northern Scout: Of the Chiefe Actions of the Malignant Party* (London, 1642), 8.
5. Quoted in *Macbeth*, ed. A. R. Braunmuller (Cambridge: Cambridge University Press, 1997), 60. Milton was also attracted to 'Duffe, & Donwald a strange story of witchcraft, & murder discover'd, & reveng'd'—material which Shakespeare drew on when composing *Macbeth*.
6. *The Tragedie of Macbeth* I.iii. TLN 148–50: V.ii. TLN 2198–200, in *The First Folio of Shakespeare: The Norton Facsimile*, ed. Charlton Hinman (London: Paul Hamlyn, 1968).
7. Alan Sinfield, '*Macbeth*: History, Ideology and Intellectuals', *Critical Quarterly*, 28 (1986): 63–77; David Norbrook, '*Macbeth* and the Politics of Historiography', in Kevin Sharpe and Steven N. Zwicker (eds.), *Politics of Discourse: The Literature and History of Seventeenth-Century England* (Berkeley: University of California Press, 1987), 78–116. Buchanan's *De jure regni apud Scotos dialogus* (1579) and *Rerum Scoticarum historia* (1582) are relevantly discussed by e.g. J. H. Burns, 'The Political Ideas of George Buchanan', *Scottish Historical Review*, 30 (1950): 60–8, and in the essays by Rebecca W. Bushnell, Roger A. Mason, and Burns, in part II of Roger A. Mason (ed.), *Scots and*

Britons: Scottish Political Thought and the Union of 1603 (Cambridge: Cambridge University Press, 1994).

8. In 1603 alone, James knighted over a hundred men (Roger Lockyer, *James VI and I* (London: Longman, 1998), 203), and contemporaries quickly inflated this to getting on for a thousand. For the satire see e.g. Ben Jonson, George Chapman, and John Marston, *Eastward Hoe* (London, 1605), 'I ken the man weel, hee's one of my thirty pound Knights' (F4r), which notoriously gave offence, and 'Verses upon the Order for making Knights of such Persons who had 40 pounds per annum in King James I. Time', British Library Additional MS 5832, fol. 206r-v ('Early Stuart Libels: An Edition of Poetry from Manuscript Sources', ed. Alastair Bellany and Andrew McRae, <http:purl.oclc.org/emls/texts/libels>): 'Knighthood & Honour are now putt to Saile'.

9. My discussion chiefly draws on Neil Cuddy, 'Anglo-Scottish Union and the Court of James I, 1603–1625', *Transactions of the Royal Historical Society*, 5th ser., 39 (1989): 107–24 and Keith M. Brown, 'The Scottish Aristocracy, Anglicization and the Court, 1603–1638', *Historical Journal*, 36 (1993): 543–76.

10. Issues of precedence could be as thorny as those of jurisdiction. The stimulus all this gave to scholarship was probably even greater than that given to satire, culminating in John Selden's historically and cross-culturally erudite *Titles of Honor* (London, 1614).

11. Keith M. Brown, *Bloodfeud in Scotland 1573–1625: Violence, Justice and Politics in an Early Modern Society* (Edinburgh: John Donald, 1986), 80, preceded by Jenny Wormald, 'Bloodfeud, Kindred and Government in Early Modern Scotland', *Past and Present*, 87 (1980): 54–97.

12. Bothwell was accused of conspiring with witches against the life of James VI (1591). The murky Gowrie plot, which involved another attempt on the king (1600), went into a now-lost play called *The Tragedie of Gowrie* which was performed twice by Shakespeare's company, The King's Men, in 1604, then apparently suppressed.

13. E.g. Arthur Melville Clark, *Murder Under Trust: Or, The Topical Macbeth* (Edinburgh: Scottish Academic Press, 1981). For richer circumstantiations, including the problems of union, see Arthur F. Kinney, *Lies like Truth: Shakespeare, Macbeth, and the Cultural Moment* (Detroit: Wayne State University Press, 2001).

14. On the change from Scottish to British kingship see e.g. Arthur H. Williamson, *Scottish National Consciousness in the Age of James VI: The Apocalypse, the Union and the Shaping of Scotland's Public Culture* (Edinburgh: Donald, 1979); Bruce Galloway, *The Union of England and Scotland, 1603–1608* (Edinburgh: Donald, 1986); Maurice Lee Jr., *Great Britain's Solomon: James VI and I in his Three Kingdoms* (Urbana: University of Illinois Press, 1990); J. P. Sommerville, 'James I and the Divine Right of Kings: English Politics and Continental

Theory', in Linda Levy Peck (ed.), *The Mental World of the Jacobean Court* (Cambridge: Cambridge University Press, 1991), 55–70; J. H. Burns, *The True Law of Kingship: Concepts of Monarchy in Early-Modern Scotland* (Oxford: Clarendon, 1996).

15. Maurice Lee, Jr., *The Road to Revolution: Scotland under Charles I, 1625–37* (Urbana: University of Illinois Press, 1985), 7.

16. *Basilikon Doron* (Edinburgh, 1599), 58–9. Cf. the London edition of 1603, 48–9, where James's reference to the *'laudable custome of England'* is naturally enough keyed in the margin.

17. This development dates from 1617 (the year of his return to Scotland). For contexts see Julian Goodare, *The Government of Scotland 1560–1625* (Oxford: Oxford University Press, 2004), chs. 8–9.

18. David Stevenson, *The Scottish Revolution 1637–1644: The Triumph of the Covenanters* (Newton Abbot: David and Charles, 1973), 35–42; Lee, *Road to Revolution*, 21–37; Allan I. Macinnes, *Charles I and the Making of the Covenanting Movement 1624–1641* (Edinburgh: John Donald, 1991), chs. 3–4.

19. Wallace can and does speak Scots, but paradoxically only when he disguises himself as a Scotsman loyal to the English during his adventure in the enemy camp. The distribution of Scots and English in *The Valiant Scot* is pragmatic, in other words grounded in cultural assumptions: intending his play for a London audience, the apparently English J. W. used English as a default, neutral idiom (much as Romeo and Juliet do not speak Italian), but, because ethnicity is an issue in the play, he needed to insert reminders of Scottishness. By giving his version of Scots to female and clerical exceptions, i.e. to Peggy and the Friar, he was able to signal difference without requiring all the Scottish characters to speak a language hard for English actors and audiences.

20. The fusing of linguistic integrity with women's sexual honour and the ownership and inheritance of land are closely related to the female gendering of nations (see above, p. 28). For Scotland as 'she/her' as well as 'it' but not 'he', see *Macbeth* IV.iii (TLN 1859–61, 1999–2002) and *The Valiant Scot*, K2r.

21. Hilary L. Rubinstein, *Captain Luckless: James, First Duke of Hamilton, 1606–1649* (Edinburgh: Scottish Academic Press, 1975), 48. That the foundational statement of Scottish independence from England, the Declaration of Arbroath (1320), was drawn up in this abbey must have enhanced the significance of this submission.

22. See e.g. Macinnes, *Charles I and the Covenanting Movement*, 85.

23. This allowed the King to avoid the statutory restriction (4 Henry IV c. 13) on the mobilizing of forces to deal with internal enemies; though his troops were drawn from East Anglia, Hamilton was mounting, in Charles's eyes, a Scottish invasion of Scotland. See Mark Charles Fissel, *The Bishops' Wars: Charles*

I's Campaigns against Scotland, 1638–1640 (Cambridge: Cambridge University Press, 1994), 21. New angles are found by John Scally, 'Counsel in Crisis: James, third Marquis of Hamilton and the Bishops' Wars, 1638–1640', in John R. Young (ed.), *Celtic Dimensions of the British Civil Wars* (Edinburgh: Donald, 1997), 18–34.

24. Fissel, *Bishops' Wars*, 13, 79.
25. Ibid. 89.
26. E.g. Rubinstein, *Captain Luckless*, 227.
27. For an account of the welcome see Anthony Nixon, *Oxfords Triumph in the Royall Entertainement of his Moste Excellent Maiestie, the Queene, and the Prince: the 27. of August last, 1605* (London, 1605), B1r-v.
28. Quoting the translation in Geoffrey Bullough (ed.), *Narrative and Dramatic Sources of Shakespeare*, vol. VII (London: Routledge, 1975), 471–2, who also gives the Latin, published at the end of Gwinn's academic play, *Vertumnus sive annus recurrens* (London, 1607). The oration may have circulated in English at the time, though the wording in Nixon does not support Bullough's claim, 429, that a translation was recited for the Queen, and the simplicity of the Latin, certainly at the point of welcome, hardly requires a gloss:

> [1]   Salve, cui *Scotia* servit.
> 2 *Anglia* cui, salve. 3 Cui servit *Hibernia*, salve.
> 1 *Gallia* cui titulos, terras dant caetera, salve.
> 2 Quem, divisa prìus, colit una *Britannia*, salve.
> 3 Summe Monarcha *Britannice, Hibernice, Gallice*, salve.

29. The 'prophetesses' also figured in a ballad version of the Macbeth story before Shakespeare's play was written. See Bullough, *Narrative and Dramatic Sources*, 429.
30. See e.g. Adrian Poole, '*Macbeth* and the Third Person', *Proceedings of the British Academy*, 105 (1999): 73–92. On the regalia of the double-crowned, three-kingdom monarchy (above, p. 53), see e.g. E. B. Lyle, 'The "Twofold Balls and Treble Scepters" in *Macbeth*', *Shakespeare Quarterly*, 28 (1977): 516–19.
31. Nixon, *Oxfords Triumph*, B1r-v.
32. For contexts see Patrick Curry, *Prophecy and Power: Astrology in Early Modern England* (Cambridge: Polity, 1989); Arthur H. Williamson, variously in his *Scottish National Consciousness* and 'Number and National Consciousness: The Edinburgh Mathematicians and Scottish Political Culture at the Union of the Crowns', in Roger A. Mason (ed.), *Scots and Britons: Scottish Political Thought and the Union of 1603* (Cambridge: Cambridge University Press, 1994), 187–212. The use of prophecy to rationalize archipelagic change recurs in the mid-seventeenth-century works of Lady Eleanor Davies and William Lilly.
33. See e.g. *Basilikon Doron*, 68, 128–9 (in the 1599 text, reproduced in the London edition at 57 and 109).
34. II.iii. TLN 911–12. III.i. TLN 1016–17.

35. See the notorious passage in the 1599 *Basilikon Doron*, 42–3, even harsher in its account of the Western Islesmen ('thinke no other of them all, then as of Wolues and Wilde Boares') than the London, 1603 text, 35–6. It is instructive to contrast Buchanan's sympathetic account in the first book of his *Rerum Scoticarum historia*.

36. Cf. Henry N. Paul, *The Royal Play of Macbeth* (New York: Macmillan, 1950), 197.

37. See e.g. Jane H. Ohlmeyer, *Civil War and Restoration in the Three Stuart Kingdoms: The Career of Randal MacDonnell, Marquis of Antrim, 1606–1683* (Cambridge: Cambridge University Press, 1993), ch. 3.

38. See pp. 166–7. When Montrose returned, in 1650 (see pp. 220–21), it was through the Orkney Isles, with Scandinavian backing.

39. The symmetry of 'Point against Point' reinforces that of 'Arme 'gainst Arme' and encourages the audience to hear 'rebellious' as qualifying both nouns within the formula.

40. See his *The True Lawe of Free Monarchies: Or, The Reciprock and Mutual Dutie Betwixt a Free King, and his Naturall Subiects* (Edinburgh, 1603), C6r–7r—reproduced in the London edition of 1603.

41. Raphael Holinshed *et al.*, *Chronicles*, enlarged edn. (London, 1587), *Historie of Scotland*, 169–70.

42. For a condensed reading list, see *Macbeth*, ed. Braunmuller, 8 *n.* 1.

43. Steve Murdoch, *Britain, Denmark-Norway and the House of Stuart, 1603–1660* (East Linton: Tuckwell, 2000), 97–8, 124.

44. *Historie of Scotland*, 171.

45. IV.iii. TLN 1930.

46. *Historie of Scotland*, 175.

47. V.iii. TLN 2222.

48. V.iii. TLN 2226. 'While then' ('until which time') and, not so plausibly, 'filed' ('defiled') have also been taken as Scotticisms (III.i TLN 1032, 1055). *Valiant Scot* B1r. Cf. Christopher Highley, 'The Place of Scots in the Scottish Play: *Macbeth* and the Politics of Language', in Willy Maley and Andrew Murphy (eds.), *Shakespeare and Scotland* (Manchester: Manchester University Press, 2004), 53–66.

49. The turning point was Charles Macklin's 1773 production at Covent Garden, though it was not well received and there were only four performances.

50. This suggests a further reason for Shakespeare not to have drawn out the Scandinavian background of Siward. He apparently had no desire to insist on the irony that Malcolme is a rebel and traitor to the incumbent monarch of Scotland, backed by an English army provided by Edward, not raised by him, nor that he is backed by Danes—Siward's men—who, at the start of the action, fought with Norway against core Scotland.

51. V.vii. TLN 2507, 2522.

52. *Coriolanus* II.iii. TLN 1517–23.

53. I.iii. TLN 147–50; on the overtones see *Macbeth*, ed. Braunmuller, note to I.iii.46.

54. 'So all haile' can mean 'That is *why* all of us now hail' as well as 'Let us all now hail'.

55. *Oxford English Dictionary*, *hale* n. 1 and 2, 'Health, well-being, welfare' and Scottish form of *heal* or *hele*, n., 'Sound bodily condition; freedom from sickness, health'.

56. Against their baleful influence are set Edward the Confessor with his power of healing and the Doctor who attends Lady Macbeth.

57. *OED hail* n.² 2, *heal, hele* n. b–c, *hale* n¹ b. Folio 'weyward/weyard' means 'Having the power to control the fate or destiny of human beings', from Old English *wyrd* 'fate, destiny' (*OED weird* a. 1 and n. 1).

58. Both Holinshed and Gwinn compare the three figures with the three classical Fates; cf. *OED weird* n. 2 pl.

59. I.iii. 201. For 'All haile' as both greeting and frozen rain see *Love's Labour's Lost* (V.ii. TLN 2265–6) and *The Valiant Scot*, F3r. *Macbeth*'s interest in *hailing* makes Rowe's generally accepted emendation of the Folio's 'thick as Tale' the more secure.

60. 'No more that *Thane* of Cawdor shall deceiue | Our Bosome interest: Goe pronounce his present death, | And with his former Title greet *Macbeth*' (I. ii. TLN 90–3).

61. 'The Bocke of Plaies and Notes therof per formane for Common Pollicie' (1611), in *The Norton Shakespeare*, gen. ed. Stephen Greenblatt (New York: Norton, 1997), 3336–8, p. 3336.

62. John Cleland, *Hero-paideia* (Oxford, 1607), bk. V, ch. 5.

63. That triple Hecate (as multiply hale/whole as the witches) is quite probably Middleton's addition to the tragedy does not disable the point.

64. TLN 1853. Braunmuller glosses the pun 'Either (1) the epithet ("tyranny") is confirmed (= "affeerred"), or (2) the valid claim and claimant are frightened ("afeared"; see *OED* Afear).'

65. George Buchanan, *The History of Scotland*, anonymously translated (London, 1690), 214.

66. *Description*, 22.

67. These edges could be, as it were, internal. James's determination to establish his Great British credentials by pacifying the Anglo-Scottish borders (above, pp. 34–5) gives a particular resonance to the English-allied peace-maker Malcolme acquiring the title Prince of Cumberland. For contexts see R. T. Spence, 'The Pacification of the Cumberland Borders, 1593–1628', *Northern History*, 13 (1977): 59–160, esp. pp. 110–14.

68. The best short accounts of 'surrender and regrant', and of 'tanistry' (officially abolished in Ireland in a test case of 1608), are by Hiram Morgan in S. J. Connolly (ed.), *The Oxford Companion to Irish History* (Oxford: Oxford University Press, 1998).

69. Michael J. Braddick, *State Formation in Early Modern England* c.*1550−1700* (Cambridge: Cambridge University Press, 2000), 374.

70. The context for James's revival of 'surrender and regrant' (and thus, it may be, for Malcolme's talk of expense and reckoning) extends to his establishment, in 1606, of a Commission for Defective Titles, which led to the confiscation of Catholic-owned land in Ireland (for the conjunction of both policies see e.g. Sir John Davies, *A Discouerie of the True Causes why Ireland was Neuer Entirely Subdued* (London, 1612), 276−80). These measures, which went back to James's contentious challenging of the titles of Highland chiefs in 1598, and his policy of making clan leaders responsible for the actions of their followers (see e.g. Allan I. Macinnes, 'Crown, Clans and Fine: The "Civilizing" of Scottish Gaeldom, 1587−1638', *Northern Scotland*, 113 (1993): 31−55), had implications for anglophone Britain and Ireland, as well as Scoto-Irish Gaeldom. They echo through the post-Revocation probing of title alluded to in *The Valiant Scot* (above, p. 96) and Wentworth's expropriations in Ireland after 1634 (p. 170).

71. Claire McEachern, 'The Englishness of the Scottish Play: *Macbeth* and the Poetics of Jacobean Union', in Allan I. Macinnes and Jane H. Ohlmeyer (eds.), *The Stuart Kingdoms in the Seventeenth Century: Awkward Neighbours* (Dublin: Four Courts, 2002), 94−112.

72. See e.g. Norman Davies, *The Isles: A History* (London: Macmillan, 1999), 554, on fears that James would become an absentee monarch, concerns about the future of the 'Auld Alliance' with France (a feature of *The Valiant Scot*), and a desire to see the English parliament engage with Scottish concerns.

73. See *Daphnis Polystephanos: An Eclog Treating of Crownes, and of Garlandes, and to Whom of Right They Appertaine* (London, 1605), A3r, B3v; compare the dedication to James, 'whom I may now call an English man' (A3v), and the incorporating comments, 'Some thinke that the word *Anglia* was sometimes vsed for the whole Isle, and… *Ion Lidgate*… asseuereth in King *Arthurs* complaint… *Great Britain now called England*' (B4r).

74. On this declaration in Star Chamber (1616) see Jenny Wormald, 'The Union of 1603', in Mason (ed.), *Scots and Britons*, 17−40, pp. 39−40.

75. Cf. Norbrook, '*Macbeth* and the Politics of Historiography', 95 and James Shapiro, '*The Scot's Tragedy* and the Politics of Popular Drama', *English Literary Renaissance*, 23 (1993): 428−49.

76. There had been kings *of England* throughout the medieval period (*rex Anglorum* was an older form); the style was extended to Ireland in 1541 (above, p. 53).

77. The last three rulers of Scotland before the 1707 Treaty of Union, Mary, William, and Anne were all styled *of Scotland*.

78. See e.g. Buchanan's account of Malcolme's efforts to limit the influence of English incomers, who spread an appetite for luxury among the Scottish nobility (*History of Scotland*, 218−19).

79. Cf. Andrew Hadfield, '*Macbeth*, IV.iii.140–58, Edward the Confessor, and Holinshed's *Chronicles*', *Notes and Queries*, 247 (2002): 234–6, which argues that Edward's failure to produce heirs or secure an English succession (cf. Elizabeth I) would raise doubts in early audiences about the practical, political merits of the saintliness attributed to him.

80. E.g. Sir Thomas Craig, *De unione regnorum Britanniae tractatus*, ed. C. Sanford Terry (Edinburgh: Scottish Historical Society, 1909), 45 [tr. 267].

81. This retitling probably goes back to nineteenth-century theatre practice, though it is sometimes (unconvincingly) argued that the play's title was avoided during Shakespeare's lifetime, or shortly thereafter. See e.g. Gabriel Egan, 'The Early Seventeenth-Century Origin of the *Macbeth* Superstition', *Notes and Queries*, 247 (2002): 236–7.

CHAPTER 3

1. Howard Brenton, *Plays: Two* (London: Methuen Drama, 1989), 20, 31.

2. Published in Basel; enlarged edns. 1546 and 1555.

3. On criticism of Geoffrey before Polydore, and the paradoxical reinvigoration of his influence brought about by the urge to defend the honour of Britain against the *Anglica Historia* during a period in which a new, Tudor ideology of 'Britishness' was emergent, see Philip Schwyzer, *Literature, Nationalism and Memory in Early Modern England and Wales* (Cambridge: Cambridge University Press, 2004), esp. ch. 1.

4. See William Camden, *Britain: Or, A Chorographicall Description of the Most Flourishing Kingdomes, England, Scotland, and Ireland*, tr. [and expanded by] Philemon Holland (London, 1610), 28–34; cf. John Clapham, *The Historie of Great Britannie* (London, 1606), 4–5; John Speed, *The History of Great Britaine* (London, 1611), 179–82; and Thomas Hariot, *A Briefe and True Report of the New Found Land of Virginia*, 2nd edn. (Frankfurt, 1590), which reproduces, by way of appendix, 'The trwe picture of one Picte', 'The trwe picture of a women Picte', and other images, after those of native Americans, '*to showe how that the Inhabitants of the great Bretannie haue bin in times past as sauuage as those of Virginia*'.

5. 24 Henry VIII c. 12; above, p. 49.

6. The boldest version of this thesis is in Willy Maley, *Nation, State and Empire in English Renaissance Literature: Shakespeare to Milton* (London: Palgrave, 2003). For reservations see my foreword to that book, xi-xvii, at pp. xii-xv, though Protestant texts, from Bible commentary to neo-Latin verse, could elide imperial with papal Rome—see e.g. John Napier, *A Plaine Discouery of the Whole Reuelation of Saint Iohn* (Edinburgh, 1593); 'In Romam', in *George Buchanan: The Political Poetry*, ed. and trans. Paul J. McGinnis and Arthur H. Williamson (Edinburgh: Scottish History Society, 1995), 250–3.

7. Anti-Roman comments can be traced through the century, in various political perspectives, from Samuel Daniel's prose history, *The First Part of the Historie of England* (London, 1612), 13–14 (lamenting 'the State of *Britayne*, whilst the *Romans* held it; induring all the calamities that a deiected nation could do, vnder the domination of strangers, proud, greedy and cruell'), through the anonymous *King and Queenes Entertainement at Richmond* (Oxford, 1636), in which a Druid speaks persuasively of 'those grand Theeues | The *Romans*' (C3v), to Charles Hopkins' play, *Boadicea* (London, 1697).

8. Camden surveys the controversy, *Britain*, 114–16.

9. Raphael Holinshed *et al.*, *Chronicles*, enlarged edn. (London, 1587); *Historie of England*, 90.

10. A. H. Dodd, 'Wales and the Scottish Succession', *Transactions of the Honourable Society of Cymmrodorion* (1938): 201–25, pp. 209–11.

11. Peter Roberts, 'Tudor Wales, National Identity and the British Inheritance', in *British Consciousness and Identity: The Making of Britain, 1533–1707* (Cambridge: Cambridge University Press, 1998), 8–42, 37.

12. Penry Williams, 'The Attack on the Council in the Marches, 1603–1642', *Transactions of the Honourable Society of Cymmrodorion* (1961), pt. 1: 1–22; R. E. Ham, 'The Four Shire Controversy', *Welsh History Review*, 8 (1977): 381–400; Peter R. Roberts, 'Wales and England after the Tudor "Union": Crown, Principality and Parliament, 1543–1624', in Claire Cross, David Loades, and J. J. Scarisbrick (eds.), *Law and Government under the Tudors: Essays Presented to Sir Geoffrey Elton* (Cambridge: Cambridge University Press, 1988), 111–38, pp. 119–33; and, in a slightly different context, the same historian's 'The English Crown, the Principality of Wales and the Council in the Marches, 1534–1641', in Brendan Bradshaw and John Morrill (eds.), *The British Problem, c.1534–1707: State Formation in the Atlantic Archipelago* (Basingstoke: Macmillan, 1996), 118–47, pp. 137–45.

13. See e.g. Roberts, 'English Crown', 142–3. For an almost contemporaneous, informative survey of the issues, see John Doddridge, *The History of the Ancient and Modern Estate of the Principality of Wales, Dutchy of Cornewal, and Earldome of Chester* (London, 1630).

14. *The Tragedie of Cymbeline* III.v (TLN 1911–1), in *The First Folio of Shakespeare: The Norton Facsimile*, ed. Charlton Hinman (London: Paul Hamlyn, 1968).

15. Caradoc of Llancarvan, *d*.1147?, *Historie of Cambria, now Called Wales*, tr. Humphrey Llwyd, corr. and cont. by Powel (London, 1584), ¶6v. This *Historie*, commissioned by Sir Henry Sidney from his chaplain, David Powel of Raubon, consists of Llwyd's translation of the old *Brut y tywysogion* (i.e. *Chronicle of the Princes*), preceded by Llwyd's revision of Sir John Price's 'Description of Cambria, now Called Wales', introduced by Powel's dedication to Sir Philip Sidney and preface 'To the Reader'.

16. *Historie of Cambria*, ¶6v; cf. e.g. George Owen, *Cruell Lawes against Welshmen*, in *Cymmrodorion Records*, ed. Henry Owen, ser. 1 part iii (London: Charles J. Clark, 1982), 120–60.

17. Humphrey Llwyd, *The Breuiary of Britayne*, tr. Thomas Twyne (London, 1573), B6r-v, E4v–5v (on the Brigantes), E8v-F2r, F6v-G7r (Cataracus, Voadicia, and much more). Boece's sources and motives are sketched by T. D. Kendrick, *British Antiquity* (London: Methuen, 1950), 67–8.

18. F6r-v, C3r. Buchanan responded to Llwyd, exposing the limits of Scoto-Cambrian humanist solidarity, in *Rerum Scoticarum historia* (1582); Roberts, 'Tudor Wales', 26, cp. Roger A. Mason, 'Scotching the Brut: Politics, History and National Myth in Sixteenth-Century Scotland', in Mason (ed.), *Scotland and England, 1286–1815* (Edinburgh: Donald, 1987), 60–84, pp. 73–4. There were even rival Merlins, 'One of *Scotland* commonly titled *Sylvester*, or *Caledonius* living under *Arthur*; the other *Ambrosius*... borne of a Nunne (daughter to the K[ing] of *Southwales*) in *Caermardhin*' (John Selden, notes to *Poly-Olbion*, Song IV, in *The Works of Michael Drayton*, ed. J. William Hebel et al., 5 vols. (Oxford: Blackwell, 1931–41), IV, 89).

19. Breandán Ó Buachalla, 'James our True King: The Ideology of Irish Royalism in the Seventeenth Century', in D. George Boyce, Robert Eccleshall, and Vincent Geoghegan (eds.), *Political Thought in Ireland Since the Seventeenth Century* (London: Routledge, 1993), 7–35, p. 11.

20. See e.g. Robert Holland's Welsh translation of King James's *Basilikon Doron* in 1604, with its recommendation that Prince Henry learn Welsh, and the associated genealogy, separately distributed, tracing James's descent through Henry VII back to the Welsh princes and ancient British kings. This move had been anticipated in the sixteenth-century claim that James's ancestor Fleance—as featured in *Macbeth*—had fled from Scotland to Wales, where he founded the Stuart dynasty by marrying a Welsh princess (e.g. Llwyd, *Breuiary*, F2v–3r).

21. E.g. Richard Verstegan, *A Restitution of Decayed Intelligence in Antiquities, Concerning the Most Noble and Renowmed English Nation* (Antwerp, 1605), dedication, +2r.

22. 'Cambria', in *Microcosmos* (Oxford, 1603), 29–38, pp. 30–1, 35. For similar, discreetly articulated tensions in Welsh-Latin writing—an important body of work—see e.g. John Owen, *Epigrammatum libri tres* (London, 1606), III.37–9.

23. 'And hath not the vnion of Wales to England added a greater strength thereto?' the King asked a reluctant parliament, 'Which though it was a great Principalitie, was nothing comparable in greatnesse and power to the ancient and famous Kingdome of Scotland': 'A Speach, as it was Deliuered in the Vpper House of the Parliament... on Munday the XIX. Day of March 1603 [1604]', in *The Workes of the Most High and Mightie Prince, Iames* (London, 1616), 485–97, p. 488.

24. Roberts, 'English Crown', 140−2.
25. E.g. confidence in the ancient dignity of the British tongue encouraged Welsh literati to produce grammars and dictionaries to instruct their new fellow-Britons. Works by John Davies of Mallwyd reached such influential readers as Ben Jonson, who used his *Antiquiae linguae Britannicae ... rudimenta* (London, 1621) in the masque *For the Honour of Wales* (1618) and received a copy of his grammar as a New Year's gift in 1630 from the Welshman James Howell, who attached a poem of his own on Welsh as 'A wild and *Wealthy* Language' ('Upon Dr Davies British-Grammar', in Howell, *Poems* (London, 1663), 71−2).
26. On Wales, the borders, and *A Maske Presented at Ludlow Castle* see e.g. Richard Halpern, 'Puritanism and Maenadism in *A Mask*', in Margaret W. Ferguson, Maureen Quilligan, and Nancy J. Vickers (eds.), *Rewriting the Renaissance: The Discourses of Sexual Difference in Early Modern Europe* (Chicago: Chicago University Press, 1986), 88−105, and Michael Wilding, 'Milton's *A Masque Presented at Ludlow Castle, 1634*: Theatre and Politics on the Border', *Milton Quarterly*, 21/4 (1987): 35−51.
27. *Breviary*, 60r. The Gaelic Irish and Scottish Highlanders shared many of these traits, but both groups were relatively distant from such places as Stratford and London; sharing a common border, and conspicuous in English towns and cities, the Welsh were arguably the Other closest to home (cf. Glanmor Williams, *Recovery, Reorientation and Reformation: Wales c.1415−1642*, History of Wales, 3 (Oxford: Oxford University Press, 1987), 464; Philip Jenkins, 'Seventeenth-Century Wales: Definition and Identity', in Bradshaw and Roberts (eds.), *British Consciousness and Identity*, 213−35, p. 216.
28. 'Address to the Welsh People by Bishop Richard Davies', tr. Albert Owen Evans, in Evans, *A Memorandum on the Legality of the Welsh Bible and the Welsh Version of the Book of Common Prayer* (Cardiff: William Lewis, 1925), 83−124, p. 85. For contexts see Glanmor Williams, 'Bishop Richard Davies' (?1501−1581)' and 'Some Protestant Views of Early British Church History', in his *Welsh Reformation Essays* (Cardiff: University of Wales Press, 1967), 155−90, 207−19, and P. R. Roberts, 'The Union with England and the Identity of "Anglican" Wales', *Transactions of the Royal Historical Society*, 4th ser., 22 (1972): 49−70, pp. 67−70.
29. Davies, 'Address', 85.
30. 'September', '*Argument*', in *The Yale Edition of the Shorter Poems of Edmund Spenser*, ed. William Oram *et al.* (New Haven: Yale University Press, 1989).
31. Contrast the view found in e.g. Holinshed that, although Joseph of Arimathea introduced the faith, paganism persisted in Britain until two Romans, Fugatius and Damianus, brought the gospel from the pope to King Lucius.
32. Robin Flower, 'William Salesbury, Richard Davies, and Archbishop Parker', *National Library of Wales Journal*, 2 (1941): 7−14, and Glanmor Williams,

'Bishop Sulien, Bishop Richard Davies, and Archbishop Parker', *National Library of Wales Journal*, 5 (1948): 215–19.

33. 'Address', 123.
34. Cf. the depiction of Winifred in the frontispiece to I. F.'s Counter-Reformation translation of Robert of Shrewsbury's early medieval *vita: The Admirable Life of Saint Wenefride: Virgin, Martyr, Abbesse* (Saint-Omer, 1635).
35. Cf. *The Gentle Craft*, where the healing properties of Winifred's well are described in the address to the reader, or *Poly-Olbion* X.139–67, which celebrates the well but through the mouth of a Welsh mountain, then calls it a 'tedious tale' (while Selden's notes denounce the 'lubberly Monkes' who profited from the Winifred cult). In 'Purity and Danger on the West Bank of the Severn: The Cultural Geography of *A Masque Presented at Ludlow Castle, 1634*', *Representations*, 60 (1997): 22–48, p. 40, Philip Schwyzer interestingly suggests that Milton uses Sabrina in *Comus* to counter Winifred's insidiously Catholic appeal. This appeal can be deduced not just from the 1635 *Admirable Life of Saint Wenefride* but from local sentiment; in *Providence in Early Modern England* (Oxford: Oxford University Press, 1999), Alexandra Walsham reports that 'When a man was found dead at Holywell in Wales in 1630 after making disparaging remarks about the marvellous healing properties of the spring a local jury seems to have brought in a verdict of death by divine judgment' (p. 99). The work of desacralizing Winifred had, however, already begun with Deloney and Rowley.
36. In *A Shoo-maker a Gentleman* (London, 1638), D3v, where a Roman leader calls Amphiabell a 'sectarist', Winifred is denounced as a 'superstitious | Virgin, that with her sorcerous devotion works miracles, | By which she drawes Christians'—a formulation which sectarists might use of moderate Protestants as well as Catholics. Differences within British Protestantism are safely flagged up by a pagan, who carries the blame of an intolerance which might as readily be found within the faith.
37. E.g. Camden, *Britain*, 49; Clapham, *Historie of Great Britannie*, bk II, ch. ii.
38. *Bonduca* IV.iv.111–12, 117–19, ed. Cyrus Hoy, in *The Dramatic Works in the Beaumont and Fletcher Canon*, gen. ed. Fredson Bowers, vol. IV (Cambridge: Cambridge University Press, 1979).
39. Holinshed, *Chronicles; Historie of England*, 38.
40. George Powell, *Bonduca: Or, The British Heroine* (London, 1696).
41. 8 July 1609, quoted by G. Dyfnallt Owen, *Wales in the Reign of James I* (Woodbridge: Royal Historical Society/Boydell, 1988), 2.
42. *Sidero-Thriambos: Or, Steele and Iron Triumphing*, lines 216–20, in *Pageants and Entertainments of Anthony Munday*, ed. David M. Bergeron (New York: Garland, 1985); cf. *Fuimus Troes: The True Troianes* (London, 1633), G1r, where ancient Britons sing in Scots of their survival of a Roman attack.

43. *The Valiant Welshman: Or, The True Chronicle History of the Life and Valiant Deedes of Caradoc the Great, King of Cambria, now Called Wales* (London, 1615), A4r-B1r.

44. Holinshed, *Chronicles; Historie of Scotland*, 45–53.

45. Hence Drummond of Hawthornden's jesting inclusion of *Albions Scotland* in a short list of imaginary books: see Robert H. MacDonald, *The Library of Drummond of Hawthornden* (Edinburgh: Edinburgh University Press, 1971), p. 228.

46. *Albions England*, first pub. 1586, rev. edn. (London, 1602), bk III, ch. 18.

47. In line with Holinshed's *Historie of Scotland*, the heroine is Voada and Caradoc's sister. She is imprisoned, though not by her husband, and released by the Welsh. Above all, the alliances between Caradoc, Gederus, and Venusius produce a war of three kingdoms against Rome, with Venusius, based in York, fighting from north of the Humber.

48. Hence the dashes substituted for oaths in the first, 1647 edition of *Bonduca*; a 1620s–30s transcript (now BL Add. MS 36758) substitutes such asseverations as 'I vowe' and 'good cozen'—see the Historical Collation in Hoy's edn.

49. *Britannia*, tr. Holland, 88.

50. Leah S. Marcus, *Puzzling Shakespeare: Local Reading and its Discontents* (Berkeley: University of California Press, 1988), 118–48.

51. E.g. as Marcus notes, his sur-addition, Leonatus, glances at the leonine iconography favoured by James as King of Scotland, and his well-born poverty and post in the King's Bedchamber recall the position of Scotsmen at court, often poor, often Gentlemen of the Bedchamber, looking for highly placed English wives.

52. See e.g. Emrys Jones, 'Stuart *Cymbeline*', *Essays in Criticism*, 11 (1961): 84–99.

53. *Tethys Festival: Or, The Queenes Wake*, in *The Order and Solemnitie of the Creation of the High and Mightie Prince Henrie, Eldest Sonne to our Sacred Soueraigne, Prince of Wales* (London: 1610), E4v.

54. William Herbert, the 'Welsh Earl'—see Michael G. Brennan, *Literary Patronage in the English Renaissance: The Pembroke Family* (London: Routledge, 1988), 132—was a local magnate as well as a power at court. Through several generations, his family had supported Welsh bards, and although the Welsh-speaking Earl wrote his own verse in English, he associated with Welsh literati. His brother (co-dedicatee of the first Folio edition of Shakespeare's plays), Philip, Earl of Montgomery was also the object of attention from Anglo-Welsh poets like William Harbert, and had Welshmen in his household.

55. On English-Scottish antagonism in the years after regal union see e.g. Jenny Wormald, 'Oh Brave New World? The Union of Scotland and England in 1603', in T. C. Smout (ed.), *Anglo-Scottish Relations from 1603–1900, Proceedings of the British Academy*, 127 (2005): 13–35.

56. Irene Scouloudi, *Returns of Strangers in the Metropolis 1593, 1627, 1635, 1639: A Study of an Active Minority*, Publications of the Huguenot Society of London Quarto Series LXII (London: Huguenot Society, 1985), 1; I owe this reference to Emma Smith.

57. II. iii (TLN 1101–14); III. v (TLN 2050–62).

58. This episode figures in Robert Chester, *Loves Martyr: Or, Rosalins Complaint* (London, 1601), H2r–3r, the Welsh-sponsored poem-cum-anthology in which Shakespeare's 'Phoenix and Turtle' first appeared. Cf. e.g. Thomas Churchyard, *The Worthines of Wales* (London, 1587), D3v-E3r, Thomas Hughes, *Misfortunes of Arthur*, ed. Brian Jay Corrigan (New York: Garland, 1992), 'The Argument of the *Tragedie*', and II. i.

59. *Eclogues* I.66, translated in Camden, *Britain*, 1, as 'And Britans people quite disjoin'd from all the world besides'.

60. Camden, *Britain*, 47. The entire selection of Latin verses, 45–7, is relevant.

61. Meenakshi Ponnuswami, 'Celts and Celticists in Howard Brenton's *The Romans in Britain*', *Journal of Dramatic Theory and Criticism*, 2/2 (Spring 1998): 69–88.

62. See e.g. J. Gwynfor Jones, 'The Welsh Poets and their Patrons, *c.* 1550–1640', *Welsh History Review*, 9 (1978–9): 245–77 and *Concepts of Order and Gentility in Wales 1540–1640* (Llandysul: Gomer Press, 1992).

63. 'Address', 107–8.

64. *Breuiary of Britayne*, 60r.

65. For Welsh angles see Garrett A. Sullivan, Jr., *The Drama of Landscape: Land, Property, and Social Relations on the Early Modern Stage* (Stanford: Stanford University Press, 1998), 135–7; Ronald J. Boling, 'Anglo-Welsh Relations in *Cymbeline*', *Shakespeare Quarterly*, 51 (2000): 33–66; and Huw Griffiths, 'The Geographies of Shakespeare's *Cymbeline*', *English Literary Renaissance*, 34 (2004): 339–58.

66. All this was well known, but is spelt out in George Owen's *Description of Penbrokshire* (comp. 1602–3)—see the edn. by Dillwyn Miles (Llandysul: Gomer Press, 1994), 41–3—a work that includes a history of the Earls of Pembroke which Shakespeare, as a client, might well have read.

67. See e.g. Sir Henry Spelman, 'Of the Union', in *The Jacobean Union: Six Tracts of 1604*, ed. Bruce R. Galloway and Brian P. Levack (Edinburgh: Scottish Historical Society, 1985), 161–84, pp. 165, 167.

68. IV.ii. TLN 2249–51, 2560–3.

69. V.iii. TLN 2933–4. See Tacitus, quoted in Holland's tr. of Camden, *Britain*, 51–2; cf. Clapham *Historie of Great Britannie*, 63.

70. Holinshed, *Chronicles; Historie of Scotland*, 155.

71. E. K. Chambers, *William Shakespeare: A Study of Facts and Problems*, 2 vols. (Oxford: Clarendon, 1930), II, 352.

72. John Morrill reminds me that, around 1610, the date of Prince Henry's inauguration as Prince of Wales, plans were afoot to negotiate a Spanish match for him.

73. See e.g. W. B. Patterson, *King James VI and I and the Reunion of Christendom* (Cambridge: Cambridge University Press, 1997).

CHAPTER 4

1. Sir Anthony Weldon, 'A Description of Scotland', in John Nichols (ed.), *The Progresses, Processions, and Magnificent Festivities of King James the First*, 4 vols. (London: J. B. Nichols, 1828), III, 338−43, p. 338.

2. Nichols, *Progresses*, III, 302, 321−2, 383−5.

3. A text was presented at Seton, home of the Earl of Winton, on 15 May 1617 (Nichols, *Progresses*, III, 306−7); published in quarto by Andro Hart (Edinburgh, 1617), the poem quickly reappeared in John Adamson's τα των μουσων εισοδια, *The Muses Welcome* (Edinburgh, 1618).

4. Lines 1−5, quoting from the text in *The Poetical Works of William Drummond of Hawthornden*, ed. L. E. Kastner, 2 vols. (Edinburgh: William Blackwood, 1913), I, 141−53.

5. 'Ben Jonson's Conversations with William Drummond of Hawthornden' (more correctly, 'Informations be Ben Johnston to W. D. when he came to Scotland upon foot') in *Ben Jonson*, ed. C. H. Herford and Percy and Evelyn Simpson, 11 vols. (Oxford: Clarendon, 1925−52), I, 132−51, p. 135.

6. Robert H. MacDonald, 'A Disputed Maxim of State in "Forth Feasting" (1619)', *Journal of the History of Ideas*, 32 (1971): 295−8, from which I quote Drummond's draft letter.

7. G. Gregory Smith (ed.), *Elizabethan Critical Essays*, 2 vols. (1904; London: Oxford University Press, 1950), I, 208−25, p. 220.

8. On these rules see e.g. Francis Cairns, *Generic Composition in Greek and Roman Poetry* (Edinburgh: Edinburgh University Press, 1972), 16−31; J. W. Binns, *Intellectual Culture in Elizabethan and Jacobean England: The Latin Writings of the Age* (Francis Cairns: Leeds, 1990), 70, 73−4.

9. Cf. Robert Cummings, 'Drummond's *Forth Feasting*: A Panegyric for King James in Scotland', *The Seventeenth Century*, 2 (1987): 1−18, esp. pp. 7−12.

10. *OED a.* and *n.* 1.

11. *Ane Schort Treatise*, 212−13.

12. See e.g. Peter Donald, *An Uncounselled King: Charles I and the Scottish Troubles, 1637−1641* (Cambridge: Cambridge University Press, 1990) and Mark Charles Fissell, *The Bishops' Wars: Charles I's Campaigns against Scotland, 1638−1640* (Cambridge: Cambridge University Press, 1994).

13. See Edwin Morgan, 'How Good a Poet is Drummond?', *Scottish Literary Journal*, 15/1 (May 1988): 14−24, the inclusion of twenty-seven items in

Alastair Fowler (ed.), *The New Oxford Book of Seventeenth Century Verse* (Oxford: Oxford University Press, 1991), and Karl Miller, *Rebecca's Vest: A Memoir* (London: Hamish Hamilton, 1993), ch. 6.

14. Against these misunderstandings see R. D. S. Jack, in the 'Introduction' to R. D. S. Jack and P. A. T. Rozendaal (eds.), *The Mercat Anthology of Early Scottish Literature 1375–1707* (Edinburgh: Mercat, 1997), vii-xxxix, pp. vii-xi.

15. Keith Brown, 'Scottish Identity in the Seventeenth Century', in Brendan Bradshaw and Peter Roberts (eds.), *British Consciousness and Identity: The Making of Britain, 1533–1707* (Cambridge: Cambridge University Press, 1998), 236–58, pp. 253–4.

16. Robert H. MacDonald, *The Library of Drummond of Hawthornden* (Edinburgh: Edinburgh University Press, 1971), 228–32, 149–228.

17. Translated from Latin in what remains the fullest biographical source, David Masson, *Drummond of Hawthornden: The Story of His Life and Writings* (London: Macmillan, 1873), 156–61.

18. 'Conversations', 135.

19. See Ronald D. S. Jack, 'Drummond of Hawthornden: The Major Scottish Sources', *Studies in Scottish Literature*, 6 (1968–9): 36–46, and *William Drummond of Hawthornden: Poems and Prose*, ed. Robert H. MacDonald (Edinburgh: Scottish Academic Press, 1976), xix.

20. R. D. S. Jack, *The Italian Influence on Scottish Literature* (Edinburgh: Edinburgh University Press, 1972), ch. 4, esp. 113–44.

21. He read, translated, and imitated Latin, Italian, French, and Spanish poetry, praised Alexander in French, and in Latin composed an elegy on King James and an eight-line poem to Drayton.

22. On the three-kingdom personnel and linguistic pluralism of James's court poets see e.g. Helena Mennie Shire, *Song, Dance and Poetry of the Court of Scotland under King James VI* (Cambridge: Cambridge University Press, 1969).

23. *Poetical Works of Drummond*, I, 35.

24. Ibid. I, ci, cx.

25. See esp. 'Commendatory Verses' and 'Posthumous Poems' in *Poetical Works of Drummond*, II.

26. *Poetical Works of Drummond*, I, 90, 224–5.

27. Quoted in *The Works of William Drummond of Hawthornden* (Edinburgh, 1711), 152–3; on the contentiously Scottish composition of the Bedchamber see Neil Cuddy, 'The Revival of the Entourage: The Bedchamber of James I, 1603–1625', in David Starkey *et al.*, *The English Court: From the Wars of the Roses to the Civil War* (London: Longmans, 1987), 173–225, esp. pp. 177, 185–204, and 'Anglo-Scottish Union and the Court of James I, 1603–1625', *Transactions of the Royal Historical Society*, 5th ser., 39 (1989): 107–24, pp. 110–11, 120–3.

28. e.g. XXVI 'A dedication of som[e] poems to Cra[i]gmiller', XXVIII, in Eloisa Paganelli, 'Lettere e Note Inedite di William Drummond of Hawthornden', *English Miscellany* (Rome), 19 (1968): 295–333, pp. 328–9.

29. Masson, *Drummond*, 34–5.

30. See his letter to William, Earl of Morton, sending madrigals, in *Works of Drummond*, 156 ('yet know I, that sometimes, to the most delicate Ear, the Warblings of the Wild Birds in the Solitary Forrests, are wont to be as delightful as the Artificial Notes of the learned Popingayes in the Guilt Cages').

31. *Poetical Works of Drummond*, II, 12.

32. 'Conversations', 132. Modern editions of this text are based on a transcript of Drummond's lost holograph made by Sir Robert Sibbald (1641–1722) collated with the reduced version published in the 1711 *Works of Drummond*. Rarely following 1711, the Oxford *Ben Jonson* prefers its 'his' over MS 'this' at this point, making Jonson's plans seem memorable to Drummond because consistently English-patriotic rather than, as 'this' would suggest, King-James-pleasingly Anglo-Scots with a provokingly insisted-upon dedication to England.

33. 'Conversations', 151.

34. Bernard H. Newdigate, *Michael Drayton and His Circle* (Oxford: Basil Blackwell, 1961), 162, 189.

35. 'Character of Several Authors' (prob. 1613–16), in *Works of Drummond*, 226–7, p. 227.

36. David Riggs, *Ben Jonson: A Life* (Cambridge, MA: Harvard University Press, 1989), 115–16, 125–6; 'Conversations', 143; letter of Jonson to Drummond (10 May 1619), quoted in Masson, *Drummond*, 109.

37. '[Sonnet: On the River Tweed]', *The English and Latin Poems of Sir Robert Aytoun*, ed. Charles B. Gullans (Edinburgh: Scottish Text Society, 1963), 167.

38. 'Courtiers and Cavaliers: Service, Anglicization and Loyalty among the Royalist Nobility', in John Morrill (ed.), *The Scottish National Covenant in its British Context* (Edinburgh: Edinburgh University Press, 1990), 155–92; 'The Scottish Aristocracy, Anglicization and the Court, 1603–38', *Historical Journal*, 36 (1993): 543–76.

39. 'Courtiers and Cavaliers', 164.

40. 'A Sonett: on Sᵣ William Alexanders harshe vearses after the Inglishe fasone', in *The Poems of James VI of Scotland*, ed. James Craigie, 2 vols. (Edinburgh: Scottish Text Society, 1955–8), II, 114. For a capable discussion see Michael R. G. Spiller, 'The Scottish Court and the Scottish Sonnet at the Union of the Crowns', in Sally Mapstone and Juliette Wood (eds.), *The Rose and the Thistle: Essays on the Culture of Late Medieval and Renaissance Scotland* (East Lothian: Tuckwell, 1998), 101–15.

41. For caveats about this terminology, though commonplace in accounts of the period, see Priscilla Bawcutt, 'James VI's Castalian Band: A Modern Myth', *Scottish Historical Review*, 80 (2001): 251–9.

42. *Works of Drummond*, 149–50, p. 150.

43. Mary Jane Wittstock Scott, 'Robert Ayton: Scottish Metaphysical', *Scottish Literary Journal*, 2/1 (July 1975): 5–16, p. 8.

44. Cp. e.g. the sonnet prefixed to Alexander's *Doomes-day* with the version in the Hawthornden MSS: *Poetical Works of Drummond*, II, 161, 371.

45. *The Poetical Works of Sir William Alexander, Earl of Stirling*, ed. L. E. Kastner and H. B. Charlton, 2 vols. (Manchester: Longmans, Green and Co., 1921–9), I, cxcvi.

46. See e.g. David Hume of Godscroft's defence of using Scots in the address 'to the Reader' that opens his *History of the Houses of Douglas and Angus,* completed in the 1620s, published partially in 1633, and quoted here from the Edinburgh edn. of 1643. That this edn. is—symptomatically enough—anglicized coheres with the defensiveness of assertions that ostensibly reverse Alexander's: 'For the Language it is my Mother-tongue, that is, Scottish: and why not, to Scottish-men? Why should I contemne it? I never thought the difference so great, as that by seeking to speak English, I would hazard the imputation of affectation. Every tongue hath [its] own vertue and grace. Some are more substantiall, others more ornate and succinct. ... For my own part, I like our own, and he that writes well in it, writes well enough to me. ... I acknowledge also my fault (if it be a fault) that I ever accounted it a mean study, and of no great commendation to learn to write, or to speak English, and have loved better to bestow my pains and time on forreigne Languages, esteeming it but a Dialect of our own, and that (perhaps) more corrupt.' For the defence of Scots as purer English than sudron, see above, p. 66.

47. *Poetical Works of Alexander*, I, cxciv-cc, II, xi-xvi

48. M. A. Bald, 'The Anglicisation of Scottish Printing', *Scottish Historical Review*, 23 (1925–6): 107–15.

49. On Scottish Presbyterianism and unionism see above, pp. 44, 49. For a sceptical investigation of the issues see Mairi Robinson, 'Language Choice in the Reformation: The Scots Confession of 1560', in J. Derrick McLure (ed.), *Scotland and the Lowland Tongue: Studies in the Language and Literature of Scotland in Honour of David D. Murison* (Aberdeen: Aberdeen University Press, 1983), 59–78.

50. This was the basis on which Hume of Godscroft arrived at a view of the relationship between Scots and English apparently at odds with Drummond and Alexander (above, n. 46). For contexts see J. Derrick McClure, 'Scottis, Inglis, Suddroun: Language Labels and Language Attitudes' (1981), rpt. in his *Scots and its Literature* (Amsterdam: John Benjamins, 1995), 44–56.

51. Cf. Deborah Howard, 'Languages and Architecture in Scotland, 1500–1660', in Georgia Clarke and Paul Crossley (eds.), *Architecture and Language: Constructing Identity in European Architecture, c.1000-c.1660* (Cambridge: Cambridge University Press, 2000), 162–77.

52. See J. Derrick McClure, 'Lowland Scots: An Ambivalent National Tongue' (1984), rpt. in his *Scots and its Literature*, 5–19.

53. 'An Elegie, Containing the Pilgrimes Most Humble Farewell to his Natiue and Neuer Conquered Kingdome of Scotland', in *The Pilgrimes Farewell to his Natiue Countrey of Scotland* (Edinburgh, 1618), H3v–4v, H4r.

54. Alexander Craig, 'Scotlands Teares', in his *Poeticall Essayes* (London, 1604), C1v–2v—though the predominant sentiment in this volume is pro-union.

55. 'On the Isle of Rhe', *Poetical Works of Drummond*, II, 245. His authorship of the satire on James I and VI's corrupted senses ('For the Kinge', *Poetical Works of Drummond*, II, 296–9), which dates from the period of Buckingham's dominance, is extremely doubtful; see Robert H. MacDonald, 'Amendments to L. E. Kastner's Edition of Drummond's Poems', *Studies in Scottish Literature*, 7 (1969): 102–22, p. 118 and the Drummond section in Peter Beal, comp., *Index of English Literary Manuscripts*, vol. I, part 2 (London: Mansell, 1980), 17–47, p. 18.

56. *Scotlands Welcome to Her Native Sonne, and Soveraigne Lord, King Charles* (Edinburgh, 1633), A3v, A4v.

57. See e.g. David Stevenson, *Scottish Covenanters and Irish Confederates: Scottish-Irish Relations in the Mid-Seventeenth Century* (Belfast: Ulster Historical Foundation, 1981).

58. *Scotlands Welcome*, C3v.

59. *The Entertainment of the High and Mighty Monarch Charles*, in *Poetical Works of Drummond*, II, 113–36, p. 123.

60. *English Civic Pageantry 1558–1642* (London: Edward Arnold, 1971), 112–31; British Library Harleian MS 4707, art. 3 (fos. 59v–60v). Cf. British Library Additional MS 40885, fos. 2r–20r; Edinburgh University Library MS D.C.4,3.

61. First published in Edinburgh, in 1633, by the John Wreittoun who produced William Lithgow's *Scotlands Welcome*.

62. Alan R. MacDonald, *The Jacobean Kirk, 1567–1625: Sovereignty, Polity and Liturgy* (Ashgate: Aldershot, 1998), 158–61, recontextualized in idem., 'James VI and I, the Church of Scotland, and British Ecclesiastical Convergence', *Historical Journal*, 48 (2005): 885–903; on ceremony, north and south, more generally, see Charles W. A. Prior, *Defining the Jacobean Church: The Politics of Religious Controversy, 1603–1625* (Cambridge: Cambridge University Press, 2005), chs. 5–6.

63. See John Spalding, *History of the Troubles and Memorable Transactions in Scotland, from 1624 to 1645*, quoted e.g. by John Morrill, 'The National Covenant

in its British Context', in Morrill (ed.), *Scottish National Covenant*, 1−30, pp. 2−3.

64. Colin Kidd, *British Identities before Nationalism: Ethnicity and Nationhood in the Atlantic World, 1600−1800* (Cambridge: Cambridge University Press, 1999), 129.

65. Cf. the early pages of Archbishop John Spottiswoode, *The History of the Church of Scotland, Beginning in the Year of Our Lord 203 and Continued to the End of the Reign of King James the VI* (London, 1655).

66. On the Revocation see above, pp. 95−6, and, on its financing of colleges and hospitals, Donald, *An Uncounselled King*, 18.

67. Allan I. Macinnes, *Charles I and the Making of the Covenanting Movement 1625−1641* (Edinburgh: John Donald, 1991), 104, notes the general scepticism about, and lack of enthusiasm for collecting, this impost, announced in 1627.

68. See e.g. Maurice Lee, *The Road to Revolution: Scotland Under Charles I, 1625−37* (Urbana: University of Illinois Press, 1985), 133−5.

69. E.g. the New World arch (designed by Thomas Dekker) that greeted King James in Fleet Street when he ceremoniously entered London—Stephen Harrison, *The Arch's of Triumph Erected in Honor of the High and Mighty Prince James* (London, 1604), H1r—and George Chapman, *The Memorable Masque* (London, 1613).

70. For evidence of his interest see the item in the Hawthornden MSS (perhaps raw material for a poem), transcribed in McGrail, *Alexander*, 236−8, and now known to derive from a report written by a Scot who went to Nova Scotia in 1629 (N. E. S. Griffiths and John G. Reid, 'New Evidence on New Scotland, 1629', *William and Mary Quarterly*, ser. 3, 49 (1992): 492−508).

71. 'Making the Empire British: Scotland in the Atlantic World 1542−1707', *Past and Present*, 155 (May 1997): 34−63, an argument now enlarged in his *Ideological Origins of the British Empire* (Cambridge: Cambridge University Press, 2000).

72. 'Memorialls', in MacDonald (ed.), *Drummond: Poems and Prose*, 193−5, pp. 193−4.

73. See Daniel Cobb Harvey, 'Sir William Alexander and Nova Scotia', Nova Scotia Historical Society, *Collections*, 30 (1954): 1−26, p. 25.

74. David Stevenson, 'The English Devil of Keeping State: Elite Manners and the Downfall of Charles I in Scotland', rpt. in his *Union, Revolution and Religion in 17th-Century Scotland* (Aldershot: Variorum, 1997), [126−44]; Lee, *Road to Revolution*, 136.

75. 'An Apologetical Letter', in William Drummond, *The History of Scotland* (London, 1656), 238−44, p. 242.

76. Bishop John Sage, 'The Life of William Drummond of Hawthornden', in *Works of Drummond*, i-xi, p. ix. For the ongoing belief, even among

NOTES TO PAGES 157—9

perceptive scholars, that Drummond only distrusted and rejected Buchanan, see MacDonald, 'A Disputed Maxim of State', 298 and Miller, *Rebecca's Vest*, 91.

77. *Works of Drummond*, 151.
78. On the poverty of the work see Gary F. Waller, 'Sir William Alexander and Renaissance Court Culture', *Aevum*, 51 (1977): 505—15, p. 514.
79. Thomas H. McGrail, *Sir William Alexander, First Earl of Stirling: A Biographical Study* (Edinburgh: Oliver and Boyd, 1940), 167; cf. Alastair J. Mann, *The Scottish Book Trade, 1500 to 1720: Print Commerce and Print Control in Early Modern Scotland* (East Linton: Tuckwell, 2000), 50.
80. Ibid., 199.
81. Ibid., 187.
82. Anne Barton, *Ben Jonson, Dramatist* (Cambridge: Cambridge University Press, 1984), 7; Ian Donaldson, *Jonson's Magic Houses: Essays in Interpretation* (Oxford: Clarendon, 1997), 19.
83. 'Anecdotes, &c. Selected from Drummond of Hawthornden's Miscellanies, Vol. II', in David Laing, 'A Brief Account of the Hawthornden Manuscripts in the Possession of the Society of Antiquaries of Scotland', *Archaeologia Scotica: Or, Transactions of the Society of Antiquaries of Scotland*, 4 ([1831] 1857), 57—116, 225—40, pp. 78—82; *Poetical Works of Drummond*, II, 208, 285—7; French Rowe Fogle, *A Critical Study of William Drummond of Hawthornden* (New York: Columbia University Press, 1952), 205, 208; MacDonald, 'Amendments', 107—11; MacDonald (ed.), *Drummond: Poems and Prose*, 141—3; 'The Country Maid', *Poetical Works of Drummond*, II, 210.
84. 'To the Reader', *Poetical Works of Drummond*, 327.
85. 'Polemo-Middinia', *Poetical Works of Drummond*, II, 321—6; there is a parallel-text translation in Allan H. MacLaine (ed.), *The Christis Kirk Tradition: Scots Poems of Folk Festivity* (Glasgow: Association for Scottish Literary Studies, 1996), 39—49. Against Drummond's authorship see MacDonald, 'Amendments', 120.
86. *Poetical Works of Drummond*, II, 245.
87. For contexts see Roger A. Mason, 'The Aristocracy, Episcopacy and the Revolution of 1638', in Terry Brotherstone (ed.), *Covenant, Charter and Party: Traditions of Revolt and Protest in Modern Scottish History* (Aberdeen: Aberdeen University Press, 1989), 7—24.
88. His religious beliefs are unfolded in *Flowres of Sion* (Edinburgh, 1623; 2nd edn. 1630), which includes the moving, eclectic meditation on death, 'A Cypresse Grove'.
89. *Poetical Works of Drummond*, II, 293—5, lines 31—40; for a similarly ventriloquized poem see 'A Character of the Anti-Couenanter, or Malignant' (II, 218—21).

90. Conrad Russell, *The Fall of the British Monarchies 1637–1642* (Oxford: Oxford University Press, 1991), 43–4, 61, 69; Joad Raymond, *Pamphlets and Pamphleteering in Early Modern Britain* (Cambridge: Cambridge University Press, 2003), ch. 5.

91. Key contexts (including the Low Countries) are established by Donald, *An Uncounselled King*, ch. 5; for one revealing career see John Coffey, *Politics, Religion and the British Revolutions: The Mind of Samuel Rutherford* (Cambridge: Cambridge University Press, 1997), 229–30, 243–6, 202–19.

92. *Works of Drummond*, 163–73, pp. 166–7, 173.

93. *Poetical Works of Drummond*, II, 206.

94. Ibid.

95. Ibid., 205. Kastner, following Masson, *Drummond*, 293, notes the poem's likely relevance to the business of the General Assembly which met in Glasgow on 21 November 1638.

96. *Works of Drummond*, 177–8, p. 178.

97. Ibid., 179–82, p. 181.

98. Jane H. Ohlmeyer, *Civil War and Restoration in the Three Stuart Kingdoms: The Career of Randal MacDonnell, Marquis of Antrim, 1609–1683* (Cambridge: Cambridge University Press, 1993), ch. 3.

99. *Poetical Works of Drummond*, II, 223.

100. This seems the likeliest occasion for 'Bold Scotes, at Bannochburne yee killd your king' and the 'Reply' attached (*Poetical Works of Drummond*, II, 207).

101. *Poetical Works of Drummond*, II, 242; my dating is again only probable.

102. *Considerations to the Parliament September 1639*, in *Works of Drummond*, 185–7, pp. 185–6.

103. *Fall of the British Monarchies*, 145.

104. *Works of Drummond*, 216–17; contrast the apologia for Covenanting Scotland in *A Relation of the Kings Entertainment into Scotland* (London, 1641).

105. Keith Brown, *Kingdom or Province? Scotland and the Regal Union, 1603–1715* (Basingstoke: Macmillan, 1992), 121–2.

106. E.g. *History of Scotland*, 5 (moderate taxation), 7 (avoidance of faction), 17 (the decadence of peace and English mores at the Scottish court), 20–2 (the English case for a league with Scotland), 114ff. (the rashness of noble rebellion), 117–19 (flaws in James III resembling those of Charles I), 210–15 (the wise counsellors of James V urge religious toleration, but, as in the 1630s, clerics prevail and create divisions); for a more generalized account see Thomas I. Rae, 'The Historical Writing of Drummond of Hawthornden', *Scottish Historical Review*, 54 (1975): 22–62, pp. 37–44.

107. *Poetical Works of Drummond*, II, 243.

108. Hawthornden MSS; National Library of Scotland MS 2062, 185r.

109. *Works of Drummond*, 190–205, p. 197.

110. David L. Smith, *A History of the Modern British Isles, 1603–1707: The Double Crown* (Oxford: Blackwell, 1998), 141.

111. *The Poems of John Cleveland*, ed. Brian Morris and Eleanor Withington (Oxford: Clarendon, 1967), 29–32.

112. See e.g. Mark Stoyle, *Soldiers and Strangers: An Ethnic History of the English Civil War* (New Haven: Yale University Press, 2005), ch. 4.

113. On these successes but also the limits of pan-Celtic solidarity see David Stevenson, *Alasdair MacColla and the Highland Problem in the Seventeenth Century* (Edinburgh: John Donald, 1980).

114. See Allan I. Macinnes, 'Scottish Gaeldom, 1638–1651: The Vernacular Response to the Covenanting Dynamic', in John Dwyer, Roger A. Mason, and Alexander Murdoch (eds.), *New Perspectives on the Politics and Culture of Early Modern Scotland* (Edinburgh: John Donald, 1982), 59–94, pp. 76–82, and parallel texts of poems by Iain Lom, 'Oran air Latha Blàir Inbhir Lóchaidh eadar Clann Dòmhnaill agus na Caimbeulaich' ('A Song on the day of the Battle of Inverlochy') and perhaps by Fionnghal, wife of Iain Garbh, 8th Maclean of Coll, 'Turas mo chreiche thug mi Chola' ('The Journey of my undoing I made to Coll') in Colm Ó Baoill (ed.), *Gàir nan Clàrsach: The Harps' Cry*, tr. Meg Bateman (Edinburgh: Birlinn, 1994), 106–17.

115. Kidd, *British Identities*, 139–41.

116. *Considerations to the Parliament*, 186.

117. Masson, *Drummond*, 404.

118. *Poetical Works of Drummond*, II, 243.

119. *Works of Drummond*, 212–15, p. 214.

120. The likely poetic influence of Drummond on Milton (e.g. H. Neville Davies, 'Milton's Nativity Ode and Drummond's "An Hymne of the Ascension"', *Scottish Literary Journal*, 12/1 (May 1985): 5–23) has been debated at least since Masson's *Drummond*, 472–4, proposed a role for Milton in the preparation of Edward Phillips's edition.

121. On Hall and Drummond see David Norbrook, *Writing the English Republic: Poetry, Rhetoric and Politics, 1627–1660* (Cambridge: Cambridge University Press, 1999), 221; on Cromwell's liking for the discourse on toleration in the James V section of the *History of Scotland*, see Derek Hirst, 'The English Republic and the Meaning of Britain' (1994), rpt. in Brendan Bradshaw and John Morrill (eds.), *The British Problem, c.1534–1707: State Formation in the Atlantic Archipelago* (Basingstoke: Macmillan, 1996), 192–219, p. 210 and *n*. 114.

122. Morgan, 'How Good a Poet is Drummond?'

CHAPTER 5

1. E.g. The events traced out in Raymond Gillespie, *Conspiracy: Ulster Plots and Plotters in 1615* (Belfast: Queen's University, Belfast, 1987).

2. O'Neill, Earl of Tyrone, led a Nine Years War against the English (1594–1603). The revolt of Sir Cahir O'Doherty, in west Ulster, in 1608,

brought out factions of the O'Cahans and O'Hanlons, though it did not turn into a full-scale rising.

3. John Clavell, *Introduction to the Sword Dance*, in Alan J. Fletcher, *Drama, Performance, and Polity in Pre-Cromwellian Ireland* (Cork: Cork University Press, 2000), 310–13.

4. Fynes Moryson's description of early seventeenth-century sword dancing in the houses of Old Irish lords brings out the element of threat that Barrymore's masque contained (the more scarcely if, as is entirely possible, Old Irish gentlemen showed their loyalty by participating as masquer-kerns): 'and it seemed to me a dangerous sport, to see so many naked swordes so neere the Lord Deputy and cheefe Commanders of the Army, in the handes of the Irish kerne, who had ether lately beene or were not vnlike to proue Rebells' (*The Irish Sections of Fynes Moryson's Unpublished Itinerary*, ed. Graham Kew (Dublin, Irish Manuscripts Commission, 1998), 112; cf. Fletcher, *Drama, Performance, and Polity*, 216).

5. The text is edited from manuscript in Albert H. Tricomi, '*A Dialogue betweene Pollicy and Piety* by Robert Davenport', *English Literary Renaissance*, 21 (1991): 190–216.

6. Letter to Lord Conway and Killultagh, rpt. in Fletcher, *Drama, Performance, and Polity*, 308–9. For the event see John Canon Begley, *The Diocese of Limerick in the Sixteenth and Seventeenth Centuries* (Dublin: Browne and Nolan, 1927), 303.

7. For reviews of the evidence, and scepticism about conversion, see William D. Wolf, 'Some New Facts and Conclusions about James Shirley: Residence and Religion', *Notes and Queries*, n.s. 29 (1982): 133–4 and Ira Clark's article on Shirley in the *Oxford Dictionary of National Biography*.

8. Allan H. Stevenson, 'Shirley's Years in Ireland', *Review of English Studies*, 20 (1944): 19–28, pp. 20–2.

9. *St Patrick for Ireland. The First Part* (London, 1640), A4r.

10. On the moving of Protestant communion tables to the east end of churches, under the 1634 Laudian reforms of the Irish Canons, spearheaded by Bramhall, see John McCafferty, '"God Bless Your Free Church of Ireland": Wentworth, Laud, Bramhall and the Irish Convocation of 1634', in J. F. Merritt, *The Political World of Thomas Wentworth, Earl of Strafford, 1621–1641* (Cambridge: Cambridge University Press, 1996), 187–208, p. 201.

11. Cf. E4v: 'this is the same *Patrick* | That was my slave once, he was a Brittan too'.

12. His views on St Patrick, scattered through his correspondence with the Counter-Reformation bishop, David Rothe — edited in William O'Sullivan, 'Correspondence of David Rothe and James Ussher, 1619–23', *Collecteana Hibernica*, 36–7 (1994–5): 7–49 — were aired in *An Epistle Written by the Reverend Father in God, James Vssher Bishop of Meath, Concerning the Religion*

Anciently Professed by the Irish and Scottish, appended to Sir Christopher Sibthorp, *A Friendly Advertisement to the Pretended Catholickes of Ireland* (Dublin, 1622), and developed in his *Discourse of the Religion Anciently Professed by the Irish and Brittish* (London, 1631).

13. On Patrick's beliefs, as extrapolated by Ussher—no prayers for the dead, no belief in purgatory, no idolatry or priestly magic, rejection of transubstantiation, marriage no sacrament—see John McCafferty, 'Saint Patrick for the Church of Ireland: James Ussher's *Discourse*', *Bullán*, 3/2 (1997−8): 87−101, p. 93.

14. Some English clerics, Bramhall among them (see Alan Ford, 'Dependent or Independent? The Church of Ireland and its Colonial Context, 1536−1649', *Seventeenth Century*, 10 (1995): 163−87, p. 176), believed that an ancient British patriarchate had included Ireland and Scotland. On the congruity sought by Laud in the 1630s, see John Morrill, 'A British Patriarchy? Ecclesiastical Imperialism under the Early Stuarts', in Anthony Fletcher and Peter Roberts (eds.), *Religion, Culture and Society in Early Modern Britain: Essays in Honour of Patrick Collinson* (Cambridge: Cambridge University Press, 1994), 209−37; for how this looked from Ireland, Amanda L. Capern, 'The Caroline Church: James Ussher and the Irish Dimension', *Historical Journal*, 39 (1996): 57−85.

15. See e.g. Alan Ford, *The Protestant Reformation in Ireland, 1590−1641* (1985; Dublin: Four Courts, 1997), 171−8. Some would later argue that the 1641 Rising was divine retribution for the Protestants having been (in Davenport's words) Politic rather than Pious in not vigorously pursuing conversion or extirpation. Ford cites Daniel Harcourt, who declared in 1643 that the English in Ireland now found 'how dearly the Israelites paid for their cruel mercy in not extirpating the idolatrous Canaanites ... teaching us ... that policy without piety is a damnable discretion' (221).

16. The debate about the chronology is summarized by Ford in *Protestant Reformation in Ireland*, 7−20 (i.e. preface to 2nd edn.). On the persistence of popular ignorance beyond the period covered by this chapter see Edward Ward, *A Trip to Ireland, Being a Description of the Country, People and Manners* (London?, 1699), 10.

17. Nicholas Canny, *Making Ireland British, 1580−1650* (Oxford: Oxford University Press, 2001), 406, and, more extensively, Tadhg Ó hAnnracháin, *Catholic Reformation in Ireland: The Mission of Rinuccini, 1645−1649* (Oxford: Oxford University Press, 2002). For a reinflection of the view that the Counter-Reformation affected Old English and mere Irish communities at different rates and in different ways, see Colm Lennon, 'The Counter-Reformation in Ireland 1542−1641', in Ciarán Brady and Raymond Gillespie (eds.), *Natives and Newcomers: Essays on the Making of Irish Colonial Society, 1534−1641* (Dublin: Irish Academic Press, 1986), 75−92.

18. For impressive fulminations by one Englishman settled in Munster see Alan Ford's edition of the long poem (c.1621) by 'Parr Lane, "Newes from the Holy Isle"', *Proceedings of the Royal Irish Academy*, 99(C) (1999): 115–56.

19. E.g. Raymond Gillespie, 'Political Ideas and their Social Contexts in Seventeenth-Century Ireland', in Jane H. Ohlmeyer (ed.), *Political Thought in Seventeenth-Century Ireland: Kingdom or Colony* (Cambridge: Cambridge University Press, 2000), 107–27, pp. 120–1 (Patrick as 'a Church of Ireland bishop [with] impeccable Laudian credentials'); Patricia Coughlan, ' "Cheap and Common Animals": The English Anatomy of Ireland in the Seventeenth Century', in Thomas Healy and Jonathan Sawday (eds.), *Literature and the English Civil War* (Cambridge: Cambridge University Press, 1990), 205–23, pp. 208–9 (Shirley was a Catholic but had a 'strictly colonising viewpoint'); cf. Deana Rankin, *Between Spenser and Swift: English Writing in Seventeenth-Century Ireland* (Cambridge: Cambridge University Press, 2005), 99–104 (*St Patrick* 'far from being an "Irish" play'). See further *n.* 31, below.

20. *The Earl of Strafforde's Letters and Dispatches*, ed. William Knowler, 2 vols. (London, 1739), I, 187–9.

21. Raymond Gillespie, *Devoted People: Belief and Religion in Early Modern Ireland* (Manchester: Manchester University Press, 1997), e.g. 94, 109.

22. Rochford (who identified himself as '*Fr. B. B. one of the Irish Franciscan Friars at Louvain*') cut fifty-four of Jocelyn's 196 chapters to bring Patrick's life into line with post-Tridentine standards of sanctity. Published at Saint-Omer in 1625, along with similarly reformed biographies of St Bridget and St Columba, this *Life* was reissued as an appendix to the Spanish Dominican Alfonso de Villegas' *Lives of the Saints* in its Saint-Omer (1627) and Rouen (1636) editions. Cf. Bernadette Cunningham and Raymond Gillespie, 'The Most Adaptable of Saints: The Cult of St Patrick in the Seventeenth Century', *Archivium Hibernicum*, 49 (1995): 82–104, p. 90.

23. The controversion of Ussher's thesis is part of an ongoing Catholic-Protestant contest over Patrick and his legacy, which Shirley's play negotiates. Cf., most forcibly, on the Counter-Reformation side, Philip O'Sullivan Beare, *Archicornigeromastix, siue Vsheri haeresiarchae confutatio* in his *Patritiana decas* (Madrid, 1629).

24. Richard Burke of Enniskillen reports an 'English book printed in the Low Countries imparting another prophecy of St Patrick' in the possession of rebels near Limerick; cited by Cunningham and Gillespie, 'Most Adaptable of Saints', 97.

25. *Life of the Glorious Bishop S. Patricke*, 16 (*contra* Gillespie, 'Political Ideas', 120–1).

26. *Life of the Glorious Bishop S. Patricke*, iv–vii; *St Patrick for Ireland*, I1v–2r.

27. 'We saw a pale man coming from the sea', 'all that were with me, … fled to this pale man', 'This pale thing shall not trouble you' (B1r)—nothing of this is in Rochford.

28. The apothegm, from Tertullian, was probably suggested by Rochford's slightly wishful 'a Martyr he was, in regard of the many conflicts he had against Kings, Magitians, Idolaters, and Diuels' (*Life*, 103−4).

29. On Bellings, see above, p. 45. His complimentary verses preface Shirley's *The Royall Master* (London, 1631).

30. Most of Shirley's nine extant prologues to Werburgh Street productions—see the 'Prologues and Epilogues' section of *Narcissus: Or, The Self-Lover* (London, 1646), 35−159—complain about small audiences, and lack of theatrical sophistication.

31. This analysis has points of contact with Sandra A. Burner, *James Shirley: A Study of Literary Coteries and Patronage in Seventeenth-Century England* (Lanham, MD: University Press of America, 1988), 121; Fletcher, *Drama, Performance, and Polity*, 274−5; and Christopher Morash, *A History of Irish Theatre 1601−2000* (Cambridge: Cambridge University Press, 2002), 7−8.

32. The process, which has deep roots, is often traced back to the pressures of the Nine Years War; see Peter Lombard's 1600 arguments for a change in sovereignty in Ireland based on shared Catholicism, *De regno Hiberniae, sanctorum insulâ, commentarius* (Louvain, 1632). For early Stuart initatives see e.g. David Rothe: P. J. Corish, 'David Rothe, Bishop of Ossory, 1618−1650', *Journal of the Butler Society*, 2 (1984): 315−23; Colm Lennon, 'Political Thought of the Irish Counter-Reformation Churchmen: The Testimony of the "Analecta" of Bishop David Rothe', in Hiram Morgan (ed.), *Political Ideology in Ireland, 1541−1641* (Dublin: Four Courts, 1999), 181−202; Thomas O'Connor, 'Custom, Authority, and Tolerance in Irish Political Thought: David Rothe's *Analecta Sacra et Mira* (1616)', *Irish Theological Quarterly*, 65 (2000): 133−56. Trends within hagiography that would prevent St Patrick from dividing Catholics along ethnic lines are brought out in another article by Thomas O'Connor, 'Towards the Invention of the Irish Catholic *Natio*: Thomas Messingham's *Florilegium* (1624)', *Irish Theological Quarterly*, 64 (1999): 157−77.

33. Hugh Kearney, *Strafford in Ireland 1633−41: A Study in Absolutism* (1959; Cambridge: Cambridge University Press, 1989), 220.

34. *Strafforde's Letters*, ed. Knowler, I, 188.

35. See e.g. Anne Laurence, 'The Cradle to the Grave: English Observations of Irish Social Customs in the Seventeenth Century', *The Seventeenth Century*, 3 (1988): 63−84, pp. 65−8.

36. John Bossy, 'The Counter-Reformation and the People of Catholic Ireland, 1596−1641', *Historical Studies*, 8, ed. T. D. Williams (Dublin, 1971), 155−69, p. 160—a pioneering article probably too much influenced by the comments of English observers; also Laurence, 'The Cradle to the Grave', 68−72.

37. Bossy, 'Counter-Reformation and the People', 161−2. On English measures following the accession of James I, see S. W. Bartholomew, 'The Origin

and Development of the Law of Bigamy', *Law Quarterly Review*, 74 (1958): 259–71.

38. I am grateful to John McCafferty for advice on the workings of the parliament.

39. To Sir John Coke (Secretary of State), 16 December 1634, *Strafforde's Letters*, ed. Knowler, I, 345–53, p. 351.

40. On the Scoto-British Ogilby, whose Dublin-London theatrical career peaked in his management of Charles II's 1661 coronation, who translated Virgil and Homer, and became best known for his road map of England and Wales, *Britannia* (London, 1675), see Katherine S. van Eerde, *John Ogilby and the Taste of his Times* (Folkestone: Dawson, 1976).

41. Fletcher, *Drama, Performance, and Polity*, 275–6, spots the topicality of the issue but gives no account of Burnell's exploration, and use, of it. Catherine M. Shaw, '*Landgartha* and the Irish Dilemma', *Éire-Ireland*, 13 (1978): 26–39 and, more securely, Rankin, *Between Spenser and Swift*, 105–8, also place the play historically.

42. 'Amours de Regner Roy de Noruege, et comme il espousa Landgerthe, et puis la repudia: et des faits louables d'icelle Princesse', Histoire 80 in François de Belleforest, *Le Quatriesme tome des histoires tragiques, partie extraites des oeuures Italiennes du Bandel, et partie de l'inuention de l'Autheur François* (Turin, 1571), 838–75.

43. *Landgartha* (Dublin, 1641), B2v.

44. Charles was not the last Stuart to be praised as an enemy of the Turks (see Waller's 'Of the late Invasion and Defeat of the Turks, &c.' [Charles II], 'A Presage of the Ruine of the Turkish Empire, Presented to His Majesty on His Birth-Day' [James VII and II]), but Burnell appears to draw on an earlier prophetic tradition, one which cast James VI and Prince Henry as latter-day Constantines, whose retaking of Constantinople—avoiding involvement in anti-Catholic warfare on the continent—would usher in apocalyptic events. For this line of thought see Arthur H. Williamson, 'An Empire to End Empire: The Dynamic of Early Modern British Expansion', *Huntington Library Quarterly*, 68 (2005): 227–56, pp. 243–4.

45. On Scottish-Swedish co-operation at this date, in support of the Covenanters, see e.g. Steve Murdoch, 'Scotland, Scandinavia and the Bishops' Wars, 1638–1640', in Allan I. Macinnes and Jane H. Ohlmeyer (eds.), *The Stuart Kingdoms in the Seventeenth Century: Awkward Neighbours* (Dublin: Four Courts, 2002), 113–34.

46. See e.g. Aidan Clarke, 'Patrick Darcy and the Constitutional Relationship between Ireland and Britain', in Ohlmeyer (ed.), *Political Thought in Seventeenth-Century Ireland*, 35–55.

47. See e.g. the 'Act for the English Order, Habite and Language', passed by the Dublin parliament in 1537 (28 Henry VIII).

48. Canny, *Making Ireland British*, 487, 523.

49. Shaw, '*Landgartha*', 35 notes that the Burnell family had estates near Dunboyne, Co. Meath, though 'te *Phip-a-Dunboyne*', as the Irish footmen call it in Ben Jonson's *Irish Masque at Court* (1613), was already an established marker of indigenous culture. Cf. *Irish Sections of Moryson's Itinerary*, ed. Kew, 112, *The Irish Hudibras: Or, The Fingallian Prince* (London, 1689), 27, 35, 101.

50. On Old English/Gaelic hybridization (adding New Irish as a category to Old Irish) see above p. 45, and on kinship e.g. Donald Jackson, *Intermarriage in Ireland 1550–1650* (Minneapolis: Cultural and Education Productions, 1970).

51. See e.g. Brian Mac Cuarta (ed.), *Ulster 1641: Aspects of the Rising* (Belfast: Institute of Irish Studies, Queen's University, 1993); M. Perceval-Maxwell, *The Outbreak of the Irish Rebellion of 1641* (Montreal: McGill-Queen's University Press, 1994); Canny, *Making Ireland British*, ch. 8; and, a qualifying perspective, Joseph Cope, 'The Experience of Survival during the Irish Rebellion', *Historical Journal*, 46 (2003): 295–316. For archipelagic angles, see Conrad Russell, 'The British Background to the Irish Rebellion of 1641', *Historical Research*, 61 (1988): 166–82.

52. Canny, *Making Ireland British*, 510.

53. My account has been informed by J. C. Beckett, 'The Confederation of Kilkenny Reviewed', in *Historical Studies*, 2, ed. Michael Roberts (London: Bowes and Bowes, 1959), 29–41; Donald F. Cregan, 'The Confederation of Kilkenny', in Brian Farrell (ed.), *The Irish Parliamentary Tradition* (Dublin; Gill and Macmillan, 1973), 102–15; and Micheál Ó Siochrú, *Confederate Ireland, 1642–1649: A Constitutional and Political Analysis* (Dublin: Four Courts, 1999).

54. Edmund Borlase, *The History of the Execrable Irish Rebellion* (London, 1653), 82, cited by Mary O'Dowd, 'Women and War in Ireland in the 1640s', in Margaret MacCurtain and Mary O'Dowd (eds.), *Women in Early Modern Ireland* (Edinburgh: Edinburgh University Press, 1991), 91–111, p. 94, and Bernadette Whelan, 'Women and Warfare, 1641–1691', in Pádraig Lenihan (ed.), *Conquest and Resistance: War in Seventeenth-Century Ireland* (Leiden: Brill, 2001), 317–43, p. 332.

55. See the extensive coverage in Alan J. Fletcher, *Drama and the Performing Arts in Pre-Cromwellian Ireland: A Repertory of Sources and Documents from the Earliest Times until c.1642* (London: Boydell and Brewer, 2001).

56. E.g. the anonymous *Aphorismical Discovery of Treasonable Faction*, in *A Contemporary History of Affairs in Ireland from 1641 to 1652*, ed. J. T. Gilbert, 3 vols. in 6 (Dublin: Irish Archaeological and Celtic Society, 1879–1880) notes, around the arrival of the Confederate general, Thomas Preston, from the Netherlands, 'dayly invitations, feasts and banquetts with the varietie as well of pallat-inticing dishes, as of gratulatorie poems, civill and martiall representations of comedies and stage playes, with mightie content' (I, 46).

57. The best account of the play is Patricia Coughlan, ' "Enter Revenge": Henry Burkhead and *Cola's Furie*', *Theatre Research International*, 15/1 (1990): 1–17, rev. in Micheál Ó Siochrú (ed.), *Kingdoms in Crisis: Ireland in the 1640s* (Dublin: Four Courts, 2001), 192–211.

58. They would remain the starting point for full-scale accounts of the rising from the New English Protestant Sir John Temple's *The Irish Rebellion* (London, 1646) to the Old English Catholic Richard Bellings, *History of the Irish Confederation and the War in Ireland, 1641–1643*, ed. John T. Gilbert, 7 vols. (Dublin: John T. Gilbert, 1882–91).

59. *A Tragedy of Cola's Furie: Or, Lirenda's Miserie* (Kilkenny, 1645), 2.

60. Alan Ford, ' "Firm Catholics" or "Loyal Subjects"? Religious and Political Allegiance in Early Seventeenth-Century Ireland', in D. George Boyce, Robert Eccleshall, and Vincent Geoghegan (eds.), *Political Discourse in Seventeenth- and Eighteenth-Century Ireland* (Basingstoke: Palgrave, 2001), 1–31.

61. 3 and 4 James I c.4, 1606; this feature was preserved in the softened version of the oath proposed for use in Ireland in the tolerant aftermath of the accession of Charles I (quoted by Ford, ' "Firm Catholics" ', 20).

62. E.g. Edward Vallance, *Revolutionary England and the National Covenant: State Oaths, Protestantism, and the Political Nation, 1533–1682* (Woodbridge: Boydell, 2005), chs. 2–7. My discussion is informed by David Martin Jones, *Conscience and Allegiance in Seventeenth-Century England: The Political Significance of Oaths and Engagements* (Woodbridge: Boydell, 1999); John Spurr, 'A Profane History of Early Modern Oaths', *Transactions of the Royal Historical Society*, 6th ser., 11 (2001), 37–63 and ' "The Strongest Bond of Conscience": Oaths and the Limits of Tolerance in Early Modern England', in Harald E. Braun and Edward Vallance (eds.), *Contexts of Conscience in Early Modern Europe, 1500–1700* (London: Palgrave, 2004), 151–65; Conal Condren, *Argument and Authority in Early Modern England: The Presupposition of Oaths and Offices* (Cambridge: Cambridge University Press, 2006), chs. 11–14.

63. For the Scottish national Covenant see Samuel Rawson Gardiner (ed.), *The Constitutional Documents of the Puritan Revolution 1625–1660*, 3rd edn. (Oxford: Clarendon, 1906), 124–34; for the Oath of Association see Bellings, *History of the Irish Confederation*, ed. Gilbert, III, 213–14.

64. Cf. Beckett, 'Confederation', 31–2; Cregan, 'Confederation', 507. The Oath anticipates division and proposes a mechanism for managing it: 'I., A. B., do profess, swear and protest before God, and His Saints, and Holy Angels, that ... I will not seek, directly or indirectly, any pardon or protection for any act done, or to be done, touching the general cause, without the consent of the major part of the ... Council'.

65. Ó Siochrú, *Confederate Ireland*. On the international dimensions of faction, especially the demands of France and Spain, see Tadhg Ó hAnnracháin, 'Disrupted and Disruptive: Continental Influences on the Confederate Catholics of Ireland', in Allan I. Macinnes and Jane H. Ohlmeyer (eds.), *The Stuart*

Kingdoms in the Seventeenth Century: Awkward Neighbours (Dublin: Four Courts, 2002), 135–50.

66. *Aphorismical Discovery*, I, 189; cf. I, 251; II, 38. Owen Roe O Neill can be identified, without name, as 'The Catholicke Generall, to his nation naturall, obseruant of his oath and couenant of Confederacie' (I, 158).

67. This depiction correlates with other Catholic accounts of Coote, a veteran opponent of Tyrone's rebellion, who responded to the 1641 rising with brutality. Against the view that he was a 'humaine-bloudsucker' (*Aphorismical Discovery*, I, 31) can be set such Protestant praise as *The Latest and Truest Newes from Ireland* (London, 1642), 'in truth he is a gallant man, full of courage and good affections' (5) and *The Souldiers Commission* (London, 1658), his 1642 funeral sermon, preached by the gifted poet Faithful Teate (father of Nahum Tate), which, like other texts, praises Coote's vigilance regarding Catholic plots (D4v). See also 'An Elegie uppon the much lamented death of that famous and late Renowned kn[igh]t and Colonell Sir Charles Coote', preserved in Ormond's papers, and edited in Carpenter, *Verse in English from Tudor and Stuart Ireland*, 228–30.

68. For radical contexts see Tomás Ó Fiach, 'Republicanism and Separatism in the Seventeenth Century', *Leachtaí Cholm Cille*, 2 (1971): 74–87. Further instances are cited in M. Perceval-Maxwell, 'Ireland and the Monarchy in the Early Stuart Multiple Kingdom', *Historical Journal*, 34 (1991): 279–95.

69. O'Mahony's book, ostensibly published in Frankfurt, but almost certainly produced in Lisbon, contains two texts: *Disputatio apologetica, de jure regni Hiberniae pro Catholicis Hibernis aduersos haereticos Anglos* and *Exhortatio ad Catholicos Hybernos*. Copies were probably circulating in Ireland by the time *Cola's Furie* was published; action was taken against the work in 1647.

70. John Lowe, 'The Glamorgan Mission to Ireland, 1645–6', *Studia Hibernica*, 4 (1964): 155–96.

71. Note the commendatory poem by William Smith ('To my loving and respected friend Mr. *Henry Burkhead* Merchant') prefixed to the printed edn. of *Cola's Furie*. This was apparently the William Smith whose association with the Ormond family is explored by Andrew Carpenter in his anthology *Verse in English from Tudor and Stuart Ireland* (Cork: Cork University Press, 2003), 273—cf. his article 'Lost and Found: Tracing Items from a Collection of Verse Presented to James Butler, first duke of Ormonde', *Butler Journal*, 4 (2003): 479–89, p. 481—and presumably the 'Mr Smith' whose verses welcomed Ormond to the confederate capital in 1646 (see Alan J. Fletcher, 'Select Document: Ormond's civic entry into Kilkenny, 29/31 August 1646', *Irish Historical Studies*, 139 (2007): 365–79). The verses chime with the subtitle of Burkhead's play when the marquis is asked to 'Pyttye decaying Irelands Myserie'.

72. William H. McCabe, *An Introduction to Jesuit Theater*, ed. Louis J. Oldani (St Louis: Institute of Jesuit Sources, 1983), 124.

73. Robert Munter, *A Dictionary of the Print Trade in Ireland, 1550–1775* (New York: Fordham University Press, 1988).

74. Within months, the Jesuits would have their own printing press in the city. Between 1646 and 1649, it turned out dozens of works for distribution in Catholic Ireland and beyond, until its effectiveness led the Council of the Confederation to commandeer it for factional ends. See James Kelly, 'Political Publishing, 1550–1700', in Raymond Gillespie and Andrew Hadfield (eds.), *The Irish Book in English 1550–1800*, The Oxford History of the Irish Book, 3 (Oxford: Oxford University Press, 2006), 194–214, pp. 201–2.

75. Louis McRedmond, *To the Greater Glory: A History of the Irish Jesuits* (Dublin: Gill and Macmillan, 1991), ch. 2; cf. Ó hAnnracháin, *Catholic Reformation in Ireland*, 241, 246, and, on the 'Englishing' of Old Irishmen who became Jesuits, Aidan Clarke, *The Old English in Ireland, 1625–42* (London: MacGibbon and Kee, 1966), 23.

76. *Titus: Or, The Palme of Christian Courage* (Waterford, 1644), text in Fletcher, *Drama, Performance, and Polity*, 302–3.

77. Even in Gaelic sources the king was rarely attacked so harshly. For a fierce exception see the anonymous 'An síogaí Rómhánach' ['The Roman Fairy'], famously translated by Henry Grattan Curran as 'The Roman Vision', in James Hardiman, *Irish Minstrelsy: Or, Bardic Remains of Ireland, with English Poetical Translations*, 2 vols. (London, 1831), II, 307–39, and retranslated in an appendix to Gilbert's edn. of *Aphorismical Discovery* (III, 190–6), which denounces, among other wrongs, Charles's persecution of Irish Catholicism:

> It was he who required them to forsake God.
> He forbade parish mass-hearing;
> He proscribed the Gaelic tongue,
> And commanded Saxon speech for all.
> By him were mass and music prohibited.
> Every horror has been wrought upon Erin;
> A perpetual deadly curse is rained upon her;
> An atom of what was done would have been woe enough.   (192)

78. McCabe, *Introduction to Jesuit Theater*, 157.

79. The time scheme of *Titus* is short, but its drawn-out depiction of the mental and physical agonies repeatedly inflicted on the protagonist and his family, the edicts and expropriations imposed upon the faithful (dealt with in the play's comic interludes), must have resonated for audiences with the experience of decades of religious oppression.

80. St Francis Xavier established Japan's first Christian mission at Kagoshima in 1579; recurrent edicts, directives, and persecutions (including the crucifixion of twenty-six Japanese and foreign Christians in 1597) climaxed

in a ban on the faith (1614); the end of the mission is usually dated 1651.

81. François Solier, *Histoire ecclésiastique des isles et royaumes du Japon* (Paris, 1627); Fletcher's attempt to connect *Titus* with the story of Don Paul in this work (*Drama, Performance, and Polity*, 194) is properly tentative, and unconvincing.

82. Tr. W[illiam]. W[right]. (Saint-Omer, 1619). The subtitle of the play I would trace to another book of Jesuit letters from 1624, João Rodrigues, *The Palme of Christian Fortitude: Or, The Glorious Combats of Christians in Iaponia* (St-Omer, 1630).

83. See e.g. the 1647 memorandum for a *Judas Maccabaeus* in Cologne, including five or six idols and at least three demountable altars (McCabe, *Introduction to Jesuit Theater*, 16) and Fletcher's *The Island Princess* (1621).

84. Rinuccini believed that he was the first papal legate since Patrick to come to Ireland; Ó hAnnracháin, *Catholic Reformation in Ireland*, 93. His formal entry into Kilkenny (November, 1645), where he was met by fifty scholars—presumably including students involved in the performance of *Titus*—armed with pistols, one of whom, garlanded with laurels, recited a eulogy to him, was made through St Patrick's Gate (G. Aizza [= Giuseppe Aiazzi] (ed.), *The Embassy in Ireland of Monsignor G. B. Rinuccini*, tr. Annie Hutton (Dublin: A. Thom, 1873), 90).

85. Ó hAnnracháin, *Catholic Reformation in Ireland*, 244.

86. The torture of leading Catholics by order of the Lords Justices, after the rising, in Dublin castle, was a keenly felt grievance; cf. the racking scene in *Cola's Fury* (D2r–3r) and the stringing up of Barbazella with burning matches between her fingers (E4r-v).

87. The medieval distinction—and connection—between the faithful in this world (church militant) and those who enjoy the glory of the risen Christ (triumphant) was re-emphasized by the Roman Catechism (1566), following the Council of Trent. Cf. R. Po-Chia Hsia, *The World of Catholic Renewal 1540–1770* (Cambridge: Cambridge University Press, 1997), 125.

88. Ó hAnnracháin, *Catholic Reformation in Ireland*, e.g. 104–11, 248–50; on the domestication of the mass, despite Tridentine priorities, see also Gillespie, *Devoted People*, 27.

89. Bossy, 'Counter-Reformation and the People', qualified by Ó hAnnracháin, *Catholic Reformation in Ireland*, 230.

90. Cf. Bossy, 'Counter-Reformation and the People', 169 and Ó hAnnracháin, loc. cit.

91. Ó hAnnracháin, *Catholic Reformation in Ireland*, 73, and, for a later phase, 228–9.

92. McRedmond, *To the Greater Glory*, 70–1.

93. See Policy's account of Ireland as 'blew Neptunes round-clipt faire one', and the economic disquisition which ends the poem, in 'Dialogue', lines 64 and

140–91, and Patrick's praise of 'This nation … this great all-nursing Iland' (I1v–2r).

94. Cf. the archipelagic account of '*Iapone*, under which name [are] conteyned diuers Ilandes lying in the east ocean of the great Kingdome of *China*' which opens 'The Preface to the Reader', *Briefe Relation*, 19.

95. The isolation of missionary exposure more readily matches the experience of the English Catholics addressed by the source translation; see *Briefe Relation*, epistle dedicatory 'To all that Suffer Persecution in England for Catholike Religion', esp. 13–15.

CHAPTER 6

1. *Poems* (London, 1664), 1–3.

2. For a full account of the parameters of his career, which often cut through Brecknockshire, now Breconshire, see R. Tudur Jones, 'The Life, Work, and Thought of Vavasor Powell (1617–1670)', D. Phil. dissertation (University of Oxford, 1947).

3. See the valuable content lists in *The Collected Works of Katherine Philips: The Matchless Orinda*, ed. Patrick Thomas *et al.*, 3 vols. (Stump Cross: Stump Cross Books, 1990–3), I, 64–8.

4. B. S. Capp, *The Fifth Monarchy Men: A Study in Seventeenth-Century English Millenarianism* (London: Faber, 1972), 68, 76.

5. Walter Cradock, *Gospel-Holiness: Or, The Saving Sight of God* (London, 1651), 65.

6. For a full text see Elizabeth H. Hageman and Andrea Sununu, ' "More Copies of it Abroad than I Could Have Imagin'd": Further Manuscript Texts of Katherine Philips, "The Matchless Orinda" ', *English Manuscript Studies 1100–1700*, 5 (1995): 127–69, pp. 128–31 (and Plate 1, from which I quote); the poem was cited earlier by Capp, *Fifth Monarchy Men*, 51. A helpful selection of Powell's verse, including 'Upon the Occasion of a Tooth ach'—which piously observes how much worse were the pains endured by Christ on the cross…—can be found in Jones, *Life, Work, and Thought of Powell*.

7. Exodus 20: 13.

8. *Life of Powell*, 11; cf. 126–7. On the local geography of Powell's early activities see R. Tudur Jones, 'Religion in Post-Restoration Brecknockshire, 1660–1688', *Brycheiniog*, 8 (1962): 1–65, pp. 13–14.

9. *Life of Powell*, 200.

10. Poetry and other evidence shows that Vaughan fought for the king in the battle of Rowton Heath, near Chester, in 1645.

11. Published in *Olor Iscanus* (London, 1651); lines 15–26, in *The Works of Henry Vaughan*, ed. L. C. Martin, 2nd edn. (Oxford: Clarendon, 1957).

12. For contexts see Christopher Hill, 'Propagating the Gospel', in H. E. Bell and R. L. Ollard (eds.), *Historical Essays 1600–1750* (London: Adam and Charles Black, 1963), 36–43; A. M. Johnson, 'Wales during the Commonwealth and Protectorate', in Donald Pennington and Keith Thomas (eds.), *Puritans and Revolutionaries: Essays in Seventeenth-Century History* (Oxford: Clarendon, 1978), 233–56; Geraint H. Jenkins, *The Foundations of Modern Wales 1642–1780*, History of Wales, 4 (Oxford: Clarendon/University of Wales Press, 1987), ch. 2; and Lloyd Bowen, 'Representations of Wales and the Welsh during the Civil Wars and Interregnum', *Historical Research*, 77 (2004): 358–76, pp. 372–6.

13. Thomas Richards, whose *Religious Developments in Wales (1654–1662)* (London: National Eisteddfod Association, 1923), is indispensable, quoted by Geraint H. Jenkins, *Protestant Dissenters in Wales, 1639–1689* (Cardiff: University of Wales Press, 1992), 17.

14. Alexander Griffith, *Mercurius Cambro-Britannicus* (London, 1652), 8.

15. *Strena Vavasoriensis, a New-Years-Gift for the Welsh Itinerants: Or, A Hue and Cry after Mr Vavasor Powell* (London, 1654), 24.

16. Vavasor Powell, *Christ Exalted above all Creatures by God His Father* (London, 1651).

17. For verse retaliation see 'A Reply to the Libellers Satyrical Rythmes' (spoken by the figure of Propagation) in the anonymous *Vavasoris Examen, et Purgamen: Or, Mr Vavasor Powells Impartiall Trial* (London, 1654), 43–6.

18. *A Welsh Narrative, Corrected, and Taught to Speak True English, and Some Latine: Or, Animadversions on an Imperfect Relation in the Perfect Diurnall* (London, 1653), 18.

19. *Strena Vavasoriensis*, 8.

20. Vavasor Powell, *The Scriptures Concord: Or, A Catechisme Compiled out of the Words of Scripture* (London, 1646), A3r. The title page describes the book as 'Intended and Translated for the good of *Wales*; and now in *English*, chiefly for the use of *Dartfords* Little-ones'. In this period the great exponents of Godly translation into Welsh—including such immediate classics as Bunyan's *Pilgrim's Progress* (i.e. *Taith neu siwrnai y pererin*)—are Stephen Hughes and Charles Edwards.

21. The author of *Vavasoris Examen* claimed that he could think of only one Welsh puritan preacher who had imperfect English, and he was so fluent in his own tongue 'that the Lord hath made him instrumental in the converting of divers Welsh people' (17–18).

22. *The Shield Single against the Sword Doubled* (London, 1653), 12.

23. Ibid.

24. The view is most extensively developed in the works of Charles Edwards. Cf. the contention of John Davies of Malwydd, in the prefaces to *Antiquiae linguae Britannicae* (London, 1621) and *Antiquiae linguae Britannicae ... dictionarium duplex* (London, 1632), that Welsh derived from Hebrew.

25. For the ramifications of millenarian Welsh-Jewishness note Menasseh ben Israel, *The Hope of Israel* (London, 1650), 21, where South American Indians are identified as a lost tribe of Israel 'forced up unto the mountaines, and the in-land countries, as formerly the *Brittaines* were driven by the *Saxons* into *Wales*' and the Welsh-British response to this tract by Arise Evans, *Light for the Iews: Or, The Means to Convert Them* (London, 1656). Evans is placed in turn by Christopher Hill, 'Arise Evans: Welshman in London', in his *Change and Continuity in Seventeenth-Century England*, rev. edn. (New Haven: Yale University Press, 1991), 48–77.

26. *Apocrypha: The Second Epistle of Paul to the Church of Laodicea*, 2; in William Erbery, *The Bishop of London, the Welsh Curate, and Common Prayers, with Apocrypha in the End* (London, 1653).

27. *Apocrypha*, 6.

28. Geoffrey F. Nuttall, *The Welsh Saints 1640–1660: Walter Cradock, Vavasor Powell, Morgan Llwyd* (Cardiff: University of Wales Press, 1957), 22, quoting the anonymous tract *A Winding-Sheet for Mr Baxters Dead* (1685).

29. Tr. L. J. Parry as *The Book of the Three Birds*, in E. Vincent Evans (ed.), *Cofnodion a chyfansoddiadau buddugol eisteddfod Llandudno, 1896/Transactions of the National Eisteddfod of Wales Llandudno, 1896* (National Eisteddfod Association: Liverpool, 1898), 195–247.

30. *Gweithiau Morgan Llwyd o Wynedd*, vol. I, ed. Thomas E. Ellis (Bangor: Jarvis and Foster, 1899), 18–31, p. 18. For a glancing discussion of the use of *penillion* for religious purposes, by Richard White the Catholic martyr, Rhys Prichard, and Llwyd himself, see Thomas Parry, *A History of Welsh Literature*, tr. H. Idris Bell (Oxford: Clarendon, 1955), 236–7.

31. Cf. Erbury, *Apocrypha*, 6, '*Wales* is a poor oppressed people, and despised also: Gentlemen and all are down already; there's Frize, and Flannen; there's Bread and Cheese, and an Oaten cake, with runing water; Oh there's a place for Christ to come', and Cradock, *Gospel-Holiness*, 159, 'I have seen poore women in the Mountaines of Wales (and I have oft thought of it) … that when they have come to a house to *beg* a little *whey* or *butter-milke*, they have been fain to beg the loane of a *pot*, or a *dish* to put it in. So we, when we come to beg mercie of God.'

32. 'All English swans that are alive and Scottish cuckowes sing | and some Welsh swallowes chirpe and chime.' These lines occur in 'The Excuse', the second section of the sequence, which justifies writing poetry (including '1648' itself) against puritan objectors.

33. Cf. the poem 'Come Wisdome Sweet', which ends—

> Sinne Death and Satan (crabbed foes) are kings of woes and wrath
> (as wind, fire, brimstone joyne in one) our Christ all conquered hath
>
> O Drymmed cri, a wnaethem ni, pe basit ti o Dduw
> heb ladd y tri, ath laddodd di, in llwyddo ni i fyw.

[O how heavy the cry, which we should have made, had not you, O
God, | slain the three, who slew you, to enable us to live.]

(*Gweithiau Morgan Llwyd*, I, 37). Also the despairing two lines 'Gwagair a
drygchwant a phrudder a sorriant [vain word and evil desire and sadness and
anger] | In soule in family in Wales & england & ever shall be & therefore', and,
from a letter of 1658–9, 'The dissemblers of these dayes exceed in that vanity,
& hyperbolically expresse it, which is too much the fashion of that countrey.
Fe ddiangodd pawb (ymron) oi calon iw tafodau [Every one (almost) has escaped from their heart to their tongues]', in *Gweithiau Morgan Llwyd o Wynedd*,
vol. III, ed. J. Graham Jones and Goronwy Wyn Owen with R. Tudur Jones
(Caerdydd: Gwasg Prifysgol Cymru, 1994), 207 and 194–5, p. 195.

34. I am grateful to M. Wynn Thomas for advice on this point.

35. The links with William Erbery are particularly suggestive. See e.g. his
'spirituall' account of the 'reign of Christ after the flesh, and of Saints after the
flesh' (written from Brecon, 26 August 1652) and his elaborate, apocalyptic
epistle to Llwyd, *The Testimony of William Erbery* (London, 1658), 162, 235–9
(cf. 113–15, from London, May 1653).

36. On Rachel see Genesis 29–30.

37. Matthew 19: 30, 20: 16, Mark 10: 31, Luke 13: 30.

38. Song of Solomon 2: 12. Apocalyptic readings of the Song correlated the
lover persona with Christ the Lamb in Revelation 21–2 coming to claim his
bride, the Church. Cf. 'Canticles. Some Select Verses of the Song of Songs,
or the Churches Hymne after Breaking Bread', 'Emyn Saesneg yn ôl Caniad
Solomon 2 | Some verses of Cant. 2', and 'As is the fruitfulle apple tree ... ' in
Gweithiau Morgan Llwyd, I, 10 and III, 16–17, 204.

39. Translated from the Welsh by M. Wynn Thomas, in his *Morgan Llwyd*
(Cardiff: University of Wales Press, 1984), 61.

40. 'Eye hath not seen, nor ear heard, neither have entered into the heart of man,
the things which God hath prepared for them that love him' (1 Cor. 2: 9).

41. *The Mount of Olives: Or, Solitary Devotions* (London, 1652), in *Works of Henry
Vaughan*, 137–90, pp. 174–5.

42. Roland Mathias, 'A New Language, A New Tradition', *Scintilla*, 6 (2002):
161–82, p. 168. For an earlier statement of the issues see his 'In Search of the
Silurist', *Poetry Wales*, 11/2 (1975): 6–35; the most persuasive counter-view
is M. Wynn Thomas, ' "No Englishman": Wales's Henry Vaughan', *The
Swansea Review*, 15 (1995): 1–19.

43. The attribution is not now accepted, but, of the twelve manuscript texts of
Englynion y misoedd recorded from the mid-sixteenth to the late eighteenth
century, four ascribe it to 'Aneurin' (as he was then called), one dated 1610
and another 1692; see Kenneth Jackson (ed.), *Early Welsh Gnomic Poems*, corr.
edn. (Cardiff: Cardiff University Press, 1961), 13.

44. Minor inaccuracies are best explained as printer's errors (Oliver Padel, personal communication): the 'mawr' supplied in square brackets is omitted, apparently by haplography, in the 1652 edn., while 'vy' appears where '[ei]' is substituted.

45. 'Vaughan quotes the first, seventh, and eighth lines of the stanza. Although he seems to have added "birds couple", the idea is actually present in the sixth line of the stanza, "pob edn a edwyn i gymar" "each bird knows its mate"' (Oliver Padel). For a translation of the whole *englyn* see Kenneth Jackson, *Studies in Early Celtic Nature Poetry* (Cambridge: Cambridge University Press, 1935), 72—5, p. 73.

46. Cf. the poet's twin brother, at the end of his treatise *Anthroposophia Theomagica*, '*English* is a *Language* the *Author* was *not born to*'; *The Works of Thomas Vaughan*, ed. Alan Rudrum (Oxford: Clarendon, 1984), 94.

47. The fullest account is in Roland Mathias, 'The Silurist Re-examined', *Scintilla*, 2 (1998): 62—77.

48. 15 June 1673, in *Works of Henry Vaughan*, 687—9, p. 688.

49. 'The Resolve', line 22 and 'The Proffer', line 43, in *Silex Scintillans*, Pts I and II (1650, 1655), quoting *Works of Henry Vaughan*.

50. 9 October 1694; *Works of Henry Vaughan*, 696—7, p. 696.

51. See the letter from Aubrey to Anthony Wood, 19 March 1681, quoted by F. E. Hutchinson, *Henry Vaughan: A Life and Interpretation* (Oxford: Clarendon, 1947), 36, 156. Though the staple of Rees's book is Latin, his discussion of the bards is, strikingly, in Welsh. Vaughan also mentions owning a manuscript by Thomas Powell of Cantref, 'Fragmenta de rebus Brittannicis: A short account of the lives, manners & religion of the Brittish Druids and the Bards &c.'; see *Works of Henry Vaughan*, 690—1, p. 690 (7 July 1673). It is in Powell's *Cerbyd jechydwriaeth* [*The Chariot of Salvation*] (London, 1657) that the following, signed Ol. Vaughan, and sometimes attributed to the poet (though 'Oliver Vaughan' would be a more natural interpretation than 'Olor Vaughan') can be found:

> Y Padcr, pan trier, Duw-tri a'i dododd
> O'i dadol ddaioni,
> Yn faen-gwaddan i bob gweddi,
> Ac athrawiaeth a wnaeth i ni.   (39)

Oliver Padel translates, literally: 'The paternoster, when it is tried, God-three provided it | of his fatherly kindness | as a foundation-stone for every prayer | and he provided instruction for us.'

52. 'Daphnis: An Elegiac Eclogue', line 61; in *Thalia Rediviva* (London, 1678), quoting *Works of Henry Vaughan*. See the atmospheric analysis by Stevie Davies, *Henry Vaughan* (Bridgend: Seren, 1995), 39.

53. 'To the Ingenious Author of *Thalia Rediviva*', lines 1—3, in *Works of Henry Vaughan*, 619—20, p. 619.

54. Cf. 'all *Bards* born after me' ('To the River Isca', line 35). As the *Oxford English Dictionary* (among other resources) shows, 'bard' remained associated with antiquity and the Celtic world at this date, only gradually acquiring its eighteenth-century use as an elevated term for 'poet'.

55. 'Mr. *George Herbert* of blessed memory; See his incomparable prophetick Poems, and particularly these, *Church-musick, Church-rents, and schisms*[,] *The Church militant.*'

56. 'The British Church', in George Herbert, *The Temple* (Cambridge, 1633), 102.

57. *Silex Scintillans I*, quoting *Works of Henry Vaughan*.

58. The complaint was familiar in Anglo-Welsh royalist writing. See e.g. Rowland Watkyns, a neighbour of Vaughan's, who began 'The New Illiterate Lay-Teachers' (later published in his *Flamma sine Fumo: Or, Poems without Fictions* (London, 1662), 43–4, p. 43):

> Why trouble you religions sacred stream,
> And tear Christs coat, which had no rent, or seam?
> And you do patch it too with ragged clouts
> Of false opinions, and phantastick doubts.

59. Walter Cradock, *Glad Tydings from Heaven; To The Worst of Sinners on Earth* (London, 1648), 50.

60. 'O Rose of the field! O lily of the valley! how are you now made food for swine', tr. in *Henry Vaughan: The Complete Poems*, ed. Alan Rudrum (Harmondsworth: Penguin, 1976), 543–4; cf. Song of Solomon 2: 1, and, for earlier lines, 4: 6 and 8: 14: 'I will get me to the mountains of myrrh, and to the hill of frankincense … Make haste, my beloved, and be thou like to a roe or a young hart, upon the mountains of spices'.

61. For the same principle reversed, see the poem 'Mount of Olives', which declares an ambition to celebrate biblical scenery as Randolph and Sir John Denham had celebrated the Cotswolds and Cooper's Hill.

62. '1654', in *Gweithiau Morgan Llwyd*, I, 92–3, printed without title in Llwyd's prose work *An Honest Discourse between Three Neighbours, Touching the Present Government in these Three Nations* (London, 1655).

63. 'White Sunday', in *Silex Scintillans II*, lines 9, 61–2.

64. See Philip West, *Henry Vaughan's 'Silex Scintillans': Scripture Uses* (Oxford: Oxford University Press, 2001), ch. 6. Such exceptions as 'The Jews', a great millenarian poem, should, however, be conceded.

65. Cf. e.g. the relative success of Rowland Watkyns, 'Solitarinesse', in *Flamma sine Fumo*, 15–16.

66. Published in *Silex Scintillans II*; lines 45–8, quoting *Works of Henry Vaughan*.

67. Cf. Alan Rudrum, 'Resistance, Collaboration, and Silence: Henry Vaughan and Breconshire Royalism', in Claude J. Summers and Ted-Larry Pebworth (eds.), *The English Civil Wars in the Literary Imagination* (Columbia, Mo: University of Missouri Press, 1999), 102–18.

68. 'To Antenor, on a Paper of Mine which J. Jones Threatens to Publish to Prejudice Him' and 'To the Truly-Competent Judge of Honour, Lucasia, Upon a Scandalous Libel made by J. Jones', *Poems*, 91–2, 87–91.

69. On this copy, in the hand of Philips's friend, Sir Edward Dering, see *Collected Works of Katherine Philips*, I, 44–5, 272–3.

70. *Collected Works of Katherine Philips*, II, 339.

71. The best account is in Jones, *Life, Work, and Thought of Powell*, 60.

72. 'On the 3. of September, 1651'.

73. See e.g. Prys Morgan, 'Wild Wales: Civilising the Welsh from the Sixteenth to the Nineteenth Centuries', in Peter Burke, Brian Harrison and Paul Slack (eds.), *Civil Histories: Essays Presented to Sir Keith Thomas* (Oxford: Oxford University Press, 2000), 265–83, pp. 274–7.

74. Quoted in *Collected Works of Katherine Philips*, ed. Thomas, I, 27.

75. On the actualities see Moelwyn I. Williams, 'Glimpses of Life in Seventeenth-Century Cardiganshire', *Ceredigion*, 12/4 (1996): 3–20 and Gerald Morgan, 'Women in Early Modern Cardiganshire', *Ceredigion*, 13/4 (2000): 1–19.

76. 'To the Right Honourable Alice Countess of Carbury, On Her Enriching Wales with her Presence', *Poems*, 31–3, p. 32, 'Parting with a Friend', in the posthumous edn. of her *Poems* (London, 1667), 159–61, p. 161.

77. Letter of 28 November 1663, in *Collected Works of Katherine Philips*, II, 117–18, p. 118. Cf. 'native Spark', above, p. 211.

78. Positive references range from such poems as 'A Retir'd Friendship', through the letter to Cotterel of 5 April 1662 ('my beloved Rocks and Rivers, which were formerly my best Entertainments', *Collected Works of Katherine Philips*, II, 25–7, p. 25), to the translation of Saint-Amant, 'La Solitude', in *Poems* (1667), 170–83.

79. 'On *Orinda's* Poems. Ode', in *Collected Works of Katherine Philips*, III, 191–5, p. 195.

80. Sir Edward Dering, Letter Book (University of Cincinnati Library, Phillipps MS 14932), Letter 3 (29 September 1662); cf. *Collected Works of Katherine Philips*, I, 377.

81. 'On the Death of the Truly Honourable Sir Walter Lloid Knight' includes the passage:

> Nay if those ancient Bards had seen this Herse,
> Who once in *British* shades spoke living Verse,
> Their high concern for him had made them be,
> Apter to weep, than write his Elogy: ...   (*Poems* (1667), 152–3, p. 152)

82. *Collected Works of Katherine Philips*, I, 377. The Welsh poet James Howell's 'Upon Dr Davies British-Grammar' comes closest in its willingness to test the ancient glories of Welsh against Quintilian and 'the *Latian* Tree': 'This is the *Toung* the *B[a]rds* sung in of old, | And *Druyds* their dark Knowledg did unfold: | *Merlin* in *this* his Prophecies did vent, | Which through the world of fame bear such extent. ...' (Howell, *Poems* (London, 1663), 71–2).

83. *Poems* (1667), 131–2.

84. I.e. She might be implying that the language has fallen upon hard times because no longer supported by the 'beauty' of an ancient civilization.

85. 'To the Most Excellently Accomplished, Mrs K. Philips', lines 13–14.

86. It was here, at Y Gelli Aur (Golden Grove), the estate of Philips's friend, Alice, Countess of Carberry, that Taylor wrote, and dedicated to the poet, *The Measures and Offices of Friendship* (London, 1657).

87. *Poems* (1664), 214–16, p. 216. Powell was more 'silenced' than 'silent' after the Restoration; he spent nine years in prison, dying there in 1670.

88. She quotes Henry Hammond—a notable opponent of contemporary applications of Revelation—in a letter of 17 May 1662 (*Collected Works of Katherine Philips*, II, 34–6, p. 35); she possessed a copy of William Chillingworth, *The Religion of Protestants* (Oxford, 1638), apparently given to her in Wales (Peter Beal, *Index of English Literary Manuscripts*, 2 vols. (London: Mansell, 1987–93), II, 125–40, p. 126, notes the indication that it was presented by 'Mrs E, Lloyd of Trevagh'); and she writes a late poem to Gilbert Sheldon (discussed at the end of this chapter). On the broad currents of thought see Frederick C. Beiser, *The Sovereignty of Reason: The Defense of Rationality in the Early English Enlightenment* (Princeton, NJ: Princeton University Press, 1996).

89. *Poems* (1664), 120–4, pp. 120–1.

90. On the dissemination of More's thought, in which Jeremy Taylor was a link for Philips, see *The Conway Letters: The Correspondence of Anne, Viscountess Conway, Henry More, and their Friends, 1642–1684*, ed. Marjorie Hope Nicholson, rev. Sarah Hutton (Oxford: Clarendon, 1992).

91. *Cupids Conflict*, attached to More's *Democritus Platonissans: Or, An Essay upon the Infinity of Worlds* (Cambridge, 1646), 1–14, p. 14.

92. This is the conclusion of Philips's poem 'The Soul'. For the anti-feminist response see *Collected Works of Katherine Philips*, I, 371–2 and Hageman and Sununu, ' "More Copies" ', 131–2.

93. *Collected Works of Katherine Philips*, II, 128–9.

94. *Poems* (1667), 166–8, p. 166.

95. See Philip Jenkins, 'Welsh Anglicans and the Interregnum', *Journal of the Historical Society of the Church in Wales*, 27 (1990): 51–9.

96. Jenkins, 'Welsh Anglicans and the Interregnum', 51, cites Aubrey the antiquarian's observation that 'Gilbert Sheldon ... and Sir John Aubrey [of Llantrithyd, Glamorgan], were *co-etanei* (fellow-students), and contracted a

great friendship at Oxford in their youth, which continued to their deaths.'
Mary Aubrey, the influential Sir John's daughter, was a friend of Katherine
Philips from childhood.

97. *Collected Works of Katherine Philips*, II, 103.
98. Philip Jenkins, ' "The Old Leaven": The Welsh Roundheads after 1660',
    Historical Journal, 24 (1983): 807–23; Geraint H. Jenkins, *Foundations of Modern
    Wales*, chs. 4–5 and *Protestant Dissenters in Wales*, chs. 5–6.

CHAPTER 7

1. George Wishart, *Memoirs of James, Marquis of Montrose, 1639–1650*, ed. Alexander Murdoch and H. F. Morland Simpson (London: Longmans, Green,
   1983), 228.
2. 'Upon the Death of King Charles the First', in Peter Davidson (ed.), *Poetry
   and Revolution: An Anthology of British and Irish Verse 1625–1660* (Oxford:
   Clarendon, 1998), 361.
3. Edward Hyde, Earl of Clarendon, *The History of the Rebellion and Civil Wars
   in England*, ed. W. Dunn Macray, 6 vols. (Oxford: Clarendon, 1888), V, 17.
4. For the diamond point, see e.g. Ronald Williams, *Montrose: Cavalier in
   Mourning* (London: Barrie and Jenkins, 1975), 387; poem in Davidson (ed.),
   Poetry and Revolution, 362–3, who doubts the received attribution.
5. 'Cumha Mhontrois' ('Lament for Montrose'), lines 35–8. Text and tr. in
   Davidson (ed.), *Poetry and Revolution*, 461–3, pp. 462–3.
6. The exchange survives patchily, though we know that Milton had written to
   Sandelands on 3 January, and a letter from him to Milton (29 January) asks
   for relief. On 11 April 1654, Sandelands told John Thurloe in a letter that
   he had employed John Phillips, Milton's nephew. See Gordon Campbell, *A
   Milton Chronology* (Basingstoke: Macmillan, 1997), 145–7, 152.
7. Milton was at Christ's College, Cambridge 1625–32; Sandelands was a
   Fellow from 1624–30, and was succeeded by Edward King, the Lycidas of
   Milton's elegy.
8. At the time, the Dutch had blocked the Danish Sound so effectively that ships
   were unable to bring naval supplies from the Baltic; Jonathan Israel, *The Dutch
   Republic: Its Rise, Greatness, and Fall 1477–1806* (Oxford, Clarendon, 1995),
   721. On shortages see J. R. Jones, *The Anglo-Dutch Wars of the Seventeenth
   Century* (London: Longman, 1996), 41.
9. *Complete Prose Works of John Milton*, gen. ed. Don M. Wolfe, 8 vols. (New
   Haven: Yale University Press, 1953–82), IV: 2, 855–8, pp. 856–8.
10. See Pieter Geyl, *Orange and Stuart 1641–72* [1939], tr. Arnold Pomerans
    (London: Weidenfeld and Nicolson, 1969); Steven C. A. Pincus, *Protestantism
    and Patriotism: Ideologies and the Making of English Foreign Policy, 1650–1668*
    (Cambridge: Cambridge University Press, 1996); and, more broadly, Keith
    L. Sprunger, *Dutch Puritanism: A History of English and Scottish Churches*

in the Netherlands in the Sixteenth and Seventeenth Centuries (Leiden: Brill, 1982); Jonathan Scott, *England's Troubles: Seventeenth-Century English Political Instability in European Context* (Cambridge: Cambridge University Press, 2000).

11. This letter to John Bradshaw follows the one to Sandelands just quoted in *Complete Prose Works of Milton*, IV: 2, 858−60.

12. The Rump Parliament imposed 'union' and 'incorporation' on Scotland and Ireland as early as 1652, but the measures were only resolved in 1654.

13. E.g. William Johnson [= Willem Jans Blaeu], *The Light of Navigation* (Amsterdam, 1612); J. Colom, *The New Fierie Sea-Colomne* (Amsterdam, 1649); the anonymous *Pas-Caert van Texel tot aen den Hoofden* (Amsterdam, 1660); and John Seller, *The Coastal Pilot* (London, 1670), *The English Pilot* (London, 1671).

14. E.g. *The Dutch Boare Dissected: Or, A Description of Hogg-Land* (London, 1665).

15. E.g. 90 (19−26 February 1652), 1425−40, pp. 1434−6; 143 (3−10 March 1653), 2277−92, pp. 2282−4.

16. E.g. 121 (23−30 September 1652), 1897−1912, p. 1910; 129 (18−25 November 1652), 2025−40, pp. 2026−32.

17. For a well-documented brief survey see Christopher A. Whatley with Derek J. Patrick, *The Scots and the Union* (Edinburgh: Edinburgh University Press, 2006), 72−80.

18. A version of Lewis Bayly's ubiquitous *Practice of Piety* went through thirty-two editions between 1620 and 1688; Maria A. Schenkeveld, *Dutch Literature in the Age of Rembrandt: Themes and Ideas* (Amsterdam: John Benjamins, 1991), 145.

19. Alastair J. Mann, *The Scottish Book Trade, 1500 to 1720: Print Commerce and Print Control in Early Modern Scotland* (East Linton: Tuckwell, 2000), ch. 3; K. L. Sprunger, *Trumpets from the Tower: English Puritan Printing in the Netherlands 1600−1640* (Leiden: Brill, 1994); and, for royalist printing, P. G. Hoftijzer, 'British Books Abroad: The Continent', in *The Cambridge History of the Book in Britain*, vol. IV, *1557−1695*, ed. John Barnard and D. F. McKenzie (Cambridge: Cambridge University Press, 2002), 735−43, p. 740.

20. E.g. Gillespie, *A Dispute against the English-Popish Ceremonies, Obtruded vpon the Church of Scotland* (Amsterdam and Leiden, 1637); Baillie, *A Review of Doctor Bramble, Late Bishop of Londenderry, His Faire Warning against the Scotes Disciplin* (Delft, 1649), *Ladensium Autokatakrisis, The Canterburians Self-Conviction: Or, An Evident Demonstration of the Avowed Arminianisme, Poperie, and Tyrannie of that Faction, by their Owne Confessions* (Amsterdam, 1640). Cf. Mann, *Scottish Book Trade*, 82−3.

21. *An Account of the Growth of Popery, and Arbitrary Government in England* ([London], 1677), 17−18.

22. On the former see Blair Worden, 'Classical Republicanism and the Puritan Revolution', in Hugh Lloyd-Jones, Valerie Pearl, and Blair Worden (eds.), *History and Imagination: Essays in Honour of H. R. Trevor-Roper* (London: Duckworth, 1981), 182–200, pp. 198–9; and, on the latter, more loosely federal scheme, Pincus, *Protestantism and Patriotism*, 150. The absorption of republican and Dutch traditions into Anglo-Scottish puritan thought, even before the 1640s, can be traced through the work of Thomas Scott; see Markku Peltonen, *Classical Humanism and Republicanism in English Political Thought 1570–1640* (Cambridge: Cambridge University Press, 1995), ch. 5.

23. For a bold, often persuasive, account, see Mark Stoyle, *Soldiers and Strangers: An Ethnic History of the English Civil War* (New Haven: Yale University Press, 2005).

24. *Complete Prose Works of Milton*, II, 485–570, p. 558. For anticipations see *Of Reformation* (1641) and *The Reason of Church-Government* (1642), in *Complete Prose Works*, I, at pp. 525–6 and 969–7, though at both points a slippage from England to 'this *Iland*' suggests an awareness of British aspects of the English Reformation.

25. Both the first and second *Defences* are more fully known as *Pro Populo Anglicano defensio*, and, like the poet's *Pro Se defensio* (1655), they are introduced by title pages headed *Joannis MiltonI ANGLI*—though how far this is a declaration of national pride, as against a mark of identification for continental readers, is open to debate.

26. The self-conscious Englishness of government at this date is explored by Sean Kelsey, *Inventing a Republic: The Political Culture of the English Commonwealth 1649–1653* (Manchester: Manchester University Press, 1997).

27. Cp. Hugo Grotius in the intellectual biography of Milton, Peter du Moulin in that of Marvell, and the republican thought of Pieter and Johan de la Court in that of Algernon Sidney.

28. See Ronald Knowles, 'The "All-Attoning Name": The Word *Patriot* in Seventeenth-Century England', *Modern Language Review*, 96 (2001): 624–43, esp. 631–5.

29. This is a natural way of reading Richard Leigh (or Samuel Butler), *The Transproser Rehears'd: Or, The Fifth Act of Mr Bayes's Play* (Oxford [London?], 1673), 30—though the polemicist's point may equally be that Donne's poems in Dutch epitomize what we would now call double-Dutch, a state of dull obscurity to which Marvell also aspires: 'methinks you might have so much studied the Readers diversion, and your own, as to have exercised your happy talent of *Rhyming*, in *Transversing* [Hales's] Treatise of *Schism*, and for the Titles *dear sake* you might have made all the Verses rung *Ism* in their several changes. I dare assure you Sir, the work would have been more gratefully accepted than *Donns Poems* turn'd into *Dutch*'. The texts referred to are those printed in Huygens's *Korenbloemen* of 1658 and 1672.

Cf. 'Aen Joff.w Luchtenburgh, met myn vertaelde dicht uyt het Engelsch van Donne' ('To the Lady Luchtenburgh, with My Poems Translated from the English of Donne'), dated 10 March 1654, in *A Selection of the Poems of Sir Constantijn Huygens (1596–1687): A Parallel Text*, ed. and tr. Peter Davidson and Adriaan van der Weel (Amsterdam: Amsterdam University Press, 1996). On authorship of the treatise, see Nicholas von Maltzahn, 'Samuel Butler's Milton', *Studies in Philology*, 92 (1995): 482–95.

30. *Selection of the Poems of Huygens*, ed. and tr. Davidson and van der Weel, app. III.

31. 'A Mad[ame] Swann' (1660), in *De Gedichten van Constantijn Huygens*, ed. J. A. Worp, 9 vols. (Groningen: J. B. Wolters, 1892–9), VI, 275–7.

32. *Selection of the Poems of Huygens*, ed. Davidson and van der Weel, 195.

33. Lawrence Lipking, 'The Genius of the Shore: Lycidas, Adamastor, and the Poetics of Nationalism', *PMLA*, 111 (1996): 205–21; Sara van den Berg, 'Two Kings and a Lady: Milton and the Irish Protestants, 1637–1649', Milton Seminar, Newberry Library, 1998.

34. E.g. Michael Wilding, 'Milton's *A Masque Presented at Ludlow Castle, 1634*: Theatre and Politics on the Border', *Milton Quarterly*, 21/4 (1987): 1–12; Philip Schwyzer, 'Purity and Danger on the West Bank of the Severn: The Cultural Geography of *A Masque Presented at Ludlow Castle, 1634*', *Representations*, 60 (1997): 22–48.

35. E.g. Thomas N. Corns, 'Milton's *Observations upon the Articles of Peace*: Ireland under English Eyes', in David Loewenstein and James Grantham Turner (eds.), *Politics, Poetics, and Hermeneutics in Milton's Prose* (Cambridge: Cambridge University Press, 1990), 123–34; Jim Daems, 'Dividing Conjunctions: Milton's *Observations upon the Articles of Peace*', *Milton Quarterly*, 33/2 (May 1999): 51–5; and Joad Raymond's sceptical 'Complications of Interest: Milton, Scotland, Ireland, and National Identity in 1649', *Review of English Studies*, 55 (2004): 315–45.

36. The perception goes back some decades, but see esp. David Loewenstein, 'An Ambiguous Monster: Rebellion in Milton's Polemics and *Paradise Lost*', *Huntington Library Quarterly*, 55 (1992): 295–315 and his *Representing Revolution in Milton and his Contemporaries: Religion, Politics, and Polemics in Radical Puritanism* (Cambridge: Cambridge University Press, 2001), 195–201; also Catherine Canino, 'The Discourse of Hell: *Paradise Lost* and the Irish Rebellion', *Milton Quarterly*, 32 (1998): 15–23.

37. 'Elegia quarta. Anno aetatis 18'. Milton's poetry is quoted from *The Riverside Milton*, ed. Roy Flannagan (Boston: Houghton Mifflin, 1998).

38. On the 'Scottish origins of the explosion of print, 1637–1642', and the publication axis that ran at this date (as later) 'between Glasgow, Edinburgh, London, Leiden and Amsterdam', see Joad Raymond, *Pamphlets and Pamphleteering in Early Modern Britain* (Cambridge: Cambridge University Press, 2003), ch. 5.

39. *Complete Prose Works of Milton*, I, 517–617, p. 597.

40. Ibid., I, 745–861, p. 798.

41. Cf. Thomas N. Corns, 'Milton and Presbyterianism', *Milton Studies* (Korea), 10 (2000): 337–54, pp. 344–53.

42. See Iain H. Murray, 'The Scots at the Westminster Assembly: With Special Reference to the Dispute on Church Government and its Aftermath', *The Banner of Truth*, 371–2 (Aug.-Sept. 1994): 6–40.

43. Cf. 'shallow *Edwards* and Scotch what d' ye call', in 'On the New Forcers of Conscience' (1646), where Milton cannot get his tongue and/or mind around the name of Robert Baillie, author of *A Dissuasive from the Errours of the Time* (London, 1645), or some other of that sort.

44. This was exactly the sort of expansionism that he had written against when urging both nations to join hands, in *Of Reformation*: 'but seeke onely *Vertue*, not to extend your Limits'; *Complete Prose Works of Milton*, I, 597.

45. *John Milton: Complete Shorter Poems*, ed. John Carey, 2nd edn. (London: Longman, 1997), 308.

46. See e.g. the playlet, *The Scottish Politike Presbyter, Slaine by an English Independent* (London, 1647).

47. Psalm 80, lines 49–50; for wider discussion see Margaret Boddy, 'Milton's Translation of Psalms 80–88', *Modern Philology*, 64 (1966): 1–9.

48. Verses 12–13: 'How art thou fallen from heaven, O Lucifer, son of the morning! ... For thou hast said in thine heart, I will ascend into heaven, ... I will sit also ... in the sides of the north'.

49. See e.g. Nedham, *The Case of the Commonwealth of England, Stated: Or, The Equity, Utility, and Necessity, of a Submission to the Present Government* (London, 1650), 38: 'Its an old saying, *nullum bonum ex Aquilone*, no good comes out of the North; and of all others, *Royallists* should be the least apt to believe any Benefit to come out of that *Nation*, from whence proceeded the Ruin and Destruction of the late *King*, and all their Party.'

50. *Complete Prose Works of Milton*, III, 190–258, p. 248.

51. *Calendar of State Papers, Domestic, 1649–1650*, 57.

52. *Observations on the Articles of Peace*, in *Complete Prose Works of Milton*, III, 259–334, pp. 308, 303–4.

53. See e.g. Corns, 'Milton's *Observations*'.

54. Phil Kilroy, *Protestant Dissent and Controversy in Ireland 1660–1714* (Cork: Cork University Press, 1994), 16–17.

55. For a different account of the Scottish axis in the *Observations*, see Willy Maley, *Nation, State and Empire in English Renaissance Literature: Shakespeare to Milton* (London: Palgrave, 2003), ch. 7.

56. *Mercurius Politicus*, 5 (4–11 July 1650): 65–80, p. 71. Cf. *Eikonoklastes*, in *Complete Prose of Milton*, III, 337–601, p. 496.

57. *Mercurius Politicus*, 1 (6–13 June 1650): 1–16, p. 3.

58. For contexts see David Stevenson, *Revolution and Counter-Revolution in Scotland, 1644–1651* (London: Royal Historical Society, 1977), chs. 3−5.

59. Thomas May, *The Changeable Covenant: Shewing in a Brief Series of Relations, how the Scots from Time to Time have Imposed upon England* (London, 1650); Cuthbert Sydenham, *The False Brother: Or, A New Map of Scotland, Drawn by an English Pencil; being a short history of the political and civil transactions between these two nations since their first friendship: wherein the many secret designs, and dangerous aspects and influences of that nation on England are discovered; with the juglings of their commissioners with the late King, Parliament, and city* (London, 1651).

60. Quoting *The Poems and Letters of Andrew Marvell*, ed. H. M. Margoliouth, 3rd edn. rev. Pierre Legouis with E. E. Duncan-Jones, 2 vols. (Oxford: Clarendon, 1971), I.

61. Cf. Marvell's attack on the Fifth Monarchists, in 'The First Anniversary of the Government under O. C.', lines 317−18: 'Oh Race most hypocrically strict! | Bent to reduce us to the ancient Pict.'

62. Or, who thinks as patchily as his ancestors were daubed with body-paint (the name of the Picts was thought to derive from Latin 'picti', 'painted, tattooed').

63. *Anglia Liberata: Or, The Rights of the People of England, Maintained against the Pretences of the Scotish King* (London, 1651), 62−3: 'no less than fifty of their Kings have been punished with death', '*Buchanan*, their own Historian ... *Rutherford* in his *Lex, Rex*'.

64. The Scottishness of the defeated army was emphasized in Commonwealth writing, to play down English disaffection with the Republic; see e.g. Payne Fisher, *Irenodia gratulatoria* ([London, 1652]), tr. Thomas Manley as *Veni; Vidi; Vici: The Triumphs of the Most Excellent and Illustrious Oliver Cromwell* (London, 1652), 53−67.

65. Pincus, *Protestantism and Patriotism*, 75.

66. It would be interesting to know whether he dealt directly with the poet and diplomat Jacob Cats, who headed a Dutch delegation to England in 1651. Milton's role in all this, explored by Leo Miller, *John Milton's Writings in the Anglo-Dutch Negotiations, 1651–1654* (Pittsburgh: Duquesne University Press, 1992) and Robert Thomas Fallon, *Milton in Government* (University Park, PA: Pennsylvania State University Press, 1993), ch. 2, is charted in Campbell, *Milton Chronology*.

67. 'In Legationem Domini Oliveri St John ad Provincias Foederatas'.

68. *Complete Prose Works of Milton*, I, 586.

69. Du Moulin's *Regii sanguinus clamor* (The Hague, 1652), with its nasty swipes at Milton (he was a worm, he was mud), was also published in Dutch.

70. *Eikonoklastes*, 394−5, 487−8 (cf. Ps 60: 7−8, 108: 8−9).

71. *Eikonoklastes*, 385, *Defence*, in *Complete Prose Works of Milton*, IV: 1, 301−537, p. 522. See above, p. 43.

72. *Defence*, 525–6.
73. *Second Defence of the English People*, in *Complete Prose Works of Milton*, IV: 1, 547–686, pp. 644, 657.
74. *Defence*, 322; *Second Defence*, 591–2 (cf. *Collected Prose of Milton*, IV: 2, 1045).
75. For an informative survey see Barbara K. Lewalski, *The Life of John Milton* (Oxford: Blackwell, 2000), 286–7.
76. Pincus, *Protestantism and Patriotism*, 70–1.
77. In the contextualizing scholarship, Blair Worden, 'John Milton and Oliver Cromwell', in Ian Gentles, John Morrill, and Blair Worden (eds.), *Soldiers, Writers and Statesmen of the English Revolution* (Cambridge: Cambridge University Press, 1998), 243–64 deserves particular attention.
78. Violet Rowe, *Sir Henry Vane the Younger: A Study in Political and Administrative History* (London: Athlone Press, 1970), 141–8.
79. Pincus, *Protestantism and Patriotism*, 24.
80. E.g. John Kenyon, 'Andrew Marvell: Life and Times', in *Andrew Marvell: Essays on the Tercentenary of his Death*, ed. R. L. Brett (Oxford: Oxford University Press, 1979), 1–35, p. 12, Annabel M. Patterson, *Marvell and the Civic Crown* (Princeton: Princeton University Press, 1978), 119–22.
81. Contrast the punitive tone of Milton's translation of Psalm 2, dated 8 August 1653, which followed a summer of defeats for the stubbornly irreconcileable Dutch: 'I on thee bestow | Th' Heathen, … them shalt thou bring full low | With Iron Scepter bruis'd'.
82. 'De uijtlandighe herder. Aenden heere Daniel Heins, Ridder etc.' ('The Exiled Shepherd: To the Lord Daniel Heinsius, Knight etc.'), in *Selection of the Poems of Huygens*, ed. and tr. Davidson and van der Weel, 64–73, pp. 64–5.
83. E.g. Highland rebels mustered near '*Ruthuen*-castle, a Garison of ours' reportedly lost heart when 'a brother of the Lord *Ogilby's* came to them, and made a relation of the conflict at sea, how that the *Dutch* were routed and run home. … immediately after they dispersed themselves' (*Mercurius Politicus*, 168 [25 August–1 September 1653]: 2687–2702, p. 2687). The threat was not insignificant: from autumn 1653 into early 1654 Sir Thomas Middleton was preparing an invasion force in Holland, with the backing of the Princess Royal and the Orangeists, to support the Highlanders.
84. For a different account of Dutch in the poem see Richard Todd, 'Equilibrium and National Stereotyping in "The Character of Holland"', in Claude J. Summers and Ted-Larry Pebworth (eds.), *On the Celebrated and Neglected Poems of Andrew Marvell* (Columbia, Mo: University of Missouri Press, 1992), 169–91, pp. 179–80, 189–90.
85. Lines 49 and 66.
86. *A Brief Character of the Low-Countries under the States* (London, 1652), 77–8.

87. They hack one other, like sculptors working stone—like Deinocrates, who wanted to cut Mount Athos into an image of Alexander—as though trying to reduce each other's bulk to human form.

88. Pincus, *Protestantism and Patriotism*, 153.

89. Hence the language of the title, *Articles of Peace, Union and Confederation, Concluded and Agreed between His Highness Oliver Lord Protector of the Commonwealth of England, Scotland and Ireland, and the Dominions thereto Belonging. And the Lords the States General of the United Provinces of the Netherlands* (London, 1654). For literary versions of this unionism see e.g. *Musarum Oxoniensium* (Oxford, 1654), 61 ('The noble *Thames*, doth now the *Texell* wed, | As old *Alphëus Arethusa* did'—from a poem by R. Gorges), 67 ('*Holland* and *Wee* are reunited *Lands*'—by Robert Mathew), 94 ('Our reunited Seas, like streams that grow | Into one River doe the smoother flow'—by the young J. Locke, then a Student of Christ Church), 97 ('*Joyn'd* by the *Isthmus* of confederate *Peace*, | We are now no more an *Isle* but *Chersonese*'—by Jo. Ailmer), 99 ('*Hermophroditus* so and *Salmacis* | (Whose Bodyes Joyn'd in a perpetuall Kisse) | With our two States receiv'd like Union; | Went *Two* into the *Streame*, Return'd but *One*'—by Will. Godolphin), and, most conceitedly, 103 ('That *Wales* and *Netherlands* should now be *one*, | Is no darke *Riddle* but a *truth* late knowne'—by Ro. Whitehall).

90. Rowe, *Sir Henry Vane*, 221.

91. *Complete Prose Works of Milton*, VII, 357.

92. *The Spirit of the Phanatiques Dissected, and The Solemne League and Covenant Solemnly Discussed in 30 Queries* (London, 1660), 7; cf. Austin Woolrych, introduction to *Complete Prose Works of Milton*, VII, 199.

CHAPTER 8

I am grateful to Alison McCann of the West Sussex Record Office for help with the Petworth House Archives and to Lord Egremont for permission to quote from them.

1. *The Dramatic Works of Roger Boyle Earl of Orrery*, ed. William Smith Clark, II, 2 vols. (Cambridge, MA: Harvard University Press, 1937), I; II.[iv.] 202–364.

2. *Dramatic Works of Roger Boyle*, I, 437.

3. *A Letter from the Lord Broghill to the Honourable William Lenthall Esq.* (London, 1651), 5.

4. For examples see Barnabe Riche, *A New Description of Ireland* (London, 1610), A3r, A4v-B2v, D2r-v, H1r-v, H4r-Ir, I2r-K1r; *The Irish Sections of Fynes Moryson's Unpublished 'Itinerary'*, ed. Graham Kew (Dublin: Irish Manuscripts Commission, 1998), 104–5. That the assumption of superiority did not protect its possessors from superstition is suggested by the medical advice sent by John [?Nunnsig] to the Countess of Orrery in 1668 (*Calendar of*

the Orrery Papers, ed. Edward MacLysaght (Dublin: Stationery Office, 1941), 61−2).

5. *Roger Boyle First Earl of Orrery* (Knoxville: University of Tennessee Press, 1965); cf. Patrick Little, 'The Political Career of Roger Boyle, Lord Broghill, 1636−1660', Ph.D. dissertation (University of London, 2000)—developed as *Lord Broghill and the Cromwellian Union with Ireland and Scotland* (Woodbridge: Boydell, 2004)—which does not, however, discuss literary material.

6. Paul Salzman, *English Prose Fiction 1558−1700: A Critical History* (Oxford: Clarendon, 1985), 190; Nigel Smith, *Literature and Revolution in England, 1640−1660* (New Haven: Yale University Press, 1994), 244, discusses *Parthenissa* as 'native heroic romance ... for English people'.

7. Mita Choudhury, 'Orrery and the London Stage: A Loyalist's Contribution to Restoration Allegorical Drama', *Studia Neophilologica*, 62 (1990): 43−59; Nancy Klein Maguire, 'Regicide and Reparation: The Autobiographical Drama of Roger Boyle, Earl of Orrery', *English Literary Renaissance*, 21/2 (Spring, 1991): 257−82, rpt in her *Regicide and Restoration: English Tragicomedy, 1660−1671* (Cambridge: Cambridge University Press, 1992).

8. It was given currency by Thomas Morrice's life of Orrery, included in the anonymously edited *Collection of the State Letters of the Right Honourable Roger Boyle* (London, 1742), 10−11.

9. See e.g. John A. Murphy, 'Inchiquin's Changes of Religion', *Journal of the Cork Historical and Archaeological Society*, 72 (January-February 1967): 58−68, and 'The Politics of the Munster Protestants', *Journal of the Cork Historical and Archaeological Society*, 76 (January-June 1971), 1−20.

10. E.g. Terence Ranger, 'Richard Boyle and the Making of an Irish Fortune', *Irish Historical Studies*, 10 (1957): 257−97.

11. On the match, see Nicholas Canny, *The Upstart Earl: A Study of the Social and Mental World of Richard Boyle First Earl of Cork, 1566−1643* (Cambridge: Cambridge University Press, 1982), 47−8.

12. 'Cuirfead cluain ar crobaing' ('I shall put a cluain'), in *Duanaire Dáibid Uí Bruadair: The Poems of David Ó Bruadair*, ed. Rev. John C. Mac Erlean, 3 vols., Irish Texts Society (London: David Nutt, 1910−17), II, 48−97, p. 53. It is a measure of Ó Bruadair's hostility to English Protestantism that he was willing to see Oliver Stephenson as Old English when his family arrived in Ireland in the same New English wave of Tudor immigration as that of Kinelmeaky himself.

13. 'Is boct mo beata' ('My life is now so poor'), *Duanaire Dáibid Uí Bruadair*, I, 50−67; 'Is olc an ceart' ('Twould be an act of shabbiness'), *Duanaire Dáibid Uí Bruadair*, I, 78−89, p. 83.

14. James G. Taafe, 'John Milton's Student, Richard Barry: A Biographical Note', *Huntington Library Quarterly*, 25 (1962): 325−36.

15. William Riley Parker, *Milton: A Biography*, 2nd edn., rev. Gordon Campbell, 2 vols. (Oxford: Clarendon, 1996), I, 572.

16. As did at least three of his brothers: see Canny, *Upstart Earl*, 127.

17. Ibid., 128; *Dánta Piarais Feiritéir*, ed. Patrick Dineen, tr. Pat Muldowney (Aubane, Co. Cork: Aubane Historical Society, 1999), 60−1, 32−3.

18. *Articles Exhibited to the Honourable House of Commons Assembled in Parliament, Against the Lord Inchiquine Lord President of Munster, Subscribed by the Lord Broghill and Sir Arthur Loftus Knight* (London, 1647), 2.

19. For these visits in the context of Boyle-family and Munster great-house entertainments more largely, see Alan J. Fletcher, *Drama, Performance, and Polity in Pre-Cromwellian Ireland* (Cork: Cork University Press, 2000), 230.

20. 'Upon my Lord Brohalls Wedding', in *The Works of Sir John Suckling, The Non-Dramatic Works*, ed. Thomas Clayton (Oxford: Clarendon, 1971).

21. 'Poem to the Earl of Orrery' (comp. 1650−57), lines 3, 553−96, in *Sir William Davenant: The Shorter Poems, and Songs from the Plays and Masques*, ed. A. M. Gibbs (Oxford: Clarendon, 1972).

22. Ted-Larry Pebworth, 'The Earl of Orrery and Cowley's *Davideis*: Recovered Works and New Connections', *Modern Philology*, 76/2 (1978): 136−48.

23. See e.g. the Dedication to Dryden's *The Rival Ladies*, published 1664.

24. *The Collected Works of Katherine Philips: The Matchless Orinda*, ed. Patrick Thomas *et al.*, 3 vols. (Stump Cross: Stump Cross Books, 1990−3), II, 57.

25. Cf. Andrew Shifflett, ' "How Many Virtues Must I Hate?": Katherine Philips and the Politics of Clemency', *Studies in Philology*, 94 (1997): 103−35.

26. Evidence of the plans to seize Dublin Castle and murder the Lord Lieutenant (of which Orrery appears to have had some intelligence) surfaced in March, May, and June 1663. *Pompey* and *Altemera* were staged in Dublin in February. Cf. Philips, 'To my Lord Duke of Ormond, Lord Lieutenant of Ireland, on the discovery of the late Plot', in *Collected Works of Katherine Philips*, I, 222−3, and *Orinda to Poliarchus*, Letter 33, in *Collected Works of Katherine Philips*, II, 95−6, p. 96.

27. Their relationship can be traced through Philips's correspondence (in *Collected Works* III), and the Welsh/Irish verse compliments they paid one another: 'Roger Boyle, Earl of Orrery to Orinda', in *Poems by Several Persons* (Dublin, 1663), which concludes 'If there be *Helicon*, in *Wales* it is. | Oh happy Country! which to our Prince gives | His title, and in which Orinda lives' and, apparently, 'The Irish Greyhound' (*Collected Works of Katherine Philips*, III, 186−8, p. 188, I, 195−6).

28. Cf. S. J. Connolly, *Religion, Law, and Power: The Making of Protestant Ireland 1660−1760* (Oxford: Clarendon, 1992), 19.

29. F. D. Dow, *Cromwellian Scotland, 1651−1660* (Edinburgh: John Donald, 1979), chs. 8−9; T. C. Barnard, 'Planters and Policies in Cromwellian Ireland', *Past and Present*, 61 (1973): 31−69, pp. 53−60; Julia Buckroyd, 'Lord Broghill and the Scottish Church, 1655−1656', *Journal of Ecclesiastical History*, 27 (1976): 359−68; David M. Walker, *A Legal History of Scotland*, vol. IV, *The Seventeenth*

Century (Edinburgh: T. and T. Clark, 1996), 69–70; Little, 'Political Career of Roger Boyle', ch. 5.

30. Little, 'Political Career of Roger Boyle', 153–4.

31. Dow, *Cromwellian Scotland*, 187–94.

32. On the complex publishing history (the Waterford connection has been challenged) see C. William Miller, 'A Bibliographical Study of *Parthenissa* by Roger Boyle Earl of Orrery', *Studies in Bibliography*, 2 (1949–50): 115–37.

33. 'The Atlantic Archipelago and the War of the Three Kingdoms', in Brendan Bradshaw and John Morrill, eds., *The British Problem, c.1534–1707: State Formation in the Atlantic Archipelago* (London: Macmillan, 1996), 172–91.

34. *The Works of the Honourable Robert Boyle*, ed. Thomas Birch, 5 vols. (London, 1744), V, 239.

35. *Parthenissa, A Romance* (London, 1655), Preface, A2r. For simplicity further quotations and references are from *Parthenissa, that Most Fam'd Romance: The Six Volumes Compleat* (London, 1676).

36. See the confession of a plotting friar before execution and the attempted betrayal of Cork to Muskerry by its Mayor and aldermen described in *A Manifestation Directed to the Honourable Houses of Parliament in England, Sent from the Lord Inchequin, the Lord Broghill [and others]* (London, 1644), 9–10, and, for a more balanced analysis, John A. Murphy, 'The Expulsion of the Irish from Cork in 1644', *Journal of the Cork Historical and Archaeological Society*, 69 (1964): 123–30.

37. BL Add. MS 25287, pp. 6–12.

38. For a nuanced account of these motives see Micheál Ó Siochrú, *Confederate Ireland 1642–1649: A Constitutional and Political Analysis* (Dublin: Four Courts, 1999), ch. 2.

39. See e.g. Colley Cibber's praise for the 'irresistably Inviting' *Parthenissa*, when introducing his adaptation from it, *Perolla and Izadora: A Tragedy* (London, 1706), A2r.

40. *The Irish Colours Displayed, In A Reply of an English Protestant to a Late Letter of an Irish Roman Catholique* (London, 1662), 6.

41. ' "Examples Are Best Precepts": Readers and Meanings in Seventeenth-Century Poetry', *Critical Inquiry*, 1 (1974): 273–90, p. 286.

42. In dialogue with the Roman Ventidius, Artabbanes presses the advantages of monarchical over republican government, but even there his emphasis is as much on the value of rule by one man (who might be Lord Protector) as it is on the merits of inheritance (II.iii, 237–72).

43. In addition to such negative depictions as T. B.'s play, *The Rebellion of Naples: Or, The Tragedy of Massenello* (London, 1649), Broghill would have access to James Howell's translations—as *An Exact Historie of the Late Revolutions in Naples* (London, 1650) and *The Second Part of Massaniello* (London, 1652)—of Alessandro Giraffi's more balanced *Le Rivolutioni di Napoli descritte dal Signor A. G.* (Venice, 1647).

44. Rosario Villari, 'Masaniello: Contemporary and Recent Interpretations', *Past and Present*, 108 (August, 1985): 117-32, pp. 125-6.

45. R. A. Stradling, *The Spanish Monarchy and Irish Mercenaries: The Wild Geese in Spain 1618-68* (Blackrock: Irish Academic Press, 1994), 38; J. H. Elliott, 'Revolts in the Spanish Monarchy', in Robert Forster and Jack P. Greene (eds.), *Preconditions of Revolution in Early Modern Europe* (Baltimore: Johns Hopkins University Press, 1970), 109-30.

46. *Calendar of State Papers, Ireland, 1663-1665*, 151.

47. H. G. Koenigsberger, 'The Revolt of Palermo in 1647', *Cambridge Historical Journal*, 8 (1944-6): 129-44.

48. A booklist in the Petworth House Archives (Orrery Papers MS 13190)— which records many theological and ecclesiastical works, Catholic as well as Protestant, the usual classical texts (e.g., 'Homers Iliads', Cicero, Sallust, Lucan), legal and political treatises (including 'Matchevills Works' in Folio), books about travel (Hakluyt), and modern literature (not least 'All Dryden's plays')—gives 'Maps' as a general heading but only specifies the map of Sicily under it.

49. Aidan Clarke, *Prelude to Restoration in Ireland: The End of the Commonwealth 1659-1660* (Cambridge: Cambridge University Press, 1999), 260-1, 263, 287.

50. Clarke, *Prelude to Restoration*, 263, on Broghill's 'approach to Robert Douglas and a number of other prominent members of the Edinburgh presbytery associated with the loyalist "Resolutioner" group with whom he had negotiated during his time as president of the Scottish council.'

51. Clarke, *Prelude to Restoration*, 292-3.

52. Ibid., 276.

53. As the king puts it: 'And, *Lucidor*, since you to armes did fly | But to preserve your mistresse' Chastitie' (V.i.389-90).

54. Hard-pressed by the Confederates, and told by Cromwell to protect English interests as best he could until an invasion was launched, the always royalist-inclined Monck exploited O'Neill's disaffection with more moderate or compromising elements in the Confederation to persuade him into a pact that allowed O'Neill to buy parliamentary gunpowder. Monck was required to explain this extraordinary deal to the Council of State, and reprimanded. The scandal was not forgotten: when Thomas Gumble wrote his biography of the General in 1671, he felt obliged to justify the pact at length, and then excused it by saying: 'This Action, little can be said for it, but the usual Arguments of Necessity and Self-preservation' (*The Life of General Monck, Duke of Albemarle* (London, 1671), 27). As for Catholic historians, the pro-O'Neill author of the *Aphorismical Discovery* was so embarrassed that he ignored the truce, merely saying that, when Ormond and Inchiquin signed an instrument for O'Neill to buy ammunition, 'he made his waies with Colonell Monke', while Richard Bellings, the Old English Ormondist, stressed the treachery to the Confederate cause which O'Neill's willingness to treat with

Monck demonstrated, though he was careful to say nothing to the detriment of Monck, who had become, thanks to the Restoration, a royalist hero (*An Aphorismical Discovery of Treasonable Faction*, in *A Contemporary History of Affairs in Ireland*, ed. John T. Gilbert, 3 vols. in 6 (Dublin: Irish Archaeological and Celtic Society, 1879–80) II, 1, 37; Richard Bellings, *History of the Irish Confederation and the War in Ireland, 1641–1643*, ed. John T. Gilbert, 7 vols. (Dublin: John T. Gilbert, 1882–91), VII, 117ff.).

55. See e.g. *Irish Colours Displayed*, 5.
56. *An Answer of a Person of Quality to a Scandalous Letter* (Dublin, 1662), 18.
57. *Irish Colours Displayed*, 12–13.
58. 'Ionnsa d'fēinn Éirionn' ("'Tis sad for Erin's Fenian bands'), *Duanaire Dáibid Uí Bruadair*, II, 8–11. For the background see James Brennan, 'A Gallican Interlude in Ireland', *Irish Theological Quarterly*, 24 (1957): 219–37 and Anthony Joseph Brown, 'Anglo-Irish Gallicanism, *c*.1635–*c*.1685', Ph.D. dissertation (University of Cambridge, 2004).
59. *A Letter Desiring a Just and Mercifull Regard of the Roman Catholicks of Ireland, Given about the End of October 1660* (Dublin?, 1662?).
60. Edmund Spenser, *A View of the State of Ireland...1596*, in Sir James Ware, *The Historie of Ireland, Collected by Three Learned Authors* (Dublin, 1633).
61. *Irish Colours Displayed*, 9–10.
62. See above, p. 24 and e.g. Connolly, *Religion, Law, and Power*, 114–24.
63. *Irish Colours Displayed*, 15.
64. *State Letters*, 198.
65. Barnard, 'Planters and Policies', 60–6.
66. An Irish Cattle Bill was narrowly passed, after heated debate, on 23 November 1666.
67. See e.g. his speech to the General Convention, held in Dublin in 1660, saying 'that rather then Ireland should bee the least Mote in the Ey of England hee would loose his right hand, but rather then England should be a beame in the ey of Ireland he would loose his head' (quoted by Clarke, *Prelude to Restoration Ireland*, 271).
68. V.[iii.]291–2; in *Dramatic Works of Roger Boyle*, I.
69. Cf. James Kelly, 'The Origins of the Act of Union: An Examination of Unionist Opinion in Britain and Ireland, 1650–1800', *Irish Historical Studies*, 25 (1986–7): 236–63, pp. 237–46; T. C. Barnard, 'Crises of Identity Among Irish Protestants 1641–1685', *Past and Present*, 127 (1990): 39–83, pp. 42–3; Jim Smyth, ' "Like Amphibious Animals": Irish Protestants, Ancient Britons, 1691–1707', *Historical Journal*, 36 (1993): 785–97, and ' "No Remedy More Proper": Anglo-Irish Unionism Before 1707', in Brendan Bradshaw and Peter Roberts (eds.), *British Consciousness and Identity: The Making of Britain, 1533–1707* (Cambridge: Cambridge University Press, 1998), 301–20.

70. See e.g. David J. Baker, *Between Nations: Shakespeare, Spenser, Marvell, and the Question of Britain* (Stanford: Stanford University Press, 1997), ch. 1; Christopher Highley, *Shakespeare, Spenser and the Crisis in Ireland* (Cambridge: Cambridge University Press, 1997), ch. 6.

71. *Irish Colours Displayed*, 83.

72. Contrast the exclusively English reading by John Butler, 'The Mirror of a King: The Earl of Orrery and Shakespeare on King Henry V', *Cahiers Élisabéthains*, 45 (April 1994): 65–75.

73. See e.g. Keith Feiling, *British Foreign Policy 1660–1672* (London: Macmillan, 1930), 63, 69, 73, 149, 218.

74. *State Letters*, 124–5.

75. Ibid., 140–1, 187, 205; cf. Liam Irwin, 'The Earl of Orrery and the Military Problems of Restoration Munster', *The Irish Sword*, 13 (1977–9): 10–19.

76. To Viscount Conway and Killulta, 17 July 1666; *CSPI 1666–1669*, 156–8.

77. *State Letters*, 297. Though Stuart claims to *mare clausum* (above, pp. 49, 240) embraced the entire archipelago, most maps (often of Dutch origin) restricted 'the British seas' to the Channel between France and England.

78. *CSPI 1666–1669*, 476–8; for anti-French sentiment more largely at this date see Steven C. A. Pincus, *Protestantism and Patriotism: Ideologies and the Making of English Foreign Policy, 1650–1668* (Cambridge: Cambridge University Press, 1996), ch. 25.

79. *CSPI 1666–1669*, 725–6.

80. Lynch, *Roger Boyle*, 140–44, 163–4; Ronald Hutton, *Charles II: King of England, Scotland, and Ireland* (Oxford: Clarendon, 1989), 298–9.

81. C. T. Atkinson, 'Charles II's Regiments in France, 1672–1678', *Journal of the Society for Army Historical Research*, 23 (1945): 53–65, 129–36, 161–72; Hutton, *Charles II*, 328–9, 363.

82. Petworth House Archives, Orrery Papers MS 13187.

83. T. C. Barnard, 'The Political, Material and Mental Culture of the Cork Settlers, c.1650–1700', in Patrick O'Flanagan and Cornelius G. Buttimer (eds.), *Cork: History and Society: Interdisciplinary Essays on the History of an Irish County* (Dublin: Geography Publications, 1993), 309–65, pp. 322–33.

84. Compare e.g. *n*. 36 above with *A Treatise of the Art of War* (London, 1677), 43.

85. *Irish Colours Displayed*, 3.

86. *Art of War*, 1, 12. There is a symptomatic split in the make-up of his last book, *Poems on Most of the Festivals of the Church* (1681); it greets the reader with preliminaries produced in London ('Printed for *Henry Herringman* at the Anchor in the Lower Walk of the *New-Exchange*') but the body of the work was apparently printed by William Smith in Cork.

87. *Parthenissa* I.iv, 351; II.viii, 755; on Spenser see above, p. 39.

88. On the persistence of such accounts see Nicholas Canny, 'Identity Formation in Ireland: The Emergence of the Anglo-Irish', in Nicholas Canny and Anthony Pagden (eds.), *Colonial Identity in the Atlantic World* (Princeton:

Princeton University Press, 1987), 159–212, pp. 198–201, but note Barnard, 'Crises of Identity', esp. 78–80.

89. See e.g. James Muldoon, 'The Indian as Irishman', *Essex Institute Historical Collections,* 111 (1975): 267–89, but also Patricia Coughlan's thoughtfully complicating 'Counter-Currents in Colonial Discourse: The Political Thought of Vincent and Daniel Gookin', in Jane H. Ohlmeyer (ed.), *Political Thought in Seventeenth-Century Ireland: Kingdom or Colony* (Cambridge: Cambridge University Press, 2000), 56–82.

CHAPTER 9

1. As the career of Marvell shows—from Cromwellian state official to Restoration MP—both dynamics were compatible with continuity and conciliation in government.

2. 'Crùnadh an dara Righ Teàrlach' ('The Crowning of King Charles II'), in Peter Davidson (ed.), *Poetry and Revolution: An Anthology of British and Irish Verse 1625–1660* (Oxford: Clarendon, 1998), 503–6.

3. *The History of My Own Time,* Part I, ed. Osmund Airy, 2 vols. (Oxford: Clarendon, 1897–1900), I, 225. Cf. the antagonistic 'Verses upon the Late Marquis of Arguille' printed from manuscript in James Maidment (ed.), *A Book of Scotish Pasquils: 1568–1715* (Edinburgh: William Paterson, 1868), 118–19.

4. Sir George Mackenzie, *Pleadings in some Remarkable Cases, before the Supreme Courts of Scotland, since the Year 1661* (Edinburgh, 1672), 172–84.

5. See e.g. William Ferguson, *Scotland's Relations with England: A Survey to 1707* (Edinburgh: Donald, 1977), 154–7—contrasting the less sceptical interpretation of court policy given in Maurice Lee, *The Cabal* (Urbana: University of Illinois Press, 1965); Burnet, *History,* I, 505.

6. Hence Charles's consistency in both unscrambling Cromwellian union and operating, from 1660 to 1667, a Scottish Council at Whitehall dominated by English politicians loyal to the crown.

7. Not all genres travelled: little drama was written in Scotland, and the performance of plays composed by Scotsmen in London is a largely eighteenth-century phenomenon, though *Tarugo's Wiles* by Thomas St Serfe—son of a Bishop of Galloway, and soldier under Montrose, who established the first Scottish (and Scots-language) newspaper in 1661—was staged at Lincoln's Inn Fields in 1667, and satirized the Covenant. Cf. Adrienne Scullion, ' "Forget Scotland": Plays by Scots on the London Stage, 1667–1715', *Comparative Drama,* 31 (1997): 105–28.

8. John Morrill, 'The British Problem, c.1534–1707', in Brendan Bradshaw and John Morrill (eds.), *The British Problem, c.1534–1707: State Formation in the Atlantic Archipelago* (Basingstoke: Macmillan, 1996), 1–38, p. 34.

9. Milton, 'On the Lord General Fairfax', explored above, pp. 229–30.

10. For discussion see Clare Jackson, 'The Paradoxical Virtue of the Historical Romance: Sir George Mackenzie's *Aretina* (1660) and the Civil Wars', in John R. Young (ed.), *Celtic Dimensions of the British Civil Wars* (Edinburgh: John Donald, 1997), 205–25.

11. Clare Jackson, *Restoration Scotland, 1660–1690: Royalist Politics, Religion and Ideas* (Woodbridge: Boydell, 2003) provides analysis and contexts.

12. See Daniela Havenstein, '*Religio* Writing in Seventeenth-Century England and Scotland: Sir Thomas Browne's *Religio Medici* (1643) and Sir George Mackenzie's *Religio Stoici* (1663)', *Scottish Literary Journal*, 25 (1998): 17–33.

13. John Evelyn, *Publick Employment and an Active Life with its Appanages, such as Fame, Command, Riches, Conversation &c Preferr'd to Solitude* (London, 1667).

14. Andrew Lang, *Sir George Mackenzie of Rosehaugh, King's Advocate 1636(?)–1691: His Life and Times* (London: Longmans, 1909), 181–2; Dryden, 'Discourse Concerning the Original and Progress of Satire' (1692), in *The Works of John Dryden*, ed. Edward Niles Hooker, H. T. Swedenberg, *et al.*, 20 vols. (Berkeley: University of California Press, 1955–2000), IV, 84–5.

15. See extensively Richard L. Greaves, *Enemies under his Feet: Radicals and Nonconformists in Britain, 1664–1677* (Stanford: Stanford University Press, 1990).

16. Ibid., 13.

17. Julia Buckroyd, *Church and State in Scotland 1660–1681* (Edinburgh: John Donald, 1980), 67.

18. See above, p. 61.

19. On the long roots of conventicle militancy, see David Stevenson, 'Conventicles in the Kirk, 1619–1637', *Records of the Scottish Church History Society*, 18 (1972–4): 99–114.

20. *History*, I, 422.

21. Maidment (ed.), *Scotish Pasquils*, 232–3. Cp. the undercurrents of admiration for the rebels in the ballad, 'The Battle of Pentland Hills', in James Maidment (ed.), *Scotish Ballads and Songs, Historical and Traditionary* (Edinburgh: William Paterson, 1868), 285–7.

22. Richard Ashcraft, *Revolutionary Politics and Locke's 'Two Treatises of Government'* (Princeton: Princeton University Press, 1986), 148.

23. Greaves, *Enemies under his Feet*, 163, cites a royalist source claiming that two-thirds of the city's population was Presbyterian.

24. To Mayor Franke, 1 December 1666; *The Poems and Letters of Andrew Marvell*, ed. H. M. Margoliouth, 3rd edn., rev. Pierre Legouis with E. E. Duncan-Jones, 2 vols. (Oxford: Clarendon, 1971), II, 46–7, p. 47.

25. Cf. Steven C. A. Pincus, *Protestantism and Patriotism: Ideologies and the Making of English Foreign Policy, 1650–1668* (Cambridge: Cambridge University Press, 1996), 414–16.

26. Ginny Gardner, *The Scottish Exile Community in the Netherlands, 1660-1690* (East Linton: Tuckwell, 2004).

27. John Foxe, *Actes and Monuments of these Latter and Perillous Dayes Touching Matters of the Church, Wherein ar Comprehended and Described the Great Persecutions [and] Horrible Troubles, that have been Wrought and Practised by the Romishe Prelates, Specially in this Realme of England and Scotlande* (London, [1563]).

28. *Naphtali: Or, The Wrestlings of the Church of Scotland for the Kingdom of Christ* (Edinburgh?, 1667), preface a8r-v.

29. Ibid., 135.

30. *A Survey of the Insolent and Infamous Libel, Entituled, Naphtali* (Edinburgh, 1668), Part I, 10. Though 'cantonize' alludes to religiously divided, weakened Switzerland, it might also seek to appeal to the anti-Cromwellian, patriotic sentiment of many Scots: England and Wales had been divided by the Lord Protector into cantons governed by twelve major-generals in 1655.

31. *A Letter to the Unknown Author of Jus Populi* (n.p., 1671), 10.

32. *Jus Populi Vindicatum: Or, The Peoples Right to Defend Themselves and their Covenanted Religion Vindicated* (London?, 1669), 371.

33. See the informative headnote in *The Poems of Andrew Marvell*, ed. Nigel Smith (London: Longman, 2003).

34. 'The Loyall Scot', lines 15-24, in *Poems and Letters of Marvell*, ed. Margoliouth, I.

35. 'Marvell and the Earl of Castlemaine', in Warren Chernaik and Martin Dzelzainis (eds.), *Marvell and Liberty* (Basingstoke: Macmillan, 1999), 290-312, p. 298.

36. This is strongly objected in, for example, 'Britannia and Rawleigh' (1674-5), which was attributed to Marvell in manuscript, though it is more likely by John Ayloffe, and survives in *Poems and Letters of Marvell*, ed. Margoliouth.

37. Dzelzainis cites contemporary testimony that 'my Lord *Douglas* and his brave *Scots*...scorn'd to receave wages of those that have declared Warr against *England*'; 'Marvell and Castlemaine', 295.

38. To William Popple, 21 March 1670; *Poems and Letters of Marvell*, ed. Margoliouth, II, 313-16, p. 314.

39. In this context I am less surprised than Dzelzainis, 'Marvell and Castlemaine', 291, to find Marvell's name on a 1669 list 'of such as may bee ingaged by the Duke of York'. The Duke, still ostensibly Protestant, but sympathetic to Catholics, was prepared to smooth the way for them by tactically supporting Dissenters against high-flying Anglicans.

40. For the big picture see John Spurr, *The Restoration Church of England 1646-1689* (New Haven: Yale University Press, 1991).

41. In *The Rehearsal Transpros'd* (London, 1672), 35, Marvell alludes to a saying attributed to Henry VII, that England need not fear Anglo-Scottish union

as the greater kingdom would draw in the lesser, to highlight the dangers in Bishop Bramhall's desire for agreement among the Christian churches: 'there is this more, which I confess was below Bishop *Bramhall's* reflexion, and was indeed fit only for some vulgar Politician, or the commissioners of *Scotland* about the late Union: Whether it would not have succeeded, as in the consolidation of Kingdoms, where the Greatest swallows down the less; so also in Church-Coalition, that though the Pope had condescended (which the Bishop owns to be his Right) to be only a Patriarch, yet he would have swoop'd up the Patriarchate of *Lambeth* to his Mornings-draught, like an egg in Muscadine.'

42. Mackenzie's views about the union (which he resisted in the Scottish parliament) can be reconstructed from his 'Discourse Concerning the Three Unions between Scotland and England', a text that found a place in *The Works of that Eminent and Noble Lawyer, Sir George Mackenzie of Rosehaugh*, ed. Thomas Ruddiman, 2 vols. (Edinburgh, 1718–22), II, 637–70, pp. 659–70. As for Stewart, he regarded the measure as cynically pursued by Lauderdale (who is most unlikely to have wanted a union) in order to enhance his 'eclipsing grandour' (*An Accompt of Scotlands Grievances by Reason of The D. of Lauderdales Ministrie* (Edinburgh?, 1672), 31).

43. Hence the ease with which the versatile Marchamont Nedham could recycle hostile material from the chapter 'Concerning the Scots' in his apology for the Republic, *The Case of the Common-wealth of England, Stated* (London, 1650), Pt II, ch. 2, to a royalist-phase *True Character of a Rigid Presbyter: With a Narrative of the Dangerous Designes of the English and Scotish Covenanters, as they have Tended to the Ruine of our Church and Kingdom* (London, 1661), 13–24.

44. *History of the Houses of Douglas and Angus* (Edinburgh, 1643), A1r.

45. First released in apparently reduced form (1633), this work was republished, after its 1643 and 1648 Edinburgh edns., in 1648–57 (again Edinburgh), 1657 (London), 1743 and 1748 (Edinburgh).

46. Michael Brown, *The Black Douglases: War and Lordship in Late Medieval Scotland, 1300–1455* (East Linton: Tuckwell, 1998).

47. Adam Fox, *Oral and Literate Culture in England 1500–1700* (Oxford: Clarendon, 2000), 1–5.

48. *A Memorable Song on the Unhappy Hunting in Chevy-Chase, Betweene Earle Piercy of England and Earle Douglas of Scotland. To the Tune of Flying Fame* (London, 1670).

49. See F. D. Dow, *Cromwellian Scotland 1651–1660* (Edinburgh: John Donald, 1979), 11 on the Scot, Sir John Hope of Craighall, proposing that Edinburgh and the Lowlands be ceded permanently to the invaders.

50. *Poems and Letters of Marvell*, ed. Margoliouth, I, 387.

51. To William Popple, 21 March 1670; *Poems and Letters of Marvell*, ed. Margoliouth, II, 313–16, p. 313—where Marvell adds the British-problem

point that it was hard to impeach Lauderdale in England because he was a Scottish peer.

52. *Poems and Letters of Marvell*, ed. Margoliouth, I, 389.

53. Mt Parnassus, sacred to the poets, has two peaks.

54. For a possible source see *Of Reformation*, in *Complete Prose Works of John Milton*, gen. ed. Don M. Wolfe, 8 vols. (New Haven: Yale University Press, 1953–82), I, 517–617, pp. 583–4.

55. Annabel Patterson, '"Crouching at Home, and Cruel when Abroad": Restoration Constructions of National and International Character', in R. Malcolm Smuts (ed.), *The Stuart Court and Europe: Essays in Politics and Political Culture* (Cambridge: Cambridge University Press, 1996), 210–27, p. 227.

56. For a judicious assessment see G. M. Yould, 'The Duke of Lauderdale's Religious Policy in Scotland, 1668–79: The Failure of Conciliation and the Return to Coercion', *Journal of Religious History*, 11 (1980–1): 248–68.

57. *History*, I, 184.

58. See e.g. *Burnet's Character*, in *Poems on Affairs of State: Augustan Satirical Verse, 1660–1714*, gen. ed. George deF. Lord, 7 vols. (New Haven: Yale University Press, 1963–75), V, 123–9, which begins:

> 'Mongst all the hard names that denote reproach,
> The worst in the whole catalogue is Scotch;
> For rascal, rakehell, vagabond, vile sot,
> Are only faint synonyms to Scot.
> To what a height then mounts that mighty he
> Who is whole Scotland in epitome!

59. *Poems on Affairs of State*, gen. ed. Lord, I, 191–203, lines 47–68.

60. Greaves, *Enemies under his Feet*, 163, 222.

61. To Sir Henry Thompson, [24 October 1674]; *Poems and Letters of Marvell*, ed. Margoliouth, II, 329–31, p. 330.

62. To Mayor Hoare, 24 August 1675; *Poems and Letters of Marvell*, ed. Margoliouth, II, 149–50. Cf. letter to William Popple, 24 July 1675; II, 341–3, p. 343.

63. See e.g. Buckroyd, *Church and State in Scotland*, 117.

64. *History*, I, 501.

65. *The Records of the Proceedings of the Justiciary Court, Edinburgh, 1661–1678*, ed. W. G. Scott-Moncrieff, 2 vols. (Edinburgh: Edinburgh University Press, 1905), II, 315.

66. Burnet, *History*, II, 141.

67. Fountainhall, quoted by James Kirkton, *The Secret and True History of the Church of Scotland*, ed. Charles Kirkpatrick Sharpe (Edinburgh: Ballantyne, 1817), 387.

68. George Hickes, *Ravillac Redivivus: Being a Narrative of the Late Tryal of Mr James Mitchel … In a Letter from a Scottish to an English Gentleman* (London, 1678), 54. François Ravaillac (1578−1610), the assassin of Henry IV of France, was invoked by Hickes both to exaggerate Mitchell's crime (he failed to kill a bishop, was not a successful regicide) and to associate a Dissenter, as so often in Anglican propaganda, with Catholic extremism (Ravaillac wanted Henry to convert the Huguenots). Ravaillac's torture and execution—scalded with burning sulphur, molten lead, boiling oil, and resin, his flesh torn apart with pincers, then drawn and quartered (pulled apart by four horses)—was also calculated to make Mitchell's treatment at the hands of the authorities look mild.

69. Playing along with the fiction of *In a Letter…*, Hickes describes them as '*Scottish* … which you will call … *English* Verses'.

70. *Idea eloquentiae forensis hodiernae* (Edinburgh, 1681), 78−106.

71. Ian B. Cowan, *The Scottish Covenanters 1660−1688* (London: Gollancz, 1976), 90.

72. *The History of the Indulgence* ([Edinburgh?], 1678).

73. Manuscript poem printed in nn. to Kirkton, *Secret and True History*, 388−9, p. 389.

74. See the powerful scene in James Robertson's best-selling novel about Mitchell as a 'justified sinner', *The Fanatic* (London: Fourth Estate, 2000), 202−13.

75. Cf. Clare Jackson, 'Judicial Torture, the Liberties of the Subject, and Anglo-Scottish Relations, 1660−1690', in T. C. Smout (ed.), *Anglo-Scottish Relations from 1603−1900, Proceedings of the British Academy*, 127 (2005): 75−101, esp. pp. 80−5.

76. Julia Buckroyd, *The Life of James Sharp Archbishop of St Andrews 1618−1679: A Political Biography* (Edinburgh: John Donald, 1987), 98.

77. Why 'Scoto-Brittannus' rather than vice versa? Usage was not consistent—James Sharp, for instance, could be satirized as 'Misanthropos, Judas, Scoto-Brittanus' (the title of a ms poem cited in the *Oxford Dictionary of National Biography* article on the Archbishop). Earlier in the century, however, as Allan I. Macinnes notes in another context, while advocates of Stuart imperial Britain employed the term 'Britanno-Scotus', 'Scoto-Britannus' ('which sustained Scottish perceptions of aristocratic republicanism and confessional confederation') was associated with a more radically Presbyterian/republican line. See his *The British Revolution, 1629−1660* (Basingstoke: Palgrave, 2005), 41 and 245 *n*.

78. *Poems and Letters of Marvell*, ed. Margoliouth, I, citing the translation in *Poems of Andrew Marvell*, ed. Smith.

79. Line 14: 'Errorem Dextrae dextera sura luat.' Latin 'Errorum' allows Mitchell to imply that his hand was in error in shooting the wrong bishop, not just, as the poem would concede, morally at fault for attempting murder.

80. Livy, *History of Rome*, II.xii-xiii.

81. Lines 19–20 read: 'Ut vacat! ut proprii sedet ad spectacula cruris | Immotus, populo commiserante, reus.'
82. Lang, *Sir George Mackenzie*, 157.
83. Burnet, *History*, II, 145–6.
84. Cf. Buckroyd, *Church and State in Scotland*, 126.
85. To Sir Edward Harley, 7 August 1677; *Poems and Letters of Marvell*, ed. Margoliouth, II, 354–6, pp. 355–6.
86. On the continuing campaign, which involved English as well as Scottish politicians, see Tim Harris, *Restoration: Charles II and His Kingdoms, 1660–1685* (London: Allen Lane, 2005), 125–9.
87. *Poems and Letters of Marvell*, II, 357.
88. See the manuscript life of Hickes quoted by William Bradford Gardner, 'The Later Years of John Maitland, Second Earl and First Duke of Lauderdale', *Journal of Modern History*, 20 (1948): 113–22, pp. 113–14, discussed in Paul Mathole, 'Marvell and Violence', Ph.D. dissertation (University of London, 2004), ch. 5. Tim Harris has found in Shaftesbury's papers a letter from Edinburgh, dated 10 September 1675, detailing Lauderdale's abuses of power and his threat 'to overthrow all our [Scotland's] liberty' (*Restoration*, 131).
89. Shaftesbury and the later Tory politician, Roger North, quoted by Jackson, *Restoration Scotland*, 73.
90. Harris, *Restoration*, 240–4.
91. See the speeches by Sir Richard Graham, Colonel John Birch, Sir Francis Winnington, and William Sacheverell cited by Harris, *Restoration*, 169.
92. *A True Account of the Horrid Murder Committed upon his Grace, the Late Lord Archbishop of St Andrews* (Dublin, 1679), 4.
93. John Northleigh, *The Parallel* (London, 1682), quoted by Harris, *Restoration*, 242.
94. 'Loudon Hill, Or, Drumclog', in Francis James Child (ed.), *The English and Scottish Popular Ballads*, 5 vols. in 3 (1882-98; New York: Folklore Press, 1957), IV, 107.
95. For fiction more sympathetic to the Covenanters see James Hogg, *The Brownie of Bodsbeck and other Tales*, 2 vols. (Edinburgh: William Blackwood and John Murray, 1818) and John Galt, *Ringan Gilhaize: Or, The Covenanters* (Edinburgh: Oliver and Boyd, 1823). As always, Scott is a perceptive but Tory-inclined historical witness.
96. Child (ed.), *English and Scottish Popular Ballads*, IV, 109–10.
97. For a ballad celebratory of Claverhouse and contemptuous of the rebels see 'The Whigs' Welcome', in Maidment (ed.), *Scotish Pasquils*, 246–8. At this date, English moderates could approve the Duke's Presbyterian sympathies; see e.g. Edmund Waller, 'On the D[uke] of Monmouth's Expedition into Scotland, in the Summer Solstice, 1678', in his *The Maid's Tragedy Altered. With Some other Pieces* (London, 1690), 53–5. Later, Tory satirists played

514 NOTES TO PAGES 289–96

on the Duke's name, James Scott, to elide him with the Covenanters; hence Aphra Behn's witty exercise in pastiche Scots, 'Silvio's Complaint: A Song, to a Fine Scotch Tune' (*c*.1683), in which Monmouth weeps 'Muckle Showers' at his folly in opposing the king and being forced into exile in the Netherlands—see her *Poems upon Several Occasions* (London, 1684), 95–8.

98. Respectively *The Indian Emperor* and *Mithridates, King of Pontus*. See Terence Tobin, 'Plays Presented in Scotland 1660–1700', *Restoration and Eighteenth-Century Theatre Research*, 12/1 (1973), 51–3, 59.

99. S. Bruce and S. Yearley, 'The Social Construction of Tradition: The Holyrood Portraits and the Kings of Scotland', in David McCrone, Stephen Kendrick, and Pat Straw (eds.), *The Making of Scotland: Nation, Culture and Social Change* (Edinburgh: Edinburgh University Press, 1989), 175–87.

100. Guy Miege, *A Relation of Three Embassies from his Sacred Majestie Charles II to the Great Duke of Muscovie, the King of Sweden, and the King of Denmark* (London, 1669), 266–7, 448; 379–80, 424–5. The whole account presents a remarkable picture of a neglected side of Marvell, as man of adventure and accomplished diplomat.

101. K. H. D. Haley, *William of Orange and the English Opposition 1672–4* (Oxford: Clarendon, 1953), 57–8, 63, 196.

102. *An Account of the Growth of Popery, and Arbitrary Government in England* (London, 1677), 145.

103. *A Letter from Amsterdam, to a Friend in England* (London, 1678), 1.

104. By Sir Roger L'Estrange.

105. Greaves, *Deliver us from Evil: The Radical Underground in Britain, 1660–1663* (New York: Oxford University Press, 1986) and *Secrets of the Kingdom: British Radicals from the Popish Plot to the Revolution of 1688–89* (Stanford: Stanford University Press, 1992) make up a trilogy with *Enemies under his Feet*; Ashcraft, *Revolutionary Politics*, is strong on the late 1670s and 1680s; Gardner, *Scottish Exile Community*.

106. 'A Mock Poem, upon the Expedition of the Highland-Host: Who Came to Destroy the Western Shires, in Winter 1678', in William Cleland, *A Collection of Several Poems and Verses, Composed upon Various Occasions* (n.p., 1697), 7–51, pp. 12–13.

107. Ibid., 38–9.

108. Kirkton, *Secret and True History*, 390–1.

109. Cleland, *Collection*, 54.

110. Hugh Ouston, 'York in Edinburgh: James VII and the Patronage of Learning in Scotland, 1679–1688', in John Dwyer, Roger A. Mason, and Alexander Murdoch (eds.), *New Perspectives on the Politics and Culture of Early Modern Scotland* (Edinburgh: John Donald, 1982), 133–55, p. 152.

111. *A Vindication of His Majesties Government, and Judicatures, in Scotland; from some Aspersions Thrown on them by Scandalous Pamphlets, and News-books* (Edinburgh, 1683), 5.

112. 'The Papers left by Mr James Mitchel', in James Stewart and James Stirling, *Naphtali* (n.p., 1693), 397–443.

113. *Poems on Affairs of State*, gen. ed. Lord, V, 275–80.

114. Excluded from *Miscellaneous Poems* (London, 1681), a short version appeared in Charles Gildon's (?) edited collection, *Chorus Poetarum: Or, Poems on Several Occasions* (London, 1694), and a longer text in George Villiers, Duke of Buckingham, *et al.*, *Poems on Affairs of State from the Time of Oliver Cromwell, to the Abdication of King James the Second* ([London], 1697); there is also an apparently late seventeenth-century pamphlet text of the poem.

115. For a trenchant account see Ian B. Cowan, 'Church and State Reformed? The Revolution of 1688–9 in Scotland', in Jonathan Israel (ed.), *The Anglo-Dutch Moment: Essays on the Glorious Revolution and Its World Impact* (Cambridge: Cambridge University Press), 163–83.

CHAPTER 10

1. The naming of Derry, Londonderry (or, as in Mitchelbourne's title, *London-Derry*) has long been problematic. I follow the practice, standard among early modern Irish historians, of using Derry for the city and Londonderry for the county, though this does not match at every point the preferences of the authors and texts under discussion.

2. Cecil Davis Milligan, *Colonel John Mitchelburne Defender of Londonderry and the Mitchelburne Club of Apprentice Boys of Derry* (Londonderry: Emery and Co., 1954), 21–2.

3. *Ireland Preserv'd: Or, The Siege of London-Derry. Together with The Troubles of the North* (London, 1705); *Troubles* and *Siege* (here quoting p. 111) are separately paginated.

4. J. G. Simms, *The Williamite Confiscation in Ireland, 1690–1703* (London: Faber, 1956), esp. chs. 8–13.

5. *Hic et Ubique: Or, The Humors of Dublin* (London, 1663), 1.

6. Probably born in Dublin *c.*1671, elder son of a bishop of Derry, Hopkins was educated at Trinity College, Dublin and Cambridge. As the events of 1688 unfolded, he returned to Ireland, where, despite some inconsistency in the sources, he seems to have fought for the Protestant cause. During the 1690s he lived a dissolute, literary life in London, but counted among his friends the Irish-born writers Thomas Southerne and William Congreve. He published poems and verse translations from Latin—*Epistolary Poems, on Several Occasions* (London, 1694)—a contribution to the debate about the morality of the theatre, *A Letter to A. H. Esq., Concerning the Stage* (London, 1698), and a series of tragedies, all published in London: *Pyrrhus, King of*

Epirus (1695), *Neglected Virtue: Or, The Unhappy Conqueror* (1696), *Boadicea, Queen of Britain* (1697), *Friendship Improv'd: Or, The Female Warriour* (1700). That Derry remained a magnet is shown by the signing of the dedication to *Friendship Improv'd* 'Londonderry, Nov. 1st. 99'. Hopkins died, allegedly overtaken by the effects of dissipation, at Templemore, Co. Londonderry, in 1700.

7. See e.g. Deborah Orr's reading of *Friendship Improv'd* in her *Empire on the English Stage 1660–1714* (Cambridge: Cambridge University Press, 2001), 204.
8. Cf. David Armitage, 'The Political Economy of Britain and Ireland after the Glorious Revolution', in Jane H. Ohlmeyer (ed.), *Political Thought in Seventeenth-Century Ireland: Kingdom or Colony* (Cambridge: Cambridge University Press, 2000), 221–43.
9. 'A Treatise of Ireland', in *The Economic Writings of Sir William Petty*, ed. Charles Henry Hill, 2 vols. (Cambridge: Cambridge University Press, 1899).
10. Irish Catholic accounts tend to be more insular (and aware that James could have sent troops to Scotland without taking Derry): e.g. *A Jacobite Narrative of the War in Ireland 1688–91* [from Nicholas Plunkett?, 'A Light to the Blind'], ed. John T. Gilbert, rpt. with an introd. by J. G. Simms (Shannon: Irish University Press, 1971), 41, 51, 66; Charles O'Kelly, *Macariae Excidium: Or, The Destruction of Cyprus*, ed. John Cornelius O'Callaghan (Dublin: Irish Archaeological Society, 1850), 33–41.
11. It is a clue to the complexity of Scottish/Irish affinities that Houston's men are identified as 'Mountaineers' (a common term for hard-line, uncivil Covenanters, though literally enough applicable to Protestant Campbells, from the West of Scotland) rather than, as one might anticipate, Lowland Presbyterians, even while, earlier in the *Troubles*, Granade pretends to be an uplander ('*Duncan Maccantosh*, the Kings Bombardier, an Highland Laird', 62) in order to pass safely through Catholic Ireland between Dublin and the north. On Ulster Presbyterianism in its Nonconforming context see esp. Phil Kilroy, *Protestant Dissent and Controversy in Ireland, 1660–1714* (Cork: Cork University Press, 1994), Kevin Herlihy (ed.), *The Religion of Irish Dissent, 1650–1800* (Dublin: Four Courts, 1996), and Richard L. Greaves, *God's Other Children: Protestant Nonconformists and the Emergence of Denominational Churches in Ireland, 1660–1700* (Stanford: Stanford University Press, 1997).
12. 21 June 1679; Historical Manuscripts Commission, *The Manuscripts of the Marquis of Ormonde*, vol. I (London: Her Majesty's Stationery Office, 1895), 102.
13. 30 June 1668; ibid., 100–1.
14. For the work see *A True Narrative of the Rise and Progress of the Presbyterian Church in Ireland (1623–1670) by the Rev. Patrick Adair. Also, The History of the Church in Ireland since the Scots were Naturalized, by the Rev. Andrew Stewart*, ed. W. D. Killen (Belfast: Aitchison, 1886); for discussion, see Kilroy, *Protestant Dissent*, 29.

15. 30 September 1679; HMC vol. cit., 102–3, corr. against National Library of Ireland MS 2505 fol. 199r–v.

16. Kathleen Menzie Lesko, 'A Critical Old-Spelling Edition of the Plays of John Wilson 1626–1695?' Ph. D. dissertation (The George Washington University, 1980), id, 4.

17. *Belphegor: Or, The Marriage of the Devil* (London, 1691), 1.

18. Historical Manuscripts Commission, *The Manuscripts of the Marquess of Ormonde*, n.s. vol. VI (London: Her Majesty's Stationery Office, 1911), 489.

19. *A Discourse of the Monarchy, More Particularly, of the Imperial Crowns of England, Scotland, and Ireland* (London, 1684), 76, 216. On this earlier conflict see the discussion of Monck's conduct at this date in Chapter 8 (*n.* 54) and W. P. Kelly, 'The Forgotten Siege of Derry, March–August, 1649', in William Kelly (ed.), *The Sieges of Derry* (Dublin: Four Courts, 2001), 31–52.

20. *Vindiciae Carolinae: Or, A Defence of Eikon Baskilike ... in Reply to a Book Intituled Eikonoklastes, Written by Mr Milton* (London, 1692), 101. The recycling helps cast doubt on the occasional attribution of this tract to Richard Hollingworth.

21. *The Royal Voyage: Or, The Irish Expedition* (London, 1690), [iii]. For an informative placing of this play, and what appears to be its equally anonymous sequel, *The Royal Flight: Or, The Conquest of Ireland* (London, 1690), in socio-political context, see Lois Potter, 'Politics and Popular Culture: The Theatrical Response to the Revolution', in Lois G. Schwoerer (ed.), *The Revolution of 1688–1689: Changing Perspectives* (Cambridge: Cambridge University Press, 1992), 184–97, p. 191.

22. *Londerias: Or, A Narrative of the Siege of London-Derry* (Dublin, 1699), 1.

23. Above, p. 69.

24. E. g. 'My Shelf did tauke [this handsome cloak] from de *English* Shentleman, and did give him my Frize Cloak, and did be aufter turn him and his Wife and Shildrens from de Fire, and I and my Comrade, did shit down in der Plaushes, and did maake him bring Mate and Drink, my Shelf and my Wife *Shuaan* did lye in de Feder Bed, and dey did lye in de Kitchin-Shamber' (*Troubles*, 55).

25. Edmund Spenser, *A View of the State of Ireland* [1596–8], pub. in Sir James Ware (ed.), *The Historie of Ireland* (Dublin, 1633), 33; Sir John Temple, *The Irish Rebellion* (London, 1646), 2. For refutation from an Irish, genealogically informed perspective, see Seathrún Céitinn [Geoffrey Keating], *Foras feasa ar Éirinn: The History of Ireland*, ed. David Comyn and P. S. Dinneen, 4 vols. (London: Irish Texts Society, 1902–14), I, 28–31, discussed by Bernadette Cunningham, *The World of Geoffrey Keating: History, Myth and Religion in Seventeenth-Century Ireland* (Dublin: Four Courts, 2000), 88.

26. On his relocation to Kilcandra see the entry by C. I. McGrath in the *Oxford Dictionary of National Biography*. Vivien Hewitt, currently researching Mitchelbourne's life, informs me that the move followed the second marriage of his father, to a very young bride in Dublin, when the future dramatist was nine.

27. E.g. Richard Cox, *Hibernia Anglicana: Or, The History of Ireland from the Conquest thereof by the English, to this Present Time*, Part 1 (London, 1689), 8, William Molyneux, *The Case of Ireland's being Bound by Acts of Parliament in England, Stated* (Dublin, 1698), 20.

28. Milligan, *Mitchelburne*, 20.

29. Mitchelbourne's life of self-justification in print began with his *Account of the Transactions in the North of Ireland, Anno Domini, 1691 ... With Particular Relation of the Manner of Besieging and Taking the town of Sligoe by Storm* (London, 1692). Later texts include *The Case of Colonel John Michelburne, Late Governor of Londonderry: and the Service of James Roach, truly Stated* (London, 1698), *Colonel Michelburne's Reply to James Roach's Answer* (London, 1703), *The Case of Col. John Michelburne, Late Governor of Londonderry; and the Regiment then under his Command* (London?, 1703?), *A Confirmation of the Losses Sustained by Colonel John Michelburne, Late Governor of Londonderry* (London?, 1704?), *The Case of Colonel John Michelburn, Late Gov[erno]r of London-Derry, further Consider'd* (London?, 1706?).

30. British Library Stowe MS 977.

31. First printed in Dublin in 1738, it appeared in Belfast in 1744, Newry 1774, and Strabane 1787.

32. Ashton's play was first published in Dublin (the 1728 edn); like *The Siege* it was published next in Belfast (1767) then in Newry and Strabane in the 1780s.

33. *The Life of William Carleton*, introd. Cashel Hoey, 2 vols. (London, 1896), I, 25-8. On the grass-roots reception and currency of *The Siege* and *The Battle of Aughrim*, see J. R. R. Adams, *The Printed Word and the Common Man: Popular Culture in Ulster, 1700-1900* (Belfast: Institute of Irish Studies, Queen's University Belfast, 1987), 27-9, 70, Niall Ó Ciosáin, *Print and Popular Culture in Ireland, 1750-1850* (Basingstoke: Macmillan, 1997), ch. 6.

34. The version on my own shelves, condensed and packaged with *The Battle of Aughrim*, Goldsmith's *Deserted Village*, John Philips's *The Splendid Shilling*, and a selection of Moore's *Irish Melodies*, claims to be the first American, from the twentieth Dublin, edn. (Rochester, NY, 1827).

35. George Walker, *A Sermon Being an Incouragement for Protestants* (London, 1689), rpt. Edinburgh in the same year; Seth Whittle, *A Sermon Preached before the Garrison of London-Derry in the Extremity of the Siege* (Edinburgh, 1689)—there was a London edn. in 1690.

36. Sam Burnside, 'No Temporising with the Foe: Literary Materials Relating to the Siege and Relief of Derry', *Linen Hall Review*, 5/3 (Autumn 1988): 4-9;

Ian McBride, *The Siege of Derry in Ulster Protestant Mythology* (Dublin: Four Courts, 1997).

37. James Sutherland, 'New Light on George Farquhar', *Times Literary Supplement*, 6 March 1937: 171.

38. *The Works of George Farquhar*, ed. Shirley Strum Kenny, 2 vols. (Oxford: Clarendon, 1988), II, 309–12, p. 309.

39. Cf. *Love and a Bottle*, III.i.193–5, where Roebuck is told, 'I suppose, Sir, you are some conceited young Scribler, who has got the benefits of a first Play in your Pocket, and are now going a Fortune hunting.'

40. See e.g. S. J. Connolly, *Religion, Law and Power: The Making of Protestant Ireland 1660–1760* (Oxford: Clarendon, 1992), 114–21.

41. L. M. Cullen, 'Economic Development, 1691–1750', in *Eighteenth-Century Ireland 1691–1800*, ed. T. W. Moody and W. E. Vaughan, A New History of Ireland, 4 (Oxford: Clarendon, 1986), 123–58, p. 135.

42. *Works of Farquhar*, ed. Kenny, I, 12.

43. E.g. 'dear Joy', 'Shild' (child), 'pouge' (bag), and 'Oh hone' (a cry of lamentation); IV.ii.146–63.

44. On Fingal see above pp. 64–5 and cp. the 'Fingall *Dance*' in Mitchelbourne, *Siege*, 14. The Oxford editor's note at this point shows that interpretations can be too archipelagic: 'Fingal's Cave, on Staffa, an uninhabited islet of the Inner Hebrides, is wild and remote. Farquhar seems to refer to the dress of the islanders.'

45. Trinity College Dublin MS 201; cited in *St Stephen's-Green: Or, The Generous Lovers*, ed. Christopher Murray (Portlaoise: Dolmen, 1980), 9.

46. Ibid, 14.

47. Composed between *c.*1618 and 1634, Keating's great contribution to Gaelic historiography crossed into English, in a version by Michael Kearney, as early as 1635, and other translations (Latin as well as English) were current by the 1670s; Peter Walsh's *A Prospect of the State of Ireland from the Year of the World 1756 to the Year of Christ 1652* ([London], 1682) draws heavily on a translation made available to the author by the Earl of Anglesey; it was finally printed in English, as *The General History of Ireland*, tr. Dermot O'Connor, in London, 1723. For the whole tradition see Cunningham, *World of Geoffrey Keating*, chs. 10–11.

48. Hugh MacCurtin, *A Brief Discourse in Vindication of the Antiquity of Ireland* (Dublin, 1717) is a reply to Cox, *Hibernia Anglicana*.

49. See the dedication to Ormond, in *The Revengeful Queen* (London, 1698), A3v.

50. 'So many St[r]ait Fellows in Red out of Employment'; *St Stephen's-Green: Or, The Generous Lovers* (Dublin, 1700), 4.

51. Patrick Kelly, 'Recasting a Tradition: William Molyneux and the Sources of *The Case of Ireland … Stated* (1698)', in Ohlmeyer (ed.), *Political Thought in Seventeenth-Century Ireland*, 83–106, pp. 84–5.

52. Philip O'Regan, 'Archbishop William King (1650−1729) and the Constitution of Church and State', 2 vols., Ph. D. dissertation (National University of Ireland, 1996), 126.

53. 6 Geo. I, c. 5.

54. See Michael Ryder, 'The Bank of Ireland, 1721: Land, Credit and Dependency', *Historical Journal*, 25 (1982): 557−82.

55. *A Proposal for the Universal Use of Irish Manufacture* (1720), in Jonathan Swift, *Irish Tracts 1720−1723 and Sermons*, ed. Herbert Davis and Louis Landa (Oxford: Blackwell, 1948), 13−22, pp. 17, 21−2.

56. 23 March 1721, to Francis Annesley; quoted in Irvin Ehrenpreis, *Swift: The Man, his Works, and the Age*, 3 vols. (London: Methuen, 1962−83), III, 157.

57. *Case of Ireland, Stated*, 148.

58. Connolly, *Religion, Law and Power*; C. D. A. Leighton, *Catholicism in a Protestant Kingdom: A Study of the Irish Ancien Régime* (Basingstoke: Macmillan, 1994).

59. Ibid., 98.

60. See Jim Smyth, ' "No Remedy More Proper": Anglo-Irish Unionism before 1707', in Brendan Bradshaw and Peter Roberts (eds.), *British Consciousness and Identity: The Making of Britain, 1533−1707* (Cambridge: Cambridge University Press, 1998), 301−20, qualified by David Hayton, 'Ideas of Union in Anglo-Irish Political Discourse, 1692−1720: Meaning and Use', in D. George Boyce, Robert Eccleshall and Vincent Geoghagan (eds.), *Political Discourse in Seventeenth- and Eighteenth-Century Ireland* (Basingstoke: Palgrave, 2001), 142−68.

61. Cf. Patrick Kelly, 'Ireland and the Glorious Revolution: From Kingdom to Colony', in Robert Beddard (ed.), *The Revolutions of 1688* (Oxford: Clarendon, 1991), 163−90, p. 188.

62. His position might be summarized by one of the 'Hints for Intelligencer Papers &c.', 'Scotch worse than Irish, but worst when partake of both nations'; Jonathan Swift, *Irish Tracts 1728−1733*, ed. Herbert Davis (Oxford: Blackwell, 1955), 306. For an overview see Christopher Fox, 'Swift's Scotophobia' *Bullán*, 6/2 (2002): 43−65.

63. *Hibernia Freed* (London, 1722), 3.

64. James Macpherson, *Original Papers; Containing the Secret History of Great Britain, from the Accession of the House of Hannover*, vol. II (London, 1775), 379; quoted by Christopher J. Wheatley, *Beneath Iërne's Banners: Irish Protestant Drama of the Restoration and Eighteenth Century* (Notre Dame: University of Notre Dame Press, 1999), 53.

65. *The Freeholder's Journal*, quoted in *The London Stage 1660−1800. Part 2: 1700−1729*, ed. Emmett L. Avery, 2 vols. (Carbondale: Southern Illinois University Press, 1960), clxiv.

66. Wheatley, *Beneath Iërne's Banners*, 60.

67. See e.g. Colin Kidd, *British Identities before Nationalism: Ethnicity and Nationhood in the Atlantic World, 1600–1800* (Cambridge: Cambridge University Press, 1999), 178–9.

68. See J. G. Simms, *William Molyneux of Dublin*, ed. P. H. Kelly (Blackrock: Irish Academic Press, 1982), 335–8, on Molyneux's relationship with the Gaelic scholar Roderic O'Flaherty.

CHAPTER 11

1. See John Robert Moore, 'Daniel Defoe: King William's Pamphleteer and Intelligence Agent', *Huntington Library Quarterly*, 34 (1971): 251–60, p. 255. On the possibility of visits in the 1680s, see James Sutherland, *Defoe*, 2nd edn. (1950; New York: Barnes and Noble, 1971), 30.

2. John Bell to [Robert Harley] (1 October 1796), Historical Manuscript Commission, Fifteenth Report, appendix, part IV, *The Manuscripts of his Grace the Duke of Portland*, vol. IV (London: Her Majesty's Stationery Office, 1897), 335.

3. See esp. David Macree, 'Daniel Defoe, the Church of Scotland, and the Union of 1707', *Eighteenth-Century Studies*, 7/1 (1973): 62–77; Spiro Peterson, 'Defoe in Edinburgh, 1707', *Huntington Library Quarterly*, 38/1 (1974): 21–33; Paula R. Backscheider, *Daniel Defoe: His Life* (Baltimore: Johns Hopkins University Press, 1989), 203–52, 264, 276–81; P. H. Scott, *Defoe in Edinburgh and Other Papers* (East Linton: Tuckwell, 1995), 3–17; Maximillian E. Novak, *Daniel Defoe, Master of Fictions: His Life and Ideas* (Oxford: Oxford University Press, 2001), ch. 13; John Richetti, *The Life of Daniel Defoe* (Oxford: Blackwell, 2005), 115–22.

4. Sir John Clerk of Penicuik, *Observations on the Present Circumstances of Scotland*, ed. T. C. Smout, in Scottish History Society, 4th series, 2, *Miscellany X* (1965), 177–212, p. 192.

5. *Memoirs of the Life of Sir John Clerk of Penicuik … 1676–1755*, ed. John M. Gray, Scottish History Society, 1st series, 13 (1892), 64.

6. *An Essay, at Removing National Prejudices, against a Union with England. Part III* (Edinburgh, 1706), 34; cf. his periodical, *A Review of the State of the British Nation* [until 6 March 1707, entitled, *A Review of the State of the English Nation*], 4/21 (29 March 1707): 82.

7. *The Review Review'd. In a Letter to the Prophet Daniel in Scotland* (1707), ed. in Maximillian E. Novak, 'A Whiff of Scandal in the Life of Daniel Defoe', *Huntington Library Quarterly*, 34/1 (1970): 35–42, p. 38.

8. *The Letters of Daniel Defoe*, ed. George Harris Healey (Oxford: Clarendon, 1955), 158–9 (26 November 1706, to Robert Harley).

9. *Letters*, 43 (July–August 1704?).

10. My attributions follow the abstemious P. N. Furbank and W. R. Owens, *Critical Bibliography of Daniel Defoe* (London: Pickering and Chatto, 1998).

11. Cf. Backscheider, *Daniel Defoe*, 234ff.

12. *The Dissenters in England Vindicated* (Edinburgh, 1707); *Passion and Prejudice, the Support of One Another, and Both Destructive to the Happiness of this Nation, in Church and State* (Edinburgh, 1707); and *A Short View of the Present State of the Protestant Religion in Britain* (Edinburgh, 1707). Cf. *A Voice from the South: Or, An Address from some Protestant Dissenters in England to the Kirk of Scotland* (Edinburgh, 1707); *An Historical Account of the Bitter Sufferings, and Melancholly Circumstances of the Episcopal Church in Scotland, under the Barbarous Usage and Bloody Persecution of the Presbyterian Church Government* (Edinburgh, 1707)—an ironical pamphlet, classed as probably canonical by Furbank and Owens; *The Scot's Narrative Examin'd: Or, The Case of the Episcopal Ministers in Scotland Stated* (London, 1709); *Greenshields out of Prison and Toleration Settled in Scotland* (London, 1710), classed as probable by Furbank and Owens.

13. Cf. the political interventions, *An Enquiry into the Disposal of the Equivalent* (Edinburgh, 1706?), *A Short Letter to the Glasgow-Men* (Edinburgh, 1706); also *Memorial to the Nobility of Scotland* (Edinburgh, 1708), classed as probable by Furbank and Owens.

14. *The Vision, a Poem* (Edinburgh, 1706); *A Reply to the Scots Answer, to the British Vision* (Edinburgh, 1706).

15. On the origins and continuity of Jacobite anti-unionism see e.g. David Daiches, *Scotland and Union* (London: John Murray, 1977), 42–3.

16. *History of the Union of Great Britain* (Edinburgh, 1709), [§*An Account of the Proceedings ... Within the Parliament of Scotland*], 98.

17. *Letters*, 211 (18 March 1707); cf. 176 (27 January 1707), to Harley.

18. The classic refutation of deterministic accounts is W. Ferguson, 'The Making of the Treaty of Union of 1707', *Scottish Historical Review*, 43 (1964): 89–110; for a richly documented nationalist analysis, see Paul Henderson Scott, *The Union of 1707: Why and How* (Edinburgh: Saltire Society, 2006); on long-term divergence see Mark Goldie, 'Divergence and Union: Scotland and England, 1660–1707', in Brendan Bradshaw and John Morrill (eds.), *The British Problem, c.1534–1707* (London: Macmillan, 1996), 220–45, and, on limited elements of convergence, Julian Goodare, *State and Society in Early Modern Scotland* (Oxford: Oxford University Press, 1999), 314–17, 337–9.

19. Christopher A. Whatley with Derek J. Patrick, *The Scots and the Union* (Edinburgh: Edinburgh University Press, 2006), 5, 29–31, 37, 79–82 *et passim*. This is also the culmination of the story told by Ginny Gardner, *The Scottish Exile Community in the Netherlands, 1660–1690* (East Linton: Tuckwell, 2004).

20. See e.g. Douglas Watt, *The Price of Scotland: Darien, Union and the Wealth of Nations* (Edinburgh: Luath, 2006).

21. *Jure Divino: A Satyr* (London, 1706), 277.

22. 'Such a Parcel of Rogues in a Nation', in *Burns: Poems and Songs*, ed. James Kinsley (Oxford: Oxford University Press, 1969), 511–12, p. 512.

23. *Review*, 3/137 (16 November 1706): 546; he more frankly told Harley, 'In short, Money Will do anything here' (*Letters*, 214 (3 April 1707)).

24. P. W. J. Riley, *The Union of England and Scotland: A Study in Anglo-Scottish Politics of the Eighteenth Century* (Manchester: Manchester University Press, 1978), 240.

25. Cf. George Ridpath, who likens the pre−1707 relationship of England and Scotland to that between Poland and Lithuania (joined by the Union of Lublin, 1569), in *Considerations upon the Union of the Two Kingdoms* (Edinburgh?, 1706), 36−8.

26. *The Dyet of Poland*, line 541, in *Poems on Affairs of State: Augustan Satirical Verse, 1660−1714*, gen. ed. George DeF. Lord, 7 vols. (New Haven: Yale University Press, 1963−75), VII, 72−132.

27. There are 535 items in W. R. and V. B. McLeod, *Anglo-Scottish Tracts, 1701−1714: A Descriptive Checklist* (Lawrence, KA: University of Kansas Libraries, 1979).

28. See John Robertson (ed.), *A Union for Empire: Political Thought and the British Union of 1707* (Cambridge: Cambridge University Press, 1995), which includes essays on Defoe by Laurence Dickey and Katherine R. Penovich.

29. John Robertson, 'An Elusive Sovereignty: The Course of the Union Debate in Scotland 1698−1707', in idem. (ed.), *Union for Empire*, 198−227, p. 225.

30. *Letters*, 176 (19 December 1706, to Harley).

31. *Caledonia, &c. A Poem in Honour of Scotland, and the Scots Nation* (Edinburgh, 1706); here quoting London edn. (1707), 25.

32. On Selkirk's Scottishness and piety see Woodes Rogers, *A Cruising Voyage Round the World* (1712), ed. G. E. Manwaring (London: Cassell, 1928), 91−2.

33. *The History and Remarkable Life of the Truly Honourable Col. Jacque Commonly Call'd Col. Jack*, ed. Samuel Holt Monk (1965; London: Oxford University Press, 1970), 308.

34. James Hodges, *The Rights and Interests of the Two British Monarchies* (Edinburgh, 1703), 64−5. For contexts see William Ferguson, 'Imperial Crowns: A Neglected Facet of the Background to the Treaty of Union of 1707', *Scottish Historical Review*, 53 (1974): 22−44.

35. E.g. Sir William Seton of Pitmedden, *A Speech in Parliament, The Second Day of November 1706* (Edinburgh, 1706), 10.

36. Cf. e.g. George Mackenzie, 1st Earl of Cromarty, *Parainesis Pacifica: Or, A Perswasive to the Union of Britain* (London, 1702), 4.

37. *Rights and Interests*, 64.

38. *Scotland's Relations with England: A Survey to 1707* (Edinburgh: John Donald, 1977), 241.

39. *Parainesis Pacifica*, 4.

40. Brian P. Levack, *The Formation of the British State: England, Scotland, and the Union 1603−1707* (Oxford: Clarendon 1987), 204−6.

41. *Review*, 4/36 (3 May 1707): 141; 4/39 (10 May 1707): 154.

42. Actual circumstances and effects (often not clear at the time) have been persuasively reassessed by Christopher A. Whatley, 'Economic Causes and Consequences of the Union of 1707: A Survey', *Scottish Historical Review*, 58 (1989): 150–81 and, reflecting on the psychology of impoverishment, 'Taking Stock: Scotland at the End of the Seventeenth Century', in T. C. Smout (ed.), *Anglo-Scottish Relations from 1603–1900, Proceedings of the British Academy*, 127 (2005): 103–25, esp. pp. 107–9.

43. *Review*, I [IX]/214 (11 June 1713); cf. the prose hymn to trade in *Review*, 4/6 (22 February 1706): 23.

44. Whatley and Patrick, *Scots and the Union*, 44.

45. *An Account of a Conversation Concerning a Right Regulation of Governments for the Common Good of Mankind* (Edinburgh, 1704), in *Andrew Fletcher: Political Works*, ed. John Robertson (Cambridge: Cambridge University Press, 1997), 175–215, p. 193. Cf. Hodges, *Rights and Interests*, 68.

46. Andrew Symson, *Sir George M'Kenzie's Arguments against an Incorporating Union Particularly Considered* (Edinburgh, 1706), 15.

47. Cf. Fletcher, *Account*, 194–5.

48. For contexts see Colin Kidd, *Subverting Scotland's Past: Scottish Whig Historians and the Creation of an Anglo-British Identity, 1689–c.1830* (Cambridge: Cambridge University Press, 1993), 43–50.

49. Riley, *Union of England and Scotland*, 285.

50. *War Betwixt the Two British Kingdoms Consider'd* (London, 1705), 85.

51. Paterson, *An Inquiry into the Reasonableness and Consequences of an Union with Scotland* (London, 1706), 73–81, 149–52; Molyneux *The Case of Ireland's being Bound by Acts of Parliament in England, Stated* (Dublin, 1698), 98.

52. *A Fourth Essay, at Removing National Prejudices* (Edinburgh, 1706), 36; III, 8; III, 18.

53. Cromarty, *Parainesis Pacifica*, 4; Defoe, *Fourth Essay*, 41–2; cf. Paterson, *Inquiry*, 88–9; and, for Seton and Clerk of Penicuik, *Andrew Fletcher: Political Works*, ed. Robertson, 196.

54. *An Essay at Removing National Prejudices against a Union with Scotland ... Part I* (London, 1706), 14.

55. *An Essay at Removing National Prejudices against a Union with Scotland ... Part II* (London, 1706), 8–9.

56. Seton, *Speech in Parliament*, 8.

57. Cromarty, *Parainesis Pacifica*, 5; cf. 22.

58. E.g. Seton, *Speech in Parliament*, 7.

59. Seton, *The Interest of Scotland in Three Essays* (Edinburgh[?], 1700), 61.

60. *Caledonia*, 18.

61. *Caledonia*, 33–5; *Essay I*, 28.

62. *Interest of Scotland*, 57.

63. See e.g. Defoe, *A Scots Poem: Or, A New-Years Gift, from a Native of the Universe, to His Fellow-Animals in Albania* (Edinburgh, 1707), 5. Cp. David

Armitage, 'Making the Empire British: Scotland in the Atlantic World 1542–1717', *Past and Present*, 155 (1997): 34–63.

64. Cf. Ian Ross and Stephen Scobie, 'Patriotic Publishing as a Response to the Union', in T. I. Rae (ed.), *The Union of 1707: Its Impact on Scotland* (Edinburgh: Blackie and Son, 1974), 94–119; George M. Brunsden, 'Aspects of Scotland's Social, Political, and Cultural Scene in the Late 17th and Early 18th Centuries, as Mirrored in the Wallace and Bruce Traditions', in Edward J. Cowan and Douglas Gifford (eds.), *The Polar Twins* (Edinburgh: John Donald, 1999), 75–113.

65. *Essay II*, 4, 31.

66. *A Tour through the Whole Island of Great Britain*, introd. G. D. H. Cole and D. C. Browning, 2 vols. in 1 (London: Dent, 1974), II, 291–2, 316.

67. 3/118 (3 October 1706): 470.

68. His concealments and distortions are summarized by Backscheider, *Daniel Defoe*, 232; for hostility see e.g. George Lockhart, *'Scotland's Ruine': Lockhart of Carnwath's Memoirs of the Union*, ed. Daniel Szcchi (Aberdeen: Association for Scottish Literary Studies, 1995), 147.

69. Sutherland *Defoe*, 168–9.

70. *Review*, 3/120 (8 October 1706): 478.

71. *Review*, 4/16 (18 March 1707): 61. Cf. *Review*, 3/139 (21 November 1706): 553; 3/145 (5 December 1706): 577–8.

72. *Review*, 4/15 (15 March 1707): 58.

73. *Review*, 4/21 (29 March 1707): 81.

74. *History* [§*An Abstract of the Proceedings*], 34.

75. *A Scots Answer to a British Vision*, lines 46–9, in *Poems on Affairs of State*, VII, 221–6. For accounts of the exchange see David Macaree, 'The Flyting of Daniel Defoe and Lord Belhaven', *Studies in Scottish Literature*, 13 (1978): 72–80, and Leith Davis, *Acts of Union: Scotland and the Literary Negotiation of the British Nation, 1707–1830* (Stanford: Stanford University Press, 1998), ch. 1.

76. Cf. B. McPhail, 'Scotland's Sovereignty Asserted: The Debate over the Anglo-Scottish Union of 1707', *Parergon*, n.s. 11/2 (December 1993): 27–44, p. 42.

77. E.g. *Review*, 3/140 (23 November 1706): 559–60; 3/147 (10 December 1706): 586; 3/150 (17 December 1706): 597–9.

78. *The Storm: Or, A Collection of the Most Remarkable Casualties and Disasters which Happen'd in the Late Dreadful Tempest, both by Sea and Land* (London, 1704), A3^{v}.

79. *History* [§*Of the Carrying on of the Treaty in Scotland*], 29.

80. 'Daniel Defoe', in *Sir Walter Scott on Novelists and Fiction*, ed. Ioan Williams (London: Routledge and Kegan Paul, 1968), 164–83, pp. 172–3.

81. *History*, 29.

82. Lom's 'Oran an Aghaidh an Aonaidh' ('A Song Against the Union') fiercely regrets the dispersal of the men who rose with the Duke of Atholl in

1707 (*Orain Iain Luim: Songs of John MacDonald, Bard of Keppoch*, ed. Annie M. MacKenzie, Scottish Gaelic Texts Society (Edinburgh: Oliver and Boyd, 1964), 222–9).

83. *Letters*, 222–3 (21 May 1707).

84. Backscheider, *Daniel Defoe*, 311; *Tour*, II, 281.

85. Daniel Szechi and David Hayton, 'John Bull's Other Kingdoms: The Government of Scotland and Ireland', in Clyve Jones (ed.), *Britain in the First Age of Party 1680–1750: Essays Presented to Geoffrey Holmes* (London: Hambledon Press, 1987), 241–80, p. 248.

86. E.g. *The Present State of the Parties in Great Britain: Particularly an Enquiry into the State of the Dissenters in England, and the Presbyterians in Scotland* (London, 1712), *Union and No Union. Being an Enquiry into the Grievances of the Scots* (London, 1713). Cf. the 'probable' texts *The Highland Visions: Or, The Scots New Prophesy* (London, 1712) and *The Second-Sighted Highlander: Or, Predictions and Foretold Events* (London, 1713).

87. Some doubt attaches to the authorship of the *View*. Cf. *A True Account of the Proceedings at Perth* (London, 1716) and the anonymous introduction to *A Journal of the Earl of Mar's Proceedings* (London, 1716), both with claims to Defoe's authorship though removed from the canon by Furbank and Owens.

88. For the attribution see John Robert Moore, *A Checklist of the Writings of Daniel Defoe*, 2nd edn. (Hamden, CT: Shoe String Press, 1971), 233. The relevant issues of the journal are distributed through May, June, August, September, and December 1716, and January 1717; cf. *An Essay upon Buying and Selling of Speeches* (London, 1716), an attack, probably by Defoe, on a House of Commons speech by Richard Steele (February 1716) recommending mercy for the Jacobite rebels.

89. *Daniel Defoe: Ambition and Innovation* (Lexington, Ky: University Press of Kentucky, 1986), 144–5.

90. Cp. *Colonel Jack*, 265, with *Tour*, II, 427–8 (referring, like the novel, to the defeat of the Germans at Cremona).

91. Lines 41–2; *Poems on Affairs of State*, VII, 209–20.

92. *Review*, 3/154 (26 December 1706): 614.

93. *Review*, 3/128 (26 October 1706): 510; cf. 3/129 (29 October 1706): 513–15.

94. *Review*, 3/149 (14 December 1706): 594, *Review*, 3/155 (28 December 1706): 618; cf. *History* [§*Of the Last Treaty, Properly Called the Union*], 56–60.

95. E.g., in the treatment of bankrupts: *Review*, 4/25 (8 April 1707): 99–100; *Review*, 4/38 (8 May 1707): 151–2.

96. *Review*, 4/38 (8 May 1707): 149.

97. See e.g. P. W. J. Riley, *The English Ministers and Scotland 1707–1727* (London: Athlone Press, 1964), 279, 286.

98. *The True-Born Englishman*, lines 334–7, in *Poems on Affairs of State*, VI, 259–309.

99. 3/122 (12 October 1706): 485.

100. No. VI; 18 January 1720.

101. On the Jacobite difficulties at Preston see Daniel Szechi, *1715: The Great Jacobite Rebellion* (New Haven: Yale University Press, 2006), 175–81.

102. Cf. J. R. Moore, Defoe's Use of Personal Experience in *Colonel Jack*', *Modern Language Notes*, 54 (1939): 362–3.

103. *Tour*, II, 85.

104. Hugh Douglas, *Jacobite Spy Wars: Moles, Rogues and Treachery* (Stroud: Sutton, 1999).

105. Opinions range from J. A. Downie, *Robert Harley and the Press: Propaganda and Public Opinion in the Age of Swift and Defoe* (Cambridge: Cambridge University Press, 1979), 76–7, who plays down Defoe's influence, through William Ferguson, *Scotland's Relations with England*, 240, who thinks his 'propaganda value ... was considerable', to Frank H. Ellis, who in *Poems on Affairs of State*, VI, 210–13, takes him at the valuation of his necessarily self-promoting letters to Harley.

CHAPTER 12

1. Sir Walter Scott, *Waverley: Or, 'Tis Sixty Years Since*, ed. Claire Lamont (Oxford: Clarendon, 1981), 32.

2. E.g. Colin Kidd, *British Identities before Nationalism: Ethnicity and Nationhood in the Atlantic World, 1600–1800* (Cambridge: Cambridge University Press, 1999), 135.

3. 'Culloden Papers: Comprising an Extensive and Interesting Correspondence from the Year 1625 to 1748 ... ', *Quarterly Review*, 14 (1815–16): 283–333.

4. Duncan Forbes, 'The Rationalism of Sir Walter Scott', *Cambridge Journal*, 7 (1953): 20–35; Peter Garside, 'Scott and the "Philosophical" Historians', *Journal of the History of Ideas*, 36 (1975): 497–512.

5. London: Methuen, 1930.

6. See e.g. Colin Kidd, 'Eighteenth-Century Scotland and the Three Unions', in T. C. Smout (ed.), *Anglo-Scottish Relations from 1603–1900, Proceedings of the British Academy*, 127 (2005): 13–35. For an overview of Scottish attitudes under the regal union itself, see Maurice Lee, Jr., 'The "Inevitable" Union: Absentee Government in Scotland, 1603–1707', in his *The 'Inevitable' Union and Other Essays on Early Modern Scotland* (East Linton: Tuckwell, 2003), 1–24.

7. Tim Harris, *Restoration: Charles II and his Kingdoms, 1660–1685* (London: Allen Lane, 2005), 347.

8. For the bigger picture see Allan I. Macinnes, *Clanship, Commerce and the House of Stuart, 1603–1788* (East Linton: Tuckwell, 1996).

9. See e.g. the concluding paragraph of William Robertson, *The History of Scotland, During the Reigns of Queen Mary and of King James VI till his Accession to the Crown of England*, 2 vols. (London, 1759), II, 260.

10. Jim Smyth, *The Making of the United Kingdom, 1660–1800: State, Religion and Identity in Britain and Ireland* (Harlow: Longman, 2001), 109.

11. On seventeenth-century sources of the Scottish enlightenment (including an exposure to English culture that long preceded 1707), see R. H. Campbell and Andrew S. Skinner (eds.), *The Origins and Nature of the Scottish Enlightenment* (Edinburgh: Donald, 1982); David Allan, *Virtue, Learning, and the Scottish Enlightenment: Ideas of Scholarship in Early Modern History* (Edinburgh: Edinburgh University Press, 1993); and Alexander Broadie, *The Scottish Enlightenment: The Historical Age of the Historical Nation* (Edinburgh: Birlinn, 2001).

12. *Scotland and Scotsmen in the Eighteenth Century from the Manuscripts of John Ramsay of Ochtertyre*, ed. Alexander Allardyce (Edinburgh: W. Blackwood and Sons, 1888), 6–7. Cf. Nicholas Phillipson, 'Politics, Politeness and the Anglicisation of Early Eighteenth-Century Scottish Culture', in Roger A. Mason (ed.), *Scotland and England, 1286–1815* (Edinburgh: Donald, 1987), 226–46.

13. Cf. the introduction, p. 72, on the establishment of the office of Postmaster General in Edinburgh in 1695 and changes in the licensing of newspapers from 1699.

14. Note esp. the patriotic James Watson's *Choice Collection of Comic and Serious Scots Poems*, 3 pts. (Edinburgh, 1706–11). For secondary discussion, see, n. 64 to Chapter 11.

15. James Thomson and David Mallet, *Alfred: A Masque. Represented before Their Royal Highnesses the Prince and Princess of Wales, at Cliffden, on the first of August, 1740* (London, 1740), 42.

16. Mary Jane Scott, 'The Manuscript of James Thomson's Scots Elegy', *Studies in Scottish Literature*, 17 (1982): 135–44.

17. Derick S. Thomson, 'Gaelic Poetry in the Eighteenth Century: The Breaking of the Mould', in Cairns Craig (gen. ed.), *The History of Scottish Literature*, vol. II, *1660–1800*, ed. Andrew Hook (Aberdeen: Aberdeen University Press, 1987), 175–89, pp. 181–2.

18. For an assessment of Scottish elements see Mary Jane W. Scott, *James Thomson, Anglo-Scot* (Athens, GA: University of Georgia Press, 1988).

19. James Sambrook, *James Thomson, 1700–1748: A Life* (Oxford: Clarendon, 1991), 16.

20. E.g. Kenneth Simpson, *The Protean Scot: The Crisis of Identity in Eighteenth-Century Scottish Literature* (Aberdeen: Aberdeen University Press, 1988).

21. Susan Manning, 'Post-Union Scotland and the Scottish Idiom of Britishness', in Ian Brown (gen. ed.), *The Edinburgh History of Scottish Literature*, 3 vols. (Edinburgh: Edinburgh University Press, 2006), II, 45–56, p. 49.

22. In about 1752 Hume anonymously published a list of *Scotticisms*. Another striking example is provided by James Beattie (author of *The Minstrel*), *Scoticisms, Arranged in Alphabetical Order* (Edinburgh, 1787). Cf. James G. Basker, 'Scotticisms and the Problem of Cultural Identity in Eighteenth-Century Britain', in John Dwyer and Richard B. Sher (eds.), *Sociability and Society in Eighteenth-Century Scotland* (Edinburgh: Mercat, 1993), pp. 81—95.

23. James Thomson, *Spring* (London, 1728), 42—3.

24. Cf. Murray Pittock, 'Historiography', in Alexander Broadie (ed.), *The Cambridge Companion to the Scottish Enlightenment* (Cambridge University Press, 2003), 258—79, p. 275.

25. 'The Tears of Scotland', lines 23—4, in Tobias Smollett, *Poems, Plays, and 'The Briton'*, ed. O. M. Brack, introd. Byron Gassman (Athens, GA: University of Georgia Press, 1993).

26. *The Monthly Review* (May, 1757), in *Collected Works of Oliver Goldsmith*, ed. Arthur Friedman, 5 vols. (Oxford: Clarendon, 1966), I, 10—14, pp. 12—13.

27. Robert Colvill, *The Field of Flowdon, A Descriptive Poem*, 9, in *Occasional Poems* (Edinburgh, 1771).

28. Geoffrey Plank, *Rebellion and Savagery: The Jacobite Rising of 1745 and the British Empire* (Philadelphia: University of Pennsylvania Press, 2006).

29. *Essays on the Superstitions of the Highlanders of Scotland: To Which are Added, Translations from the Gaelic*, 2 vols. (London: Longman, 1811).

30. *Eighteen Hundred and Thirteen: A Poem, in Two Parts* (Edinburgh: Ballantyne for Longman, 1814), 80.

31. '*Culloden Papers*', 331—3.

32. Cf. Jane Dawson, 'The Gaidhealtachd and the Emergence of the Scottish Highlands', in Brendan Bradshaw and Peter Roberts (eds.), *British Consciousness and Identity: The Making of Britain, 1533—1707* (Cambridge: Cambridge University Press, 1998), 259—300, esp. pp. 268—72, 287—300; Michael J. Braddick, *State Formation in Early Modern England c.1550—1700* (Cambridge: Cambridge University Press, 2000), 356—7.

33. For potent early statements see the antiquarian and ballad-forger, John Pinkerton's *Dissertation on the Origin and Progress of the Scythians or Goths* (London, 1787) and *Enquiry into the History of Scotland Preceding the Reign of Malcolm III, or the Year 1056* (London, 1789).

34. See e.g. Franklin E. Court, *Institutionalizing English Literature: The Culture and Politics of Literary Study, 1750—1900* (Stanford: Stanford University Press, 1992), ch. 4.

35. John Morrill, 'The War(s) of the Three Kingdoms', in Glen Burgess (ed.), *The New British History: Founding a Modern State 1603—1715* (London: Tauris, 1999), 65—91, p. 69.

36. Pittock, 'Historiography', 268.

37. *The History of Great Britain*, vol. I (Edinburgh, 1754), 17. Cf. his disapproval of Charles II's failure 'to effectuate a union' in 1670: *History of Great Britain*, vol. II (London, 1757), 199.

38. Colin Kidd, *Subverting Scotland's Past: Scottish Whig Historians and the Creation of an Anglo-British Identity, 1689-c.1830* (Cambridge: Cambridge University Press, 1993), chs. 1–6.

39. Susan Manning, *Fragments of Union: Making Connections in Scottish and American Writing* (Basingstoke: Palgrave, 2002), ch. 1.

40. *History of Scotland*, II, 254, 260.

41. *History of Great Britain*, I, 298–9.

42. *History of Great Britain*, I, 137–8. II, 125–6, 453.

43. See Blair's *Lectures on Rhetoric and Belles Lettres*, published in London as well as Edinburgh in 1783, after his retirement from the Regius chair of Rhetoric and Belles Lettres at the University of Edinburgh which had been created for him in 1762.

44. Crawford, *Devolving English Literature*, ch. 1; cf. idem. (ed.), *The Scottish Invention of English Literature* (Cambridge: Cambridge University Press, 1998).

45. Some are noted by Crawford; for the others, see D. J. Palmer, *The Rise of English Studies: An Account of the Study of English Language and Literature from its Origins to the Making of the Oxford English School* (London: Oxford University Press for the University of Hull, 1965), app. 1; Richard Terry, *Poetry and the Making of the English Literary Past, 1660–1781* (Oxford : Oxford University Press, 2001), 196–206; and Cairns Craig, 'The Study of Scottish Literature', in Brown (gen. ed.), *Edinburgh History of Scottish Literature*, I, 16–31, pp. 24–5.

46. Palmer, *Rise of English Studies*, app. 1; Crawford, *Devolving English Literature*, 41.

47. *The Works of Jonathan Swift*, ed. Walter Scott, 19 vols. (Edinburgh: Constable, 1814), IV, 424–5.

48. *The Poems of Jonathan Swift*, ed. Harold Williams, 3 vols., 2nd edn. (Oxford: Clarendon, 1958), 96.

49. *Jonathan Swift: The Complete Poems*, ed. Pat Rogers (Harmondsworth: Penguin, 1983), 627.

50. 'Maxims Controlled in Ireland: The Truth of Some Maxims in State and Government, Examined with Reference to Ireland', in Jonathan Swift, *Irish Tracts 1728–1733*, ed. Herbert Davis (Oxford: Blackwell, 1955), 131–7, p. 132.

51. On his 'unseemly' dependence on John Nichols' edns. of Swift (1801 and 1808) see John Sutherland, *The Life of Walter Scott: A Critical Biography* (Oxford: Blackwell, 1995), 166–7, citing Lee H. Potter, 'The Text of Scott's Edition of Swift', *Studies in Bibliography*, 22 (1969): 240–55.

52. On an early Petty catamaran (there were several prototypes) see 'In Laudem Navis Geminae E Portu Dublinij ad Regem Carolum IIdum Missae' (1663), in Andrew Carpenter (ed.), *Verse in English from Tudor and Stuart Ireland* (Cork: Cork University Press, 2003).

53. Richard Head, *Hic et Ubique: Or, The Humors of Dublin* (London, 1663), 4.

54. On Petty's 'hopelessly chimerical and virtually unimplementable' proposals for union see James Kelly, 'The Origins of the Act of Union: An Examination of Unionist Opinion in Britain and Ireland, 1650–1800', *Irish Historical Studies*, 25 (1986–7): 236–63, pp. 238–40.

55. See his 'Ode to the King: On his Irish Expedition and the Success of his Arms in General'.

56. *A Letter from a Member of the House of Commons in Ireland to a Member of the House of Commons in England, Concerning the Sacramental Test* (1709), in Jonathan Swift, *Bickerstaff Papers and Pamphlets on the Church*, ed. Herbert Davis (Oxford: Blackwell, 1940), 109–25, p. 113.

57. Katie Trumpener, *Bardic Nationalism: The Romantic Novel and the British Empire* (Princeton, NJ: Princeton University Press, 1997), 137.

58. Cf. Swift's poems 'The Description of a Salamander' (1705) and 'An Excellent New Ballad: Or, The True En[gli]sh D[ea]n to be Hang'd for a R[a]pe' (1730).

59. See e.g. in Scotland, William Wright, *The Comical History of the Marriage betwixt Fergusia and Heptarchus* (Edinburgh, 1706), and, in England, on a parliamentary committee: 'Sir John Packington disapproved of this incorporating union, which he likened to a marriage with a woman against her consent' (Tobias Smollett, *A Complete History of England, Deduced from the Descent of Julius Caesar, to the Treaty of Aix la Chapelle*, 4 vols. (London, 1757–8), IV, 329).

60. *The Story of the Injured Lady: Being a True Picture of Scotch Perfidy, Irish Poverty, and English Partiality* (1707, pub. 1746), in Jonathan Swift, *Irish Tracts 1720–1723 and Sermons*, ed. Herbert Davis and Louis Landa (Oxford: Blackwell, 1948), 1–12, p. 3.

61. 'Marginalia 12', in Jonathan Swift, *Miscellaneous and Autobiographical Pieces, Fragments and Marginalia*, ed. Herbert Davis (Oxford: Blackwell, 1962), 295–320; cf. his 'Short Remarks on Bishop Burnet's *History*' and 'Marginalia 11' on Burnet's *History of his Own Times* (1724–34), in the same volume (183–4, 266–94)—also contemptuous though less tediously rabid.

62. 'Letter IV. To the Whole People of Ireland', in Jonathan Swift, *The Drapier's Letters and Other Works 1724–1725*, ed. Herbert Davis (Oxford: Blackwell, 1941), 51–68, pp. 61–2.

63. *A Letter to the Right Honourable the Lord Viscount Molesworth* (1724), in *Drapier's Letters and Other Works*, ed. Davis, 77–94, p. 86.

64. From an essay published in the *Dublin Magazine*, 1931–2, quoted by Roy Foster, *W. B. Yeats: A Life*, vol. II, *The Arch-Poet 1915–1939* (Oxford: Oxford

University Press, 2003), 411. Yeats had been writing his play about the ghost of Swift, *Words upon the Window-Pane*.

65. *Swift's Irish Pamphlets: An Introductory Selection*, ed. Joseph McMinn (Gerrards Cross: Colin Smyth, 1991), 18.

66. 'To Quilca: A Country House in No Very Good Repair' (c.1725), quoting line 2.

67. Vivian Mercier, 'Swift and the Gaelic Tradition', in A. Norman Jeffares (ed.), *Fair Liberty was All His Cry: A Tercentenary Tribute to Jonathan Swift 1667–1745* (Macmillan: London, 1967), 279–89; Alan Harrison, *The Dean's Friend: Anthony Raymond 1675–1726, Jonathan Swift and the Irish Language* (Dublin: Éamonn de Búrca, 1999), ch. 5.

68. *An Answer to Several Letters Sent Me from Unknown Hands*, in *Irish Tracts 1728–1733*, 83–90, p. 89.

69. 'The Description of an Irish-Feast, Translated almost Literally out of the Original Irish' (1720, pub. 1735). Of the ninety-six lines of Irish, Swift translated 1–40 and 45–72; in his edn., XIV, 135–41, Scott reprinted the version of lines 41–4 given in a c.1782 translation of the poem by Charles Henry Wilson, and his own lively rendering of the rest. See Andrew Carpenter and Alan Harrison, 'Swift's "O'Rourke's Feast" and Sheridan's "Letter": Early Transcripts by Anthony Raymond', in Hermann J. Real and Heinz J. Vienken (eds.), *Proceedings of the First Münster Symposium on Jonathan Swift* (Munich: Wilhelm Fink, 1985), 27–46.

70. As the story goes: 'The Dean admired Carolan's genius, had him frequently at the Deanery House in Dublin, and used to hear him play and sing the *pléaráca* [i.e., *Pléaráca na Ruarcach*, 'O'Rourk's Feast']. He was particularly struck with the happy and singular onomatopoeia in several passages of the original, particularly that which represented the sound of the wet in the dancers' shoes, "*glug-glug i n-a mbróg*". This was thought to be inimitable by English words, till Carolan bade him send his servant to walk over shoes in a pool of water and then dance before him. This coincided with the Dean's own whimsical fancy. The experiment was made, and the Dean caught the sound and expressed it by "*Splish, splash in their pumps, etc.*" ' Quoted from an 1818 *History of the City of Dublin* by Carpenter and Harrison, 'Swift's "O'Rourke's Feast" ', 32, who note the inaccuracy of the Irish.

71. See Swift's poem, 'My Lady's Lamentation and Complaint against the Dean', lines 159–62.

72. See e.g. his *Proposal for Correcting, Improving and Ascertaining the English Language* (1712), in Jonathan Swift, *A Proposal for Correcting the English Tongue, Polite Conversation, Etc.*, ed. Herbert Davis with Louis Landa (Oxford: Blackwell, 1957), 3–21.

73. E.g. Blair, *Lectures on Rhetoric and Belles Lettres*, lect. x, though lect. xxiv has some acute reservations about the style of Swift's *Proposal for Correcting ... the English Language*.

74. Tony Crowley, *Wars of Words: The Politics of Language in Ireland 1537−2004* (Oxford: Oxford University Press, 2005), 80−1.

75. James Kelly, 'Origins of the Act of Union', 242−5, and his 'Public and Political Opinion in Ireland and the Idea of an Anglo-Irish Union, 1650−1800', in D. George Boyce, Robert Eccleshall, and Vincent Geoghegan (eds.), *Political Discourse in Seventeenth- and Eighteenth-Century Ireland* (Basingstoke: Palgrave, 2001), 110−41, pp. 115−21; Jim Smyth, ' "Like Amphibious Animals": Irish Protestants, Ancient Britons, 1691−1707', *Historical Journal*, 36 (1993): 785−97, ' "No Remedy More Proper": Anglo-Irish Unionism before 1707', in Bradshaw and Roberts (eds.), *British Consciousness and Identity*, 301−20, pp. 311−20, and his *Making of the United Kingdom*, 207−10. For scepticism about the sincerity of aspirations to union, see D. W. Hayton, 'Ideas of Union in Anglo-Irish Political Discourse, 1692−1720: Meaning and Use', in Boyce *et al.* (eds.), *Political Discourse*, 142−68.

76. Wills Hill, Marquis of Downshire, *A Proposal for Uniting the Kingdoms of Great Britain and Ireland* (Dublin, 1751).

77. *An Answer to the Late Proposal for Uniting the Kingdoms of Great Britain and Ireland; in Some Occasional Remarks upon the Proposal Itself* (Dublin, 1751), 33−4, 31, 48.

78. Robert Mahony, *Jonathan Swift: The Irish Identity* (New Haven: Yale University Press, 1995), chs. 2−3.

79. Jonathan Swift, *Gulliver's Travels*, ed. Harold Williams (Oxford: Blackwell, 1941), 138.

80. See the stringent critique by S. J. Connolly, 'Precedent and Principle: The Patriots and Their Critics', in idem. (ed.), *Political Ideas in Eighteenth-Century Ireland* (Dublin: Four Courts, 2000), 130−58, pp. 155−8.

81. E.g. Connolly, 'Introduction: Varieties of Irish Political Thought', in *Political Ideas in Eighteenth-Century Ireland*, 11−26, esp. 14−21.

82. *A Proposal for the Universal Use of Irish Manufacture*, in *Irish Tracts 1720−1723*, 13−22, p. 21.

83. There was a reprint at the time of Anglo-Scottish union, during the controversy over Wood's halfpence in the 1720s, and again in 1749, before the decade of troubles in America (1770, 1773, 1776).

84. Patrick Kelly, 'William Molyneux and the Spirit of Liberty in Eighteenth-Century Ireland', *Eighteenth-Century Ireland*, 3 (1988): 133−48; Jacqueline R. Hill, 'Ireland without Union: Molyneux and his Legacy', in John Robertson (ed.), *A Union for Empire: Political Thought and the British Union of 1707* (Cambridge: Cambridge University Press, 1995), 271−96.

85. Gerard O'Brien, 'The Grattan Mystique', *Eighteenth-Century Ireland*, 1 (1986): 170−94, pp. 190−4.

86. Note (f), to line 11.

87. E.g. Jacqueline R. Hill, 'Popery and Protestantism, Civil and Religious Liberty: The Disputed Lessons of Irish History, 1690−1812', *Past and Present*, 118 (1988): 96−129, pp. 104−5.

88. Eamonn O Ciardha, *Ireland and the Jacobite Cause, 1685−1766: A Fatal Attachment* (Dublin: Four Courts, 2002). The fullest account is in Irish: Brendán Ó Buachalla, *Aisling ghéar. Na Stíobhartaigh agus an t-aos léinn 1603−1788* (Baile Átha Cliath: An Clóchomhar Tta, 1996).

89. 'Popery and Protestantism', 105−6.

90. On Macpherson's use of Gaelic material, gathered on a tour of the Highlands in 1760, see Derick Thomson, *The Gaelic Sources of Macpherson's 'Ossian'* (Edinburgh: Oliver and Boyd, 1952); in relation to historiography, see Ian Haywood, *The Making of History: A Study of the Literary Forgeries of James Macpherson and Thomas Chatterton* (Rutherford: Fairleigh Dickinson University Press, 1986).

91. Clare O'Halloran, *Golden Ages and Barbarous Nations: Antiquarian Debate and Cultural Politics in Ireland, c.1750−1800* (Cork: Cork University Press/Field Day, 2004), 5.

92. Cf. Deana Rankin, 'Historical Writing, 1750−1800', in Raymond Gillespie and Andrew Hadfield (eds.), *The Irish Book in English 1550−1800*, The Oxford History of the Irish Book, 3 (Oxford: Oxford University Press, 2006), 282−300, p. 289.

93. Toby Barnard, '"Parlour Entertainment in an Evening?": Histories of the 1640s', in Micheál Ó Siochrú (ed.), *Kingdoms in Crisis: Ireland in the 1640s* (Dublin: Four Courts, 2001), 20−43.

94. Temple's book was rpt. at least ten times between the two Popish Plot-related, London edns. of 1679 and 1812, including additional London issues just after the '45 (two, in 1746) and a series in Dublin and Cork (1766). King's appeared over a dozen times, sometimes abridged and printed with Temple, between London edns. of 1691 and a Cork edn. of 1768, inc. one dated 1745 *Plainly Shewing Us*—as its title page puts it—*What we Are to Expect in Case of a Revolution at Present*. On the occasions of republication and links between the 1766 *Irish Rebellion*, the 1768 *State of the Protestants*, and Catholic, Whiteboy disturbances, see Thomas P. Power, 'Publishing and Sectarian Tension in South Munster in the 1760s', *Eighteenth-Century Ireland*, 19 (2004): 75−110.

95. As the only major Catholic account to appear between 1691 and the mid-eighteenth century, the *Impartial History* accumulated, in later editions, other documents illustrating grievances, including the text of the Treaty of Limerick (betrayed by William III under Irish Protestant pressure), the last speech of Oliver Plunkett, executed in 1681, and a 1724 case in support of Irish papists by Cornelius Nary. See Niall Ó Ciosáin, *Print and Popular Culture in Ireland, 1750−1850* (Basingstoke: Macmillan, 1997), 102−6.

96. Crouch, who published under the names Robert and Richard Burton, was a prolific writer of chapbooks, specializing in the production of historical epitomes. He was so successful—and we shall hear of him again (p. 392)—that, on both sides of the Irish sea, chapbooks were often known as 'Burton books'. Cf. Ó Ciosáin, *Print and Popular Culture in Ireland*, 106–7.

97. Jacqueline R. Hill, '1641 and the Quest for Catholic Emancipation, 1691–1829', in Brian Mac Cuarta (ed.), *Ulster, 1641: Aspects of the Rising* (Belfast: Institute of Irish Studies, Queen's University of Belfast, 1993), 159–71.

98. E.g. John Curry, *A Brief Account from the Most Authentic Protestant Writers of the Causes, Motives, and Mischiefs, of the Irish Rebellion, on the 23d day of October 1641, Deliver'd in Dialogue between a Dissenter, and a Member of the Church of Ireland* (London, 1747); Charles O'Conor, *A Counter-Appeal, to the People of Ireland* (Dublin, 1749).

99. O'Conor's full-length study never appeared, but Curry was persistent: in addition to his *Brief Account*, see his *Historical Memoirs of the Irish Rebellion in the Year, 1641* (London, 1758), and *An Historical and Critical Review of the Civil Wars in Ireland* (Dublin, 1786), a posthumous publication prepared for the press by O'Conor. Their most influential collaboration was the anonymously published *Observations on the Popery Laws* (Dublin, 1771), in which the seventeenth century is a zone into which the past rebelliousness of 'Papists' is securely consigned (33–6).

100. Norman Vance, 'Celts, Carthaginians and Constitutions: Anglo-Irish Literary Relations, 1780–1820', *Irish Historical Studies*, 22 (1981): 216–38; Francis G. James, 'Historiography and the Irish Constitutional Revolution of 1782', *Eire-Ireland*, 18 (1983): 6–16.

101. 'An Historical Sketch, of the Constitution, and Government of Ireland, From the Most Early Authenticated Period, Down to the Year 1783', in his *Strictures on the Ecclesiastical and Literary History of Ireland* (Dublin, 1789), 336–82,

102. Thomas Dermody, 'The Union', in his *Harp of Erin*, 2 vols. (London, 1807).

103. O'Halloran, *Golden Ages and Barbarous Nations*, 156–7. See esp. Sir Richard Musgrave, *Memoirs of the Different Rebellions in Ireland from the Arrival of the English, with a Particular Detail of that which Broke out the 23d. May, 1798* (Dublin: n.p., 1801), which ran through three edns. in two years.

104. Sources include G. C. Bolton, *The Passing of the Irish Act of Union* (Oxford: Oxford University Press, 1966); Patrick M. Geoghegan, *The Irish Act of Union: A Study in High Politics, 1798–1801* (Dublin: Gill and Macmillan, 1999); Dáire Keogh and Kevin Whelan (eds.), *Acts of Union: The Causes, Contexts and Consequences of the Act of Union* (Dublin: Four Courts, 2001); and Michael Brown, Patrick M. Geoghegan, and James Kelly (eds.), *The Irish Act of Union, 1800: Bicentennial Essays* (Dublin: Irish Academic Press, 2003)—the last of

which includes an authoritative review of 'The Historiography of the Act of Union' by Kelly, 5–36.

105. William Hamilton Drummond, *The Giant's Causeway: A Poem* (Belfast: J. Smith for Longman, 1811), 26.

106. W. J. McCormack, *The Pamphlet Debate on the Union between Great Britain and Ireland 1797–1800* (Dublin: Irish Academic Press, 1996) lists more than 300 items, the great bulk of them published in Dublin.

107. Henry James Pye, *Carmen Seculare for the Year 1800* (London, 1800), 43.

108. In addition to a full rpt. McCormack lists—for the busy Dubliner—*Extracts from de Foe's History of the Union* (68pp.), both published by John Exshaw in 1799.

109. For discussion of these courtship-as-union stories, see Trumpener, *Bardic Nationalism*, 134–7. Cf. Nicholas Robinson, 'Marriage against Inclination: The Union and Caricature', and Jane Elizabeth Dougherty, 'Mr and Mrs England: The Act of Union as National Marriage', in Keogh and Whelan (eds.), *Acts of Union*, 140–58, 202–15.

110. McCormack, *Pamphlet Debate*, 8–9.

111. 'General Preface' to the 1829 edn. of the Waverley Novels, in *Waverley*, ed. Lamont, 349–61, pp. 352–3.

112. Paul Henderson Scott, *Walter Scott and Scotland* (Edinburgh: William Blackwood, 1981), 21; Caroline McCracken-Flesher, *Possible Scotlands: Walter Scott and the Story of Tomorrow* (Oxford: Oxford University Press, 2005), 73–107.

113. E.g. 'I am very glad I did not live in 1745 for though as a lawyer I could not have pleaded Charles's right and as a clergyman I could not have prayed for him yet as a soldier I would I am sure against the convictions of my better reason have fought for him even to the bottom of the gallows.' To Miss Clephane, 13 July 1813, in *The Letters of Sir Walter Scott*, ed. H. J. C. Grierson, 12 vols. (London: Constable, 1932–7), III, 301–3, p. 302.

114. *Letters to the Editor of the Edinburgh Weekly Journal, from Malachi Malgrowther, Esq., on the Proposed Change of Currency*, in Sir Walter Scott, *Miscellaneous Prose Works*, 28 vols. (Edinburgh: Robert Cadell, 1834–6), XXI, 267–402, p. 270.

115. Above, p. 102.

116. The first printing of the letters uses the stanza of an old Scottish song as epigraph—'When the pipes begin to play | *Tutti taittie* to the drum, | Out claymore, and down wi' gun, | And to the rogues again'—but this was demoted to a half-apologetic footnote when the work was reprinted (332).

117. Christopher A. Whatley with Derek J. Patrick, *The Scots and the Union* (Edinburgh: Edinburgh University Press, 2006), 8.

118. Smollett, *Complete History of England*, IV, 327.

119. James Boswell, *The Journal of a Tour to the Hebrides, with Samuel Johnson, LL.D.* (London, 1785), 19–20.

120. T. C. Barnard, 'The Uses of 23 October 1641 and Irish Protestant Celebration', *English Historical Review*, 106 (1991): 889—920.

121. Pocock, 'Empire, State and Confederation: The War of American Independence as a Crisis in Multiple Monarchy', in Robertson (ed.), *A Union for Empire*, rpt. in Pocock's *The Discovery of Islands: Essays in British History* (Cambridge: Cambridge University Press, 2005), 134—63, p. 145.

122. Tobias Smollett, *Complete History of England*, IV, 313.

123. Pocock, 'Empire, State and Confederation', in *Discovery of Islands*, 153.

124. E.g. the permutations of union in Adam Ferguson, *An Essay on the History of Civil Society* (Edinburgh, 1767); on the reverberations of Scottish thought about union in North American writing, see Manning, *Fragments of Union*.

125. 'The Union in British History', *Transactions of the Royal Historical Society*, 6th ser., 10 (2000): 181—96, rev. in his *Discovery of Islands*, 164—78, p. 177.

126. *The Journal of Sir Walter Scott*, ed. W. E. K. Anderson (Oxford: Clarendon, 1972), 525—6. It is Anderson who notes, at this point, that 'His Irish visit had moderated Scott's opinion on this question.'

127. E.g. David Hempton, *Religion and Political Culture in Britain and Ireland: From the Glorious Revolution to the Decline of Empire* (Cambridge: Cambridge University Press, 1996).

128. E.g. 'Empire, State and Confederation', in *Discovery of Islands*, 138.

129. Nahum Tate, *The Triumph of Union: With the Muse's Address For the Consummation of it in the Parliament of Great Britain*; C[harles] D[arby], *Union: A Poem Humbly Dedicated to the Queen*; Mary Pix, *A Poem, Humbly Inscrib'd to the Lords Commissioners for the Union of the Two Kingdoms*; Elkanah Settle, *Carmen Irenicum: The Union of the Imperial Crowns of Great Britain. An Heroick Poem*; Lewis Theobald, *A Pindarick Ode on the Union*; Edward Vernon, *The Union: A Poem*—all published in London within months of the union. (Sermons in praise of the Treaty, often close in argument to the poems, were published even more abundantly in 1707.) Despite a predictable falling-off, union-related panegyric continued to appear, or be reprinted; e.g. Settle's *Eusebia Triumphans: The Protestant Succession as Now Establish'd, and Inviolably Secur'd, by the Happy Union of the Imperial Crowns of Great Britain* (London, 1709); Joseph Trapp, *Peace. A Poem* (London, 1713); William Oldisworth, 'On the Union: A Poem to the Queen', in Joseph Browne (ed.), *State Tracts: Containing Many Necessary Observations and Reflections on the State of our Affairs at Home and Abroad*, 2 vols. (London, 1715), II, 162—8; Nicholas Rowe, 'Epigram, On the Union', in his *Poetical Works* (London, 1715), 27—8.

130. Dustin Griffin, *Patriotism and Poetry in Eighteenth-Century Britain* (Cambridge: Cambridge University Press, 2002).

131. See his *Poems on Several Occasions* (London, 1717), 41—5.

132. Ann Yearsley, 'The Genius of England, On the Rock of Ages: Recommending Order, Commerce and Union to the Britons', in her collection *The*

Rural Lyre (London: G. G. and J. Robinson, 1796), 94–9; Charles Dibdin (the Younger), 'The Four Saints', in his *Mirth and Metre* (London: Vernor, Hood, and Sharpe, 1807).

133. 'Relinquishes his Bow and Arrows, and Deposits them Within the British Standard', in Thomas Park, *Cupid Turned Volunteer* (London: E. Harding, 1804), 2.

134. Cf. *The Fall of Cambria: A Poem*, 2 vols. (London: Longman, 1808).

135. *Malvern Hills, with Minor Poems*, 4th edn. (London: T. Cadell, 1829), 217, 220.

136. *A Congratulatory Poem on the New Parliament Assembled on this Great Conjuncture of Affairs* (London, 1701), 14.

137. *The Queen an Empress, and her Three Kingdoms One Empire: Or, Brief Remarks upon the Present; and a Prospect of the Future State of England* (London, 1706), 9. Cf. Kidd, *British Identities*, 77.

138. Samuel Kliger, *The Goths in England: A Study in Seventeenth and Eighteenth Century Thought* (Cambridge, MA: Harvard University Press, 1952); J. G. A. Pocock, *The Ancient Constitution and the Feudal Law: A Study of English Historical Thought in the Seventeenth Century*, reissue with retrospect (1957; Cambridge: Cambridge University Press, 1987); R. J. Smith, *The Gothic Bequest: Medieval Institutions in British Thought, 1688–1863* (Cambridge: Cambridge University Press, 1987).

139. *British Identities*, 91.

140. On the phenomenon, and its limits, see Peter Mandler, *The English National Character: The History of an Idea from Edmund Burke to Tony Blair* (New Haven: Yale University Press, 2006), ch. 3.

141. Morrill, 'War(s) of the Three Kingdoms', 69.

142. See e.g. 'The Most Remarkable Transactions of the Third Year of the Reign of King Charles the Second, Anno Dom. 1651', in *The History of the Grand Rebellion; Containing, The Most Remarkable Transactions from the Beginning of the Reign of King Charles I to the Happy Restoration ... Digested into Verse*, 3 vols. (London, 1713)—reissued in 2 vols. in 1715.

143. *The Works of Lord Bolingbroke*, 4 vols. (Philadelphia: Carey and Hart, 1841), I, 292–455, p. 389.

144. The extent to which Jacobitism kept English historiography open to British and Irish aspects requires further investigation, but note e.g. the inclusiveness of Thomas Carte's *A General History of England*, 4 vols. (London, 1747–55)—even though the author is proudly identified as 'an Englishman' on the title page of each volume.

145. See Blair Worden, *Roundhead Reputations: The English Civil Wars and the Passions of Posterity* (London: Allen Lane, 2001), chs. 1–6, which includes a fascinating account of how the Irishman John Toland (above, p. 89), wrote biography of, and edited works by, Milton, Harrington, and probably Ludlow, Algernon Sidney and others; also Melinda S. Zook, 'The Restoration

Remembered: The First Whigs and the Making of their History', *The Seventeenth Century*, 17 (2002): 213–34.

146. Contexts had been established by his *Memoirs of North Britain* (London, 1715) and *Memoirs of Ireland from the Restoration, to the Present Times* (London, 1716).

147. *The History of England from the Accession of James I to that of the Brunswick Line*, 8 vols. (London, 1763–83), VIII, 328.

148. Quoted by Geraint H. Jenkins, 'Historical Writing in the Eighteenth Century', in Branwen Jarvis (ed.), *A Guide to Welsh Literature, c.1700–1800* (Cardiff: University of Wales Press, 2000), 23–44, p. 23.

149. See the vision of Liberty prophesying the spread of union 'Thro' the whole Isle' to a sleeping St David in *The Leek: A Poem on St David's Day* (London, 1717), 27.

150. *The Leek* itself climaxes in a panegyric on George I and the Hanoverian succession, valued by the Society of Ancient Britons—a group of Welshmen in London—to whom the poem is addressed (27–8). Cf. the related materials in Sir Thomas Jones, *The Rise and Progress of the Most Honourable and Loyal Society of Antient Britons, Established in Honour to Her Royal Highness's Birth-day* (London, 1717), and the work of Jane Brereton (née Hughes) discussed by Sarah Prescott, 'The Cambrian Muse: Welsh Identity and Hanoverian Loyalty in the Poems of Jane Brereton (1685–1740)', *Eighteenth-Century Studies*, 38 (2005): 587–603.

151. E.g. *The Foundations of Modern Wales 1642–1780*, History of Wales, 4 (Oxford: Clarendon/University of Wales Press, 1987), 241–53.

152. Lewis Morris insisted that the Welsh medieval translation of Geoffrey's *Historia* was the original from which the Latin derived. The correspondence of Morris and his brothers in London and Anglesey is the best witness to Welsh antiquarianism in this period: *The Letters of Lewis, Richard, William and John Morris of Anglesey (Morrisiaid Môn) 1728–1756*, ed. J. H. Davies, 2 vols. (Aberystwyth: J. H. Davies, 1907–9), *Additional Letters of the Morrises of Anglesey (1735–1786)*, ed. Hugh Owen, *Transactions of the Honourable Society of Cymmrodorion*, 49 (1947–9).

153. Evan Evans, *Love of Our Country: A Poem, with Historical Notes*, 2nd edn. (Carmarthen, 1773), v.

154. George Lyttelton, 1st Baron Lyttelton, *The History of the Life of Henry the Second* (London, 1767).

155. *Love of Our Country*, 15, 24.

156. Evans was the holder of at least eighteen curacies, and never received advancement. His name does not appear on the title-page page of *Love of Our Country*, which is said to be 'By a CURATE from Snowdon'.

157. On Evans and Williams, the invention of the past and Welshness, see Prys Morgan, *The Eighteenth Century Renaissance* (Llandybie: Christopher Davies, 1981), chs. 3–4.

158. The poet's own description, quoted from National Library of Wales MS 21285E/826 in the best account of his career: Damian Walford Davies, *Presences that Disturb: Models of Romantic Identity in the Literature and Culture of the 1790s* (Cardiff: University of Wales Press, 2002), ch. 4, at p. 158.

159. On the cult, see Gwyn A. Williams, *Madoc: The Making of a Myth* (London: Eyre Methuen, 1979).

160. Edward Williams, *Poems, Lyric and Pastoral*, 2 vols. (London: 1794), II, 49–69, p. 54.

161. Jenkins, *Foundations*, 222.

162. See Gerard Carruthers and Alan Rawes (eds.), *English Romanticism and the Celtic World* (Cambridge: Cambridge University Press, 2003).

163. Serious composition began in 1769.

164. Thomas Warton (ed.), *The Union: Or, Select Scots and English Poems* ([Oxford], 1753), Preface.

165. D. Nichol Smith, 'Thomas Warton's Miscellany: *The Union*', *Review of English Studies*, 19 (1943): 263–75, p. 270.

166. Pieces of Lindsay had appeared, for the first time in an English book, in Thomas Hayward (ed.), *The British Muse: Or, A Collection of Thoughts Moral, Natural, and Sublime, of our English Poets*, 3 vols. (London: 1738).

167. Craig, 'The Study of Scottish Literature', 20.

168. Terry, *Poetry and the Making of the English Literary Past*, 43–4: apps 1–2.

169. Terry, *Poetry and the Making of the English Literary Past*; cf. René Wellek, *The Rise of English Literary History* (Chapel Hill: University of North Carolina Press, 1941), Jonathan Brody Kramnick, *Making the English Canon: Print-Capitalism and the Cultural Past* (Cambridge: Cambridge University Press, 1998), and David Fairer's introd. to his facsimile edn. of Warton's *History of English Poetry*, 4 vols. (London: Routledge/Thoemmes, 1998), I, 1–70.

170. Cf. Philip Connell, 'British Identities and the Politics of Ancient Poetry in Later Eighteenth-Century England', *Historical Journal*, 49 (2006): 161–92, pp. 182–9. As he notes, Joseph Ritson pungently dismissed Warton as 'a thorough-bred Oxonian rory-tory High-churchman', in *Observations on the First Three Volumes of the History of English Poetry* (London, 1782), 12.

171. *The History of English Poetry, from the Close of the Eleventh to the Commencement of the Eighteenth Century*, 4 vols. (1774–81), II, 257.

172. Despite his liking for the old Scots poets, Warton probably would have taken the anglicizing as evidence of English 'improvement' (though he evidently remained unsure when, how, and why Scottish poetry took the path it did). As he says of 'The Thistle and the Rose' (a poem now explicitly read in relation to 1707, as celebrating 'an event … which ultimately produced the union of the two crowns and kingdoms' (II, 257)): 'Another general observation, immediately resulting from the subject of this poem, may be here added, which illustrates the present and future state of the Scotch poetry. The

marriage of a princess of England with a king of Scotland, from the new communication and intercourse opened between the two courts and kingdoms by
such a connection, must have greatly contributed to polish the rude manners,
and to improve the language, literature, and arts, of Scotland' (II, 264).

173. Jenkins, *Foundations*, 309−12.
174. Paul Langford, 'South Britons' Reception of North Britons, 1707−1820', in
     Smout (ed.), *Anglo-Scottish Relations*, 143−69.
175. Smyth, *Making of the United Kingdom*, 156.
176. 26 June 1762, rpt. in *The North Briton*, 2nd edn., 3 vols. (Dublin, 1763), I,
     27−35, pp. 29−30.
177. Charles Churchill, *The Prophecy of Famine: A Scots Pastoral ... Inscribed to John
     Wilkes* (London, 1763), 14−15.
178. Tobias Smollett, *The Expedition of Humphrey Clinker*, 3 vols. (London, 1771),
     III, 99−112; Robert Fergusson, 'The Ghaists: A Kirkyard Eclogue', in *The
     Poems of Robert Fergusson*, ed. Matthew P. McDiarmid, 2 vols. (Edinburgh:
     Scottish Texts Society, 1954−6), II, 141−5, p. 143.
179. *Genius and Valour: A Scotch Pastoral* (London, 1763), 14−15.
180. E.g. J. G. Lockhart, *Memoirs of the Life of Sir Walter Scott* (Edinburgh: Cadell,
     1850), 37−8 quotes the novelist relating how, when he was a lad of fifteen,
     he met Burns for the only time—an emblematic encounter—in a room
     which contained a print illustrating Langhorne's poem *The Country Justice*.
     Scott drew a look of approval from Burns when he identified the quotation
     on the print.
181. E.g. Samuel Johnson, *A Journey to the Western Islands of Scotland* (London,
     1775), 14−15, 40−1; Boswell, *Journal of a Tour to the Hebrides*, 50, 138, 302−3.
     Cf. Boswell's report of Johnson's anti-Scottish banter in a 1776 encounter
     with Wilkes: *The Life of Samuel Johnson, LL.D.*, 2 vols. (London, 1791), II,
     88−91.
182. On the specifics see M. J. Robinson, 'Cumbrian Attitudes to Union with
     Scotland: Patriotism or Profit?', *Northern History*, 39 (2002): 227−44; on
     the general point, Alexander Murdoch, *British History, 1660−1832: National
     Identity and Local Culture* (Basingstoke: Macmillan, 1998).
183. Caroline Robbins, *The Eighteenth-Century Commonwealthman* (Cambridge,
     MA, Harvard University Press, 1959), chs. 4, 8. Christine Gerrard, *The Patriot
     Opposition to Walpole: Politics, Poetry, and National Myth, 1725−1742* (Oxford :
     Clarendon, 1994), chs. 1−2.
184. Christopher Hill, 'The Norman Yoke', *Puritanism and Revolution: Studies
     in Interpretation of the English Revolution of the Seventeenth Century* (London:
     Secker and Warburg, 1958), 50−122.
185. E.g. *The Butiad: Or, Political Register* (London, 1763), 5.
186. Cf. Kathleen Wilson, *The Island Race: Englishness, Empire and Gender in the
     Eighteenth Century* (London: Routledge, 2003), 13.
187. Quoted by Jenkins, *Foundations*, 313.

188. See e.g. Connell, 'British Identities and the Politics of Ancient Poetry', 167–75.

189. Gerald Newman, *The Rise of English Nationalism: A Cultural History, 1740–1830*, rev. edn. (Basingstoke: Macmillan, 1997), 227.

190. For the complications and contradictions in perceptions of English national character see Paul Langford, *Englishness Observed: Manners and Character, 1650–1850* (Oxford: Oxford University Press, 2000) and Mandler, *English National Character*, chs. 1–2.

191. See e.g. the critique of Newman offered as part of an argument that 'Englishness' is a late nineteenth-century phenomenon, in Krishan Kumar, *The Making of English Identity* (Cambridge: Cambridge University Press, 2003), ch. 7.

192. Linda Colley, *Britons: Forging the Nation, 1707–1837* (London: Pimlico, 1994). On the psychology of heightened allegiance to *both* England and Britain at this date see Jacqueline Rose's gloss on Colley's *Britons*, in her *States of Fantasy* (Oxford: Clarendon, 1996), 62.

193. See e.g. Tony Claydon and Ian McBride (eds.), *Protestantism and National Identity: Britain and Ireland, c.1650-c.1850* (Cambridge: Cambridge University Press, 1998); Smyth, *Making of the United Kingdom*; J. C. D. Clark, 'Protestantism, Nationalism, and National Identity, 1660–1832', *Historical Journal*, 43 (2000): 249–76.

194. E.g. Murray Pittock, *Inventing and Resisting Britain: Cultural Identities in Britain and Ireland, 1685–1789* (Basingstoke: Macmillan, 1997).

195. Howard D. Weinbrot, *Britannia's Issue: The Rise of British Literature from Dryden to Ossian* (Cambridge: Cambridge University Press), 1, 479.

196. E.g. Dafydd Moore, *Enlightenment and Romance in James Macpherson's Poems of Ossian* (Aldershot: Ashgate, 2003).

197. For the claim that warfare facilitated British identity-construction in Ireland—even among Catholics, who began to serve in large numbers in the British army during the Seven Years War—see Stephen Conway, *War, State, and Society in Mid-Eighteenth-Century Britain and Ireland* (Oxford: Oxford University Press, 2006), 200–2.

198. William Drennan, *Letters of an Irish Helot, signed Orellana: Republished by Order of the Constitution Society of the City of Dublin* (Dublin, 1785), 7–8.

199. In his *Fugitive Pieces in Verse and Prose* (Belfast: F. D. Finlay, 1815), 1–2.

Primary Sources

MANUSCRIPTS

British Library
Broghill's Letter Book, BL Add. MS 25287.
Drummond's *Entertainment*, BL Harleian MS 4707, BL Add. MS 40885.
Draft of Mitchelbourne's *Siege of London-derry*, BL Stowe MS 977.

Edinburgh University Library
Drummond's *Entertainment*, MS D.C.4.

National Library of Scotland
Rewritten poem by Drummond in the Hawthornden MSS, NLS MS 2062.

Petworth House Archives
Booklist, Orrery Papers MS 1319.
Orrery's 'A Vision', Orrery Papers MS 13187.

National Library of Ireland
Letter by John Wilson, 30 September 1679, NLI MS 2505 fol. 199r-v.

University of Cincinnati Library
Sir Edward Dering, Letter Book, Phillipps MS 14932.

CALENDARED PAPERS

Calendar of the Orrery Papers, ed. Edward Maclysaght (Dublin: Stationery Office, 1941).
Calendar of the State Papers relating to Ireland, ed. Robert Pentland Mahaffy, 4 vols. [1660–2, 1663–5, 1666–9, 1669–70 plus addenda] (London: His Majesty's Stationery Office, 1905–10).
Historical Manuscripts Commission, Fifteenth Report, Appendix, Part IV, *The Manuscripts of his Grace the Duke of Portland*, vol. IV (London: Her Majesty's Stationery Office, 1897).
—— *The Manuscripts of the Marquess of Ormonde*, n.s. vol. VI (London: Her Majesty's Stationery Office, 1911).
—— *The Manuscripts of the Marquis of Ormonde*, vol. I (London: Her Majesty's Stationery Office, 1895).

PRINTED AND ELECTRONIC

ADAIR, PATRICK, *A True Narrative of the Rise and Progress of the Presbyterian Church in Ireland (1623–1670) by the Rev. Patrick Adair. Also, The History of the Church in Ireland since the Scots were Naturalized, by the Rev. Andrew Stewart*, ed. W. D. Killen (Belfast: Aitchison, 1886).

ADAMSON, JOHN (ed.), Τα των μουσων εισοδια, *The Muses Welcome to the High and Mightie Prince James by the Grace of God King of Great Britaine France and Ireland* (Edinburgh, 1618).

AICKIN, JOSEPH, *Londerias: Or, A Narrative of the Siege of London-Derry* (Dublin, 1699).

AIZA, G. (= Giuseppe Aiazzi) (ed.), *The Embassy in Ireland of Monsignor G. B. Rinuccini*, tr. Annie Hutton (Dublin: A. Thom, 1873).

ALEXANDER, SIR WILLIAM, EARL OF STIRLING, *An Encouragement to Colonies* (London, 1624).

—— *Recreations with the Muses* (London, 1637).

—— *The Mapp and Description of New-England* (London, 1630).

—— *The Poetical Works of Sir William Alexander, Earl of Stirling*, ed. L. E. Kastner and H. B. Charlton, 2 vols. (Manchester: Longmans, Green and Co., 1921–9).

ANON, *A Character of France to which is added, Gallus Castratus: Or, An Answer to a Late Slanderous Pamphlet, called the Character of England* (London, 1659).

—— *A Letter from Amsterdam, to a Friend in England* (London, 1678).

—— *A Letter to the Unknown Author of Jus Populi* (n.p., 1671).

—— *A Memorable Song on the Unhappy Hunting in Chevy-Chase, Betweene Earle Piercy of England and Earle Dowglas of Scotland. To the Tune of Flying Fame* (London, 1670).

—— *A Relation of the Kings Entertainment into Scotland* (London, 1641).

—— *A Second Discovery by the Northern Scout: Of the Chiefe Actions of the Malignant Party* (London, 1642).

—— *A True Account of the Horrid Murder Committed upon his Grace, the Late Lord Archbishop of St Andrews* (Dublin, 1679).

—— *A Welsh Narrative, Corrected, and Taught to Speak True English, and Some Latine: Or, Animadversions on an Imperfect Relation in the Perfect Diurnall* (London, 1653).

—— *An Accompt of Scotlands Grievances by Reason of The D. of Lauderdales Ministrie* (Edinburgh?, 1672).

—— *An Answer to the Late Proposal for Uniting the Kingdoms of Great Britain and Ireland; in Some Occasional Remarks upon the Proposal Itself* (Dublin, 1751).

—— *An Aphorismical Discovery of Treasonable Faction*, in *A Contemporary History of Affairs in Ireland from 1641 to 1652*, ed. J. T. Gilbert, 3 vols. in 6 (Dublin: Irish Archaeological and Celtic Society, 1879–80).

—— *Anglia Liberata: Or, The Rights of the People of England, Maintained against the Pretences of the Scotish King* (London, 1651).

ANON, *Articles of Peace, Union and Confederation, Concluded and Agreed between His Highness Oliver Lord Protector of the Common-wealth of England, Scotland and Ireland, and the Dominions thereto Belonging. And the Lords the States General of the United Provinces of the Netherlands* (London, 1654).

—— *Bogg-Witticisms: Or, Dear Joy's Common-places* (London, 1682).

—— *Fuimus Troes: The True Troianes* (London, 1633) [by Jasper Fisher?].

—— *Musarum Oxoniensium* (Oxford, 1654).

—— *Pairlement Chloinne Tomáis*, ed. N. J. A. Williams (Dublin: Dublin Institute for Advanced Studies, 1981).

—— *Pas-Caert van Texel tot aen den Hoofden* (Amsterdam, 1660).

—— *The Anti-Union* (Dublin, 1798–9).

—— *The Butiad: Or Political Register* (London, 1763).

—— *The Dutch Boare Dissected: Or, A Description of Hogg-Land* (London, 1665).

—— *The Dutch-mens Pedigree: Or, A Relation, shewing how they were first Bred, and Descended from a Horse-turd, which was enclosed in a Butter-box* (London, 1653).

—— *The History of the Rebellion and Civil Wars in Ireland* (Dublin, 1719–20) [attrib. Edward Hyde, Earl of Clarendon].

—— *The Irish Hudibras: Or, The Fingallian Prince* (London, 1689).

—— *The Irish Rendezvous: Or, A Description of T[yrconne]ll's Army of Tories and Bog-Trotters* (London, 1689).

—— *The King and Queenes Entertainement at Richmond* (Oxford, 1636).

—— *The Latest and Truest Newes from Ireland* (London, 1642).

—— *The Queen an Empress, and her Three Kingdoms One Empire: Or, Brief Remarks upon the Present; and a Prospect of the Future State of England* (London, 1706).

—— *The Review Review'd. In a Letter to the Prophet Daniel in Scotland* (1707), ed. in Maximillian E. Novak, 'A Whiff of Scandal in the Life of Daniel Defoe', *Huntington Library Quarterly*, 34/1 (1970): 35–42.

—— *The Royal Flight: Or, The Conquest of Ireland* (London, 1690).

—— *The Royal Voyage: Or, The Irish Expedition* (London, 1690).

—— *The Scotch Echo to the English Legion: Or, The Union in Danger* (Edinburgh, 1707).

—— *The Scottish Politike Presbyter, Slaine by an English Independent* (London, 1647).

—— *The Whole Prophesie of Scotland, England, and Some-part of France, and Denmark, Prophesied bee Meruellous Merling, Beid, Bertlingtoun, Thomas Rymour, Waldhaue, Eltraine, Banester, and Sibbila, All According in One* ([London?], 1603).

—— *Titus: Or, The Palme of Christian Courage* (Waterford, 1644).

—— *Vavasoris Examen, et Purgamen: Or, Mr Vavasor Powells Impartiall Trial* (London, 1654).

—— 'Verses upon the Order for making Knights of such Persons who had 40 pounds per annum in King James I. Time', British Library Additional MS 5832, fol. 206r-v, in 'Early Stuart Libels: An Edition of Poetry from Manuscript Sources', ed. Alastair Bellany and Andrew McRae <http:purl.oclc.org/emls/texts/libels>.

ARMIN, ROBERT (?), *The Valiant Welshman: Or, The True Chronicle History of the Life and Valiant Deedes of Caradoc the Great, King of Cambria, now Called Wales* (London, 1615).

ARNOLD, MATTHEW, *On the Study of Celtic Literature* (London, 1867).

ASHTON, ROBERT, *The Battle of Aughrim* (Dublin, 1728).

ATWOOD, WILLIAM, *The Superiority and Direct Dominion of the Imperial Crown of England over the Crown and Kingdom of Scotland* (London, 1704).

AUBREY, JOHN, *Brief Lives*, ed. Oliver Lawson Dick (London: Secker and Warburg, 1950).

AYTOUN, SIR ROBERT, *The English and Latin Poems of Sir Robert Aytoun*, ed. Charles B. Gullans (Edinburgh: Scottish Text Society, 1963).

B., T., *The Rebellion of Naples: Or, The Tragedy of Massenello* (London, 1649).

BACON, FRANCIS, *The Works of Francis Bacon*, ed. James Spedding, Robert Leslie Ellis, and Douglas Denon Heath, 15 vols. (London: Longmans, 1857–74).

BAILLIE, ROBERT, *A Dissuasive from the Errours of the Time Wherein the Tenets of the Principall sects, especially of the Independents, are Drawn together in One Map* (London, 1645).

—— *A Review of Doctor Bramble, Late Bishop of Londenderry, His Faire Warning against the Scotes Disciplin* (Delft, 1649).

—— *Ladensium Autokatakrisis, The Canterburians Self-Conviction: Or, An Evident Demonstration of the Avowed Arminianisme, Poperie, and Tyrannie of that Faction, by their Owne Confessions* (Amsterdam, 1640).

BARBOUR, JOHN, *The Acts and Life of the Most Victorious Conqueror Robert Bruce, King of Scotland* (Glasgow, 1672).

BARRY, GERAT, *A Discourse of Military Discipline, Devided into Three Boockes, Declaring the Partes and Sufficiencie Ordained in a Private Souldier, and in Each Officer* (Brussels, 1634).

BEATTIE, JAMES, *Scoticisms, Arranged in Alphabetical Order, Designed to Correct Improprieties of Speech and Writing* (Edinburgh, 1787).

—— *The Minstrel: Or, The Progress of Genius. A Poem*, Book I (London, 1771).

—— *The Minstrel: Or, The Progress of Genius. A Poem*, Book II (London, 1774).

BEHN, APHRA, *Poems upon Several Occasions* (London, 1684).

BELLEFOREST, FRANÇOIS DE, *Le Quatriesme tome des histoires tragiques, partie extraites des oeuures Italiennes du Bandel, et partie de l'inuention de l'Autheur François* (Turin, 1571).

BELLINGS, RICHARD, *History of the Irish Confederation and the War in Ireland, 1641–1643*, ed. John T. Gilbert, 7 vols. (Dublin: John T. Gilbert, 1882–91).

BEN ISRAEL, MENASSEH, *The Hope of Israel* (London, 1650).

BLAIR, HUGH, *Lectures on Rhetoric and Belles Lettres*, 2 vols. (London, 1783).

BOSWELL, JAMES, *The Journal of a Tour to the Hebrides, with Samuel Johnson, LL.D.* (London, 1785).

—— *The Life of Samuel Johnson, LL.D.*, 2 vols. (London, 1791).

BOYLE, ROBERT, *The Works of the Honourable Robert Boyle*, ed. Thomas Birch, 5 vols. (London, 1744).

BOYLE, ROGER, LORD BROGHILL, EARL OF ORRERY, *A Letter from the Lord Broghill to the Honourable William Lenthall Esq.* (London, 1651).

—— *A Treatise of the Art of War* (London, 1677).

—— *An Answer of a Person of Quality to a Scandalous Letter* (Dublin, 1662).

—— *Articles Exhibited to the Honourable House of Commons Assembled in Parliament, Against the Lord Inchiquine Lord President of Munster, Subscribed by the Lord Broghill and Sir Arthur Loftus Knight* (London, 1647).

—— *A Collection of the State Letters of the Right Honourable Roger Boyle* (London, 1742).

—— *English Adventures* (London, 1676).

—— *Parthenissa, A Romance* (London, 1655).

—— *Parthenissa, that most Fam'd Romance: The Six Volumes Compleat* (London, 1676).

—— *Poems on Most of the Festivals of the Church* (London/Cork, 1681).

—— *The Dramatic Works of Roger Boyle Earl of Orrery*, ed. William Smith Clark, II, 2 vols. (Cambridge, MA: Harvard University Press, 1937).

—— *The Irish Colours Displayed, In A Reply of an English Protestant to a Late Letter of an Irish Roman Catholique* (London, 1662).

—— et al., *A Manifestation Directed to the Honourable Houses of Parliament in England, Sent from the Lord Inchequin, the Lord Broghill [and others]* (London, 1644).

BRATHWAITE, RICHARD, *Panthalia: Or, The Royal Romance* (London, 1659).

BRENTON, HOWARD, *The Romans in Britain*, in his *Plays: Two* (London: Methuen Drama, 1989).

BROOKE, CHARLOTTE, *Reliques of Irish Poetry: Consisting of Heroic Poems, Odes, Elegies, and Songs, Translated into English Verse* (Dublin, 1789).

BROWN, JOHN, *An Apologeticall Relation of the Particular Sufferings of the Faithful Ministers and Professours of the Church of Scotland, since August, 1660* ([Edinburgh?], 1665).

—— *The History of the Indulgence* ([Edinburgh?], 1678).

BUC, SIR GEORGE, *Daphnis Polystephanos: An Eclog Treating of Crownes, and of Garlandes, and to Whom of Right They Appertaine* (London, 1605).

BUCHANAN, GEORGE, *De jure regni apud Scotos: Or, A Dialogue, Concerning the Due Priviledge of Government in the Kingdom of Scotland, Betwixt George Buchanan and Thomas Maitland*, tr. 'Philalethes' (n.p., 1680).

—— *George Buchanan: The Political Poetry*, ed. and trans. Paul J. McGinnis and Arthur H. Williamson (Edinburgh: Scottish History Society, 1995).

—— *Rerum Scoticarum historia* (Edinburgh, 1582).

—— *Rerum Scoticarum historia ... De iure regni apud Scotos dialogus* (Antwerp, 1583).

—— *The History of Scotland*, anonymously tr. (London, 1690).

BURKHEAD, HENRY, *A Tragedy of Cola's Furie: Or, Lirenda's Miserie* (Kilkenny, 1645).

BURNELL, HENRY, *Landgartha* (Dublin, 1641).

BURNET, GILBERT, *History of My Own Time*, Part I, ed. Osmund Airy, 2 vols. (Oxford: Clarendon, 1897–1900).

BURNS, ROBERT, *Burns: Poems and Songs*, ed. James Kinsley (Oxford: Oxford University Press, 1969).

CAMDEN, WILLIAM, *Britannia* (London, 1586); tr. Philemon Holland (London, 1610), enlgd. with new tr. by Edmund Gibson (London, 1695), inc. 'The Union' (London, 1722).

CAMPBELL, THOMAS, *Strictures on the Ecclesiastical and Literary History of Ireland* (Dublin, 1789).

CARADOC OF LLANCARVAN, *Historie of Cambria, now Called Wales*, tr. Humphrey Llwyd, corr. and cont. by David Powel (London, 1584); rev. William Wynne (London, 1697).

CAREW, THOMAS, *The Poems of Thomas Carew with his Masque 'Coelum Britannicum'*, ed. Rhodes Dunlap (Oxford: Clarendon, 1949).

CARLETON, WILLIAM, *The Life of William Carleton*, introd. Cashel Hoey, 2 vols. (London, 1896).

CARPENTER, ANDREW (ed.), *Verse in English from Tudor and Stuart Ireland* (Cork: Cork University Press, 2003).

CARTE, THOMAS, *A General History of England*, 4 vols. (London, 1747–55).

Catechismus ex decreto Concilii Tridentini ad parochos (Rome, 1566).

CAVENDISH, MARGARET, DUCHESS OF NEWCASTLE, *The Life of William Cavendish Duke of Newcastle*, ed. C. H. Firth, 2nd edn. (London: Routledge, 1907).

CÉITINN, SEATHRÚN [Geoffrey Keating], *Foras feasa ar Éirinn: The History of Ireland*, ed. David Comyn and P. S. Dinneen, 4 vols. (London: Irish Texts Society, 1902–14); tr. Dermot O'Connor as *The General History of Ireland* (London, 1723).

CHAPMAN, GEORGE, *The Memorable Masque* (London, 1613).

CHESTER, ROBERT, *Loves Martyr: Or, Rosalins Complaint* (London, 1601).

CHILD, FRANCIS JAMES (ed.), *The English and Scottish Popular Ballads*, 5 vols. in 3 (New York: Folklore Press, 1957).

CHILLINGWORTH, WILLIAM, *The Religion of Protestants* (Oxford, 1638).

CHURCHILL, CHARLES, *The Prophecy of Famine: A Scots Pastoral … Inscribed to John Wilkes* (London, 1763).

CHURCHYARD, THOMAS, *The Worthines of Wales* (London, 1587).

CIBBER, COLLEY, *Perolla and Izadora: A Tragedy* (London, 1706).

CLAPHAM, JOHN, *The Historie of Great Britannie* (London, 1606).

CLAVELL, JOHN, *Introduction to the Sword Dance*, ed. in Alan J. Fletcher, *Drama, Performance, and Polity in Pre-Cromwellian Ireland* (Cork: Cork University Press, 2000), 310–13.

CLELAND, JOHN, *Hero-paideia* (Oxford, 1607).

CLELAND, WILLIAM, *A Collection of Several Poems and Verses, Composed upon Various Occasions* (n.p., 1697).

—— *Disputatio juridica de probationibus* (Utrecht, 1684).

CLERK OF PENICUIK, SIR JOHN, *Memoirs of the Life of Sir John Clerk of Penicuik ... 1676–1755*, ed. John M. Gray, Scottish History Society, 1st series, 13 (1892).

—— *Observations on the Present Circumstances of Scotland*, ed. T. C. Smout, in Scottish History Society, 4th series, 2, *Miscellany X* (1965), 177–212.

CLEVELAND, JOHN, *The Poems of John Cleveland*, ed. Brian Morris and Eleanor Withington (Oxford: Clarendon, 1967).

COLLIER, JEREMY, *A Short View of the Immorality, and Profaneness of the English Stage* (London, 1698).

COLLINE, WILLIAM, *The Spirit of the Phanatiques Dissected, and The Solemne League and Covenant Solemnly Discussed in 30 Queries* (London, 1660).

COLOM, J., *The New Fierie Sea-Colomne* (Amsterdam, 1649).

COLVILL, ROBERT, *The Field of Flowdon*, in his *Occasional Poems* (Edinburgh, 1771).

CONWAY, ANNE, VISCOUNTESS CONWAY AND KILLULTAGH, *et al.*, *The Conway Letters: The Correspondence of Anne, Viscountess Conway, Henry More, and their Friends, 1642–1684*, ed. Marjorie Hope Nicholson, rev. Sarah Hutton (Oxford: Clarendon, 1992).

COTTLE, JOSEPH, *Malvern Hills, with Minor Poems*, 4th edn. (London: T. Cadell, 1829).

—— *The Fall of Cambria: A Poem*, 2 vols. (London: Longman, 1808).

COWLEY, ABRAHAM, *The Civil War*, in *The Collected Works of Abraham Cowley*, ed. Thomas O. Calhoun, Laurence Heyworth, Allan Pritchard (Newark: University of Delaware Press, 1989—), vol. I.

COX, RICHARD, *Hibernia Anglicana: Or, The History of Ireland from the Conquest thereof by the English, to this Present Time*, Part 1 (London, 1689).

CRADOCK, WALTER, *Glad Tydings from Heaven; To The Worst of Sinners on Earth* (London, 1648).

—— *Gospel-Holiness: Or, The Saving Sight of God* (London, 1651).

CRAIG, ALEXANDER, *Poeticall Essayes* (London, 1604).

CRAIG, SIR THOMAS, *De unione regnorum Britanniae tractatus*, ed. C. Sanford Terry (Edinburgh: Scottish Historical Society, 1909).

CROMWELL, OLIVER, *The Writings and Speeches of Oliver Cromwell*, introd. and ed. Wilbur Cortez Abbott, 4 vols. (Oxford: Clarendon, 1937–47).

CROUCH, NATHANIEL *The History of the Kingdom of Ireland* (London, 1693).

—— *The Wars in England, Scotland and Ireland, ... From the Beginning of the Reign of King Charles I in 1625, to His Majesties happy Restauration, 1660* (London, 1681).

CURRY, JOHN, *A Brief Account from the Most Authentic Protestant Writers of the Causes, Motives, and Mischiefs, of the Irish Rebellion, on the 23d day of October 1641,*

Deliver'd in Dialogue between a Dissenter, and a Member of the Church of Ireland (London, 1747).

CURRY, JOHN, *An Historical and Critical Review of the Civil Wars in Ireland* (Dublin, 1786).

—— *Historical Memoirs of the Irish Rebellion in the Year, 1641* (London, 1758).

D[ARBY], C[HARLES], *Union: A Poem Humbly Dedicated to the Queen* (London, 1707).

DANIEL, SAMUEL, *Tethys Festival: Or, The Queenes Wake*, in *The Order and Solemnitie of the Creation of the High and Mightie Prince Henrie, Eldest Sonne to our Sacred Soueraigne, Prince of Wales* (London: 1610).

—— *The First Part of the Historie of England* (London, 1612).

DAVENANT, SIR WILLIAM, *The Shorter Poems, and Songs from the Plays and Masques*, ed. A. M. Gibbs (Oxford: Clarendon, 1972).

DAVENPORT, ROBERT, 'Dialogue betweene Pollicy and Piety', ed. in Albert H. Tricomi, '*A Dialogue betweene Pollicy and Piety* by Robert Davenport', *English Literary Renaissance*, 21 (1991): 190–216.

DAVIDSON, PETER (ed.), *Poetry and Revolution: An Anthology of British and Irish Verse 1625–1660* (Oxford: Clarendon, 1998).

DAVIES OF HEREFORD, JOHN, *Microcosmos* (Oxford, 1603).

DAVIES OF MALLWYD, JOHN, *Antiquiae linguae Britannicae ... rudimenta* (London, 1621).

—— *Antiquiae linguae Britannicae ... dictionarium duplex* (London, 1632).

DAVIES, RICHARD, *Chesters Triumph in Honor of her Prince* (London, 1610).

DAVIES, RICHARD (BISHOP), *Epistol at y Cembru*, 'Address to the Welsh People by Bishop Richard Davies', tr. Albert Owen Evans, in Evans, *A Memorandum on the Legality of the Welsh Bible and the Welsh Version of the Book of Common Prayer* (Cardiff: William Lewis, 1925), 83–124.

DAVIES, SIR JOHN, *A Discouerie of the True Causes why Ireland was Neuer Entirely Subdued* (London, 1612).

DEFOE, DANIEL (?), *A True Account of the Proceedings at Perth* (London, 1716).

—— (?), *An Essay upon Buying and Selling of Speeches* (London, 1716).

—— (?), *An Historical Account of the Bitter Sufferings, and Melancholly Circumstances of the Episcopal Church in Scotland, under the Barbarous Usage and Bloody Persecution of the Presbyterian Church Government* (Edinburgh, 1707).

—— (?), *Greenshields out of Prison and Toleration Settled in Scotland* (London, 1710).

—— (?), introduction to *A Journal of the Earl of Mar's Proceedings* (London, 1716).

—— (?), *Memorial to the Nobility of Scotland* (Edinburgh, 1708).

—— (?), *Mercurius Politicus* (London, 1716–20).

—— (?), *The Highland Visions: Or, The Scots New Prophesy* (London, 1712).

—— (?), *The Second-Sighted Highlander: Or, Predictions and Foretold Events* (London, 1713).

DEFOE, DANIEL, *A Fourth Essay, at Removing National Prejudices* (Edinburgh, 1706).

—— *A Reply to the Scots Answer, to the British Vision* (Edinburgh, 1706).

DEFOE, DANIEL, *A Review of the State of the British Nation* [until 6 March 1707 *A Review of the State of the English Nation*] (London, 1704–13); vol. VI into VII also pub. in Edinburgh.

—— *A Scots Poem: Or, A New-Years Gift, from a Native of the Universe, to His Fellow-Animals in Albania* (Edinburgh, 1707).

—— *A Short Letter to the Glasgow-Men* (Edinburgh, 1706).

—— *A Short View of the Present State of the Protestant Religion in Britain* (Edinburgh, 1707).

—— *A Tour through the Whole Island of Great Britain*, introd. G. D. H. Cole and D. C. Browning, 2 vols. in 1 (London: Dent, 1974).

—— *A Trumpet Blown in the North, and Sounded in the Ears of John Eriskine, Call'd by the Men of the World, Duke of Mar* (London, 1715).

—— *A View of the Scots Rebellion: With Some Enquiry What we Have to Fear from Them? and What is the Properest Method to Take with Them?* (London, 1715).

—— *A Voice from the South: Or, An Address from some Protestant Dissenters in England to the Kirk of Scotland* (Edinburgh, 1707).

—— *An Enquiry into the Disposal of the Equivalent* (Edinburgh, 1706?).

—— *An Essay at Removing National Prejudices against a Union with Scotland ... Part I* (London, 1706).

—— *An Essay at Removing National Prejudices against a Union with Scotland ... Part II* (London, 1706).

—— *An Essay, at Removing National Prejudices, against a Union with England. Part III* (Edinburgh, 1706).

—— *Caledonia, &c. A Poem in Honour of Scotland, and the Scots Nation* (Edinburgh, 1706; London, 1707).

—— *Jure Divino: A Satyr* (London, 1706).

—— *Memoirs of a Cavalier*, ed. James T. Boulton (London: Oxford University Press, 1972).

—— *Memoirs of the Church of Scotland* (London, 1717).

—— *Passion and Prejudice, the Support of One Another, and Both Destructive to the Happiness of this Nation, in Church and State* (Edinburgh, 1707).

—— *The Commentator* (London, 1720).

—— *The Dissenters in England Vindicated* (Edinburgh, 1707).

—— *The Fortunes and Misfortunes of the Famous Moll Flanders*, ed. G. A. Starr (London: Oxford University Press, 1971).

—— *The History and Remarkable Life of the Truly Honourable Col. Jacque Commonly Call'd Col. Jack*, ed. Samuel Holt Monk (1965; London: Oxford University Press, 1970).

—— *The History of the Union of Great Britain* (Edinburgh, 1709).

—— *The Letters of Daniel Defoe*, ed. George Harris Healey (Oxford: Clarendon, 1955).

—— *The Life and Strange Surprizing Adventures of Robinson Crusoe of York, Mariner*, ed. J. Donald Crowley (London: Oxford University Press, 1972).

DEFOE, DANIEL, *The Mercator: Or, Commerce Retrieved, being Considerations on the State of the British Trade* (London, 1713–14).

—— *The Present State of the Parties in Great Britain: Particularly an Enquiry into the State of the Dissenters in England, and the Presbyterians in Scotland* (London, 1712).

—— *The Scot's Narrative Examin'd: Or, The Case of the Episcopal Ministers in Scotland Stated* (London, 1709).

—— *The Scots Nation and Union Vindicated* (London, 1714).

—— *The Shortest-Way with the Dissenters* (London, 1702).

—— *The Storm: Or, A Collection of the Most Remarkable Casualties and Disasters which Happen'd in the Late Dreadful Tempest, both by Sea and Land* (London, 1704).

—— *The Vision, a Poem* (Edinburgh, 1706).

—— *Union and No Union. Being an Enquiry into the Grievances of the Scots* (London, 1713).

DEKKER, THOMAS (?), *The Welsh Embassador*, in *The Dramatic Works of Thomas Dekker*, ed. Fredson Bowers, vol. IV (Cambridge: Cambridge University Press, 1961).

DELONEY, THOMAS, *The Gentle Craft*, in *The Works of Thomas Deloney*, ed. Francis Oscar Mann (Oxford: Oxford University Press, 1912).

DENNIS, JOHN, *Liberty Asserted* (London, 1704).

DERMODY, THOMAS, *The Harp of Erin*, 2 vols. (London, 1807).

DIBDIN, CHARLES (the Younger), *Mirth and Metre* (London: Vernor, Hood, and Sharpe, 1807).

DODDRIDGE, JOHN, *The History of the Ancient and Modern Estate of the Principality of Wales, Dutchy of Cornewal, and Earldome of Chester* (London, 1630).

DOYLE, RODDY, *The Commitments* (Dublin: King Farouk, 1987).

DRAYTON, MICHAEL, *The Works of Michael Drayton*, ed. J. William Hebel et al., 5 vols. (Oxford: Blackwell, 1931–41).

DRENNAN, WILLIAM, *Fugitive Pieces in Verse and Prose* (Belfast: F. D. Finlay, 1815).

—— *Letters of an Irish Helot, signed Orellana: Republished by Order of the Constitution Society of the City of Dublin* (Dublin, 1785).

DRUMMOND OF HAWTHORDEN, WILLIAM (attrib., more likely composed by Scot of Scotstarvit), 'Polemo-Middinia', in *Poetical Works of Drummond*, II, 321–6; tr. in Allan H. MacLaine (ed.), *The Christis Kirk Tradition: Scots Poems of Folk Festivity* (Glasgow: Association for Scottish Literary Studies, 1996), 39–49.

—— 'Anecdotes, &c. Selected from Drummond of Hawthornden's Miscellanies, Vol. II', in David Laing, 'A Brief Account of the Hawthornden Manuscripts in the Possession of the Society of Antiquaries of Scotland', *Archaeologia Scotica: Or, Transactions of the Society of Antiquaries of Scotland*, 4 ([1831] 1857): 57–116, 225–40.

—— *Poems* (London, 1657).

—— *The Works of William Drummond of Hawthornden* (Edinburgh, 1711).

DRUMMOND OF HAWTHORDEN, WILLIAM, *The History of Scotland* (London, 1656).

—— *The Poetical Works of William Drummond of Hawthornden*, ed. L. E. Kastner, 2 vols. (Edinburgh: William Blackwood, 1913).

—— *William Drummond of Hawthornden: Poems and Prose*, ed. Robert H. MacDonald (Edinburgh: Scottish Academic Press, 1976).

DRUMMOND, WILLIAM HAMILTON, *The Giant's Causeway: A Poem* (Belfast: J. Smith for Longman, 1811).

DRYDEN, JOHN, *The Works of John Dryden*, ed. Edward Niles Hooker, H. T. Swedenberg, *et al.*, 20 vols. (Berkeley: University of California Press, 1955–2000).

DU MOULIN, PETER, *England's Appeal from the Private Cabal at White-Hall to the Great Council of the Nation* ([London], 1673).

—— *Regii sanguinus clamor ad coelum adversus paricidas Anglicanos* (The Hague, 1652).

ECHARD, LAURENCE, *The History of England*, 3 vols. (London, 1707–18).

—— *The History of the Revolution, and the Establishment of England, in the Year, 1688* (London, 1725).

ERBERY, WILLIAM, *The Bishop of London, the Welsh Curate, and Common Prayers, with Apocrypha in the End* (London, 1653).

—— *The Testimony of William Erbery* (London, 1658).

—— *The Welsh Curate* (1652).

EVANS, ARISE, *Light for the Iews: Or, The Means to Convert Them* (London, 1656).

EVANS, EVAN, *Love of Our Country: A Poem, with Historical Notes*, 2nd edn. (Carmarthen, 1773).

—— *Some Specimens of the Poetry of the Antient Welsh Bards* (London, 1764).

EVELYN, JOHN (?), *A Character of England. As it was Lately Presented in a Letter, to a Noble Man of France* (London, 1659).

EVELYN, JOHN, *Publick Employment and an Active Life with its Appanages, such as Fame, Command, Riches, Conversation &c Preferr'd to Solitude* (London, 1667).

FALKINER, C. LITTON (ed.), *Illustrations of Irish History and Topography, Mainly of the Seventeenth Century* (London: Longmans, 1904).

FARQUHAR, GEORGE, *The Works of George Farquhar*, ed. Shirley Strum Kenny, 2 vols. (Oxford: Clarendon, 1988).

FEIRITÉIR, PIARAIS, *Dánta Piarais Feiritéir*, ed. Patrick Dineen, tr. Pat Muldowney (Aubane, Co. Cork: Aubane Historical Society, 1999).

FELLTHAM, OWEN, *A Brief Character of the Low-Countries under the States* (London, 1652), rpt. as *Batavia: Or, The Hollander Displayed* (1672).

FENTON, ELIJAH, *Poems on Several Occasions* (London, 1717).

FERGUSON, ADAM, *An Essay on the History of Civil Society* (Edinburgh, 1767).

FERGUSSON, ROBERT, *The Poems of Robert Fergusson*, ed. Matthew P. McDiarmid, 2 vols. (Edinburgh: Scottish Texts Society, 1954–6).

FISHER, PAYNE, *Irenodia gratulatoria* ([London, 1652]), tr. Thomas Manley as *Veni; Vidi; Vici: The Triumphs of the Most Excellent and Illustrious Oliver Cromwell* (London, 1652).

FLETCHER, ANDREW, *Political Works*, ed. John Robertson (Cambridge: Cambridge University Press, 1997).

FLETCHER, JOHN, *Bonduca*, ed. Cyrus Hoy, in *The Dramatic Works in the Beaumont and Fletcher Canon*, gen. ed. Fredson Bowers, vol. IV (Cambridge: Cambridge University Press, 1979).

FORD, JOHN, *The Chronicle Historie of Perkin Warbeck: A Strange Truth* (London, 1634).

FOWLER, ALASTAIR (ed.), *The New Oxford Book of Seventeenth Century Verse* (Oxford: Oxford University Press, 1991).

FOXE, JOHN, *Actes and Monuments of these Latter and Perillous Dayes Touching Matters of the Church* (London, [1563]).

GALT, JOHN, *Ringan Gilhaize: Or, The Covenanters* (Edinburgh: Oliver and Boyd, 1823).

GARDINER, SAMUEL RAWSON (ed.), *The Constitutional Documents of the Puritan Revolution 1625–1660*, 3rd edn. (Oxford: Clarendon, 1906).

GERNON, LUKE, 'A Discourse of Ireland, Anno *1620*', in Falkiner (ed.), *Illustrations of Irish History and Topography*, 348–62.

GILDON, CHARLES (?) (ed.), *Chorus Poetarum: Or, Poems on Several Occasions* (London, 1694).

GILL, ALEXANDER, *Logonomia Anglica (1619)*, tr. Robin C. Alston, ed. Bror Danielsson and Arvid Gabrielson (Stockholm: Almqvist and Wiksell, 1972).

GILLESPIE, GEORGE, *A Dispute against the English-Popish Ceremonies, Obtruded vpon the Church of Scotland* (Amsterdam and Leiden, 1637).

GIRAFFI, ALESSANDRO, *Le Rivolutioni di Napoli descritte dal Signor A. G.* (Venice, 1647), tr. James Howell as *An Exact Historie of the Late Revolutions in Naples* (London, 1650).

GOLDSMITH, OLIVER, *Collected Works of Oliver Goldsmith*, ed. Arthur Friedman, 5 vols. (Oxford: Clarendon, 1966).

GORDON, JOHN, *A Panegyrique of Congratulation for the Concord of the Realmes of Great Britaine in Unitie of Religion, and under One King* (London, 1603).

GRANT, ANNE, *Eighteen Hundred and Thirteen: A Poem, in Two Parts* (Edinburgh: Ballantyne for Longman, 1814).

——— *Essays on the Superstitions of the Highlanders of Scotland: To Which are Added, Translations from the Gaelic*, 2 vols. (London: Longman, 1811).

——— *The Highlanders, and Other Poems* (London: Longman, Hurst, Rees, and Orme, 1808).

GREENE, ROBERT, *The Scottish Historie of Iames the Fourth, Slaine at Flodden* (London, 1598).

GRIFFITH, ALEXANDER, *Mercurius Cambro-Britannicus* (London, 1652).

GRIFFITH, ALEXANDER, *Strena Vavasoriensis, a New-Years-Gift for the Welsh Itinerants: Or, A Hue and Cry after Mr Vavasor Powell* (London, 1654).

GRIFFITHS, NEHEMIAH, *The Leek: A Poem on St David's Day* (London, 1717).

GUMBLE, THOMAS, *The Life of General Monck, Duke of Albemarle* (London, 1671).

HALL, EDWARD, *The Vnion of the Two Noble and Illustrate Famelies of Lancastre [and] Yorke beeyng long in Continual Discension for the Croune of this Noble Realme* (London, 1548).

HARDIMAN, JAMES, *Irish Minstrelsy: Or, Bardic Remains of Ireland, with English Poetical Translations*, 2 vols. (London, 1831).

HARRINGTON, JAMES, *The Common-wealth of Oceana* (London, 1656).

HARRISON, STEPHEN, *The Arch's of Triumph Erected in Honor of the High and Mighty Prince James* (London, 1604).

HAYWARD, THOMAS (ed.), *The British Muse: Or, A Collection of Thoughts Moral, Natural, and Sublime, of our English Poets*, 3 vols. (London: 1738).

HEAD, RICHARD, *Hic et Ubique: Or, The Humors of Dublin* (London, 1663).

—— *The English Rogue Described, in the Life of Meriton Latroon* (London, 1666).

—— *The Western Wonder: Or, O Brazeel, an Inchanted Island Discovered* (London, 1674).

HEMANS, FELICIA, *Poems* (Edinburgh: William Blackwood, 1868).

HENRY, THE MINSTREL [BLIND HARRY], *The Life and Acts of the Most Famous and Valiant Champion, Sir William Wallace Knicht of Ellerslie, Maintainer of the Libertie of Scotland* (Edinburgh, 1611).

HEYWOOD, THOMAS, *An Apology for Actors* (London, 1612).

HICKES, GEORGE, *Ravillac Redivivus: Being a Narrative of the Late Tryal of Mr James Mitchel ... In a Letter from a Scottish to an English Gentleman* (London, 1678); (Dublin, 1679).

HILL, WILLS, MARQUIS OF DOWNSHIRE, *A Proposal for Uniting the Kingdoms of Great Britain and Ireland* (Dublin, 1751).

HODGES, JAMES, *The Rights and Interests of the Two British Monarchies* (Edinburgh, 1703).

—— *War Betwixt the Two British Kingdoms Consider'd* (London, 1705).

HOGG, JAMES, *The Brownie of Bodsbeck and other Tales*, 2 vols. (Edinburgh: William Blackwood and John Murray, 1818).

HOLINSHED, RAPHAEL, *et al.*, *The First and Second Volumes of Chronicles, Comprising 1 The Description and Historie of England, 2 The Description and Historie of Ireland, 3 The Description and Historie of Scotland*, enlarged edn. (London, 1587).

HOLLAND, HUGH, *Pancharis* (London, 1603).

HOME, HENRY, LORD KAMES, *Sketches of the History of Man* (Edinburgh, 1774).

HOME, JOHN, *Douglas: A Tragedy* (London, 1757).

HONEYMAN, ANDREW, *A Survey of the Insolent and Infamous Libel, Entituled, Naphtali* (Edinburgh, 1668).

HOPKINS, CHARLES, *A Letter to A. H. Esq., Concerning the Stage* (London, 1698).

—— *Boadicea, Queen of Britain* (London, 1697).

—— *Epistolary Poems, on Several Occasions* (London, 1694).

—— *Friendship Improv'd: Or, The Female Warriour* (1700).

—— *Neglected Virtue: Or, The Unhappy Conqueror* (1696).

—— *Pyrrhus, King of Epirus* (1695).

HOWELL, JAMES, *Poems* (London, 1663).

HUGHES, JOHN and KENNETT, WHITE, *A Complete History of England*, 3 vols. (London, 1706).

HUGHES, THOMAS, *Misfortunes of Arthur*, ed. Brian Jay Corrigan (New York: Garland, 1992).

HUME OF GODSCROFT, DAVID, *The British Union: A Critical Edition and Translation of David Hume of Godscroft's 'De Unione Insulae Britannicae'*, ed. Paul J. McGinnis and Arthur H. Williamson (Aldershot: Ashgate, 2002).

—— *The History of the Houses of Douglas and Angus* (Edinburgh, 1643).

HUME, ALEXANDER, *Of the Orthographie and Congruitie of the Britan Tonge*, ed. H. B. Wheatley (London: Early English Text Society, 1865).

HUME, DAVID, *Scotticisms* (Edinburgh, 1752).

—— *The History of England, from the Invasion of Julius Caesar to the Revolution in 1688*, 6 vols. (London, 1762).

—— *The History of Great Britain, Vol. I: Containing the Reigns of James I and Charles I* (Edinburgh, 1754).

—— *The History of Great Britain, Vol. II: Containing the Commonwealth, and the Reigns of Charles II and James II* (London, 1757).

HUYGENS, SIR CONSTANTIJN, *A Selection of the Poems of Sir Constantijn Huygens (1596–1687): A Parallel Text*, ed. and tr. Peter Davidson and Adriaan van der Weel (Amsterdam: Amsterdam University Press, 1996).

—— *De Gedichten van Constantijn Huygens*, ed. J. A. Worp, 9 vols. (Groningen: J. B. Wolters, 1892–9).

HYDE, EDWARD, EARL OF CLARENDON, *The History of the Rebellion and Civil Wars in England*, ed. W. Dunn Macray, 6 vols. (Oxford: Clarendon, 1888).

JACK, R. D. S. and P. A. T. ROZENDAAL, (eds.), *The Mercat Anthology of Early Scottish Literature 1375–1707* (Edinburgh: Mercat, 1997).

JACKSON, KENNETH (ed.), *Early Welsh Gnomic Poems*, corr. edn. (Cardiff: Cardiff University Press, 1961).

JAMES VI AND I, *Basilikon Doron* (Edinburgh, 1599); (London, 1603); incomplete Welsh tr. by Robert Holland, *Basilikon Doron: neu, Athrawiaeth i fawredh yw anwylaf fab Henri'r tywyfog* (London, 1604).

—— *Ane Schort Treatise, Conteining Some Reulis and Cautelis to be Obseruit and Eschewit in Scottis Poesie* (1584), in G. Gregory Smith (ed.), *Elizabethan Critical Essays*, 2 vols. (1904; London: Oxford University Press, 1950), I, 208–25.

JAMES VI AND I, *The Poems of James VI of Scotland*, ed. James Craigie, 2 vols. (Edinburgh: Scottish Text Society, 1955–8).

—— *The Progresses, Processions, and Magnificent Festivities of King James the First*, ed. John Nichols, 4 vols. (London: J. B. Nichols, 1828).

—— *The True Lawe of Free Monarchies: Or, The Reciprock and Mutual Dutie Betwixt a Free King, and his Naturall Subiects* (Edinburgh, 1603).

—— *The Workes of the Most High and Mightie Prince, James by the Grace of God, King of Great Britaine, France and Ireland* (London, 1616).

JAMES, HENRY, *Roderick Hudson* [New York Edition] (Harmondsworth: Penguin, 1969).

JOCELYN OF FURNESS, tr. and adapted by B. B. [Robert Rochford], *Life of the Glorious Bishop S. Patricke* (Saint-Omer, 1625).

JOHNSON, SAMUEL, *A Dictionary of the English Language*, 2 vols. (London, 1756).

—— *A Journey to the Western Islands of Scotland* (London, 1775).

JOHNSON, WILLIAM, [= Willem Jans Blaeu], *The Light of Navigation* (Amsterdam, 1612).

JONES, SIR THOMAS, *The Rise and Progress of the Most Honourable and Loyal Society of Antient Britons, Established in Honour to Her Royal Highness's Birth-day* (London, 1717).

JONSON, BEN, 'Ben Jonson's Conversations with William Drummond of Hawthornden' (more correctly, 'Informations be Ben Johnston to W. D. when he came to Scotland upon foot') in *Ben Jonson*, ed. C. H. Herford, Percy and Evelyn Simpson, 11 vols. (Oxford: Clarendon, 1925–52), I, 132–51.

—— *The Fortunate Isles and their Vnion* (London, 1625).

—— *The Workes of Beniamin Jonson* (London, 1616).

—— *The Workes of Benjamin Jonson* (London, 1641).

——, GEORGE CHAPMAN and JOHN MARSTON, *Eastward Hoe* (London, 1605).

KELTON, ARTHUR, *A Commendacyon of Welshmen* (London, 1546).

KING, WILLIAM, *The State of the Protestants of Ireland under the Late King James's Government* (London, 1691).

KIRK, ROBERT, *The Secret Commonwealth* (1691), ed. in Michael Hunter, *The Occult Laboratory: Magic, Science and Second Sight in Late Seventeenth-Century Scotland* (Woodbridge: Boydell, 2001).

KIRKTON, JAMES, *The Secret and True History of the Church of Scotland*, ed. Charles Kirkpatrick Sharpe (Edinburgh: Ballantyne 1817).

LANE, PARR, 'Newes from the Holy Isle', ed. Alan Ford, in 'Parr Lane, "Newes from the Holy Isle"', *Proceedings of the Royal Irish Academy*, 99(C) (1999): 115–56.

LANGHORNE, JOHN, *Genius and Valour: A Scotch Pastoral* (London, 1763).

LARKIN, JAMES F. and PAUL L. HUGHES (eds.), *Stuart Royal Proclamations*, vol. I (Oxford: Clarendon, 1973).

LEIGH, RICHARD (or Samuel Butler), *The Transproser Rehears'd: Or, The Fifth Act of Mr Bayes's Play* (Oxford [London?], 1673).

LELAND, THOMAS, *The History of Ireland from the Invasion of Henry II* (London, 1773).

L'ESTRANGE, SIR ROGER, *An Account of the Growth of Knavery under the Pretended Fears of Arbitrary Government and Popery with a Parallel betwixt the Reformers of 1677, and those of 1641, in their Methods, and Designs* (London, 1678).

LEWIS OF LLYNWENE, JOHN, *The History of Great-Britain, from the First Inhabitants Thereof, 'till the Death of Cadwalader, Last King of the Britains* (c.1610) (London, 1729).

LHUYD, EDWARD, *Archaeologia Britannica* (Oxford, 1707).

LITHGOW, WILLIAM, *Scotlands Welcome to Her Native Sonne, and Soveraigne Lord, King Charles* (Edinburgh, 1633).

—— *The Pilgrimes Farewell to his Natiue Countrey of Scotland* (Edinburgh, 1618).

LLWYD, HUMPHREY, *Commentarioli Britannicae descriptionis fragmentum* (Cologne, 1572).

—— *The Breuiary of Britayne*, tr. Thomas Twyne (London, 1573).

LLWYD, MORGAN, *An Honest Discourse between Three Neighbours, Touching the Present Government in these Three Nations* (London, 1655).

—— *Gweithiau Morgan Llwyd o Wynedd*, vol. I, ed. Thomas E. Ellis (Bangor: Jarvis and Foster, 1899).

—— *Gweithiau Morgan Llwyd o Wynedd*, vol. III, ed. J. Graham Jones and Goronwy Wyn Owen with R. Tudur Jones (Caerdydd: Gwasg Prifysgol Cymru, 1994).

—— *Llyfr y tri aderyn* (1653), tr. L. J. Parry as *The Book of the Three Birds*, in E. Vincent Evans (ed.), *Cofnodion a chyfansoddiadau buddugol eisteddfod Llandudno, 1896/Transactions of the National Eisteddfod of Wales Llandudno, 1896* (National Eisteddfod Association: Liverpool, 1898), 195–247.

LOCKHART, GEORGE, *'Scotland's Ruine': Lockhart of Carnwath's Memoirs of the Union*, ed. Daniel Szechi (Aberdeen: Association for Scottish Literary Studies, 1995).

LOCKHART, J. G., *Memoirs of the Life of Sir Walter Scott* (Edinburgh: Cadell, 1850).

LOMBARD, PETER, *De regno Hiberniae, sanctorum insulâ, commentarius* (Louvain, 1632).

LORD, GEORGE DeF. (gen. ed.), *Poems on Affairs of State: Augustan Satirical Verse, 1660–1714*, 7 vols. (New Haven: Yale University Press, 1963–75).

LUIM, IAIN [Iian Lom], *Orain Iain Luim: Songs of John MacDonald, Bard of Keppoch*, ed. Annie M. MacKenzie, Scottish Gaelic Texts Society (Edinburgh: Oliver and Boyd, 1964).

LYTTELTON, GEORGE, BARON LYTTELTON, *The History of the Life of Henry the Second* (London, 1767).

MACAULAY, CATHARINE, *The History of England from the Accession of James I to that of the Brunswick Line*, 8 vols. (London, 1763–83).

MACCURTIN, HUGH, *A Brief Discourse in Vindication of the Antiquity of Ireland* (Dublin, 1717).

MACHIAVELLI, NICCOLÒ, *The Florentine History in VIII Books*, anonymously tr. (London, 1674).

MACKENZIE, GEORGE, EARL OF CROMARTY, *Parainesis Pacifica: Or, A Perswasive to the Union of Britain* (London, 1702).

MACKENZIE, SIR GEORGE, *A Moral Essay, Preferring Solitude to Publick Employment* (Edinburgh, 1666).

—— *A Vindication of His Majesties Government, and Judicatures, in Scotland; from some Aspersions Thrown on them by Scandalous Pamphlets, and News-books* (Edinburgh, 1683).

—— *A Vindication of the Government in Scotland during the Reign of King Charles II* (London, 1691).

—— *Aretina: Or, The Serious Romance* (Edinburgh, 1660).

—— 'Discourse Concerning the Three Unions between Scotland and England', in *The Works of that Eminent and Noble Lawyer, Sir George Mackenzie of Rosehaugh*, ed. Thomas Ruddiman, 2 vols. (Edinburgh, 1718–22), II, 637–70.

—— *Idea eloquentiae forensis hodiernae* (Edinburgh, 1681).

—— *Jus Regium: Or, The Just and Solid Foundations of Monarchy* (London, 1684).

—— *Pleadings in some Remarkable Cases, before the Supreme Courts of Scotland, since the Year 1661* (Edinburgh, 1672).

—— *Religio Stoici* (Edinburgh, 1663).

MACPHERSON, JAMES, *An Introduction to the History of Great Britain and Ireland* (London, 1771).

—— *Fingal, An Ancient Epic Poem, in Six Books: Together with Several other Poems, Composed by Ossian the Son of Fingal. Translated from the Galic* (London, 1762).

—— *Temora, An Ancient Epic Poem, in Eight Books: Together with Several other Poems, Composed by Ossian, the Son of Fingal. Translated from the Galic* (London, 1763).

—— *The Works of Ossian, the Son of Fingal*, 2 vols. (London, 1765).

MAIDMENT, JAMES (ed.), *A Book of Scotish Pasquils: 1568–1715* (Edinburgh: William Paterson, 1868).

—— (ed.), *Scotish Ballads and Songs, Historical and Traditionary* (Edinburgh: William Paterson, 1868).

MARVELL, ANDREW, *An Account of the Growth of Popery, and Arbitrary Government in England* (Amsterdam [London], 1677).

—— *Miscellaneous Poems* (London, 1681).

—— *The Poems and Letters of Andrew Marvell*, ed. H. M. Margoliouth, 3rd edn. rev. Pierre Legouis with E. E. Duncan-Jones, 2 vols. (Oxford: Clarendon, 1971).

—— *The Poems of Andrew Marvell*, ed. Nigel Smith (London: Longman, 2003).

—— *The Rehearsal Transpros'd* (London, 1672).

MAY, THOMAS, *The Changeable Covenant: Shewing in a Brief Series of Relations, how the Scots from Time to Time have Imposed upon England* (London, 1650).

Mercurius Politicus. Comprising the Summ of All Intelligence, with the Affairs, and Designs now on Foot, in the Three Nations of England, Ireland, and Scotland. In Defence of the Common-wealth, and for Information of the People, ed. Marchamont Nedham and John Hall, then Nedham alone, and finally John Canne (London, 1650–60).

MERITON, GEORGE, *A Yorkshire Dialogue* (York, 1683).

MIEGE, GUY, *A Relation of Three Embassies from his Sacred Majestie Charles II to the Great Duke of Muscovie, the King of Sweden, and the King of Denmark* (London, 1669).

MILTON, JOHN, *Complete Prose Works of John Milton*, gen. ed. Don M. Wolfe, 8 vols. (New Haven: Yale University Press, 1953–82).

—— *The Riverside Milton*, ed. Roy Flannagan (Boston: Houghton Mifflin, 1998).

MITCHELBOURNE, JOHN, *A Confirmation of the Losses Sustained by Colonel John Michelburne, Late Governor of Londonderry* (London?, 1704?).

—— *An Account of the Transactions in the North of Ireland, Anno Domini, 1691 ... With Particular Relation of the Manner of Besieging and Taking the town of Sligoe by Storm* (London, 1692).

—— *Colonel Michelburne's Reply to James Roach's Answer* (London, 1703).

—— *Ireland Preserv'd: Or, The Siege of London-Derry. Together with The Troubles of the North* (London, 1705).

—— *The Case of Col. John Michelburne, Late Governor of Londonderry; and the Regiment then under his Command* (London?, 1703?).

—— *The Case of Colonel John Michelburn, Late Gov[erno]r of London-Derry, further Consider'd* (London?, 1706?).

—— *The Case of Colonel John Michelburne, Late Governor of Londonderry: and the Service of James Roach, truly Stated* (London, 1698).

—— *The Case of the Governor, Officers and Soldiers actually concerned in the Defence of London-Derry* (London, 1698).

MOLYNEUX, WILLIAM, *The Case of Ireland's being Bound by Acts of Parliament in England, Stated* (Dublin, 1698).

MORE, HENRY, *Cupids Conflict*, attached to his *Democritus Platonissans: Or, An Essay upon the Infinity of Worlds* (Cambridge, 1646).

MORYSON, FYNES, 'The Description of Ireland', in Falkiner (ed.), *Illustrations*, 214–32.

—— *The Irish Sections of Fynes Moryson's Unpublished Itinerary*, ed. Graham Kew (Dublin, Irish Manuscripts Commission, 1998).

MORRIS, LEWIS, et al., *Additional Letters of the Morrises of Anglesey (1735–1786)*, ed. Hugh Owen, *Transactions of the Honourable Society of Cymmrodorion*, 49 (1947–9).

—— *The Letters of Lewis, Richard, William and John Morris of Anglesey (Morrisiaid Môn) 1728–1756*, ed. J. H. Davies, 2 vols. (Aberystwyth: J. H. Davies, 1907–9).

MUNDAY, ANTHONY, *Pageants and Entertainments of Anthony Munday*, ed. David M. Bergeron (Garland: New York, 1985).

NEDHAM, MARCHAMONT, *The Case of the Commonwealth of England, Stated: Or, The Equity, Utility, and Necessity, of a Submission to the Present Government* (London, 1650).

—— *The True Character of a Rigid Presbyter: With a Narrative of the Dangerous Designes of the English and Scotish Covenanters, as they have Tended to the Ruine of our Church and Kingdom*, 2nd edn. (London, 1661).

NICCHOLS, HENRY, *The Shield Single against the Sword Doubled* (London, 1653).

NIXON, ANTHONY, *Oxfords Triumph in the Royall Entertainement of his Moste Excellent Maiestie, the Queene, and the Prince: the 27. of August last, 1605* (London, 1605).

NORTHLEIGH, JOHN, *The Parallel: Or, The New Specious Association* (London, 1682).

Ó BAOILL, COLM (ed.), *Gàir nan Clàrsach: The Harps' Cry*, tr. Meg Bateman (Edinburgh: Birlinn, 1994).

O'CONOR, CHARLES, *A Counter-Appeal, to the People of Ireland* (Dublin, 1749).

—— and JOHN CURRY, *Observations on the Popery Laws* (Dublin, 1771).

O'FLAHERTY, RODERIC, *Ogygia seu, rerum Hibernicarum chronologia: Ex pervetustis monumentis fideliter inter se collatis eruta* (London, 1685).

OGILBY, JOHN, *Britannia…: Or, An Illustration of the Kingdom of England and Dominion of Wales by a Geographical and Historical Description of the Principal Roads Thereof* (London, 1675).

O'KELLY, CHARLES, *Macariae Excidium: Or, The Destruction of Cyprus*, ed. John Cornelius O'Callaghan (Dublin: Irish Archaeological Society, 1850).

OLDISWORTH, WILLIAM, 'On the Union: A Poem to the Queen', in Joseph Browne (ed.), *State Tracts: Containing Many Necessary Observations and Reflections on the State of our Affairs at Home and Abroad*, 2 vols. (London, 1715), II, 162–8.

OLDMIXON, JOHN, *History of England*, 3 vols. (London, 1730–5).

—— *Memoirs of Ireland from the Restoration, to the Present Times* (London, 1716).

—— *Memoirs of North Britain* (London, 1715).

O'MAHONY, CONOR, *Disputatio apologetica* (Frankfurt [Lisbon], 1645).

O'RAHILLY, CECILE (ed.), *Five Seventeenth-Century Political Poems* (Dublin: Dublin Institute for Advanced Studies, 1952).

O'SULLIVAN BEARE, PHILIP, *Archicornigeromastix, siue Vsheri haeresiarchae confutatio* in his *Patritiana decas* (Madrid, 1629).

—— *Historicae Catholicae Iberniae compendium* (Lisbon, 1623).

OWEN, GEORGE, *Cruell Lawes against Welshmen*, in *Cymmrodorion Records*, ed. Henry Owen, ser. 1 part iii (London: Charles J. Clark, 1982), 120–60.

—— *Description of Pembrokeshire*, ed. Dillwyn Miles (Llandysul: Gomer Press, 1994).

OWEN, JOHN, *Epigrammatum libri tres* (London, 1606).

PARK, THOMAS, *Cupid Turned Volunteer* (London: E. Harding, 1804).

PATERSON, WILLIAM, *An Inquiry into the Reasonableness and Consequences of an Union with Scotland* (London, 1706).

PEDRO, MOREJON, *A Briefe Relation of the Persecution Lately Made against the Catholike Christians, in the Kingdome of Iaponia… Taken out of the Annual Letters of the Fathers of the Society of Iesus, and other Authenticall Informations*, tr. W[illiam]. W[right]. (Saint-Omer, 1619).

PERCY, THOMAS, *Reliques of Ancient English Poetry: Consisting of Old Heroic Ballads, Songs, and Other Pieces of our Earlier Poets*, 3 vols. (London, 1765).

PETTY, SIR WILLIAM, *The Economic Writings of Sir William Petty*, ed. Charles Henry Hill, 2 vols. (Cambridge: Cambridge University Press, 1899).
—— *The Political Anatomy of Ireland* (London, 1691).
PHILIPS, GEORGE, *The Interest of England in the Preservation of Ireland* (London, 1689).
PHILIPS, KATHERINE, *Poems* (London, 1664); 2nd edn. (London, 1667).
—— *The Collected Works of Katherine Philips: The Matchless Orinda*, ed. Patrick Thomas *et al.*, 3 vols. (Stump Cross: Stump Cross Books, 1990–3).
PHILIPS, WILLIAM, *Hibernia Freed* (London, 1722).
—— *St Stephen's-Green: Or, The Generous Lovers* (Dublin, 1700).
—— *St Stephen's-Green: Or, The Generous Lovers*, ed. Christopher Murray (Portlaoise: Dolmen, 1980).
—— *The Revengeful Queen* (London, 1698).
PINKERTON, JOHN, *A Dissertation on the Origin and Progress of the Scythians or Goths* (London, 1787).
—— *An Enquiry into the History of Scotland Preceding the Reign of Malcolm III, or the Year 1056* (London, 1789).
PIX, MARY, *A Poem, Humbly Inscrib'd to the Lords Commissioners for the Union of the Two Kingdoms* (London, 1707).
PLUNKETT OF DUNSOGHLY, OLIVER, *A Light to the Blind*, edited as *A Jacobite Narrative of the War in Ireland 1688–91*, ed. John T. Gilbert, rpt. with an introd. by J. G. Simms (Shannon: Irish University Press, 1971).
POWEL, DAVID, *Historie of Cambria*, see Caradoc of Llancarvan.
POWELL, GEORGE, *Bonduca: Or, The British Heroine* (London, 1696).
POWELL, THOMAS, *Cerbyd jechydwriaeth* (London, 1657).
POWELL, VAVASOR, *Christ Exalted above all Creatures by God His Father* (London, 1651).
—— *The Scriptures Concord: Or, A Catechisme Compiled out of the Words of Scripture* (London, 1646).
PRISE, SIR JOHN [Syr Siôn ap Rhys], *Yny lhyvyr hwnn y traethir* (London?, 1546).
PUTTENHAM, GEORGE, *The Arte of English Poesie* (1589), ed. Gladys Doidge Willcock and Alice Walker (Cambridge: Cambridge University Press, 1936).
PYE, HENRY JAMES, *Carmen Seculare for the Year 1800* (London, 1800).
RALEIGH, SIR WALTER, *The History of the World* (London, 1614).
RAMSAY OF OCHTERTYRE, JOHN, *Scotland and Scotsmen in the Eighteenth Century from the Manuscripts of John Ramsay of Ochtertyre*, ed. Alexander Allardyce (Edinburgh: W. Blackwood and Sons, 1888).
RAMSAY, ALLAN, *Tartana: Or, The Plaid* (Edinburgh, 1718).
—— *The Tea-Table Miscellany*, 4 vols. (Edinburgh/London/Dublin, 1724–37).
RAMSAY, ALLAN (ed.), *The Ever Green, being a Collection of Scots Poems* (Edinburgh, 1724).
RANDOLPH, THOMAS, *Hey for Honesty, Down with Knavery: Translated out of Aristophanes his Plutus* (London, 1651).

RAPIN DE THORYAS, PAUL DE, *Histoire de l'Angleterre*, 8 vols. (The Hague, 1724).

RAY, JOHN, *A Collection of English Words Not Generally Used* (London, 1674), 2nd edn. (London, 1691).

REILLY, HUGH, *Ireland's Case Briefly Stated: Or, A Summary Account of the Most Remarkable Transactions in that Kingdom since the Reformation* (Paris?/Louvain?, 1695), later published as *The Impartial History of Ireland*.

RICHARDS OF HELMDON (?), WILLIAM, *Wallography: Or, The Britton Describ'd* (London, 1682).

RICHE, BARNABE, *A New Description of Ireland* (London, 1610).

RIDPATH, GEORGE, *Considerations upon the Union of the Two Kingdoms* (Edinburgh?, 1706).

RITSON, JOSEPH, *Observations on the First Three Volumes of the History of English Poetry. In a Familiar Letter to the Author* (London, 1782).

ROBERT OF SHREWSBURY, tr. and adapted by I. F. [John Falconer], *The Admirable Life of Saint Wenefride: Virgin, Martyr, Abbesse* (Saint-Omer, 1635).

ROBERTSON, JAMES, *The Fanatic* (London: Fourth Estate, 2000).

ROBERTSON, WILLIAM, *The History of Scotland, During the Reigns of Queen Mary and of King James VI till his Accession to the Crown of England*, 2 vols. (London, 1759).

RODRIGUES, JOÃO, *The Palme of Christian Fortitude: Or, The Glorious Combats of Christians in Iaponia* (St-Omer, 1630).

ROGERS, WOODES, *A Cruising Voyage Round the World* (1712), ed. G. E. Manwaring (London: Cassell, 1928).

ROWE, NICHOLAS, *Poetical Works* (London, 1715).

—— *The Royal Convert* (London, 1708).

ROWLEY, WILLIAM, *A Shoo-maker a Gentleman* (London, 1638).

RUTTER, SAMUEL, *Archdeacon Rutter's Song Book*, ed. Roger Dickinson, in David George, ed., *Lancashire*, Records of Early English Drama (Toronto: University of Toronto Press, 1991), app. 5.

—— 'To the Glorious Memory of the Blessed Martyr, James, Earle of Derby', in *The Stanley Papers*, III. 2, Chetham Society, 67 (1867), app. 15.

SALES, SIR WILLIAM, *Theophania: Or, Severall Modern Histories Represented by Way of Romance and Politickly Discours'd Upon* (London, 1655).

SCOT OF SCOTSTARVIT, SIR JOHN, LORD SCOTSTARVIT, *et al.*, *Delitiae poetarum Scotorum*, 2 vols. (Amsterdam, 1637).

SCOTT, SIR WALTER, 'Culloden Papers: Comprising an Extensive and Interesting Correspondence from the Year 1625 to 1748 ...', *Quarterly Review*, 14 (1815–16): 283–333.

—— 'General Preface' to the 1829 edn. of the Waverley Novels, in *Waverley*, ed. Lamont, 349–61.

SCOTT, SIR WALTER, *Letters to the Editor of the Edinburgh Weekly Journal, from Malachi Malgrowther, Esq., on the Proposed Change of Currency*, in Sir Walter Scott, *Miscellaneous Prose Works*, 28 vols. (Edinburgh: Robert Cadell, 1834–6).

—— *Old Mortality*, ed. Jane Stevenson and Peter Davidson (Oxford: Oxford University Press, 1993).

—— *Redgauntlet*, ed. G. A. M. Wood with David Hewitt (Edinburgh: Edinburgh University Press, 1997).

—— *Rob Roy*, ed. Ian Duncan (Oxford: Oxford University Press, 1998).

—— *The Black Dwarf*, ed. Peter Garside (Edinburgh: Edinburgh University Press, 1993).

—— *The Heart of Midlothian*, ed. Claire Lamont (Oxford: Oxford University Press, 1982).

—— *The Journal of Sir Walter Scott*, ed. W. E. K. Anderson (Oxford: Clarendon, 1972).

—— *The Letters of Sir Walter* Scott, ed. H. J. C. Grierson, 12 vols. (London: Constable, 1932–7).

—— *Waverley: Or, 'Tis Sixty Years Since*, ed. Claire Lamont (Oxford: Clarendon, 1981).

SELDEN, JOHN, *Titles of Honor* (London, 1614).

SELLAR, W. C. and R. J. YEATMAN, *1066 and All That: A Memorable History of England* (London: Methuen, 1930).

SELLER, JOHN, *The Coastal Pilot* (London, 1670).

—— *The English Pilot* (London, 1671).

SETON OF PITMEDDEN, SIR WILLIAM, *A Speech in Parliament, The Second Day of November 1706* (Edinburgh, 1706).

—— *The Interest of Scotland in Three Essays* (Edinburgh?, 1700).

SETTLE, ELKANAH, *Carmen Irenicum: The Union of the Imperial Crowns of Great Britain. An Heroick Poem* (London, 1707).

—— *Eusebia Triumphans: The Protestant Succession as Now Establish'd, and Inviolably Secur'd, by the Happy Union of the Imperial Crowns of Great Britain* (London, 1709).

SHAKESPEARE, WILLIAM, *Chronicle Historie of the Life and Death of King Lear* (London, 1608).

—— *Macbeth*, ed. A. R. Braunmuller (Cambridge: Cambridge University Press, 1997).

—— *The First Folio of Shakespeare: The Norton Facsimile*, ed. Charlton Hinman (London: Paul Hamlyn, 1968).

—— *The Norton Shakespeare*, gen. ed. Stephen Greenblatt (New York: Norton, 1997).

—— et al., *Edward III*, ed. Giorgio Melchiori (Cambridge: Cambridge University Press, 1998).

—— *The Raigne of King Edward the Third* (London, 1596).

SHEPARD, THOMAS, *New Englands Lamentation for Old Englands Present Errours and Divisions* (London, 1645).

SHIRLEY, JAMES, *Narcissus: Or, The Self-Lover* (London, 1646).

SHIRLEY, JAMES, *St Patrick for Ireland. The First Part* (London, 1640).

SMOLLETT, TOBIAS, *A Complete History of England, Deduced from the Descent of Julius Caesar, to the Treaty of Aix la Chapelle*, 4 vols. (London, 1757–8).

——— *Poems, Plays, and 'The Briton'*, ed. O. M. Brack, introd. Byron Gassman (Athens, GA: University of Georgia Press, 1993).

——— *The Expedition of Humphrey Clinker*, 3 vols. (London, 1771).

SOLIER, FRANÇOIS, *Histoire ecclésiastique des isles et royaumes du Japon* (Paris, 1627).

SPALDING, JOHN, *The History of the Troubles and Memorable Transactions in Scotland and England, from 1624 to 1645*, ed. James Skene, 2 vols. (Edinburgh: Ballantyne, 1828–9).

SPEED, JOHN, *The History of Great Britaine under the Conquests of the Romans, Saxons, Danes and Normans* (London, 1611).

——— *The Theatre of the Empire of Great Britaine: Presenting an Exact Geography of the Kingdomes of England, Scotland, Ireland, and the Iles Adioyning* (London, 1612).

SPENSER, EDMUND, *A View of the State of Ireland ... 1596*, in Ware, *Historie of Ireland*.

——— *The Faerie Queene*, ed. A. C. Hamilton (London: Longman, 1977).

——— *The Yale Edition of the Shorter Poems of Edmund Spenser*, ed. William Oram *et al.* (New Haven: Yale University Press, 1989).

SPOTTISWOODE, JOHN, *The History of the Church of Scotland* (London, 1655).

ST JOHN, HENRY, VISCOUNT BOLINGBROKE, *The Works of Lord Bolingbroke*, 4 vols. (Philadelphia: Carey and Hart, 1841).

ST SERFE, THOMAS, *Tarugo's Wiles: Or, The Coffee-House* (London, 1668).

STARKEY, GEORGE, *The Dignity of Kingship Asserted: In Answer to Mr. Milton's Ready and Easie Way to Establish a Free Common-wealth* (London, 1660), rpt. as *Monarchy Triumphing over Traiterous Republicans* (London, 1661).

STEVENSON, JANE and PETER DAVIDSON (eds.), *Early Modern Women Poets (1520–1700): An Anthology* (Oxford: Oxford University Press, 2001).

STEWART, JAMES, *Jus Populi Vindicatum: Or, The Peoples Right to Defend Themselves and their Covenanted Religion Vindicated* (London?, 1669).

——— and JAMES STIRLING, *Naphtali: Or, The Wrestlings of the Church of Scotland for the Kingdom of Christ* (Edinburgh?, 1667).

SUCKLING, SIR JOHN, *The Works of Sir John Suckling, The Non-Dramatic Works*, ed. Thomas Clayton (Oxford: Clarendon, 1971).

SWIFT, JONATHAN, *A Proposal for Correcting the English Tongue, Polite Conversation, Etc.*, ed. Herbert Davis with Louis Landa (Oxford: Blackwell, 1957).

——— *Bickerstaff Papers and Pamphlets on the Church*, ed. Herbert Davis (Oxford: Blackwell, 1940).

——— *Gulliver's Travels*, ed. Harold Williams (Oxford: Blackwell, 1941).

——— *Irish Tracts 1720–1723 and Sermons*, ed. Herbert Davis and Louis Landa (Oxford: Blackwell, 1948).

SWIFT, JONATHAN, *Irish Tracts 1728–1733*, ed. Herbert Davis (Oxford: Blackwell, 1955).

—— *Miscellaneous and Autobiographical Pieces, Fragments and Marginalia*, ed. Herbert Davis (Oxford: Blackwell, 1962).

—— *The Complete Poems*, ed. Pat Rogers (Harmondsworth: Penguin, 1983).

—— *The Drapier's Letters and Other Works 1724–1725*, ed. Herbert Davis (Oxford: Blackwell, 1941).

—— *The Poems of Jonathan Swift*, ed. Harold Williams, 3 vols., 2nd. edn. (Oxford: Clarendon, 1958).

—— *The Works of Jonathan Swift*, ed. Walter Scott, 19 vols. (Edinburgh: Constable, 1814).

SYDENHAM, CUTHBERT, *The False Brother: Or, A New Map of Scotland, Drawn by an English Pencil* (London, 1651).

SYMSON, ANDREW, *Sir George M'Kenzie's Arguments against an Incorporating Union Particularly Considered* (Edinburgh, 1706).

TATE, NAHUM, *A Congratulatory Poem on the New Parliament Assembled on this Great Conjuncture of Affairs* (London, 1701).

—— *The Triumph of Union: With the Muse's Address For the Consummation of it in the Parliament of Great Britain* (London, 1707).

TAYLOR, JEREMY, *The Measures and Offices of Friendship* (London, 1657).

TAYLOR, JOHN, *The Pennyles Pilgrimage: Or, The Money-lesse Perambulation* (London, 1618).

TEATE, FAITHFUL, *The Souldiers Commission* (London, 1658).

TEMPLE, SIR JOHN, *The Irish Rebellion* (London, 1646).

The Records of the Proceedings of the Justiciary Court, Edinburgh, 1661–1678, ed. W. G. Scott-Moncrieff, 2 vols. (Edinburgh: Edinburgh University Press, 1905).

The Statutes at Large, from Magna Charta, to the Thirtieth Year of King George the Second, ed. H. B. Cay, 6 vols. (London, 1758).

The Statutes at Large, Passed in the Parliaments held in Ireland … A. D. 1310 to … A. D. 1800, 21 vols. (Dublin, 1786–1804).

THEOBALD, LEWIS, *A Pindarick Ode on the Union* (London, 1707).

THOMSON, JAMES, *Spring* (London, 1728).

—— and DAVID MALLET, *Alfred: A Masque. Represented before Their Royal Highnesses the Prince and Princess of Wales, at Cliffden, on the first of August, 1740* (London, 1740).

TRAPP, JOSEPH, *Peace. A Poem* (London, 1713).

UÍ BRUADAIR, DÁIBID, *Duanaire Dáibid Uí Bruadair: The Poems of David Ó Bruadair*, ed. Rev. John C. Mac Erlean, 3 vols., Irish Texts Society (London: David Nutt, 1910–17).

URQUHART, SIR THOMAS, *The Works of Sir Thomas Urquhart of Cromarty*, ed. Thomas Maitland (Edinburgh: Maitland Club, 1834).

USSHER, JAMES, *A Discourse of the Religion Anciently Professed by the Irish and Brittish* (London, 1631).

USSHER, JAMES, *An Epistle Written by the Reverend Father in God, James Vssher Bishop of Meath, Concerning the Religion Anciently Professed by the Irish and Scottish; Shewing it to be for Substance the Same with That which at This Day is by Publick Authoritie Established in the Church of England*, appended to Sir Christopher Sibthorp, *A Friendly Advertisement to the Pretended Catholickes of Ireland* (Dublin, 1622).

—— 'Correspondence of David Rothe and James Ussher, 1619–23', ed. William O'Sullivan, *Collecteana Hibernica*, 36–7 (1994–5): 7–49.

VAUGHAN, HENRY, *The Complete Poems*, ed. Alan Rudrum (Harmondsworth: Penguin, 1976).

—— *The Works of Henry Vaughan*, ed. L. C. Martin, 2nd edn. (Oxford: Clarendon, 1957).

VAUGHAN, THOMAS, *The Works of Thomas Vaughan*, ed. Alan Rudrum (Oxford: Clarendon, 1984).

VERGIL, POLYDORE, *Anglica historia* (Basel, 1534).

VERNON, EDWARD, *The Union: A Poem* (London, 1707).

VERSTEGAN, RICHARD, *A Restitution of Decayed Intelligence in Antiquities, Concerning the Most Noble and Renowmed English Nation* (Antwerp, 1605).

VILLERS, GEORGE, Duke of Buckingham, *et al.*, *Poems on Affairs of State from the Time of Oliver Cromwell, to the abdication of King James the Second* ([London], 1697).

W., J., *The Valiant Scot* (London, 1637).

—— *The Valiant Scot*, ed. George E. Byers (New York: Garland, 1980).

WALKER, GEORGE, *A Sermon Being an Incouragement for Protestants* (London, 1689); rpt. (Edinburgh, 1689).

—— *A True Account of the Siege of London-derry* (London, 1689).

WALLER, EDMUND, *A Panegyrick to my Lord Protector* (London, 1655).

—— *The Maid's Tragedy Altered. With Some other Pieces* (London, 1690).

WALSH, PETER, *A Letter Desiring a Just and Mercifull Regard of the Roman Catholicks of Ireland, Given about the End of October 1660* (Dublin?, 1662?).

—— *A Prospect of the State of Ireland from the Year of the World 1756 to the Year of Christ 1652* ([London], 1682).

—— *The Irish Colours Folded: Or, The Irish Roman-Catholick's Reply to the (Pretended) English Protestants Answer to the Letter Desiring a Just and Mercifull Regard of the Roman Catholicks of Ireland* (London, 1662).

WARD, EDWARD, *A Trip to Ireland, Being a Description of the Country, People and Manners* (London?, 1699).

—— *The History of the Grand Rebellion; containing, The Most Remarkable Transactions from the Beginning of the Reign of King Charles I to the Happy Restoration ... Digested into Verse*, 3 vols. (London, 1713).

WARE, SIR JAMES, comp., *The Historie of Ireland, Collected by Three Learned Authors* (Dublin, 1633).

WARNER, WILLIAM, *Albions England*, rev. edn. (London, 1602).

WARTON, THOMAS, *The History of English Poetry, from the Close of the Eleventh to the Commencement of the Eighteenth Century*, 4 vols. (1774–81).

—— (ed.), *The Union: Or, Select Scots and English Poems* ([Oxford], 1753).

WATKINS, ROWLAND, *Flamma sine Fumo: Or, Poems without Fictions* (London, 1662).

WATSON, JAMES (ed.), *A Choice Collection of Comic and Serious Scots Poems both Ancient and Modern*, 3 pts. (Edinburgh, 1706–11).

WEDDERBURN, ROBERT, *Complaynt of Scotland* (Paris, 1550).

WELDON, SIR ANTHONY, 'A Description of Scotland', in *Progresses, Processions, and Magnificent Festivities of King James the First*, ed. Nichols, III, 338–43.

WENTWORTH, THOMAS, EARL OF STRAFFORD, *The Earl of Strafforde's Letters and Dispatches*, ed. William Knowler, 2 vols. (London, 1739).

WHITTLE, SETH, *A Sermon Preached before the Garrison of London-Derry in the Extremity of the Siege* (Edinburgh, 1689).

WILKES, JOHN and CHARLES CHURCHILL, *The North Briton*, 2nd edn., 3 vols. (Dublin, 1763).

WILLIAMS, EDWARD, *Poems, Lyric and Pastoral*, 2 vols. (London: 1794).

WILLIAMS, ROGER, *The Hireling Ministry None of Christs: Or, A Discourse Touching the Propagating the Gospel of Christ Jesus* (London, 1652).

WILSON, JOHN, *A Critical Old-Spelling Edition of the Plays of John Wilson 1626–1695?*, ed. Kathleen Menzie Lesko, Ph.D. dissertation (The George Washington University, 1980).

—— *A Discourse of the Monarchy, More Particularly, of the Imperial Crowns of England, Scotland, and Ireland* (London, 1684).

—— *Belphegor: Or, The Marriage of the Devil* (London, 1691).

—— *To His Excellence Richard Earle of Arran &c. Lord Deputy of Ireland* (Dublin, 1682).

—— *Vindiciae Carolinae: Or, A Defence of Eikon Baskilike … in Reply to a Book Intituled Eikonoklastes, Written by Mr Milton* (London, 1692).

WILSON, THOMAS, *The Arte of Rhetorique* (London, 1553).

WISHART, GEORGE, *Memoirs of James, Marquis of Montrose, 1639–1650*, ed. Alexander Murdoch and H. F. Morland Simpson (London: Longmans, Green, 1983).

WRIGHT, WILLIAM, *The Comical History of the Marriage betwixt Fergusia and Heptarchus* (Edinburgh, 1706).

YEARSLEY, ANNE, *The Rural Lyre* (London: G. G. and J. Robinson, 1796).

Index